Introduction to Early Childhood Education
Preschool through Primary Grades

SIXTH EDITION

Jo Ann Brewer
University of Massachusetts Lowell

PEARSON
and

Boston • New York • San Francisco
Mexico City • Montreal • Toronto • London • Madrid • Munich • Paris
Hong Kong • Singapore • Tokyo • Cape Town • Sydney

Series Editor: Kelly Villella Canton
Series Editorial Assistant: Angela Pickard
Executive Marketing Manager: Krista Clark
Production Editor: Annette Joseph
Editorial Production Service: Omegatype Typography, Inc.
Development Editor: Sue Freese
Composition Buyer: Linda Cox
Manufacturing Manager: Megan Cochran
Electronic Composition: Omegatype Typography, Inc.
Interior Design: Carol Somberg
Photo Researcher: Annie Pickert
Cover Administrator: Linda Knowles
Cover Designer: Studio Nine

For related titles and support materials, visit our online catalog at www.ablongman.com.

Between the time website information is gathered and then published, it is not unusual for some sites to have closed. Also, the transcription of URLs can result in typographical errors. The publisher would appreciate notification where these errors occur so that they may be corrected in subsequent editions.

Library of Congress Cataloging-in-Publication Data

Brewer, Jo Ann.
   Introduction to early childhood education : preschool through primary grades / Jo Ann Brewer.—6th ed.
     p. cm.
   Includes bibliographical references and index.
   ISBN 0-205-49145-6
    1. Early childhood education—United States. 2. Early childhood education—History. 3. Child development—United States. I. Title. II. Title: Early childhood education.

LB1139.25.B74 2007
372.21—dc22

                                2006044824

Printed in the United States of America

10 9 8 7 6 5 4 3 2 1   RRD-OH   11 10 09 08 07 06

Photo credits appear on page 552, which constitutes an extension of the copyright page.

*To my family with love
and especially to my husband Bill*

Brief Contents

PART ONE: FOUNDATIONS OF EARLY CHILDHOOD LEARNING 1

1 Young Children Growing, Thinking, and Learning 2

2 Designing Schools for Young Children 38

3 Creating an Environment for Learning 76

4 Planning Learning Activities 104

5 Play: Learning at Its Best 140

6 Guiding Behavior 174

7 Assessment and Reporting 200

8 Working with Parents and Paraprofessionals 236

PART TWO: THE CURRICULUM CHAPTERS 265

9 Celebrating the Magic of Language 266

10 Developing Literacy 302

11 Manipulation and Discovery through Mathematics 348

12 Manipulation and Discovery through Science 384

13 Encouraging the Creative Arts 414

14 Living Together: The Social Studies 452

15 Promoting Wellness: Physical Education and Health, Nutrition, and Safety Education 480

Contents

Features   xv
Preface   xvii

PART ONE: FOUNDATIONS OF EARLY CHILDHOOD LEARNING   1

CHAPTER 1

Young Children Growing, Thinking, and Learning   2

Developmentally Appropriate Practice   4
Theories of Development   5
  Behaviorist Theory   6
  Maturationist Theory   7
  Constructivist Theory   8
  Multiple Intelligences Theory   10
  Social Learning Theory   12
  Ecological Systems Theory   13
  Theoretical Influences on Teaching   13
  Theoretical Influences on Observations   15
Children's Development   15
  Physical Development   15
  Social Development   20
  Emotional Development   27
  Intellectual Development   29
  Child Development and Curriculum Planning: An Example   33
  CHILDREN WITH SPECIAL NEEDS   35
  CELEBRATING DIVERSITY   35
SUMMARY   36
REFLECTIONS   36
EXPLORATIONS AND ACTIVITIES   37

CHAPTER 2

Designing Schools for Young Children   38

Early Schools for Young Children   40
  Key People in Early Childhood Education   40
  Other Influential People in Early Childhood Education   44
Changes in Early Childhood Education   46
  The Child-Care Movement   46
  Kindergarten   46
  Head Start   47
  Programs for Children with Special Needs   47
  Early Intervention Programs   49

Contemporary Models of Early Childhood Programs   49
   The Montessori Model   50
   The Behaviorist Model   57
   The Constructivist Model   60
   Summaries and Comparisons   69

Research on Program Models   70

CHILDREN WITH SPECIAL NEEDS   72

CELEBRATING DIVERSITY   73

SUMMARY   73

REFLECTIONS   74

EXPLORATIONS AND ACTIVITIES   75

CHAPTER **3**

Creating an Environment for Learning   **76**

Planning a Learning Environment   78

Structuring the Physical Environment   79
   Room Arrangement   80
   Physical Climate   82
   Assessing the Environment   83

Instructional Materials   85
   Learning Areas   87
   Beginning the Year   94
   Managing Learning Areas   94

Planning the Outdoor Environment   96

Planning for Safety—Inside and Out   98

CHILDREN WITH SPECIAL NEEDS   101

CELEBRATING DIVERSITY   102

SUMMARY   102

REFLECTIONS   103

EXPLORATIONS AND ACTIVITIES   103

CHAPTER **4**

Planning Learning Activities   **104**

Curriculum Design   106

Curriculum Organization   108

Developmentally Appropriate Curriculum   108
   Rationale for an Integrated Curriculum   110
   Selecting a Theme   111
   Implementing the Theme   112
   Evaluating the Theme   114

Learning Plans   116
   Mandated Lessons and Goals   118
   Multicultural Education and Antibias Curriculum   119

Computers in Early Childhood Programs   122
    Teaching and Learning with Computers   124
    Young Children Online   126
Scheduling   128
    Details of the Schedule   129
    Simplifying Routines   133
    Adapting the Schedule   133
    Kindergarten: Half-Day, Full-Day, and Alternate-Day
      Programs   134
    Other Scheduling Issues   134
    CHILDREN WITH SPECIAL NEEDS   135
    CELEBRATING DIVERSITY   136
SUMMARY   137
REFLECTIONS   138
EXPLORATIONS AND ACTIVITIES   139

CHAPTER **5**

Play: Learning at Its Best   **140**

Defining Play   142
    Types of Play   142
    Characteristics of Play   142
    Levels of Play   144
Purposes of Play   148
    Intellectual Development   148
    Social and Emotional Development   150
    Physical Development   150
Development of Play Behaviors   151
    Infancy   151
    Preschool   151
    Early Primary Grades   151
    Middle Childhood   152
Play in School Settings   153
    Roles of the Teacher   156
    Play in Primary Classrooms   157
    Benefits of Play at School   158
    Selecting Materials for Play   159
    Play as a Teaching Strategy   160
    Communicating the Benefits of Play   162
    Play and Academic Learning   164
Outdoor Play   167
    CHILDREN WITH SPECIAL NEEDS   168
    CELEBRATING DIVERSITY   170
SUMMARY   171
REFLECTIONS   172
EXPLORATIONS AND ACTIVITIES   172

CHAPTER 6

Guiding Behavior   174

Defining Discipline, Punishment, and Guidance   176
Punishment   177
Guidance   177

Planning for Guidance in the Classroom   178
Preventing Behavior Problems   180

Strategies for Guiding Behavior   186
Teaching Skills and Behaviors   186
Guiding Groups   188
Making Guidance Decisions   190

Behavior-Management Systems   192
Assertive Discipline   192
Glasser Model   195
Ginott Model   195
Dreikurs Model   195
Assessing Behavior-Management Systems   196

CHILDREN WITH SPECIAL NEEDS   197

CELEBRATING DIVERSITY   198

SUMMARY   198

REFLECTIONS   199

EXPLORATIONS AND ACTIVITIES   199

CHAPTER 7

Assessment and Reporting   200

Defining Assessment and Testing   202
Types of Assessment   203
Types of Tests   203

Testing Young Children   204
High-Stakes Testing   205
No Child Left Behind (NCLB) Act   206

Strategies for Assessment   207
Tallies   207
Running Narratives or Logs   208
Incident Records   208
Narratives   209
Anecdotal Records   210
Checklists and Rating Scales   213
Records of Conversations, Conferences, and Interviews   214
Rubrics   215
Parent Questionnaires   217
Self-Evaluations   217

Organizing Assessment Data   217
Portfolios   219

Reporting Assessment Data   223
Report Cards   223
Conferences   225

Student-Led Conferences   228
Narrative Reports   228
Telephone Calls   229
Casual Conversations   229
Newsletters   229
Videotapes   229
Evaluating Assessment and Reporting   229

Program Assessment   230

■ CHILDREN WITH SPECIAL NEEDS   231

■ CELEBRATING DIVERSITY   232

SUMMARY   233

REFLECTIONS   234

EXPLORATIONS AND ACTIVITIES   234

CHAPTER **8**

Working with Parents and Paraprofessionals   **236**

Parent Involvement   238
Realities of Parent–Teacher Relationships   238
Implications for Teachers   239

Encouraging Parent Involvement   240
Strategies for Teachers and Schools   240
Parent Roles   242
Activities for Involving Parents   244

Communicating with Parents   246
School Handbooks   246
Home Visits   247
Parent Visits to School   248
Letters and Notes   251
Telecommunication   252
Community Resources   253

Volunteers in the Classroom   253

Working with Paraprofessionals   256

■ CHILDREN WITH SPECIAL NEEDS   260

■ CELEBRATING DIVERSITY   262

SUMMARY   262

REFLECTIONS   263

EXPLORATIONS AND ACTIVITIES   263

PART TWO: THE CURRICULUM CHAPTERS   265

CHAPTER **9**

Celebrating the Magic of Language   **266**

Defining Language   268
Characteristics of Language   268

    Systems of Language   268

Learning Language   271
    Sequence of Language Development   272
    Theoretical Models of Language Learning   273

Teaching Language   276
    Creating an Effective Environment   276
    Standards for Language Development   282
    Observing Language Learners   283
    Providing Activities That Encourage Language Growth   283

CHILDREN WITH SPECIAL NEEDS   289

CELEBRATING DIVERSITY   293

SUMMARY   299

REFLECTIONS   301

EXPLORATIONS AND ACTIVITIES   301

CHAPTER **10**

Developing Literacy   302

Defining Literacy   304

Teacher Qualities That Support Literacy   304
    Evaluating the Research   304
    Understanding How Literacy Develops   305
    Standards for Reading Teachers   309

Program Elements That Support Literacy   309
    Goals for Literacy Instruction   311
    Standards for Literacy Development   312
    Providing a Supportive Classroom Environment   314
    Oral Language and Listening Skills   315
    Music as a Literacy Activity   316
    Reading Aloud and Storytelling   317
    Learning about Print   319
    Attending to Sound   319
    Presenting Selected Text   324
    Commercial Programs for Literacy Instruction   326
    Helping All Children Feel Successful as Literacy Learners   327

Learning to Write   329
    Development of Writing   329
    Conventions of Written Language   334
    The Writing Process with Young Children   335

Assessing the Development of Literacy   337
    Observing Oral Language   337
    Observing Writing   337
    Determining Knowledge of Books and Print   339
    Observing Reading   339

CHILDREN WITH SPECIAL NEEDS   340

CELEBRATING DIVERSITY   341

SUMMARY   345

REFLECTIONS   345

EXPLORATIONS AND ACTIVITIES   346

CHAPTER 11

Manipulation and Discovery through Mathematics

348

Defining Mathematics   350
Learning Mathematics   350
Teaching Mathematics   352
  Standards for Mathematics Education   353
  The Strand Model   354
Materials for Mathematics Instruction   372
  Manipulatives   372
  Calculators and Computers   374
Integrating Mathematics into the Curriculum   374
  Mathematics and Play   374
  Mathematics and Literacy   376
  Mathematics and Literature   378
Assessment of Mathematics   378
CHILDREN WITH SPECIAL NEEDS   380
CELEBRATING DIVERSITY   381
SUMMARY   382
REFLECTIONS   383
EXPLORATIONS AND ACTIVITIES   383

CHAPTER 12

Manipulation and Discovery through Science

384

Defining Science   386
Learning Science   386
  Manipulation, Observation, and Discovery   386
  The Scientific Process   388
Teaching Science   391
  Ensuring Safety   392
  Teaching Basic Concepts and Encouraging Positive Attitudes   393
  Planning the Sequence of Activities   393
  Standards for Science Education   395
Integrating Science into the Curriculum   405
  Science and Literacy   407
CHILDREN WITH SPECIAL NEEDS   410
CELEBRATING DIVERSITY   411
SUMMARY   411
REFLECTIONS   412
EXPLORATIONS AND ACTIVITIES   412

CHAPTER 13

Encouraging the Creative Arts   414

The Importance of Arts Experiences   416
Goals of Arts Education   417
Standards for Arts Education   419

Visual Arts   419
Stages in Development   420
Goals of Visual Arts Experiences   422
Standards for Visual Arts Education   424
Suggested Visual Arts Experiences   425
Art versus Craft Activities   427

Music   428
Goals of a Music Program   429
Standards for Music Education   430
Singing   431
Playing Instruments   433
Listening Experiences   434
Approaches to Music Instruction   434

Movement and Dance   436
Movement Experiences   436
Dance Education   437
Standards for Dance Education   437

Drama   438
Encouraging Drama   439
Standards for Drama Education   440

Roles of Specialists   441

Assessing Experiences in the Arts   442

Integrating the Arts into the Curriculum   443

CHILDREN WITH SPECIAL NEEDS   445

CELEBRATING DIVERSITY   448

SUMMARY   450

REFLECTIONS   450

EXPLORATIONS AND ACTIVITIES   451

CHAPTER 14

Living Together: The Social Studies   452

Defining Social Studies   454

Learning Social Studies   455
A Constructivist View   455

Teaching Social Studies   456
Multiple Views of the Social Studies Curriculum   456
Current Expectations   461
Standards for Social Studies Education   462
Planning Social Studies Experiences   464

Integrating Social Studies into the Curriculum   468
Social Studies Themes   470

Celebrating Holidays 472

▨ CHILDREN WITH SPECIAL NEEDS 477

▨ CELEBRATING DIVERSITY 477

SUMMARY 478

REFLECTIONS 479

EXPLORATIONS AND ACTIVITIES 479

CHAPTER **15**

Promoting Wellness: Physical Education and Health, Nutrition, and Safety Education **480**

Physical Education 482
Encouraging Motor Development 482
Goals of Physical Development Programs 484
Standards for Physical Education 486
Physical Education Activities 487

Health, Nutrition, and Safety Education 490
Health Education 490
Nutrition Education 494
Safety Education 498

Integrating Physical Education and Health, Nutrition, and Safety Education into the Curriculum 503

▨ CHILDREN WITH SPECIAL NEEDS 504

▨ CELEBRATING DIVERSITY 505

SUMMARY 506

REFLECTIONS 507

EXPLORATIONS AND ACTIVITIES 507

Glossary 509

Resources for Further Reading 515

Children's Books 523

References 526

Index 545

Features

DEVELOPMENTALLY APPROPRIATE PRACTICE

Young Children Growing, Thinking, and Learning   32
Designing Schools for Young Children   71
Creating an Environment for Learning   93
Planning Learning Activities   116
Play: Learning at Its Best   155
Guiding Behavior   184
Assessment and Reporting   226
Working with Parents and Paraprofessionals   258
Celebrating the Magic of Language   294
Developing Literacy   324

Manipulation and Discovery through Mathematics   354
Manipulation and Discovery through Science   403
Encouraging the Creative Arts   443
Living Together: The Social Studies   474
Promoting Wellness: Physical Education and Health, Nutrition, and Safety Education   492

INTEGRATING THE CURRICULUM

Language-Learning Activities   289
Literacy Experiences   340
Mathematical Experiences   375

Science Activities   408
Art Experiences   444
Social Studies Experiences   469
Wellness Experiences   503

LEARNING PLAN

Teaching Classification Skills to Three- and Four-Year-Olds   117
Teaching Measurement and Descriptive Writing Skills to Six- and Seven-Year-Olds   118
Teaching How to Recognize and Use Descriptive Words to Six- and Seven-Year-Olds   119
Teaching Discrimination of Plane Geometric Shapes to Prekindergarten and Kindergarten Children   162

Vocabulary Development for Grades 1–2   286
A Learning Plan on Writing: First Grade   334
Displaying and Analyzing Data: Grade Two   370
Writing Cinquains in First- or Second-Grade Science   409
Exploring Artists and Their Styles: First- and Second-Graders   428
Social Studies for Kindergarteners   466
Creating a Class Cookbook: First Grade   499

A **Teacher** SPEAKS

Using Developmental Knowledge in Planning 34
Darla Wood-Walters, *Elk Meadow Elementary, Bend, Oregon*

Montessori Schools 56
Cary Williams, *Keystone Montessori School, North Chelmsford, Massachusetts*

Planning the Classroom Environment 86
Kate McLaughlin, *Demonstration School, Lowell, Massachusetts*

Planning for Success 120
Beth Peter, *Neill Elementary School, Burnsville, Minnesota*

Respecting Children's Play 165
Megbe Hughes, *Isidore Newman School, New Orleans, Louisiana*

Helping Children Learn to Manage Their Own Behavior 181
Rick Coxen, *Pringle Elementary, Salem-Keizer District, Oregon*
Pam Coxen, *James R. Schirle Elementary, Salem-Keizer District, Oregon*

Assessment Practices for Primary-Age Children 224
Mary Giard, *Center for Teaching and Learning, Edgecomb, Maine*

The Relationship between Teachers and Teaching Assistants 261
Margaret Egenhoefer, *Dixon Elementary School, New Berlin, Wisconsin*

Teaching Content and Language Together 300
Jennifer Rosholt, *Stevenson Elementary School, Seattle, Washington*

Reading in the Literacy Classroom 338
Sandy Bjorklund, *Madison Camelview School, Phoenix, Arizona*

A Kindergarten Teacher's Approach to Mathematics Assessment 381
Karen Yourd, *Bon Meade Elementary School, Moon Township, Pennsylvania*

Engaging First-Graders in Science 391
Pamela Pottle, *Happy Valley Elementary School, Bellingham, Washington*

Integrating Art and Social Studies 446
Carol Schroeder, *Town Center Elementary, Plainsboro, New Jersey*

Promoting the Home–School Connection 473
Emilie Rodger, *Sedona Elementary School, Sedona, Arizona*

Doing It All 506
Ellen Bissallion, *Perley Elementary School, Georgetown, Massachusetts*

AN **Expert** SPEAKS

Computers in the Early Childhood Program 128
Suzanne Thouvenelle, *Johns Hopkins University*

Instruction for English Language Learners 137
Jana Echevarria, *California State University, Long Beach*

Play at School 153
Jim Johnson, *Pennsylvania State University*

Guidance Personified: Liberation Teaching 193
Dan Gartrell, *Bemidji State University, Minnesota*

Assessment in Early Childhood Education 218
Ann Benjamin, *University of Massachusetts Lowell*

Involving All Parents 254
Michaela Wyman-Colombo, *University of Massachusetts Lowell*

Bilingual Education 297
Jim Cummins, *University of Toronto*

Becoming Literate 328
Mary Renck Jalongo, *Indiana University of Philadelphia*

Let's Face the Facts 362
Susan Sperry Smith, *Cardinal Stritch University*

Science Education 406
Gregory Potter, *University of the Pacific*

Art in the Curriculum 418
Susan Wright, *Queensland University of Technology*

The Social Studies 463
Carol Seefeldt, *University of Maryland*

The Immediate and Long-Term Benefits of Recess 489
Judith Kieff, *University of New Orleans*

Preface

Being an early childhood teacher has never been easy and, as I have said in the prefaces of previous editions, it continues to be a challenging and complex task. More teachers teach more children who are poor, who speak languages other than English, who have social and emotional needs that reflect the stress on modern families, and who are trying to cope with the social changes of life today. It is the skill, knowledge, and dedication of our teachers that give us hope for the future of this country.

Teachers of young children have always needed a solid foundation of knowledge on which to base their educational decisions. They have to know about children and their development, about learning and how it takes place, and about the content of the academic disciplines and how to make it accessible to young learners. In addition, early childhood teachers must work sensitively with families and communities that are diverse in many different ways. And as if these demands were not enough, today's teachers of young children also must cope with the pressures of testing and the decisions that are made based on test results.

If the challenges are enormous, then so are the rewards of helping children as they learn about themselves and their communities and as they develop a concept of themselves as successful learners.

Plan for the Text

This book defines *early childhood* as the period from birth through age eight and focuses on the school experiences of children in this age range. The early childhood years are more important than any other eight-year period in the life of a human being in terms of the learning that occurs, the attitudes about learning and school that develop, and the social skills that are acquired that will enable the individual to succeed in today's world. The problems of the future will be solved by today's children only if they value learning, know how to cooperate with others, and appreciate a democratic way of life. Teachers can help young children develop these attitudes and skills.

The primary goal of this text is to provide a comprehensive knowledge base for teachers of young children so they can make decisions that are founded on more than educational traditions and their own experiences as students. This text is also designed to encourage early childhood teachers to consider the child, the family, and the community when planning experiences for each individual. Finally, this text will help readers prepare for the Praxis exam, which some states require teachers pass before they can become certified. The content of each chapter reflects the newest standards and research coupled with practical suggestions and activities.

This book is organized into two main parts. The first eight chapters, which comprise Part I, are grouped as foundational chapters and thus offer basic information that guides good teaching practice:

- Chapter 1 gives a brief overview of child development. This material is presented first in the text because knowing about how children's growth and development are related to providing appropriate experiences for them is basic to teaching young children.

- Chapter 2 provides a historical context for the schools of today and describes what are currently the most common approaches to early childhood education, including the Reggio Emilia schools of Italy.

- Chapter 3 offers guidelines for making good decisions when planning learning environments for children.

- Chapter 4 provides suggestions for planning appropriate learning activities and experiences.

- Chapter 5 focuses on play and the critical role it has in how young children learn.

- Chapter 6 explores the topic of discipline, with the emphasis on guiding children's behavior and teaching them self-control.

- Chapter 7 on assessment has sections on observing young children, including techniques for recording observations (including electronic recording) and using them to inform instruction. Observation, assessment, and reporting are discussed as complementary processes. Information on the No Child Left Behind Act has been added to this chapter.

- Chapter 8 offers strategies for promoting parent involvement and for working well with paraprofessionals and volunteers in the classroom.

Part II is comprised of Chapters 9 through 15, which are the content-area chapters:

- Chapter 9 highlights the development of language and the strategies for incorporating language development into all elements of a program.

- Because literacy is a critical component in today's early childhood programs, Chapter 10 offers brief overviews of the various programs designed for teaching literacy that are common in modern schools. It also discusses phonics and phonemic awareness and how children develop as readers and writers.

- In Chapters 11 and 12, the mathematics and science chapters (respectively), the emphasis is on hands-on activities that are intellectually challenging for and interesting to children.
- Chapter 13 addresses four areas of the arts: visual arts, music, movement and dance, and drama. Goals are considered for planning instruction in each of these areas, and a range of developmentally appropriate activities are provided.
- Chapter 14, on social studies, presents multiple views of the social studies curriculum and recommends how to plan relevant social studies experiences for young children.
- Chapter 15 discusses three areas related to the wellness of young children: physical education and health, nutrition, and safety education.

Each of these chapters considers the place of this content area in the early childhood curriculum. New to this edition is information about the professional standards established for each content area, which are intended to provide a framework for curriculum planning.

Even though the content areas are presented in separate chapters, the emphasis is always on designing an integrated, meaningful curriculum. To that end, each of the content chapters contains a section on integrating the curriculum around a theme. The theme illustrated in this edition is *spaces*. It was selected because it connects with all the major content areas in meaningful ways and because children are quite interested in exploring spaces, both natural and humanmade. Each chapter provides suggestions for connecting the content to the theme of *spaces;* even so, the expectation is that the teacher will find many more ways to help children make connections through a meaningful curriculum.

Many activities appropriate for children of various ages are recommended throughout the text, and these activities have been tried by real teachers in real classrooms. They are presented not as isolated units or events (something to do on Monday) but as applications of theory. When teachers understand theory, they can design their own learning activities and evaluate other activities presented in the many publications aimed at teachers of young children.

Included at the end of the book are four useful sections:

- The **Glossary** lists key terms along with their definitions. Each chapter opens with a list of the key terms found within it, and the terms are bolded in the text where they are discussed.
- The **Resources for Further Reading** includes individual chapter lists of sources of additional information, each related to the content of that chapter. Useful annotations identify the key features of the sources. By using these lists, readers can begin to build their own professional libraries.
- The **References** section lists the professional works and children's literature cited and discussed in the text.
- A comprehensive **Index** provides ready access to specific topics covered in the text.

Features of This Edition

The features of this sixth edition of *Early Childhood Education* reflect the many challenges faced by teachers of young children in today's world:

◄ Developmentally Appropriate Practice

In this edition, as well as in previous editions, the goal has been to help readers view *developmentally appropriate practice (DAP)* as the process of choosing learning experiences that are individually appropriate for each child, that recognize the strengths of each learner, and that involve children actively in their own learning. In each chapter, readers are presented with a **Developmentally Appropriate Practice** box that asks them to respond to questions or statements designed to help build a strong understanding of DAP and what it means when implemented in the classroom setting.

◄ Integrating the Curriculum

Another focus of this text has been to demonstrate the importance of integrating subjects within the early childhood curriculum. As mentioned earlier, the theme of *spaces* is developed in each content-area chapter (Chapters 9 through 15) in a feature called **Integrating the Curriculum.** This feature demonstrates that any well-chosen topic can incorporate all the content areas and that young children learn best when the experiences and activities planned for them are not divided into discrete subject-matter areas.

A Teacher Speaks ►

All the chapters have boxed pieces called **A Teacher Speaks.** Written by practicing teachers, these pieces reflect the day-to-day realities of working with real children in real classrooms. Each piece is introduced with one or more questions or suggestions to help readers reflect on the content of the essay. The goal is to make these pieces more interactive for readers. Hearing the thoughts and advice of seasoned professionals will give readers new perspective on the chapter content. Except for length, these pieces have not been edited, so their authors have freely expressed their opinions.

An Expert Speaks ➤

Similarly, most chapters have boxed pieces called **An Expert Speaks,** written by established professionals. Like the "Teacher" boxes, each of these expert essays is introduced with a question or a suggestion that helps readers become engaged in the content. And again, except for length, these pieces have not been edited.

Parents Sidebars ➤

Short **Parents** boxes, found throughout each chapter, provide suggestions for teachers on communicating with the parents of children in their classrooms. Although such communication has always been the responsibility of teachers, it can no longer be discharged simply by sending home report cards every six weeks. These boxes offer innovative ways to help parents understand what is happening at school and why.

AN **Expert** SPEAKS: Let's Face the Facts
Susan Sperry Smith
Cardinal Stritch University

[expert essay text partially obscured]

Parents and School Design
● Provide parents and other visitors to your school with references for articles or books that support your program philosophy and perhaps explain the differences between your program and others.

Children with Special Needs ➤

Near the end of each chapter, a section entitled **Children with Special Needs** relates the given chapter content to teaching children with a variety of disabilities and exceptionalities, ranging from language delays to physical limitations.

CHILDREN WITH SPECIAL NEEDS

In response to Public Law 94-142 and the extension of this law by Public Law 99-457, most children with special needs are now enrolled in regular classes. The enrollment in these *inclusive classes* is typically about one-half children with special needs and about one-half typically developing children. Often, the total enrollment for an inclusive class is lower than that for a class at the same level that is not inclusive. Teachers of inclusive classes are often teamed to include a teacher certified in special needs education and a regular classroom teacher, at least for part of the day.

The premise underlying inclusion is that all children will benefit from the interaction. Namely, typically developing children will serve as models

Celebrating Diversity ➤

Following the Children with Special Needs section is a section entitled **Celebrating Diversity,** which encourages teachers of young children to think about the benefits of diversity in their classrooms and to ensure that they are sensitive to the diversity in their schools and communities.

CELEBRATING DIVERSITY

Being responsive to children's diverse needs is a goal of almost all programs. Some programs would argue that meeting the needs of each child would, by definition, mean meeting the needs of children from diverse backgrounds. Other programs might argue that equipping children with the skills and abilities they need to succeed in mainstream schools is the best outcome for any child, regardless of cultural or ethnic differences. Teachers of young children must learn about the individuals in their programs and make the best programming decisions possible to help all children learn and develop in the best ways for them.

Until 1954, when the U.S. Supreme Court ruled in *Brown v. Board of Education* that "separate but equal" schools were not equal and that schools had to be racially integrated, most children of color attended segregated schools. Although some school districts have "resegregated" themselves by tracking students or creating neighborhood schools, the classrooms of today are much more diverse than at any time in U.S. history (Kozol 2005). Not too long ago, most teachers in the United States could expect to teach in schools that were somewhat homogeneous in terms of cultural background. That is no longer true. Not only do public schools today enroll children from all racial and ethnic groups, but most also enroll many children whose first

A second group of features will help readers understand the organization and content of each chapter:

Young Children Growing, Thinking, and Learning

When you enrolled in the program to become a teacher of young children, you knew that you had much to learn about planning activities for children, keeping records of children's progress, and handling all the other responsibilities of a teacher. You were pleased when your first observation was to be focused on children's growth and development because that seemed to you to be basic information that every teacher would need to know.

You selected a second-grade classroom in a school where the population was diverse and the school was in a low socioeconomic area of the city. After your observation, when you looked over your notes, you found many indicators of development in all areas. The children in this classroom exhibited their physical development through skillful ball throwing and catching, jumping rope, hanging by their knees from bars, and other physical skills. They also had the fine motor skills to make writing, drawing, and painting easy for them to manage. You noted evidence of social growth as children settled a disagreement about who was responsible for cleaning up the art center by talking about their points of view and listening to one another's perception of the problem. You noted that indications of frustration or anger were rare in this classroom. You also found that these children could attend to a task for an extended period of time. You watched in amazement as they worked on their research projects for an hour.

◀ **Chapter-Opening Vignette**

Each chapter opens with a **vignette** that asks readers to imagine visiting a classroom to observe and then to regroup with classmates to discuss what everyone has seen. The vignette engages readers in the content of the text that follows.

Focus Questions ▶

Focus Questions preview the main sections in the chapter. Reviewing these questions will give readers an overview of the chapter content. The answers to these questions, presented as concise bulleted points, can be found in the chapter-ending Summary.

FOCUS QUESTIONS

● What is *developmentally appropriate practice (DAP)?*

● What are the five major theories that describe child growth and development?

● What patterns make up the physical, social, emotional, and intellectual development of young children?

● How can knowledge about child development be used to identify children with special needs?

● What is the relationship between child development and diversity?

3

KEY TERMS you'll find in this chapter:

- Cognitive development, 29
- Developmentally appropriate practice (DAP), 4
- Early childhood, 4
- Ecological systems theory, 13
- Maturationist theory, 7
- Metaknowledge, 9
- Multiple intelligences theory, 10
- Operant conditioning, 6
- Social learning theory, 12
- Stimulus-response theory, 6
- Zone of proximal development (ZPD), 10

◀ **Key Terms**

Each chapter opening also includes a list of **Key Terms** that identifies the primary topics of the chapter along with new vocabulary. So that readers can look at each term in context, the page number on which the bolded term will be found is included in this list. As noted earlier, all the terms are defined in the Glossary at the end of the text.

Reflections *and* Explorations and Activities ➤

New to this edition are chapter-ending sections called **Reflections** and **Explorations and Activities.** The Reflections questions engage students in critical thinking, asking them to consider, for instance, possible practice situations or dilemmas. The Explorations and Activities involve hands-on classroom experience and are appropriate both for teachers and student teachers.

REFLECTIONS

1. Explain how knowing about the history of early childhood education can help teachers recognize the roots of various program goals and activities.
2. Describe the three major models of early childhood programs currently found in the United States, and explain the strengths and weaknesses of each.
3. From your understanding of the research on program models, what conclusions can you draw and apply in making the best curriculum decisions for your own classroom?
4. Which of the models do you think fits your vision of teaching and school most closely? Why?
5. Is there a best model of early childhood education that every school should endorse? If so, what is it and why is it the best? If not, why?

My LabSchool ➤

Each chapter ends with a reference to **MyLabSchool,** an online collection of tools that will aid readers not only in completing their coursework but in taking licensure exams and practicing as early childhood educators.

mylabschool

MyLabSchool is a collection of online tools for your success in this course, your licensure exams, and your teaching career. Visit **www.mylabschool.com** to access the following:

■ Online Study Guide
■ Video Cases from real classrooms
■ Help with your research papers using Research Navigator
■ Career Center with resources for:
  —Praxis and Licensure Preparation
  —Professional Portfolio Development
  —Job Search and Interview Techniques
  —Lesson Planning

Finally, three types of marginal notes have been added to this edition to flag materials for readers:

NAEYC Criteria Correlations ➤

Notes labeled **NAEYC Criteria** identify the relevant performance criteria from the program standards of the National Association for the Education of Young Children (NAEYC). Specifically, each note provides the number or numbers of the criteria that pertain to the topic being discussed in the adjacent text. The full text of the NAEYC standards is available from that organization.

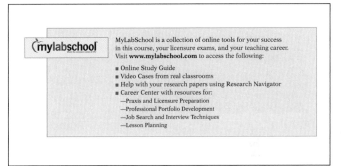

NAEYC CRITERIA
3.6, 3.7, 3.8

WWW.

http://teacher.scholastic.com/ products/ect/froebel.htm

Part of a series on the Roots of Education; provides a biography of Froebel and a description of his work

Annotated Website Addresses ➤

Marginal notes also identify **websites** that are relevant to the topic at hand. Along with the web address is a short description of what the site provides. Readers can use these notes to find more information about the topics presented in text.

PRAXIS

Be able to explain the importance of transitions and routines in meeting the needs of young children

Praxis Preparation ➤

As often as possible, marginal notes are used to align the examples in the chapters with the **Praxis** exam. This gives readers the opportunity to think about the questions that are asked on the exam and how they might answer them.

Supplements to the Text

To get the most use out of *Introduction to Early Childhood Education: Preschool through Primary Grades,* sixth edition, a number of useful supplements are available for students and instructors. **Speak with your representative about obtaining these supplements for your class.**

- **Instructor's Manual with Test Bank** An instructor's manual with test questions is available to adopters of this text.
- **Companion Website** Found at www.ablongman.com/brewer6e, this site provides weblinks, essay questions, and practice tests for each chapter.
- **Power Point™ Presentation** Designed around the framework of the sixth edition text, these slides may be downloaded by adopters.
- **MyLabSchool** Where the classroom comes to life! With videoclips of teachers and students interacting, sample lessons, a portfolio and lesson builder tool with state and national standards, and hundreds of articles from major journals, MyLabSchool provides resources students need to succeed in the education field.

Every teacher makes important decisions every day. This book is designed to help teachers of young children make wise decisions that will benefit the children they teach and, therefore, all of us.

Acknowledgments

No book can be completed without the work of many people, and this one is no exception. Many teachers have helped me with ideas and offered me opportunities to be in their classrooms. I wish that I could list all their names, but I cannot. I also want to thank all my students, who push me to think of new ways to explain concepts and see applications of theory in the classroom. I am also grateful for the contributions of the various people who wrote the An Expert Speaks pieces and the classroom teachers who contributed A Teacher Speaks pieces for this edition. There is no reward for doing this work other than my appreciation and the knowledge that they are helping other teachers.

The editorial staff at Allyn and Bacon also has provided support and encouragement at every stage of producing this book. I wish especially to thank Kelly Canton for her work in guiding and supporting the publication of this sixth edition and Sue Freese who did an outstanding job as development editor.

Without the help of reviewers, it would be difficult to choose direction and focus for a new edition; therefore, I am very appreciative of the work of the reviewers who helped with this edition: Funsho Akingbala, the University of Texas at Austin; Susan Johnston, University of Utah; Barbara Morgan-Fleming, Texas Tech University; Josie Rivera, University of Houston–Victoria; and Barbara Weiserbs, Kingsborough Community College.

Finally, I appreciate the love and support of my husband and colleague, Bill Harp. Bill keeps the household running and is always generous with his advice and praise.

PART I

Foundations of Early Childhood Learning

The beginning chapters of this book (Chapters 1 through 8) are designed to help you develop a knowledge base about children, schools, families, guidance, and play. These chapters are also intended to help you develop the basic concepts of planning and assessing a program for young children.

As you begin your career as a teacher of young children, you will join a profession that has a long history and you will recognize the historical roots of many ideas about how children think and learn. You must have knowledge of child development in order to plan appropriately for any child in your program. Your planning also will be influenced by what you know about the cultural backgrounds of the children and their families.

The most successful programs have the strongest foundations: knowledgeable teachers, carefully designed places in which children can learn, and families that both feel supported and can support their children. Going to school is a big step in the life of any child. You can make it a successful and happy experience for the children and yourself.

CHAPTER 1

KEY TERMS you'll find in this chapter:

- Cognitive development, 29
- Developmentally appropriate practice (DAP), 4
- Early childhood, 4
- Ecological systems theory, 13
- Maturationist theory, 7
- Metaknowledge, 9
- Multiple intelligences theory, 10
- Operant conditioning, 6
- Social learning theory, 12
- Stimulus-response theory, 6
- Zone of proximal development (ZPD), 10

Young Children Growing, Thinking, and Learning

FOCUS QUESTIONS

- What is *developmentally appropriate practice (DAP)?*

- What are the five major theories that describe child growth and development?

- What patterns make up the physical, social, emotional, and intellectual development of young children?

- How can knowledge about child development be used to identify children with special needs?

- What is the relationship between child development and diversity?

When you enrolled in the program to become a teacher of young children, you knew that you had much to learn about planning activities for children, keeping records of children's progress, and handling all the other responsibilities of a teacher. You were pleased when your first observation was to be focused on children's growth and development because that seemed to you to be basic information that every teacher would need to know.

You selected a second-grade classroom in a school where the population was diverse and the school was in a low socio-economic area of the city. After your observation, when you looked over your notes, you found many indicators of development in all areas. The children in this classroom exhibited their physical development through skillful ball throwing and catching, jumping rope, hanging by their knees from bars, and other physical skills. They also had the fine motor skills to make writing, drawing, and painting easy for them to manage. You noted evidence of social growth as children settled a disagreement about who was responsible for cleaning up the art center by talking about their points of view and listening to one another's perception of the problem. You noted that indications of frustration or anger were rare in this classroom. You also found that these children could attend to a task for an extended period of time. You watched in amazement as they worked on their research projects for an hour.

When you talked with the teacher, she explained that for children ages seven and eight, she plans many activities that give the children a choice about what they will do to achieve a goal, she invites children to share their ideas and discoveries with one another, she plans regular sessions in which classroom problems are solved, and she is sensitive to the cultural expectations of the parents. She knows that second-graders still need to move around and talk to one another. ■

Developmentally Appropriate Practice

This chapter is meant to be a review of the principles of child development, not a comprehensive treatment of the topic. A basic knowledge of child development is critical to appropriate planning, teaching, and evaluating in programs for young children. Just as we would never plan a meal or vacation without knowing something about the ages and tastes of the participants, we cannot plan curricula without knowing what children of a given age will likely be able to do and be interested in doing.

The National Association for the Education of Young Children (NAEYC) defines **early childhood** as the period from birth to age eight (Bredekamp 1987). Some child-care programs serve infants and toddlers as well as pre-schoolers (three- and four-year-olds) and primary children (five-, six-, seven-, and eight-year-olds). Most of this chapter will discuss normal growth and development. Keep in mind that to determine the average age when a child is able to perform a task or behave in a certain way, some children must perform that task earlier than the average and some later than the average.

You will meet many children in your teaching career who have special needs, ranging from severe mental or physical challenges to slight delays in the development of language. You also will meet children who are gifted and talented in a variety of ways, who have attention deficits, and who are wise beyond their years in relating to people. Children come in all sizes, colors, and places on the developmental continuum. Our job as teachers is to recognize each child's abilities and growth and plan for the next steps as she grows physically, intellectually, socially, and emotionally.

The term **developmentally appropriate practice (DAP)** will be used throughout this book to mean practice that is age and individually appropriate for each child in a program. Planning a developmentally appropriate curriculum means that teachers have to know each child—where he is developmentally and what his individual talents and interests are. DAP also requires that teachers think about children's basic needs for play and rest, that they focus on children's development in all areas, that they plan an inclusive program that honors the cultural differences each child brings to school, and that they work to support parents and families (Bredekamp 1987, 1996).

Programs for young children can vary widely and still be considered DAP programs. However, some practices are not appropriate for young children. These practices include timed tests, a focus on academic skill devel-

www.
www.naeyc.org
Several statements about developmentally appropriate practice along with resources for teachers

A variety of developmentally appropriate toys should be provided in the preschool classroom.

opment through worksheets or workbooks, and a schedule that ignores a young child's need to move physically and expects her to sit for extended periods of time.

The chapters that follow will provide more detail about developmentally appropriate practice and ask you to reflect on what makes one choice developmentally appropriate and another inappropriate. Please remember that although some basic guidelines help define DAP, in classrooms across the United States, DAP looks quite different. DAP requires that teachers and children work continuously to determine the best practice for a group of children at a given time. DAP is dynamic, not static. It cannot be the same for all children or all groups of children.

The purpose of this chapter is to review briefly some theoretical lenses through which child development is seen and to outline typical patterns of development. This knowledge is most useful when it can be consciously applied to selecting and organizing curriculum experiences. Often, teachers choose activities and organize those activities in ways that can be traced to the different theories of child growth and development, but they are unaware of these connections. As a teacher, you need to recognize why you choose one activity over another or one organizational scheme over another.

Theories of Development

Children's growth and development can be described from several theoretical points of view. Each of these points of view has its supporters among practitioners in early childhood education, and each offers explanations of human growth and development. These theoretical positions include behaviorism, maturationism, constructivism, multiple intelligences theory,

Parents and Development

● Each month, find an article on some aspect of child development related to the age of children you teach. Make the article available to parents by summarizing it in the class newsletter or letting those who are interested check it out.

social learning theory, and ecological systems theory. Throughout your career, as you read and think about children and about planning programs that will be beneficial to them, reflect on the points of view expressed by authors of articles and reports, and notice how their suggestions differ depending on what they believe about children's development.

Behaviorist Theory

www.
www.sil.org/lingualinks/
literacy/implement
ALiteracy/Behaviorist
TheoriesofLearning.htm

Information and links to resources on behaviorism and its important theorists

www.
http://web.cocc.edu/cbuell/
theories/behaviorism.htm

More information about behaviorism

PRAXIS

Be able to describe various theories of child development

Behaviorist theory suggests that behavior can be shaped by the response that follows any particular action. John B. Watson (1878–1958), Edward Thorndike (1874–1949), and B. F. Skinner (1904–1990) are well-known behaviorists.

Skinner is the best known of the modern behaviorists. He wrote extensively about learning as controlled by a system of rewards and punishments. His name is synonymous with the terms **stimulus-response theory** and **operant conditioning** (W. F. Hill 1977). The basic elements of stimulus-response theory include reinforcements, punishments, operant conditioning, and extinguishing behavior.

In *classical conditioning*, a learner is presented with a stimulus and a reward and learns to expect the reward whenever the stimulus is presented. This type of conditioning is exemplified by the classic Pavlovian experiment of ringing a bell and immediately presenting a dog with food until the dog salivates at the sound of the bell. *Operant conditioning* differs from classical conditioning in that the behavior precedes the reinforcement. For example, a pigeon may learn to push a lever to get a food pellet. Presenting a reward after a response provides positive reinforcement of the behavior. Negative reinforcement can also be used to elicit behavior. If the floor of the pigeon's cage were electrified and pushing the lever stopped the shock, the pigeon would learn to press the lever to avoid an unpleasant stimulus; that is negative reinforcement. Behavior can also be punished rather than reinforced. A pigeon might be punished by an electric shock for failing to push a lever on a set schedule.

In the classroom, reinforcements are often used to shape behaviors. Reinforcements in the classroom can be positive or negative. A *positive reinforcement* is something the learner views as desirable. If a child completes a task or exhibits a behavior that is desirable, the teacher may positively reinforce that behavior by verbal praise, a token such as a sticker, or some other treat. *Negative reinforcement* involves allowing a child to avoid or escape from an undesirable consequence or situation if certain behaviors are exhibited. For example, the teacher might give a child the option of leaving the "time-out" chair more quickly if she does not talk at all for five minutes. Finally, *punishment* in the classroom need not necessarily be corporal (physical) punishment but can be time-outs, exclusion from the group, withdrawal of privileges, and so on.

In a classroom, operant conditioning might be used to shape children's performance on an academic task. For example, suppose a class of second-graders has been assigned the task of completing twenty arithmetic problems. Those children who complete the task promptly and correctly get tokens, which can be redeemed for objects in the class store on Friday. With those children who do not complete the task either promptly or correctly, the teacher may take one of several approaches. If he knows that three of the children have never completed twenty problems, he may choose to reward their performance if they complete more than they have completed before. He may choose to provide neither positive nor negative reinforcement to children who complete the same number of problems they have completed in the past. If he believes that some children deliberately did not attempt the task for some reason, he might punish them by reducing their recess time.

Operant conditioning can be used to shape behavior by providing reinforcements when the learner's behavior moves closer to the target behavior. Shaping behavior involves the following components (Pellegrini 1987):

1. targeting the desired behavior
2. fixing a behavioral baseline
3. selecting reinforcers
4. analyzing the task and sequencing the segments
5. systematically applying the reinforcers (p. 113)

In the classroom example just discussed, by rewarding a child who completes more problems than in previous assignments, the teacher is rewarding closer approximations to the target behavior of completing twenty problems. Teachers often use such techniques to help children gain control of their classroom behaviors. If a child is hitting other children, for example, the teacher will first collect baseline data through observations to determine how often the child is hitting and then provide rewards as the hitting behavior decreases.

Behaviors can be extinguished by failing to provide reinforcements for them. If a child is behaving in ways the teacher deems inappropriate, then the teacher can ignore the less desirable behaviors while consistently rewarding the more desirable behaviors.

The goal of employing behavioristic techniques is for the desired behavior to become rewarding to the child so that the teacher or parent need not continue to provide extrinsic rewards. Most teachers, even those who believe strongly in other theories of development employ some behavioristic strategies as they ignore some behaviors and praise others. Most teachers have had experience with children who prefer negative attention—that is, punishment—to no attention; the usual strategy for dealing with such children is to make every effort to ignore their misbehavior and to reward their appropriate behavior.

Behaviorist theory does not say much about physical development because most authorities agree that physical development is genetically determined and thus does not affect a child's behavior, at least in an optimal environment that includes good nutrition, lack of disease, and safety. Behaviorists are more concerned with how children develop socially, emotionally, and intellectually.

Maturationist Theory

The roots of the **maturationist theory** are found in the work of Jean-Jacques Rousseau (1712–1778), who believed that children should be allowed to "unfold." A child is like a seed that contains all the elements to produce a wonderful apple if given the proper amounts of nutrients from the soil and water along with sunshine and an ideal climate. The modern maturationist point of view is most often associated with the work of the Gesell Institute (Ilg and

www.

www.ncrel/org/sdrs/areas/ issues/students/earlycld/ ea7lk18.htm

Explanations of maturationist theory

Ames 1955). The Gesellian literature describes growth and development in terms of children's maturity.

Experience plays a much less important role in development in the maturationist point of view than it does in the behaviorist point of view. Maturationists believe that each child's physical, social, emotional, and intellectual development follows an individual schedule that is basically predetermined. They believe that a child will develop to his potential when placed in an optimal environment and that his development will be slowed or retarded if the environment is not optimal.

Maturationists believe that a child's developmental level is the most important determiner of social and intellectual success, especially in school settings. They suggest that the child will have difficulty in school if he is "overplaced," that is, placed in settings where the requirements do not match his developmental level. Maturationists emphasize the child's own schedule of maturation rather than rewards and punishments, experiences, or interactions with the environment. Experience, in the maturationist point of view, is always filtered by the child's maturation level.

Even though this theoretical position has been criticized, many schools continue to screen children for entry into programs on the basis of developmental tests developed by the Gesell Institute (Meisels 1987).

Constructivist Theory

The constructivist, or developmentalist, theory is founded on the work of Jean Piaget (1896–1980) and Lev Vygotsky (1896–1934). Modern constructivists—such as Jerome Bruner, George Forman, and others—continue to refine the theories of Piaget and to clarify concepts about children's development.

Jean Piaget

Piaget believed that children create knowledge through interactions with the environment. Children are not passive receivers of knowledge; rather, they actively work at organizing their experience into more and more complex mental structures. Piaget and Inhelder's (1969) descriptions of children's thinking include the concepts of assimilation, accommodation, and equilibrium.

Assimilation is fitting information into existing schemas or categories. If a child has developed a schema for "dog" and is presented with a new example of a dog, such as a St. Bernard, the new example can be assimilated, or included, in the existing schema. If presented with a cat, the child may create a new schema for "furry pets that are not dogs." Creating a new category is the process of *accommodation*. Through a series of repeated assimilations and accommodations, the child eventually creates a mental structure that will account for all animals.

Equilibrium is the balance achieved whenever information or experience is fitted into a schema or a new schema is created for it. This balance is very short lived, as the child constantly encounters new experiences and information. *Disequilibrium* describes the mental state in which there is an imbalance between assimilation and accommodation. Disequilibrium is motivating in that it drives the learner to achieve equilibrium.

Equilibration is the process of moving from disequilibrium to equilibrium. Equilibration allows the learner to employ assimilation and accommodation as tools for achieving equilibrium (Piaget 1985). In the "dog"

www.

www.nvcc.edu/home/Kludlow/ theories/default.htm
www.ncrel/org/sdrs/areas/ issues/content/cntareas/ science/sc5model.htm

Both offer explanations of constructivist theory and its major theorists

www.

http://chiron.valdosta.edu/ whuitt.col.cogsys/piaget.html

A biography of Piaget and an explanation of his theories

example, if the child is presented with a basenji, a dog that rarely barks, disequilibrium may result as the child is confronted with a dog that does not exhibit one of the usual dog behaviors. The child must then assimilate this dog into her schema of dogs. Some theorists agree that equilibration is one process that contributes to cognitive growth but question the idea that one process can account for all cognitive development.

Piagetians categorize knowledge as physical, social, or logico-mathematical. Forman and Kuschner (1983) postulate a fourth kind of knowledge: knowing what one knows. The term used in the literature to describe this category of knowledge is **metaknowledge.** If a child knows about the number system, for instance, then his knowing that he knows the system is another type of knowledge that is not social, physical, or logico-mathematical.

Wadsworth (1989) describes the definition of *learning* in Piagetian terms as follows:

> Two usages or meanings of the word learning are differentiated by Piagetians. The first usage can be called learning in the broad sense, and it is synonymous with development. It is appropriate to talk about the development of, or the learning of, physical knowledge, logical-mathematical knowledge, and social knowledge. The second usage of learning is narrower. It refers to the acquisition of specific information from the environment, learning that is assimilated into an existing schema. Most content learning is the second kind. Both forms of learning imply comprehension.
>
> Rote memory, or memorization, is not considered learning because it does not involve assimilation and comprehension. Some theories, such as behaviorism, consider rote memory as a form of learning and do not differentiate between it and the two kinds of learning defined here. For Piagetians, learning always involves construction and comprehension. (p. 156)

Wadsworth goes on to explain that even though rote memory is not considered by Piagetians to be a kind of learning, it is valuable. Rote memory is certainly useful for knowing one's address or telephone number, for example, but comprehension is not necessarily a component of memorization. A child who comprehends place value is intellectually different from one who has simply memorized the algorithm for solving addition problems that require regrouping.

Lev Vygotsky

Lev Vygotsky was a contemporary of Jean Piaget, and the two men agreed on many points about human growth and development. Whereas Vygotsky died as a young man, Piaget lived into his early eighties and thus produced a greater volume of work. Moreover, Vygotsky's work remained relatively unknown for many years, as U.S. scholars rarely read the work of Soviet scholars during the cold war era. In more recent years, Vygotsky's work has been translated and studied, such that his *sociocultural theory* is now influential in our understanding of children.

Vygotsky (1978) described learning as the construction of knowledge within a social context. He believed that development could not be separated from its social context and that learning could lead development. Vygotsky viewed the learner as an active participant in constructing his own learning within the context of interactions with caregivers, a family or community, and a society. For example, a child in a society that depends on technology

www.
www.indiana.edu/~intell/ vygotsky.shtml
A brief biographical sketch of Vygotsky and an explanation of his most important ideas

www.
www.psy.pdx/PsiCafe/ Keytheorists/Vygotsky.htm
Information about Vygotsky and links to other sites about related topics

will learn to think differently than a child in a society that depends on agriculture.

Vygotsky also believed that language plays a central role in cognitive development, as learning language influences the way a person thinks about the world. For example, a child who learns the scientific language of classification will think differently about classification tasks than one who has not learned such language. Vygotsky agreed with Piaget that learning is dependent on the child's development, but he believed that learning new strategies (when presented at the appropriate level for the child) could lead to increased development.

Bodrova and Leong (1996) describe a three-year-old child who is learning to classify objects but cannot keep the categories straight. When the teacher helps her by providing two boxes, one labeled "big" and one labeled "little," the child is able to keep the categories straight. Learning to classify in terms of *big* and *little* will aid the child's development of categorical thinking. As summarized by Bodrova and Leong (1996):

> The highest level of development is associated with the ability to perform and self-regulate complex cognitive operations. Children cannot reach the level through maturation or the accumulation of experiences with objects alone. The emergence of this higher level of cognitive development depends on the appropriation of tools through formal and informal instruction. (p. 19)

For early childhood educators, one of the most significant elements of Vygotsky's theory is the **zone of proximal development (ZPD).** The ZPD is the gap between what the child can do independently and what he cannot do even with the assistance of someone (such as an adult or peer) who is more skilled than he is. For example, if a child can independently solve addition problems involving regrouping, then he does not need instruction in solving these types of problems but could learn to solve subtraction problems that require regrouping. However, he probably would not be able to solve problems that involve long division, even with assistance. The skill range in which the child *can* work successfully with some assistance is the ZPD. Clearly, it is a waste of time to teach children what they already know as well as what they cannot do, even with assistance.

Piaget and Vygotsky agreed that learning involved "major, qualitative transformations in thinking" (Berk and Winsler 1995, p. 111). And even though Piaget and Vygotsky did not agree on other points, both of their theories are valuable to early childhood educators. Namely, both can help us understand that teachers must recognize the development of individual children, provide activities and experiences that will enhance children's thinking, and remember that all learning takes place in a social context.

Multiple Intelligences Theory

Howard Gardner

The theories of Howard Gardner (1943–   ) in explaining the growth of human intelligence are very important to the work of early childhood teachers. In his **multiple intelligences theory,** Gardner has identified nine intelligences that meet the strict criteria for being labeled as such. Gardner (1997a) describes these multiple intelligences as follows:

NAEYC CRITERIA

3.61

www.thomasarmstrong.com/
multiple_intelligences.htm

Information about multiple intelligences and links to other sites with related topics

1. ***Linguistic intelligence*** is the individual's capacity to use language— her native language and perhaps other languages—to express herself and to understand other people. A poet really specializes in linguistic intelligence, but any kind of writer, orator, speaker, lawyer, or person for whom language is important to her trade demonstrates a high level of linguistic intelligence.

2. ***Logical-mathematical intelligence*** is highly developed in someone who understands the underlying principles of some kind of causal system— the way a scientist or a logician does—or who can manipulate numbers, quantities, and operations—the way a mathematician does.

3. ***Spatial intelligence*** refers to a person's ability to represent the spatial world internally in her mind—the way a sailor or airplane pilot navigates the large spatial world or the way a chess player or sculptor represents a more circumscribed spatial world. Spatial intelligence can be used in the arts or in the sciences. If someone is spatially intelligent and oriented toward the arts, she will more likely become a painter, sculptor, or architect than, say, a musician or writer. Similarly, certain sciences, such as anatomy and topology, require spatial intelligence skills.

4. ***Bodily-kinesthetic intelligence*** is the capacity to use the whole body or parts of it—hands, fingers, arms—to solve a problem, make something, or put on some kind of production. The most evident examples of people with well-developed bodily-kinesthetic intelligence are those in athletics or the performing arts, particularly dance and drama.

5. ***Musical intelligence*** is the capacity to think in musical terms—to be able to hear patterns, recognize them, remember them, and perhaps manipulate them. People who have a strong musical intelligence do not just remember music easily—they cannot get it out of their minds, it is so omnipresent. Some critics argue that musical ability is a talent, not an intelligence. However, the genius of individuals such as Mozart and Beethoven would seem to demonstrate the existence of musical intelligence.

6. ***Interpersonal intelligence*** is understanding other people. It is an ability everyone needs, but it is vital to success for anyone who is a teacher, clinician, salesperson, or politician. Anybody who deals with other people has to be skilled in the interpersonal sphere.

7. ***Intrapersonal intelligence*** refers to a person's understanding himself—knowing who he is, what he can do, what he wants to do, how he reacts to things, which things to avoid, and which things to embrace. People are drawn to individuals who have a good understanding of themselves because they tend to be confident and successful. They know what they can and cannot do, and they know where to go if they need help.

8. ***Naturalist intelligence*** is the human ability to discriminate among living things (such as plants, animals) and to be sensitive to other features of the natural world (such as clouds, rock formations). This ability was clearly of value in humans' evolutionary past as hunters, gatherers, and farmers; it continues to be central in such roles as botanist and chef. Much of consumer society also seems to exploit naturalist intelligence in discriminating among goods such as cars, sneakers, kinds of makeup, and the like. The kind of pattern recognition valued in certain of the sciences may also draw on naturalist intelligence.

www.infed.org/thinkers/ gardner.htm
Information about Gardner and his theories

> **If we understand the mind of the five-year-old we will understand human nature.**
>
> —*Howard Gardner*

9. *Existentialist intelligence* is the most recent type of intelligence proposed by Gardner. He describes this intelligence as the "proclivity to ask fundamental questions about life: Who are we? Where do we come from? Why do we die?" (1999). Questions such as these underlie much of religion, art, science, and philosophy. Children are often intrigued by these questions, as well.

In a classroom for young children in which the teacher believes that the theory of multiple intelligences is a meaningful guide to making curriculum decisions, the program would include various ways of learning material, but lessons would not be repeated to address every type of intelligence. At least once during each week, however, information would be presented through each of the intelligences so that every child could learn through her strongest skills some of the time. For example, if the children were investigating simple machines, they would take apart old appliances looking for the simple machine parts, work in small groups to invent their own appliances using simple machines, write descriptions of their appliances, and present their appliances to the class and try to persuade others to buy them. On another day, the children would learn about the life cycle of the frog through watching a video, put together a puzzle depicting the life cycle, listen to a recording of the sounds of various kinds of frogs, and examine the back legs of a frog on a computer simulation that compares the frog's leg muscles to those of a human being, measuring the distance each can jump from a standing start, and so on.

The significance of multiple intelligences theory for early childhood teachers is that it gives them the opportunity to look for learning strengths in all children and to justify providing a wide variety of learning experiences so that each child will have the chance to learn through areas of strength. Gardner explains that all learners need all the intelligences and opportunities to grow intellectually in all areas. However, initial learning or entry-point learning is most easily achieved through employing individuals' personal areas of strength. In sum, by understanding and applying multiple intelligences theory, teachers affirm that every child has abilities that can be recognized and honored.

Social Learning Theory

Albert Bandura

www.psy.pdx.edu/PsiCafe/ KeyTheorists/Bandura.htm
www.ship.edu/~cgboeree/ bandura.html
Both have information about Bandura and social learning theory

Albert Bandura (1925–) is one of the major theorists who describes **social learning theory** (Bandura 1977), which emphasizes imitation, or social learning, in children's development. This theory suggests that children observe their caretakers performing certain actions and then imitate those actions themselves. In more recent years, social learning theory has emphasized cognition, suggesting that children begin to think about what they are imitating and become more selective about the elements in their environments that they choose to imitate (Bandura 2001). Although Bandura comes from a behaviorist tradition, he believes that children take an active role in their development.

The most important element of social learning theory for teachers is the idea of modeling desired behaviors so that children will have an example to follow. Such modeling is most prominent in the area of social development. Teachers commonly model kindness, turn taking, and other behaviors that they wish children to emulate. Even in the area of intellectual development, teachers often try to model curiosity and interest so that children will follow their example.

Ecological Systems Theory

Urie Bronfenbrenner

www.psy.pdx.edu/PsiCafe/ KeyTheorists/Bronfenbrenner. htm
Information about Bronfenbrenner's theories and links to other useful sites

Urie Bronfenbrenner's (1917–2005) **ecological systems theory** explains that a child develops within a complex system of relationships and that all these relationships are themselves influenced by multiple levels of the surrounding environment (Bronfenbrenner and Evans 2000). For example, a child has a relationship with a parent, and that relationship is set within a family structure of some kind. In some families, the child and a single parent make up the family. In other cases, the child and parent are set within a family that consists of grandparents, aunts, uncles, cousins, and so on—an extended family model.

However the family is structured, it is also set within various cultural environments. The cultural milieu may expect that the parent has complete responsibility for the child or that all the family or even the "village" is responsible for childrearing. The cultural group itself may be set in another layer of environments. For instance, it might be the dominant culture in a given area or a minority culture, such that its cultural beliefs are very different from those of the dominate culture or even in direct conflict with them. This layer also may be complicated by various laws (e.g., laws about what constitutes child abuse), customs (e.g., circumcision), and values (e.g., attending formal school or learning skills at home).

Further complicating the nature of ecological systems is the fact that they are not static but dynamic, or always changing (Spencer and Schöner 2003; Thelen and Smith 1998). As children get older, they have varying degrees of opportunity to create their own settings and experiences. The dynamic systems view is that a child's mind and body and physical and social worlds form an integrated whole that guides the development of new skills and knowledge. If a change occurs in one part of the system, then the system must be reorganized so that the components work together again but in a more complex manner. For example, a child of about eight may discover that her parents do not know everything. This knowledge will change the way she and her parents interact. They must learn to interact in new ways that reflect the new knowledge.

Theoretical Influences on Teaching

PRAXIS

Be able to plan instruction from various theoretical points of view

The theoretical stance a teacher takes will influence the way she plans and implements instruction. In the following sections, we will examine how a teacher might teach one-to-one correspondence from each theoretical point of view.

One-to-one correspondence means that a child knows that each item he is counting has only one number tag and that if two sets are equivalent numerically, then the objects in one set can be matched to the objects in the other set. An example that indicates that the concept is understood is for the teacher to ask a child to pass out one piece of paper to each child in the class. If the child can count the number of children and then count the number of pieces of paper without having to physically match each piece of paper to each child, then that child has mastered the concept of one-to-one correspondence.

How will this concept be taught according to the various theories we have discussed?

Behaviorist   The teacher will first determine whether the child has a grasp of the concept. If needed, the teacher will provide direct instruction by asking the child to connect one set of objects to another and determine that the sets are equivalent. The teacher might supply a worksheet with a set of dogs and a set of bones and ask the child to draw lines from the dogs to the bones; the teacher would then tell the child that these sets have the same number of items because there is one bone for each dog. In various ways, the teacher will ask the child to practice matching sets until he can say that sets are equivalent if there is one item in one set for each item in another set. Rewards such as "happy faces" and tokens will be given each time the child succeeds on the worksheet.

Maturationist   The teacher will determine if the child is mature enough to learn this concept by observing his physical development for the ability to sit still long enough for instruction and his interest in counting and numbers by observing how often he plays with magnetic numerals and other math materials at choice time. Once the teacher decides that the child is ready for this concept, she will place objects on a table that can be matched one to one and ask the child to match them. Then she will explain that these sets are the same numerically if there is one ball for each bat. This might be repeated several times until the child can state that the sets are equivalent.

Constructivist   Knowing that the child will have to develop his own understanding of one-to-one correspondence, the teacher will provide many different materials that the child can match into equivalent sets (e.g., dolls and dollclothes, paintbrushes and paint containers, unit blocks and half units, lids and jars, and so on). As the child plays with the materials, the teacher will question him about what he is doing and ask him to explain what it means if the sets are the same numerically.

Multiple Intelligences   Knowing that some children would find mathematics more meaningful than others, the teacher would determine who understood the concept of one-to-one correspondence and then set up situations that would help children understand the concept. For example, a child who learns best through visual means could be encouraged to create matching sets in paintings; another might be encouraged to create matching movements such as taking a step for each bounce of a ball; another might be encouraged to create two strings of musical notes that match in number; and so on. However the child creates the sets, the teacher would help the child make the connection from one set to the matching set. Such experiences would be repeated until the child grasped the concept.

Social Learning   Knowing that children learn by observing in a social context, the teacher would model the concept of one-to-one correspondence many times. This modeling would happen in many daily interactions. For example, when passing out paper to each child the teacher would comment that each child had one piece of paper so that the number of sheets of paper was equal to the number of children. At snack time, similar modeling could be done as each child got one serving of juice, one plate, one set of silverware, and so on. After modeling many times, the teacher would expect the child to begin noting the comparisons between sets when gathering materials or creating sets that were equivalent in their cardinal numbers.

Ecological Systems   The teacher will arrange an environment in which the child can be taught the concept of one-to-one correspondence. The teacher might demonstrate the concept several times and then ask the child to demonstrate his understanding with a different set of materials. The teacher will point out such correspondences in the school environment, ask the parents to call attention to the concept at home, and demonstrate social applications, such as one voter, one vote in the classroom. Once the child can demonstrate understanding of the concept, then the teacher will help him apply the skill to counting and other mathematical experiences.

Theoretical Influences on Observations

The different theories of development provide points of view through which to interpret observations of children as they grow and develop. Depending on our theoretical orientation, we will look at examples of children's development differently. If a child is observed throwing a ball at a target, a behaviorist might point out the reinforcements that make the child seek closer approximations to the most effective throwing techniques. The maturationist observing the same child might focus on the child's physical maturity, as indicated by her ability to grasp and release the ball appropriately. The constructivist will view repeated attempts to hit the target as evidence that the child is actively seeking information about velocity and angle of release in order to hit the target (although the child will not be expected to verbalize these concepts).

A child develops as a whole. Development in one area certainly influences development in other areas. For example, when a child becomes mobile, he opens up many more possibilities for exploration and learning about the environment. Children who feel that they are learning successfully or who feel confident about their physical abilities develop more positive self-esteem. Children who learn to control their impulsive behaviors may be able to sustain interactions with people and materials longer than children who do not, which affects their intellectual development. A child's social, physical, emotional, and intellectual development are always interrelated.

Children's Development

This section provides brief overviews of patterns in children's physical, social, emotional, and intellectual development. Table 1.1 summarizes and gives examples of these patterns.

Physical Development

Patterns of Development

Physical development is orderly, not random. Infant development is marked by the change from undifferentiated mass activity to controlled activity. It

NAEYC CRITERIA
4.12

www.pbs.org/wholechild/abc/physical.html
Milestones in physical development for the typically developing child

www.childdevelopmentinfo.com/health_safety/physical_development.shtml
Information about the physical development of children

TABLE 1.1 Overview of Patterns in Children's Development

	BIRTH TO THREE YEARS OLD	THREE TO FOUR YEARS OLD	FIVE TO SIX YEARS OLD	SEVEN TO EIGHT YEARS OLD
Physical Development	Physical skills develop rapidly Sits and crawls Walks and begins to run Fine motor skills develop; can stack and pick up small objects Manages spoon or fork for feeding Grasps and releases objects	Physical skills increase Rides a tricycle Walks up and down stairs, alternating feet Runs Jumps with both feet Walks on balance beam Climbs on playground equipment Undresses and dresses self Catches ball with arms extended Walks backward and on tiptoe Holds crayon with fingers	Skips on alternate feet Rides two-wheel bike Skates Throws fairly accurately Catches ball with hands Turns somersaults Participates in games requiring physical skills Small muscle development increases; eye–hand coordination develops Fine muscle control increases; can use hammer, pencil, scissors, etc. Copies geometric figures Cuts on lines Prints some letters Pastes and glues Begins to lose teeth Handedness is well established	Physical skills become important in self-concept Energy level is high Rate of growth slows Fine muscle control is good; can form letters well Permanent teeth appear Body proportions, facial structure change More mature throwing and catching pattern Increases accuracy in throwing and kicking
Social Development	Responds to others Enjoys company of other children Can maintain involvement with another for a very short period Is unable to share without coaxing Shows very little ability to postpone gratification Imitates actions of others Begins to engage in parallel play	Becomes more aware of self Develops more altruistic feelings Becomes aware of racial/ethnic and sexual differences Is able to take direction, follow some rules Has strong feelings toward home and family Shows a growing sense of self-reliance Parallel play is common; cooperative play begins Imaginary playmates are fairly common	Expresses rigid ideas about sex roles Has best friends but for short periods of time Quarrels often but anger is short lived Is able to share and take turns Is eager to participate in school experiences Considers teacher very important Wants to be first Becomes possessive	Is more competitive with peers Depends on parents for expansion of interests, activities Is influenced by peer opinions Plays with opposite sex less often Needs teacher approval Is able to share Wants to please Is more independent at work and play Forms more enduring friendships Peer groups begin to form

TABLE 1.1 Continued

	BIRTH TO THREE YEARS OLD	THREE TO FOUR YEARS OLD	FIVE TO SIX YEARS OLD	SEVEN TO EIGHT YEARS OLD
Emotional Development	Cannot tolerate frustration	Can tolerate some frustration	Expresses and labels feelings	Expresses reactions to others
	Cries easily	Develops some self-control	Controls aggression better	Is sensitive to ridicule and criticism
	Is often unable to control impulses	Appreciates surprises and novel events	Expresses less concern when separated from parents	Expresses more worries: war, loss of parents
	Begins to express affection	Begins to show sense of humor	Expresses sense of humor in jokes, nonsense words	Shows more persistence
	Needs routines and security	Needs overt expressions of affection	Learns right from wrong	Expresses more empathy; is able to see others' viewpoints
	Begins to perceive emotions of others	Fears the dark, being abandoned, strange situations	Develops a conscience	
	Expresses self, sometimes emphatically			
Cognitive Development	Sensorimotor investigation of environment is predominant	Follows instructions of two commands	Shows a growing attention span	Differences in reading and language abilities widen
	Development of concepts is rapid	Makes impulsive judgments and frequent mistakes	Is able to seriate objects	Transition to concrete operational thinking begins
	Develops a sense of object permanence	Develops vocabulary rapidly	Is able to group objects	Talking and discussion are important
	Develops language	Uses numbers without understanding	Is more deliberate, less impulsive in judgments	Is able to plan
	May use some number and color words but may not understand them	Has difficulty differentiating fantasy and reality	Differentiates between fantasy and reality	Can sustain interest over long periods of time
		Begins to classify, especially by function	Uses language aggressively, in categorization	Begins to understand cause and effect
		Begins to use some functional abstract words	Is aware that words and pictures represent real objects	Develops a growing understanding of time, money
		"Why?" questions are constant	Becomes interested in numbers and letters	Uses slang and profanity
		Thinking is very egocentric	Knows names of colors	Understands and uses more abstract terms
			Does not spontaneously use rehearsal in memory tasks	Expresses more awareness of community, world
			Follows three unrelated commands	
			May begin to conserve number, length	

Sources: Association for Supervision and Curriculum Development 1975; Berk 2006; Tudor 1981.

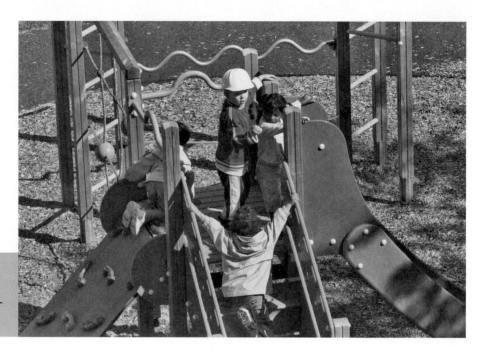

Gross motor development is aided by providing play activities that involve climbing, jumping, and so on.

is easy to observe undifferentiated mass activity in an infant. If she is excited, her whole body moves and her arms and legs flail. Gradually, the baby becomes more capable of differentiated movements, such as deliberately reaching for and grasping a rattle.

Movements that become controlled and deliberate also become organized into patterns, such as pulling oneself to a standing position, releasing the hands, and moving the legs and feet to walk. The patterns then become available to the child as possible responses to different situations. If the child wants a toy that is across the room, at first the only option for getting there is scooting and rocking. As development progresses, crawling and finally walking and running become patterns of physical movement available to the child.

The physical development of children in the infant stage proceeds rapidly. The child learns to control head position, to grasp objects, and perhaps to stand and walk in the first year. As children grow, the development of their motor skills is not quite as rapid as it is in infancy, but it continues throughout childhood.

Observations of physical development reveal that growth is *cephalocaudal* (it proceeds from head to tail) and *proximodistal* (it proceeds from the center of the body outward) and that gross motor movements are developed before fine motor movements. Control of the head and arm muscles is achieved before control of the leg muscles. Similarly, children are able to control the muscles of their arms before they can control the fine muscles in their hands that are needed for tasks such as writing and cutting with scissors.

The rate of children's physical development is variable and related to environmental features such as nutrition and the freedom to practice movements. Some behaviors, such as walking, tend to emerge at about the same time in children, even if they have been confined as infants; others, such as throwing, seem to depend more on practice opportunities. Most children are encouraged to practice their developing skills through interactions in daily life. The parent may encourage the child to progress from letting go of support, to standing alone, to walking a step or two, and finally to walking several steps across the room. Children give their caretakers clues about what to encourage at any given time by attempting the behaviors. Thus, for example, most caretakers would not attempt to encourage walking in children who are not yet showing they are ready to walk by pulling themselves to a standing position.

By the time they are three, most children can walk backward and on tiptoe and can run. They can throw a ball and catch it with their arms extended. They can also ride a tricycle and hold a crayon or pencil with their fingers rather than their fists. Four-year-olds continue to refine their skills; they can bounce a ball, hop on one foot, climb a ladder, alternate feet while walking downstairs, and jump from a standing position. Some five-year-olds can skip, and some learn to jump rope. By the time children are six, most can throw fairly accurately, and many learn to ride a two-wheel bike.

Children seven and eight continue to refine the skills they have acquired and learn new skills. They are physically active, running, skipping, hopping, and climbing—rarely just walking. Their fine motor abilities increase so that they can draw, write, and learn to play musical instruments. Practice in motor skills is important in this period, especially for newly acquired skills such as swimming. Age and practice have more effect on the development of motor skills in this period than does gender. Girls can run as fast and throw as far and as accurately as boys during this period.

Implications for the Curriculum

During the preschool and early elementary school years, children need to have many opportunities for engaging in physical activities. Three-year-olds are in a constant state of motion, and it is important that teachers and parents provide opportunities for safe physical activity and not expect motor control that is beyond what children can achieve. Fours and fives still need much more movement in their programs than sitting, although they can sit still for short periods for such activities as story time.

Teachers and parents need to think carefully when planning activities for young children. For example, writing on a line requires excellent fine motor control, and most fives and sixes cannot perform this task without considerable difficulty. Children who engage in organized sports such as tee-ball and soccer when they are very young may face the same sort of difficulties. Some parents and coaches expect coordination beyond what five- to eight-year-olds are capable of. If children do participate in organized activities, parents and coaches need to be aware of the abilities that the activities require and match their expectations to children's capabilities.

All young children need vigorous physical activity every day, and no child should be deprived of the opportunities for such activities because he must complete other tasks or because he is being punished. There is a growing concern that children in the United States today are less physically fit than previous generations of children (Berk 1996). This trend seems to reflect the time that children spend in passive activities, such as watching television and sitting quietly at desks, and the lack of vigorous exercise in their daily lives.

The following suggestions may help teachers plan activities that encourage the physical development of children:

- Provide outside play every day that it is possible. Equipment should encourage climbing, running, jumping, and so on.

- Make sure children have access to an inside play area that contains a tumbling mat, Velcro balls and targets, and other materials to encourage movement.

- For very young children, indoor equipment for physical development can include rocking boats, steps, and low slides and tunnels. As children mature, appropriate equipment includes more complex climbing apparatus, balance beams, and so on.

- Provide balls that are age appropriate. For very young children, balls should be large and made of soft materials such as foam and yarn. As children learn to catch and throw more easily, they can use balls made of soft rubber. Durable rubber balls should be provided for children of about five and six who are learning to kick a ball.

- Beginning around five years of age, children can use jump ropes and hula hoops for experimenting with movement and control.

- Many classroom activities help children gain fine muscle control: painting, cutting with scissors, manipulating clay, stringing beads, sewing cards, using pegs and pegboards, and so on. Teachers must encourage these activities as the children's development indicates.

Social Development

Patterns of Development

www.ambpeds.org/
socialdevelopment.cfm
www.gifteddevelopment.com/
Articles/Social%20
Development.html

Both provide descriptions of the typical social development of children

As noted in the section on physical development, the child's first physical actions are not differentiated—she moves all over, all at once when excited. The infant's social and emotional development is also undifferentiated, in the sense that responses to stimuli such as being cold or hungry evoke crying behaviors that are not specific to the stimuli.

In a matter of weeks, the child's crying becomes differentiated so that the primary caregiver can distinguish between the cries that indicate that the child is hungry, bored, or in pain. By six weeks or two months, the infant is able to respond to an adult by smiling and begins to imitate behavior such as sticking out her tongue or closing her eyes. By eight months or so, the child has developed a strong attachment to the primary caregiver and is anxious about separation from that person. Toddlers begin to develop attachments to their families. Two-year-old children are trying to establish their own identities, and "Me do it" is one of their most frequent statements.

> **Children are remarkable for their intelligence and ardor, for their curiosity, their intolerance of shams, the clarity and ruthlessness of their vision.**
>
> —*Aldous Huxley*

By the time they are three, children have established relationships with their families and with others outside their families. They have also developed some strategies for achieving what they want and some ideas about sex-role identification.

http://psychology.about.com/
library/weekly/aa091500a.
htm
http://facultyweb.cortland.
edu/~ANDERSMD/ERIK/
welcome.HTML
www.childdevelopmentinfo.
com/development/erickson.
shtml

All have information about the theories of Erik Erikson

Development of Personality One element of social development is development of personality. Erik Erikson (1902–1994), a psychoanalytic theorist, concentrated on studying the development of the *ego*—a sense of self (Ambron 1978). His description of stages in ego development are especially useful to teachers. Erikson viewed the child's developing identity as a reflection of relationships with parents and family within the broader context of society.

Teachers who think about children's behavior in Erikson's terms will plan programs that provide many opportunities for children to build trust and to make choices and feel successful in the choices they make. Building friendships is important in early childhood. Cooper and McEvoy (1996) state that forming friendships offers children the chance to learn skills in negotiation and compromise that are necessary for mature social interactions as adults. In addition, having good peer relationships as a child is an excellent predictor of achieving adequate social adjustment as an adult.

Helping children recognize their own needs and the feelings and emotions of others are important steps in building trust. The child must feel

Erikson's Stages of Psychological Development

Basic Trust versus Basic Mistrust (first year of life)

Experiences and sensations that give the infant a sense of familiarity and inner certainty provide him with a sense of self. He feels that the world is benevolent or at least reliable, and he likewise trusts himself and his own capacities. He has established basic trust. If the individual develops basic mistrust instead, he may tend to behave irrationally or to withdraw into schizoid or depressive states in later life.

Autonomy versus Shame and Doubt (second year of life)

During the second year of life, the infant develops muscular control; she moves about and begins toilet training. She needs firmness now, as a protection against the potential anarchy of her own impulses. The sense of self-control (autonomy) learned at this stage leads to a lasting sense of goodwill and personal pride. A failure to achieve well-guided autonomy can lead later in life to compulsive neurosis (a pervasive sense of shame before the world) and compulsive doubt of the self and others.

Initiative versus Guilt (the preschool years)

During the preschool years, the child has a boundless supply of energy, which permits him to learn all kinds of activities and ideas quickly and avidly. He concentrates on successes rather than failures and does things for the simple pleasure of the activity. Autonomy becomes more focused and effective. The child becomes "more himself." The danger in this period is that the child's exuberant and aggressive explorations and conquests may lead him into frustration. His new physical and mental strengths encourage ambitions that may turn out to be beyond his abilities—inevitably, he sometimes fails or is defeated. Unless he can come to terms with these disappointments, he may be overwhelmed by resignation, guilt, and anxiety.

Perhaps the best way to help the child at this age is to encourage him to play constructively, to do some chores around the house, or to help care for younger children. In this way, the conflict between initiative and guilt may be resolved by the establishment of a constructive moral sense; it can set the individual on the road to goals that are not only possible for him but also deeply satisfying. If the conflict remains unresolved, in adult life the individual may be inhibited or impotent (socially as well as sexually), or he may overreact by compulsive showing off.

Industry versus Inferiority (middle childhood)

Building on the previously developed trust, autonomy, and initiative, the child can achieve a sense of industry. In school, she learns the basic tools of literacy and cooperation that will enable her to become a productive member of society, and a sense of achievement becomes important to her. She learns the satisfaction of persisting at a task until it is completed and of using her skills to perform according to her own and others' expectations. In a culture like that in the United States, in which achievement is often measured in terms of doing better than someone else, she also learns to compete and to measure her productivity in relation to that of others.

The dangers of this period are twofold. On the one hand, the child may learn to value achievement in work above all else; she may alienate her peers by excessively competitive behavior. On the other hand, she may feel unable to perform the tasks required of her and develop a sense of inferiority that prevents her from trying. Experiences of failure may lead to the child's feeling that she is inadequate, that she cannot be successful as a worker. In extreme cases, this sense of inferiority can affect the child's attitude toward work for life.

Source: Adapted from Erikson 1963.

that his ideas are good ideas and that others respect them. If too much of the time spent in school or child care is directed by the teacher, children will begin to feel that their ideas are unacceptable. For example, four- and five-year-olds need to know that if they suggest activities, the teacher will listen and help them carry out their ideas, if possible. If the activity cannot be incorporated into the classroom, the teacher will still treat the idea with respect and perhaps help the child modify the idea or accomplish some part of the activity. Older children need to be able to participate in activities in which their achievements are obvious and celebrated.

Development of Self-Esteem   Another element of the social development of the young child is the development of self-esteem. The concept of self is developed gradually; the young child develops a concept of himself as a separate individual over a period of years. Through interactions first with the parents and family and then with peers and others outside the family, children gradually develop a concept of who they are and what they are like. In a classic study of children's self-esteem, Coopersmith (1967) found that children, especially boys, with high self-esteem had parents who were accepting, affectionate, and genuinely concerned about their child. The parents also enforced rules carefully and consistently and insisted on high standards of behavior but used noncoercive methods of discipline. They also demonstrated more democratic interactions with their children.

Teachers of young children often plan experiences in which improving self-esteem is the primary goal. However, such plans for activities often ignore the pervasive nature of the development of self-concept. Katz (1986) discusses the futility of planning an activity based on "me" (a booklet about my favorite food, my pet, my favorite dress, my best skill, and so on) as a means of improving self-esteem. Such an activity might contribute to the child's self-esteem if it is conducted in the context of a classroom environment in which children have choices and opportunities to participate in a variety of activities in which they can feel successful and in control. But if the classroom environment is generally structured so that children feel unable to be successful, then even a series of self-esteem lessons will not be effective.

Kostelnik et al. (1993) state that "fifteen-minute activities or the adult's gushing remarks will not infuse children with a sense of well-being or inoculate them against negative self-perceptions. Because esteem-influencing experiences pervade all aspects of children's lives and are ever-present, authentic esteem enhancing efforts must be pervasive too" (p. 78). Therefore, a teacher who wishes to build self-esteem in children will consider how children are treated all through the day. The kinds of experiences regularly provided for them are much more important in the process of building self-esteem than isolated lessons or activities designed to focus on positive feelings about oneself.

The Role of Play   Play experiences are very important in the social and emotional development of young children. Children can "play" various roles and behaviors and get feedback about the appropriateness of the behaviors in play. They can play "bully" or "baby" and find out what kinds of responses their behavior elicits in nonthreatening situations. They can also play various adult roles. Young children often play the roles of family members, and with experience, they begin to play roles of those outside the family. They

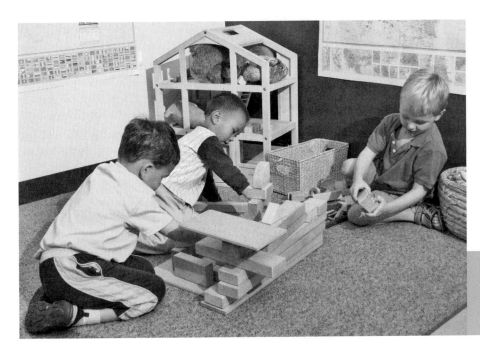

Playing with construction toys provides opportunities for social, emotional, physical, and intellectual growth.

might play "grocery clerk," "filling station attendant," "dentist," or "garbage worker" and explore the behavior patterns that they believe are appropriate for those individuals.

Because play is so important in the lives of children, an entire chapter will be devoted to the topic of play (see Chapter 5).

Social Skills and Social Relationships Research continues to emphasize the importance of fostering children's social development in the early childhood years. In summarizing the effects of peer relationships in childhood, Hartup (1992) states that these relationships contribute greatly to our successful adaptation as adults:

> Indeed, the single best childhood predictor of adult adaptation is not IQ, not school grades, and not classroom behavior but rather the adequacy with which the child gets along with other children. Children who are generally disliked, who are aggressive and disruptive, who are unable to sustain close relationships with other children, and who cannot establish a place for themselves in the peer culture are seriously at risk. (p. 1)

Rogers and Ross (1986) describe *social skill* as the "ability to assess what is happening in a social situation; skill to perceive and correctly interpret the actions and needs of the children in the group at play; ability to imagine possible courses of action and select the most appropriate one" (pp. 14–15). Children who are popular and most successful socially demonstrate these abilities, but children who lack social skills may need direct instruction through modeling, role-playing, or the use of puppets to help them develop these abilities. Roopnarine and Honig (1985), in a review of research on the unpopular child, add that teachers can help children become more popular by helping their families focus on more positive discipline techniques and making sure that positive social development is a major program goal. Katz and McClellan (1997) believe that the child's capacity for developing close, caring friendships, not just her popularity, is the best indication of a social competence.

Teachers and parents are concerned with the development in young children of *prosocial behaviors:* helping, cooperating, and empathizing. Kostelnik et al. (1993) report that prosocial behaviors increase rapidly during the preschool years. In the classroom setting, teachers can help children develop these behaviors through modeling the desired behaviors, setting up situations that require cooperation, and suggesting specific ways that children can be cooperative or helpful. Some play equipment should be selected that can be used by more than one child, such as telephones, jump ropes, and board games. Teachers can model caring and empathy for each child and discuss with the children how some actions make others feel. Teachers can also demonstrate how to be cooperative by helping build a block construction or helping dig in the garden.

Katz and McClellan (1997) suggest that building prosocial behaviors has several components. One is to alert children to other people's feelings and interests. Teachers can help children think about others who share their interests or help children think about how others might feel. Another component of building prosocial behaviors is to encourage children to accept alternative interpretations of others' behaviors. For example, if one child accidentally knocks over another child's block structure, the teacher may need to help both children recognize the difference between accidental and purposeful behavior.

Teachers may also need to help children develop verbal skills by providing them with models for what to say to facilitate interactions. For instance, the sensitive teacher can encourage taking turns through teaching the child who wants a turn how to ask and through appealing to the resisting child's sense of generosity and reason. If the child continues to resist, the teacher may have to intervene. The resisting child needs to be offered some other interesting choices of activities so that the resistance does not become a significant behavioral style.

Aggression Another aspect of social development that receives attention is aggression. Teachers and parents are concerned with children's aggressive behavior. The results of studies indicate that aggressive behavior in the classroom can be reduced by providing enough space and materials so that children do not have to compete with one another. These studies also suggest eliminating toys that lend themselves to aggressive themes and not allowing children to benefit from aggressive behavior by either controlling the victim or getting the teacher's attention. It is also important to model cooperative behavior and discuss and demonstrate solutions to problems other than aggression (Potts, Huston, and Wright 1986; Yarrow 1983).

Aggression also seems to be gender related in some ways. Giles and Heyman (2005) studied preschool-age children and found that girls were less likely than boys to be physically aggressive but more likely to threaten not to play with others. However, Mayeux and Cillessen (2003) found that boys who were rated more highly by their peers tended to be less aggressive and that younger children viewed aggression as an acceptable means of solving peer conflicts.

Aggression can be manifested as either a reactive or a proactive action. A *reactive* action is usually accompanied by anger, as when a child defends himself or his belongings through aggressive actions. A *proactive* action is not always accompanied by anger but involves the child's use of aggressive behavior to get something he wants, such as a toy from another child. Bullying is usually proactive aggression.

Helping children manage their anger will help eliminate much aggressive behavior. Marion (1997) suggests teachers take these measures to help children manage their anger:

1. Create a safe emotional climate.
2. Model responsible anger management.
3. Help children develop self-regulatory skills.
4. Encourage children to label feelings of anger.
5. Encourage children to talk about anger-arousing interactions.
6. Use appropriate books and stories about anger to help children understand and manage anger.
7. Communicate with parents. (pp. 65–66)

Stopping the behavior of a bully can be especially complex. It may involve helping the child make the connection between her behavior and her rejection by the other children. The teacher may need to directly intervene and then indicate her dislike for the bullying child's behavior. Asking the child how it would feel to be bullied requires a cognitive analysis that the child may be unable to perform, so direct action is usually more successful (Katz and McClellan 1997).

Farver (1996) found that aggressive children tend to play with other aggressive children and suggests that regrouping the children for projects or outings might change the aggressive patterns. Hektner, August, and Realmuto (2000) found that aggressive children who choose other aggressive children for playmates often do so because they have been rejected by other more nonaggressive children. Teaching children how to become friends with nonaggressive playmates can reduce the amount of aggressive behavior.

Violence in schools is an area of growing concern. There is evidence that aggression and violent behavior begin early in children's lives; therefore, many schools have adopted violence prevention programs. Anderson (2001) suggests that schools can help prevent violence by providing experiences that do the following:

- Help build and foster relationships that support learning
- Promote social and emotional competence
- Provide frequent and positive interactions between adults and children
- Strengthen children's skills to interact meaningfully with others
- Demonstrate good and positive role models
- Foster problem solving with respectful words and actions (p. 60)

One of the assumptions in early childhood care is that aggressive behavior will increase if there are not enough toys or attractive activities for the number of children in the group. Blair and Kwang-Sun (2000) found that the incidence of aggression was lowered after children were trained in social skills even when the number of toys was not adequate. Reducing aggressive behavior in situations in which such behavior is frequently demonstrated lends strong support for teaching social skills.

Bullies and their victims can both benefit from what Shure (2000) calls "problem-solving dialogue." In lieu of providing punishment for bullying, she suggests helping bullies learn more positive interaction patterns and helping victims learn to be more assertive. Shure believes that children from

Parents and Development

● If parents are interested, ask a speaker to focus on the relationships among child development, discipline, and routines or some other area of development.

ages four to seven can learn to solve interaction problems and that by about age eight, children gain new skills in understanding the points of view of others. She suggests that teachers should get children actively involved in questioning their behavior and finding solutions rather than simply telling them what to do (as in "Tell him with words what you want"). Leff et al. (2001) examined violence prevention programs for young children and found that teaching positive social skills was an effective means of reducing violence.

Sex-Role Identification Sex-role identification is yet another important element of social development. Before they are three, children begin to identify themselves as boys or girls, and at around three years of age, they can identify others as boys or girls. They continue to develop their concepts of sexual identity and their attitudes about appropriate roles for males and females. In fact, preschoolers may be quite rigid about what is appropriate play or an appropriate task for males or females.

Teachers will want to structure the classroom and activities so that both boys and girls have equal opportunities and encouragement to participate. The literature selected for use in the classroom should contain models of behaviors that are not stereotyped by sex, and teachers should avoid assigning tasks in a stereotypical manner (such as consistently having boys do heavy work and girls do verbal or artwork). Bigler and Liben (1990, 1992) have found that direct instruction can help children broaden their ideas about what constitutes appropriate behaviors for boys versus girls.

Implications for the Curriculum

Teachers do not usually plan activities in which the sole purpose is social development; instead, they think about social development as one facet of children's participation in a variety of classroom experiences. Teachers who want to help children develop socially will be aware of children's social abilities and take advantage of classroom routine to further their development. Activities should encourage children to cooperate, to develop their self-esteem, and to gain skill in interacting with other children. The following are only a few suggestions of ways to promote growth in social abilities:

NAEYC CRITERIA

3.62

■ Provide dress-up corners where children can take on a variety of roles. Simple costumes such as aprons and hats can help children explore new roles. Threes and fours need more family-oriented props; older children need more props for roles found in the larger community. Sixes, sevens, and eights may respond to props that help them reenact stories from literature.

■ Involve primary children in solving social problems in the classroom through role-play and discussions of how to find alternative solutions, how to disagree without being aggressive, and how to make changes in rules they believe are inappropriate or unfair.

■ For threes, popular play materials should be plentiful so that fewer arguments arise and children do not have to wait long for a turn. As children mature, teachers may help them work out approaches to taking turns and sharing toys and equipment, such as using a waiting list or a timer.

- Use puppets to model appropriate techniques for entering a play group. For example, the teacher could use a puppet to demonstrate how a child might ask a group playing with blocks if she could play, too.

- Encourage children to make as many decisions as possible. In free play, allow children to choose activities and experiences. In more directed times of the day, such as music or story time, encourage children to choose songs or stories.

- Model empathy and caring behaviors, and encourage children to display these behaviors.

- Role-play solutions to problems in social interactions. For example, children might role-play how to make an introduction when a guest comes to the classroom or how to ask another child to share materials.

Emotional Development

Patterns of Development

Emotional development, like physical and social development, follows fairly predictable stages of growth (Berk 2006). The infant responds to any emotion with undifferentiated crying. As the baby grows, this crying becomes differentiated to reflect various emotions. By the time the baby is a few months old, he may scream in anger but produce none of the tears that accompany crying caused by physical pain. Infants have almost no capacity to wait for someone to attend to their needs; their reactions to feelings are immediate.

Some researchers (Thomas and Chess 1977) have found that children have distinct temperaments early in life and that temperament tends to be stable over time. Other researchers (DeVries and Sameroff 1984) believe that temperament is responsive to environmental influences. If a baby is difficult and irritable, for example, the parents may not handle the baby as much as they might have handled a more responsive or easy-going baby—and this, in turn, will further affect the baby's temperament.

Toddlers are compulsive in their behaviors. They have little control of their impulses and are easily frustrated. By the time children reach three years of age, they have developed some tolerance for frustration. They can wait for short periods of time. If their mother explains that dinner will be ready very soon, they can manage to wait for it. They are also developing some self-control; they do not respond to every impulse. Three-year-olds have been observed talking themselves out of doing things they would have done without thinking a year earlier.

Threes and fours like surprises and novel events. They need the security of knowing that there is structure to their day—that they are going to play, have a snack, and so on—but they respond well to some surprises in the day. When someone dressed as Mother Goose stops by the classroom to share some nursery rhymes, they can handle the change. Three- and four-year-olds are also beginning to develop a sense of humor. They often laugh when they hear a word that sounds funny to them or when they see something incongruous. They are not embarrassed when they laugh at inappropriate moments because they cannot analyze their own behavior in order to determine that it was inappropriate.

www.

www.pbs.org/wholechild/abc/social.html
www.parentingme.com/emotdev.htm

Information for parents and teachers on the emotional development of children and activities to help children become more emotionally mature

By the time children are in kindergarten and first grade, they are able to express and label a wide variety of emotions. They can describe their own sad, angry, and happy feelings and can describe situations that produce given emotions in others. These children become more capable of controlling their aggressive feelings and, with some guidance, can learn to work out their frustrations with other children using words rather than hitting. Five- and six-year-olds also begin to develop a conscience and a sense of right and wrong.

Fives and sixes express their sense of humor in jokes and nonsense words. They often tell jokes without punch lines and still laugh at their own stories. They repeat jokes they have heard, often without understanding them. "Knock-knock" jokes are favorites, and children frequently make up their own versions. They also have great fun creating nonsense words and making rhymes with other words. These tend to be especially funny if they are a little naughty.

Children in the primary years, seven- and eight-year-olds, continue to gain even more control of their emotional responses. They are much less impulsive than younger children. They have strong responses to other individuals and usually like or dislike them immediately. Children in this age group are quite sensitive to criticism or ridicule. They demonstrate embarrassment at their own behavior. They tend to have more worries than younger children as they become more aware of world conditions and attend more to news stories they see on television or hear being discussed by adults. They worry about war, about things happening to their parents (death or divorce), and about accidents.

Seven- and eight-year-olds demonstrate persistence in trying to achieve their goals. This often drives their parents mad, as the child asks to do something again and again after it has been denied. Children this age develop much more empathy for other people and feel bad when someone else is hurting, either physically or emotionally. They offer comfort to family and friends without being prompted to do so.

Implications for the Curriculum

Emotional growth can be encouraged through typical classroom experiences if the teacher is aware of the child's level of development and what can be done to encourage that development. The following are examples of classroom activities that can help children:

- Have children dramatize situations in which anger or frustration are handled appropriately.
- Use puppets to model appropriate responses to emotions. For example, with younger children, the teacher might use puppets to model the use of language rather than hitting to express anger. With older children, the teacher might model different responses to frustrations, such as not winning a race or a game.
- Help children learn to acknowledge and label their feelings as they participate in classroom activities.
- Choose literature in which the characters respond to emotions appropriately, and discuss how they felt and how they acted.
- Provide empathy for children's fears and concerns. They are real to the child and should not be belittled.

- Allow children to share their humor; appreciate the growth in their sense of humor.
- Primary children may be helped to express their feelings through writing. Select examples from literature that illustrate how children have written about their frustrations or stresses and learned to cope more effectively with them through the writing process.

Intellectual Development

Patterns of Development

Berk (2006) defines *cognition* as "the inner processes and products of the mind that lead to 'knowing.' It includes all mental activity—remembering, symbolizing, categorizing, problem-solving, creating, fantasizing, and even dreaming" (p. 219). **Cognitive development,** then, refers to the development of the child's thinking and reasoning abilities.

http://classweb.gmu.edu/awinsler/ordp/cogdev.html
www.psy.pdx.edu/PsiCafe/Areas/Developmental/CogDev-child/index.htm
Both have basic information on the cognitive development of children

Theories of Development   The cognitive development of young children is described by different theorists in different terms. The behaviorist point of view is that children grow intellectually through accumulating more and more information. Most measures of intelligence are based on this idea of accumulating knowledge. Another point of view is that of the constructivists, or developmentalists, who describe knowledge as being constructed from children's interactions with the environment. According to this viewpoint, intellectual development is influenced by both maturation and experience (Piaget and Inhelder 1969). Cognitive development is indicated by a growing ability to plan, to employ strategies for remembering, and to seek solutions to problems.

Piaget and Inhelder (1969) described the cognitive development of children as progressing in several stages, including the *sensorimotor stage,* the *preoperational stage,* and the *concrete operational stage* (see box). The stages evolve with the child's growing maturity and experience. Although approximate ages have been attached to these stages, the rate at which individuals pass through them is variable; the sequence of stages, however, is invariant. In other words, a child must pass through each stage, but different children may pass through the stages at different ages. The transition time between stages is lengthy. Children do not move suddenly from one stage of thinking to another—changes may take months or years, as the child constructs and integrates knowledge. A child may be performing some tasks in ways that indicate preoperational thinking while performing other tasks in very stable operational ways.

> **The human mind is our fundamental resource.**
>
> *—John F. Kennedy*

Vygotsky (1978) believed that children's intellectual development is influenced more by social context than by individual experiences. His theory places a great deal of emphasis on effective social interaction. One characteristic of such effective interactions is what Vygotsky called *intersubjectivity,* which describes a process in which two people are engaged in a task and begin it with different understandings but come to a shared understanding. With infants, this process is illustrated when the caregiver follows the infant's gaze and talks about or hands the object of the gaze to the child. The nature of these encounters changes over time, especially with the development of language.

Piaget's Stages of Development

Sensorimotor Period (birth to two years)

The sensorimotor period is characterized by interactions with the environment based on the child's reception of sensory input and muscular reactions. The period begins with reflexive actions, which are gradually controlled by the child, and ends with the child's having developed a concept of separateness from others and the beginnings of symbolic thinking. The task of this period is to develop the concept of *object permanence,* the idea that objects exist even when they cannot be seen or heard.

Preoperational Period (two to seven years)

The beginning of the preoperational period is characterized by emergence of the ability to represent objects and knowledge through imitation, symbolic play, drawing, mental images, and spoken language. One outstanding characteristic of preoperational thinking is lack of conservation. *Conservation* is defined as the knowledge that the number, mass, area, length, weight, and volume of objects are not changed by physically rearranging the objects.

Children whose thinking is preoperational are egocentric in that they cannot easily take the points of view of others. A preoperational child believes that everyone thinks as she does and that everyone thinks the same things she does. *Egocentrism* is not exclusive to the thinking of preoperational children but is most prominent then. Egocentrism is a factor in the child's reasoning at this stage because children do not question their own thinking and therefore do not change schemata readily.

Another characteristic of preoperational thinking is *centration.* The preoperational child tends to pay attention to one element of a problem at a time and cannot coordinate information from multiple sources. Centration is related to classification, seriation, and other such tasks. The following anecdote describes an example of centration:

> A child was visiting with a family friend, and they were going out in a boat. The friend's boat was beside an identical boat at the dock. One boat was tied up about three feet farther in the slip than the other one. The child walked up and down the pier several times, observing the two boats. After a few minutes, he remarked, "Your boat is longer on this end, and that boat is longer on the other end."

A fourth characteristic of preoperational thinking is the difficulty a child has in trying to reverse thinking.

NAEYC CRITERIA
3.62

Scaffolding Another hallmark of effective interactions is *scaffolding:* the support given the learner in the social context, which changes with the growing ability of the child or with the situation. In scaffolding physical skills, an adult helping a child learn to cut may hold the scissors with his hand over the child's hand and help the child move them, pointing out what happens when they are moved in a certain way. As the child becomes more skilled, the adult offers less help and more challenging cutting tasks.

Scaffolding for intellectual abilities might include such experiences as numerous sorting activities. The materials offered for sorting will be obviously different in the beginning, such as large and small objects that are the same except for size. As the child's skill increases, the materials offered for sorting will require finer discriminations. For example, the child might need to sort by color or style and finally by function. Observing the process of learning to read reveals a great deal of scaffolding, as the reader moves from being read to, to learning to recognize some elements of print, and finally to reading independently. At each stage, the teacher or parent offers the assistance that the child needs at the time.

Make-Believe Vygotsky (1978) also emphasized the role of make-believe play in children's cognitive development. Children involved in pretend play learn to act in accordance with their internal ideas, not just their external environment. Children must also follow the rules of the social situation they are playing—for example, riding on a train, going to church, and so on.

Reversibility is defined as the ability to follow a line of reasoning back to the beginning point. In the problem of conserving numbers, a child is presented with two rows of eight plastic chips and observes that they are equal. When the space between the chips is lengthened, the preoperational child believes that the number has been changed because the row is longer. When the child is able to reverse the reasoning process, he will be able to determine that moving the chips does not affect the number. A child may be able to reverse an operation physically before being able to reverse operations mentally.

Preoperational children have difficulty in reasoning logically about transformations. The child tends to concentrate on the elements of change and not on the transformations of objects or materials from one state to another. Piaget found that children had difficulty thinking about successive changes in states and about the relationship of one event to another. Piaget made this observation when walking with a child through the woods and drawing the child's attention to the snails that could be seen at various points along the path. The child could not determine if the snails were all the same snail or different snails. Children can observe the beginning point and the ending point of transformations, but they often have difficulty following all the points in between. If a child is asked to draw what happens to a pencil as it falls off a table, she can draw the pencil on the table and on the floor but not all the steps between the table and the floor.

Concrete Operational Period (seven to eleven or twelve years)

Children begin making the transition from preoperational thinking to operational thinking at various times. In most kindergarten classrooms, a few children will be beginning to think operationally. In the primary grades, more children will be operational thinkers, even though many may still be preoperational on some tasks. Piaget and Inhelder (1969) describe the operational thinker as one who employs "identity or reversibility by inversion or reciprocity" (p. 99) in solving problems.

Concrete operational thinkers are able to solve problems of conservation and reversibility. They can *decenter*, or coordinate information from more than one source, in solving problems. They are not as egocentric in their thinking. Because they are aware that others may come to conclusions that differ from theirs, they are much more likely to examine their own conclusions.

Sources: Piaget and Inhelder 1969; Wadsworth 1989.

Current Brain Research In addition to the theoretical explanations of cognitive growth, an increasing amount of knowledge is available from biology as scientists study the human brain. Using sophisticated imaging techniques and other investigative strategies, scientists can determine how the electrical activity in the brain differs from one experience to another. This is the beginning of a revolution in the field of education. When we have answers about how the brain works, teaching will radically change.

At this time, however, our knowledge of the brain is limited. Some proponents of so-called brain-based learning are making claims that cannot be proven. For example, Bruer (1999) argues against the generally accepted belief that the two hemispheres of the brain have different functions, such as the processing of music and math. He believes that scientific evidence proves that different areas of the brain do different kinds of processing; however, it is much more refined than the proponents of left- and right-brain teaching would have us believe, and both hemispheres are involved in almost every processing task. He also finds no scientific support for the idea that learning takes place more quickly and easily when children are young. According to Bruer, there is no evidence that a five-year-old brain learns more quickly than a fifteen-year-old brain.

What we *do* know about the brain is that it is "wired" to process information in different ways. Some of this wiring happens prenatally when cells differentiate into the different areas of the brain. Human brains are prewired for some capabilities, such as oral language (Brandt 1999), and some of this wiring happens because of experience or need. For example, people can learn to interpret the messages from the nerves in the eyes differently, as

http://bdl.uoregon.edu/Links/ links.html

The website for the brain study lab at the University of Oregon, with links to several of its projects

www.zerotothree.org/ brainwonders

Information for parents and caregivers about recent studies of how the brain grows and develops

www.facsnet.org/tools/ sci_tech/biotek/eliot.php

Technical information about brain growth and development, but it is explained well when they learn to wear one contact lens to correct for distance vision. In doing so, the pattern from one eye is always fuzzy, either at a distance or close up. After a few weeks, the brain learns to ignore the fuzzy message and interprets only the clear message.

It is also safe to say that providing an enriched environment encourages many more connections between the neurons of the brain, creating more possibilities for solving problems (Jensen 1998; Sylwester 1995). It cannot be said for certain, however, just what an *enriched environment* is and what cultural biases limit the descriptions of enriched environments currently being published. In a review of current brain research as it applies to young children and their environment, Gallagher (2005) believes that an enriched environment is developmentally appropriate in that it offers many stimulating experiences that provide for increased connections in the brain and for a reduced level of stress hormone. (The production of too much stress hormone can lead to lower cognitive functioning.)

Even though we have much to learn about the brain and its functioning, we can observe children's development and offer them opportunities for many kinds of experiences under emotionally comfortable circumstances. If we do this and continue to read and learn about the biology of the brain, we can make schools better and learning more accessible to all children.

Implications for the Curriculum

Planning for the intellectual growth of children must be based on the knowledge of children's cognitive development. A child who is preoperational, for instance, would not be expected to solve problems in the same way that an older child would solve them. Also, children need chances to learn in ways that are active and that provide opportunities to learn in ways that suit their individual techniques for organizing and remembering information.

DEVELOPMENTALLY APPROPRIATE PRACTICE

Knowing the child or the learner is absolutely necessary for planning a developmentally appropriate program. Several questions about DAP are directly related to children's development:

- Are the activities planned usually of interest to children of the age for which they are intended?

- Can most children complete the activities successfully?

- Will some children be allowed to choose more challenging activities?

- Will some children be allowed to choose activities that require less skill without being censured?

- Will expectations for performance reflect knowledge of child development?

One challenge for teachers is to avoid what Lilian Katz (1986) describes as "learned stupidity," which occurs when children are given tasks that they cannot do and, through failure at those tasks, learn to believe that they are stupid. No young child has the life experience to evaluate an inappropriate task and determine that it was the task that was at fault, not the learner.

Young children learn best through manipulating objects and being reflective about those manipulations, not through passive experiences in which they listen to someone tell them how something works. Young children need the stimulation of their peers in solving problems, and they need to be able to use what they already know in learning new information. Throughout this book, you will find suggestions for encouraging the intellectual growth of children; the following activities are merely a small sample of the endless possibilities:

NAEYC CRITERIA
3.59

- Provide old machines (toasters, TVs, radios, and so on) that children can dismantle and explore. (Be sure to remove the electrical connections and any springs that could be unsafe.)

- Set up problems to be presented to the class in ways that encourage divergent thinking and multiple right answers. For example, ask children how many different ways they can sort the blocks, rather than ask them to sort the blocks by color.

NAEYC CRITERIA
3.57

- Give children the opportunity to choose as many of their own activities as possible. Children can learn to classify by playing with blocks, leaves, keys, items from the supermarket, and articles of clothing. When children are given a choice, they are more likely to learn.

- Provide materials that are open ended so that the challenge and complexity can be increased as the children grow. For example, given beads, children at different ages can string them, use them to create patterns, or use them to create models and designs.

- Encourage children to follow their interests. Jacque Wuertenburg (1993) calls it "leading through life." If a child is interested in spiders or snakes or computers, use that interest to help build skills and concepts.

- Assist children in understanding the application of what they are learning in school to real life. Learning without a purpose is difficult.

Child Development and Curriculum Planning: An Example

In her short essay on using knowledge of development in planning for instruction, Darla Wood-Walters mentions handwriting instruction (see A Teacher Speaks). Handwriting instruction is a good example of an activity that forces teachers to think of all areas of development.

For instance, a child cannot learn to form letters without having the physical ability to hold the pencil and to control the movements necessary to write. It is also difficult to learn handwriting until one has a social need for handwriting. If writing did not exist in our society, we would have no need for handwriting. Social development is required for handwriting, since part of learning to form letters in the agreed-on forms comes from the

A **Teacher** SPEAKS: Using Developmental Knowledge in Planning

Darla Wood-Walters

Elk Meadow Elementary
Bend, Oregon

My classroom brings together children who are assigned to a specific grade level. However, whether I am teaching kindergarten or first grade for a given school year, my focus is always on the developmental needs of the individual children in my classroom, not their grade-level placement.

It is my challenge to identify and celebrate what a child can do well, build a foundation of confidence and pride, and from there guide and support him as he takes the next step. Although I can present lessons and activities that are well prepared, organized, and appropriate for my grade-level curriculum, if they are not within reach of my students' present understandings, they are nothing more than a lesson taught, not a lesson learned.

The concept of developmental appropriateness has received much attention in past years, with general definitions being assigned to each of the primary grades. However, I teach the child, not the grade level. It is as developmentally inappropriate to fail to challenge students as it is to frustrate other students. My goal is always to match instruction to the developmental needs of my students, providing a task that is just beyond what they think they can do and giving them the support they need not only to be able to do it but also to do it well.

For example, I want young writers to know that writing is talking on paper. Rather than spoon-feeding them with fill-in-the-blanks and specific structures to make them all sound like writers, I want to recognize each child's first steps to becoming a writer as she shares her thinking and talking voice through an illustration, letterlike marks, random letters, phonetic spelling, con-

ventional spelling, or edited writing and revising. As I conference with a young writer, I applaud what she does well and focus her attention on what she can do to make her next writing even better. For one child, this might be to put spaces between words, for another it might be how to use a word card to edit for spelling, and for yet another it might be how to extend the story to make it more interesting.

Just as the instructional focus reflects the writing development of the student, the book size and format also reflect the writer's needs. Emergent writers need large, blank paper, providing space for the untamed pencil and crayon. Developing and fluent writers use smaller formatted, lined paper, as the illustration becomes less important and the print carries more of the message. A variety of writing materials would be used in kindergarten and first grade, providing each child with the support she needs for success.

There is no set time in the year when I begin instruction on handwriting. Until a student has a good grasp of directionality, spatial awareness, and motor control, learning to make letters correctly is unnecessarily difficult. I focus a student's attention on handwriting when these concepts and skills are in place, when a child is confident in putting pencil to paper, and when he has had enough writing experiences to understand that good writing is much more than how the print looks. I teach handwriting on an individual basis, embedding it in meaningful print, beginning with a child's name, pulling letters out of his daily writing, and then attending to capitals/lowercase as needed to support understandings of punctuation. This focus on handwriting might begin with one student the first month of kindergarten; it might begin with another midyear of first grade. Always, instruction is based on the development of the child.

recognition that one needs to write in order to communicate with others. Children must also have a sufficient level of emotional development to take direction from the teacher and to continue to try to match the model provided by the teacher, even when it is frustrating. Finally, the child must have the intellectual capacity to recognize what letters are and how they are used to send messages to other humans.

Do you agree that handwriting instruction is a good example of planning that depends on knowledge of child development? Why or why not?

CHILDREN WITH SPECIAL NEEDS

One of the most common ways of informally diagnosing the special needs of a child is to observe that the child is not meeting the usual developmental benchmarks. These benchmarks allow for wide variation in development. For example, Berk (2006) notes that 90 percent of children learn to walk between nine and seventeen months of age. This is a rather long period of time for a young child, and it illustrates how development varies with individual children. However, knowing this benchmark will help parents and other observers to recognize that if a child has not learned to walk by about seventeen months, some screening may be in order to determine if there are problems in development. All the areas of development are subject to wide variation, but knowing the general schedule for development will aid parents and teachers as they observe children.

Children with special needs such as learning disabilities may not display any unusual developmental signs; in fact, their problems may not be discovered until they are asked to learn school-related tasks. Other children with special needs can be identified much earlier than the beginning of school experiences. Most states now have public programs for children beginning at age three who have been identified with language delays, physical disabilities, cognitive issues, and other special needs. Some states even have early identification programs for all children from birth to three years of age and offer assistance to any child who has special needs.

CELEBRATING DIVERSITY

The work of Vygotsky supports the notion that children from different cultures learn different things at different ages. Teachers need to recognize that children learn to use language in ways that are appropriate for their own culture and to perform tasks that are significant in their culture. For example, some Asian children can manipulate chopsticks successfully long before their European counterparts have the fine motor control to do so.

Cultural expectations certainly have an influence on child development. In some cultures, children are expected to assume more responsibilities than children of the same age in other cultures. In some cultures, for instance, children are expected to contribute to the care of younger children and to perform household chores, while in other cultures, children are expected to play and to do only simple chores, such as helping to pick up their own toys. It is wise for teachers to learn about what parents in their community believe about child development and the ages at which certain behaviors are expected. You can do this best by carefully observing the children in your class and by asking parents what children are expected to do at home and at school.

Parents and Development

- Communicate with parents about their children's accomplishments in all four areas of development: physical, social, emotional, and cognitive. For each child, keep a column in a notebook or a file of observations labeled with the four areas so that you can tell at a glance if you are not observing growth in one area as much as in others. Share this information with parents, and ask them to provide information across all areas as well—particularly cultural expectations.

Your job is to set the stage for children to develop in all areas and to be sensitive to the expectations of the families represented in your classroom. If you are providing children with opportunities to grow in physical, social, emotional, and intellectual ways, then you are likely helping them develop skills and abilities that will serve them well in all cultural settings.

SUMMARY

● *Developmentally appropriate practice (DAP)* is defined as teaching that considers a child's developmental levels, cultural background, previous experiences, and interests when planning activities and experiences. Developmentally appropriate practice is constantly changing as the teacher and children work out the best possible learning environments and experiences. One cannot say that any single activity or experience is developmentally appropriate or not without knowing the children well, observing their behaviors and interests, and recognizing how that activity or experience fits into the whole of the program.

● Many theories offer ideas about child growth and development. Some theories are much more complete than others, as they attempt to explain all areas of development. Other theories focus on one area without giving much attention to other areas of development. The behaviorist, maturationist, constructivist, multiple intelligences, social learning, and ecological systems theories all provide unique lenses for viewing child growth and development and for describing normal growth in the domains of physical development, social development, emotional development, and intellectual development.

● Each domain of development follows predictable patterns and allows for individual variations as part of the predictability. Physical growth and development proceeds from the head down and the middle out and from gross motor development to fine motor development. This means that children learn to control their heads before they can control their legs. Movements typically progress from all-over responses, such as waving the arms and kicking the legs, to more refined responses, such as climbing stairs and controlling the movement of a marker. Both social and emotional development are marked by full-body responses at first and then more discrete responses. Much of this development takes place in the preschool years, but it continues throughout life. Intellectual development is quite rapid in the early years, as children move from learning about their world through sensory experiences to being able to use language and to create a framework for organizing their growing knowledge. Intellectual development follows a continuum and is constantly changing.

● Children with special needs are often identified when they fail to develop according to what is considered a normal timeframe for specific behaviors. For example, a child may not sit up or walk at the usual time or may not develop the use of language that is typical for his chronological age. Knowing the general benchmarks of child development will help teachers and parents of young children recognize variations that may need further observation or intervention by a specialist.

● Child development must always be viewed within a framework of cultural expectations. Children may be expected to perform certain tasks at different times, depending on their culture. We might naturally expect language and social and emotional development to be reflective of culture, but physical development may also reflect some cultural expectations. For instance, children in one culture might be asked to use chopsticks at an age much younger than would seem reasonable in another culture.

REFLECTIONS

1. What does *developmentally appropriate practice (DAP)* mean to you? Compare DAP to your own school experience. What differences and similarities can you identify?

2. The theories of child development described in this chapter provide different ways of seeing children and their behavior. Why are there so many theories of

development? Why do different theorists see children from different points of view?

3. The development of young children is often described in terms of physical development, social development, emotional development, and intellectual development. Give an example of how development in one area might influence development in other areas.

4. Suppose that you have children from several different cultural backgrounds in your classroom. Would you assume that the cultural experiences of the children have no influence on their development? Some influence but not enough to affect decisions about the curriculum? A great deal of influence that you would need to understand in order to plan the curriculum most successfully?

5. Think about a child you know well. What are the characteristics of that child's development at this point? Why are these characteristics interesting to you? What do they mean to you as a teacher?

EXPLORATIONS AND ACTIVITIES

1. Select two children who are very close in chronological age. Compare the development of these two children across a range of developmental milestones, such as motor skills, language skills, and social/emotional skills. What different needs might these two children have in terms of activities and experiences in an early childhood classroom? Think about how you could modify a common classroom activity, such as reading aloud, to meet the needs of these two children.

2. Plan how to modify a common learning area (such as blocks or art) to allow for children's developing skills in motor control, social/emotional abilities, and intellectual abilities. What changes would you make to support such development?

MyLabSchool is a collection of online tools for your success in this course, your licensure exams, and your teaching career. Visit **www.mylabschool.com** to access the following:

- Online Study Guide
- Video Cases from real classrooms
- Help with your research papers using Research Navigator
- Career Center with resources for:
  —Praxis and Licensure Preparation
  —Professional Portfolio Development
  —Job Search and Interview Techniques
  —Lesson Planning

CHAPTER 2

KEY TERMS you'll find in this chapter:

- **Child care,** 46
- **Direct instruction,** 57
- **Emerging curriculum,** 42
- **Head Start,** 47
- **Kindergarten,** 46
- **Least restrictive environment (LRE),** 48
- **Mainstreaming,** 48
- **Mastery learning,** 45
- **Montessori model,** 50
- **Progressive education movement,** 42

Designing Schools for Young Children

FOCUS QUESTIONS

- What should teachers today know about the history of early childhood education?

- What changes in early childhood education have been the most significant?

- What are the three major models of early childhood education programs?

- What does research say about the effectiveness of the different program models?

- How has the education of children with special needs changed in response to improved knowledge and legislation in this area?

- What is the nature of diversity in schools today?

When you entered the kindergarten classroom in which you observed this week, a child asked, "Do you want to see my book?" You admired the child's book and were then invited to observe other children's accomplishments: a replica of the fire station they had visited several days ago; a painting of a bird's nest; a melody played on bells; and a plant along with a growth chart, starting from the day the seed was planted. Everybody in this busy classroom seemed to be doing something interesting, but you did not see anyone doing the lessons you had expected to see.

When you shared your observations with members of your class, you found that the school settings your peers had observed varied a great deal. Some had observed lessons in which small groups of students were learning the alphabet and the sounds represented by the letters. Others had observed in classrooms in which children worked independently with materials they selected from neatly arranged shelves.

When you finished sharing observations with your peers, you did discover some elements that the programs had in common. For example, all the programs were promoting learning in children. Even so, the content of the learning and how the instruction was delivered varied greatly.

You have many questions now: Who makes the decisions about how programs are organized? Who determines the focus of the instruction? Who determines what role the teacher in the program will play? What is the best kind of program for young children? ■

Early Schools for Young Children

As an early childhood educator, you will be asked to make many decisions in your career. Many of those decisions will be about the programs and activities that you will provide for the children you teach. The decisions you make will reflect your own view of how children learn best and the most effective ways to teach them. You will want to know that early childhood education has a long history and that for many years philosophers and teachers have been thinking about these same questions.

Early childhood programs today can trace their development back to early philosophers. For example, Martin Luther (1483–1546) believed that all boys should be educated (a radical thought in his day) and insisted that music and physical education should be integral parts of the curriculum (Frost and Kissinger 1976). A century later, John Comenius (1592–1670) suggested that all children should attend school, and he recommended an integrated, hands-on curriculum. He believed that children should learn to speak by speaking, to write by writing, and to reason by reasoning (Comenius 1642; reprinted 1969). Later educators such as John Dewey, Maria Montessori, and Jean Piaget have echoed Comenius's call for active learning.

Two other philosophers, Jean-Jacques Rousseau (1712–1778) and Johann Pestalozzi (1746–1827), also made important contributions to early childhood education. Rousseau thought that educational decisions should be made on the basis of the child's nature. He also developed a stage theory of child development based on his belief that children from birth to age five learn best from physical activity and that children from five to twelve learn best by direct experience and exploration of the environment (Rousseau 1780; reprinted 1950). When educators advocate hands-on learning, they are agreeing with Rousseau. Pestalozzi wanted to rid the schools of cruel punishment and rote learning. He believed in having children participate in real, meaningful activities and in grouping children of various ages so that the older ones could help the younger ones (Pestalozzi 1885, 1894).

Key People in Early Childhood Education

Friedrich Froebel

http://teacher.scholastic.com/products/ect/froebel.htm

Part of a series on the Roots of Education; provides a biography of Froebel and a description of his work

Friedrich Froebel (1782–1852) is credited with founding *kindergartens:* "children's gardens." He studied with Pestalozzi but believed that Pestalozzi did not go far enough in matching teaching to the nature of the child. Froebel began his school for young children in Blankenburg, Germany, in 1837. He believed that everything in the universe functions in relationship to God and that each person has a specific purpose to fulfill in this life. He wrote, "Education should lead and guide man to clearness concerning himself and in himself, to peace with nature, and to unity with God" (Froebel 1826, ch. 5). The importance of the individual and the respect that must be accorded to each person is central to Froebelian thinking.

Froebel believed that play is the foundation for children's learning and envisioned the kindergarten as the child's bridge between home and school. He believed that appropriate play helps children think about the interactions between "life and self-activity, thought and action, representation and cognition, and ability and understanding" (Ransbury 1982, p. 104). Froebel believed that materials in forms found in nature—spheres, cubes, cylinders, squares, triangles, circles, and lines—help children explore the properties of matter and understand the relationships in the universe. He called these materials "gifts," and they can be purchased today from many online sources.

Froebel also designed sequences of activities that he called "occupations"; they included folding paper, drawing, and weaving. He distinguished between what he called "thoughtless copying" and "deliberate imitation." He believed that when children perform the occupations, they restructure their own ideas and do not merely copy actions without thinking about them. In Froebel's school, children often learned verses to accompany the occupations. Froebel encouraged these "Mother rhymes," which were what we would call *fingerplays* today. Children said the rhymes while they performed actions with their hands or bodies. Froebel believed that to teach young children, it was necessary to arouse and maintain interest and attention, use the child's curiosity, and plan for motivation to learn.

Although Froebel's structured approach to kindergarten instruction has been discarded, modern teachers of young children do employ fingerplays and play materials designed to encourage learning. Modern teachers also recognize the value of play as a mode of learning and the importance of recognizing the individual child. All these ideas can be traced to Froebel and his kindergarten.

Patty Smith Hill

Patty Smith Hill (1868–1946) was trained as a Froebelian but soon challenged the rigid Froebelian curriculum. Her most important contributions to the profession of early childhood education include her dedication to the scientific study of children; her belief in play as a way of learning; her insistence on creative approaches to art and music; and her commitment to the goal of an individualized curriculum.

Hill's belief in the value of play was articulated in a speech she gave at her college graduation ceremonies, when she commented that Adam and Eve deserved sympathy because they never had an opportunity to play as children. Others have continued to develop her ideas about the meaning of play in children's lives. She designed "hollow blocks"—big blocks that children can use to build structures large enough to play inside—that were later manufactured commercially. She also invented other play materials that encouraged children to construct a variety of items (Garrison 1926).

In addition to promoting free play as a valuable learning experience, Hill believed in free expression in art and music. She and her sister introduced children to bells, triangles, and other instruments to "call the children's attention to the beauty of sounds" (qtd. in Fowlkes 1984, p. 48). One of the songs created by the Hills is the song most frequently sung in English, "Happy Birthday to You." (The rights to this song sold for about 12 million dollars in 1988.) Hill also rejected the formal art lessons that were standard in her time. In these lessons, children were instructed to draw horizontal lines followed by diagonal lines and were told that when all the lines were

www.kdp.org/about/laureates/
laureates/pattyhill.php

A short biography of Patty Smith Hill and information about her work drawn correctly, they could be combined into a house. Hill believed that children should express themselves in their artwork and that formal lessons in which all the products were the same were not appropriate.

The curriculum that grows out of observation of the children and their needs, along with the interactions between the teacher and the children, is described by leaders in early childhood education today as the **emerging curriculum.** Patty Smith Hill would approve of current efforts to fit the curriculum to the child.

Another of Hill's contributions to early childhood education was her emphasis on the importance of the child's home and the learning that took place there. In 1926, she wrote an article (Hill 1926; republished 1987) in which she described the function of the kindergarten teacher as ministering to the natures and needs of children by looking forward to their needs as they develop through the sixth year and looking backward to the home to study the experiences and types of learning that have taken place there. She also wrote an article entitled "The Home and the School as Centers of Child Life" (1928), in which she defined the differences between home learning and school learning and advised teachers to pay attention to home learning and use information about it in their own teaching.

Hill founded the National Association for Nursery Education (NANE) in 1926. This organization is now the National Association for the Education of Young Children (NAEYC).

John Dewey

www.siu.edu/~deweyctr

A center for the study of Dewey's work; a biography and other information are available

John Dewey (1859–1952) is most often connected with the **progressive education movement.** He was the most influential educational philosopher in the United States in the early 1900s, and his influence is still being felt—and debated—in U.S. schools. Dewey established a laboratory school at the University of Chicago in 1903 and implemented his educational theories in the school. The progressive movement gained momentum until the time of the Great Depression and then lost credibility with the public, but many of the ideas of the movement are now considered traditional, especially those in early childhood education.

Education for children in Dewey's time was very teacher centered, in that the teacher had absolute control of the activities in the classroom and selected those in which each child would participate. Most schools relied on a subject-matter orientation in selecting curriculum experiences and on rote learning as the teaching method. For example, facts in biology were learned from a text and teacher lectures. Students were then expected to repeat the information either orally or in writing. Dewey and the other leaders of the progressive movement believed that curriculum experiences should be based on children's interests and should involve children in active experiences. In learning about biology, children might explore a limited area of their schoolyard, collect specimens of the plant and animal life, learn to classify these specimens, compare their collections with the collections of others, learn about how their specimens fit into larger ecological systems, and so on. In the process of investigating their own areas of the schoolyard, they would read, write, solve mathematical problems, and learn to work successfully with others.

Dewey's ideas have often been misinterpreted to mean that children should do only what they are interested in and that any kind of experience is valuable for learning. In fact, Dewey believed that activity itself was not enough for learning. He believed that children needed to be engaged in real and meaningful activities that would lend themselves to a wide variety of learning possibilities and that would be vehicles for learning to think and reflect. In his day, Dewey was concerned that in the democratic United States, the schools failed to reach large segments of the population and that the teaching methods stifled individual growth and development (Dewey 1900, 1902).

Early childhood education has benefited from Dewey's work in developing an active curriculum for young children that is integrated, rather than divided into subject-matter segments. Dewey's influence is also evident in curricula that reflect the interests of the children. Such curricula cannot be set ahead of time but must be built on knowledge of children and their interests. Teachers are responsible for achieving the goals of the school, but the specific topics to be studied to meet those goals cannot be determined in advance. Children are also encouraged to learn to work in groups and to learn about the interdependence of people in a community and a nation.

Lucy Sprague Mitchell

Lucy Sprague Mitchell (1878–1967) founded the Bureau of Educational Experiments in 1916. The bureau eventually grew into the Bank Street College of Education, a leading institution in the study of children and play and the development of curriculum materials.

www.bankstreet.edu/sfc/ history.html

A history of Bank Street and its founder, Lucy Sprague Mitchell

Mitchell was a student of John Dewey, who greatly influenced her work. When the progressive movement began, typical school conditions involved harsh punishments, a curriculum that was established without regard for the individual child, teaching methods that relied on rote memory, and a subject-matter orientation to learning. Those involved in the progressive movement emphasized the needs of the individual child, believed that children learned best when they were interested in the materials, felt that learning was best achieved through active involvement with materials, and were concerned with the development of the whole child—physically, socially, intellectually, and emotionally. "Whole child" was one of Mitchell's phrases.

Mitchell's philosophy of education proposed that the education of young children should be based on these principles:

- stimulating each child to unfold as fully as possible, but at her or his own pace;
- welcoming individual children's conversation and other forms of self-expression (art, music and movement, story creating, etc.);
- promoting learning through play (always child-initiated and child-directed) and through meaningful self-initiated or teacher-initiated planned experiences and projects (e.g., attending to how young children learn);
- individualizing; and
- avoiding teacher-given external rewards, because the reward of learning through meaningful activity is in seeing a challenge and solving the problem *oneself*. (Greenburg 1987, p. 73)

Although Mitchell did not create any of these principles, she served as a leader in promoting them. For instance, she opened a laboratory school to implement and experiment with the teaching principles in which she believed. She also organized a laboratory to study how and why children function as they do and a teacher's college to educate teachers about these principles. She organized a workshop for writers of children's literature— a field not recognized as important in that time—and published bulletins to inform people about what she and others in the progressive movement were accomplishing. Like Dewey, Mitchell believed that the education of the young is important in a democratic society, and she placed great importance on helping children learn cooperation and group skills.

Mitchell was also a leader in educational research. When she began her work, psychology was a new field of study and psychologists were just beginning to try to explain human behavior. Mitchell's goals were to bring together researchers from a broad range of disciplines to study normal children in a setting in which they were offered a curriculum made up of experiences as well as information. She wanted to support educational experiments and make information about these experiments available to the public.

Lucy Sprague Mitchell was an influential leader in early childhood education because of her contributions in developing and implementing a hands-on curriculum and because of her dedication to the scientific study of education (Antler 1987).

Other Influential People in Early Childhood Education

New ways of thinking about children have evolved from the research of leading educators such as G. Stanley Hall, J. McVicker Hunt, Benjamin Bloom, Abraham Maslow, and Jerome Bruner. The results of their research and child study have certainly had an impact on thinking in the field of early childhood education.

G. Stanley Hall

G. Stanley Hall (1844–1924) was an advocate of the scientific study of children and adolescents in the late 1800s. He urged psychologists to study education and teaching, which were not especially interesting topics to most psychologists of that time. He also wanted to create a professional base of knowledge for education. Although Hall's studies focused on the nature of the child, he never tested his conclusions in real school settings. His work would not meet current standards for scientific studies.

Hall was very critical of the Froebelian approach to kindergarten and wanted more emphasis on free play and attention to physical health than was common in the traditional kindergarten. His real concern for the study of children contributed to the development of the field of educational psychology. He and his many students pushed educators to learn more about children and the psychology on which teaching decisions are based (Ross 1972).

J. McVicker Hunt

Historically, educators had believed in the fixed nature of intelligence. It had been believed for years that the intelligence of each child was fixed at birth and could not be altered. Building on earlier studies, J. McVicker Hunt (1906–1991) demonstrated in the late 1950s that at least what we *measure* as intelligence is not fixed but rather responsive to experience.

This finding gave added impetus to the early childhood education movement, especially to intervention programs such as Head Start (which is discussed in more detail later in this chapter). Such programs were designed to provide experiences for children who might otherwise miss out on what is available to middle-class children. For example, children in intervention programs who had never seen a farm would be stimulated through field trips to a farm and follow-up language experiences revolving around the trip. The idea that a child's measured intelligence quotient (IQ) could be raised by participation in given experiences provided early childhood educators with support for the importance of their programs (Hunt 1961).

Benjamin Bloom

The research of Benjamin Bloom (1913–1999) also had an impact on early childhood education programs. One of Bloom's major studies, *Stability and Change in Human Characteristics* (1964), looked at intelligence over a period of time and concluded that much of what can be measured as IQ at age seventeen is developed in the child's early years. His findings, like Hunt's, gave early childhood educators more reasons to be concerned with the quality of educational experiences for young children and more support for the importance of experience in children's early years.

Bloom developed a taxonomy of objectives by which experiences and questions can be ordered in a hierarchy. *Bloom's taxonomy* ranges from simple recall, to understanding, to applying, to analyzing, to evaluating, and finally to creating. This taxonomy helps teachers think about what kinds of questions they ask students as well as what kinds of thinking will result from various planned experiences (Bloom 1956).

Also important is Bloom's concept of **mastery learning.** He believed children could master the tasks presented to them at school, but that some children would need more time and more activities or guidance in order to do so. He proposed that curricula be organized so that each learner could move at his own pace in mastering the objectives.

Abraham Maslow

In 1954, Abraham Maslow (1908–1970) published the book *Motivation and Personality,* in which he proposed a theory of learning that focused on the learner's needs. According to this theory, unless the needs that Maslow described as *basic needs* were met, learning would be very difficult or not happen at all. The *hierarchy of needs* that Maslow proposed placed shelter, food, air, and water at the very bottom, or most basic level of needs. The next level was for safety and security followed by love and belonging. The top two levels of his hierarchy were self-esteem and self-actualization.

Much of what Maslow believed is common sense in that a child who is hungry is not likely to be very interested in learning; likewise, a child who does not feel secure is not likely to be motivated to learn. For early childhood teachers, Maslow's work underscores the importance of helping children meet their basic needs (e.g., offering a breakfast program at school) and providing a safe (physical and psychological) learning environment. Children also need to feel that they are cared for and that they belong to the group for learning to be most effective.

Jerome Bruner

It is difficult to summarize the work of Jerome Bruner (1915–) because he has been involved in so many kinds of educational research over the years. He has studied the development of language, play, thinking, and curriculum.

Bruner wrote that "any subject can be taught effectively in some intellectually honest form to any child in any stage of development" (Bruner 1960, p. 32). This statement has often been misinterpreted, leading some people to believe that he meant that children of any age can learn any subject—that all teachers need to give them is more practice or more drill and they can master anything.

Bruner believes the key to good teaching is to understand the child's development and how she views the world and then to translate the subject to some form that fits the child's current views. A teacher who understands development would not believe that two-year-olds should be taught multiplication but would help young children begin to recognize that some objects in their environment, such as their shoes, come in sets. This concept of sets is the basis for learning multiplication.

Changes in Early Childhood Education

The Child-Care Movement

The earliest **child care** was established in the settlement houses of big U.S. cities at the turn of the twentieth century "to provide a shelter for the children of mothers dependent on their own exertions for their daily bread; [but] also to rear useful citizens among the class represented by the children we reach" (Steinfels 1973, p. 29). Even though most mothers who worked outside the home did so for economic survival, the belief persisted that mothers should take care of their own children, so the availability of child care declined as the century progressed.

Other efforts at providing child care have been in response to national emergencies. During the Great Depression, the Works Progress Administration created nursery schools to provide teaching positions for unemployed teachers, and during World War II, the Lanham Act established nursery schools so that mothers could participate in the war effort. At the end of each of these periods, the federal funding ended, and so did the programs (Grubb 1989).

During the 1970s, there were repeated efforts to pass legislation to support child care. Progress on child-care legislation stalled during the 1980s, but some positive steps were made in the 1990s, such as providing more federal funding for programs that benefit children. Currently, efforts are being made to support child care for poor families through block grants to states and grants for those families on assistance programs.

Kindergarten

Kindergarten—defined as "a specialized school adapted to the nature and needs of young children from the fourth to the sixth year" (Hill 1992)—began with the Froebel kindergarten in Germany in 1837. The first kindergarten in the United States was opened in 1855 by Margaretha Schurz, and the first English-speaking kindergarten was opened by Elizabeth Peabody in 1860. The first publicly supported kindergarten was opened by Susan Blow in St. Louis in 1873 (Frost and Kissinger 1976).

Publicly supported kindergarten is now available in almost all the states, and many states provide funding for public school programs for four-year-olds, especially those deemed at risk of failing in public school for any

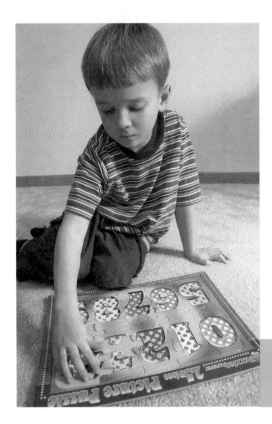

Playing alone as well as with others is important in well planned programs.

reason. In a few states, attendance in kindergarten is compulsory; that is, state law requires that parents send their children to school at five years of age. In most states, even though school districts are required to *offer* kindergarten, attendance is not mandated by law.

Head Start

The charity schools of the early 1800s (nursery schools supported by philanthropists to save children from poor families from disadvantaged environments) and the settlement house programs of the early 1900s shared the goal of trying to change the lives of young poor children. Modern-day programs continue this effort.

One component of the War on Poverty in the early 1960s was **Head Start,** a compensatory program that was a major feature of the plan to break the cycle of poverty in the United States. Head Start provides educational, social, medical, dental, nutritional, and mental health services to low-income preschool children. In 2000, Head Start celebrated its thirty-fifth anniversary, but the program continues to be able to serve only a portion of the eligible children.

Many different programs have been developed and evaluated as part of Head Start, and much research in early childhood education has been undertaken in Head Start programs. Thus, Head Start has been beneficial not only to the millions of children who have attended programs but also to the profession of early childhood education.

Programs for Children with Special Needs

The education of children with special needs has undergone radical changes in the last few decades. Early in the twentieth century, children with

www.

www2.acf.dhhs.gov/ programs/hsb

The national website for Head Start with links to many related topics disabilities were often excluded from school experiences. Later, they were identified but segregated into special classes in schools. Often, all children with disabilities from a given school district were housed in a special school so that they had no contact with typically developing children.

In 1975, Public Law (PL) 94-142, the Education for All Handicapped Children Act, was passed in the United States. This law is often called the "mainstreaming law," but it does not mention the word **mainstreaming.** What the law does say is that every child is entitled to an education in the **least restrictive environment (LRE).** Separate schools or classes are appropriate only when the "nature or severity of the handicap is such that education in regular classes with the use of supplementary aids and services cannot be achieved satisfactorily" (PL 94-142 20 U.S.C. 1412, 5, B).

Public Law 99-457, enacted in 1986, reauthorized PL 94-142 and extended its provisions to younger children. The intent of the original law had been to provide services to children with disabling conditions from birth to school age, but the law had been written so that states were not required to provide services to children younger than school age. PL 99-457 extended the services to children from ages three to five and added incentives for states that served children from birth to age two, as well. Services can be provided by public or private agencies, but providers must demonstrate quality and integration. Key elements in PL 99-457 are its emphasis on the role of parents and its recognition of the importance of the family in the child's development.

Recognizing that labeling young children can be a harmful practice, PL 99-457 does not require or emphasize categorical labels. Safford (1989) states the following reasons for avoiding labeling:

> Young children's needs are difficult, if not impossible, to categorize with traditional labels.
>
> Especially during the early years, these needs change rapidly.
>
> Categorical labels have no utility for young children, since categorical programs may not be appropriate.
>
> Early labeling of children may limit and restrict them, since others may respond to these labels in limiting and restricting ways.
>
> Labels tend to follow the child, even after they are no longer applicable or appropriate. A label is a hard thing to lose!
>
> Least restrictive services for young children, required by P. L. 99-457, are intended to foster the interaction of handicapped and nonhandicapped children. Labels tend to impede that interaction. (p. 10)

Federal law also requires that a minimum of 10 percent of the children enrolled in Head Start programs be children with disabilities and that services be provided to meet their special needs (Head Start, Economic Opportunity and Community Partnership Act of 1974, PL 93-644, 1974). To meet enrollment quotas, children who are disabled but not otherwise eligible for Head Start may be admitted (Safford 1989).

PL 94-142 was updated in 1990 and is now known as the Individuals with Disabilities Education Act (IDEA). IDEA expanded the categories of children eligible to receive special education services to include those with autism and traumatic brain injury. The new law continues to mandate parental involvement in educational decisions, education in the least restrictive environment, and individualized education programs (Hardman et al. 1993).

An updated version of IDEA was signed into law in December of 2004. It aligns IDEA closely with the No Child Left Behind (NCLB) Act, "helping to ensure equity, accountability and excellence in education for children with disabilities" (U.S. Department of Education 2006). A series of public meetings were held throughout 2005 to gather ideas about how to implement programs according to the provisions of the new law. While specific instructions for implementing IDEA 2004 are being prepared, those from the 1997 law remain in effect, as long as they are consistent with the new statute. (For the most current information on the new provisions of IDEA 2004, go to www.ed.gov/policy/speced/guid/idea/idea2004.html.)

Early Intervention Programs

Most states have programs for children deemed at risk for any number of factors. Many of these children are identified because their mothers are poor, received little or no prenatal care, or are substance abusers. Other children who qualify for intervention are those with disabilities or other special needs. Many states have programs that seek to identify eligible children at birth and to provide home-based services to these children from birth to age three. At age three, most states provide center- or school-based programs for children with special needs.

The support for early intervention programs is based on the idea that preventing a problem from occurring is more efficient than trying to correct a problem that already exists. In other words, if children who are at risk can be identified and provided with needed services early in their lives, many problems can be prevented. Early intervention specialists usually focus on helping the family provide an environment that promotes healthy growth—both physically and intellectually. For example, caretakers are aided in planning children's diets and visits to physicians for immunizations as well as taught how to talk to children to promote language development.

Available services, procedures for identifying children, and funding vary widely across the states. Some states attempt to provide services for a broad range of conditions, whereas others provide services only for children with identified disabilities.

Contemporary Models of Early Childhood Programs

Today, many models describe goals, materials, teacher roles, and appropriate instructional practices for early childhood education. Roopnarine and Johnson (2000) describe thirteen models, including home-based models. It is not a simple task to group the programs commonly found in early childhood into model designations. Goffin and Wilson (2001) discuss models in four basic categories. All of these authors believe that knowledge of the models can lead to a more professional approach to developing curriculum and activities for young children.

Models can serve as guidelines for planning and organizing experiences, but they are rarely, if ever, implemented totally. Uncritical acceptance of any model certainly does not encourage the professional growth and development of teachers and curriculum planners. As teachers use models and theories, they construct their own understanding of the teaching–learning

www.
www.ed.gov/policy/speced/ guid/idea/idea2004.html
A government site about special education law and the IDEA regulations

PRAXIS

Be able to define the Montessori model and compare the Montessori model to other models of teaching processes and should be able to incorporate their experiences into any model to make it a more cohesive or complete explanation of how children develop and learn.

Most knowledge of models in early childhood education grew out of work done in the late 1960s and early 1970s in Head Start programs. Financial support for developing and testing models has been much more difficult to obtain since then; therefore, fewer models have been developed. Of the thirteen models described by Roopnarine and Johnson (2000), the center-based models fall roughly into three categories: Montessori models, behaviorist models, and constructivist models.

In this chapter, we will describe each of these three basic approaches to early childhood education. Although some of the models have been extended to address both younger and older children, for the sake of comparison each program in this chapter will be described as it applies to four- and five-year-olds; notes about applying programs to younger or older children will be included. Each section will include a description of the theoretical foundation of the model, the beliefs about teaching and learning on which the model is based, the goals of the model, a typical day in a school based on the model, and a brief evaluation of the model.

The Montessori Model

www.montessori.edu

A website with many links to information about Montessori education

Maria Montessori left her mark on the world in many ways. She was the first woman in Italy to become a doctor of medicine and the first woman to earn a doctorate in anthropology. She established the method of education that bears her name and continues to be used today in schools all over the world. Even schools that do not claim any particular kinship to Montessori education use materials and methods of teaching that were influenced by Montessori and her inventions (Kramer 1976).

Montessori became interested in education as she worked with children who were labeled "feebleminded." She soon discovered that her methods of teaching could also be applied to children who did not have mental retardation. She opened her first school in a poor district in Rome in 1907 and in a very short time drew worldwide attention to Montessori education.

Interest in the **Montessori model** of education in the United States was very strong in the early 1900s. Montessori came to lecture at Carnegie Hall as the guest of Thomas Edison, and shortly afterward the Montessori Society was formed, with Alexander Graham Bell as its first president. Montessori schools, at both the preschool and elementary levels, are now common in most U.S. communities. Although most Montessori schools are private, some public school systems offer Montessori programs as alternative schools.

How Children Learn: Montessori

Some key elements of Montessori philosophy include the ideas of the absorbent mind, the prepared environment, autoeducation, sensitive periods, and the principle of freedom for the child. Each of these elements is a factor in explanations of how children grow and develop.

The concept of the *absorbent mind* is important in Montessori philosophy. The prevailing idea in Montessori's time was that children do not do anything mentally during infancy. Montessori, however, believed that infants unconsciously absorb all that is around them and that gradually this process becomes conscious. As the child becomes conscious, he begins to organize experiences and make generalizations. For example, after several experiences with cups of various kinds, the child comes to understand "cup" as a category that includes not only all existing cups but also all possible cups. Montessori philosophy also holds that the child's construction of a sense of self is accomplished if he is free to develop the pattern inherent in him (Standing 1962).

In a Montessori program, the teacher is responsible for the *prepared environment:* that is, for selecting and arranging the materials that make learning possible. Materials for learning must be carefully chosen and displayed to catch the child's interest. The tables and chairs must be child sized and lightweight so that a child can arrange them in the way that is most comfortable for her. The environment must be orderly so that the child develops a sense of order and control. It must also be attractive so that the child develops a respect for beauty. Most Montessori classrooms are decorated with plants and objects from nature as well as colorful displays and tasteful pieces of art.

The teacher is responsible for sequencing the child's experiences so that he learns concepts logically. The materials for instruction are arranged so that the child can select from among them the ones in which he is interested, but it is the teacher's role to bring out and demonstrate new materials at the optimal time in the development of each child. Once the teacher has demonstrated the procedures for using materials, the child can choose to work with them.

It is within this carefully planned framework that *autoeducation*—the organizing of information into logical patterns—takes place. Children learn to clarify their perceptions and organize their experiences through certain activities. The teacher's role is not to present information through direct instruction but to demonstrate the materials and guide the child's selection of materials and activities.

A basic premise of the Montessori philosophy is that the child copies reality rather than constructs it. From watching and then doing activities, the child organizes the world and her own thinking. One of the primary roles of a Montessori teacher is to demonstrate how materials are to be used and tasks are to be completed. These demonstrations are very specific in that there is an exact procedure for using each set of materials; children are not allowed free expression with the materials until they have mastered the exact procedures (Montessori 1914).

Most Montessori materials are self-correcting in that they are designed to give the child feedback on the correctness of his actions. An example of self-correcting material is the Pink Tower, which is a set of cubes of graduated sizes. The child begins building the Tower by placing the largest cube on the bottom; each additional cube is placed on the Tower in order by decreasing size, such that the smallest cube is placed on the top. In demonstrating how to use the Tower, the teacher first shows how it is constructed; then he takes it apart and allows the child to construct it. The teacher does not supply information or cues to the child while he is attempting this construction. If the Tower is constructed correctly, each cube will be used and every cube placed on the Tower will be smaller than the preceding cube. If the child makes an error in construction, one or more cubes will be left over or will not fit properly. The purpose of the Pink Tower is to help the child

> **Assume that children are basically good and provide opportunities for this goodness to flourish.**
>
> —*Jean-Jacques Rousseau*

NAEYC CRITERIA
3.19

develop abilities in seriation. Once the child has mastered the Tower, other materials are introduced in a careful sequence to aid him in transferring the ability to seriate from one situation to another and to further his thinking and reasoning abilities.

Montessori materials and exercises are basically divided into four categories that promote the development of daily-living skills and sensorial, academic, cultural, and artistic abilities:

1. **Daily-living exercises** involve the physical care of oneself and the environment and include tasks such as washing a table and polishing shoes. The purpose of these tasks is not simply to develop a skill but also to aid the "inner construction of discipline, organization, independence, and self-esteem through concentration on a precise and completed cycle of activity" (Lillard 1972, p. 71).

2. **Sensorial materials** are designed to encourage refinement of the senses for the purpose of aiding the child in developing intelligence. Montessori believed that intelligence is developed as the child organizes and categorizes perceptions into a mental order. An example of sensorial materials is a collection of seven different fabric samples: velvet, silk, wool, fine linen, coarse linen, fine cotton, and coarse cotton. The teacher is to take care that these samples are pure. The child is encouraged to play with the samples, to learn the names of the fabrics, and then to identify a given sample by touch.

3. **Academic materials** include the movable alphabet, sandpaper letters, and plane geometric insets. After the child has learned to recognize the individual letters of the alphabet and to compose some words with help from the teacher, she is presented with the movable alphabet. There are several duplicates of each letter, and the child is encouraged to compose words with them. The child is freed from the difficulty of forming letters by hand and so can progress more quickly in composing and recognizing words.

4. **Artistic or cultural materials** and exercises are designed to help children learn to love and appreciate music and to learn to control movements of their hands and feet in preparation for dance. Rhythm and then harmony and melody are introduced. Children are taught how to use musical instruments and to recognize musical sounds through the sensorial exercises. Although drawing is never taught directly, children are taught about line and color before painting is introduced.

Freedom to choose activities and when to change activities is very important in Montessori education. The teacher may guide the child by demonstrating new materials she thinks might interest or challenge the child, but the child must choose which materials to use. The choice of materials is the child's, but how the materials are used is clearly defined. If the child chooses to use materials in unacceptable ways, the teacher may remove the materials and ask the child to make another choice. Freedom of choice is related to the concept of autoeducation; the child must educate himself. Standing (1957) summarizes this concept in the following statements:

1. The child must learn by his own activity.
2. He must be granted a mental freedom to take what he needs.

NAEYC CRITERIA
3.20

3. He must not be questioned in his choice—since the "teacher should answer the mental needs of the child, not dictate them." (p. 364)

Another important concept in Montessori education is that of *sensitive periods,* which are periods when a child is capable of and interested in learning specific things. This concept is much like that of *readiness.* For example, if a child is in a sensitive period in which she is fascinated with details, the teacher might supply materials that have many small parts to put together. Montessori teachers are trained to observe these sensitive periods and provide experiences appropriate for each period.

Montessori believed that young children want to be obedient and that they desire order in their environments. If a child becomes agitated or experiences "brainstorms" of activity, then he is to be removed silently and gently from the environment and encouraged to rest quietly until he has calmed down. Teachers in a Montessori school maintain discipline by expecting children to respect one another's work and workspaces and by removing children who lose control of their impulses.

NAEYC CRITERIA
3.21

Goals of Montessori Education

The most important goal of Montessori education is to develop the individual. The facts a child learns are not as important as her mental or intellectual development. Therefore, the goals of Montessori programs emphasize development of general intellectual skills and general, rather than particular, subject-matter concepts. As stated by the American Montessori Society (1984), the goals of Montessori programs include development of the following:

NAEYC CRITERIA
3.44

- Concentration
- Observation
- Awareness of order and sequence
- Coordination
- Perceptual awareness and practical skills
- Mathematical concepts
- Language skills
- Writing and reading skills
- Familiarity with the creative arts
- Understanding of the world of nature
- Experience with and understanding of the social sciences
- Experience with critical-thinking skills through problem-solving techniques

Montessori programs are concerned with children's development physically, socially, emotionally, and intellectually. The importance of physical development is reflected in an emphasis on outdoor play and participation in rhythmic activities. Social development is emphasized in discussions of appropriate behavior on the playground and in the focus on respecting the individual's work and space in the classroom. Intellectual development is achieved through activities designed to help children organize, classify, seriate, and heighten their perceptual awareness.

A Typical Day in a Montessori Preschool

9:00– 9:20	Arrival, group time
9:20–10:20	Choice time
10:20–10:45	Outdoor play
10:45–10:55	Group time, preparation for snack
10:55–11:10	Snack
11:10–11:30	Story time, one group in rhythms

In Susan's group, there are twenty-eight children, a head teacher, and two assistant teachers. The children in this group are between three and five years old. As Susan enters the light and airy classroom, she goes immediately to the area with open cupboards containing hooks and hangs up her coat while her mother signs her in for the day. Susan waves good-bye to her mother and joins the children who are gathered on the "blue line," a line of blue tape that forms a square in the middle of the largest room in the building. Susan is greeted by her teacher and says hello to her friend, who is already sitting on the line.

When all the children are gathered, the teacher sits at a small table containing a plastic mat, blue and brown clay, a rolling pin, and two identical trays about five by eight inches in size. The teacher tells the children they are going to learn about the words *island* and *lake*. She tells them that an island is land surrounded by water and that a lake is water surrounded by land. She then asks about the colors of water and land, and the children respond "blue" and "brown." She makes a model of a lake by rolling out some of the blue clay and some of the

brown clay and placing the brown clay around the blue clay on one of the trays. She repeats the process to make an island on the other tray. Then various children are called on to come up and point to the representations of the island and the lake. At the conclusion of the lesson, the teacher tells the children that this material will be available in the art room so that they can construct their own lakes and islands today.

The head teacher then tells the children that they may choose to work today in the solarium, the art room, or the large room. One of the teachers will be in each of these areas. The head teacher asks the children to go one at a time to choose their favorite things to work on and to get started working. All the children go immediately to an area and choose an activity.

One boy chooses a carpet square, places it on the floor, and selects from the shelves a tray containing a corkboard, a small hammer, and small wooden shapes, each with a hole drilled through it. Using the pegs on the tray, the child begins to attach each shape to the corkboard.

Susan takes a circular felt mat from a stack and places it on a nearby table. She then selects a basket containing a wooden board divided into six squares, with a picture of an animal on each square. She finds small squares with matching pictures and places one on each square. When she has completed this task, she places the pieces back in the basket, places the basket on the shelf, places the mat back on the stack, and chooses a carpet square, which she

NAEYC CRITERIA
3.40

NAEYC CRITERIA
3.42

In the classroom described in the box, some children are developing perceptual abilities by matching pictures or completing puzzles. Others are learning the difference between lakes and islands by constructing models with clay. The outcomes expected from each of the experiences differ. Not all children share the same experiences, but all are guided to learn some concepts and to develop some abilities. Subject-matter concepts, such as the vocabulary to describe islands and lakes or the names of the letters of the alphabet, are conveyed through group or individual instruction. Content areas such as science and social studies are included in the program in the form of materials or equipment such as scales and maps. Math concepts are also developed through materials such as the Tower and beads. Literacy is promoted through materials such as alphabet letters of different textures and the movable alphabet. Some activities, such as listening for syllables in names, are also designed to promote the development of literacy. Stories are read daily to encourage children's interest in books.

When children younger than three are accepted in Montessori programs, they usually attend two or three mornings each week, and the programs are modified by having smaller groups and fewer choices for the puts on the floor. She selects a puzzle from the shelf and begins to work on the carpet.

Meanwhile, some children have chosen to work in the solarium, where many science-oriented activities are available. Some children are working with the teacher using a scale to weigh various objects and find out whether they are heavier, lighter, or the same weight as other objects. Other children are filling containers with water from a tub; some are sorting objects based on the materials they are made of. In the art room, some children don painting smocks and paint at easels; one works with the clay to make islands and lakes; and other children choose paper and clay for drawing and molding experiences.

A few children in the large room are working with the teacher on recognizing letters. The teacher places white letters (upper- and lowercase) on a black background and tells the children the name of each letter and its sound. Then they look at a small set of pictures of objects whose names begin with that sound and name each one, emphasizing the sound. Another teacher moves around the room, working with individual children, for example, asking them the names of colors after they have matched color strips. Each child works with an activity as long as she chooses.

The children work with their activities for about an hour and are then instructed to put their materials away and get their coats for outdoor play. They play outside for about twenty minutes on the swings, a climber/slide, and balance beams and also with some large outdoor toys.

Susan walks the balance beam several times. One of the teachers holds her hand the first time, and then she walks with the teacher walking beside her but not touching her. Then Susan joins a group playing on the climber/slide and plays there until it is time to go inside.

As the children return to the room, they are instructed to wash their hands for a snack and to sit on the blue line again. As the children are washing up, one of the assistant teachers beats the rhythm of a child's name on a drum, and then all the children clap the rhythm. Each child called on is asked what name to beat—some supply only their first names, some their full names. When all the children are on the line, the head teacher discusses a problem that occurred outdoors: Someone threw a rock. She asks the children to explain why they cannot throw rocks and concludes by having them think of things they *can* throw outdoors. The children are dismissed to have their snack by getting up one by one as the teacher describes their clothing.

After the snack each day, one group stays in the large room for movement exercises. Susan goes with a small group to one of the small rooms for story reading. The small groups are selected on the basis of maturity and experience in listening to stories. The teachers read the stories and ask questions about them. They then read stories selected by the children, if there is more time.

By this time, parents are beginning to arrive. Susan's father signs her out, helps her collect her coat, and takes her home.

children. The Montessori approach also includes elementary programs (and a limited number of secondary programs). Programs for children in the primary grades are fundamentally the same as preschool programs in that children are presented with materials and allowed to work with those they select. In the primary grades, there is much more emphasis on literacy, as children create words from the movable alphabet. They begin writing by copying words and then move on to writing sentences and stories. Instruction in reading often emphasizes a phonetic approach. Many Montessori materials are available for helping children develop concepts in mathematics, social studies, and science.

Two publications offer additional information about Montessori education: *Montessori Life*, a journal published by the American Montessori Society, and *Public School Montessorian*, published by Jola Publications (2933 North 2nd Street, Minneapolis, MN 55411). Montessori Internationale also publishes a small journal once a year.

Cary Williams, the subject of the following A Teacher Speaks box, founded and directs a Montessori school and describes its essential features. What do you think would be the advantages of a Montessori program for a child that you know?

A **Teacher** SPEAKS: *Montessori Schools*

Cary Williams

Keystone Montessori School
North Chelmsford, Massachusetts

As the founder and director of a Montessori school that offers programs from preschool through grade six, I am very familiar with the question "What is Montessori, anyway?" In answering, I describe a complex mix of thought and practice that I have come to know as the Montessori method of education.

Maria Montessori was very interested in how learning happens. Her research led her to two French physicians: Jean Itard and Edouard Seguin. Through their research and observations, they had questioned what portion of human intelligence is hereditary and what portion is learned. Montessori's clinical observations led her to analyze how children learn by actually constructing themselves through what they find in their immediate environment. Her research and studies helped change the course of education. Those who studied with her and went on to make their own major contributions include Anna Freud, Jean Piaget, Alfred Adler, and Erik Erikson.

Montessori's scientific observation of children's almost effortless ability to absorb knowledge from their environment, as well as their tireless interest in manipulating materials, led to the creation of her method and materials. In other words, the Montessori classroom helps children do in a more perfect way what they are seeking to do on their own. Early childhood educators today have come to accept what Maria Montessori discovered a hundred years ago: that children under the age of six have an incredible universal ability to absorb knowledge from their surroundings. Montessori called this "the absorbent mind."

Montessori also observed what are called "sensitive periods." When a child passes from one stage to another, she observed that the child becomes fascinated with certain kinds of experiences. If the child is allowed to engage in the activities that fascinate him, the interaction leads to full development in that area. This experience also results in less frustration and boredom, and the children tend to behave very calmly. This explains why observers in a Montessori classroom exclaim in amazement "that so many children in one room are so peaceful!"

Montessori also observed that if a child is denied this opportunity to pursue spontaneous interests during this sensitivity, he would not develop those skills as easily later in life. This I see so thoroughly in my own experiences with three- to six-year-olds. Watching them delight in language activities at the age of four and begin to read before five is just a natural process in a Montessori classroom. The sensitive periods for the three- to six-year-old child include order, manners (self-confidence and consideration for others), refinement of the senses, writing, movement, culture (art, music, and dance), geography and maps, and language. The child also experiences the development of the mathematical mind in this period.

The Montessori classroom is designed around these specific characteristics of a young child's development. So, what else goes into creating the actual classroom? First and foremost is a Montessori-trained teacher: one who has trained at an accredited Montessori training college and who can function as a designer of the environment, role model, record keeper, parent communicator, and observer. Because the classroom spans a three-year age range, the children can stay with a teacher for several years and the teacher becomes an important partner in the life of that child.

Second, the classroom should be equipped with a full complement of Montessori materials. They are multisensory, sequential, and self-correcting. In each of the four main areas of the curriculum (practical life, sensorial, math, and language), there are specific materials that isolate each concept. The teacher prepares, presents, and records the usage of each material by the child, making available a new extension or particular lesson when the child is ready.

Montessori is a whole-child approach, which helps the child reach his full potential in all areas of life. Social skills, conflict resolution, physical coordination, development of work and learning style, emotional growth, as well as academic areas are covered in the curriculum. The prepared environment allows the child to make choices, act independently, and move freely. In this encouraging atmosphere, the child develops independence, confidence, and self-esteem.

The Behaviorist Model

The behaviorist model of schools for young children is based on the learning theories of Edward Thorndike and B. F. Skinner (described in Chapter 1). Basically, these theories explain behavior in terms of a stimulus and a response and operant conditioning. Three other key components in the behaviorist model—also known as **direct instruction**—are reinforcement schedules, shaping of behavior, and extinction of behavior:

- A *reinforcement schedule* is established after a specific response has been achieved; at that point, the learner is rewarded on a schedule rather than for every response. The learner might be rewarded for every two responses, then every four responses, and so on; eventually, the learner will not need a reward to continue the response.

- *Shaping of behavior* is changing behavior by controlling the rewards and punishments. If a child is disruptive to the group, the teacher might decide to change the child's behavior by ignoring all disruptive behavior and rewarding more appropriate behavior. Even calling the child's name when she is disruptive can be rewarding to a child seeking attention.

- Behaviors can be *extinguished* just as they can be encouraged. For instance, if a child throws a temper tantrum in order to get something that has been denied, the teacher can ignore that behavior until it is no longer exhibited. If a behavior does not result in the child's getting what he wants, he will try another behavior.

www.nifdi.org
A detailed explanation of direct instruction

PRAXIS

Be able to define the behaviorist model and compare it to other models of teaching

How Children Learn: Behaviorist

In the behaviorist view, a child acquires knowledge as the result of repeated interactions with the environment. The consequences of the interactions—reward or punishment—determine whether the interaction will be repeated. The most effective teaching presents a carefully selected stimulus and then controls the rewards or punishments connected with the child's response to the stimulus. The behaviorist view is that a child accumulates knowledge through repeated exposures to stimuli and that the learning process is directed by the adult who controls the sequence of stimuli and the reward system (Roopnarine and Johnson 2000).

In the direct instruction model, the focus is on achievement of academic goals, especially in reading, arithmetic, and language. The lessons presented to children are designed to be conducted in small groups and are carefully sequenced. Each lesson includes an activity designed to motivate students and attract their attention. Following this part of the lesson, new information is presented and responses are elicited from students. If their responses are correct, the students are rewarded. If their responses are incorrect, the students repeat the lesson until the correct responses have been elicited and then rewarded.

The children's behavior is also controlled by a system of rewards and punishments. For example, when a child comes into the room in the morning and hangs up his coat without being reminded, the teacher might reward the child by giving him a token. Tokens can be redeemed later for extra play time or special activities or used to purchase items from a class store. Children who fail to follow the rules may receive no tokens or have tokens taken away.

Teachers who follow the direct instruction model are expected to understand and be able to use reinforcement schedules, shaping of behavior, and extinction of behavior in achieving academic and behavioral goals. Bereiter and Engelmann describe the hallmarks of their method as follows:

1. *Fast pace.* During a twenty-minute period as many as 500 responses may be required of each child. Usually five or more different kinds of tasks are presented during a single period.
2. *Reduced task-irrelevant behavior.* The teacher controls the session relying only incidentally on spontaneous exchanges to dictate the direction of instruction. Efforts of both teacher and children are focused on the tasks being studied.
3. *Strong emphasis on verbal responses.* These are often produced in unison, so that each child's total output can be maximized.
4. *Carefully planned small-step instructional units with continual feedback.* The teacher is not receptive to irrelevant exchanges but is very sensitive to possible areas of difficulty, possible ambiguities that arise from her presentation. She quickly corrects mistakes. She tries to anticipate and avert them.
5. *Heavy work demands.* Children are required to pay attention and to work hard. They are rewarded for thinking; half-hearted or careless performance is not tolerated. (qtd. in Spodek 1973, pp. 177–178)

With the direct instruction model, the classroom is simplified and the number of activities is limited. Bereiter and Engelmann (1966) offer this rationale for setting these limitations:

An object-rich environment stimulates a culturally deprived child to attend to a glitter of superabundant stimuli. He darts from one object to another, treating each only in terms of sensory gratification. When the toy no longer "feels good," another one is selected. By minimizing the inducement of noise in the environment, the preschool can be far more effective in directing the child not to the vehicle of the concept but to the concept itself. Sterilizing the environment is a firm requirement of the work-oriented preschool. Toys should be limited to form boards, jigsaw puzzles (which are usually favorites with the children), books, drawing and tracing materials, Cuisenaire rods (to be handled during free time under the direction of the teacher), and a miniature house, barn and set of farm animals. Paper, crayons, and chalk (but no paint) should be available for expressive play. Motor toys, such as tricycles and wagons, and climbing equipment are not necessary for the program. (p. 72)

More recently, Neisworth and Buggey (1993) have summarized the basic procedures of the teacher in a behaviorist program:

- Reward constructive behavior; ignore undesirable behavior. The best rewards are those that are natural or intrinsic to an activity. Add-on, contrived rewards (e.g., tokens, extra praise) should only be used when necessary, much as crutches should be used.
- Teach skills in simulated settings or in the actual circumstances in which the skills are expected.
- Practice what you teach. Children will imitate teacher behavior.
- Behavioral teaching is by definition individualized. Plan developmentally appropriate sequences for each child.
- Choose rewards that are appropriate and motivating to the child. Children's preferences differ; not all children enjoy the same activities, rewards, or circumstances.

- Learning occurs when the child is interacting with the environment; maximize interaction.
- Plan for generalization; use shaping and stimulus-control. Evaluate acquired skills across settings, time, and persons.
- Make sure that children have opportunities to practice (and experience reinforcement for) learned skills periodically to maintain them. Optimally, what children learn at one time is used as part of more sophisticated behavior learned later. (p. 130)

Goals of Behaviorist Models

The most important goals of behaviorist models are to achieve academic competencies in language, reading, and arithmetic. Children are also expected to learn to answer questions from the teacher articulately and in complete sentences and to perform on cue. The developers of direct instruction models believe that children who are academically capable will have improved self-concepts. Motor development is not among the primary goals of direct instruction models.

In the description on pages 60–61 of a typical day in a behaviorist preschool, the children are engaged in activities designed to teach content knowledge or facts and to help them develop the skills necessary for success in school settings, such as answering questions posed and responding to cues provided by the teacher. Other activities are included to accomplish specific academic goals, to complement the teacher's instruction, or to reward performance.

The behaviorist models focus primarily on *intellectual development*, which is defined as the learning of content and facts, not as the development of generalized intellectual abilities. Physical development is not a primary goal of this type of instruction, nor are social and emotional development. Behaviorists believe that children will achieve more positive self-esteem if they feel that they are successful learners. Children are assumed to develop emotionally as they learn to control their impulsive behaviors and respond appropriately in school settings.

Subject-matter content in language, mathematics, and reading is broken down into small, discrete steps, which children must master in sequence before going on. These subject-matter areas are emphasized because they are considered basic to the children's success. The curriculum is tightly sequenced but not integrated. Children learn each subject without regard for what is being learned in other subjects. Science and social studies are rarely included in the curriculum, and the arts are included in a limited fashion as part of the choice activities.

When implemented with older children, the fundamental behaviorist model remains intact. Basically, the changes for older children are found in the content of the lessons presented in subject-matter areas.

Many elements of behaviorist models are evident in current elementary programs. Specification of limited objectives, emphasis on the sequence of materials and activities, and mastery of small steps as a method of achieving larger goals are all behavioristic in origin. In many elementary schools that do not claim to be behavioristic, tokens or stickers are used as reinforcers, and grades are often viewed as rewards or punishments.

Parents and School Design

- Provide parents and other visitors to your school with references for articles or books that support your program philosophy and perhaps explain the differences between your program and others.

A Typical Day in a Behaviorist Preschool

9:00– 9:15	Arrival, group time
9:15–10:00	Rotating instructional groups
10:00–10:25	Outdoor play
10:25–10:45	Snack
10:45–11:10	Instructional groups
11:10–11:25	Choice of activities
11:25–11:30	Dismissal

The school Alan attends has separate classes for fours and fives. The classroom in which five-year-old Alan works each day is a large room with three smaller rooms that open off it. For Alan's group of thirty children, there is a teacher and two assistant teachers.

The teacher greets Alan at the door with a smile and tells him how glad she is that he is at school. As Alan hangs up his coat, the teacher slips him a red token, and with a grin he puts it into his pocket. Alan joins the other children sitting in a circle on the floor. In a few minutes, when all the children are present, the teacher joins the group and calls the roll. Alan responds to his name with "I am present." Then the teacher reviews the days of the week and the months of the year. Alan raises his hand to say the days of the week. He repeats the names successfully and receives another token. He also gets a smile and praise from the teacher. After a child

is selected to pin the correct numeral on the calendar and move pointers on the weather chart to indicate today's weather, Alan is instructed to go to the language room with his group. Alan's group membership is based on his ability level. There are high, middle, and low groups.

One of the assistant teachers conducts Alan's language lesson for twenty minutes. Alan and the other members of his group sit on small risers to be as close as possible to the teacher and to facilitate their choral responses. The first part of the lesson is a warm-up in which the teacher tells the children that when she taps her pencil three times, they should clap their hands. Some children do not clap on cue, and the exercise is repeated. The children are reminded that paying close attention and responding quickly are very important.

Today's lesson is on the use of pronouns: *I, he, she, we*. The teacher opens a paper bag and removes a comb. She says, "I comb my hair." The children are instructed to pretend combing their hair and to repeat, "I comb my hair." Each child who responds correctly is rewarded with a token. The teacher then goes through sentences using the pronouns *he, she,* and *we* with descriptions of other self-care actions, such as brushing the teeth, washing the face, and so on. When the lesson is com-

www.piaget.org

A biography of Piaget and an explanation of his stage theory

PRAXIS

Be able to define the constructivist model of teaching and compare it to other models

The Constructivist Model

The constructivist model is based on the learning theories of Jean Piaget (1896–1980) and Lev Vygotsky (1896–1934). Examples of constructivist programs include the High/Scope program, developed by David Weikart; the Bank Street College of Education, developed by Lucy Sprague Mitchell; the Reggio Emilia programs in Italy; and the Project Approach, developed by Lilian Katz and Sylvia Chard. There are points of agreement among constructivist programs as well as some differences. Among the points of agreement are the following:

1. All contend that a basic objective to be drawn from Piaget's work is to foster structural change in children's reasoning in the direction of operational thought.
2. All emphasize the fundamental importance of the child's action for learning and development.
3. All borrow ideas from the child-development tradition in early education for materials, equipment, and activities that permit children to be active (for example, painting and other art activities, blockbuilding, pretend play, singing, and sand and water play).
4. None of the . . . Piagetian programs is just "Piagetian." Each recognizes certain limitations in using Piaget's theory alone as a basis for educational practice. (DeVries and Kohlberg 1987b, p. 51)

Programs differ in their definitions of action, the extent of emphasis on logic in language, the extent of reliance on child development traditions, and pleted, Alan and his group leave their room and walk with the teacher to the next room for their arithmetic lesson.

In this lesson, Alan's group is learning to recognize and complete simple addition equations. As the teacher holds up flashcards showing equations such as 3 + 1, the group responds, "Three plus one equals four." Today, the teacher repeats combinations whose sums do not exceed six. When the children have reviewed these sums, they are given a worksheet, listing the same equations, and asked to complete it. Alan mumbles something to Brad, who is sitting beside him at the table. The teacher quickly reminds him that this is work time and that talking to friends is not appropriate now. She tells Alan that a token will be taken away if he talks again. Alan writes the answers to the problems and is rewarded when he does them correctly.

For the next twenty-minute period, Alan and his classmates play outside. The playground has swings, climber/slides, tire swings, and climbers. Alan chooses to swing and takes turns with Brad.

When the children return to the classroom, they are instructed to wash their hands before the snack. The snack today consists of apples cut into fourths and crackers scored into fourths. The teachers introduce and rein-force the use of the fractional terms as the children eat their snacks.

After the snack, Alan's group goes into a small room for the reading lesson. Again, the teacher gets the children's attention with a warm-up exercise, and when all have responded correctly, he begins the lesson. Today's lesson is on the sounds represented by the letters *b*, *m*, *l*, and *d*. The teacher presents a letter on a card and says, "This letter is *b* and its sound is 'buh.'" The children repeat the name and the sound several times. They already know the long vowel sounds, and today's letters are combined with each of the vowels in succession and pronounced.

When the reading lesson is finished, Alan and his group return to the large room, where all the children are gathered. They now have the opportunity to spend their tokens on some special activities. Alan chooses to spend three of his tokens for drawing with paper and markers. When he completes his drawing, he spends three more tokens to play with the jigsaw puzzles. Then he and the assistant teacher build some sets with the Cuisenaire rods. The teacher blinks the lights to indicate that it is time to put away all the materials and get ready to go home.

In a few minutes, the room is clean and orderly, and the children have put on their coats and are out the door.

how cooperation and interest are fostered. Some developmentalists define *action* as physical action; some broaden the definition to include mental action. Some programs place more emphasis on children's being able to articulate their understanding; others emphasize performance. Some programs allow more time for free play and free expression than others. Some programs rely on free-play activities to help children develop cooperative behaviors; others specifically plan for interventions in behavior cycles.

How Children Learn: Constructivist

Recall from Chapter 1 that Piaget and Vygotsky described *learning* as a process that is under the control of the learner, or intrinsically motivated. According to Piaget, not all knowledge is acquired in the same way. Some kinds of knowledge, such as the concept of *hot*, can be learned only by experience with objects. We don't learn *hot* until we are burned. Thus, the properties of objects—texture, shape, function, and so on—are learned through experiencing them. Language and social customs, however, cannot be learned from experience but only from other people. Logico-mathematical knowledge—which includes what we know about mathematics, seriation, classification, and so on—can only be acquired by interacting mentally with physical objects.

For example, if you let a three-year-old loose in your classroom, he would explore everything about the desks. He would soon know that they have hard, smooth surfaces; that they balance on four legs; that they are heavy; and so forth. However, no amount of exploration would help the child discover the label "desk" that we apply to this piece of furniture. He would have to learn the word from someone in his social group who knows what we have agreed to call this thing.

Vygotsky (1978) recognized that children learn a great deal about their environments from manipulating objects; he called this kind of learning *spontaneous*. He also identified another kind of learning—what we typically think of as school learning (the freezing point of water, for example)—as *scientific* learning. Vygotsky believed that all learning is mediated by the social group, so if counting is important in the social group, then the child will learn to count.

NAEYC CRITERIA
3.19

Recall from Chapter 1 that Vygotsky also believed that children are only capable of learning certain things, even with assistance, at given ages or skill levels; this notion is the foundation of the zone of proximal development (ZPD). An application of the ZPD is shown in the description of a typical day in a constructivist school (see pages 68–69), when the teacher sends two children to the library to find information about the praying mantis. The teacher must know whether these children can use materials from the library to further their own learning. If they cannot use printed materials or other library information, then this strategy will not be appropriate for them.

Constructivists believe that children want to learn and are, in fact, always learning. They also believe that children construct their own understandings and are continually refining them in terms of new experiences and knowledge. For example, at age two, most children have no concept of *time*. By age four, however, most know that a watch or clock tells time and that certain things are done at certain times of the day, such as eating breakfast in the morning and going to bed at night. By age six, the child may be able to read a watch or clock or to say the time on a digital clock. Children become increasingly aware of time and by about age ten or eleven have developed a stable concept of time, in which they know that time passes at an even rate that is not related to activities. Developing this concept of *time* as a constant takes several years and probably thousands of experiences.

NAEYC CRITERIA
3.21

Instruction in a constructivist program is provided primarily to individual children and to small groups; whole-group instruction occurs less often. Also, instruction rarely involves the teacher giving information to the students. More frequently, the teacher has arranged an experience in which to engage the learners and then asks them questions as they participate in the task. Supplying students with answers is not the goal in a constructivist program; in fact, unanswered questions are important in terms of continued interest and continued learning.

In a contructivist program, curricula are planned and learning experiences are selected to follow children's interests or expose them to new areas in which their interest might be aroused. The process of finding information, analyzing data, and reaching conclusions is considered more important than learning facts. An emphasis on process does not mean that content is lacking, however. Children learn a great many facts and concepts, but they are always embedded in meaningful contexts.

NAEYC CRITERIA
3.23

For example, children who are learning about trees might "adopt" a tree and visit it on a regular basis in order to record changes over time. They might learn to identify and classify leaves of various trees and participate in experiments to discover the function of leaves. The children might examine the rings in a tree stump, draw conclusions about their observations, and so on. They might locate books about trees in the library, and the teacher might

In the constructivist classroom, children are often instructed in small groups.

read to them about trees. In other words, the curriculum experiences would focus on children's learning how to find, analyze, and evaluate information, but facts would be presented in the process.

Constructivists believe that it is important to select curriculum experiences containing content that can be acted on in various ways. The teacher must also consider the developmental stage of the learner and the complexity of the tasks required to be successful in learning the material.

Goals of Constructivist Programs

The goal of any constructivist program is to stimulate children in all areas of development. Physical development, social and emotional development, and cognitive (intellectual) development are all important. Language development and an emphasis on the process of learning are also important. Programs attempt to keep a balance so that all areas of development are addressed and none are neglected. Encouraging children to become actively involved in their own learning and developing children's desire to continue to learn are also important goals.

Piaget on Early Education Kamii and DeVries (1977) state that education must be based on the long-term objective of developing the entire personality, with particular emphasis on intellectual and moral autonomy. Their emphasis on intellectual development is based on Piaget's own statements:

> The principal goal of education is to create [people] who are capable of doing new things, not simply of repeating what other generations have done—[people] who are creative, inventive, and discoverers. The second goal of education is to form minds which can be critical, can verify, and not accept everything they are offered. The great danger today is of slogans, collective opinions, ready-made trends of thought. We have to be able to resist individually, to criticize, to distinguish between what is proven and what is not. So we need

We must see that every child has equal opportunity, not to become equal, but to become different—to realize the unique potential he or she possesses.

—*John Fischer*

pupils who are active, who learn early to find out by themselves, partly by their own spontaneous activity and partly through material we set up for them; who learn early to tell what is verifiable and what is simply the first idea to come to them. (Piaget 1964, p. 5)

In the short term, constructivist programs also strive to help children achieve the following socioemotional goals:

1. To feel secure in a noncoercive relationship with adults
2. To respect the feelings and rights of others and begin to coordinate different points of view (decentering and cooperating)
3. To be independent, alert, and curious; to use initiative in pursuing curiosities; to have confidence in his ability to figure things out for himself, and to speak his mind with conviction. (Day and Parker 1977, p. 393)

Finally, such programs encourage children to achieve cognitive objectives:

1. To come up with interesting ideas, problems, and questions
2. To put things into relationships and notice similarities and differences. (Day and Parker 1977, p. 394)

Despite their general similarities, the goals of different constructivist programs can vary. The descriptions that follow will help clarify some of the differences in programs based on Piagetian theory.

WWW.

www.highscope.org
The website for the High/ Scope foundation with links to information about this program

PRAXIS

Be able to define the key characteristics of the High/Scope program

NAEYC CRITERIA

3.21

High/Scope The High/Scope program, developed by David Weikart, is known for emphasizing careful and systematic observations of the child and for organizing the curriculum around key experiences. *Key experiences* have been identified in the categories of social and emotional development, movement and physical development, and cognitive development:

Key experiences provide a composite picture of early childhood development, are fundamental to young children's construction of knowledge, take place repeatedly over an extended period of time, and describe the concepts and relationships young children are striving to understand. They occur in active learning settings in which children have opportunities to make choices and decisions, manipulate materials, interact with peers and adults, experience special events, reflect on ideas and actions, use language in personally meaningful ways, and receive appropriate adult support. (Hohmann and Weikart 1995, p. 299)

The categories of key experiences are creative representation, language and literacy, initiative and social relations, movement, music, classification, seriation, numbers, space, and time.

Most activities lend themselves to several key experiences. For example, a child might choose to paint. Such a choice would give the teacher the opportunity to observe how the child was able to understand the routine of getting paper, paint smocks, and so on and then putting away the paper when she was finished. If the child needed instruction, it could be provided. Painting would also be an activity that allowed the teacher to observe how the child represented objects and related to other children involved in the same task.

Key experiences provide teachers with a basis for planning and organizing the curriculum so that activities are not random. Through observing individual students, teachers are also able to assess how children are growing in their abilities, as categorized by key experiences (Bredekamp 1996).

The Bank Street College of Education   The Bank Street program grew out of the work of Lucy Sprague Mitchell, who had been a student of the famous educator John Dewey. Mitchell began a school for young children in which play would be taken seriously—namely, one in which children could play and researchers could study them doing so in a naturalistic setting. The Bank Street program is dedicated to fostering children's development, not simply to promoting specific learning. The following principles are the framework of the program:

1. Development is not a simple path from less to more; and it is not an unfolding, like the unfolding of a flower. Development involves changes or shifts in the way a person organizes experience and copes with the world, generally moving from simpler to more complex, from single to multiple and integrated ways of responding. The concept of stages of development is crucial, and is also a convenient way of talking and thinking about developmental change and growth. Stages are approximate and are only loosely related to age. . . .

2. Individuals are never at a fixed point on a straight line of development, but operate within a range of possibilities. Earlier ways of organizing experience are not erased, but become integrated into more advanced systems. While people will want to function at the highest possible level, they are also able to use less mature ways appropriately. (Even after a child knows how to hop and jump, there are times when it is a good idea to crawl; even adults find moments when it is appropriate to be silly.) . . .

3. Developmental progress involves a mix of stability and instability. A central task for the educator is to find a balance between helping a child consolidate new understandings and offering challenges that will promote growth. . . .

4. The motivation to engage actively with the environment—to make contact, to have an impact, and to make sense of experience—is built into human beings. The growing child gradually adds more ways of actively engaging with the world as she develops. Generally, the progression is from more physical, body-centered ways of responding to perceptual and then more conceptual, symbolic ways. . . .

5. The child's sense of self is built up from his experiences with other people and with objects; knowledge of the self is based on repeated awareness and testing of one's self in interaction. . . .

6. Growth and maturing involve conflict—conflict within the self, and conflict with others. Conflict is necessary for development. The way conflicts are resolved depends on the nature of the interaction with significant figures in the child's life and the demands of the culture. (Mitchell and David 1992, pp. 16–17)

The Reggio Emilia Schools   In recent years, the thinking of early childhood educators has been influenced by the Reggio Emilia schools of northern Italy. These community preschools are based on the following principles:

■ All children construct their own learning and are capable of learning.

■ The community is an integral force in the school, providing both monetary support and involvement with programs and children.

■ Collaboration, sharing, and personal relationships are valued.

NAEYC CRITERIA
3.23

www.latelier.org/usefullinks
A site with links to all kinds of information about the Reggio Emilia schools

NAEYC CRITERIA
3.19

PRAXIS

Be able to define the key
characteristics of the
Reggio Emilia Schools

- The environment—the "third teacher"—is important in stimulating interest and encouraging creativity.

- A child's personal sense of time is respected, and the pace of the day is determined by the children.

- Teachers consider themselves learners and work with other teachers and parents.

- Children have access to a wide variety of media materials that foster creativity; the emphasis is on the arts as a way of knowing.

- The curriculum is emergent, as children select projects, continue with them by choice, and return to them as they gain new insights.

- Documenting children's work is crucial to the success of the program (Cadwell 1997; Edwards, Gandini, and Forman 1993; Gandini 1993).

The Reggio Emilia schools are housed in beautiful and well-cared-for spaces that invite children to engage in activities. Each school has teachers, a *pedagogista*, and an *atelierista*. The *pedagogista* works with teachers to consider what experiences mean to children, how to help children learn more, and what additional experiences should be planned. The *atelierista* is the art director, who helps teachers and children express their interests and knowledge in many different media. For example, children studying flowers might create paintings, drawings, clay models, sculptures, and so on. Each time they create something in a new medium, they are expected to think about what they know so that each new representation will express their growing understanding. Teachers usually stay with the same group of children for several years, which allows them to get to know the children and their families very well.

> *Let early education be a sort of amusement; you will then be better able to discover the child's natural bent.*
>
> —Plato

One of the key elements of the Reggio Emilia schools is the documentation of children's learning:

> Careful consideration and attention are given to the presentation of the thinking of the children and the adults who work with them. Teachers' commentary on the purposes of the study and the children's learning process, transcriptions of children's verbal language (i.e., words and dialogue), photographs of their activity, and representations of their thinking in many media are composed in carefully designed panels or books to present the process of learning in the schools. (Cadwell 1997, p. 6)

This documentation, which is shared with parents and the community, creates a history of the child's learning and is used by teachers to explore possibilities for future experiences.

Another key element of the Reggio Emilia schools is the ongoing nature of the projects. Typical projects in U.S. schools tend to be rather short lived—for instance, a study of animals will go on for two weeks and be followed by a study of plants for another two weeks (or less, in some schools). In a Reggio Emilia school, the projects often last for months and the children continue to add to and revisit them again and again.

Educators in the United States have wondered how the Reggio Emilia model can be implemented in U.S. schools. Some have actually attempted to transform the model and use it in their own schools (Cadwell 1997; Staley 1998). There are several obstacles to such a transformation, however. One is money. Most school budgets do not have the funds for hiring an *atelierista* and *pedagogista* to help teachers. Another obstacle is the pressure in U.S. schools to cover a wide range of content material rather than focus on one or two projects for a year. Lack of community support and parent involvement are other obstacles for implementing the model in U.S. schools. Nonetheless, some educators continue to try to implement as much as they can of the model, believing that it is a worthwhile endeavor and that the results are well worth the effort (Cadwell 1997; Gerson 2000; Staley 1998).

Project Approach Although the Project Approach is not usually classified as a program model, it is another way of organizing the curriculum. This approach was inspired by the success of the Reggio Emilia schools, and it is constructivist in philosophy. The Project Approach was introduced by Lilian Katz and Sylvia Chard in their publication *Engaging Children's Minds* (1989).

In the Project Approach, a topic for a project is selected with input from the children, and the children also help to decide what they will learn about that topic. This topic must be meaningful to the children and have sufficient depth to engage them intellectually as they investigate it. Most of the investigations are hands-on, active inquiries into various aspects of the topic. At the conclusion of the project, the teacher helps the children develop a culminating experience, in which they can share what they have learned with others. This culminating experience may take many forms, but each will engage the children in evaluating their learning and in making decisions about how best to share their work with others.

Overview of Constructivist Programs

Although the goals or emphases of these constructivist programs are not identical, they are all concerned with the development of children's thinking and reasoning abilities and their abilities to represent experiences in meaningful ways. Each program depends on children's active involvement with materials and teachers' guidance in helping children reflect on their experiences.

In examining the activities of a typical day (see pages 68–69) in a constructivist classroom, we find that playing with blocks offers children opportunities to develop concepts in mathematics, such as length and equivalence. The addition of the pulley provides opportunities for developing concepts related to simple machines. Representation of experience is achieved through building the model of an apartment building. Several activities offer children opportunities to use their developing skills in literacy (signing in on arrival, recording comments about the painting, recording observations on the walk in the neighborhood) and to represent understandings. In exploring the numerical patterns in the room, the teacher attempts to aid children in the development of number concepts. Other activities require children to solve problems using reasoning (taking apart the toaster, deciding who can play in the new area).

Constructivist programs focus on the development of physical, social, emotional, and intellectual competence. The curriculum is based on children's interests and is integrated so that content is not arranged by subject-matter areas. Many activities and experiences are selected to help children think about solutions to social as well as cognitive problems. The

www.
www.project-approach.com
Information about the Project Approach, including a thorough, step-by-step description of planning and many sample projects that teachers and children have completed

NAEYC CRITERIA
3.19, 3.21

PRAXIS
Be able to define key elements of the Project Approach

PRAXIS
Be able to describe the various program models and how teaching–learning varies according to their principles

NAEYC CRITERIA
3.44

A Typical Day in a Constructivist Preschool

9:00–10:00	Arrival, choice time
10:00–10:15	Group time
10:15–10:40	Outdoor play
10:40–10:55	Snack time
10:55–11:10	Group time for optional activities
11:10–11:30	Story time and dismissal

Michelle bounces into her classroom, carrying a milk carton with a praying mantis in it. In Michelle's class of four-, five-, and six-year-olds, there are twenty-four children, a teacher, and an assistant teacher.

The classroom she enters has only one area large enough for all twenty-four children to sit down at once. The rest of the space is filled with areas arranged for different explorations or interactions. There is a large area for blocks; an area for dramatic play that contains dolls, child-sized kitchen equipment, dress-up clothes, and costumes; an area that contains easels and many kinds of art supplies; an area that contains a water table and sand table; an area that contains puzzles and games; an area for reading books that is furnished with two rocking chairs and some floor pillows; an area with many kinds of paper and writing utensils; an area that has baskets of math manipulative materials; an area that, at the moment, is filled with a large collection of old clocks and other small appliances; and another area where there is a table, which today is covered with paper and has some blocks and cardboard milk cartons on it.

Michelle's teacher notices her entry into the classroom and smiles a greeting. She notes that Michelle has signed in on the clipboard by the door and that she has hung her coat in the cubby labeled with her name. The teacher is helping two girls find a way to remove the levers and springs from an old toaster but turns her attention to Michelle and her box when Michelle approaches. The teacher listens while Michelle tells how she and her brother caught the praying mantis and made a container

for it. She suggests that Michelle place the container on a display table near the door for other children to observe, if they choose.

Michelle does so and then decides to spend some time in the blocks area. She selects a tagboard circle with her name on it and places it on one of the pegs beside a picture of blocks on a pegboard near the door. When she gets to the blocks area, she tells her friend Amy that she would like to build an apartment building. They decide to work on it together and find that it needs a strong base to support the ten stories that they want to add to it. The teacher observes their construction and offers them a pulley, a small box, and some cord so that they can make an elevator for their building.

After about thirty minutes of animated block building, the girls put away the blocks and Michelle checks on her praying mantis. She finds three children at the table and tells them about catching the insect and making the milk carton container for it. She takes her name from the "blocks" peg and moves it to the "art" peg. She gets a friend to help her fasten her paint smock and attaches paper to an easel. She paints a picture of her praying mantis. When the teacher observes her painting, she suggests that perhaps Michelle would like to write about the insect. After Michelle has cleaned the painting area, she goes to a table where there are many kinds of paper, pencils, and markers. She finds her journal in a basket and writes about the insect and draws pictures of it. The teacher helps her date her paper and painting. The teacher and her assistant have been moving from area to area in the classroom, asking questions, providing guidance, and suggesting activities to individual children.

The teacher rings a little bell, which is the signal for the children to finish their work and clean up the areas. After that has been done, the children meet on the rug, where the teacher is leading some fingerplays and songs. When all the children have gathered, the teacher asks

interrelationship of all areas of development is important in developing the *whole child*. The content areas of science, social studies, mathematics, the arts, and health and safety are all integrated into themes of interest to the children. Literacy is taught in the context of children's other activities, as they extend their language to reading and writing. Constructivists assume that literacy skills are best learned within a context in which they can be applied.

Because the selection of materials and experiences is based on the children's developmental level, extending the program to younger or older children requires adapting materials and experiences; nonetheless, the basic tenets of choice, intrinsic motivation in learning, and a balanced program remain constant. With younger children, the choices of activities are more limited and the guidance of the teacher is more apparent. Projects for them to think about some of the things they learned this morning. A few children tell about the parts they found in the appliances. Others tell about how they solved some problems in their play. The teacher says that she noticed that not everyone who wanted to do so could play in one of the areas where a new set of materials was available. She asks if they can think of some ways to solve the problem. The children finally decide to take a survey to determine who has already had a turn with the new materials and to make a sign-up sheet for those who have not yet had a turn. Some children make comments about the praying mantis and ask questions about it. The teacher asks how they could find out more about these insects. Two children decide that they could go to the library and ask the librarian for help in locating information. The teacher suggests a good time later in the morning for them to go.

Next, the children review the calendar for any special celebrations that are coming up and for the symbol that indicates the day the eggs in the incubator are expected to hatch. They recall their trip to the bakery last week and their plans for sharing time the next day.

After these activities have been finished, the children go outside to play. They can choose riding toys, swings, climber/slides, climbers, and some large blocks and tunnels for play. Michelle and a small group of friends climb and swing, shouting joyfully most of the time.

After about twenty-five minutes, the teacher signals the children to return to the room. As the children enter, each is asked to choose a snack: apple juice, orange juice, apple slices, or orange slices. They wash their hands and begin to help serve the snack. When they have finished their snack, the children construct a graph of their snack choices with help from the teachers and discuss all the relationships that are illustrated on the graph.

After the graph has been finished, the children get their coats again because today they are going on a walk around the neighborhood. Each child has a clipboard and pencil and chooses something to look for. Some will observe the number and kinds of houses they pass; others will observe the number and kinds of businesses. A few children want to record the number and kinds of plants they see, and some will look for all the printed words that they can find. They know that tomorrow they will begin to transfer the information they collect to the map of their immediate neighborhood that they are building on the table.

When the class returns from the walk, the children gather on the rug again for singing and movement. Two children go off to the library to get praying mantis information; the others learn some new songs and review the lyrics to other songs that are printed on large charts. The children also use some little books in which they have illustrated a few of the songs.

The teacher then shares a story from a "big book," with large illustrations and type so that all the children can see while the teacher reads. As the teacher reads the story a second time, some children join in on the words that they recognize. The teacher tells them that they may choose to write their own stories tomorrow.

The two children return from the library with several books and some posters. The teacher places these books on the display table with the praying mantis. Several children are really interested in the insect, and the teacher promises that they will have time to observe it and read about it tomorrow.

As the children gather their coats and papers and get ready for dismissal, they review patterns and arrange themselves in line according to their coat colors. It takes some time, but they form a pattern of red, blue, green, and yellow coats; then they add the children who do not fit that particular pattern. Michelle has on a red jacket and gets in line to help complete the pattern. She has her painting in her hand and hurries to share it with her mother when the teacher dismisses the class.

older children are selected so that in-depth explorations of topics is possible. Teachers make a conscious effort to teach subject-matter content in meaningful contexts and to select experiences in which children can apply skills being learned.

Summaries and Comparisons

The program models described in this chapter have some common goals, but each has a different view of what is the best and most appropriate learning environment for young children (see Table 2.1). One goal common to all three models—Montessori, behaviorist, and constructivist—is for children to learn. The models differ, however, on the means used to reach this goal:

TABLE 2.1 Overview of Program Models

	PHYSICAL DEVELOPMENT	SOCIAL/EMOTIONAL DEVELOPMENT	COGNITIVE DEVELOPMENT	OTHER EMPHASES
Montessori	Emphasizes fine motor tasks	Focuses on individual, self-control	Emphasizes individual; tasks are selected by child	Shows great respect for child's work; teacher observes more than talks
Behaviorist	Gives little attention	Believes self-esteem is developed as child gains cognitive competence	Focuses on learning facts and responding to questions; lessons are highly sequenced	Emphasis is on learning; environment is controlled to avoid distractions
Constructivist	Focuses on both gross and fine motor development	Believes social interactions are critical; emphasizes peer learning and problem solving in relationships	Focuses on skills needed at the time and on teaching skills through projects child chooses	Believes knowledge is constructed by learner; teacher is facilitator

- Educators who follow the Montessori philosophy believe that children learn best through interactions with materials in a prepared environment; there is little child–child interaction.
- Behaviorists believe that children learn best in a highly structured environment in which the information presented is carefully sequenced and the rewards are controlled.
- Those who hold a constructivist view of learning also believe that children learn through interactions with objects and people but that children must reflect on their actions, as well.

Parents and School Design

- In the school's entry or main hallway, post your teacher's certification, accompanied by a short statement of your philosophy of teaching.

Other goals of the programs also vary. An additional goal of Montessori programs is to develop the child's intellect and control. Constructivist programs focus on development in all areas: physical, social, emotional, and intellectual. Behaviorists generally focus on academic knowledge and place less emphasis on physical and social development. These differing views of how children learn (and the varied program goals based on these views) translate into very different experiences for children who attend these programs.

Research on Program Models

Attempts to compare the effectiveness of different program models have been inconclusive. It is not an easy task to control all the variables that influence such research. For example, we could argue that it is invalid to compare the academic achievement of children who attend preschools based on the different program models just described because the focuses of some of the programs are much broader than academic achievement. Proponents of such broadly focused programs would argue that even if their children did not score as well on standardized tests as children from more academic

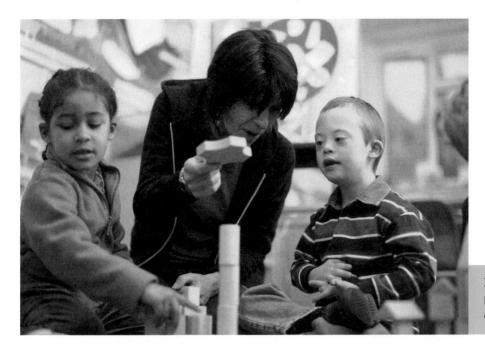

In effective programs, teachers provide instruction to individuals and small groups.

programs, they learned other things that such tests do not measure. It is difficult to assess the academic achievement of young children accurately. It is also difficult to control for family involvement, teacher effectiveness, children's motivation, and so forth in studies that compare different program models.

Attempts to find differences between program models have produced mixed results. Children who show initial gains in skill levels as the result

DEVELOPMENTALLY APPROPRIATE PRACTICE

In Chapter 1, we introduced the concept developmentally appropriate practice (DAP). *Although DAP may look very different in different situations, some basic criteria are critical to such practice, including choice, activities based on children's interests, and activities appropriate for individual children. Think about the critical elements of DAP as you respond to the following questions:*

■ Are all the program models described in this chapter equally developmentally appropriate? Why?

■ Some people argue that a kind and nurturing teacher is the most important element in any program. No one would suggest that teachers should be other than kind and nurturing, but is such behavior enough to counterbalance a lack of choice or a lack of individual appropriateness? Why?

■ Must a program for young children give up academic goals in order to be developmentally appropriate? Why?

■ Are the guidelines for developmentally appropriate practice a good yardstick for measuring programs? Why?

of a particular preschool experience may later show declines. Lilian Katz (1988) suggests that educators attend to the long-term, cumulative effects of programs, as evidenced by children's interest in learning. Not many long-term studies have been done, but one of the most significant research studies on the effects of preschool experience is the Perry Preschool High/Scope research (Schweinhart 2005).

Researchers at the High/Scope foundation have been following the children who were enrolled in the program for many years and have collected data on them at various ages (15, 27, and 40 years old). Each time these children have been compared to children who attended a direct instruction model or no program at all, the findings have indicated that the High/Scope children did better in school and were more prosocial (holding offices in school, participating in sports). Moreover, at later ages, the High/Scope children were more likely to have graduated from high school, earned more money, used social services less often, were more likely to own their own homes, and had been arrested less frequently (Schweinhart 2005).

Criticism has been made against some of the earlier High/Scope studies that found positive results for children who had attended the program. For instance, Engelmann (1999) suggests that the numbers are too small to be conclusive and that there are errors and discrepancies in the data reported. He argues that the amount of time a student spent in the program was not considered and that individuals' experiences in later years of school varied considerably yet were not considered when reporting the study results.

The conclusion we *can* draw from research is that much remains to be learned about the development and learning of young children. Teachers and parents must think carefully about program choices and expectations for children. And researchers must continue to attempt to solve the complex problem of evaluating different approaches to instruction for young children.

Parents and School Design

- Create a brochure or welcome letter to share with parents your philosophy about learning in a school setting.

CHILDREN WITH SPECIAL NEEDS

In response to Public Law 94-142 and the extension of this law by Public Law 99-457, most children with special needs are now enrolled in regular classes. The enrollment in these *inclusive classes* is typically about one-half children with special needs and about one-half typically developing children. Often, the total enrollment for an inclusive class is lower than that for a class at the same level that is not inclusive. Teachers of inclusive classes are often teamed to include a teacher certified in special needs education and a regular classroom teacher, at least for part of the day.

The premise underlying inclusion is that all children will benefit from the interaction. Namely, typically developing children will serve as models of speech, play, and other behaviors for their special-needs peers while also learning to respect the strengths and abilities of these peers.

Most public school systems offer programs for children with special needs beginning at three years of age. Typically developing children are added to these classes through a lottery. Some school systems contract with local preschools to offer services to special-needs students younger than five, although this practice is becoming less common as more and more schools offer their own preschool programs.

Advocates for children with special needs are interested in programs that individualize expectations, activities, and experiences for all children. Teachers must think about the needs, interests, and abilities of every child in the program, including every child with special needs. Some children will require modifications in the physical environment (e.g., space to maneuver a wheelchair), while others will need more time, direction, and attention in order to complete given activities. Teachers who think about all children as individual learners will be able to plan for them in all the developmental domains.

CELEBRATING DIVERSITY

Being responsive to children's diverse needs is a goal of almost all programs. Some programs would argue that meeting the needs of each child would, by definition, mean meeting the needs of children from diverse backgrounds. Other programs might argue that equipping children with the skills and abilities they need to succeed in mainstream schools is the best outcome for any child, regardless of cultural or ethnic differences. Teachers of young children must learn about the individuals in their programs and make the best programming decisions possible to help all children learn and develop in the best ways for them.

Until 1954, when the U.S. Supreme Court ruled in *Brown v. Board of Education* that "separate but equal" schools were not equal and that schools had to be racially integrated, most children of color attended segregated schools. Although some school districts have "resegregated" themselves by tracking students or creating neighborhood schools, the classrooms of today are much more diverse than at any time in U.S. history (Kozol 2005). Not too long ago, most teachers in the United States could expect to teach in schools that were somewhat homogeneous in terms of cultural background. That is no longer true. Not only do public schools today enroll children from all racial and ethnic groups, but most also enroll many children whose first language is not English.

Diversity can be a bonus for a school and make it stronger, or it can be a detriment if a school fails to meet the needs of all its children. Teachers of young children can help make schools welcoming to all children by creating a positive learning environment.

SUMMARY

● Today's early childhood teachers need to know the sources of the various ideas and models that have influenced early childhood education. The ideas of mixed age groups, learning from real experiences, and playing as a way of learning are not new. Likewise, many of the materials and types of equipment commonly in use in early childhood programs are based on the ideas of early figures in early childhood education, such as Maria Montessori, Friedrich Froebel, and Patty Smith Hill. A program that advocates an active curriculum of real experiences is following the ideas proposed by John Dewey and Lucy Sprague Mitchell. Many researchers also have contributed to modern thought about young children.

- Early childhood education has certainly changed over the years, from the nursery schools in the tenements of large U.S. cities, to public kindergartens in almost every state, to Head Start programs designed to break the cycle of poverty, to programs for children with special needs who might have been excluded from schools in earlier times, to early intervention programs that attempt to prevent problems before children are of school age. All these changes represent efforts to serve young children better and to provide opportunities for all children to grow and develop in the best environment possible.

- The early childhood education programs of today follow three major models: Montessori, behaviorist, and constructivist. A school will usually identify with one of these models but may incorporate elements of all the models in varying degrees. Montessori programs value the individual child and plan instruction in a sequence to fit each child. The focus of Montessori programs is individual choice and the presentation of tasks from which the child may choose. Behaviorist programs typically focus on academic progress and offer instruction in a carefully sequenced and teacher-directed set of lessons. Constructivist programs focus on the development of the whole child and the idea that children must construct their own understandings of some concepts. Constructivist programs attempt to follow the child's

interests while achieving the goal of producing increased knowledge and skill.

- Researchers have been unable to make definitive statements about the effectiveness of any of the program models when compared to the other models. High/Scope has collected information on children in their programs over longer periods of time than any of the other models and their data would indicate that children who attended their programs are more successful socially and academically than children who attended direct instruction models. However, their conclusions are based on small numbers of children and the groups used in the studies may not be comparable.

- Children with special needs are much more likely to attend regular public schools today than they were in the past. Historically, many children with special needs either did not attend school at all or were sent to specialized schools. Today, only children with severe special needs are sent to specialized schools. Most children are enrolled in mainstream classrooms.

- Diversity is now commonplace in U.S. public schools. Almost every school will have some children who are diverse across many demographic features: race, ethnicity, language, religion, gender, and socioeconomic status. Diversity can add to the richness of any program if teachers and administrators learn about each child and make adaptations to meet each child's needs.

REFLECTIONS

1. Explain how knowing about the history of early childhood education can help teachers recognize the roots of various program goals and activities.
2. Describe the three major models of early childhood programs currently found in the United States, and explain the strengths and weaknesses of each.
3. From your understanding of the research on program models, what conclusions can you draw and apply in making the best curriculum decisions for your own classroom?
4. Which of the models do you think fits your vision of teaching and school most closely? Why?
5. Is there a best model of early childhood education that every school should endorse? If so, what is it and why is it the best? If not, why?

1. In the Yellow Pages of the phone directory, look at the advertisements for schools in your local area. Can you determine the model that characterizes each school? What are the key words that indicate the model or approach followed? Are some schools more or less open than others about their philosophies, as indicated in their advertisements?

2. Not even schools that follow the same model will be exactly alike. Many schools choose elements from several models to put together their curriculum and activities. Observe two schools based on one model (e.g., Montessori) and compare them. How are they alike and different?

MyLabSchool is a collection of online tools for your success in this course, your licensure exams, and your teaching career. Visit **www.mylabschool.com** to access the following:

- Online Study Guide
- Video Cases from real classrooms
- Help with your research papers using Research Navigator
- Career Center with resources for:
    —Praxis and Licensure Preparation
    —Professional Portfolio Development
    —Job Search and Interview Techniques
    —Lesson Planning

CHAPTER 3

KEY TERMS you'll find in this chapter:

- **Adaptive equipment**, 96
- **Complex unit**, 83
- **Instructional materials**, 78
- **Learning areas**, 87
- **Learning environment**, 78
- **Room arrangement**, 78
- **Simple unit**, 83
- **Super unit**, 83
- **Traffic patterns**, 81
- **Vertical space**, 80

Creating an Environment for Learning

FOCUS QUESTIONS

- What are the key considerations in planning a classroom environment?

- How will you make decisions about arranging the furniture and materials in the classroom?

- How does a teacher select instructional materials that are appropriate for a given group of children?

- How will I plan an outdoor learning environment?

- How will I promote safety in classroom and on the playground?

- What adaptations in the environment will I make for children with special needs?

- How will I reflect respect for cultural differences in the classroom environment?

Your assignment this week was to focus your observations on the physical environment of the classroom. To do so, you needed to sketch the arrangement of the furniture and list the materials and equipment available to the children. When you went to the first-grade classroom where you were to observe, you found about what you had expected: The children all had desks, which were arranged in a *U* shape around the classroom. There were shelves along one wall, where materials such as art supplies and books were stored. The teacher's desk was at the front of the classroom and to one side. There were chalkboards on two walls and bulletin boards on the other two.

When you got back to your own class and heard from your classmates, you found that the physical environments everyone had observed varied greatly. Some had tables and chairs and no desks. Some had been arranged in work areas for art, blocks, sand and water, and so on, plus a library. Some had many materials readily available to the children; others had almost none.

Now you are much more interested in the physical environment provided for children. You have questions about how teachers make decisions about furniture and room arrangements, and you also want to know how such decisions affect the children's learning and behavior. ■

The environments where we live and work are important. They can enhance our work and home lives, or they can detract from the quality of our life experiences. Important questions about the environment include the following:

- Is the setting a place of beauty? Beautiful places are pleasing and even comforting to all of us, and an environment that speaks to all the senses should be a priority for all children.

- Does the setting promote strong families? Is there a place for adults to meet, get information, and discuss their children in a comfortable setting?

- Does the environment encourage community? Is there a place for gathering and for supporting the learners individually and in groups?

- Are there places for listening and conversations? Are there spaces for work and play as individuals and groups?

- Does the environment challenge children to explore and learn? Are there inviting materials and spaces to use these materials? Are new materials added on a regular basis that will invite children to use them? (Greenman, 2005).

As you think about the space in which you and the children will spend a great deal of time, keep these questions in mind. Most spaces can be made attractive and comfortable with thought, planning, and hard work.

Planning a Learning Environment

The first task in creating a **learning environment** that works is planning the physical space of the classroom. Some planning decisions can be made before the children arrive. Teachers can decide on the basic learning areas to be set up, the basic materials to be used, and the initial room arrangement. Other planning decisions must be made after the teacher and children become acquainted. Planning is never really finished. It is a continual cycle of making and implementing plans, observing, evaluating the effectiveness of your plans, and using that information for more planning.

The decisions you make about **room arrangement** and **instructional materials** and equipment will reflect your goals and expectations for the children. It is fairly common during an interview for a principal to ask a prospective teacher of young children to sketch a room arrangement that she would use. Much of what a principal wants to know about a candidate's curriculum priorities is reflected in how the prospective teacher chooses to arrange the room. If your program goals include encouraging children's exploration of a variety of materials and investigation of the phenomena around them, then you will not choose to set up your room with a desk for each child and the teacher's desk as the focal point of the classroom.

Environmental decisions reflect the philosophy and goals of the teacher. Thus, you will find contrasts among the instructional materials and room arrangements designed to accomplish various sets of objectives. For example, assume that one of Teacher A's beliefs is that children become more literate through participating in a broad range of activities that include read-alouds, journal writing, exploring books, playing games such as Go Fish, and reading interactive stories on the computer. Given this belief, this

www.ncrel.org/sdrs/areas/
issues/students/earlycld/
ea4lk24.htm

Several different aspects of classroom environments

PRAXIS

Be able to design an environment that is socially stimulating and positive teacher will make sure that his classroom has a comfortable library area, that the children can access many materials without asking for them, and that they have table space for playing games. Suppose that Teacher B, on the other hand, believes that children need to have lessons on various skills. Her classroom might be arranged in a more traditional way, with a separate desk for each child, a space where a small group could sit for instruction (horseshoe tables were once common in primary classrooms), and fewer spaces open to the children.

As noted in Chapter 2, the teachers of the Reggio Emilia schools consider the environment the "third teacher," in that many explorations and ideas can be inspired by the environment itself. Of course, the opposite is true, as well. A dull, uninteresting environment can stifle children's imaginations.

The general goals of many programs include helping children to do these things:

1. Learn that they are capable learners, that they can make choices, and that their ideas are respected
2. Learn and apply skills in a meaningful context
3. Explore a variety of materials
4. Become able to communicate their needs and feelings
5. Learn to use and appreciate many sources of information—people, printed materials, visual materials
6. Become able to express themselves creatively

In order to meet these goals, teachers have many decisions to make. Be aware that the decisions you make about the learning environment can either foster or hinder achievement of these goals.

Structuring the Physical Environment

NAEYC CRITERIA
3.9

Often, many of the physical characteristics of the classroom in an early childhood program do not reflect the choices of the teacher—the room may be too small for the number of children, have a sink that the children cannot reach, have a bathroom down the hall, have chalkboards on every wall, or have only one electrical outlet. However, teachers can make other decisions about the physical environment, including how the furniture is arranged. Although teachers may not be able to choose the furnishings for the room at the outset of a program, they may be able to make changes over time. Teachers should also keep in mind that children need to be involved in planning the space, as well. Teachers should make preliminary plans and arrangements, but they must always address the needs of the children once they are working in the classroom.

The furniture selected must be of appropriate size for children and should be easy to rearrange to meet changing classroom needs. The most flexible furniture includes tables and chairs and shelf units on wheels. Rarely will every child need to sit at a table at once, so there need not be places at tables for everyone. Every child does need a space for her own things; this could be a cubby or a portable tub of some kind. Figure 3.1 shows one design for storage cubbies.

FIGURE 3.1

Storage Cubbies

Room Arrangement

The way the furniture is arranged and the way the room looks communicate to children what they are expected to do and how they are expected to behave. Furniture or the lack of furniture provides all of us with clues about what is expected of us. Think of bank lobbies that are cold and hard, telling us to get our business done and leave; a typical college classroom telling us to sit, listen, and take notes; and a comfortable family room that invites sitting or lounging and participation in a variety of activities such as watching television, playing games, snacking, reading, and relaxing.

For years, studies have shown that the environment affects children's behavior and attitude. As the quality of the environment (as measured by adequate space and materials) decreased, the number of rules imposed by the adults and the amount of conflict among the children increased (C. B. Hill 1989; Midjaas 1984; Prescott, Jones, and Kritchevsky 1967; Weinstein 1979).

It is clear from the research that the environment is important and that environmental influences are strong. In fact, Hubbard (1998) states that "access to a range of spaces, access to materials, access to other children and other adults; in short, the ability to access their own creative process" (p. 30) is the key to successful classroom arrangements in which children can think.

In choosing how to arrange furniture in the classroom, the first consideration—beyond the locations of doors and windows—is the locations of electrical outlets. In new schools, outlets are usually plentiful; outlets are often in short supply in older buildings, however. Areas that require electricity obviously must be located next to outlets. Usually, this means that videocassette recorders (VCRs), computers, tape recorders, aquariums, and other items that use electricity must be placed in the classroom first. Teachers should keep in mind these general guidelines for room arrangements:

1. Space must accommodate multiple uses. Few classrooms and centers have enough space for each activity to have its own area; therefore, areas must serve more than one purpose. For example, blocks can be placed in a corner that is also used for story time during another part of the day.

2. Areas in which water is used should be as close to the water supply as possible. These include art, science, and water table areas.

3. Quiet areas should be close together so that children who want to work quietly can do so. *Quiet* does not mean that children cannot talk, but activities in such areas as the library, the writing table, and a listening station are quieter by nature than activities in some other areas.

4. Noisy areas, such as the blocks and dramatic play areas, should be grouped on the other side of the room from quiet areas.

Vertical space is often overlooked in classrooms for young children. The backs of room dividers, walls, and other vertical surfaces can be used for interactive activities, such as matching activities, in which children match dresses to dolls or cookie monsters to cans; dressing activities, in which children lace, tie, zip, and button various pieces of clothing; flannelboard or magnetic story activities, in which children create and retell stories; and so

www.
www.ncrel.org/sdrs/areas/
issues/students/earlycld/
ea1lk4-5.htm

Criteria for evaluating indoor and outdoor environments

PRAXIS

Be able to explain why a classroom needs to be planned carefully

NAEYC CRITERIA
3.6, 3.7, 3.8

FIGURE 3.2

Room Arrangement for a Preschool Classroom

on. By using vertical spaces, teachers can provide an extra activity or two in areas that would otherwise be decorative or perhaps even wasted (Readdick and Bartlett 1994/1995).

Figure 3.2 shows an example of a room arrangement for a preschool or kindergarten classroom, and Figure 3.3 shows one for a primary-grade classroom. Evaluate these plans in terms of use of space, how well they would accommodate your objectives, and what **traffic patterns** you think would develop. Please note that these room arrangements do not have a teacher's desk. Most teachers of young children do not need a desk; they just need a shelf or table to store supplies and to keep their records together. Teacher's desks take up an extraordinary amount of floor space that can be put to better use.

PRAXIS

Be able to arrange the classroom environment to promote individual, and group activities

FIGURE 3.3

Room Arrangement for a Primary-Grade Classroom

Teacher's Storage

Bookshelves

Doorway to Outside Play

Sink

Cabinets

Sofa

Rug

Art Center

Bookshelves

Science Center

Computer Center

Writing Center

Bookshelves

Bookshelves

Math Center

Rug

Easel

Listening/ Media Center

Doorway to Hall

Cubbies

Physical Climate

In thinking about the physical environment in your classroom, you must think about more than just furniture and electrical outlets. Researchers have recommended softer spaces (Vergeront 1987), more natural light (Grangaard 1995; Schreiber 1996), and the use of ethnic colors in the environment (Caples 1996).

Lyons (2001) points to studies of poor air quality in schools and the lack of appropriate ventilation as problematic, especially for the ever-increasing number of students with asthma and other breathing problems. He also notes that good acoustics are critical for the best learning environment. In most schools, the floors and walls are hard and so the sound quality is often very poor. Lyons suggests that at some time in the instructional day, at least 15 percent of the children have difficulty hearing what is being said. He also supports the use of full-spectrum lighting, rather than the fluorescent lighting most common in schools. Hathaway (1993) found that full-spectrum lighting had both positive physical and performance effects on children.

Finally, it is important for the temperature of the classroom to be comfortable. If it is either too hot or too cold, children will not be able to concentrate as well or be as productive as they would with an optimal temperature. In sum, the research makes it clear that the classroom environment is important and that environmental influences are strong.

You can improve the classroom climate even in an older building by adding paint in appropriate colors and by reducing noise with area rugs, fabric coverings on bulletin boards, soft furniture, and felt pads on chair legs. To improve air quality, try to keep windows open as often as you can, and when you cannot open windows, push for adequate ventilation (which often means cleaning and repairing air conditioning and heating units). You can also overcome the effects of fluorescent lights by replacing the typical bulbs with full-spectrum bulbs and by using as much natural light as possible.

Assessing the Environment

One method of assessing the learning environment is to examine activity areas in terms of their simplicity or complexity (Kritchevsky and Prescott 1969):

> **What the best and wisest parent wants for his own child, that must the community want for its children.**
>
> —*John Dewey*

NAEYC CRITERIA
3.12

- A **simple unit** for play or activity has one obvious use and does not have subparts for children to manipulate or improvise with; examples include rocking horses, swings, and vehicles.
- A **complex unit** has subparts made of two essentially different play materials that children can manipulate or improvise with. A sand table with tools is a complex unit; art activity tables with paint or clay and tables with books are also classified as complex.
- A **super unit** has three or more play materials juxtaposed. Examples include a tunnel with movable boards and boxes, a sand table with tools and water, and a blocks area with hollow blocks, unit blocks, and block accessories.

A super unit is about eight times as effective in holding children's attention as a simple unit; a complex unit is about four times as effective.

In analyzing your own room plans, count the variety of possible activities and the amount of things to do per child. Table 3.1 may help you analyze your own space. It shows Kritchevsky and Prescott's (1969, p. 13) analysis, in which the number of play spaces represents the number of children who can comfortably play in a given unit. Divide the total play spaces by the number of children to find the ratio of play spaces to children. If there are at least two play spaces for each child, children will be much more likely to find play spaces for themselves without teacher help than if the ratio were smaller. If the number of play spaces is less than the number of children, children will have difficulty finding something to do, other than grabbing something from someone else. An analysis of your room will provide information about whether there are adequate activities for the number of children and how you might rearrange the environment to make it more complex.

In addition to determining the number of play spaces and the complexity of the activities, assess your classroom space from both aesthetic and practical points of view. To begin your assessment, take photographs of your classroom. (It is amazing what the camera can see that the naked eye

TABLE 3.1 **Analysis of Play Spaces**

NUMBER OF PLAY UNITS	TYPE OF UNIT	NUMBER OF PLAY SPACES
12 vehicles	Simple	12
1 rocking boat	Simple	1
1 tumble tub	Simple	1
1 jungle gym with boxes and boards	Complex	4
1 dirt area plus scoop trucks	Complex	4
1 equipped sand table with water	Super	8
		Total Play Spaces = 30

Source: Kritchevsky and Prescott 1969, p. 13.

PRAXIS

Be able to design a classroom to meet the needs of all children

cannot!) Second, get down and look at your classroom from the children's eye level. What do they see? Finally, invite a colleague to examine your classroom with a critical eye and give you feedback on what could be improved. In conducting this assessments, develop and answer some questions, such as these:

1. Could a stranger who walked into your classroom tell what was valued in this environment?
2. From what is displayed in the classroom, what seem to be the topics of study?
3. Does the arrangement of the furniture make sense in terms of quiet/noisy and messy/neat activities?
4. Can the children get what they need to carry out their ideas without adult help?
5. Is it immediately clear from classroom displays that the work of the children is valued?
6. Do the materials and decorations in the classroom reflect the many cultures and ethnicities of the classroom and beyond?
7. Is the classroom aesthetically pleasing? Is the use of colors, fabrics, plants, and other materials arranged so that the room is appealing and interesting?
8. Can a child who needs a quiet space find it in this room?
9. Are the table and floor spaces adequate so that children who want to work with materials in a given area can do so easily?
10. Is the level of visual stimulation appropriate? Is the classroom too cluttered? Are enough interest areas and decorative pieces provided to invite interest?
11. If you were a child, would walking into this room make you feel good? Excited? Dreary? Bored? Anxious? (Harms 1970; Isbell and Exelby 2001; Wilford, 2005).

In assessing the environment for a primary-grade classroom, the teacher must think about adequate space and materials for completion of projects such as a study of animals or birds. Ask questions such as these about a primary environment:

1. Can a child or small group get materials (paper, markers, scissors, and so on) and find a space to work comfortably?

2. Is it possible to move around the room without disturbing the work of others?

3. Is there a quiet place for a child or small group to read or think?

4. Is the furniture arrangement flexible enough to allow moving from large group to small group to individual instruction without major disruptions and loss of time?

5. Are necessary items (such as a pencil sharpener) placed in the room so that a child needing to use them can do so without disturbing others?

6. Have the children been involved in solving any problems they encounter in getting their work done?

Most classrooms are not ideal, and you will have to do some thoughtful planning to make the space work for you and the children. You may have to think about combining some centers, finding ways to move some centers to the middle of the room, and generally using the space you have in creative ways. If you keep in mind what your goals are for the children and for a space that helps them be comfortable and happy, then you will be able to solve most problems. All teachers want more space. Good planning will not achieve that, but it will help you make the best use of the space you have.

In the box A Teacher Speaks, Kate McLaughlin discusses her process of classroom design in terms of working through the physical constraints of the room and then learning to look at pieces of furniture as functionally flexible, rather than functionally fixed. She would probably add, "What in this room can I not change?" to the list of questions for assessing a space. What other questions would you add to the list?

Instructional Materials

Materials for the classroom can be quite expensive. In addition to purchasing materials, most teachers ask for contributions from parents, go to garage sales, and scrounge materials from community sources. For example, some teachers get boxes and scrap paper from businesses that generate numerous computer printouts or wood scraps from local construction sites or cabinet shops.

The following guidelines will be helpful when you are selecting materials for the classroom:

1. Choose materials that can be used for more than one experience. Single-use materials like windup toys do not invite children to use them again and again, each time in a new or creative manner.

2. Select materials sturdy enough to withstand use by many active children.

3. Select materials that serve many instructional purposes, such as small blocks that can be used for constructing, for counting, for sorting by color, for arranging into patterns, and so on.

Education is not the filling of a pail, but the lighting of a fire.

—*William Butler Yeats*

A **Teacher** SPEAKS: Planning the Classroom Environment

Kate McLaughlin

Demonstration School

Lowell, Massachusetts

One of the ongoing struggles I have had as a classroom teacher is the design and maintenance of the ever-evolving physical environment of the classroom. I consistently ask myself how I can ensure that all students have a safe, productive place to learn and grow. If only the answer were simple and clear cut!

Every year, I seem to go through the same process of questioning the design of my classroom, in part to improve on the previous design and in part because I have not had the same room for more than one year. I first begin by reviewing the curriculum goals for the grade level along with the needs of the students. I also must take into account how both of these variables might change throughout the year. From there, I decide which learning areas will be necessary to meet those goals and needs.

With the list of essential learning areas, I can proceed through the numerous sketches of floorplans. During this phase, I take into consideration research and expert advice. For instance, I know that each learning area needs a workspace for students, a storage space for materials, and a display area for artifacts, essential information, and student work. I also need to group learning areas based on the noise level of the activities to be completed in those areas. Although experts provide a clear, logical method of designing classroom space, I struggle with conditions that may not be ideal.

When I read about classroom arrangement, the possibilities seem endless, but when I step into the classroom, the possibilities seem to dwindle. One example

from my current classroom is that the furniture arrangement seems to be more fixed. The computer area must be against one whole wall because of the Internet hookups. Therefore, the writing center must be adjacent to the computer area so that it can also serve as the publishing area. If I group together quiet learning areas, then the reading area needs to be in close proximity. Although I have read many articles and books on physical environment, I must base the arrangement of a large portion of the room on the location of the computer wiring. Every teacher must work through these types of constraints. Classroom design is a compromise between the ideal and reality, but with effort, creativity, and thought, it can be successful.

Throughout my journey in classroom design, I have found that the key to creating better student-centered classrooms is overcoming functional fixedness. When I first started teaching, I looked at a desk and saw only a space for an individual student to work and to store materials. Now I see a desk in many more capacities: as part of the work surface and storage space of a learning area, as a base for student mailboxes, or as a shelf in a closet. An open space with an area rug that was once just a meeting area could now be strewn with pillows or beanbags to create a reading nook or could be an area for building with engineering sets during science.

Sometimes the only limits we have in classroom design are the ones we place on ourselves and on the materials and space we have available to us. Although it is sometimes difficult to view the classroom and its contents with a fresh eye, I have found that overcoming functional fixedness leads to new and bountiful ideas that can grow and evolve into even better ideas when I start the process all over again the next year.

4. Select materials that can be used by children of varying ages and abilities. Sand, for example, can be used by very young children, who like to feel it and pour it from container to container. Older preschoolers can use sand to compare quantities and to measure. Primary-age children will be more sophisticated in their sand play. Barbour, Webster, and Drosdeck (1987) report observing one group of second-graders creating a desert environment after listening to their teacher read *The Desert Is Theirs* (Baylor 1970).

5. Choose safe materials; those with broken parts or rough edges should be discarded.

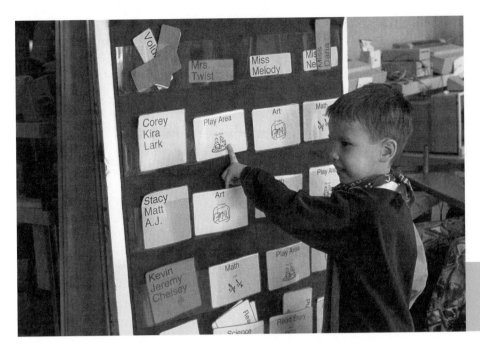

Children should have opportunities to make choices in the learning environment.

Learning Areas

One common technique for organizing instructional materials in classrooms is to place materials into learning centers or **learning areas.** Use of the phrase *learning centers* is sometimes criticized because it seems to imply that learning takes place only in those specific centers. The assumption underlying this discussion is that learning takes place all over and outside the classroom.

The phrase *learning area* will be used to indicate a specific location where related materials are arranged in a classroom. The basic learning areas in early childhood classrooms include areas for art, music, library/listening/writing activities, blocks, dramatic play, science/discovery activities, manipulatives/mathematics/games, woodworking, sand and water tables, and quiet activities. If space and equipment allow, an area for physical education is also important. These areas should reflect the children's ages, development, growing abilities, and changing interests; learning areas are not static.

See the panel on pages 88–89 for an overview of what materials and equipment should go in the basic learning areas. The following sections will discuss these areas in more detail.

Art Area

Teachers who want to encourage children in art experiences will think carefully about the materials and classroom environments that promote participation in art activities. If the goals of an art program are to be achieved, materials for many art experiences must be readily available to children.

In choosing a place in the classroom for art, consider sources of light and access to water. An area with a sink is ideal so that children can clean up easily, but a container of warm water will serve if no sink is available. Low shelves for storage of materials, easels for painting, and tables for working with other materials are also important.

Traffic patterns must be considered when deciding where the art area will be located. If the area cannot be in a corner, other pieces of furniture

www.
www.eduplace.com/rdg/res/classroom.html
Suggestions for setting up learning areas or centers and some possible center ideas

NAEYC CRITERIA
3.11, 3.13, 3.14, 3.15

PRAXIS

Be able to explain how the learning environment can provide children with opportunities to play, explore, and discover

Materials and Equipment for Early Childhood Classrooms

Some materials will not be appropriate for all age groups. The teacher must select those most appropriate for his group of students.

Basic furniture in any classroom should include tables and chairs of appropriate size, shelf units, storage units, an adult-sized rocking chair, sofas, child-sized rocking chairs, floor pillows, and a full-length mirror. The following lists include additional materials that teachers in preschool and primary grades have found to be useful. Teachers will also want to provide other materials to enhance the presentations of specific topics or themes.

Dramatic Play

- Child-sized kitchen equipment (with pots and pans)
- Dishes and silverware
- Tables and chairs
- Telephones
- Child-sized ironing board and iron
- Child-sized cleaning equipment (brooms, mops, dustpan, and so on)
- Assorted dolls
- Dollclothes
- Doll bed, carriage
- Dollhouse, furniture
- Assorted tubs, buckets, dishpans
- Assorted dress-up clothing and costumes

Block Play

- Blocks (unit and hollow)
- Block accessories (people, cars, safety signs, and so on)
- Small blocks (sets of cubes, small colored blocks)
- Sturdy wooden vehicles (cars, trucks, boats, planes, tractors, fire engines, buses, helicopters)

Art

- Adjustable easels
- Brushes (half-inch to one-inch widths)
- Liquid tempera paint (in a variety of colors)
- Painting smocks (purchased or homemade)
- Crayons
- Colored chalk
- Clay
- Scissors
- Glue, paste
- Paper (glazed for fingerpainting, newsprint, white drawing paper, construction paper in a variety of colors, tissue paper)
- Drying rack for paintings
- Miscellaneous supplies (fabric scraps, rickrack, yarn, ribbon, glitter, buttons, natural materials)

Library/Listening/Writing

- Computer and printer
- Typewriter

can be used to isolate the space so that children do not walk through it to get from one part of the classroom to another.

Setting up an art area also includes deciding on smocks and floor coverings that will help children be most comfortable as they explore art materials. Smocks can be made from plastic or from old shirts. The point is to protect the children's clothing so that they are free from the worry of getting their clothes dirty. Floor coverings should be tile, if possible, so that floors can be cleaned easily (see Figure 3.4). Floors can be covered with newspapers to aid in cleanup. Materials for cleanup—water, sponges, a small broom and dustpan—should also be readily available to the children.

In selecting materials for art experiences, teachers must think about developmental appropriateness and possibilities for multiple uses. Chalk, markers, and crayons should be easy to grasp and should not break easily. Children should be allowed to use materials in a variety of ways. For example, some teachers allow children to use crayons only as they would pencils. But the wrappers can be removed from crayons so they can be rubbed across the surface of a paper on their sides. The fewer rules that are attached to materials, the more children will be encouraged to think for themselves and be creative in using them.

Just because art materials are arranged in one place in the classroom does not mean that art experiences cannot take place in other areas. Be open

- Paper (various colors, sizes, shapes) and writing instruments (pencils, markers)
- Tape recorder, tapes, books with tapes
- Record player
- Flannelboard with stand and flannel pieces
- Books (professional and published by classroom authors)
- Magazines

Manipulatives/Games

- Hand puppets
- Puzzles
- Games (Lotto, checkers, chess, dominoes, Candy Land, Chutes and Ladders, Hi-Ho Cherry O, and so on)
- Beads and strings
- Sewing cards
- Manipulative materials (ranging from stacking rings to very complex materials)
- Tinkertoys (regular size and large size)
- LEGO blocks, bristle blocks

Science/Discovery

- Aquarium
- Terrarium
- Magnets of various kinds
- Magnifying glasses
- Prism
- Metric measuring equipment, test tubes, slides, petri dishes

- Pattern blocks
- Pegs and pegboards
- Geoboards
- Geoblocks
- Base 10 blocks
- Unifix cubes
- Scales (balance and other types)
- Rhythm instruments
- Sandbox
- Water table with top
- Workbench with equipment

Physical Education

- Balance beam
- Tumbling mat
- Rocking boat
- Steps
- Walking boards
- Jungle gym
- Fabric tunnel
- Sawhorses (sturdy metal)
- Climbing ladder, climbing rope
- Balls of various sizes
- Ropes
- Hula hoops
- Bowling set
- Outdoor equipment (wheeled toys, gardening tools, sandbox)

to a variety of places and possibilities for art activities. In nice weather, children might be offered the chance to do art outside; for example, they might do rubbings on outside surfaces. They might also choose to draw in other places in the classroom. On the other hand, even though art activities are not limited to one area of the room, it is convenient for all the supplies to be stored together in the art area so that children always know where to find what they need. Figure 3.4 is a sketch of an art area that illustrates some of the suggestions in the preceding paragraphs.

Music Area

A piano is often the center of the music area. If you are lucky enough to have a piano and can play a simple tune, you can use it in many different ways to encourage children's music skills. Although a piano is still very valuable in an early childhood classroom, many teachers today use guitars and autoharps. These instruments are much easier to

FIGURE 3.4

Art Area

play and allow the teacher to face the children while playing. Still, many teachers like to have CD players or tape recorders in the music area to be used in group music experiences or by individual students.

Exploration of music can be encouraged by making a limited number of musical instruments available to children. If the classroom is equipped with a piano, a low shelf area near the piano is adequate for storing other selected instruments. A listening center with headphones gives children opportunities to listen to CDs and tapes without disturbing the rest of the class.

The teacher might also keep a file of songs that children know along with charts of the lyrics. When these materials are made available, children can select songs for group singing or review songs they especially like.

Usually, the space used for movement experiences is used for other purposes during other parts of the day. If possible a space can be provided for movement during the time children choose their own activities. A shelf with scarves, hula hoops, large circles made of elastic (often known as *Chinese jump ropes*), a small drum, and ankle bells will encourage explorations of movement.

Library/Listening/Writing Area

An area for language arts activities should be located in a quiet part of the classroom and should have open shelves for storing books and a table for writing activities. Children may or may not need chairs for the listening center; sometimes the unit can be placed so that children sit on the floor to use it.

It is better to display books standing up, with their covers showing, than to store them stacked on a shelf. Storing books standing up takes more space than stacking them, but children are much more likely to be enticed to choose a book if they can see its front cover. Because the number of books that can be displayed at once in this manner is limited, the books on display will need to be rotated frequently and selected to support topics of study.

In addition to a table for writing, a storage area for different writing papers and writing instruments is necessary. Pencils, pens, markers, and so on should be stored in small baskets or cans to make it easy for children to choose the ones they need. Paper in different colors and sizes should be available and can easily be stored in open boxes. Dictionaries should also be kept in this area. Picture dictionaries are especially useful for young writers. Children's personal dictionaries can be kept in a basket in the writing area.

Typewriters and computers can also be housed in the library/listening/writing area. Children working with such equipment need the same supplies (word lists, dictionaries, and the like) that other writers need, so it is sensible to locate such equipment in this area. Use of typewriters and computers can generate a lot of talking and interaction, so they should be placed where students using them will disturb those in the quiet reading area as little as possible.

Block Play Area

Blocks require storage shelves and a large floor area for construction. A smooth carpet can help reduce the noise in this area and will not interfere with balancing the blocks. Larger blocks, such as hollow blocks, can be stored directly on the floor rather than on shelves. As Hirsch (1984) reminds us, the block storage area should be neither too neat nor too messy. If it's too neat, children will be intimidated and worry about cluttering the area when they use the materials; if it's too messy, children will find it difficult to locate the exact blocks they need, which is frustrating. Unit blocks should not be stored in carts or boxes. Such storage makes finding the needed block almost impossible and encourages children to toss the blocks back into the box, thereby denting them and reducing their useful life.

You will have to decide if you want to mark the block shelves (for example, with silhouettes of the blocks to be stored on each shelf) or if you want the children to determine the storage. Children do learn to recognize the shapes of the blocks and match them to the silhouettes, but they learn more about size relationships and classification when they are responsible for making storage decisions. Figure 3.5 illustrates a block play area.

FIGURE 3.5

Block Play Area

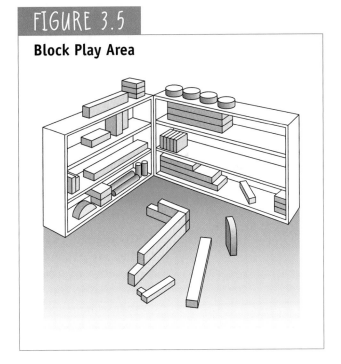

Dramatic Play Area

The dramatic play area is often called the *housekeeping corner* or the *doll corner*. It is an area that will reflect the development and changing interests of the children as they grow. For example, threes and fours may need child-sized kitchen equipment, dishes and pans, dolls and doll beds, and other materials for acting out the roles in a family. As children grow and develop, they are able to assume the roles of people outside the family. Although they may still enjoy the kitchen equipment, they will often use the dramatic play area to act out roles of people in such locations as a grocery store, a gas station, a beauty or barber shop, a doctor's office, a hospital, an airport, and other areas that are part of their experience.

The teacher will need to be flexible in providing the materials and assistance to support children's ideas. Primary-grade children often use this area for dramatizing characters in stories they have heard or read. They will need a variety of costumes, dress-up clothes, and props to support their play as their knowledge expands. If the dramatic play area stays the same throughout the year, then the teacher will need to take special steps to encourage children to develop and expand their interests.

Science/Discovery Area

Science activities do not take place only in the science or discovery area, of course, but the tools for investigations are kept on shelves in this area. Most teachers also like to have a table where interesting displays can be arranged and where children can explore materials—plants, soils, rocks, shells, leaves, or whatever. The area should be equipped with shelves that contain magnets, magnifying glasses, measurement containers, and other materials for investigating scientific topics. Teachers often include an invention corner in this area, where old appliances such as television sets, radios, toys, clocks, and toasters can be dismantled and reassembled, perhaps even using the parts to create new objects.

Manipulatives/Mathematics/Games Area

The math area is another area that will need to change to meet the needs and interests of children. This area should be the storage place for puzzles, beads, sewing cards, and other materials designed to help younger children develop fine motor skills. Older children will still be interested in puzzles and manipulative games and will also begin using pattern blocks, Unifix cubes, base 10 blocks, and other manipulatives used in mathematics. All ages will need construction toys and tabletop blocks. Games designed for individuals or small groups are often stored in this area. Playing cards, dice, and other game materials should also be available here; children will not only play with them but also use them for inventing games. This area needs shelves for storage and a table on which to work with the materials.

Woodworking Area

The woodworking area requires a workbench, storage areas for wood scraps, and shelves or a pegboard for holding tools. Young children who have not had much experience with woodworking are often satisfied with a sturdy log or other large piece of wood into which they can hammer nails. Children do not necessarily need to be able to make something until they have had more experience. Tools should be real tools designed on a small scale and sturdy enough to work well. Saws should really cut wood, and hammers should really drive nails.

Sand and Water Tables Area

Good-quality sand and water tables are available from supply catalogs, but they are expensive. A sand table can be constructed by adding a frame to the edge of a low table. Sometimes teachers substitute rice or cornmeal for sand in order to make cleanup easier. However, in addition to the fact that some teachers may be reluctant to use food in activities that render it inedible, neither of these materials has the same qualities that sand offers. For example, children cannot add water to these materials and mold them. Teachers should also recognize that individuals from some cultures may be offended by this use of food.

Many sand and water tables are equipped with covers so they can be used for other purposes when not being used for sand and water play. Accessories for sand and water tables depend on the developmental level of the children using them. Younger children may only pour and scoop, so precise measuring equipment is not needed. Older children will need materials to make measuring, comparing, and other investigations possible. Storage for accessories is often in boxes under the tables.

Water tables are more difficult to make than sand tables. The newest models of water tables are made of clear plastic and are often round with drains in the bottom that allow for easy draining and cleaning. Teachers often substitute a tub or a child's wading pool for a water table. These substitutes are better than not having water tables, but because children lean over them rather than stand around them and could easily fall in, even more supervision is required. The water in water tables should be replaced daily, so draining and filling conditions should be considered when purchasing a table. Water play accessories should include objects for filling and pouring, tubes and connectors, and materials that sink and float. Specific materials can be added to sand and water tables to help children explore topics in the curriculum.

Physical Education Area

An area where children can use a tumbling mat and engage in other physical activities is important. Some teachers like to place equipment that encourages gross motor development around the room, rather than in one area, because it takes up so much space. For example, balance beams and tunnels can be placed so that children can use them to get from one area of the room to another. Physical development is enhanced with beanbags, Velcro darts, Nerf balls, tunnels, bowling pins and balls, and so on. These materials should be stored on shelves or in a closet near an area large enough for children to use them without disturbing the work of others.

Quiet Area

Every classroom needs a small area where a child can go to be alone for a time. This area needs no special equipment—perhaps just a chair or a floor pillow. Some teachers like to make the quiet area inviting with flowers (nothing elaborate, just one or two), a piece of sculpture, or a drape of fabric. A child should be able to take a game or a book to this quiet area whenever she needs to.

Specialized Learning Areas

Some learning areas are set up for specific purposes and are not designed to be part of the classroom all year. Such specialized centers might be used for activities such as following up on stories, sorting and classifying objects, and demonstrating skills.

DEVELOPMENTALLY APPROPRIATE PRACTICE

Reflect on different classroom environments you have observed in terms of what you now know about planning a learning environment:

- Do any elements of the classroom environment indicate developmentally appropriate practice? Why?

- Can a classroom environment be developmentally appropriate when the desks are arranged in rows, with each child facing the teacher's desk in the front of the room? Why?

- Could a more flexible furniture arrangement fail to be developmentally appropriate? Why?

- In addition to furniture arrangement, what else in the environment would indicate DAP? Why?

Activities to follow up on stories include placing pictures from the story in correct sequence, listening to a tape recording of the story while following along in the book, drawing a picture of a favorite part of the story, and so on. Sorting and classifying or problem-solving centers might offer collections to be sorted and explained (shells, keys, leaves, and so on) or materials to be grouped (paper and pencils, stamps and envelopes, keys and locks). Skill activities might be finding pictures of sets of objects whose names rhyme or finding the matching cylinders in a sound game. (Canisters from 35-mm film containing beans, rice, nails, stones, or other materials and having the lids taped on work well for this activity.)

Many magazines for teachers describe learning activities such as these. Teachers have to decide how they fit the program goals, if they suit the individual needs of children, and if so, where to locate the activities in the room.

Storage Areas

Each classroom needs an area in which materials not currently in use can be stored. A closet lined with shelves is ideal. If no storage facilities are built into the classroom, perhaps a storage unit can be purchased from a school supply firm. If the room contains no closet and a unit cannot be purchased, the teacher may have to improvise a storage area in one corner. Fabric can be used to cover the front of a shelf unit so that the contents are out of sight.

Beginning the Year

Teachers can begin the year by arranging materials in basic areas, knowing that they will make changes as soon as the children actually begin to work in the classroom. Teachers should try to simplify areas so that only the very basic materials and equipment are available for the first few days or weeks of the schoolyear. Materials that are easy to put away should be used until the children learn the routines of cleaning up work areas. Some materials should also be kept back initially and brought out later to add interest and novelty throughout the year; for example, large blocks and a few unit blocks can be put out in the blocks area right away, but other unit blocks and accessories can remain put away for use later.

For the first few days of school, activities in the art center should be limited to the use of crayons, paper, and clay. Unless classroom assistance is available—such as a parent volunteer or paraprofessional who can help children learn where to find paint smocks and paint, where to place their paintings until they dry, and how to clean up the art area—paint and easels should be brought out only after children have learned to handle the materials in other areas. Similarly, such areas as music, water tables, and carpentry can be set up when the teacher knows the children better and feels they do not require such close supervision.

Managing Learning Areas

More often than not, children will distribute themselves among learning areas without any problems of overcrowding. If new materials are added, the teacher may have to help children solve the problem of who has a turn first. If some areas do not attract children, the teacher's responsibility is to determine what the area needs and why it is not interesting to the children. The youngest children will need teacher guidance in choosing areas for play; older pre-

www.ilovethatteachingidea.
com/ideas/subj_learning_
centers.htm

Several tips for managing learning areas and learning area ideas schoolers may be able to plan their activities more independently, with the help of a few guidelines for managing the learning areas; and primary-grade children can take most of the responsibility for distributing themselves.

Many teachers have an activity time when children first arrive for the day; this allows children to choose an area and begin their activities without waiting for everyone else to arrive. Other teachers begin activity time after a group meeting, during which they have reviewed the calendar or completed other discussions with the group.

To avoid having everyone trying to get to an area at once, many teachers use some scheme for deciding who chooses first and how choices are made during the play period. Some teachers group children randomly into two or three groups and rotate the group that gets to choose first. For example, the groups might be labeled red, yellow, and blue; if the red group has first choice today, the yellow group will have first choice tomorrow, and the blue group, the day after.

Teachers of very young children should try to allow them to play where they choose. When their choices cannot be honored, then the teacher should suggest another area and perhaps play there with the children for a few minutes. Some teachers of older preschoolers manage the number of children in each area by posting a number that defines how many can be in that area at a time. A child is free to join others in that area if the number of children allowed will not be exceeded. For example, if the blocks area will hold six children comfortably, a 6 is posted on one of the shelves. A child coming to the blocks area must decide if she can play with the blocks, given the number of children already in the area.

Other teachers like to use a pegboard system (see Figure 3.6). A pegboard is prepared so that the learning areas are displayed down the left side. Pictures representing learning areas are added to aid the children in identifying each area. The number of pegs for each area is determined by the number of children that area can accommodate easily; pegs are placed in the row beside each picture to indicate how many children can use that area at one time.

Again, if six children can use the blocks area, there will be six pegs beside the picture of blocks. Each child will have a tag with his name on it; he will place his tag on a peg when he wants to play with the blocks. If there are no empty pegs for the blocks area, he will have to make another choice. There should be more total pegs than there are children in order to give children as many choices as possible. And when an area is not available for some reason, the pegs for that area can be removed for the day.

Such a pegboard system also allows some subtle guidance in helping children make new choices. For example, if a child always chooses the art area and the teacher feels that she has developed enough confidence to work in another area, the teacher might limit the number of art pegs so that the child will have to make another choice. The teacher should make sure that choices are available that will interest the child and perhaps go there with her to play for a few minutes.

Teachers may want to involve primary-age children in more formal planning. One way to do this is to provide each child with a planning sheet on which the scheduled events for the day are listed (see Figure 3.7). After reviewing the events, each child can check what he plans to do that day.

FIGURE 3.6

Pegboard

FIGURE 3.7

Planning Sheet

Name: _____

☐ Independent Reading/Writing

☐ Writing Conference with Teacher

☐ Reading Conference with Teacher

☐ Buddy Reading

☐ Special Activity

☐ Math Activity

☐ Outdoor Play

☐ Work on Project with Group

☐ Library

☐ Listening Center

☐ Games Center

☐ Special Lesson

www.whitehutchinson.com/
children/articles/outdoor.
shtml

An explanation of why children need to be exposed to nature as well as advice for planning a playground

Parents and Playgrounds

● Invite parents to observe children playing on the playground. Provide a guide sheet that will help parents identify various kinds of play and activities.

● Provide resources so that parents can read about what makes playgrounds challenging, fun, and safe for children of various ages.

NAEYC CRITERIA

3.3, 3.29

Planning the Outdoor Environment

Outdoor environments, like indoor environments, require planning if they are to achieve the best results for the children (Herlein 1995). Ideally, outdoor play areas should be adjacent to indoor areas, with easy access to toilet facilities. Outdoor areas should be securely fenced and should have covered sections for play on rainy or very hot days.

Outdoor areas should include sections with different surfaces: grass, concrete, areas for digging, and sand. Play areas should include different terrains when possible; hills and inclines provide interesting terrains for riding toys, rolling downhill, and so on, as well as visual interest. Paved paths and large areas are ideal for wheel toys or riding toys. In addition to the physical exertion required by riding toys, they offer children many opportunities for dramatic play.

Apparatus for swinging, climbing, sliding, and crawling should also be provided in the outdoor environment. Some apparatus should have higher bars for swinging while hanging by the hands and lower bars for hanging by the knees or elbows. Studies have shown that children develop more upper-body strength when they play on playgrounds equipped with overhead ladders (Gabbard 1979). In selecting apparatus, the teacher should think about providing a balance of equipment so that children will use all the large muscles as they play. The hull of a rowboat or the body of an old car can stimulate dramatic play and offer something to climb on. Boards for walking and balance beams are also useful pieces of equipment.

Many playgrounds leave nothing for children to use in planning, arranging, or creating. Elizabeth Jones (1989) recommends that play areas have "loose parts" that children can move around and with which they can build and be creative. With movable equipment, children can construct their own play environment; boxes, boards, barrels, sawhorses, and short ladders work well. Tires and tubes are also useful for rolling around and stacking.

An outdoor play space should include a gardening area, a sandbox, a water play area or water table, a storage area for tools and toys, and tables or easels. (If need be, portable easels can be moved from the classroom for outside use.)

Having a gardening area does not mean that the entire area must be used for planting. At least some of the space should be reserved for impromptu digging. When children dig, they learn about the composition of soil, the differences between dry and damp soil, the insects and worms that live in the soil, and the pieces of organic matter that decompose to produce soil. A garden that includes an area for planting and caring for the plants, in addition to a digging area, can extend many classroom experiences.

An outside sandbox has advantages that an indoor sand table cannot offer. Children can climb into a sandbox, sit in the sand while playing in it, and create play areas on a much larger scale. An outdoor sandbox should have a cover to keep the sand clean, preferably one that folds back in sections to make handling easier. In many areas of the United States, a sandbox also should have some kind of roof so that the sand does not get too hot or stay wet all the time. Baker (1966) observed that the sandbox was frequently the place children started playing while they watched the more vigorous play around them. When they gained enough confidence, they joined the more active play.

Opportunities for water play outdoors can be provided with a small wading pool or a water table. Pools of water must be carefully supervised. Children can use the water outside much as they do in the classroom—pouring, measuring, and comparing. The differences are that outside, much more splashing is acceptable, and water can be carried all over the play area. Practically everything outdoors can be "painted" with water. A few large paintbrushes and some buckets are essential water play accessories outdoors.

Outdoor play is an important means of achieving social development goals.

Finally, many fine arts activities can be conducted outdoors if portable easels or tables are available for painting, creating collages, and other art projects. When the weather is pleasant outdoors, art experiences can be especially satisfying because children do not have to be as concerned about paint spills or drips. Cleanup is simple.

A shed for storing outdoor materials is a must. It can hold garden and digging tools, sandbox and water toys, riding toys, balls, and other materials used outdoors. Teachers tend to be much more relaxed about allowing children to dig in sand and mud when they know that the tools do not have to be clean enough to take back indoors when the play ends. A shed will also protect the toys and tools from exposure to the elements and prolong the life of materials.

Odoy and Foster (1997) suggest that teachers extend indoor play activities to the outdoors by using play crates, which are large, plastic boxes that hold materials used in various kinds of play. For example, a collection of shovels, watering cans, buckets, and scoops will encourage children to dig and garden. Other boxes might hold PVC pipes and elbows from which children can construct systems for carrying water or sand. Hoops, streamers, and scarves will encourage movement and imaginative play. The number and kind of crates is limited only by the teacher's imagination.

Playgrounds should be planned to help children with different physical abilities. A study by Barbour (1999) found that playgrounds designed primarily for exercise activities were not appropriate for all children. In particular, those children who are not as capable physically cannot use the equipment and have few or no other options for interacting with their peers. Children who have limited physical competence therefore fall further behind those peers who can accomplish physical feats.

Figure 3.8 is a diagram of a playground appropriate for children in preschool through second grade. Analyze this playground using the same criteria used earlier for analyzing room arrangements (see page 78). How well is the space used? What developmental objectives can be met using this playground? What traffic patterns do you predict?

Planning for Safety—Inside and Out

In choosing any room arrangement or collection of instructional materials, one of the critical criteria is safety. Teachers must make every effort to provide a safe learning environment, both inside the classroom and on the playground. In addition to the safety considerations already mentioned for individual pieces of equipment, the following list will help you analyze the environment for safety:

A Safety Checklist

1. Check the environment, both inside and outside, for any hazards. Check electrical outlets and cords; make sure children cannot pull over any equipment (television sets, projectors, and so on); remove dangerous plants; cover sharp edges; make sure fences are sturdy and exit gates are childproof; and eliminate any other hazards to children's safety.

2. Practice emergency procedures on a regular basis. Children's and teachers' responses to fire drills (and in some areas, tornado and earthquake procedures) must become automatic.

3. Make sure that the classroom contains a fire extinguisher and that all staff (and children who are old enough) know how to use it.

FIGURE 3.8

Playground for Children in Preschool through Second Grade

4' chain-link fence around entire area

Covered Area

Sandbox

Gardening Area

Digging Area

Water Play Area

Play Structures

Door to Classroom

Grassy Area

50 feet

Steps

Table

Raised Area

Playhouse

Storage Area

30 feet

4. All teachers and staff members should be trained in first aid and cardio-pulmonary resuscitation (CPR). At minimum, one person with such training should be present at all times. Staff should be required to have special training for CPR with infants, if the program accepts children that young.

5. Post a list of the names of all children and a map of fire exit routes near each exit.

6. Keep a first aid kit adequately stocked at all times. Keep it in a specific place so that any staff member can locate it quickly.

7. Keep an up-to-date list of emergency phone numbers (parents, relatives, doctors, and hospitals) for each child.

8. Keep the number for the nearest poison control center posted near the telephone.

9. Post a list of children's allergies (including reactions to wasp or bee stings) so that it can be checked before planning any food experiences or outdoor activities.

10. Keep a list by the door of the adults authorized to pick up each child. Do not release a child to any unauthorized person.

11. Make all posted information readily available to substitute teachers.

Teachers must consider a number of factors in assessing playground safety. Frost and Wortham (1988) devised the following checklist, which you may find helpful:

- A fence (minimum four feet high) protects children from potentially hazardous areas (e.g., streets, water).
- Eight to twelve inches of noncompacted sand, pea gravel, shredded wood, or equivalent material is in place under and around all climbing and moving equipment.
- Resilient surface is properly maintained (e.g., in place, noncompacted, free of debris).
- The equipment is sized to the age group served, with climbing heights limited to the reaching height of children standing erect.
- There are no openings that can entrap a child's head (approximately four to eight inches).
- Swing seats are constructed of lightweight material with no protruding elements.
- Moving parts are free of defects (no pinch, shearing, or crush points; bearings are not excessively worn).
- Equipment is free of sharp edges, protruding elements, broken parts, and toxic substances.
- Fixed equipment is structurally sound—no bending, warping, breaking, or sinking.
- Large equipment is secured in the ground, and concrete footings are recessed in the ground.
- All safety equipment (e.g., guard rails, padded areas, protective covers) is in good repair.
- The area is free of electrical hazards (e.g., unfenced air conditioners and switchboxes).
- The area is free of debris (e.g., sanitary hazards, broken glass, and rocks). (p. 24)*

The National Playground Safety Institute (NPSI) notes that 40 percent of injuries are directly related to lack of supervision. Be alert and engaged with the children at all times. The Consumer Product Safety Commission does not recommend heavy swings, multiple-occupancy gliders, free-swinging ropes, exercise rings, or trapeze bars for public playgrounds.

The Americans with Disabilities Act (ADA) requires that playgrounds be accessible to children with disabilities and that schools and programs

---

*From Joe L. Frost and Sue C. Wortham, "The Evolution of American Playgrounds," *Young Children* 43 (July 1988): 19–28. Reprinted with permission from the National Association for the Education of Young Children.

modify playgrounds to make them accessible. Sorohan (1995) suggests that the following elements should be considered when thinking about playground adaptations:

- *Support:* Some children need back supports to play in sandboxes or with spring toys.
- *Reach:* Avoid placing elements too high or too low for children in wheelchairs to reach.
- *Diversity:* Think about materials that will enhance development of social and cognitive skills as well as gross motor skills. Materials that can be manipulated and those that require two or more children to play are both useful.
- *Cues:* Provide visual, tactile, and auditory cues to help children move around the playground safely.
- *Getting on and off:* Ramps and transfer platforms might be needed for some students. Think about equipment that will allow a child to return to his wheelchair without assistance after use.
- *Location:* Place playgrounds close to buildings for easier access.

Although many schools have attempted to make playgrounds accessible and enjoyable for all children, much is still needed to achieve the goal of fully integrated playgrounds. Malkusak, Schappet, and Lawrence (2002) remind us that one in ten children has some type of disability that usually prevents him from having a full play experience. They state,

> Playgrounds for children of all abilities are essential to the healthy development of all children. Play is how children learn to navigate the world. All children need outdoor play environments to build their strength and socialization skills, learn to be independent, take turns and meet challenges, gain a sense of self-determination and esteem and enhance cerebral/motor development. (p. 71)

CHILDREN WITH SPECIAL NEEDS

Some areas and materials may need to be adapted for children with special needs, for instance, to make them wheelchair accessible or to add visual or auditory information to help all children work as independently as possible. Teachers should analyze the room arrangement and material storage areas in terms of the needs of all children in the class. Some spaces may need to be enlarged or more clearly defined to facilitate children's movement, some materials may need to be placed on more accessible shelves so they are within children's reach, or some materials may need to be organized so that children who have trouble hearing receive the maximum visual information.

For example, Sheldon (1996) recommends making **adaptive equipment** available in the dramatic play area so that children will experience what adaptive equipment actually feels like and be less wary of it. Of course, the children using these materials will require close supervision so the materials are not damaged and no children are injured. Bromer (1999) suggests that teachers find diverse props and play materials and that props be tailored to meet children's needs, such as having dress-up clothing that opens in the front, has large openings, and fastens with Velcro closures.

Clutter may be distracting for children with perceptual difficulties. Some common supplies may need to be stored in several locations throughout the

PRAXIS

Be able to design a classroom to accommodate children with special needs room so that children who have problems moving around have easy access to them. Room arrangements, materials, and schedules must be adapted for each group and for each individual child.

CELEBRATING DIVERSITY

Teachers can show respect for the community and the cultures of children in their classrooms by asking for information and help from various school patrons and parents. Some special materials can be selected for learning areas that will help children feel more at home. For example, the dress-up center could include several pieces of clothing that are typical of those worn by ethnic groups in the community. Some traditional clothing may be too rare or expensive to use for children's play, but if it can be obtained, it will be valuable for the children. Pictures can be taken around the community and used as illustrations in student-made books or as posters for the classroom.

Play materials, such as puzzles and dolls, also need to reflect the various cultures of the community. If they are not available commercially, perhaps some members of the community would be willing to help make them. Sears and Medearis (1993) describe a project in which community members helped schools develop materials, art projects, science activities, and so on that were culturally appropriate for local American Indian groups. With some effort, teachers could replicate the work of this project with their own local cultural groups.

Huber (2004) suggests that teachers should not only find appropriate multicultural materials but that they should also leave them in the classroom for several weeks so that children will be able to interact with them. She goes on to recommend that teachers participate with children in using these materials, rather than just put them out. Huber also suggests that teachers should think about everyday activities and include multicultural materials in areas common to all cultures, such as pretend food, cooking utensils, menus from ethnic restaurants, and chairs, futons, hammocks, or whatever else is common in children's homes.

> **No one has yet realized the wealth of sympathy, the kindness and generosity hidden in the soul of a child. The effort of every true education should be to unlock that treasure.**
>
> —*Emma Goldman*

SUMMARY

- The key considerations in planning a learning environment include the nature of the physical space, achieving an environment that challenges children to explore while keeping materials available, the goals of the program, and achieving a beautiful space for the children.

- The arrangement of furniture in a classroom reflects the goals and objectives of the teacher. Furniture and equipment should be selected and arranged to achieve the best working environment for the children. The teacher also needs to think about the classroom in terms of color, lighting, temperature, and air quality to maximize children's comfort and productivity.

- Instructional materials must be selected for flexibility and durability and with an eye toward multiple possibilities for use. The materials in a classroom are typically arranged in various learning areas, such as an art area; a music area; a library/listening/writing area; a block play area; a dramatic play area; a science or discovery area; an area for manipulatives, games, and math materials; a woodworking area; an area for sand and water tables; a physical education area; a quiet area; and specialized learning areas.

- An outdoor environment requires careful planning to be safe and productive. Outdoor learning areas might include a gardening area, a digging area, a water play area, a gross motor development area, a sand play area, a stage, a playhouse, and open areas. Many indoor activities, such as art, can be moved outdoors when the weather permits. Ideally, children should be able to play indoors or outdoors, but supervision issues and the location of some playgrounds distant from the classroom often preclude this option.

● The teachers and staff are responsible for making sure that all children are safe in the school environment, both inside and outside. Safety procedures must be in place and followed carefully, including conducting frequent inspections of equipment and providing safe surfaces under any equipment where children might fall.

● The classroom arrangement and materials may need to be adapted for children with special needs, so that they have access to all classroom learning areas as well as materials and equipment.

● In selecting materials for their classrooms, teachers must consider the diversity of the families represented in the school. Materials should reflect the variety of cultures in the community and also the world at large, regardless of the school population.

REFLECTIONS

1. Sketch a diagram of your ideal classroom, and justify the arrangements that you have made.
2. Creating learning areas is one way of arranging materials in a classroom. Is it the best way? Why or why not?
3. Explain at least two adaptations that you might make in a classroom to make sure that all children have access to learning areas and equipment.
4. Explain the benefits of outdoor play. Is it important enough to you that you will spend time planning it? Or is it just recess with supervision, requiring no real planning?
5. Does the environment of the classroom actually influence children's behavior for better or for worse? What about their learning? Can it be influenced by the environment? Explain your answers.

EXPLORATIONS AND ACTIVITIES

1. Look through a catalog of supplies and equipment for an early childhood classroom, and choose the ten most important pieces of equipment (excluding furniture) that you would want in your room. Justify your choices.

2. As you observe in classrooms, look for instances of environmental elements that seem to enhance or detract from the children's learning. What could you do to change those elements that detract from learning?

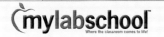

MyLabSchool is a collection of online tools for your success in this course, your licensure exams, and your teaching career. Visit **www.mylabschool.com** to access the following:

■ Online Study Guide
■ Video Cases from real classrooms
■ Help with your research papers using Research Navigator
■ Career Center with resources for:
 —Praxis and Licensure Preparation
 —Professional Portfolio Development
 —Job Search and Interview Techniques
 —Lesson Planning

CHAPTER **4**

KEY TERMS you'll find in this chapter:

- **Antibias curriculum,** 119
- **Curriculum,** 106
- **Daily class schedule,** 128
- **Incidental learning,** 117
- **Integrated curriculum,** 110
- **Learning plan,** 116
- **Mandated goals,** 118
- **Multicultural education,** 119
- **Pull-out programs,** 134
- **State standards,** 111
- **Theme,** 111
- **Transitions,** 132

Planning Learning Activities

FOCUS QUESTIONS

- How is *curriculum* defined and organized?

- What does *developmentally appropriate practice (DAP)* mean in terms of curriculum planning?

- What are the benefits of organizing curriculum thematically?

- How will I make plans for children's learning?

- How will my curriculum reflect the principles of multicultural education?

- How will computers be used in my curriculum?

- What are some options for the daily schedule?

- How will I plan for children with special needs?

- How will I celebrate diversity in my planning?

You observed in a kindergarten this week. You were amazed at the variety of activities the children had to choose from during most of the morning. You noticed that the teacher encouraged children to choose a project that interested them and that some children continued to work on the same activity for the entire time. One child built an elaborate block structure to represent the harbor the class had visited last week. She labeled all the parts with signs. She smiled happily when the teacher photographed her construction, asked the teacher for a blank book in which to mount the photograph, and told you that tomorrow she would write about the construction in the book. You wondered how building this block structure fit in with the teacher's goals and objectives for the class. Other children were involved in such activities as creating animals from cardboard boxes, painting at easels, observing and recording the behavior of a large frog, and following the directions in a book for making an appropriate home for a box turtle.

The teacher showed you his plan book, and you found lesson plans that did not follow the outline you learned in your first education class. How do teachers select learning activities? What does a learning plan that includes many different activities look like? How does a teacher evaluate a program? ■

Curriculum Design

In designing a **curriculum** for young children, the teacher must select objectives, select and organize content, choose the appropriate learning experiences, determine the most appropriate sequence for the learning activities, and determine how to assess both children's growth and the program itself. *Curriculum* is a term that has many definitions: It can mean all experiences that happen at school; a written plan for learning; a syllabus that lists learning topics and the order in which they will be presented; or a program, such as a drug abuse prevention program, that specifies a sequence of activities. In this chapter, *curriculum* is defined as a written plan for learning experiences in which children will be involved.

In designing a curriculum, the teacher must begin by thinking about the goals of the program. What will children know or be able to do when they finish the program? Will the focus of the program be on learning specific information or on learning how to find information? Will the focus be on academic learning or broader goals of development and growth as a whole child? If we assume that the program sets broad goals for development in all areas—physical, social, emotional, and intellectual—that will be the framework for the curriculum.

Next, the teacher should analyze the options for achieving the goals. For the broad goals described, the options would include taking field trips, having classroom visitors, conducting demonstrations and experiments, and participating in activities such as classifying, problem solving, reading aloud, doing hands-on projects, and others. Over the course of a year, each of these options might be selected several times.

For example, suppose the children are learning about the life cycles of plants. A seed specialist might be invited to the class to share information about seeds with the children, or the children might take a field trip to a nursery or arboretum and classify seeds and plants in a variety of ways. The children might also plant seeds and care for the seedlings, or they might chart the growth of their plants and check the parts of their plants against

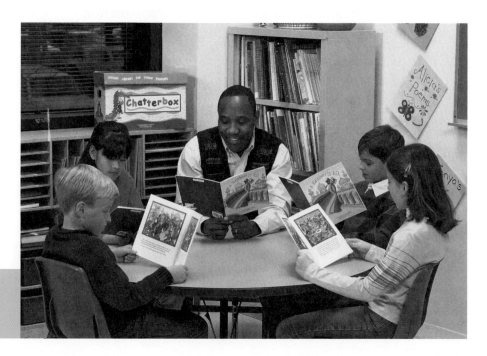

Small-group instruction is an important component of a well planned program.

a diagram provided on the computer. The outcomes of the study of plants would be intellectual development in learning facts about plants and seeds; physical development in planting and recording plant growth; social development in learning how to behave on a field trip or how to interact with a visitor; and emotional development in learning how to inhibit impulsive responses or develop control in a group setting.

For each part of a study of plants, the teacher would select objectives that would help achieve the purpose of the specific study and be related to the overall program goals. Objectives should not be too broad or vague (e.g., "The children will learn to love reading") nor should they be so narrow that they limit the possibilities for children's success (e.g., "Every child will learn to count to ten").

Suppose that our objective is as follows: "Children will develop increased skill in classification and in communicating their own criteria for classification categories." Assume that various classroom materials are usually available to the children for classification, such as buttons, keys, seashells, and so on, but for this experience, children also will be provided with collections of seeds that can be classified in a variety of ways. The children might also classify leaves; if they are responsive to the leaves, they might invite a botanist to explain how scientists classify leaves.

After choosing the content (knowledge of plants) and the objectives (increased skill in classification and communication), the teacher should select possible activities that will help children achieve the goals of the program. Knowledge of the content area is critical here, as the teacher must decide the sequence of activities and experiences that will be most beneficial to the children. Will going on a field trip to get an overall view of plants be more beneficial at the beginning of the plant study, when children are introduced to the subject; in the middle of the study, when they will have had some experiences with plants; or at the end, when children may need help consolidating their knowledge? Some experiences must precede others. For example, children could not be expected to communicate their criteria for classifying leaves without having had some experience in actually classifying leaves.

In short, when designing the curriculum, the teacher is responsible for selecting the objectives and the content, determining how it is organized, selecting the learning activities, and then assessing the activities. The teacher must also consider the interests of the children when selecting curriculum experiences. If the teacher who selects plants as content finds, after a few days, that the children have absolutely no interest in plants, she should select another topic.

Suppose the children had expressed interest in the caterpillars they found on the playground. Caterpillars and other insects could be just as useful as plants in helping children understand and apply classification abilities. Children should also be encouraged to choose what they would like to do from the many learning activities available and to make some choices about what they would like to learn about any given topic.

Although the sequence of designing a curriculum has been presented as a linear process, in reality it is usually more recursive: Teachers plan

Parents and Planning

● Keep parents informed about the topics studied at school. Provide suggestions for activities they might do at home to enhance the projects being done at school. For example, if the children are studying how plants change, you might suggest that parents gather seeds and other materials from plants and make a collage of them or that they take a family walk, looking for changes in plants.

content and activities, adapt them for individual children, select other activities, evaluate, and plan again. All the steps are there, but the process is rarely completely linear.

Curriculum Organization

When designing a curriculum, teachers have several options for choosing how to organize learning experiences. The most common approaches for young children are a facts approach and a skills approach. With a *facts approach,* experiences are arranged so that children learn a given set of factual information, such as the days of the week or the names of colors. With a *skills approach,* experiences are selected and arranged so that children learn to cut on a line, to share, or to find information in a selection of reference books.

In elementary schools, the most common organization has been the *subject-matter approach,* whereby children learn reading or math or social studies. Another approach is *thematic organization,* in which skills, facts, and subject-matter knowledge are integrated around a unifying theme, such as community.

> Do not train children to learning by force and harshness, but direct them to it by what amuses their minds, so that you may be better able to discover with accuracy the peculiar bent of the genius of each.
>
> —*Plato*

www.ncrel/org/sdrs/areas/ issues/earlycld/ea7lk.htm

A discussion of developmentally appropriate curriculum and how it can be implemented

www.tr.wou.edu/train/cdcDAP. htm

An explanation of developmentally appropriate curriculum and what it means in the classroom

NAEYC CRITERIA
3.46, 3.70

Developmentally Appropriate Curriculum

In 1987 the National Association for the Education of Young Children (NAEYC) issued a statement defining developmentally appropriate practice (DAP) in *Developmentally Appropriate Practice in Early Childhood Programs Serving Children from Birth through Age 8* (Bredekamp 1987). In order to provide examples of what developmentally appropriate practice should look like in the early childhood classroom, two more volumes were published: *Reaching Potentials: Appropriate Curriculum and Assessment for Young Children,* volume 1 (Bredekamp and Rosegrant 1992), and *Reaching Potentials: Transforming Early Childhood Curriculum and Assessment,* volume 2 (Bredekamp and Rosegrant 1995). Furthermore, the original statement on developmentally appropriate practice has been revised and issued in *Developmentally Appropriate Practice in Early Childhood Programs,* revised edition (Bredekamp and Copple 1997). All of these titles are mentioned here so that you can appreciate the long struggle to define and explain frameworks for programs in early childhood education.

Remember that the NAEYC represents a broad spectrum of professionals in the field of early childhood education; therefore, you should consider the following statements of guidelines as distillations of the thinking of all these people, not simply statements of single points of view:

Guidelines for Developmentally Appropriate Practice

A. Developmentally appropriate curriculum provides for all areas of a child's development: physical, emotional, social, linguistic, aesthetic, and cognitive.

B. Curriculum includes a broad range of content across disciplines that is socially relevant, intellectually engaging, and personally meaningful to children.

An important part of planning is ensuring that the activities and objectives are developmentally appropriate.

C. Curriculum builds upon what children already know and are able to do (activating prior knowledge) to consolidate their learning and to foster their acquisition of new concepts and skills.

D. Effective curriculum plans frequently integrate across traditional subject-matter divisions to help children make meaningful connections and provide opportunities for rich conceptual development; focusing on one subject is also a valid strategy at times.

E. Curriculum promotes the development of knowledge and understanding, processes and skills, as well as the dispositions to use and apply skills and to go on learning.

F. Curriculum content has intellectual integrity, reflecting the key concepts and tools of inquiry of recognized disciplines in ways that are accessible and achievable for young children, ages 3 through 8. . . . Children directly participate in study of the disciplines, for instance, by conducting scientific experiments, writing, performing, solving mathematical problems, collecting and analyzing data, collecting oral history, and performing other roles of experts in the disciplines.

G. Curriculum provides opportunities to support children's home culture and language while also developing all children's abilities to participate in the shared culture of the program and the community.

H. Curriculum goals are realistic and attainable for most children in the designated age range for which they are designed.

I. When used, technology is physically and philosophically integrated in the classroom curriculum and teaching. (Bredekamp and Copple 1997, pp. 20–21)

Support for an active, center-based curriculum comes from many sources. Among those who have looked at such a curriculum recently are Bottini and Grossman (2005), who found that children in center-based learning did not learn less academically and in fact benefited from the active curriculum in many ways, including engagement, independence in learning, and the integration of the arts. Geist and Baum (2005) found that teachers have some "Yeah, buts," or concerns that keep them from embracing a more active curriculum even when they agree that it will be better for the children. Some of these concerns are as follow:

- The teacher in the next grade will not teach in a developmentally appropriate manner.
- They are required to use a prepared curriculum.
- They have to get through an entire textbook.
- They think parents will not believe that they are really teaching.
- They will not be sure that children are learning.
- It is a lot of work.

All of these concerns can be answered by thinking about what is best for the child as a learner, communicating effectively with parents, conducting ongoing assessment to guide instruction, helping children achieve the required benchmarks through appropriate instruction, and becoming more efficient with time by rethinking what the teacher has to do. DeVault (2003) suggests that teachers can hold on to the practices that are best for young children if they have support from their administrators and a strong knowledge base about how children learn.

Although at times, a content-area study might be appropriate, the DAP guidelines support an integrated, thematic approach to curriculum. As explained in the next section, this approach is believed to be the most productive in helping teachers design a developmentally appropriate curriculum.

> If I trust the capacity of the human individual for developing his own potentiality, I can provide him with many opportunities and permit him to choose his own direction in his learning.
>
> —*Carl Rogers*

www.nwrel/org/scpd/sirs/8/c016.htm

A site for school improvement research and a discussion of integrated curriculum

www.geocities.com/Athens/Olympus/7123/integrate.html#what

An example of an integrated unit with links to brief explanations about how to create an integrated theme and plan for integration

PRAXIS

Be able to explain the value of an integrated curriculum

NAEYC CRITERIA

3.55

Rationale for an Integrated Curriculum

The idea of integrating the curriculum is not a new one. At the turn of the century, John Dewey (1859–1952) (1902) advocated the organization of curriculum around projects that would interest and involve children. The most common approach to curriculum organization in schools in the United States, however, continues to be subject-matter organization, in which learning is segmented into math and science and language arts (Jacobs 1989).

You probably remember that in elementary school, you had reading first thing in the morning, math right before lunch, and science in the afternoon. Yet when children learn outside school, they learn in wholes. For example, a child visiting tide pools can learn about many things at once: language arts (learning vocabulary for the animals and plants of the tide pools); physical skills (staying on top of the slippery rocks); classification (noticing which animals are related); the environment (noticing pollution or litter); family stories (hearing parents tell about when they visited these tide pools as children); and so on. A child's learning experiences outside school are not divisible into subject-matter areas.

An **integrated curriculum** can help a child make sense of the world more easily. If a child is learning the names of the letters of the alphabet, that knowledge must be placed in a context that makes sense to him. When the child learns the names of the letters by hearing the teacher read alphabet books and by exploring the forms of the letters in writing, he knows that the names of the letters communicate information about the printed form of language. He recognizes that this information is personally useful, not something learned to please an adult but that has no other utility for him.

An integrated curriculum provides opportunities for the following:

1. In-depth exploration of a topic and learning that is more than just superficial coverage
2. More choices and therefore more motivation to learn and greater satisfaction with the results
3. More active learning
4. An opportunity for the teacher to learn along with the children and model lifelong learning
5. A more effective use of student and teacher time

> A method may help or hinder, facilitate or complicate, but not create learning. Obtaining knowledge is a result of the learner's own activity.
> —*Emilia Ferreiro and Ana Teberosky*

Organizing learning experiences around a **theme** can be productive, but if thematic teaching is to be successful, the theme must be carefully selected, activities carefully planned, and evaluation of the theme and of individual children's progress carefully monitored.

Selecting a Theme

The selection of a worthwhile theme is critically important if thematic instruction is to be successful. There are several considerations in selecting a theme:

- The topic must be worthy of study. It should be an important topic that would be studied even if you were not doing thematic instruction. A theme will take several weeks to complete, and the topic should be worth the time.
- Meeting **state standards** and goals is facilitated with a good theme.
- The topic should be of interest and relevant to the learners. Children must find the learning applicable to their world outside of school. For example, children who have no experience with deserts will not be able to apply what they are learning to their lives outside of school. If children live in the desert, they will see the plants and the animals of the desert, and what they learn about the desert will be useful every day.
- There must be opportunities for the application of skills the children are learning. If the children are learning to cut with scissors, to take research notes, to put words in alphabetical order, or to write a poem, the theme study should allow them to use the skills they are learning.
- There must be adequate resources to support the topic of study with realia, people in the community who can be guest speakers or resource people, and places in the community for field trips that will add to the study.

Thematic instruction can be done poorly. If teachers choose a theme with no real content, if they apply a theme without considering the previous knowledge of the children, or if every child is required to complete the same activities, then thematic instruction will not be any better than a poorly conceived curriculum organized by subject matter. Teachers can be tempted to do cute themes, such as apples or teddy bears, but such topics rarely offer any real learning for children that will be useful to them in their lives. Some early childhood programs send out a list of their themes for each week before school begins each year. But thematic instruction cannot be done well if the themes are planned before the teacher even knows the children or their needs. Themes are often available on the Web or in teacher supply stores, but themes planned by someone who does not know your children and that do not involve children in the planning cannot achieve the goals of good thematic instruction.

One of the major reasons for selecting a thematic organization is to offer children the opportunity for in-depth rather than superficial study of various topics. Therefore, the theme selected must be one for which the activities are worthwhile. Thematic organization alone does not guarantee a well-planned, thoughtful curriculum. There are trivial approaches to thematic organization as well as to other types of curriculum organization.

For instance, a teacher could decide to focus on *mice* as a theme and provide meaningful activities in which children learned about nutrition, training, building mazes, genetics, and so on. Or the teacher could choose *mice* as a theme and focus on it simplistically: covering the container where the children place their work with paper to represent cheese, decorating the bookmarks children use to mark their places in the reader with mice, using pictures of mice to enliven math worksheets, and having children make paper mice in art. A theme cannot be implemented solely through classroom decorations.

Implementing the Theme

Once a theme has been selected, the teacher (and the children, if they are old enough) will brainstorm areas of interest related to that particular theme. Older children will be able to see more relationships than younger ones.

After a topic and related subtopics have been chosen, the next step is to select activities that will help children learn content and apply their skills in meaningful contexts. What can be learned on a field trip? What can resource people share with the children? What play experiences can be facilitated? Are there construction possibilities? What skills can be applied in this study? What curriculum goals can be met through the study of this topic?

Let's assume that one of the teacher's curriculum goals is to help children become familiar with a variety of reading materials: narrative, poetry, expository writing, and so on. In studying *corn*, for instance, the children can read (or listen to the teacher read) information books about corn and perhaps stories and poems about the importance of corn to some American Indian groups. Another goal might be for children to participate in the writing process on a daily basis. They can write records of the growth of corn plants, describe in writing what happens to corn when it is popped, or create their own informational books about corn. Yet another goal might be for children to increase their ability to recall and retell significant details. Participating in activities such as popping corn can be the basis for recalling and retelling meaningful details.

Once a theme has been tentatively selected, the teacher and children can create webs of things the children know and might want to know (see Figure 4.1). Jones and Nimmo (1994) describe the value of webbing:

FIGURE 4.1

Web for the Theme *Spaces*

Inside Spaces

What kinds of spaces are inside?
    Buildings?
    Blocks?
Does everything have a space inside?
    Rocks?
    Woods?

Outside Spaces

What kind of spaces are outside?
    Parks?
    Streets?
What grows outside?
    Trees?
    Grass?

Spaces

Little Spaces

What are the smallest spaces in the
    classroom?
How can you make little spaces?
What toys have little spaces?

Big Spaces

What are the largest spaces in the
    classroom?
How can you make big spaces?
What toys have big spaces?

It gives a staff of adults the chance to explore the possibilities of any material or idea in order to make decisions about use: Is it worth doing? Is it likely to generate developmentally appropriate activities? What are the ways we might want to enrich the activity by being prepared with other materials or questions? How long might children's interest continue?

A web is a tentative plan. It doesn't tell you exactly what will happen or in what order. That depends in large part on the children's response. So, first you plan and then you start trying your ideas, *paying attention to what happens,* evaluating, and moving on with further activities. (p. 11)

Once curriculum goals have been reviewed, the teacher and children can determine activities that will be possible in this study. Not every child will participate in every activity; choices will be available to the children. The teacher must think about the objectives of each activity and the relationship of the objectives to the curriculum goals. If an activity cannot contribute to the curriculum goals, it should be eliminated as a choice.

Classroom learning areas should be used to enhance particular themes. For example, in a study of *plants,* materials such as flowers (not poisonous), leaves, and seedpods could be placed in the art center; books and computer software about plants could be available in the library; puzzles with plant content could be available in the manipulatives area; and accessories could be added to the blocks area so that the children could create a farm. Enhancing learning areas in these ways does not mean that children will be assigned to do certain tasks in the areas; rather, materials will be available to help children complete their investigations or follow up on their interests.

Many teachers try to follow the children's lead in planning curriculum. If the children are interested in a certain topic, then the teacher will

> **NAEYC CRITERIA**
> 2.5, 2.6

> **PRAXIS**
> Be able to develop plans for appropriate topics in early childhood education

help them explore that topic and develop their interests until their questions and activities lead them to another topic. Several authors have described this emerging curriculum approach and their own ways of implementing it (Byrum and Pierce 1993; Edwards, Gandini, and Forman 1993; Jones and Nimmo 1994). These teachers believe that the best curriculum is one in which the children are fully engaged and their interests are fully explored. The challenge, however, is to build a curriculum that not only follows the children's interests but also meets the goals of the program.

The most famous of the emerging curriculum schools are those of Reggio Emilia, which are municipal schools in a city in northern Italy. As noted in Chapter 2, much has been written about these schools and the project approach that they use (Bredekamp 1993; Edwards et al. 1993; Gandini 1993; Kennedy 1996; Malaguzzi 1993; McCarthy 1995). These projects grow out of simple experiences, such as the children's visit to a poppy field. The children examined the flowers, drew them, painted them, sculpted them, discussed them, created murals of them, and otherwise continued to focus their activities on the poppies for a long period of time. The teachers continued to guide the children by asking questions, offering new materials, and helping the children refine and rethink their work.

The quality of the work that the Reggio Emilia children have produced is what has led to so much investigation of the processes employed in these schools. The teachers who implement this sort of emerging curriculum have support from colleagues and administrators. In Reggio Emilia, they also have support from parents, who often attend teacher planning meetings and feel comfortable making suggestions. (These parents also know how hard the teachers work!)

A child-centered curriculum that produces outstanding products while focusing on the process of learning and doing is the ideal in early childhood education. A teacher, especially a new teacher, who wants to implement a child-centered curriculum should find a colleague who also wants to implement such a program. That way, all of the questions, problems, failures, and successes can be shared with someone else struggling to achieve the same goals. A solitary teacher without support will find implementing such a program nearly impossible.

Evaluating the Theme

NAEYC CRITERIA
2.11, 2.12

Teachers will want to evaluate their thematic instruction in a variety of ways. First, teachers must always be accountable for the progress of individual children. Assessment strategies for monitoring the progress of children will be discussed in detail in Chapter 7, but you will want to keep records that help you know what curriculum goals have been met and what kinds of instruction have been provided.

One way to accomplish this is to keep a chart such as the one illustrated in Figure 4.2. Prepare a sheet for each child with the curriculum goals listed down the left side and columns for each topic of study on the right. As the child meets various goals, you record the progress. You need a sheet for each child because not all children will choose the same activities during the theme. (Assessment possibilities are described in Chapter 7.) In evaluating the theme, the teacher would observe the children's interest and record the contributions of the theme to overall goals.

FIGURE 4.2

Evaluation Checklist

Child's Name _____ Jamie _____

	Plants	Insects	
Reads a variety of materials: reference materials, narrative stories, poetry	10/6	11/15 11/20	
Participates in writing process: personal writing, letter writing, narratives, expository writing	10/8	11/10 12/1	
Recognizes adaptation as a factor in all plant and animal life (habitat, camouflage, food chain)	10/12 10/15 10/16	11/20 11/23 11/24	
Uses computation to solve problems			
Uses the scientific process to solve problems			

Although a teacher may choose to repeat a theme another year, rarely can a theme be repeated in the same form. The interests and experiences of different groups of children vary considerably, and some themes that work well with one group are not at all interesting to other groups. Even if topics are repeated, the activities chosen by the children are likely to vary so much that one year's implementation of the theme will not be the same as that of a previous year. When a teacher simply applies a theme to the children, it becomes mechanical, and the classroom routine fails to reflect children's interests and experiences. Theme studies require considerable investments of time and energy by the teacher, but the result—meaningful experiences for the children through which they gain not only knowledge and skills but also the disposition to learn—is well worth the effort.

As you read the chapters in this book about language, literature, literacy, math, science, social studies, the arts, and health and physical education, remember that although these content areas are presented in discrete chapters, the underlying assumption is that knowledge of each subject-matter area will help you integrate curriculum. You do need to understand the goals and objectives in each area in order to plan appropriately, but you should use this knowledge to plan meaningful and conceptually important themes. Throughout the content-area chapters of this book (Chapters 9 through 15), the theme of *spaces* will be the focus. So even though the discussion in each chapter will be about a discrete subject (math, science, music, and so on), the emphasis will be on an integrated curriculum.

However the curriculum is organized, teachers are responsible for developing the plans for learning experiences in their classrooms. The following section provides some advice on creating those plans.

Learning Plans

A **learning plan** differs from a lesson plan in that often a lesson plan outlines only one lesson. In early childhood programs, however, learning experiences are not usually confined to single lessons. As Elkind (1982) reminds us, "Clearly children learn in many different ways and what mode of learning is employed depends very much upon what is to be learned" (p. 7). Learning plans involve long-term planning, unit or theme planning, and short-term goals. Each day's activities should contribute to the unit or theme goals, and each unit or theme should contribute to the overall goals of the program.

As the teacher of the program, you may not have much control over the program goals. They are often established by the administration of the center or school—hopefully, with the collaboration of the teachers. These are the kinds of goals that centers advertise on their consumer brochures and that are printed in the curriculum guides of school districts. However, goal statements do not define how goals are to be achieved. The "how" is up to the teacher and should reflect knowledge of the children's development, the children's abilities and interests, and the teacher's own interests.

A daily learning plan may indicate the materials to be placed in the learning areas, include notes about guiding specific children's learning, and suggest plans for evaluation of activities. If one of the daily goals is learning to use the concept *line* in talking about art, the learning plan would note the pieces of art to be displayed, specify that strings and strips of paper should be made available in the art area, and call for an emphasis on line in movement experiences. Teachers would work with individual children as they participated in art or movement to emphasize the concept of *line* and would talk with those who were looking at the art examples about how the artists had used lines. This plan would fit into the larger theme of *lines and space* being explored in a variety of areas and support the overall goals of increasing children's ability to communicate effectively and to explore a variety of materials.

DEVELOPMENTALLY APPROPRIATE PRACTICE

Reflect on plans for learning experiences for children. Review the framework for a developmentally appropriate curriculum as you think about these questions:

- Can a teacher of young children purchase a curriculum that is developmentally appropriate? Why?

- Given what you know about developmentally appropriate practice, can a teacher plan the topics of study for the year before meeting the children? Why?

- Can a teacher incorporate the topics/goals of the school curriculum guide into a developmentally appropriate curriculum? Why?

- If a first-grade teacher wanted to study transportation with her students, would that be developmentally appropriate? If your answer is no, under what conditions would the topic be appropriate? If yes, explain why the topic is appropriate.

Teaching Classification Skills to Three- and Four-year-Olds

Program Goals: Increased skill in classification

Theme: Spaces

Topic: Inside and outside spaces

Objectives: Children will be able to classify spaces as being inside spaces or outside spaces. For children who have a clear concept of *inside and outside,* introduce the idea of spaces that can be either inside or outside.

Activity Time:

- *Art:* Talk to children about the spaces in their paintings or drawings that are open spaces and filled spaces. Provide plastic blocks for printing and wood scraps for construction.
- *Fine motor:* Make available small blocks (wooden blocks, Duplos, and so on), Popsicle sticks, twigs from outside, paper strips, and other materials that will require fine motor coordination. Talk about the spaces that children create.
- *Blocks:* Make hollow blocks available for building spaces that children can get inside. Put out small models of animals that children can build spaces for with unit blocks or other small blocks.
- *Library:* Display books such as *The Indoor Noisy Book* (Brown, 1994) and *The Noisy Book* (Brown, 1993).
- *Dramatic play:* Make available costumes and tools for inside spaces (cooks, office workers, and so on) and outside spaces (gardeners, construction workers, and so on).
- *Movement:* Create spaces to step over, jump over, step around, walk through, and crawl through inside and outside.
- *Read Aloud:* *A House Is a House for Me* (Hoberman 1978); *Right Outside My Window* (Hoberman 2002).
- *Small Groups:* Invite each group to draw objects on a large piece of paper labeled "Inside" on one side and "Outside" on the other. Ask the children to then share what they drew and why they chose these objects.
- *Evaluation:* Observe children as they participate in the various activities, noting who has a clear concept of *inside and outside.*

Three daily learning plans for preschool and primary children are presented in the boxes on pages 117, 118, and 119. Take some time to review them, and as you do, keep this in mind: Learning plans should always be as complete as possible but should never be so rigid that **incidental learning** cannot be included in the day's schedule. For instance, if a child brings a pet rabbit to school, obviously time must be allotted to observing and discussing the rabbit. If the children are really interested in the rabbit, then the teacher might make some plans for additional experiences with rabbits in a few weeks.

The point is to take advantage of what the children want to know now as you keep the overall goals in mind. When Alice came to the Cheshire Cat and asked which road to take, he told her that it did not make any difference, because she did not know where she was going. Teachers of young children need to know where they are going—and they need to plan which road to take but be prepared to take another one if it appears to be better for the children.

Although learning plans are more appropriate than isolated lesson plans in terms of planning for instruction, lesson plans may sometimes be designed to teach specific elements of a broader learning plan. Some plans will provide for whole-class activities, others for small groups, and still others for individual children. For example, in the learning plan that asks students to describe their own secret or favorite place (see page 118), the teacher will read aloud one selection to the whole group, ask the children to work in pairs to find the descriptive words in the next selection, and ask them to work individually to find descriptive words in their own writing.

Teaching Measurement and Descriptive Writing Skills to Six- and Seven-year-Olds

Program Goals: Increased skill in measurement and using descriptive words in writing

Theme: Spaces

Topic: Our own favorite space

Objectives: Children will be able to do these things:
- Measure their favorite space (length, width, and height). They will choose the unit of measure and explain why they selected it.
- Describe their own favorite or secret place.

Group Time/Read Aloud: Read one each day: *Your Own Best Secret Place* (Baylor 1979); *Secret Place* (Bunting 1996); *A Place for Ben* (Titherington 1999); *Evan's Corner* (Hill 1993). After all the books have been read, discuss how the authors described their favorite places. List the elements that made the places interesting (descriptive words, personal narrative, unique elements of their space, common need of all to have a space of our own, and so on). Encourage children to write about their own secret or favorite places.

Activity Time:

- *Art:* Provide paper for children to draw their favorite spaces. Also display paintings, drawings, and sculptures that help children think about using space in representation.
- *Library:* Ask children to map the library space and then work in groups to suggest better arrangements for the area. Make sure they provide justifications for their suggestions.

- *Social Studies:* Choose a space such as the schoolground or park, and determine who it belongs to, such as the city or county. Also discuss spaces that belong to states, countries, and continents. Make a list of spaces that cannot belong to anyone, such as oceans, the underground, and the atmosphere. Who is responsible for these spaces?
- *Math and Science:* Experiment with the displacement of water to demonstrate that a given space can be occupied by only one thing at a time. Is there a relationship between the size of an object placed into water and the amount of water it displaces? Fill a container to a given depth, and estimate how many objects of a given size and shape it will take to raise the water level to the capacity of the container. Try different beginning depths and sets of different objects. Record the findings.
- *Movement:* Experiment with movements that take up large spaces and movements that take up small spaces. Experiment with placing blocks to create passages, and determine what is the smallest space one can pass through without touching a block.
- *Language Arts:* Create a list of what children would like to keep in their own favorite spaces. Then determine what the requirements are for the classroom spaces designated for the computer center, listening center, and so on. Have children write descriptions or poems about their favorite spaces or imaginary spaces they would like to have.

Note: This theme of *spaces* will continue for several weeks, as the children explore spaces in their lives.

A learning plan should include a balance of whole-group activities, small-group activities, and individual activities.

Mandated Lessons and Goals

If the school district has **mandated goals** and corresponding materials to be used, the professional teacher must decide if the materials are appropriate for his particular group of children and, if not, how the children could achieve the mandated goals in a more appropriate manner. For example, in one school district, kindergarten teachers were told that all kindergarten children should master eighteen basic sight words from the adopted basal reader by the end of kindergarten. A professional teacher would be accountable for teaching the sight-word vocabulary to all the children for whom this goal was reasonable, but given his knowledge of emerging literacy, he would choose a meaningful context for helping children learn to recognize the sight words. These basic words (*boy, girl, I, ran, look,* and so forth) are

Teaching How to Recognize and Use Descriptive Words to Six- and Seven-year-Olds

Objective: Children will be able to recognize descriptive words in the writing of others and use descriptive words in their own writing.

Materials:

Books: *Your Own Best Secret Place* (Baylor 1979) and *Secret Place* (Bunting 1996)
Markers and whiteboard or chartpaper

Procedure:

1. Read *Your Own Best Secret Place* aloud.
2. Select several pages and read them aloud; then discuss the descriptive words used on each page. Make a list of these descriptive words on the whiteboard or chartpaper.
3. Reread pages of *Secret Place*. (This book was read aloud on the previous day.) With their partners, ask the children to make lists of the descriptive words they hear. Compare the lists.
4. Ask each child to select one piece of her own writing where she uses descriptive words and one that could be improved by using more descriptive words.

Accommodations: Provide children with individual help in finding descriptive words in their own writing samples. Demonstrate the power of descriptive words with a simple sentence, such as *The hen ate the corn*. Ask the children to visualize the meaning of this sentence. Then add descriptive words and ask them to visualize the meaning again.

Evaluation: Note the use of descriptive words in children's writing. Compare this writing to previous writing samples.

---

common in children's writing and in the stories and poems that a teacher uses in the classroom. The teacher would use the words as they occurred naturally and help children recognize them in these contexts. Keeping good records of the children's work helps the teacher discuss the learning that is taking place and the reasons that the choice of instructional materials is important to the children's success.

The professional teacher of young children depends on assessment of program goals and the growth of individual children to make decisions about what instruction is most appropriate for them. Materials and programs must be carefully evaluated in terms of children's needs before they are used for instruction. Most goals can be reached by many routes; the teacher must choose the one that suits the children best.

In the following A Teacher Speaks, Beth Peter discusses her planning as daily but within a framework of a clear picture of where students are going and how to get them there. Do you think standards for learning can help you by providing the framework for where children are going?

Multicultural Education and Antibias Curriculum

In addition to organizing the curriculum and selecting learning experiences, teachers of young children must also plan for a curriculum that is multicultural and antibias in nature. **Multicultural education** and **antibias curriculum** are terms used to describe educational programs that attempt to teach children respect for all people and their cultures. Multicultural education involves learning about one's own and other cultures in an integrated way. A multicultural or antibias curriculum is not achieved by superficial lessons; it is achieved by sensitive and knowledgeable teachers who help children learn in a context in which all cultures are appreciated. These issues are not confined to one topic or one subject matter but are important in all curriculum decisions.

> **NAEYC CRITERIA**
> 3.24

A Teacher SPEAKS: Planning for Success

Beth Peter

Neill Elementary School

Burnsville, Minnesota

My classroom is a multiage classroom that houses first- through fourth-graders who are constantly in different places on the continuum of learning development. However, meeting a wide variety of needs and matching different stages of development in the classroom is a challenge that is not unique to multiage. I've taught in single-grade classrooms where the needs of the students are also quite diverse.

I'm certain there are many "teachable moments" that happen throughout my day, but the majority of my instruction is carefully planned ahead of time. I believe that planned instruction is a vital element in taking a student to his next learning step. This planning takes a variety of forms and a variety of time frames, but it all has a common thread of building upon a student's strengths in the area in which I want new learning to occur.

I plan on a daily basis. Each day, for as many students as I am able, I examine what he has done today to enable me to plan his instruction for tomorrow. Let me use writing as an example. My students write daily. As I look through their writing for that day, I record in a notebook what I see them doing successfully in regard to the content of their writing, the surface features like their spelling and structure, and their handwriting skill. I carefully examine their writing for evidence that they are attempting to gain control over these same areas. Common strengths, attempts, and needs can be seen, from which I plan writing conference groups, editing conferences, modeled writing lessons, spelling lessons, handwriting groups, and reading material that might take them to the next learning step. I also need to have a strong understanding of the writing process, the broad stages of writing development, the reading process, and the stages that readers go through. My students become the guides of what will be next in my instruction.

I also use observation of their reading and writing behaviors to ask myself if there is a part of the process that needs instruction. I cannot wait until the teacher's manual tells me that it is time to teach contractions, because I think teaching at the point of a student's need is where true learning occurs. You might think that it would be an impossible task time-wise to meet individual learning needs, but I find that students naturally fall into groups with common needs. These groups change as fluidly as the needs of the learners change. Obviously, I do not have the time to meet with each of my students individually on a daily basis, but through small-group *and* individual instruction, I am able to see each of my students daily.

I use "running records" and the information I receive from their analysis to guide my reading instruction and to form groups for guided and shared reading experiences. The information from a running record allows me to meet the learner with a text that is at her instructional level and will allow her to build on what she is currently doing as a reader. Again, my students fall into groups that have common needs.

Even though the majority of my planning for instruction takes place on a daily basis, I still need to have a strong picture of where I want my students to go and how I am going to get them there. This planning is more global and is the umbrella for what I plan on a daily basis. I keep in mind the skills that a lifelong learner needs as I plan and write down what I expect to see happening with a student as a result of my instruction.

The National Council for Accreditation of Teacher Education (1987) defines *multicultural education* as a perspective that recognizes "(1) the social, political, and economic realities that individuals experience in culturally diverse and complex human encounters and (2) the importance of culture, race, sex and gender, ethnicity, religion, socioeconomic status, and exceptionalities in the education process" (p. 57).

The effort to eliminate racism and prejudice by helping students and teachers become more aware and accepting of the cultural diversity in the United States is relatively new. Recent U.S. demographic information indicates that cultural and ethnic minority populations are growing rapidly and will likely continue to do so. Consequently, multicultural education is also gaining importance.

Whaley and Swadner (1990) argue for beginning multicultural education in infant and toddler programs. Very young children learn to discriminate differences and classify things and feelings; they can also learn to be more empathetic than was once believed. Programs that support multicultural education are important as very young children begin to learn about people other than family. Teachers of preschoolers can make sure that materials (books, music, dolls, and so on) represent a variety of cultures, use pictures of different cultural and ethnic groups involved in a variety of experiences, and take every opportunity to help children learn to care for one another.

Education that is multicultural will be reflected in the teacher's choices of books and literature, in the signs posted in the classroom, in holiday celebrations, and in planned activities—in short, throughout the curriculum. For example, children can learn about different languages and different systems of writing through language arts activities. They can learn about foods contributed to their diets by North and South American cultures (corn), Eastern cultures (rice), and European cultures (wheat).

Children's families also are a valuable source of information and support for a multicultural or antibias curriculum. Teachers can bring families into the classroom to share traditions, expectations, and stories (McCracken 1993; Neuman and Roskos 1994; Swick et al. 1995; Swick, Boutte, and Van Scoy 1995/1996; Wardle 1996). To develop strong relationships with families, teachers need to consider who speaks for the family and how they make decisions on a case-by-case basis. Even though it may be typical of some cultures that the father makes the decisions, there are as many differences within groups as between groups, so knowing each family personally is critical (Bruns and Corso 2001).

Another factor in teaching successfully in an environment that supports a multicultural and antibias curriculum is the teacher attitudes toward the children and the cultures represented in the classroom. If teachers believe that children are lacking in certain attributes that lead to success in school, they will plan the curriculum and treat the children in certain ways. This deficit view has colored the thinking of many teachers over the years. On the other hand, if teachers view children and their families as different but not lacking in skill or knowledge, they will plan and organize experiences that honor and appreciate each child and the culture of each family (Pattnaik 2003; Wardle 2001).

Goals of Multicultural Education

As summarized by Banks and Banks (1997), "Multicultural education incorporates the idea that all students—regardless of their gender and social class and their ethnic, racial, or cultural characteristics—should have an equal opportunity to learn in school" (p. 3). Ramsey (1998) identifies these specific goals of multicultural education:

1. Children will develop a strong identity of themselves, as members of a group, and as living beings on this planet.
2. Children will develop a sense of solidarity with all people and the natural world.

www.nameorg/org

The home page for the National Association for Multicultural Education, with links to many resources

www.ncrel/org/sdrs/areas/ issues/educatrs/presrvce/ pe3lk1.htm

A discussion of the integrated curriculum, a rationale for integration, and other issues in using an integrated curriculum

3. Children will become critical thinkers.
4. Children will be confident and persistent problem solvers.
5. Children will gain the academic skills that will give them access to the knowledge of our society and power to make a difference. (pp. 6–7)

Teachers should plan all activities with an eye for including a multicultural dimension. Figure 4.3 is a checklist designed to help teachers analyze their classrooms and materials.

Multicultural Program Characteristics

Derman-Sparks (1999) states that a program with the following characteristics is well on the way to providing quality multicultural/antibias education:

- Staff actively incorporate their children's daily life experiences into daily curriculum.
- Staff tailor curriculum and teacher-child interactions to meet the cultural, as well as individual, developmental needs of their children, actively using parents' or family caregivers' knowledge about their home cultures.
- Daily classroom life and curriculum incorporate diversity and justice issues related to gender, disabilities, socioeconomic status, and the many ways of being a family, as well as issues related to ethnicity and culture.
- Staff use a variety of strategies to involve parents actively and regularly in the program, including provisions for languages other than English.
- Staff intentionally encourage children's development of critical thinking and tools for resisting prejudice and unfair behaviors directed at themselves or others. Parents and other neighborhood people share what they do to improve the quality of life and social justice in their communities.
- Staff reflect the cultural and language diversity of the children and families they serve and the communities of their centers and schools.
- Staff engage in intentional and regular reflections about their practice and the influences of their cultural backgrounds, and they openly help each other uncover and change biases and hurtful (even if unintentional) behaviors. (p. 43)

The ability of children now in early childhood classes to cope with life in this century may well depend on the quality of their educational experiences. Quality education must include multicultural experiences.

Just as multicultural and antibias principles should underlie planning for all children's experiences, so, too, should computers and their use in the early childhood classroom be integrated all through the day.

Computers in Early Childhood Programs

In today's world, computers are a part of almost every early childhood program. Having one or many computers in the classroom may mean that the children are frequent and active users of computers, that children who are "good" get to use computers as a reward, that children use computers to reinforce skills lessons, or that the computers are gathering dust because none of the adults feels comfortable using them. It is obvious that computers are a vital part of modern life. So the question is: How can they be used in early childhood programs to benefit children?

http://ecrp.uiuc.edu/v6n1/gillespie.html

A descriptive study of Head Start and kindergarten students in a discovery-based, logo-rich classroom

www.naeyc.org/ece/2001/01/asp

An issues paper defending the use of computers in early childhood education

FIGURE 4.3

Multicultural Checklist

Use this checklist to help you focus on individual aspects of your classroom environment, take a closer look at your curriculum, and highlight areas that need improvement. Try to answer each question as it pertains to your classroom.

Language arts	1. Does your classroom have a wide variety of age-appropriate and culturally diverse books and language arts materials? Look for examples.	☐	☐
	2. Are the cultures in your class and community represented in your books and materials?	☐	☐
	3. Are there any books that speak of people of diverse cultures in stereotypic or derogatory terms? What are they? Should they be removed, or is there a way to use them with children to broaden their concepts and encourage them to share their experiences?	☐	☐
	4. Are the pictures of people on the walls representative of a multicultural community?	☐	☐
Social studies	5. Does the curriculum help children increase their understanding and acceptance of attitudes, values, and lifestyles that are unfamiliar to them? If so, how? If not, what can you do to change it?	☐	☐
	6. Are materials and games racially or sex-role stereotypic? If so, how can you change your collection to give strong, positive images?	☐	☐
Blocks	7. Are the accessories in the blocks area representative of various cultural groups and family configurations? If not, how can you change them?	☐	☐
	8. Are the people blocks accessories stereotypic in terms of sex roles? If so, how can you change them?	☐	☐
Dramatic play	9. Is there a wide variety of clothes (everyday garments, not exotic costumes) from various cultural groups?	☐	☐
	10. Are the pictures on the walls and the props representative of a diversity of cultures?	☐	☐
	11. Are the dolls representative of the major racial groups in our country, not just in colors but in features?	☐	☐
Music and games	12. Do music experiences reinforce children's affirmation of cultural diversity? How?	☐	☐
	13. Do you use fingerplays, games, and songs from various cultural groups?	☐	☐
Cooking	14. Do cooking experiences encourage children to experiment with foods they aren't familiar with?	☐	☐
	15. Are these experiences designed to give children a general notion of the connections between cultural heritage and the process of preparing, cooking, and eating food? If so, how?	☐	☐

Source: Adapted from Frances E. Kendall, Ph.D., "Creating a Multicultural Environment," *Pre-K Today* (November/December 1988): 34–39. Reprinted with permission of the author.

NAEYC CRITERIA
2.13

Teaching and Learning with Computers

The National Association for the Education of Young Children (NAEYC) has recognized that computers are common features in early childhood classrooms and thus issued a position statement on technology and young children. The statement assumes that computers can be misused, as can any other learning tool. The tenets are as follow:

1. A professional judgment by the teacher is required to determine if a specific use of technology is age appropriate, individually appropriate, and culturally appropriate. . . .
2. Used appropriately, technology can enhance children's cognitive and social abilities. . . .
3. Appropriate technology is integrated into the regular learning environment and used as one of many options to support children's learning. . . .
4. Early childhood educators should promote equitable access to technology for all children and their families. Children with special needs should have increased access when this is helpful. . . .
5. The power of technology to influence children's learning and development requires that attention be paid to eliminating stereotyping of any group and to eliminating exposure to violence, especially as a problem-solving strategy. . . .
6. Teachers, in collaboration with parents, should advocate for more appropriate technology applications for all children. . . .
7. The appropriate use of technology has many implications for early childhood professional development. (NAEYC 1996)

Computers are not necessary for very young children (Haugland 1999), and some educators believe that computers are harmful to young children's learning (Healy 2003). Computer use needs to be carefully planned and observed. Computers should not be used as electronic workbooks, and they should not be used as a reward for good behavior. Computer use should be child initiated, not teacher directed, and children should be allowed to leave the computer when they choose. Davidson and Wright (1994) believe that computer use is likely to be more appropriate for children if the following assumptions and attitudes are followed:

1. Computer use is a social activity.
2. Computer use is a child-initiated and child-directed activity.
3. Computer software allows children to explore, experiment, and problem solve.
4. Computers offer new learning opportunities when unexpected things happen.
5. Computers are one of many materials in a developmentally appropriate classroom. (p. 78)

Children generally prefer using computers with other children. Both language development and social skills can be improved when children explain to each other what to do to achieve certain results and negotiate turns. According to Kent and Rakestraw (1994), "Computers appear to be a

PRAXIS
Be able to explain how technology can enhance the learning experiences of young children

Children often prefer—and should be encouraged—to use computers in groups.

valuable tool for facilitating language use within the classroom. When used appropriately, they can provide a genuine, real world context for children's exploration" (p. 336).

Computers in early childhood classrooms should be one of many materials offered for children to explore and use as tools to accomplish their goals. Computers, especially those with voice synthesizers that read what has been keyed in, can help children make discoveries about written language. Computers are much more effective in classrooms where they can be integrated into the curriculum, rather than in a lab where instruction is not related to classroom activities.

The question of how many computers are enough must be answered by deciding how the computers will be used in the program and what children will actually do with them. Many teachers find that one computer is adequate and that they can schedule time for every student to use the computer weekly.

Computers can be used in ways that are inappropriate for young children. For example, research has shown (Clements, Nastasi, and Swaminathan 1993) that the use of drill-and-practice programs can lead to children's loss of creativity. The use of skills programs might increase ability in some areas, but the importance of obtaining such skills is not consistent with a more wholistic view of how children learn to read and write. A better use of computers in early childhood classrooms is to create stories and pictures, as opposed to practicing discrete skills. Teachers can help individual children meet their own learning goals through adapting their interactions with computers (Samaras 1996).

Selecting Software

Teachers need to carefully evaluate software before purchasing it for their classrooms. Clements and Sarama (2003) suggest that teachers select high-quality, research-based software that makes a unique contribution to children's learning.

Parents and Computers

● Share the list of software programs you have found to be appropriate for young children so that they can use them at home or at the library.

Several guides and newsletters are available for helping teachers as well as parents make good decisions about their purchases. Isenberg and Rosegrant (1995, p. 29) suggest that teachers should think carefully about software that is purchased for classroom use. They recommend that teachers keep the following features in mind as they evaluate any computer program:

- *Technical features* include how function keys are used, how learners can manipulate the program, and whether learners' work can be saved or printed.
- *Learning features* include the voice or visual supports provided, the rate at which items are presented, and the amount and types of feedback available.
- *Content features* include what children learn—information, processes, or skills—and the level of difficulty within each area.
- *Developmentally appropriate features* include whether the program is suitable for the given children's ages, how complex the activities are, and whether children can be playful with the program.

Teachers should use these evaluation criteria not only before ordering software but also after observing children actually using the programs.

Adaptations in technology for special-needs children might include modifying the standard keyboard or providing touch-sensitive screens or voice-input capabilities. Stickers on keyboards can be used to help children learn which keys to use for particular programs. And for children who have difficulty with the keyboard, solutions include providing a template that allows only certain keys to show or a keyguard that allows use of only one key at a time. All children should be allowed to participate in open-ended activities so that special-needs children can interact with their classmates in positive play situations at computers (Sheldon 1996).

Young Children Online

In addition to making decisions about computer use in general, teachers today must make decisions about children's use of the World Wide Web. Haugland (2000) recommends that teachers install one of several screening devices before children are allowed to use the Web—for instance, Kid Desk: Internet Safe, Net Nanny, or Cyber Patrol. She also recommends that for safety reasons, children should use pen names or the names of pets on the Web and never give out any information about their home addresses, parents' names, or phone numbers.

Burriss (2003) agrees with these cautions and also suggests that computers be placed with the monitors facing into the classroom so teachers can see what the children are seeing. The NAEYC (1998), in their *Child Health Alert* bulletins, offers the same precautions plus two additional suggestions: Children should be taught that (1) not everything on the Internet is necessarily true, and (2) they should report it immediately if they get a threatening or inappropriate message. Figure 4.4 is a checklist you can use

FIGURE 4.4

Teacher Technology Assessment

Basic Operation of the Computer and Related Components
- Do you know how to turn everything on and off?
- Can you make the computer do what you want it to do?
- Do you know how to troubleshoot solutions when a problem occurs?
- Can you use software shortcuts that save you time?

Choosing Appropriate Software for Young Children
- How does the software support children's age-appropriate developmental skills?
- In what ways does the software reflect your organization's curriculum goals and objectives?
- How does the software avoid gender, racial, and ethnic stereotypes?
- Will the software easily integrate with ongoing curriculum activities and materials?
- What characteristics does the software share with other quality early childhood materials?
- How does the software serve as a learning tool, rather than as an electronic worksheet?
- How does the software support English-language learners?

Using the Computer for Instruction with Young Children
- How does your current curriculum support learning with computers?
- What would you say if a parent or colleagues asked about controversial issues regarding technology and children, such as teaching toddlers about computers?
- How does the physical environment affect children's social, emotional, and cognitive development when they use computers: Does the arrangement and location of the computer center support peer learning and teaching? Can children easily collaborate with each other?
- Are you familiar with basic research related to young children's learning with computers?
- What strategies do you use to effectively introduce the computer to young children so that it becomes an ongoing and independent learning center?
- How do you plan and implement curriculum activities based on the computer?

Using Computers for Instructional Support
- Do you know how to make instructional materials (labels, games, pictures, newsletters, stories, and so forth)?
- Can you keep records and create reports about the children or classroom activities?
- How does your computer help you assess children's learning?
- Can you communicate with parents and/or other professionals via e-mail?
- Can you locate Internet resources for lesson planning and ideas for best teaching practices?
- Can you create or add educational information to a classroom-based website?
- Can you develop and print photographs from digital cameras?

Source: Cynthia J. Bewick and Marjorie Kostelnik, "Educating Early Childhood Teachers about Computers," *Young Children* 59(3) (May 2004): 26–29. Reprinted with permission from the National Association for the Education of Young Children.

to assess your own knowledge about computers and their use in early childhood classrooms.

In the following An Expert Speaks box, Dr. Suzanne Thouvenelle describes how the potential of computers in programs for young children

AN **Expert** SPEAKS: Computers in the Early Childhood Program

Suzanne Thouvenelle, Johns Hopkins University

The debate over computer use with young children rages on. Advocates for computers maintain that even young children can benefit educationally from their use (Becker 2000; Clements and Samara 2002; Wright and Shade 1994). Just look at how children gravitate to the computer—surely their curiosity and motivation count for something! Nonbelievers say that computers are just one more high-priced fad that promises a quick fix for educational ills and that computers for young children destroy creative thinking and social interactions (Alliance for Childhood 2000; Cuban 2000; Elkind and Whitehurst 2001; Healy 2000).

As with many educational issues, the truth lies somewhere between these distant positions. When school budgets shrink and technology begins to consume a greater proportion of resources in schools, we early childhood educators are forced to seriously consider the implications of acquiring and using technology in our classrooms. We need to question the impact and effectiveness of instructional technology for young learners. The research in this area offers little real help in settling the issue. For the most part, we educators tend to be optimistic about the value of educational technology, yet we often act based on incomplete information.

Children at home and in school already spend extended periods daily with computers and other technology-based devices. Still, we do not know exactly how technology affects children's cognitive, social, emotional, and physical development. There are large gaps in published literature in all these areas. Small sample size and limited research designs are characteristic of studies that involve young children. Little research has focused on the impact of computers in classrooms of young children, those between the ages of three and eight years old.

So what should we early childhood educators do about classroom computer use? I believe a balanced use of computers can be effective for young children. In the last decade, I have visited hundreds of classrooms where many teachers used technology with young children in outstanding and educationally meaningful ways. These classrooms incorporate two common elements: (1) quality software and (2) an educator who takes responsibility for mediating the computer learning experience for young children. I am confident that in time, the formal research studies will document these exciting events and provide clear evidence that appropriate use of computers does make a difference for young children. Regardless of the educational medium used, effectiveness still depends on what teachers have students do with the materials. This applies to technology, too.

Only when early childhood educators accept the challenge of learning how to integrate computers into their classrooms, through thoughtful software selection and creative use with children, will we begin to develop a base of effective professional practice. Educators can advance everyone's knowledge by documenting and sharing their own successful technology practices. I encourage you to adopt effective practices and take the risks required to learn—even if it's about classroom computers and you remain skeptical.

depends on the knowledge, skill, and creativity of the teacher. What will you expect of yourself in terms of learning more about technology and its use with young children?

Scheduling

One professional task that helps the teacher manage the activities of the class in an appropriate manner is setting up the **daily class schedule.** Like room arrangements, furniture, and choices of areas, the schedule can be planned before the teacher knows the children, but plans should be made with the knowledge that the schedule will change to reflect the needs of the group and of individuals.

A schedule must allow children to move around and select materials and activities as easily as possible. In planning a schedule, the teacher should begin by noting any fixed times, such as the time the class can use the outdoor play area, lunchtime, or time with specialists (music, physical education, or art). The teacher should try to arrange for a large block of the time to be a period in which children have a choice of activities and materials. Other activities that the teacher wants to include can then be added: a story time, a music time, a group time, and a snack time.

The time allotted for these activities will depend on the children's ages. Threes and fours need much shorter story and music times than older children and probably do not need group time at all. Fives and sixes can benefit from longer story and music times and from group time, as well. Teachers in primary grades experience more intrusions in their schedules (fixed recess periods, visits from various specialists, and so on), but they still have long periods during which they can schedule activities. One source of tension in planning any schedule for young children is attempting to balance large-group times and times for self-selected activities.

One purpose of a schedule is to provide routine and structure for children so that they know basically what to expect each day (Lund and Bos 1981). Another purpose is to provide balance in the day. For instance, activities in which children are relatively passive should not be scheduled back to back so that children have to sit quietly for long periods of time.

Table 4.1 shows samples of schedules for younger children and older children in half-day programs, a full-day program for kindergarten children, and a full-day schedule for primary-grade children. Note that none of these schedules includes time for cleanup or toileting. Teachers should involve children as much as possible in cleaning up the room and putting away materials before moving to other activities. Ideally, all rooms for early childhood programs should have bathrooms attached so that children can just go to the bathroom when they need to. Teachers in some older buildings (where this arrangement is often not the case) may have to arrange to take the class to the restrooms in groups. If possible, the teacher should send a few children at a time with an aide or volunteer while other children continue working.

Details of the Schedule

Activity Time

Experiences that are appropriate for children will be discussed in more detail in the content-area chapters (Chapters 9 through 15). Children usually participate in these experiences during activity times. For example, if the topic is a study of how insects change, children might work puzzles depicting insects in the manipulatives area; observe insects on display in the science area using a magnifying glass and record their observations; read (or look at pictures in) books about insects in the library; sort pictures of insects; examine sequence boards showing the life cycles of insects in the language arts area; or play with puppets and flannelboard cutouts of insects in the language arts area. Children might paint or draw insects or build insect homes in the art area. Whatever the topic, it should be incorporated into as many content areas as possible and reasonable. Activity times are scheduled so that children can participate in small-group and individual activities.

NAEYC CRITERIA
2.10

NAEYC CRITERIA
3.35

TABLE 4.1 Schedules for Various Programs

PROGRAM	TIMES	ACTIVITIES
Half-day program for younger children	9:00–10:00	Activity time
	10:00–10:10	Music time
	10:10–10:40	Outdoor play
	10:40–11:00	Snack time
	11:00–11:10	Quiet time
	11:10–11:20	Movement activities
	11:20–11:30	Story time
Half-day program for older preschoolers	9:00–10:00	Activity time
	10:00–10:20	Music and movement
	10:20–10:40	Group time (calendar, weather, discussions)
	10:40–11:00	Outdoor play
	11:00–11:10	Snack
	11:10–11:30	Story, poetry
Full-day kindergarten	9:00–9:15	Opening, singing, planning for the day
	9:15–10:15	Activity time
	10:15–10:45	Snack
	10:45–11:15	Outdoor play (gross motor play indoors in bad weather)
	11:15–11:45	Story time, literature study
	11:45–12:30	Lunch and recess
	12:30–1:30	Rest period
	1:30–1:40	Group time (discussions, planning for afternoon)
	1:40–2:15	Activity time
	2:15–2:45	Library, music, art, or physical education
	2:45–3:00	Evaluations of activities, dismissal
Primary children	9:00–9:15	Opening, singing, planning for the day
	9:15–10:15	Reading workshop
	10:15–10:30	Recess/snack
	10:30–11:30	Writing workshop
	11:30–12:30	Lunch and recess
	12:30–1:30	Theme activities and math
	1:30–2:00	Library (alternating with art or music specialists)
	2:00–2:30	Physical education, outdoor play
	2:30–2:45	Read-aloud, creative dramatics
	2:45–3:00	Sharing events of day, discussions, plans for next day, dismissal

Group Time

Some traditional group time experiences are not especially meaningful to children. As noted earlier, threes and fours probably do not need group time at all. Trying to get them to learn about the calendar is not the best use of their time. Fives and sixes can review the calendar and daily weather, but these should be brief reviews, not extended drills. Other activities appropriate for group time for fives and sixes include planning and evaluating their experiences during activity time, participating in some short group experiences (such as viewing a videotape that relates to a theme topic), listening to a resource person, discussing a problem in the room, having specific instruction in fire safety rules, and so on. Whole-group instruction is not an appropriate teaching strategy for the content areas; lecturing on a topic to children of this age is of little value.

Group time with primary children may be used for some of the same activities as those suggested for fives and sixes. It may also be used to help children recognize the choices they can make for their theme studies and to do more formal planning of their day. Some limited group instruction with primary children is useful. For example, the teacher may teach the whole group to recognize story structure or to recognize particular strategies that an author has used in a story the children are reading. Group discussions of books the children are reading are also important. Likewise, having children present work they have completed can be a valuable component of group time in the primary grades.

Show-and-tell, or sharing, is often a regular part of group time, especially with five- to eight-year-olds. Show-and-tell often becomes "bring-and-brag," as children bring their newest toy to show off. The teacher usually controls the audience for the speaker and directs the children while they speak or ask questions. If sharing time is to achieve the goal of promoting more effective communication, however, the teacher must structure the time so that children do the talking and organizing, rather than the teacher.

One technique is to have the sharing focus on the children's work, rather than on objects brought from home. Children may also need to share something especially meaningful to them from time to time, but not every child needs to share something every day. Another technique is to organize sharing time into small groups so that children share with three or four others and do not have to sit while twenty-five children share, one at a time. It is important to evaluate sharing experiences on the basis of what the children are actually learning, rather than simply to state that sharing is an important means of children learning to communicate more effectively.

Snack Time

Very young children need a snack during the morning or afternoon. Snack time should be considered a teaching time, as children learn about new foods, learn to carry on conversations, and learn how to help prepare and serve the snack. Snacks should always be nutritious and help children learn about good nutrition.

Snack time for fives and sixes can be time consuming in a half-day program when time is so limited. By the time all the children have washed their hands, been served, eaten their snacks, and cleaned up, twenty to thirty minutes out of a two-and-a-half-hour day have been used up. Therefore, some teachers prefer to have snacks available on a table so that two or

| NAEYC CRITERIA |
| 3.56 |

| NAEYC CRITERIA |
| 3.33, 3.34 |

three children can serve themselves and then go back to their activities. Other teachers prefer to incorporate snack time into activity time by making food preparation one of the activities. In this way, activity time can be extended.

Transitions

PRAXIS

Be able to explain the importance of transitions and routines in meeting the needs of young children

Transitions from one activity to another are the most likely times for behavior problems or disruptions in any program. What can the teacher do when one or two children are ready to begin a new activity and the others are still cleaning up their work areas? Or what can the teacher do when the class is ready to go to the cafeteria for lunch and the principal asks her to hold her class for exactly two more minutes? The teacher can have children who have completed their cleanup help others finish. Those who have finished can then sit in the group area and listen to a tape recording of nursery rhymes, folk songs, or fingerplays; others will join as they finish. With older children, one child can begin a rhyme, the second can say the next line, and so on; the last child can begin another rhyme.

When moving children from one area to another, the teacher should try having them move in groups by color or kind of clothing (all children wearing yellow, all children wearing sandals, and so on). Playing a rhythm on a drum or piano also helps in moving children from one area to another; they can march around the room and then out the door to go outside or to the lunchroom. There are many memory games that children can play in line, such as Going on the Train, in which the first player takes something beginning with the letter *a,* the second something beginning with *b,* and on through the alphabet. Children can also play guessing games, such as Twenty Questions and Who's in My Family? or they can listen to tapes of jokes or short pieces of poetry.

The teacher should involve the children in solving transition problems. If it is time to go outdoors, the children might be asked to think of ways they can all get their coats without bumping into anyone or crowd-

The transition times between activities need to be planned just as carefully as the activities themselves to avoid disruptions in the schedule.

ing. It is also helpful to have the activity that follows cleanup be something the children are anxious to do; dawdlers are not encouraged to finish their tasks when what they are going to do next is not exciting to them (Alger 1984).

Simplifying Routines

The routines of checking attendance, counting the children who will purchase milk, and so on can take up a lot of time. Some teachers choose to make these routines learning experiences for the children and as simple as possible for themselves. One way to check attendance is to have the children sign their names on a paper attached to a clipboard by the door. The teacher can see from the child's signature what he knows and is learning about writing.

Another technique is to divide a board in half, labeling one half "Present" and the other half "Absent." Nails or pegs are added below the label on each half, enough for all the children in the class. Each child is given a nametag with a hole in it, which he will hang on the board, or a name on a magnet and a magnetic board. As the children come in every day, they move their nametags from the "Absent" side to the "Present" side of the board. In preparation for the next day, the teacher reverses the "Present" and "Absent" headings.

Taking a count for milk can be accomplished by having each child who is purchasing milk place a marker with her name on it in a pocket marked "Milk." The same technique works for lunch counts.

Adapting the Schedule

For the first two weeks or so of the new schoolyear, the schedule may be adapted to help children make a more comfortable adjustment to school. Some schools have only half of the children assigned to each classroom come each day for the first week; the other half of the class comes to school the second week. This way, children have a chance to learn about school routines and get more attention from the teacher while they adjust. Some schools for younger children divide groups in half and ask each half to attend for half of each day for the first two or three weeks; other schools begin the year on a staggered schedule, so that there are five children the first two days, ten the next two days, and fifteen on the fifth day. Teachers should work with the administration and parents to make the beginning of school successful for all involved; sometimes parents are willing to help more at the beginning of the year to ensure a good start for all children.

Teachers may also have to adapt schedules to fit the children's developing abilities. Children may not be able to sustain their play for as long as the teacher predicted at the beginning of school and may need two short play periods rather than one long one. Children also may need more rest than was predicted, or they may be able to engage in activities of their choice for longer than might have been predicted. Teachers, with input from the children, may need to adapt schedules to fit individuals' needs.

Parents and Planning

- Make sure that parents are aware of your typical daily schedule. Invite them to come to class at different times of day so they can observe individual activities as well as small- and whole-group activities.

Kindergarten: Half-Day, Full-Day, and Alternate-Day Programs

www.lib.csufresno.edu/ subjectresources/curriculum juvenile/kindergarten

A site with many links to resources, book lists, and other useful information for kindergarten teachers

www.nkateach.org

The National Kindergarten Alliance home page, which offers many links to sites of interest to kindergarten teachers

This section applies specifically to kindergarten because there is so much debate about the values of different schedules for kindergarten children. The schedule for threes and fours is generally either a morning or an afternoon session of about two and a half or three hours, whereas the schedules for primary grades are usually set to match the full-day elementary school schedule. Some schools have two sessions of kindergarten each day. Because of transportation problems and the need for full-day child care, some schools have adopted an alternate-day schedule, so that kindergartners attend for a full day but only on alternate days. Other schools provide full-day programs for some kindergartners, especially those deemed at risk of academic failure. What does the research say about these different schedule patterns?

The research on the various programming choices for kindergarten remains mixed. It is difficult to keep constant the skill of the teacher, the child's motivation and interest, the parents' support, and the kind of measure used to judge success as well as other factors that can influence the outcomes of studies. Clark (2001), in her review of the research, states that studies from the 1990s are more positive about all-day kindergartens, but she admits that many of those studies had serious problems.

Several studies have shown that attending an all-day kindergarten is beneficial for academic achievement, especially for children deemed at risk of school failure (Elicker and Mathur 1997; Fusaro 1997; Hough and Bryde 1996). Nelson (2000) looked at half-day and full-day kindergarten, multiage grouping, and class size as influences on achievement. She concluded that for low-income, urban schools, a full-day program with smaller classes was the best choice. The findings of del Gaudio Weiss (2002), in a study that followed children into the fourth grade, also supported a full-day program.

On the other hand, Finn and Pannozzo (2004) looked at measures of student behavior, academic progress, and engagement in learning and concluded that children from all-day kindergarten programs scored more poorly than children from half-day programs. Brannon (2005) found that when parents had the choice of a full-day or half-day program, they made the decision based primarily on their assessment of their child's maturity and their comfort level with helping their child at home. Although Brannon only used one measure of phonemic awareness, she found that children from full-day programs scored higher in this area at the end of kindergarten, but by the end of first grade, there was no difference between the full-day and half-day scores.

When evaluating schedules, the best approach is to determine what is best for the children involved, to plan for excellent experiences no matter when the children are in school, and to evaluate continuously. A full-day program that involves children in inappropriate activities will not be beneficial to children, even though they will be there longer than children in half- or alternate-day programs. Decisions should not be made on the basis of convenience; rather, the guideline should be to provide optimal environments for children.

Other Scheduling Issues

An ongoing problem for kindergarten and primary teachers is **pull-out programs,** in which children are removed from class at certain times for special lessons and activities, such as speech therapy. Removing children from the class makes it difficult to schedule large-group activities and also complicates having all children participate in small-group or individual activities.

One solution to the problem, which is being used in an ever-increasing number of schools, is to have the special teachers come to the regular classroom to work with individual students, rather than have the students go to the teachers. In schools in which this solution has not yet been implemented, the regular classroom teachers might approach the special teachers with the idea and agree to help solve any problems that arise.

If this solution is not applied and pull-out programs remain a fact of life, regular classroom teachers should try to arrange activity time for that part of the day when the most children will be in the room. Classroom teachers should also try to work with the schedules of the special teachers in order to achieve a more reasonable day for the class. Regardless, there does not seem to be an easy solution to the problem of pull-out programs.

CHILDREN WITH SPECIAL NEEDS

Many children with special needs will have an *individualized education plan (IEP)* or an *individualized family service plan (IFSP)*, each of which must be made in accordance with federal regulations. However, neither plan will specify the daily learning activities for the child; instead, it will detail specific goals for the child.

Taking the IEP or IFSP into account, the teacher must translate the goals that are stated into activities that will move the child toward achieving those goals. The goals may be social, emotional, physical, or academic:

- *Social goals* often require the teacher to plan small-group activities so that the child can interact with other children.
- *Emotional goals* may be met through daily routines of cleaning up play materials, eating a snack with others, and following general classroom procedures.
- *Physical goals* may be met through planning indoor or outdoor activities that encourage gross motor movements or fine motor movements.
- *Academic goals* may be met by making adaptations in materials, time to use materials, assessments chosen, or projects selected.

Planning for children with special needs may also require teachers to think of ways to challenge learners for whom certain activities are not appropriate. Just as adaptations for some learners will require more time or different materials, adaptations for gifted children will require activities that are appropriate for their more advanced abilities.

An integrated, thematic curriculum can be easily adapted for all learners because they don't all have to do all the possible activities. For example, a theme of *zoo animals* might have children classify animals in the zoo that are related. Some children might use models of zoo animals for classification, some might make a list of related animals, and some might use the Internet to learn more about the families of zoo animals and produce a report on a selected family of animals.

Planning for children with special needs will also require assessment to be an ongoing process. In addition, assessment must provide information that teachers can use when making instructional decisions for individual children.

NAEYC CRITERIA

2.4

CELEBRATING DIVERSITY

To celebrate the diversity of the classroom, teachers should plan for experiences and activities that reflect the diversity of society. For example, in selecting themes, teachers should think carefully about the meanings of the activities for the children involved. For example, what will a two-week theme with a focus on St. Patrick's Day mean to a class of three- and four-year-olds who are Hispanic or Southeast Asian? On the other hand, St. Patrick's Day may be an important holiday to a child from an Irish household. Perhaps implementing a theme about this holiday could be justified if there were Irish children in the class and the theme focused on the holidays of all the ethnic groups represented in the class. In sum, the themes selected must be relevant to the lives of the children. Teachers should consider that by focusing on holidays, they may be denying children experiences with more interesting and relevant themes, such as those focusing on animals, insects, plants, and other interests.

Diversity can be celebrated in many of the activities and experiences that teachers plan for young children. For example, when planning cooking experiences, teachers can prepare foods that are typical of the various ethnic groups represented in the class. Members of the community can be invited to share special ethnic foods and traditional clothing, stories, and games. Community members whose work is nontraditional for their gender also can be invited to share information about their work with the class. Teachers should not advocate a curriculum that simply adds a "diversity feature." Rather, their goal should be the authentic integration of people and other resources that will help children explore topics in ways that naturally include diversity.

Experiences with literature can enhance children's knowledge and appreciation of racial and ethnic differences if they are planned carefully by teachers. Namely, teachers should select pieces of literature to add information or interest to themes, ensuring that the works of authors and illustrators of various racial/ethnic groups and both genders are included. Books, both fiction and nonfiction, and poetry that include a wide variety of characters should also be selected. In one second-grade boy's reading-response journal, he explained that he really liked a particular book because he was Hispanic and had never known about a book with Hispanic characters before. Children should be able to find characters like themselves in books that are part of the classroom experience.

The next An Expert Speaks box presents Dr. Jana Echevarria, who describes instruction for English language learners that can help these children succeed in school. How do you feel about your responsibility to plan instruction for English language learners?

AN **Expert** SPEAKS: Instruction for English Language Learners

Jana Echevarria, California State University, Long Beach

Young English language learners arrive at school eager to learn. They are excited about being at school and want to gain the teacher's approval. For most English language learners, their parents have talked very positively about school and the opportunities an education will bring. Our challenge as educators is to build on their enthusiasm by providing interesting, relevant learning experiences they can participate in fully and feel success. One way to ensure that teaching is comprehensible for these youngsters is to use sheltered instruction.

Sheltered instruction (also called SDAIE in some regions) is a set of techniques and activities that are used to make instruction understandable for English language learners. The features of sheltered instruction share many of the characteristics of high-quality instruction for all children, but it pays particular attention to English language learners' unique second-language acquisition needs. These children are learning new information, concepts, and skills at the same time they are learning a new language. So, many of the classroom procedures and words used during instruction are known by other students but are completely new to these students. Therefore, sheltered instruction is more than just good instruction. It must take into account English language learners' unique linguistic situation.

Many English language learners are able to assess content information through sheltered lessons but may not make adequate progress in learning English. Developed through a research grant, the SIOP (Sheltered Instruction Observation Protocol) model of sheltered instruction is intended to provide educators with a model for consistently implemented high-quality instruction as well as providing systematic English language development (Echevarria, Vogt, and Short 2004). The SIOP model

is a means for making content (math, social studies, language arts, science) comprehensible for English language learners while at the same time developing their English language proficiency. Rather than teachers picking and choosing among a variety of techniques, the SIOP model promotes consistent implementation of specific features of instruction that, when taken together, improve students' academic achievement. The model is a tool that empowers classroom teachers to meet the academic and language needs of their students. The booming growth of English language learners in U.S. schools dictates that all teachers become equipped to provide high-quality instruction for these learners.

Effective lessons for English language learners begin with standards-based content objectives as well as language objectives. Content objectives are usually known to teachers, but language objectives are equally important and ensure that attention to language isn't haphazard but regularly builds academic English proficiency. SIOP lessons take into consideration students' background experiences and make lessons meaningful by linking the content to those experiences. Supplementary materials are used to a high degree to make the lesson's concepts clear and meaningful. Further, comprehension is increased when young English language learners have the opportunity to practice the lesson's language and concepts through hands-on activities and grouping configurations that promote discussion.

With intentional planning and systematic implementation of features known to be effective for English language learners, lessons will offer these youngsters the learning opportunities they need to participate fully in learning, make adequate academic progress, and meet high academic standards.

SUMMARY

- *Curriculum* has multiple definitions, but in this chapter, it means a written plan for learning experiences in which children will be involved. A curriculum can be organized many different ways: by subject (which is most common), by skills (such as cutting on a line, placing words in alphabetical order, counting to ten, and so on), and thematically (so that learning activities are related to a theme that connects the experiences).

- Curriculum planning based on developmentally appropriate practice (DAP) provides for development in all areas: social, emotional, physical, and intellectual. The content is relevant to the children's lives and intellectually engaging. Such a curriculum builds on what children know and can do, integrates learning across subject-matter lines, supports children's home cultures, and is attainable for most children in the program.

- An integrated curriculum helps teachers plan for in-depth learning, supports choices for children, depends on active learning, and is an effective use of student and teacher time. A thematic curriculum alone does not guarantee good instruction; the teacher must involve the children in the planning and respond to their needs. An effective curriculum cannot simply be purchased and applied.

- Learning plans are broader and more comprehensive than lesson plans. Whereas a lesson plan outlines what the teacher plans to do in a specific part of the day (such as a demonstration of safety procedures), a learning plan outlines what the teacher plans for each learning center in the room as well as what lesson plans will be implemented. Both learning and lesson plans need to reflect accommodations to be made for specific children.

- The goals of multicultural education and an antibias curriculum include helping each child develop a strong identity as a member of a group, a knowledge of and respect for other cultures, an ability to empathize with others, and a willingness to engage in activities to solve problems of discrimination and/or bias in any form. Diversity is a fact of life in U.S. schools today, and both teachers and children can learn to view diversity as a strength of U.S. society.

- The use of computers in programs for young children can support learning if the teacher gives careful thought to the software selected for the children's use, teaches children to be safe online, and uses this technology as an aid in solving problems, promoting creativity, and encouraging social interaction. Computers can be used in ways that are harmful to children—for instance, using them as worksheets for drill-and-practice on isolated skills or in lieu of activities with real objects and materials.

- Scheduling activities is important, as young children need to know that a regular routine will be followed during the day. Activities should be scheduled so that children are not forced to sit quietly or to be quiet for too long. Teachers should schedule activities that involve physical movements between quiet activities, and children need adequate time for planning and implementing their own ideas in the classroom.

- Children with special needs can be accommodated in a program of activities that offers many choices of how to reach given goals. Teachers may need to make adaptations in materials, time allotments, and group sizes to accommodate children who might need more or less of a challenge than most of the others in the program.

- Celebrating diversity through various activities is a reasonable objective for early childhood programs. Children can be involved in manipulating materials common to a given culture, preparing and sharing food from a given culture, interacting with families to learn about their traditions, learning some words of another language, and recognizing art and music from other cultures. The most important goals in planning to celebrate diversity are to ensure that all children feel positive about their own culture and respect the cultures of others.

REFLECTIONS

1. What do you think is the purpose of having a curriculum?
2. Do learning plans/lesson plans benefit the children? If yes, how? If no, why not? Do they benefit the teacher? If yes, how? If no, why not?
3. The author of this book advocates planning and scheduling activities. Does doing so sound too rigid for the classroom you envision for yourself? If so, how would you organize the day for the children? If not, how will you take advantage of the so-called teachable moments in a day?
4. Is it important for teachers of young children to learn about the cultures of the children in their classes so they can adapt their teaching for those children, or is good teaching the same for all children? Provide examples to support your answer.

5. Why would you want to plan instruction around themes, as opposed to using a subject-matter organization, especially since the subject-matter approach is most common in elementary schools?

EXPLORATIONS AND ACTIVITIES

1. Unfortunately, many documents of state standards are written so that one has to look in separate subject documents to find the standards for prekindergarten (Pre-K), kindergarten (K), and elementary students. Locate the standards in several subject documents for Pre-K, K, or grade 1 or grade 2. Do these standards seem reasonable to you? Do you think the people who prepared them are knowledgeable about young children and how they learn? Do you see any evidence that only academic standards really matter in your state, or do the standards encourage physical and social/emotional growth as well as academics?

2. Choose an interesting theme or topic of study, and determine how many of the state standards could be met by implementing such a study. How would you document that you had actually engaged the children in learning that met the various standards?

MyLabSchool is a collection of online tools for your success in this course, your licensure exams, and your teaching career. Visit **www.mylabschool.com** to access the following:

- Online Study Guide
- Video Cases from real classrooms
- Help with your research papers using Research Navigator
- Career Center with resources for:
  - —Praxis and Licensure Preparation
  - —Professional Portfolio Development
  - —Job Search and Interview Techniques
  - —Lesson Planning

CHAPTER **5**

KEY TERMS you'll find in this chapter:

- **Directed play,** 142
- **Egocentric thought patterns,** 150
- **Exploratory play,** 148
- **Free play,** 142
- **Games of construction,** 146
- **Games with rules,** 145
- **Guided play,** 142
- **Illicit play,** 155
- **Instrumental play,** 155
- **Open-ended materials,** 159
- **Play,** 142
- **Practice play,** 145
- **Rule-governed play,** 148
- **Social play,** 145
- **Sociodramatic play,** 146
- **Symbolic play,** 145
- **Teaching strategies,** 160

Play: Learning at Its Best

FOCUS QUESTIONS

- How would you define *play*?
- What are the purposes of play?
- What play behaviors are typical for children of different ages?
- Why is play important in school?
- How should you plan for outdoor play?
- How should you plan for the play of children with special needs?
- How can you celebrate the diversity of your children in play experiences?

This morning you visited a second-grade classroom to observe children's play. You found the children busily working on various projects. One group had written the script for a play and were making the puppets they would need to present their drama. Another small group was constructing a habitat for an insect collection using the directions they found in several reference books. They were also creating small posters that described the care the various insects would need. Another small group was working on a three-dimensional map of their community made from cereal boxes. Four children were playing a board game they had created based on the story *The Lion, the Witch, and the Wardrobe* (Lewis 1951). Two pairs of children were using computers to create final copies of the stories they had composed earlier. Several other individual children were involved in tasks such as building a dodecahedron from Popsicle sticks and putting a colorwash on paper to be used for mounting poetry selections.

You were amazed that these children were playing in second grade. However, as you observed more closely, you realized they were learning academic as well as social skills through their play. You want to know how the teacher manages all these play activities and how play can help achieve the goals of a developmentally appropriate program.

Back in your campus class, the discussion of play in the classroom was a lively one. Many of your classmates felt children should play in school, but they were worried about justifying play when teachers are held accountable for achieving so many academic standards these days. You want to find answers to your questions about the nature of play and how it can contribute to realizing curriculum goals. ■

Defining Play

Teachers, parents, and administrators need continued support in their efforts to include **play** in the curriculum and to defend its use to those not as knowledgeable in early childhood education. Almy (1984) has published statements in several sources about the child's right to play. She writes that the distinguishing characteristics of play make it essential to the child's development. She believes that adults must provide opportunities for children to play and to learn from observations and actions as well as from being told things.

In a position paper approved by the Association for Childhood Education International (ACEI), Isenberg and Quisenberry (1988) state that "play—a dynamic, active and constructive behavior—is a necessary and integral part of childhood, infancy through adolescence." The ACEI also asserts that teachers must take the lead in articulating the need for play in children's lives, especially as a part of their school life.

> It would be wrong to think he does not take his play seriously; on the contrary, he takes his play very seriously and he expends large amounts of emotion on it.
>
> —*Sigmund Freud*

www.acei.org/playpaper.htm
Includes the position paper supporting the right of the child to play from the Association for Childhood Education International

www.kidsource.com/kidsource/content2/nature.of.childs.play.html
The article "The Nature of Children's Play," which describes kinds of play and the importance of play in the life of the child

http://fun.familyeducation.com/outdoor-activities/play/35262.html
The article "Rethinking Children's Play," which supports play for children and suggests that children's play is not getting the attention it deserves; also discusses new toys for children and makes suggestions for creative play

Types of Play

Play in a school setting can be described on a continuum that runs from free play to guided play to directed play:

- **Free play** can be defined as play in which children have as many choices of materials as possible and in which they can choose how to use the materials (within bounds, of course; for example, they cannot hit others with the blocks).
- **Guided play** is defined as play in which the teacher has selected materials from which the children may choose in order to discover specific concepts. If the goal is to learn to classify objects as large or small, then the teacher will provide several sets of objects to play with that could be classified as such.
- **Directed play** is play in which the teacher instructs the children in how to accomplish a specific task. Singing songs, engaging in fingerplays, and playing circle games are examples of directed play (Bergen 1988).

Characteristics of Play

In addition to thinking about the types of play, we can define *play* according to its characteristics. These include personal motivation, active involvement, nonliteral meaning, no extrinsic goals, meaning that is supplied by the players, and no extrinsic rules.

Play Is Personally Motivated

In order for an activity to be called *play*, the player must choose to participate. If a child chooses an activity, it is usually play, although what is being done may appear to be work. For example, a child may load up a wheelbarrow with sand, move it across the playground to a new sandbox, and dump it. Similarly, children often "work" for hours gathering materials and building forts. The difference between play and work is that a play activity is self-chosen: The child controls how long she will participate and defines the goals of the activity.

Ceglowski (1997) found that kindergartners had no trouble in identifying activities that were play versus work. Children described as *play* only those activities they selected and directed. Activities that were teacher selected or teacher directed were described as *work*. Play is always pleasurable to the participants. The feelings may be the satisfaction of having achieved internal goals or the pure joy of running freely. The player experiences pleasure in play.

Play Is Active

All play experiences require some active involvement on the part of the player. Play is *not* a passive activity, such as watching television, although play does not require active physical involvement. Children are playing when they participate in a "tea party" or investigate the hardness of rocks. Children playing are engaged in thinking, organizing, planning, and interacting with the environment. If the involvement is passive, then the activity is probably not play.

> ## Parents and Play
> ● Ask parents to keep a play diary for a few days, recording the time their child spends in active play and the materials used in the play.
> ● Arrange for a speaker to talk with parents about the need for active play in a child's life and to help them find a strategy to increase play if the child is not engaging in active play. Be sure that the parents make the distinction between active play and passive activity, such as watching TV.

Play Is Often Nonliteral

Children at play can suspend reality, usually with the magic words "Let's pretend." The time, setting, and characters involved in play can be negotiated at the moment and are not tied to reality. They need not even be possible; children might pretend to fly, to be from outer space, or to be monsters.

Play Has No Extrinsic Goals

Suppose a child is arranging and rearranging a set of letters on a magnetic board. If this task has been assigned for the purpose of helping her learn alphabetical order, then it is not play. If the child is arranging the letters to suit goals that are her own, then it is play. In playing, the process, or means, not the end result, is most important. The outcome of play is not as important as the *participation* in it.

Players Supply Meaning to Play

Children sometimes explore or use materials in ways specified by others, but when they play, they provide their own interpretations of materials. A child might use base 10 blocks to build models of numbers if directed to do so by an adult. But if allowed to use the materials freely during another portion of the day, the child might use the blocks to build houses or roads.

Play Has No Extrinsic Rules

If an activity is to be considered play, the players must be able to alter the rules of the activity as needed. In a game of tag, for example, the players negotiate where the "safe" areas will be. Similarly, children playing with blocks may establish rules about spaces for building, but these rules are negotiated by the players.

Levels of Play

We can also define *play* by considering the various levels that children engage in, including social play, play with objects, and sociodramatic play. Learning about the theories of Lev Vygotsky will also point to the meaning and importance of play.

www.

www.ericdigests.org/2002–2/ play.htm

A digest entitled "Pretend Play and Young Children's Development," which supports play for social and linguistic competence

Social Play

Teachers who observe children playing will notice several different levels of involvement with other children in play episodes. In her classic study, Parten (1932) describes these levels as *solitary, onlooker, parallel, associative,* and *cooperative play*. Table 5.1 summarizes Parten's descriptions of levels of social play.

TABLE 5.1 Levels of Social Play

LEVEL	DESCRIPTION
Solitary play	Play in which children play without regard for what other children around them are doing. A child may be constructing a tower with blocks and be completely oblivious to what other children in the room are doing.
Onlooker play	Play in which the child who is playing individually is simultaneously observing those playing in the same area. The child may be talking to peers. Children who watch other children play may alter their own play behavior after watching. Children engaged in onlooker play may seem to be sitting passively while children around them are playing, but they are very alert to the action around them.
Parallel play	Play in which several children are playing with the same materials, but each is playing independently. What one child does is not dependent on what others do. Children working puzzles are usually engaged in parallel play. They usually talk to one another, but if one leaves the table, the others continue playing.
Associative play	Play in which several children play together but in a loosely organized fashion. Several children might decide to play "monsters," for example, and run around the playground, chasing each other. But there are no definite roles, and if one child does not run and chase, the others can continue to play.
Cooperative play	Play in which each child accepts a designated role and is dependent on others for achieving the goals of the play. When children want to play "store," for instance, one child must accept the role of store clerk and others must be shoppers. If a child refuses to play unless she can be the storekeeper, the play episode will end.

Source: Based on Parten 1932.

Children of different ages exhibit different levels of **social play.** Very young children are not cognitively capable of assuming different roles and playing cooperatively. They do not possess enough information about roles or enough social skills to work together for a single purpose. Older children do not engage in cooperative play exclusively. They may engage in any of the levels of play; they simply have a much broader repertoire of possible play behaviors.

Play with Objects

There are levels of play with objects as well as levels of social play. Piaget (1962) and Piaget and Inhelder (1969) have described different types of play with objects, including practice play, symbolic play, games with rules, and games of construction.

Practice play, or functional play, is play in which children explore the possibilities of materials. Even adults engage in practice play when the materials presented are new to them. For instance, children using dominoes in practice play would stack them and stand them on end.

After playing with the dominoes for some time, children might begin to use them in **symbolic play.** They would use a domino to represent something else. Perhaps they would make a corral of blocks and pretend that the dominoes were cattle in the corral.

In a **game with rules,** children might play according to rules they have made up themselves or according to the rules that are generally agreed on for playing the game. If the children were playing with dominoes, for example, they might decide that the rules were to match all the ends but not play the doubles across; if they know the conventional rules for playing dominoes and keeping score, they might follow those rules instead. Anyone who has ever tried to play a game with rules (such as Candy Land or Concentration) with a three- or four-year-old knows that a child this age will usually play the way she wants to and that following the rules is almost impossible.

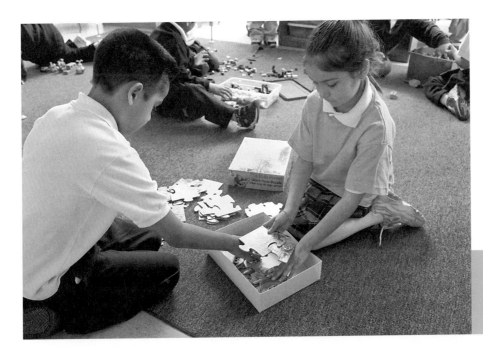

The children playing here are developing skills in fine motor control, language use, and social interaction.

Games of construction are described by Piaget as growing out of symbolic play "but tend later to constitute genuine adaptations (mechanical constructions, etc.) or solutions to problems and intelligent creations" (Piaget and Inhelder 1969, p. 59). Levels of object play depend on the children's maturity and experience. As children mature, they become more capable of using materials symbolically and of playing a game with accepted rules.

Sociodramatic Play

www.

http://ecrp.uiuc.edu/v4n1/ bergen.html

Doris Bergen's article "The Role of Pretend Play in Children's Cognitive Development," which shares her research on play in early childhood and her concern about the loss of play in this age of accountability

Sociodramatic play involves a small group of participants playing defined roles that they have chosen. Called *fantasy play* by some, this type of play allows children to engage intellectually with many aspects of their own lives. For example, after a disaster, children may play what to do in such a situation. They may also play mundane parts of their lives, such as how to shop for clothes, or they may play imaginatively, such as how to travel in space.

Smilansky (1971) has studied sociodramatic play for many years. She and her colleague (Smilansky and Shefatya, 1990) have determined that sociodramatic play requires time and space as well as interesting objects for play. They also note that such play is cooperative and that players must agree on the themes and characters before the play can be successful. In addition, they note that such play is pretense and make-believe, while at the same time being grounded in reality.

Sociodramatic play is especially important in the development of creativity, intellectual growth, and social skills. Not all children will have had experience with sociodramatic play. Therefore, teachers may need to assume more responsibility in fostering such play with these children. Teachers can look carefully for the elements of sociodramatic play and encourage it by intervening and helping children achieve any missing elements.

Research findings support the value of sociodramatic play:

> A vast amount of research indicates that imaginative play (symbolic play) is a significant causal force in the development of a multitude of abilities, including creativity, sequential memory, group cooperation, receptive vocabulary, conceptions of kinship relationships, impulse control, spatial perspective-taking skill, affective perspective-taking skill, and cognitive perspective-taking skill. (Gowen 1995, p. 78)

Paley (2004) believes that sociodramatic play is the foundation of early childhood education. The abilities to take on the role of another person and to shift perspective are important basic skills for academic learning. Research provides ample support for the effects of such play on the development of cognitive skills. In addition, Elias and Berk (2002) found that children who were impulsive benefited from sociodramatic play in learning to self-regulate their behavior.

For some children, sociodramatic play occurs if time is allowed for it; for others, the teacher may have to be much more involved to get children to participate. This can be accomplished by providing time and often props to get children started in sociodramatic play. The dramatic play area and the housekeeping center are often settings that encourage sociodramatic play by providing costumes, furniture, and other props. If children have ideas about play themes, the teacher can help them carry out these ideas by providing needed props.

Teachers might consider asking parents to help them collect materials that could be used for any number of play situations. Materials for given situations might then be stored in individual boxes so that they are available when the children's interests dictate use. Such boxes might include materials for playing "repairperson," "beauty shop," "office," and so on. Myhre (1993) suggests prop boxes containing materials to recreate a bakery, a flower shop, and a beach party, as well as a jewelry and accessory box and "dentist," "police," and "firefighter" boxes.

In addition to providing time and props, the teacher might have to model appropriate play behavior for children with little or no experience in sociodramatic play. He may have to assume a role and play it for a few minutes, at least long enough to demonstrate the behavior so that children will understand and be able to perform the behavior themselves. The teacher might also suggest roles others could play or ask questions to get the children started on a play episode. The line between assisting children and dominating play is a fine one. Teachers must develop skills in listening to and responding to children, following their lead, rather than imposing their ideas about what children should be playing.

Reifel and Yeatman (1993) urge teachers to think of play in broader categories than those described by Parten and Piaget. They note, for example, that rough-and-tumble play, word play, and jokes are not covered in either theorist's description of play, although these behaviors are certainly part of children's play experiences. A play episode may begin with one type of play, move to another, and then back again, so teachers need to think about how children are relating to materials and to one another throughout play episodes, rather than make quick judgments based on short, isolated observations.

Finally, teachers should look for opportunities to encourage sociodramatic play that stems from real events in children's lives. For example, suppose one of the children has been in the hospital. When she returns to school and tells of her experience, the children will likely be anxious to play "being in the hospital." The teacher might ask some questions to help the children think about what they need to play "hospital" and then help them find appropriate props, such as clipboards to use for patient charts, stethoscopes, boxes for furniture, and so on.

Vygotsky on Play

In their important work on the theories of Lev Vygotsky, Bodrova and Leong (1996) have summarized his views on play. In sum, play develops from the manipulative play of toddlers to the socially oriented play of older preschoolers and kindergartners and finally to games.

Vygotsky would label as play behavior by toddlers in which they begin to use objects in imaginary situations and label the actions with words. For example, using a spoon to bang on a table is not play, but using a spoon to feed a teddy bear and asking the bear to eat is play. Most five-year-olds focus on the social roles of their play rather than on the objects. For example, they can pretend to have a pad of paper and pen for taking orders if they are playing "waiter" or "waitress." Games, as a type of play, emerge in children's play behavior around age five. Games involve explicit and detailed rules in which the imaginary situations are hidden. For example, soccer is a game in which the players agree not to use their hands, although they could use them (Bodrova and Leong 1996).

Vygotsky believes that play is extremely important in the child's development in three ways:

1. *"Play creates the child's zone of proximal development."* In a play setting, a child can control behavior such as attending to a task before she is able to control that behavior in another setting.

2. *"Play facilitates the separation of thought from actions and objects."* In play, the child can pretend that a block is a boat; this separation of object from meaning is critical to the development of abstract thinking.

3. *"Play facilitates the development of self-regulation."* In developing self-regulation, children in play are required to make their behavior match the role they have accepted. For example, a child playing "dog" can stop barking or sit still on command (quotes from Bodrova and Leong 1996, p. 126).

According to Vygotsky:

> Play creates a zone of proximal development in the child. In play, the child always behaves beyond his average age, above his daily behavior; in play it is as though he were a head taller than himself. As in the focus of a magnifying glass, play contains all developmental tendencies in a condensed form and is itself a major source of development. (1978, p. 102)

Purposes of Play

Play contributes to cognitive growth, aids social and emotional development, and is essential to physical development. Many of the abilities required to succeed in school settings are gained through play experiences.

Eheart and Leavitt (1985) state that play offers young children opportunities "to master many fundamental physical, social, and intellectual skills and concepts" (p. 18). Other researchers have come to similar conclusions about both younger and primary-age children (Garvey 1977; Sylva, Bruner, and Genova 1976). Fantuzzo, Sekino, and Cohen (2004) studied two groups of Head Start children and found that those who demonstrated a high level of peer interaction also demonstrated more competent emotional regulation, initiation, self-determination, and receptive vocabulary skills. The children who played well also scored higher on cognitive, social, and movement/coordination outcomes than children with less skill in interacting. Thus, the phrase "Plays well with others," often used in jest or sarcasm, seems to provide a serious assessment of a range of abilities.

Parents and Play
- Emphasize the value of play in your reports to parents. Mention play activities that children especially enjoy in school and what they learn from such play. Select a type of play for each issue of the newsletter, and explain how this play contributes to a child's cognitive, social/emotional, and physical growth.

Intellectual Development

Both **exploratory play**—play in which the child has no objective other than exploration—and **rule-governed play**—play in which the child has objectives such as finding solutions to problems or determining cause and effect—contribute to cognitive growth. *Cognitive growth* is defined as an increase in the child's basic store of knowledge (Lunzer 1959); it occurs as a result of experiences with objects and people (Piaget 1952b).

Many studies support the positive relationship between play experiences and the development of children's cognitive abilities. Cognitive abilities include identifying, classifying, sequencing, observing, discriminating, making predictions, drawing conclusions, comparing, and determining cause-and-effect relationships. These intellectual abilities underlie children's success in all academic areas.

Play helps children develop organizing and problem-solving abilities. Children playing must think about organizing materials in order to meet their play goals. For example, a child who wants to play "visiting the doctor" must decide where the doctor's office and the waiting room will be, what will be used for a stethoscope, and so on. Children must also organize tasks, deciding how to move and arrange materials so that they can play. Some of these organization tasks require very fine discriminations, such as sorting by size, shape, or color. Children playing must also think about the other players involved. Older children playing the roles of characters in books they have read must think about the roles being assumed by other players and take those into consideration when creating their own roles.

Children playing are often engaged in problem-solving behavior. They might experiment with adding water to sand to make it the proper consistency for holding its shape when molded, or they might search the room to find suitable materials for something needed in play. Children playing "riding on the bus," for example, might look for things to use for seats and perhaps something to be the steering wheel of the bus. They might also look for props to serve as tickets and baggage. They might find old purses in the dress-up area to be suitcases or a pie pan to be the steering wheel.

Because they will also need people to participate as passengers, the children playing "riding on the bus" will have to solve the problem of how to persuade enough other children to join the play. Sylva et al. (1976) found that children who played with materials were as capable of solving a problem as children for whom the solution had been demonstrated. Children who play with materials are more likely to assume that there are many possible solutions to a problem and to continue trying to solve a problem longer than children for whom a solution has been demonstrated.

Older children, as well as younger ones, are actively engaged in problem solving when they attempt to create a structure to match the image they plan. For example, children learning about triangles might build structures supported with triangles and test their strength; children learning about hexagons might build dodecahedrons from Popsicle sticks.

Children at play certainly demonstrate creative thinking and creative problem solving. During play, children must put together information from previous experience, from the real world, and from other play participants. Frank (1968) concludes that play "is a way of learning by trial and error to cope with the actual world" (p. 436). In a review of current research on play, Stegelin (2005) states that the connection between play and cognitive development is clear for children under age five but is less clear for primary-grade children. Very little research linking play and cognitive development for primary-grade children has been done. It is worrisome to

> **Man does not cease to play because he grows old; man grows old because he ceases to play.**
>
> —*George Bernard Shaw*

NAEYC CRITERIA
3.41

see play time reduced as the push for more academics for younger children gets stronger.

Social and Emotional Development

In the Piagetian view, play pushes children out of **egocentric thought patterns** (Piaget 1962). That is, children in play situations are forced to consider the viewpoints of their playmates and therefore become less egocentric. If Susan and Juan are pretending to cook dinner, each may have definite ideas about how the task should be done. They will each have to accommodate the other's thinking in order to continue their play. Children learn to cooperate to achieve some group goals during play. They also have opportunities during play to learn to delay their own gratification for a few minutes—for instance, while someone else finishes playing with a drum.

Children often play out their fears and concerns. One study reports the reactions of a group of children after they witnessed an accident on their playground and describes how they worked out stress through their play (N. Brown, Curry, and Tittnich 1971). Children in different age groups (threes, fours, and fives) incorporated the accident into their play differently, but each group revealed some fear and tried to relieve it through "hospital" play or other play involving someone being injured. In another instance, children who had experienced a tornado played various forms of "hiding from the tornado" or "the tornado is coming" for a long time after the experience. Barnett (1984) found that children who were anxious showed reduced anxiety after enacting their fears in play episodes.

Although most teachers are not trained to be play therapists, they can be aware of how children explore different emotions (anger, sadness, and so on) and different social roles in their play. For example, children might "try on" the role of "bully" in a play situation; after they get feedback about how other people react to them in that role, they can alter their behavior.

Stegelin (2005) summarizes the benefits of play in social development: "Social competence, largely developed by age six, is best nurtured in young children through sociodramatic and pretend play with peers, social interactions in small group settings, and assimilation of routines and reciprocal engagement with peers and caring adults" (p. 84).

Physical Development

Children achieve both fine and gross motor control through their play. They can practice all the gross motor skills of running, jumping, and hopping while playing. Children at play can be encouraged to lift, carry, and walk or hop, spin, and move in response to rhythms. They can also practice fine motor skills as they string beads, fit together puzzles, hammer nails into wood, or paint at easels.

Not only young children need active play; older children should participate in this type of play, too. They can throw, catch, kick, bat, balance on two-wheel bikes, and skate. Today's children often spend a great deal of time in passive behavior, such as watching television or videos. These children especially need to have the chance to climb, swing, pull, push, run, hop, jump, and walk in order to gain control of their bodies.

Development of Play Behaviors

As described in the following sections, children's play behaviors develop from infancy through middle childhood. Each age is characterized by different types and purposes of play.

Infancy

The play of infants is *sensorimotor:* They explore objects and people and investigate the effects of their actions on these objects and people. At about the end of the first year, children begin to exhibit play behaviors such as pretending to eat or sleep (Rubin, Fein, and Vanderberg 1983). They are also able to begin playful interactions with others, such as playing peek-a-boo.

Preschool

Preschoolers spend most of their play time in exploratory or practice play. They are focused on the process, rather than the product, of their play. For example, they might mix the colors of paint or the colors of clay, but their interest is in what happens to the materials, not in the painting or sculpture that later results.

Preschoolers often engage in sociodramatic or fantasy play, but it is generally focused on their own experiences. For example, they may play "Mommy" and "Baby" or other family roles. In fantasy play, they like to have materials that resemble the real things in the fantasy setting, such as a small broom for sweeping or a play telephone or grocery scanner that resembles the actual equipment.

Threes and fours also begin to involve others in their play. For instance, they may want someone to drink the tea or eat the cookie. This involvement gradually becomes sociodramatic play, which depends on others for the success of the play episode.

The play of preschoolers is vigorous; they like to chase one another and climb and jump. But they are not usually very interested in games with rules. They need a great deal of support in playing simple games such as Duck, Duck, Goose and have difficulty following rules about turns and procedures.

Early Primary Grades

Kindergartners and first-graders engage in sociodramatic play that involves several children in the play episode, and they play without needing the objects they use to be so realistic. A block, for example, can be whatever they need it to be. At this age, fantasy play likely focuses less on home roles and more on roles observed in the community, such as "police officer," or on stories heard or read, such as "Three Billy Goats Gruff."

Practice play and the time spent exploring new objects decrease during the early primary grades until only about 15 percent of play can be labeled as practice (Ellis 1979). Most play of primary-grade children is constructive play,

Parents and Play

- For children in primary grades, plan homework that involves family play, such as thirty minutes of playing a board game or creating a puppet with materials from around the house. For younger children, encourage parents to set aside some time each week to play with their children.

The play of older children can often increase their understanding of the subject-matter areas.

involving building or making something. They like to punch holes with the hole puncher, but they also like to glue the cutouts on a piece of paper to create a design or greeting card. Children may begin their play with the goal of constructing a boat or an airplane. Unlike threes and fours, who just move the materials around, fives and sixes like to have their play result in products.

Games with rules become more important in the play of early primary students. They may believe that the rules are made by some unknown authority and are usually very rigid in enforcing them. Children of this age cannot adapt rules to account for present conditions, such as the number of cards each person gets when playing with different numbers of players. They need adult help in learning to apply and understand rules.

Middle Childhood

Sevens and eights still enjoy constructive play with LEGOs and other construction materials, although they usually play less with blocks than younger children. Less construction play may be observed simply because children have less access to construction materials in the classroom.

Practice play becomes more cognitive as children learn to use their literacy skills to create stories and learn information. Sociodramatic play tends to disappear and be replaced with creative drama, such as acting out stories or scenes. Children in middle childhood may act out historical scenes or create dramas to help them understand scientific facts, such as the molecular behavior of gases, solids, and liquids.

Games with rules dominate the play of sevens and eights. Board games, computer games, and athletic games, such as soccer and baseball, become important parts of the play experience. Children of this age can apply the rules of games more flexibly and can integrate their growing cognitive knowledge and social abilities more easily.

AN **Expert** SPEAKS: Play at School

Jim Johnson, Pennsylvania State University

Play has a privileged status in early childhood education (ECE). Indeed, some view play as the "gasoline" needed to get the "engine" of developmentally appropriate curriculum and teaching for young children "all revved up"! Before you step on the accelerator, however, please consider the following precautions.

ECE teachers need to take care to distinguish play from other behaviors that are related to play—but that are not play itself. Consider the difference between play and exploration and the difference between play and imitation. Exploring and playing often go hand in hand. Sometimes you see a child engaged in exploratory play, sometimes in playful exploration. A well-known pattern is the so-called "examine, reexamine, transform (play) cycle." First, a child explores a new object or situation in a general way, then in more specific ways, and then finally begins to act on or change the object to make something different. For example, a child approaches a new puzzle, checking the pieces and board to see how they look and feel, and then investigates particular pieces and the relations among them. Only then will the child begin to engage in the constructive play of putting the puzzle together, or maybe even turning the pieces over and pretending they are something else all together. In either case, playing (What can I do with this?) follows exploring (What is this?).

Imitating and playing are also distinguishable and serve different purposes. A child can playfully imitate another, as in a lighthearted game of copycat. At other times, the child imitates a model, not in a playful way but in earnest, as a way to learn how to do or say something new. In general, quality playing is transformative and generative of new learning or realizations and emanates from within the child acting on and assimilating experiences, whereas imitation is accommodation to ex-ternal stimulation in order to learn something new or to practice or to repeat what is already known.

Children learn by playing, by exploring, and by imitating, yet the processes and purposes of playing, exploring, and imitating differ. It does not help to lump them all together. If you do, you run the risk of stretching the meaning of play and giving too much credit or blame to play.

Sometimes you hear early educators referring to simplistic slogans such as "Play is the business of childhood" and "Play is the child's way of learning." The teachers voicing them are perhaps unaware of the important conceptual distinctions noted above. Inadvertently, these teachers are inviting those who are opposed to play in education (and who prefer a nonplay traditional didactic approach) to dismiss the case for the use of play on the grounds that the idea seems too broad and vague to be a valid basis for ECE. Many of these play opponents are already convinced, based on seeing too many low-level, unchallenging activities called "play" occur in ECE settings.

Except for pretend play and group games, behaviors at school should be called "activities." Perhaps restricting the use of the word *play* in this way is too radical, that ECE as a profession is not ready for this yet—and maybe never will be or should be. Perhaps it is sufficient to always use the adjective *educational* in front of the word *play,* assuming this expression is only used to refer to high-quality activities. As a way of putting this idea across, please remember that developmentally appropriate and enhancing practices in ECE are not based on low- or even medium-grade but on high-grade, superpremium "educational play gasoline"!

Before reading the following section on play in school, consider what Jim Johnson says in the An Expert Speaks box. Should it be called *play* or *activities* in school? Try to answer that question for yourself.

Play in School Settings

Play at school usually differs from play at home in several ways. Generally, there are larger numbers of children in play groups at school than in play groups at home. The materials at school are often different from those at home; only a few children will have access to unit blocks or easels for painting at home. Toys and play materials also differ in the degree to which they must be shared. In a large group, children must learn to work cooperatively with others.

Some of the differences between play at home and play at school are summarized in Table 5.2. Thinking of play at home and at school along these dimensions will also help teachers explain to parents why play at school is necessary and not a duplication of children's play at home.

Play is often more restricted at school than at home. Play activities at school tend to be more guided and more closely observed. Teachers are more likely to plan specific ways of enhancing play than are most parents. For example, if the teacher observes a group of children attempting to build a space rocket, he may collect materials from around the room, such as boxes or paints, that will assist the children in achieving their goal. He may also find books in the library, pictures of spacecraft, or websites or videotapes to extend the play to other activities.

Teachers will select play experiences that match the goals of their programs. If program goals emphasize discovery, then free play is most appropriate. If objectives require children to explore concepts, then guided play is most appropriate. Finally, directed play experiences are best if the teacher wants children to demonstrate specific skills.

In learning concepts about sound, a child in a free-play situation might discover that he can produce sound by striking a surface. The alert teacher would help the child verbalize his discovery and continue to explore sounds, if he still showed interest. Guided play would be appropriate for teaching children the concept that the pitch of sound varies with the length and size of the string that is vibrated. The teacher might display cigar boxes with rubber bands of various lengths and thicknesses stretched over them. Whenever

TABLE 5.2 Differences between Play at Home and at School

	HOME	SCHOOL
Peers	Mixed ages Self-selected	Age peers Selection within the group
Group Size	Alone or small group	Large group
Materials and Equipment	Restricted by expense, space, messiness	Larger selection Less restricted
Guidance and Supervision	Often focused on safety	Guides development of specific concepts Models play behaviors Questions about learning
Adult–Child Interactions	Purchases materials Listens to child's requests Attends to safety issues	Facilitates play Interacts with individual children Determines child's goals
Time Commitments	Must fit family schedule Shorter periods	Regularly scheduled time Longer periods
Planning	Guided by family budget "Go play" is common direction	Choices of materials, equipment Evaluation of experience
Space	Typical bedroom, family room, or living room space	Larger spaces for blocks, climbing, etc.

Source: Jo Ann Brewer and Judith Kieff, "Fostering Mutual Respect for Play at Home and School," *Childhood Education* 73 (February 1996/1997): 95.

a child expressed interest in these materials, he would be encouraged to discover the differences in sounds produced by the various rubber bands. In directed play, the teacher might have the children listen to sounds produced by various instruments and indicate with hand movements the changes in pitch.

Van Hoorn et al. (1993) describe play at school as instrumental or illicit. **Instrumental play** is that which the teacher plans and encourages, such as the sociodramatic scenarios of playing "hospital" and "shoe store," described earlier. **Illicit play** is not sanctioned and may even be expressly forbidden by the teacher. Examples of illicit play include children creating guns from Tinkertoys or passing secret notes behind the teacher's back. Although such play may make the teacher uncomfortable, Sutton-Smith (1988) reminds us that it also contributes to a child's developing social skills.

Should illicit play be banned from early childhood classrooms? There are no clear-cut answers to this question. Teachers who try to ban "war" play or "superhero" play realize that children find ways to engage in these activities anyway. It tends to go underground but not stop. The teacher then loses any opportunity to influence children's ideas about violence and how to manage power in a social community (Boyd 1997). The result is more tension and management problems. On the other hand, some educators believe that "war" play stimulates children to believe that violence is an acceptable means of solving problems. "Sociopoliticalists argue that war play and war toys glamorize fighting and killing, promote excessive materialism, and foster unnecessary aggression" (Isenberg and Jalongo 1993, p. 246).

Some teachers recommend redirecting "war" play or "superhero" play to focus on the positive things that soldiers or heroes can do, such as saving people who are trapped by natural disasters and building hospitals to help people who are hurt. Teachers must also help children learn to solve their everyday conflicts peacefully (Levin 2003; Rogers and Sharapan 1991). Parents should be involved in making decisions about how to handle "war" toys and

DEVELOPMENTALLY APPROPRIATE PRACTICE

Reflect on the importance of play in a developmentally appropriate classroom:

- How does play contribute to a developmentally appropriate program?

- Would it be possible to have a DAP classroom without play? Why?

- Would it be possible to have a play session that was not developmentally appropriate? Why?

- If play is important in developmentally appropriate practice, what are the most effective means of facilitating it?

- Does all play contribute to DAP? What about rough-and-tumble play? Solitary play? Explain your answers.

- What aspects of play that are developmentally appropriate for eight-year-olds would not be appropriate for four-year-olds? Why?

other types of violent play in the classroom so that teachers will have their understanding and support.

Roles of the Teacher

The roles of the teacher in play within the classroom setting are very important. The teacher must be an observer, an elaborator, a model, an evaluator, and a planner of play (Bjorkland 1978).

Observer

In *observing*, the teacher should watch children's interactions with other children and with objects. He should observe the length of time that children can maintain play episodes, and he should look for any children who have trouble playing or joining play groups. These observations should then be used in planning additional play experiences, in making decisions about whether to enter play situations, and in making assessments of the play of individual children. In a review of studies concerning the effects of the physical environment on children's behavior in preschool settings, Phyfe-Perkins (1980) concludes that if a setting is to provide support for developmentally appropriate activities, the teacher must engage in systematic observation of children at play.

Elaborator

Another aspect of the teacher's role is that of *elaborator*. If the children are playing "going to the hairdresser," the teacher might help them collect items that could be used to represent those found at a hairdresser's shop. She might find photographs or magazine illustrations that would help the children construct a beauty salon. The teacher might even join in the play briefly and ask questions that would guide the children in thinking through their roles or their conceptions of a trip to the hairdresser. If older children were involved in a study of insects, the teacher might supply a film or videotape of insects so that the children could recreate insect movement or sounds in their play.

Modeler

NAEYC CRITERIA
1.20, 1.21

Teachers who value play are often *modelers* of appropriate behaviors in play situations. For instance, a teacher may choose to sit in the blocks area for a brief time and join children in building in order to model ways in which the blocks might be used. Or he might choose to join dramatic play in order to model behaviors that are useful in entering a play group and responses that are useful for helping play continue.

Sometimes, the teacher might model play behaviors that will get a play episode started or back on track if it has gone in a direction he considers negative. For example, children playing characters from a television program might begin to chase and catch one another rather aimlessly. The teacher might ask some questions about the purposes of the characters and demonstrate how they might handle interactions without running and chasing inside the room.

Evaluator

As an *evaluator* of play, the teacher has to be a careful observer and diagnostician to determine how different play incidents serve the needs of individual children and what learning is taking place as children participate in play. It is the teacher's job to recognize the academic, social, cognitive, and physical growth that takes place during play and to be able to communicate these changes to parents and administrators. Evaluation means that materials, environments, and activities must be carefully considered in light of the curriculum goals, and changes must be made if needed.

Planner

Finally, the teacher has to serve as a *planner.* Planning involves all the learning that results from observing, elaborating, and evaluating. The teacher must plan for new experiences that will encourage or extend children's interests.

For example, a parent who was a shoe clerk could come to the classroom to share her occupation. She might measure the children's feet and demonstrate that part of her job is to show the customers several choices of shoes in the proper sizes and to help them try on shoes. In planning to continue the children's obvious interest, the teacher might do several things: gather a collection of many kinds of shoes, find a rack suitable for storing them, borrow several of the instruments used for measuring feet, and so on. The teacher's careful planning will result in days of active play involvement by the children as they arrange chairs to make a shoe store, write up sales, and bag shoes to send home with the "customers." The teacher can encourage the children to talk about the different kinds of shoes and who wears them, to draw shoes, to create signs for their shoe store, and even to write stories about shoes. When the children tire of the shoes and no longer demonstrate interest in playing with them, the shoes should be removed. By that time, the teacher will have already planned other experiences that will pique the interest of the children and can be extended in play (Ford 1993).

Parents and Play

- Invite parents to observe a play time at school. Provide a guide sheet that will encourage parents to look for those academic skills being learned in play. For example, list classification, grouping, seriating, analyzing, and so on to help parents notice these skills. On the back of the sheet, you might describe examples of these skills in housekeeping play, block play, and other play areas. The guide sheet might also list social skills, such as sharing, turn taking, cooperating, and others.

In planning for play that contributes to development, teachers should consider the following guidelines:

1. Make sure children have sufficient time for play.
2. Help children plan their play.
3. Monitor the progress of play.
4. Choose appropriate props and toys.
5. Provide themes that can be extended from one day to the next.
6. Coach individuals who need help.
7. Suggest or model how themes can be woven together.
8. Model appropriate ways to solve disputes. (Bodrova and Leong 1996, p. 132)

Play in Primary Classrooms

Most teachers are aware that play is much more acceptable in classrooms of preschoolers and kindergartners than it is in classrooms of primary-grade children. The expectation that only serious learning should take place in to make discoveries about the relationships among the block shapes and sizes and about the physics of stacking blocks. These children can experience the aesthetic pleasure of the feel of blocks and the symmetry of their constructions.

Children playing with sand and water are free to explore the properties of the materials and to learn how the materials respond under different conditions. They are in charge of the outcomes and derive satisfaction from playing to meet their own goals. Sand and water allow for individual experimentation and also group interactions. Children using sand and water establish their own goals and feel satisfaction when those goals are met.

Materials that allow children to make play choices and allow multiple outcomes are necessary for the best play environments. Many materials can be considered open ended if it is possible for children to use them in different ways. For example, teachers might supply rollers, boxes, balls, and targets that will help children develop concepts in physical science (Kamii and DeVries 1978). These materials are open ended to the extent that children have choices in exploring the arrangements and outcomes that can be achieved with them. Many commercial materials, on the other hand, are limited in terms of what children are able to do with them, providing only one or two options. When dollars for purchasing materials are limited, open-ended materials are the best investment.

Play as a Teaching Strategy

Teachers have choices when deciding how to present new information or concepts to children. Some information must be presented in a teacher-directed format. For example, safety rules, such as those about fire, cannot be explored; they must be stated firmly. But generally speaking, *telling* is the least successful strategy for presenting information to young children. Even young children can repeat words or phrases, but verbal responses only indicate that they have learned the words; such responses do not measure children's understanding at all.

Play is one of the **teaching strategies** available to teachers as they plan for children's learning. The following examples illustrate goals that could readily be achieved through play:

- To encourage children to learn about appropriate clothes for the weather, provide many different pieces of clothing in the dress-up area.

- To encourage children to learn how to create secondary colors, provide paints in primary colors.

- To encourage children to demonstrate the ability to classify, provide leaves, shells, keys, buttons, and models of farm and zoo animals.

- To encourage children to learn the characteristics of three-dimensional shapes, provide the shapes in boxes, geoblocks, and regular building blocks.

- To encourage children to learn about water erosion on landforms, provide water in containers (so that the flow can be varied) in the sandbox or gardening area.

www.
www.usask.ca/education/
coursework/mcvittiej/
methods/play.html

An explanation of the teaching strategy play–debrief–play and how to implement it in the classroom

PRAXIS

Be able to describe how play can be used as a teaching strategy to teach specific concepts

NAEYC CRITERIA
3.16

Using play experiences as teaching strategies requires that the teacher observe how children use materials and that he ask questions to guide children's thinking and reflections. As Sutton-Smith (1986) reminds us,

> Although we use play in various ways in the classroom for our own purposes, we need to remember that the children have purposes of their own, and need to deal with purposes largely by themselves (even if under distant supervision), making use of this vital and universal kind of communication [play]. (p. 13)

Teachers can make plans for play experiences, but children's needs must be honored and they must be allowed to use play for their own learning. In other words,

> Play, then, offers the child the opportunity to make sense out of the world by using available tools. Understanding is created by doing, by doing with others, and by being completely involved in that doing. Through play, the child comes to understand the world and the adult comes to understand the child. (Chaille and Silvern 1996, p. 277)

Vygotsky's belief that representational play includes rules for behavior is obvious even to untrained observers when they watch children who assign or accept roles and are then chastised if they fail to behave according to those roles. For example, the child playing "dog" cannot go to work nor can the "baby" watch television. As summarized by Berk,

> From this perspective, the fantasy play of the preschool years is essential for further development of play in middle childhood—specifically, for movement toward game play, which provides additional instruction in setting goals, regulating one's behavior in pursuit of those goals, and subordinating action to rules rather than impulse—in short, for becoming a cooperative and productive member of society. Play, in Vygotsky's theory, is the preeminent educational activity of early childhood. (1994, p. 33)

Teachers have many opportunities to plan environments and materials so that learning goals can be achieved in playful activities. Observations of children at play will guide teachers in choosing other play materials that will help children learn concepts and clarify and extend their understandings.

Selecting guided play as a teaching strategy does not imply that play is assigned; it means that careful thought is put into the selection of materials and intervention in children's play. A teacher might put out an assortment of materials that she expects will invite children to explore a new concept. If children do not learn the concept from interacting with the materials, then the teacher must choose other materials or select a different approach. Assigning a child to complete a task means that he no longer has a choice and that the teacher has chosen a strategy other than play.

Cooper and Dever (2001) found that sociodramatic play was an excellent vehicle for integrating the curriculum. They asked children to choose a theme for the dramatic play area and then used that theme to engage children in writing, oral language development, mathematics, and other content areas. Through their work, the children developed and enjoyed the selected theme.

Thus, teachers must be thoughtful when intervening in children's play and avoid trying to force their own agendas on the children. For example,

Teaching Discrimination of Plane Geometric Shapes to Prekindergarten and Kindergarten Children

Framework Goals: Name, describe, sort, and draw simple two-dimensional shapes.

Objectives: When presented with a collection of plane geometric shapes, children will be able to discriminate among the shapes. (Some children may be able to name the shapes.)

Procedure:

1. Arrange a collection of plane geometric shapes of many colors in a box on a low table.
2. As children play with the shapes, many will naturally sort them in some way. If the children sort them by color, ask if there is another way to sort them. You may need to show children an example of two shapes that are the same shape but different colors.
3. If children sort the shapes by shape, help them to describe the shapes (three sides, four equal sides, a circle, etc.).
4. Add other colors and sizes of shapes as children become more skillful in their sorting and describing. (Be sure to add triangles that are not equilateral triangles.)
5. Add plane shapes to other play areas, such as the blocks area, the dramatic play area (pizzas, square plates, rectangular trays, and so on), the music area (triangles, tambourines, drums, etc.), and the art area (sponges cut in shapes for printing).

the teacher can begin to play with a small group and propose a theme for the play, but the children must be allowed to reject that theme or convert it to one following their own interests. The teacher can also assume a role in sociodramatic play, such as the "neighbor coming over for lunch," but such an intervention must be done carefully. Moreover, the teacher will need to think about how to leave the play so that the children can continue on their own (Ward 1996).

Communicating the Benefits of Play

Teachers have an obligation to explain to parents and administrators the benefits of the time children spend playing during the schoolday. Teachers are and should be accountable for children's learning. Part of that responsibility is to be able to provide specific information about individual children and their play experiences. The following section applies specifically to assessment of play; a more comprehensive discussion of assessment is included in Chapter 7.

One form of data to be shared is the *anecdotal record*. With this type of record keeping, the teacher or another adult records the child's behavior and verbalizations for a brief period of time. Judgments about the child's intentions or motivations should be clearly labeled as such in the record and distinguished from descriptions of the child's overt behaviors. At the end of the day, these notes are placed in the child's file. Over a period of time, the notes should reveal some patterns that will help the teacher talk to others about the child's growth through play.

For example, the teacher might have noted that Jennifer played alone with the blocks and made horizontal patterns with them. A few weeks later, an observer might note that Jennifer had started to use vertical patterns along with the horizontal ones. Later, Jennifer might be seen building a vertical structure with a friend. Still later, she might build a vertical and symmetrical structure. An observer might note that Jennifer had talked about her building before she began the construction and completed a structure that matched her plans. These records would clearly reveal

Jennifer's growth in building more complex structures and in planning her activities.

Another technique for recording play is to record where the children are in the classroom at given time intervals. For example, every ten minutes, the teacher or an adult records on a grid which children are playing with blocks, in dramatic play, in art, or in reading. Over time, these *time–activity records* will reveal children's patterns of choice and, in combination with anecdotal records, will be useful in planning other activities. Figure 5.1 is an example of such a record.

A third technique is to keep several *checklists* scattered throughout the room. As an adult observes a child engaged in particular behavior, he notes it on the record. For example, the following behaviors might be listed across the top of the form: "Completes puzzles with 10 pieces," "Strings beads in a pattern," "Plays cooperatively with at least 2 others," and so on. The children's names are listed down the side of the form. Whenever a child is observed completing a puzzle with ten pieces, the date is recorded on the form. Such records are helpful because they offer flexibility in selecting what to look for in observations and make it quick and easy to record information. Figure 5.2 is an example of such a record.

Finally, teachers can keep samples of products from some play activities. Selected paintings, for instance, can be kept in a file for comparison with previous artwork. Obviously, it is impossible to keep samples of block constructions or sand play. Some results of these activities can be recorded in photographs, but most will have to be described in anecdotal records. As children talk about their experiences each day, the teacher can record some of the students' own evaluations. The teacher will also want to

FIGURE 5.1

Sample of Time–Activity Record

Date _____ 4/17 _____

	9:00	9:10	9:20
Unit Blocks	Sara Carlos Hillary Jason	Sara Hillary Brian Michael	Sara Michael Brad Gretchen
Easels	Cheri Karen Phil Juanita	Dolores Cheri Juanita Jason	
Clay			
Dress-up			

FIGURE 5.2

Sample Record of Behavior

	Completes puzzles with 10 pieces	Strings beads in a pattern	Plays cooperatively with at least 2 others	
Geoffrey				
Judith				
Leslie				
Michael				

add to each child's file her own insights and interpretations of the child's play.

Before a teacher can share what children are learning in play experiences, he must be actively involved while the children are playing. If the teacher is busy doing other tasks while the children are playing, he will miss chances for observations and insights. We cannot share what we haven't seen or heard; therefore, play time is a very busy time for the teacher of young children.

Megbe Hughes, a preschool teacher, discusses her assessment of play in the following A Teacher Speaks box. She uses photographs and videotaping as well as anecdotal records, such as those just recommended. Think about other ways that play in the classroom might be assessed to help parents understand its value.

Play and Academic Learning

Sometimes observers of young children think that children will not learn academic skills if they spend their time playing. The truth is that play contributes to the development of academic ability. Children who are ordering objects by length or size in free-play situations, learning rhymes and chants in directed play, or exploring rhythms or constructing with LEGOs in guided play are all involved in activities that contribute to reading ability.

Reading is a complex process that involves eye coordination, visual and auditory discrimination, and the cognitive ability to work with parts of wholes. Play is an important means of developing such abilities. Collier (1983) found that play assists the development of representational skills and the formation of the symbolic foundations that are necessary for reading.

**www.kidsource.com/kidsource/
content5/studies.play.html**

The paper "Academic Studies and Play on a Collision Course and Play Is Losing," which describes a survey that revealed parents' attitudes about play were mixed (at best) and suggests that parents need to support play

**www.edu-cyberpg.com/
Literacy/play.asp**

Play's the Thing is the title of this site, which provides quotes, essays, and links to other sites in support of play

Megbe Hughes
Isidore Newman School
New Orleans, Louisiana

Respecting the complexity, value, and form in children's play takes much more from adults than just making time in the daily schedule for play to take place. Respecting children's play implies that we, as teachers, do not know all of the answers and that children can be counted on for some of these answers. Respect also implies children's right to privacy.

> It is true that if we are interested in children we must look to them and listen to them as a matter of course. And as we pay attention to their play, we must never violate its complexity by presuming to "decode" or oversimplify it. (Koste 1987, p. 44)

In my pre-K classroom, children learn by playing. Watching four- and five-year-olds play allows me to expand on their interests, their knowledge, and their play. Watching children play on the playground and providing them with different balls, bats, and/or building tools enables me to facilitate learning and enables the children to build new knowledge on their existing knowledge. Watching children interact in the dramatic play center and providing new and different props allows me to extend students' language and play without "telling" them what to do. Being the audience in a library corner as children act out their favorite story using puppets, costumes, or flannelboard pieces allows children to demonstrate their knowledge in a playful manner and gives me the opportunity to talk with them about the story. Paying attention to my students, their individual interests, and their varied skills allows me to build on what they know in supportive ways, fostering a love of learning in every student.

Assessing children's play by observing, taking anecdotal records, videotaping, and taking photographs allows me to give parents accurate information about the nature of their children's play and opportunities to extend play in my classroom. I observe my students interacting with each other and often initiate games with them; then I back away and observe them continue to play these games. I take anecdotal records daily on computer labels that I can file in each child's folder. This enables me to look at each child every day and compile an ongoing record of the child's play behaviors. Using videotapes and photographs is the best way that I have found to bring the classroom home. Parents enjoy seeing their children in action, and often these forms of assessment provide insight into how much learning is accomplished through play. Assessment is key when it comes to helping parents value play as an avenue for learning in the classroom.

I feel that we must respect our children's play and trust them to learn from their play. I see it as my job as a pre-K teacher to show parents how important play is to their children, and the most effective way to do this is through sharing my observations and talking with parents about what their child is learning as he or she is playing.

The following list provides only a few examples of the many kinds of academic learning that children develop during play:

NAEYC CRITERIA
3.45, 3.58, 3.68

Language Arts

- Develop oral language abilities (vocabulary, language in different situations such as arguing and explaining, and imaginative language)
- Develop visual discrimination skills as they sort, compare, classify
- Develop auditory discrimination skills as they listen to others, explore sounds produced by different materials, and engage in musical play
- Create stories for puppets, create signs to use in their play, and make books related to their play
- Take the perspectives of others
- Develop the fine motor skills needed for writing through painting, drawing, cutting, shaping clay, building with LEGOs, and assembling puzzles

- Write as part of the play experience as they take orders at the restaurant, fill out a patient information form at the doctor's office, make signs for their buildings, and so on

PRAXIS

Be able to use discovery as a teaching strategy for a specific concept

Science

- Develop the science skills of observing, making predictions, gathering data, and testing hypotheses
- Learn physics as they build with blocks and learn about stress, mass, and weight
- Learn about simple machines as they experiment with ramps, levers, and gears
- Learn earth science as they play in the sand and observe the weather
- Learn biology as they observe classroom animals and their life cycles
- Learn chemistry as they observe the mixing of materials in a solution, the effect of salt on ice, and the results of the application of heat to various compounds
- Investigate the various consistencies of paint and the results of using these on different kinds of paper with different brushes or painting techniques

Mathematics

- Learn about equal lengths, open and closed spaces, topography, and solid geometric shapes as they play with blocks
- Learn about set theory as they group, sort, and classify
- Learn to compare sets, develop one-to-one correspondence, and solve problems using mathematics (such as counting the pieces needed for each child to play a game)

Primary-age children engaged in project work can be involved in play experiences that will help them consolidate their learning and explore possibilities in given topics. Children learning about seeds can sort, group, and classify seeds; pretend to be sprouting seeds; create board games with facts about seeds; create models of seeds from clay or other materials; paint seeds; use seeds in counting and other mathematics activities; and so forth. Play should not be limited to the preschool years, as it is also an important tool for teaching children in the primary grades (Stone 1995/1996).

In planning for play experiences that enhance the curriculum, teachers must be careful to make play available, not to assign experiences that they perceive as playful. Many playful experiences can be offered that correspond with themes of instruction, such as sorting rocks to accompany a theme of *rocks* (Stone 1995/1996). If such an experience is provided as a choice and children choose to participate, it is play; however, if the teacher assigns the task, it is not play. As mentioned earlier, one of the criteria for determining whether an activity is play is the element of choice. If choice is not present, then by definition the activity is not play.

Children understand this. Consider how often children classify what they do at school as "play" or "work." The usual definition is that *work* is something assigned by the teacher, although older children may say it was *play* if it was fun (Perlmutter and Burrell 1995).

Outdoor Play

Outdoor play offers children many opportunities to solve intellectual problems, such as how to make the water flow down the rows in the garden, and also how to solve social and emotional problems. Children on the playground have many opportunities to problem solve ways to move from one place to another, ways to use various materials, and ways to help other children achieve their goals (Rivkin 2001). Children playing outdoors often have more freedom than is typical of indoor play.

Many teachers have observed that leadership in play activities is more readily observable outdoors than in the small-group play in a classroom. Thompson, Knudson, and Wilson (1997) found that recess provided for social growth. They held group meetings to help children learn to solve problems, to interact more successfully with their peers, and to negotiate with their classmates more successfully. Even though some schools have reduced or eliminated recess, teachers of young children should remind administrators that it is not developmentally appropriate to do so and should provide them with good reasons why children need to play outdoors. (Refer back to An Expert Speaks on page 153 to review the importance of play at school.)

In order to be productive, outdoor play needs the planning, observation, and evaluation accorded to indoor play. Outdoor play may offer benefits that are not available in the classroom, such as large muscle activities and less teacher control of shouting, running, jumping, rolling, and climbing. These activities can be encouraged outdoors where the children will be safe and other children will not be in danger, as they might be indoors. Theemes (1999) describes the benefits of outdoor play as "contact with nature, opportunities for social play, and freedom of movement and active physical play" (p. 4).

Many indoor activities can be taken outdoors, given the right materials. For example, children might set up easels and paint pictures outdoors, or they might use water to "paint" buildings and sidewalks, using big brushes that encourage large, sweeping strokes. Children might enjoy block building outdoors when provided with large plastic or weatherproof blocks, ramps, ladders, and other equipment. Such materials lend themselves to building structures that are large enough for children to get inside.

Although teachers of young children often discourage or forbid rough-and-tumble play because they believe it turns into negative or aggressive behavior, research reveals that such play is age related. Specifically, the incidence of rough-and-tumble play increases as children move from preschool into kindergarten and the primary years and then decreases as children reach middle childhood (Kostelnik et al. 1993). Other research shows that children who are typically rejected by their peers are more likely to misinterpret rough-and-tumble play and to participate aggressively.

Popular children, on the other hand, are more likely to participate in a playful, unaggressive manner (Pellegrini and Boyd 1993). In a recent study, Smith, Smees, and Pellegrini (2004) found that children from about age five

> Playgrounds—facilitating environments—afford a viable alternative for TV and boredom and a major vehicle for learning.
>
> —Joe Frost

Parents and Play

● Provide parents with information about the importance of outdoor play, and ask them to help you make sure that recess and other outdoor play times are not reduced or eliminated in your school.

and up could identify which play episodes were play fighting and which were real fighting when shown videotapes of the episodes.

Even though children may know the difference between these types of encounters, teachers must help them stop the play if it turns into real fighting. Teachers should be aware that rough-and-tumble play is developmental in children's play lives. When such play becomes aggressive, teachers should intervene and help children modify inappropriate behavior (Bergen 1994; Carlsson-Paige and Levin 1995).

Ideally, children should be able to play either indoors or out. However, lack of supervision and the fact that few schools have outdoor play areas connected to classrooms make such choices difficult.

www.

http://kcsos.kern.org/cccc/ stories/storyReader$830

The article "Helping Special Children Learn through Play," along with links to a resource library and guidelines for choosing toys for special-needs children

CHILDREN WITH SPECIAL NEEDS

To plan play experiences for children with special needs, teachers must think about the developmental levels of individual children and make play available that matches those levels.

Typically developing children learn to play in cooperative ways beginning at about age three. Children who are not developing typically may need more time to play in solitary play and then be helped to move into cooperative play with one child. Murata and Maeda (2002) suggest that teachers should think about using structured play for children with developmental delays as a way of helping them gain useful skills. Their recommendations include:

Arrange the environment to engage preschoolers into various motor activities.
Allow preschoolers to explore and engage the physical activity through guided discovery.
Allow preschoolers with and without developmental delays to interact.
Change the environment to promote generalization. (p. 239)

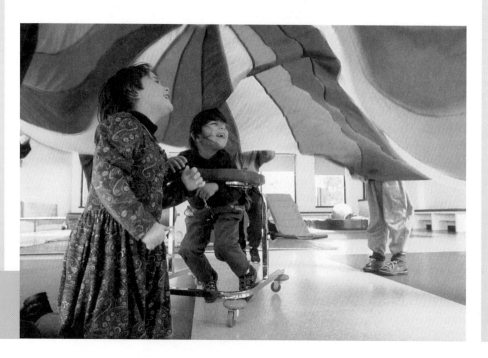

Play experiences must be carefully planned to meet the special needs of all children.

All children can benefit when teachers provide appropriate materials and encourage children to explore what they can do with their bodies. As with any other children, teachers need to think about children with special needs in terms of their individual needs. Special-needs children vary as much as do typically developing children.

Figure 5.3 is a list of possible adaptations that might be needed for children with special needs in the outdoor play area.

FIGURE 5.3

Adaptations for Children with Special Needs

POSSIBLE ADAPTATIONS

. . . for the child who is blind or has low vision

- Orient the child to the major playground features (e.g., the walkway, climbing equipment, water table, sandbox, garden, and fence) that can be used as points of reference. Take a tour of the playground. With adult supervision, a sighted friend can assist the child by offering her arm/elbow to guide the child who is blind.

- Describe what is happening in different areas to help the child who is blind find her friends and join in their play. When the child enters the playground, tell her which children are playing on the climbing structure, which are in the sandbox, and which are gardening or playing on riding toys.

- Use the child's name when verbally directing activities, as he will not be able to see a physical gesture such as pointing.

- Make certain the walking space is free from toys left unattended or other potential falling hazards.

- Mark the location of different outdoor areas or structures with audible cues. Different types of wind chimes or bells can help a child locate a particular area. For example, hang a wind chime from a tree branch above the sandbox. At first, physically assist the child to move into a desired area. Gradually decrease physical assistance and use verbal prompts to direct the child.

- Place toys underneath the child's hands to encourage exploration rather than pulling the child's hands forward to touch or hold the toys.

- Provide outdoor toys that use the senses of hearing, touch, smell, and movement and encourage activities that other children enjoy. Toys that address the sense of hearing are balls that beep or have noisemakers inside. Toys and materials that promote exploration through touch are those with interesting textures such as Koosh balls and bumpy balls. Smell can be incorporated into many materials by adding extracts/flavorings to paints and water. Movement can be experienced through swinging. Additional support to ensure safety and comfort may include the use of an adaptive swing.

. . . for the child who is deaf or has hearing loss

- Obtain a child's attention through touch or gestures before giving a direction.

- Make sure the child can see your face and your lips with no shadows obscuring them when giving directions. Be sure the child who is deaf and the other children are positioned so that their faces and gestures can be easily seen by one another.

- Use gestures, prompts, and visual cues to communicate information. Gestures may include pointing and sign language. Prompts may include physically assisting. Visual cues may include the use of concrete materials and modeling (e.g., demonstrating digging with a shovel in the garden).

- Learn basic signs and teach them to the other children if sign language is the child's mode of communication.

- Make sure that the child can see most areas of the playground from any given spot. Remove extraneous walls, fences, or hedges that might block her view of the other children's play and further isolate her.

- Provide outdoor toys and materials that use the other senses available to the child, including touch, smell, and movement, and encourage activities that other children enjoy.

. . . for the child who has physical challenges

- Position a child with physical challenges so that he can achieve maximum range of motion, muscle control, and visual contact with materials and other children. A child may need to lie on his side or use a bolster to access materials and interact with other children during activities such as gardening and painting.

- Furnish specifically adapted play and recreation equipment when necessary. This may include modified swings, tricycles, and tables for independent participation in activities.

- Encourage the child to use her own means of getting around—whether a wheelchair, walker, or scooter—

(continued)

FIGURE 5.3

Continued

to participate in the activities and games of the other children.

- Provide activities for the lower body and feet, such as foot painting, splashing in a wading pool, digging in the garden or sand, and kicking a ball, for a child with limited use of his hands and upper body.

- Provide activities including painting, water table, sandbox, and gardening that a child with limited use of her feet, legs, and lower body can do independently and successfully with her upper body. Always ensure correct positioning of the child's torso.

- Increase the width of balance beams and modify slippery surfaces to support better balance.

- Use softer balls (e.g., foam balls) or lightweight objects to facilitate throwing and catching when a child lacks strength and endurance.

- Use large balls (e.g., beach balls) and other large objects to make catching easier for a child who is unable to grasp smaller objects.

. . . for the child who has autism spectrum disorder

- Be aware of situations and events, such as inconsistent and unstructured environments, new situations, overstimulation, and internal changes including illness or extreme fatigue, that may trigger undesired behaviors.

- Make sure the child is aware of playground modifications prior to experiencing the change. For example, if a flat-bottomed swing is removed from the swinging tree and a tire is put in its place, tell the child ahead of time about the change. Show her a picture of the new swing and describe it before going out onto the playground. If the child is willing, accompany her to the new swing and allow her to touch it, push it, and perhaps take a turn at swinging on it.

- Limit the number of outside rules, communicate them clearly and in multiple ways, and enforce them firmly, kindly, and consistently.

- Provide extra support during new or difficult tasks and break playground activities into simple, sequential steps.

- Increase predictability and consistency in outside routines and prepare the child for what comes next through verbal and concrete prompts. For example, put a ball in a child's hand to indicate it is time to go outside while simultaneously using words to describe the next change. When it is time to transition inside, ring a bell on the playground, tell the child it is time to go inside, and put an inside toy in his hands to carry.

- Include repetition and modeling when giving directions to children who have difficulty with perception and sensory input.

- Provide structured activities that are away from distractions for children who have difficulty paying attention or controlling bodily movements.

- Organize sections of the playground that provide physical boundaries for the child. These may include a tunnel, large barrel, tent, or huge cardboard box made into a playhouse.

- Include pets in the outside play area. Some children may interact with pets before they will interact with people. Including pets in the outside play area allows children to touch the animals, feed and water them, clean their cages, and be responsible for their welfare.

. . . for the child who has cognitive delays

- Keep vocabulary at the child's level and keep sentence structure simple.

- Remind the child of the various types of play activities available and offer choices rather than determining places for the child to play.

- Adapt materials or vary the difficulty of an activity so that the child can succeed. For example, modify or shorten an obstacle course to encourage independent, successful completion.

- Lead the children in noncompetitive games so that the child can feel successful and enjoy her individual achievements.

- Reduce the number of concepts presented at one time.

- Use repetition and examples to explain an idea.

- Teachers, family members, and other team members should determine the most appropriate modifications for each child. . . . Not all activities require modifications. Adaptations are used only when necessary to support the child's optimal level of outside play.

Source: Linda L. Flynn and Judith Kieff, "Including *Everyone* in Outdoor Play," *Young Children* 57 (May 2002): 20–26. Reprinted with permission from the National Association for the Education of Young Children.

CELEBRATING DIVERSITY

Play is a part of every culture, but there are cultural variations in how children participate in play and at what ages they are expected to play in certain ways. Some families may believe that play is not appropriate at school; therefore, their children may play in less complex ways (Kieff and Casbergue 2000). Other children may not recognize the play materials offered if they have no experience with the materials or the materials are arranged in new ways.

Researchers suggest that the themes of dramatic or pretend play vary by culture. For example, Farver and Shin (1997) found that Korean American children played more everyday activities compared to European American children, who played more fantasy and suspected danger in the environment. The Korean American children also used more polite requests and fewer commands than their European American playmates.

Teachers should think about providing culturally appropriate play materials, such as dress-up clothing, musical instruments, and household items. According to Retting (2002), "One of the most natural ways of promoting cultural awareness among young children is through the use of play. In fact, throughout history and across cultures, play is a way in which societies communicate cultural values to children in both direct and indirect play" (p. 198).

Teachers should encourage parents to share the common play materials of their native countries and of their own childhoods. If these materials need to be demonstrated, then it will provide an opportunity for the parents to play with all the children. Parents also might also be asked to demonstrate some of the games played in their native countries. Playing these games will help children appreciate that cultures all over the world share some similar games and play activities.

Be sure that parents understand specifically what their children are learning as they are engaged in classroom activities. Doing so will help parents appreciate the activities and feel that their children are benefiting from the time spent playing.

SUMMARY

- *Play* can be defined by looking at its characteristics, types, and levels. In order to be classified as play, activities have to be personally motivated, active, usually nonliteral, not related to extrinsic goals, and meaningful in the mind of the players. Play is often described as ranging across a continuum from free play, which is play as just described; to guided play, in which the teacher puts out materials to help children reach given goals; to directed play, in which the children play a game, sing a song, or repeat a finger rhyme. Finally, there are several levels of play. Play with people is social play and ranges from solitary play to playing with a group. Play with objects can be described as practice play, symbolic play, games with rules, and games of construction. Vygotsky believed that play helps teachers define each child's zone of proximal development. Moreover, it helps children separate objects from thought and learn to regulate their own behavior.

- In terms of purpose, play has value in intellectual development, social and emotional development, and physical development. Children learn many skills and develop many concepts while playing. They also learn how to take turns, wait for gratification of their own desires, and hone their skills in moving and controlling their bodies.

- Observers of children's play have noted developmental trends in play behaviors. Younger children exhibit much more exploratory play, preschoolers engage in sociodramatic play and constructive play, and elementary-age children will most likely be involved in games with rules.

- Teachers must guide the play in school settings by observing, elaborating, modeling, evaluating, and planning play experiences. These responsibilities require skill in knowing when to make suggestions and when to allow children to solve their own problems and think about their own play themes. Play is beneficial to children learning various skills and concepts. Teachers need practice in communicating the value of play to parents and administrators.

- Carefully planned outdoor play experiences can provide many of the same benefits of indoor play and often allow children more freedom than play indoors.

- Planning play experiences for children with special needs may include adapting the physical environment; providing special instruction in play skills may also be necessary. Children who are developmentally delayed may exhibit play behaviors that are typical of much younger children.

- Play is an excellent means of helping children understand their own culture and the cultures of others. Play materials can include materials from the cultural or ethnic groups represented in the class, and culturally relevant games may help children understand the similarities among people and cultures.

REFLECTIONS

1. Does playing with a computer game or other electronic game fit the criteria of *play*? Why or why not?

2. Is one kind of play (social, play with objects, sociodramatic, practice, and so on) *better* than another? Is there a hierarchy of play behaviors? Use examples to explain.

3. Describe the possible intellectual, social, emotional, and physical benefits of four children playing at a water table.

4. If a parent complains about his child playing at school, what might you do to explain the importance of play at school?

5. In this era of pushing children to achieve given academic goals, is there room for play in the schoolday? Why or why not?

EXPLORATIONS AND ACTIVITIES

1. Observe a small group of children playing in a well-equipped setting for at least a half hour. Note their activities, the length of time spent in one activity, the language used, and so on. After making these observations, code your notes with highlighter pens, using one color for academic or intellectual development, another color for language development, another color for social/emotional development, and another color for physical development. What can you say about children's development based on your observations? Was spending these thirty minutes of the children's time in play worthwhile? Why or why not?

2. Plan a play experience for which you intend to achieve a specific goal. For example, if you want children to be able to sort a collection of items into the categories "big" and "little," how can you arrange the materials that children choose to play with to encourage them to perform the sorting? What questions can you ask? What if the children have misconceptions, such as "All wooden objects are big" or "All plastic objects are little"? What will you do for an extension activity if the children can sort by "big" and "little" easily?

CHAPTER **6**

KEY TERMS you'll find in this chapter:

- **Arrival time,** 184
- **Autonomy,** 184
- **Behavior-management systems,** 192
- **Corporal punishment,** 177
- **Departure time,** 185
- **Discipline,** 176
- **Dispositional learning,** 188
- **Guidance,** 178
- **Punishment,** 176
- **Social knowledge,** 188
- **Social skills,** 186
- **"Time out,"** 177
- **Transitions,** 185
- **Verbal skills,** 186
- **Withitness,** 191

Guiding Behavior

FOCUS QUESTIONS

- What are the definitions of *discipline, guidance,* and *punishment?*

- How can a teacher plan for guidance?

- What strategies can teachers use for guiding behavior?

- What are behavior-management systems?

- What guidance strategies are appropriate for children with special needs?

- Should the diversity of the classroom influence the teacher's guidance choices?

Your most recent observation assignment was to look at discipline strategies in the classroom. You were excited about this observation because all your classmates had been worrying about how they were going to control the behavior of the children in their charge more than they worried about any other element of teaching. You have also noticed how often discipline is a topic in journals for teachers and how many sessions at conferences for teachers of young children focus on the topic of discipline, so you know that even experienced teachers have concerns about classroom discipline.

You chose to visit a first-grade classroom. When you entered the classroom, you could not find the teacher for a few minutes. She was helping a small group of children with their plans to construct a display of what they had learned about penguins. In the two hours you spent in the classroom, the only interaction you would have called discipline was when the teacher reminded one youngster to remember that other people needed to hear and that he needed to use a quieter voice when speaking to his partner. You were thinking that discipline was highly overrated as a problem.

Discussion with your peers after the observation made it clear that other people had not shared your experience. Some people reported that they had observed teachers who made a checkmark beside the child's name if the child disobeyed a rule. This system had been adopted by the entire school. Another observed a chart with each child's name and a pocket, like those in library books, under the name. If the child was being good, a card with a green dot was under his name; if the child had committed one infraction of the rules, his card had a yellow dot; and if the child had more than one infraction, the dot was red. A red dot meant that the child was not allowed to participate in recess or any other class activity that was not academic work. Other students reported that they had observed a "time-out" chair, where students were asked to sit if they misbehaved.

Discipline was the topic of a lively discussion with your peers, and you know that it will continue to be an important issue. ■

Defining Discipline, Punishment, and Guidance

Discipline and **punishment** are not synonymous terms. Often, members of the public and even teachers use the word *discipline* when what they are referring to is *punishment* designed to enforce obedience to those in authority. Table 6.1 contrasts discipline and punishment.

The title of this chapter uses the word *guiding* because the best discipline consists of guiding children in developmentally appropriate ways to achieve self-control and eventually become self-disciplined individuals.

TABLE 6.1 Discipline versus Punishment

DISCIPLINE	PUNISHMENT
Children are *disciplined* when . . .	Children are *punished* when . . .
they are shown positive alternatives rather than just told "no"	their behavior is controlled through fear
they see how their actions affect others	their feelings are not respected
good behavior is rewarded	they behave to avoid a penalty or get a bribe
adults establish fair, simple rules and enforce them consistently	the adult only tells them what not to do
Children who are disciplined . . .	Children who are punished . . .
learn to share and cooperate	feel humiliated
are better able to handle their own anger	hide their mistakes
are more self-disciplined	tend to be angry and aggressive
feel successful and in control of themselves	fail to develop control of themselves

Source: Helping Children Learn Self-Control: A Guide to Discipline (brochure). (Washington, DC: National Association for the Education of Young Children, 1998). Reprinted with permission from the National Association for the Education of Young Children.

Guidance is not punishment—it is helping children learn. Teachers must consider carefully how to guide children's behavior. Just as teachers would think about children's needs and developmental levels in planning for growth in literacy or any subject-matter area, they must think about how children can best learn to achieve self-control.

Punishment

Corporal punishment is physical punishment; when the term is used in schools, it almost always refers to spanking. Ramsburg (1997) has reviewed the research on spanking and concluded that other disciplinary alternatives are more beneficial to children than corporal punishment.

The Association for Childhood Education International issued a position paper supporting a ban on corporal punishment (Cryan 1987). The paper traces the historical and legal perspectives on corporal punishment and then briefly cites the research on the effects of such punishment. The effects are so negative, especially over the long term, that it is clear that corporal punishment is not an effective method of discipline and does not help children learn self-control.

Punishment is not always corporal punishment, however. Children can be punished by being confined to their rooms, by having privileges restricted, or by a variety of other means. Some punishments are natural consequences of behavior. If a child breaks the crayons, then he will not have any when he wants to draw. If a child bullies her friends, no one will want to play with her. A later section of the chapter will discuss the use of natural consequences in a system of discipline (see "Dreikurs Model").

"Time Out"

One type of punishment commonly meted out by early childhood teachers to control children's behavior is being confined to the "time-out" chair. The original theory behind **"time out"** was sound: Taking time out gives children an opportunity to gain control of their own behavior and to choose when they are ready to return to the group.

Unfortunately, that is not the way time out is used in most classrooms. In many classrooms, the time-out chair is clearly punishment that is overused to obtain obedience. Betz (1994) states that he has "seen it misused so often that it has become unbearably trivialized" (p. 11). Although many experts in early childhood education have criticized the use of time out as a discipline strategy (Betz 1994; Katz 1984; Miller 1984), many teachers continue to use it.

Guidance

Gartrell (2001, 2002) suggests that teachers replace time out with strategies focused on building an "encouraging classroom." He suggests that teachers begin by using the four guidance basics of conflict management, class meetings, guidance talk, and comprehensive guidance. *Conflict management* is used when there are two or more children involved, and *class meetings* are employed when a conflict may affect the whole class. *Guidance talk* is used for dealing with conflicts with the adult or when additional work is needed after a conflict is solved.

NAEYC CRITERIA
1.19

www.
www.nccic.org/poptopics/
behavior.pdf
The homepage of the National Child Care Information Center, with many links related to discipline and guidance

Gartrell (2002) recommends these five steps for providing *comprehensive guidance:*

1. *Cool down*—The teacher and all the children involved take a few minutes to cool down as preparation for talking.
2. *Identify the problem*—The children agree on what the problem is and put it into words. (They may need help doing this.)
3. *Brainstorm solutions*—Children come up with possible solutions. (They may need help here, too.)
4. *Go for it*—The solution is tried.
5. *Follow-up*—The teacher continues to monitor, encourage, and guide the children involved.

The work of **guidance** is important in helping children learn how to handle conflicts and disappointments. Children have to be taught what to do when faced with conflicts, and punishing them, with or without a time-out chair, does not teach them what to do the next time.

Punishment may stop a behavior temporarily, but it may also interfere with teaching children appropriate behavior (Schickedanz, Schickedanz, and Forsyth 1982). Punishment may reduce children's initiative if they do not know which behaviors will be punished, and it may result in children's avoiding new situations in order to avoid punishment (Clewett 1988).

Discipline is important—how teachers respond to children's behavior is crucial in helping them grow and feel competent. No one would suggest that discipline be ignored; chaos in the classroom is not healthy for children or for teachers. Neither would anyone be naive enough to suggest that discipline is easy.

There are no clear-cut rules to follow in providing guidance because every situation and every child are different. The same behavior from two different children might (and probably should) elicit different responses from the same teacher. So much depends on the child's age, development, previous experience, and present situation that no rules will ever apply to all situations. Providing guidance helps children gain self-esteem, learn to be cooperative, and gradually learn the skills necessary for taking responsibility for their own behavior.

Planning for Guidance in the Classroom

Every teacher has faced or will face situations in which children's behavior is inappropriate or hurtful. It would be unrealistic to expect children who are still growing and learning to behave in ways that always please the other people around them. A professional teacher knows that some behavior management will be required when working with children and thinks about how different situations can be handled most successfully.

Teachers must consider the long-term effects on children's self-esteem, rather than just the immediate results, when making discipline decisions. Teachers must also think of discipline situations as teaching opportunities—opportunities to help children learn how to solve problems, how to negotiate differences, how to handle frustrations, and so on. Effective discipline requires thinking and planning, not only to prevent problems but also to prepare reactions that will be most appropriate when problems do occur.

A knowledgeable teacher also understands what is normal behavior for children of different ages and does not have unrealistic expectations. For example, very young children may scream or throw tantrums; four-year-olds may use foul language; five-year-olds may call each other cruel names; and eight-year-olds may form tight groups that gang up on outsiders. Children in one kindergarten class were often punished for lying. A sound knowledge of child development would have helped the teacher understand that many five-year-olds do not have well-developed concepts of truth and that most will deny any deed to protect themselves. Teachers have to think about what lying and other behaviors mean to the children they are teaching.

Guiding the behavior of young children is related to building self-concept, to curriculum design and organization, and to teachers' beliefs about how children learn best. Guidance requires that teachers make decisions about individual and group behaviors. In some teaching situations, guidance may also require that teachers make decisions about discipline plans that are adopted by the school. The goal of all of this decision making is to plan carefully in order to prevent as many problems as possible.

The following scenarios illustrate the difference between a teacher who focuses on guidance and one who focuses on punishment. Assume that the children are four to five and that the teachers know Tommy and Susan well.

Parents and Guiding Behavior

● Make sure that parents are aware of your program goals in terms of developing appropriate social skills, and highlight the guidance strategies that lead to achievement of those goals.

> **When you are dealing with a child, keep your wits about you and sit on the floor.**
> —*Austin O'Malley*

PRAXIS

Be able to explain what support could be provided to a child with challenging behaviors

Scenario 1

Tommy throws a block and hits Susan on the leg.

Teacher A sends Tommy to the time-out chair and tells him he must sit there until she tells him to get up. He is instructed to think about his behavior and how the block hurt Susan.

Teacher B removes Tommy from the blocks area and discusses with him the rule against throwing blocks, emphasizing the reason for that rule. If Tommy threw the block in anger, then she helps him think of acceptable outlets for his anger. If he threw the block to see how far he could throw it, she may help him think of better materials to throw and places to throw them. The teacher helps Tommy understand that Susan was hurt by the block. She helps him make a decision about what to do now in terms of behavior.

Scenario 2

Susan yells words that are deemed unacceptable in the classroom.

Teacher A removes Susan from the classroom and puts her in a chair in the hall for fifteen minutes with instructions to think about her behavior.

Teacher B moves close to Susan and tries to determine why she used inappropriate language: Was she angry at another child? Frustrated by her inability to complete some task? Playing a role? Depending on the reason for the outburst, the teacher will ask Susan to find more acceptable words to express her anger, help her think of what to do when she is frustrated (ask for help, choose another play material, and so on), or help her think about other words that a character might use.

In sum, neither teacher ignores inappropriate behavior nor lets it continue. But Teacher A's approach is to punish without teaching, which will not help the children make better decisions in the next situations. Discipline, when interpreted as *guidance*, focuses on teaching children what to do and helping them make better choices in the future.

In the following A Teacher Speaks box, Rick and Pam Coxen emphasize the ideas of modeling behaviors they want children to emulate and helping children treat each other fairly and with respect. The Coxens see good discipline as helping children learn to solve their own problems. Does what they say help you think about how you might handle discipline issues in your own classroom?

Preventing Behavior Problems

When teachers are faced with the challenging behaviors of children, they often look first to the children involved to determine the nature of the problem. Before trying to associate the problem with the children, teachers need to examine the program or activities presented for the children, the materials and room arrangement, the classroom routines, and the daily schedule. Not until all of these factors have been examined is it appropriate to look at the behaviors of the children.

Qualities of Programs and Activities

In planning programs and activities, teachers must ensure that they are interesting and engaging for children. When caught in dull or boring situations, adults can play mental games, plan what they are going to do later, do

NAEYC CRITERIA
2.15, 2.16, 2.17

www.

http://childcare.about.com/
od/behaviors/a/kidfighting.
htm
Advice about handling children's fighting for both teachers and parents

NAEYC CRITERIA
1.28

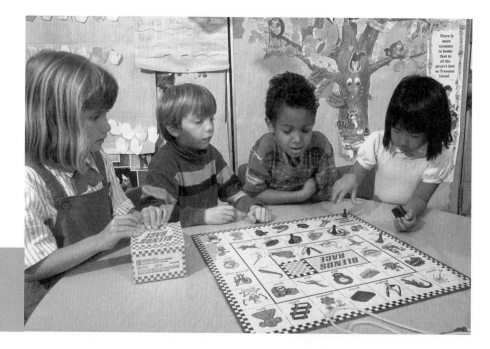

Activities in which several children participate can help children gain control of their behavior.

A **Teacher** SPEAKS: *Helping Children Learn to Manage Their Own Behavior*

Rick Coxen
Pringle Elementary
*Salem-Keizer
District, Oregon*

Pam Coxen
James R. Schirle Elementary
Salem-Keizer District, Oregon

It's the beginning of a new schoolyear for us; time to reflect on the past and plan for the future. When we think about classroom management issues, we look at the outcomes and then determine what we need to do in order to achieve them. As we choose our adult friends, we know we enjoy people who are respectful, empathetic, cooperative, honest, good problem solvers, and show integrity. Assuming that others enjoy these qualities as well, we look at how to help children build these traits.

Guiding our whole philosophy is the underlying tone of the classroom. We work to maintain a positive, safe environment for children. We expect children to become risk takers and to celebrate success, as well as learn from mistakes. We celebrate positive social choices and help children learn to compliment others (and receive compliments) for good choices.

One of the most important things we do as teachers is to model what it is we expect of children. This applies not only to academic areas but to social and emotional arenas as well. When children observe us interacting with other adults—staff members, parents, student teachers—they watch us show respect and display a cooperative nature. When we work to solve problems that arise, they see how cooperation and problem solving are applied. When we follow through on our commitments and maintain high personal standards, they understand integrity.

Beyond modeling the behaviors we want, we directly teach skills that will help children build the traits that will help them throughout life. Discussions about real classroom situations or discussions built around photos representing social problems begin most lessons. Role-play of difficult situations that result in problem solving, compromise, and solution play a big part in helping children apply what they have discussed. In just the same way that woodworking or sewing can be explained to you but not fully understood until you actually have to perform the task, social skills can be discussed but not really understood and made usable until the application process. Role-plays help children apply skills in nonthreatening, neutral situations before they are called on to apply the skill when the circumstance is a bit more personal and possibly filled with emotion.

In the same way that we show children, through our daily interactions, that all of their classmates are treated fairly, we also guide children to treat others fairly and equally. Since "fair" is often in the eye of the beholder, we often must have conversations about what really does constitute fairness in various situations. Compromise often plays a significant role, and helping children negotiate is part of our role.

To the extent possible, we try to let children become independent problem solvers. We must give them the skills to verbalize a problem, to see possible solutions, and to negotiate settlement along the way. When adult intervention is the only option, we intervene in order to help reach a compromise, rather than to provide the solution.

Taking the time to plan for and teach social skills benefits everyone. There are fewer classroom problems and more time for academics, and we have helped children develop the traits that will help them throughout their lives.

something else (as when college students study for upcoming tests during boring lectures), or at least pretend not to be bored (as when employees chat politely with the boss at a dull office party). But children simply do not have the skills to look attentive while they are doing something else. When bored or frustrated, they pinch their neighbors, fall out of their chairs, or get out of their seats.

> **What office is there which involves more responsibility, which requires more qualifications, and which ought, therefore, to be more honorable than that of teaching?**
>
> —*Harriet Martineau*

http://ceep.crc.uiuc.edu/ eecearchive/digests/1997/ marion97.html
Research from the clearing-house on Early Education and Parenting, which deals with helping children manage anger; also provides links to other sites with resources about discipline

In one second-grade classroom, two children were disrupting the teacher's lesson on the basic food groups. Their behavior resulted in being removed from the classroom. Later, the teacher admitted that these boys were gifted and already knew all the information being presented. If the curriculum had been more individualized, these two boys would have done their own experiment involving food, which would have engaged them intellectually and eliminated their disruptions and the need for punishment.

To prevent challenging behaviors, Loomis and Wagner (2005) suggest that teachers pay particular attention to activities in which behavior problems are likely to occur. Many teachers have found that such problems occur more often during teacher-directed activities than during activities that give children more choices in what to do. These authors recommend that teachers determine the following:

- The purpose of the activity
- How long it will take
- How they might incorporate children's ideas and interests in the activity
- If it is important that every child sit
- If it is a bad time in the day (i.e., the children are hungry)
- How they will respond if there is a display of inappropriate behavior

An example Loomis and Wagner offer is circle time. Teachers who carefully evaluate circle time may find that it does not serve the purpose for which it is intended, that it may last too long, that it may not be meaningful for some children, and that it may result in challenging behavior.

Materials and Classroom Arrangement

In addition to examining programs and activities for appropriateness, teachers also need to examine materials and classroom arrangements. If, for example, only two wheel toys are available for a large group of children, there will be disputes because of the unreasonable amount of time children must wait for a turn. Similar problems will arise if there are not enough blocks for several children to be building with them at one time. Children become extremely frustrated when they start a project and then find they do not have enough materials to complete it or when storage areas are so congested and unorganized that they cannot get the materials they need.

The room arrangement is also important in preventing discipline problems. If the blocks are in an area through which children must walk to get from one part of the room to another, the teacher will spend an inordinate amount of time mediating disputes over toppled structures. In primary classrooms, the pencil sharpener often seems to be a source of contention. The pencil sharpener should be located where users will not disturb other children and disrupt the class as little as possible yet allow children to sharpen their pencils when needed. Nagging and making rules about such little things

PRAXIS
Be able to explain how to design an environment that will provide children with positive feelings and help prevent discipline problems

as using the pencil sharpener seems a waste of teacher energy in comparison to the time it would take to prevent the problem in the first place.

One technique to discover traffic patterns or areas of congestion is to make a map of children's movements. The teacher should make a copy of the floorplan of the classroom and draw lines to show the paths children take during given five-minute periods; observations should be repeated every thirty minutes to show patterns throughout the day. These traffic maps will help teachers make decisions about where to locate storage and program areas.

The arrangement of the classroom space should also make it possible for the teacher to scan the room frequently in order to deal with problems before they escalate. For example, if the teacher sees too many children playing in the housekeeping corner, she should redirect some of them into another activity. Perhaps this is the time to get out some new materials and encourage several children to use them. If the number of children in the housekeeping center continues to be too large, a more lasting solution may be needed. If the teacher sees the children are getting too rowdy for indoor play, she should move to the area and help the children regain self-control by offering play suggestions for quieter activities. For example, she might ask two or three children to join her in a plan for building a robot at the art center.

Large, open spaces sometimes invite children to run or to get more exuberant than the teacher would like. To avoid this, the classroom furniture can be arranged so as to break up the large spaces into several smaller spaces. Bookshelves on wheels and lightweight tables can be moved easily if a larger space is needed at another time of the day.

Careful observation of children at play can help teachers plan for assistance in controlling their behavior.

Classroom Routines

Once the teacher has examined the curriculum and the room arrangements in an effort to prevent problems, another step is to establish routines so that children feel safe and know what to expect. We would all be exhausted if we had to start from scratch to organize our time each day. We know that most of what we do is routine, and we do not have to put energy into deciding about most of our activities (eating, working, sleeping, and so on).

Children also need routines in which activities are predictable but not rigidly set. Children need to know that there will be play time, snack time, outdoor play time, and other basic elements in their day. A mentally healthy person can change daily routines without undue stress. When they are secure about basic routines, children, too, can adjust to changes—the arrival of a guest speaker, a field trip, and so on. Complete lack of routine, however, leads to frustration, insecurities, and behavior problems.

Teachers might also need to examine their attitudes and feelings about autonomy and what constitutes obedient behavior from children. Kamii (1982) describes **autonomy** as the ability to make decisions for ourselves. She believes that schools generally reinforce children when they obey without thinking and therefore "unwittingly prevent them from developing autonomy" (p. 85). Having autonomy does not mean that children do not have to obey rules or respect other people and their property. It does mean that children learn to make decisions and think clearly about their behavior and their learning.

Daily Schedule

Experienced teachers will agree that discipline problems are more likely at certain times of day than others, including arrival times, transition times, and departure times. Planning for these key times is essential.

For **arrival time,** the teacher might ask that children wait until everyone has arrived or until a set time has been reached before activities begin.

DEVELOPMENTALLY APPROPRIATE PRACTICE

Reflect on the connections between discipline and developmentally appropriate practice as you respond to the following questions:

- Can discipline be developmentally appropriate if it is not based on understanding the child and what is normal behavior for her given stage of development? Why?

- Should a system of discipline be instituted without considering the match between the child and the curriculum? Can discipline be appropriate if the curriculum is not? Explain your answers.

- Discipline must be considered as an opportunity for teaching. If it is not, can it be developmentally appropriate? Why?

- If you read about a conference presentation called "Developmentally Appropriate Discipline," what information would you expect to be covered?

The fact is, though, that children are not good at waiting. Alternatives to waiting might be to plan an activity to occupy children who arrive early or to allow these children to begin working in learning areas.

Music and fingerplays can be used to help children make **transitions** from one activity to another without nagging and reminding by the teacher. Often, children will put away toys and materials if the teacher helps and makes up a simple song ("This is the way we put blocks on the shelf" or "This is the way we wash the paintbrushes"). Playing a record or tape of a march song will encourage the children to march around the room until they come to the area for group activities; while marching, they will have no time to become bored and get into trouble.

If the children are old enough, one child can begin to lead either a song or a fingerplay, and each child can join when she is ready. Fingerplays led by the teacher can encourage children to do what is necessary without being reminded. For example, the fingerplay "Two Little Hands Go Clap, Clap, Clap" ends with the line "And one little child sits quietly down." By the end of this fingerplay, all the children will be sitting, and the teacher will not have nagged anyone to do so.

Departure time also needs to be planned. Teachers need to think about how to distribute notices and work at the end of the day so that children do not have to wait too long. A routine of getting coats, distributing materials to take home, and delivering some short closing message can help keep children on track during departures.

On occasion, an activity might be appropriate for most of the group but not for an individual child. If a child is having difficulty, it is usually appropriate to allow him another choice. The teacher might whisper to a child, "You can stay here if you choose, or you may work quietly with the puzzles or books if you want." Individualizing the curriculum means attending to the needs of different children. The sensitive teacher is usually aware of when a child may need to leave a group and tries to arrange for that before an incident happens.

In sum, many discipline problems can be avoided by anticipating when they are likely to occur and planning to circumvent them. Crosser (1992) uses the acronym BASIC to describe such planning:

> Before school begins
> Arrival and departure times
> Schedule transitions
> Interactions with equipment and materials
> Conflict management (p. 23)

In addition to planning for key times during the day, teachers must think about the schedule in terms of how long children are asked to sit still and how much physical activity is allowed. Quiet, sitting-down activities must be alternated with more active activities. Often just a few minutes of vigorous movement will alleviate problems before they arise. King and Gartrell (2003) note that boys, in particular, need a great deal of large motor and whole-body movement as well as less sitting still and more blocks play, woodworking activities, and sensory exploration and experimentation activities than girls of the same chronological age. To ask young boys to sit still and be quiet for long periods of time is simply not appropriate.

NAEYC CRITERIA

**1.23, 1.25, 1.26,
1.33, 1.34, 1.35,
1.36, 1.37, 1.38**

> **I see the mind of the
> 5-year-old as a volcano with
> two vents: destructiveness
> and creativeness.**
>
> —*Sylvia Ashton-Warner*

NAEYC CRITERIA

1.11, 1.30

Strategies for Guiding Behavior

As discussed in the preceding sections, the teacher plans the environment, plans for special times in the day, plans to help children learn to work with classroom equipment and materials, and teaches children how to settle conflicts that arise. Figure 6.1 is a checklist of planning strategies that can be used to support positive behaviors.

Teaching Skills and Behaviors

Professional teachers should also respond to problem situations by analyzing what can be taught in them. Katz (1984) categorizes what can be taught as social skills, verbal skills, social knowledge, and dispositional learning.

Social skills include taking turns, negotiating, and coping. Taking turns is not limited to sharing toys but is important in all social situations. During language activities, for example, children must learn to read the signals from a speaker that tell them when they can have a turn talking—eye contact, body language such as inclining the head, and so on. Children must also learn when the speaker is not willing to give up the floor—when he says "ah, ah, ah," avoids eye contact, and so on (Wells 1981).

A similar kind of reading of the situation is helpful when one child wants a toy that another child has. The teacher might suggest that the child who wants the toy observe the child who has it and look for signs that he is tiring of it and might be ready to give it up. The teacher might help by modeling language to be used in negotiation, such as "I'll pull you in the wagon later if you'll let me have the truck now."

Children also need to learn coping skills because not every request that they make will be honored. The teacher might say, "Well, perhaps you can play with the truck tomorrow. For now, you might want to listen to a record or draw a picture." We have all seen adults who cannot cope with not getting what they want, when they want it. Teaching children to cope gives them a valuable life skill.

Verbal skills that can be taught in problem situations include making appropriate assertive statements and talking about disagreements. For example, a child who has just had a toy snatched from her can learn to say firmly, "I was not finished playing with that boat. Please give it back." Being able to be assertive without being aggressive is a skill that will serve the child well for the rest of her life.

Carrying on conversations about disputes is often difficult for children because they lack the words to continue the discussion. Teachers may have to model the conversations by speaking for both children, as described by Katz (1984):

> Using this technique, the teacher might say to Leslie, "Robin really wants a turn," to which Leslie might grunt a refusal. The teacher might then say to Robin something like, "Leslie does not want to give up the tricycle yet." Robin might respond to this with a whining protest, in which case the teacher can paraphrase to Leslie what Robin is feeling by saying, "Robin really would like a turn now," and so on. In short, the teacher keeps up the conversation, verbalizing to each child what she infers to be the feelings of the other. (p. 31)

FIGURE 6.1

Checklist for Supporting Positive Behaviors

Strategy	Yes/No	Notes
Physical Environment		
1. Design clearly designed areas		
Interest areas		
Group meeting time		
Pathways		
2. Provide adequate space for interest areas		
Set limits for number of children using area		
Discuss rules with children		
3. Monitor potential problem areas		
Blocks		
Dramatic play		
Sand/water play		
Woodworking		
Other		
4. Maintain relaxed, calm, interesting environment		
Engaging activities every day		
Images/words at eye level		
Materials on low, open shelves		
Neatly organized items		
Labeled shelves and containers		
Programmatic Environment		
5. Assess structure of activities		
Open-ended activities		
Balance between unstructured/structured activities		
6. Follow age-appropriate schedule		
Alternate active and quiet times		
Group times short		
Group times spread throughout the day		
Children's cues used to assess group time limits		
Adequate choice time		
7. Establish routines		
Consistent yet flexible		
No wait times		
Posted schedule with pictures and words		
8. Plan transitions		
Use consistent signal for end of choice time		
Allow 5 or more minutes for ending activities/cleanup		
Give verbal warning to all children		
Plan and use transitions every day		

Source: Nancy Ratcliff, "Use the Environment to Prevent Discipline Problems and Support Learning," *Young Children* 56 (September 2001): 84–89. Reprinted with permission from the National Association for the Education of Young Children.

www.washburn.org/aboutus/
programs/OutreachArticles/
BehaviorGuidance.html

Several strategies for helping children learn positive behavior without using punishment; interesting information on using praise

PRAXIS

Be able to explain how language and tone affect children's behavior

Parents and Guiding Behavior

- Talk with parents about the growth of their child in terms of self-control as well as academics.
- Help parents appreciate the positive qualities of their child's behavior, such as curiosity and enthusiasm.

Social knowledge includes the ability to put incidents into perspective and an initial understanding of the concept of *justice*. If one child fails to get a turn on the swing, the teacher might say, "I know that you are disappointed, but there are other things you can do." The tone of voice should be empathetic but not tragic. Children who hit learn about justice when they are restrained from hitting and told, "I won't let you hit anyone. If anyone else hits, I will stop them from hitting, too." The child then begins to feel safer and to feel that the environment is a just one.

Dispositional learning in discipline situations includes learning to be more empathetic, to try different techniques, and to avoid negative dispositions (sulking, temper tantrums, whining, and the like). Children can be taught to be more empathetic (Honig 1985; Marantz 1988). One of the best strategies for teaching empathy is modeling accompanied by discussion. For example, if one child falls and hurts himself, the teacher can model appropriate empathy in her response. Concern for the feelings of others must be a priority in the early childhood classroom.

Children can also learn that problem-solving strategies can be applied in conflicts with others. The teacher might recommend a strategy to a child and then follow the recommendation by saying, "If that doesn't work, come back, and we'll think of something else to try." Children must learn to accept that their first efforts may not always be successful while realizing that they can try again.

Sometimes, a child may have adopted a negative behavior that the teacher would like to help her change—for example, tattling or complaining. The teacher must make a decision about how best to respond to a child's complaints to help her learn that complaining is not always successful and to learn when an adult should be told about an incident. Children are usually six or seven before they can understand the difference between tattling to get someone in trouble and telling the teacher about something that it is important for an adult to know.

For children in primary classrooms, one strategy suggested by Rightmeyer (2003) is to have a daily group meeting. At this meeting, the children take up any issue put on the agenda by a class member. That child explains the problem, and the class then offers solutions. The child who raised the problem chooses one of the solutions to try for a week, and that solution is recorded in a book. After a week, the child evaluates the solution to determine if it is working or not. If not, the child comes back to the group and explains why it is not working.

This strategy meets the criteria for good discipline because the children are respected and responsible for solving the problems. However, the teacher will have to model and demonstrate more than once how to make this strategy work.

Guiding Groups

Children in groups must be given some rules. The fewer and more flexible these rules, the better. As soon as children are old enough, they should have a part in making group rules. Some children as young as three can be involved in rule making.

Rules must be clearly stated. Leatzow, Neuhauser, and Wilmes (1983) observe that many early childhood educators have only one rule: "You may not hurt yourself or anyone else" (p. 83). This kind of rule covers many situations and is understood by the children. Other teachers add a rule that children cannot destroy property.

Sometimes, the teacher must manage the group in addition to guiding individual children. The younger the children, the fewer the group-management techniques that should be needed. As children are able to participate in more group activities, group-management techniques will become more useful to the teacher.

One rule for group management is not to call attention to an individual child. For example, a teacher might say, "You all need to sit on your bottoms so that everyone can see the pictures while I read the story," rather than "Julian and Hope must sit down so that others can see." It also helps in this particular situation to reassure some children that they will get to see a book later if they are very excited about it. The teacher might say, "You all need to sit flat on your bottoms now, but after I read the story, I'll leave the book here on the table if you want to look at the pictures more closely." With older children who are anxious to see something, the teacher might say, "When you leave this table, put your name on the list if you want to see the book again later."

Just as public criticism is to be avoided, so, too, is public praise inappropriate in group-management situations. For example, the teacher might say, "Almost everyone is ready for the story; in just a minute, we will begin," rather than "Sara and Randy are sitting nicely, waiting for the story."

In using group-management strategies, teachers must be careful to preserve children's self-esteem and to use techniques that help children learn acceptable behaviors—the same concerns that apply when guiding individual behavior. Gartrell (1987b) acknowledges that learning these techniques takes commitment and practice on the part of teachers. Teachers must "deal with the young child's need to feel safe and secure, through personal acceptance, sensible limits, gentle correction, and genuine encouragement" (p. 55).

The same considerations of appropriateness of activity must be applied to group-management situations as to individual guidance situations. When

www.

www.naeyc.org/resources/ eyly/1999/11.htm
Understanding children's behavior is a key component in effective discipline

children are in group situations too long or when group activities are inappropriate, behavior problems will result. One teacher of five-year-olds had a group lesson on the beginning sound of "r." The teacher had twenty-three children sit in a circle to listen to a recording about the letter *r*. The teacher held an inflatable figure representing *r*. During the thirty-minute lesson, the teacher had to discipline children many times—"Stop leaning back in your chair," "Don't pull her hair," "Pay attention," and so on.

Clearly, this activity was inappropriate for five-year-olds, and the time spent on it was too long. The teacher could have saved much frustration for himself and the children by choosing other teaching strategies.

Making Guidance Decisions

When teachers are confronted with misbehavior, they must make decisions about whether to respond, how to respond, and how to evaluate the growth of the children involved. The following sections provide strategies for making these types of guidance decisions.

Weighing the Situation

In some situations, the most effective response is no response at all. Children sometimes behave in ways that are not appropriate but are not harmful to anyone and are not disruptive if they are ignored.

For example, suppose the teacher asks the children to come to group time and sit on the floor for a story. Maria comes to the group but stands instead of sits. The teacher comments to the group that she is almost ready to start reading and makes eye contact with Maria, who remains standing. Rather than call her name and force her to sit, the teacher should do nothing and begin reading, as if Maria were sitting quietly. Maria may soon sit down and join the group, or she may keep standing, but as long as she is not interfering with others, little will be gained from making her sit. If Maria continually refuses to do anything that she is asked, the teacher will need to take steps privately to find out what makes Maria feel so defiant.

Effective teachers know when to ignore behavior and when to deal with it. No rules determine what to ignore and when—only professional judgment provides the answers. In weighing a given situation, the teacher should ask herself these questions: What will be gained in terms of teaching and increased self-control by responding to the behavior? What will be lost in terms of the child's self-concept or feeling of autonomy?

Making the Choice to Respond

Once a teacher has decided to respond to a child's behavior, she must decide how. In this case, there are certain rules to follow:

1. The response should be private, if at all possible. A child who is hitting another child will have to be restrained immediately, but then he can be removed and the behavior can be dealt with privately.

2. The response should be developmentally appropriate—for example, redirecting a toddler, appealing to the empathetic feelings of a five-year-old, or explaining rationally to an eight-year-old.

3. The response should be aimed at helping the child increase her self-control. The teacher should express acceptance of the child's feelings

and provide guidance in finding a socially acceptable way of expressing them.

4. The response should demonstrate caring for the child but firmness in rejecting the behavior: "I'm sorry that you are frustrated because you can't have the doll now, but you cannot spit on anyone. You can spit in the sink."

5. The response should involve as much knowledge about the child and his situation as the teacher can summon in the split second that is often available for making a decision. For instance, suppose that the teacher knows that Derek's father has just moved out and that his family is under stress. When Derek behaves in a way that is not typical for him, such as throwing sand on a friend, the teacher can quietly take him aside and explain gently that she knows that Derek feels like throwing something, that he can tell her how he feels if he wants to, but that he cannot hurt other children.

Withitness is a term that has become popular in the literature on discipline; it was derived from the work of Jacob Kounin, a well-known educational researcher (Charles and Barr 1989). Withitness is knowing what is going on in the classroom at all times. If students observe that the teacher chooses to correct the wrong child's behavior, they will assume that the teacher does not know what is going on. Teachers with withitness also know to stop misbehavior before it spreads to others; timing such as this requires that teachers observe carefully.

Examples of Effective Responses

The following scenarios demonstrate effective responses to real-life problems in the classroom:

NAEYC CRITERIA
2.18, 2.19, 2.20

NAEYC CRITERIA
1.31

PRAXIS
Be able to offer responses to a given behavioral issue

■ You are reading a story to a small group. Several children start to whine that they do not like the story. One child puts her hands over her ears. Others notice and start to put hands over their ears. You could ignore the behavior and do a little editing of the story to finish it quickly. Or you could stop reading and say, "I know that some of you like other books better. Perhaps we will read a book that you like better tomorrow. But some people like this book, so I'm going to finish reading it now. You can wait quietly for the few minutes it will take."

■ You find several children in the bathroom exposing themselves. You could say, "I see that you are interested in the differences between boys and girls. Would you like to have me read this book to you that explains some of the differences?"

■ One child pulls all the blocks off the shelf and refuses to help put them away. You might say, "I know that it is much more fun to pull these blocks off the shelf than it is to put them away. We all have to do things that are not much fun sometimes. I'll help you begin, and you can finish." If the child still refuses to help, you could say, "I'm going to put away these blocks now. Then you and I must talk about why you are not feeling like helping today."

■ A child bites another child. First, you must restrain the child so that no more biting can occur. Then you might say, "You cannot bite Sidney. You know that biting hurts very much, and the rule is that you cannot hurt anyone. I will not let you hurt anyone, and I will try not to let anyone hurt you. I know that you are angry, and I know that Sidney grabbed your toy. You must tell Sidney that you do not like it when he grabs your toy. Use words to tell him how angry you are."

Evaluating Growth

Evaluating children's growth in handling conflicts and in managing their own behavior requires that teachers keep anecdotal records of children's behavior over time and be able to document their growth in behaving in more acceptable ways. Gartrell (1995) relates the story of a child who said "You damm sunnamabitch" to another child. When the teacher got to the children, she comforted the second child briefly and then whispered, "I'm proud of you" in the ear of the swearing child. She explained later to an observer that until last week, this child had hit or kicked others whenever he was angry; his teachers had been trying to get him to use words to express himself in these situations. When the teacher whispered in the boy's ear to congratulate him on his language use, she also supplied him with some words that would not bother people as much as the swear words.

Children's growth usually takes time and comes in little steps, but teachers need to be able to see the changes, even when they are small. Teachers must also evaluate their own growth in responding to children's behavior. Teachers must remember that both children and adults get tired and become angry. If teachers occasionally respond in ways that are less than professional, they should forgive themselves and learn from their experience.

Dan Gartrell, in the An Expert Speaks box, tells the story of Brian and a group of teachers who thought that if Brian were not in their school, all their discipline problems would be solved. As you read this story, think about how you might handle your own Brian someday (because every teacher will have one!).

Parents and Guiding Behavior

- Help parents evaluate possible solutions to their children's difficult behaviors. It might be helpful to provide some guidelines that include thinking about long-term goals for behavior and possible outcomes (Heath 1994).

Behavior-Management Systems

Several **behavior-management systems** have been designed to help teachers control children's behavior. The following sections will describe assertive discipline, the Glasser model, the Ginott model, and the Dreikurs model.

Assertive Discipline

www.

www.behavioradvisor.com/
AssertiveDiscipline.html
www.humboldt.edu/~tha1/
canter.html

Both sites offer information on assertive discipline

Designed by Lee Canter (1976), *assertive discipline* is a system in which the rules for classroom behavior are established by the teacher and posted in the classroom. The consequences for breaking any of the rules are also posted. If a child breaks the rule against speaking out in class, for example, her name is written on the chalkboard. (In subsequent publications, Canter has recommended that the names be written on a clipboard or in a book, rather than on the board [D. Hill 1990].) Another offense results in a checkmark being placed after the child's name. Usually, the consequence of receiving two checkmarks is being sent to the principal's office or having the teacher call the child's parents.

AN **Expert** SPEAKS: Guidance Personified: Liberation Teaching

Dan Gartrell, Bemidji State University, Minnesota

Guidance means teaching children to learn from their mistakes, rather than punishing them for the mistakes they make, and helping children learn to solve their problems, rather than punishing them for having problems they cannot solve. But what of that child who is always bullying and making trouble? The one kid you flat out don't care for?

Many years ago when I was in graduate school, our major advisor assigned four of us "experienced" students to work with a large, urban child-care center. The purpose of our practicum was to assist the preschool staff in improving their program. The program for the three- to five-year-olds was in the basement of a large church: forty kids, grey-painted cement floor, big pipe pillars with worn padding. The one positive was that all six of the staff were receiving credits for their efforts—a college class that allowed for weekly discussion, planning, and evaluation.

We encouraged the staff to create family groups, so that each teacher worked with the same six or seven children during time blocks each day. We got the basement set up in learning centers, including an active play center, and regularly rotated groups out of the classroom for vigorous activity in another room. We established themes, which rekindled the interest of the staff in their teaching. We coached the staff toward replacing "time outs" with conflict resolution. One night in class, the staff informed us that there was just one problem we hadn't tackled: the problem of Brian.

Brian was a veteran four-year-old. He was a leader, boisterous, usually got what he wanted, and often had conflicts. Brian was the topic of the entire class session. The teachers insisted that "something had to be done." (We had the feeling they meant removing Brian from the program.) Well, we started by asking the staff to list positive things about Brian. The list kind of petered out after "When he is gone, the whole program runs better"! The assignment for the next week was to note positive qualities in Brian and to try to understand nonblaming reasons for when he had conflicts.

The next week's class was amazing! After sharing their lists, the staff concluded that Brian's behavior had improved so much that he was no longer an issue! We discussed the fact that Brian's behavior really hadn't changed that much. It was just that his teachers were taking a new attitude toward him—and seeing new qualities in him. From then on, Brian became much less of an issue. Occasionally, the staff even remarked about positive things that Brian had done.

Sometimes, we resign ourselves to the behavioral disposition of a particular child. We come to expect certain behaviors—and are not surprised when that is what we see (Ginott 1972). In education, the danger of labeling a child and actually reinforcing the negative behaviors that we are on guard for is real. The labels can stick. The research of J. D. Coie (1996), among others, indicates that children who have conflicts often and are neither liked nor helped in the early childhood classroom tend to show these problems for years to come.

In the classic little book *Caring: Supporting Children's Growth,* Warren (1977) states that teachers need not love every child and need not feel guilty when they have unpositive thoughts. But as professionals, teachers do need to figure out how to form a *positive relationship* with each child; accept each child as a worthy member of the class; and teach each child the skills to negotiate and get along so he doesn't have the conflicts. (No doubt about it, this most important level of teaching takes persistence and smarts.)

So, what is it about your kid that really bothers you? Is it his behavior? His appearance? His temperament? Her relative immaturity? Her family background? Often it is easier *not* to think about our feelings and just tolerate the child for the time he is with us. But this denial really means rejection. If we want to help this child for the long term (really for the child's whole life), we will explore our feelings—and observe closely to discover what about the child we can understand, care for, and like. We will reflect these positives back to the child—every day, in every way—and teach the child what he needs to get along.

Liberation teaching means assisting young children to make their problems more solvable. Liberation teaching means finding qualities we can appreciate in every girl and boy. Liberation teaching means helping all children see themselves as worthy individuals and contribution members of our class. Liberation teaching means never giving up on any child. Liberation teaching is at the heart of guidance and is the purest expression of our belief in this approach.

Because disruptions prevent teachers from teaching effectively, Canter believes that use of the assertive discipline system enables teachers to be more effective and solves the management problems in any classroom. This system is in use in many elementary schools, which means that many early childhood teachers are required to follow assertive discipline. Administrators who believe that the system helps teachers feel more comfortable about discipline are likely to promote its use.

One of the first things any teacher of young children must do is assess the validity of the assumptions of any behavior-management program. Canter based the assertive discipline system on the assumption that children want to disrupt the teacher and prevent teaching (Canter 1988; Hitz 1988). Teachers who believe that children have an inherent desire to learn and who have observed the eagerness with which young children approach learning will find this assumption invalid.

Another problem with assertive discipline is that it assumes that young children can operate according to rules. Experienced teachers know that young children can learn that some behaviors are acceptable at school and others are not. They also know that this learning usually takes time, guidance, and repeated experience. The assertive discipline system assumes that telling children that there is a rule and punishing them for breaking the rule will prevent unacceptable behavior. This approach may prevent the behavior at a given moment, but children will not know why the behavior is unacceptable, nor will they learn to make better judgments about how to behave in future situations.

Behavior-management systems that enforce rules established by adult authority do not help children learn to be responsible. Such systems do, however, teach children to obey authority that is exercised through "power assertion" (Hitz 1988). There are situations in which adults must assert their power and demand instant obedience—for example, in order to prevent injury or cope with an emergency, such as a fire. Adults exert such control until children are old enough to learn rational reasons for controlling their own behavior in like situations.

However, controlling children by power and demanding instant obedience should not be typical means of behavior management. Gartrell (1987a) expresses concerns that assertive discipline damages children's self-concepts and turns teachers into "managing technicians" (p. 11). Perhaps a larger concern is the danger that children will not be able to determine appropriate behavior and to develop a sense of responsibility for their actions.

The assertive discipline model also fails to examine the causes of disruptive behavior. The system is applied regardless of the curriculum, the room arrangement, or the schedule. No system of discipline should ever be applied without careful assessment of all the factors and individuals involved in a teaching situation.

Jones and Jones (1990) report that some schools that began assertive discipline programs several years ago have moved away from them, for several reasons:

> Many teachers are frustrated because problem students seem to be relatively unaffected by the procedures, and students who do not need such repressive methods tend to find the method insulting or anxiety provoking. Our own concern is that too frequently the method creates a "sit down, shut up, or get out" philosophy in classrooms in which teaching methods are failing to meet students' basic personal and academic needs. Too often teachers use the Assertive

Discipline procedures rather than examining their own teaching methods to consider how to prevent disruptive behavior. (p. 412)

Glasser Model

The Glasser model (Glasser 1997) is based on providing good choices for children and handling disruptions that do occur in a calm and logical manner. Glasser believes that good choices produce good behavior and bad choices produce bad behavior. He believes that behavior represents individuals' attempts to meet their needs and that if schools are to have better discipline, they will have to become places where fewer children and teachers are frustrated in getting what they need. Some of the important needs that Glasser identifies are the needs to belong, to have power, to be free, and to have fun. Schools in which children do not feel a sense of belonging or have no power to make choices are schools in which discipline problems are common.

Glasser recommends that teachers structure learning experiences so that children have high motivation to work on behalf of the group and that stronger students help weaker students, thus fulfilling the stronger students' need for power and the weaker students' need to contribute to the group. One of the hallmarks of Glasser's model is the class meeting, in which students discuss class rules and behavior.

Although Glasser's model is used more often with older children than with young children, his focus on problem solving, on the choices provided by teachers and on teachers' persistence in helping children with problems is appropriate for young children. More recently, Glasser (2000) has written about violence prevention programs in schools. Even though this work is focused on older children, the same principles of respect and thoughtful guidance apply to young children as well.

www.brains.org/classroom_management.htm
Information about Glasser and his theories

Ginott Model

The Ginott model (Ginott 1972) is based on setting up a classroom climate that is conducive to good discipline through effective communication between teachers and children. Ginott believes that discipline is an ongoing process that is achieved over time.

One of the principles of this model is that corrective messages to children should attack the problem and not the child. Ginott uses the term *congruent communication* to describe responses that are in harmony with children's feelings about situations or themselves. He also advocates inviting cooperation, not demanding it. Teachers applying Ginott's recommendations do not label children and communicate their willingness to help children solve problems.

Charles and Barr (1989) report that even teachers who are sympathetic with Ginott's views feel that more structured management is needed in many teaching situations. Nonetheless, Ginott's emphasis on the ability to communicate well with children is of value to early childhood teachers. Another component of Ginott's model that is of value to early childhood teachers is its emphasis on the self-esteem of the child and the importance of the teacher's behavior.

www.humboldt.edu/~tha1/discip-options.html#seven%20models
www.kingsleyschool.ca/who_was_haim_ginott.htm
Both sites provide more information about Ginott and his theories

Dreikurs Model

The Dreikurs model (Dinkmeyer and Dreikurs 2000) is best known for its emphasis on logical consequences. Dreikurs defines *discipline* as teaching students to impose limits on themselves. He believes that all children want to belong and that their behaviors represent efforts to achieve a sense of belong-ing. Misbehaviors are the result of mistaken goals, such as seeking attention, power, or revenge or wanting to display another child's inadequacy. Dreikurs suggests that the best method of discipline is encouraging positive behavior.

When teachers encounter behavior problems, Dreikurs recommends that they point out to students the logical consequences of their actions. In describing *logical consequences,* Charles and Barr (1989) use examples that apply to older children, but their explanation will suggest applications for younger children, as well:

> Logical consequences must be differentiated from punishment. Punishment is action taken by the teacher to get back at misbehaving students and show them who is boss. Punishment breeds retaliation and gives students the feel-ing that they have the right to punish in return. Logical consequences, on the other hand, are not weapons used by the teacher. They teach students that all behavior produces a corresponding result: good behavior brings rewards and unacceptable behavior brings unpleasant consequences. If a student throws paper on the floor, that student must pick it up. If a student fails to do work as assigned, that student must make up the work on his or her own time. (p. 83)

Gartrell (2002) believes that the terminology used can influence the mind-set of the teacher toward guiding children's behavior; thus, he promotes using the term *mistaken behavior,* rather than *misbehavior. Misbehavior* makes teach-ers think of punishing, whereas *mistaken behavior* encourages thinking about guiding and teaching. Gartrell credits Dreikurs's thinking about behavior as the stepping stones that led to development of the concept *mistaken behavior.*

In evaluating different models for managing behavior, Charles and Barr (1989) state that "Dreikurs' views have the greatest potential for bringing about genuine attitudinal change among students, so that they ultimately behave better because they consider it the proper thing to do" (p. 85).

Assessing Behavior-Management Systems

It is the teacher's responsibility to assess any behavior-management system or discipline policy based on the following criteria:

■ *Respect for children*—Not every teacher will love every child, but each child deserves respect as a human being. If it is hard to respect the child be-cause of constant problems, the teacher should seek help from co-teachers, counselors, parents, or administrators. Using a behavior-management sys-tem that does not respect the individual child will cause more harm than it attempts to address.

■ *Knowledge of individual children*—Discipline cannot be applied fairly if it is applied without knowledge of the individual child. For exam-ple, enforcing a rule against bad language with the child discussed earlier, who swore instead of hitting, would leave him without an acceptable way to express his frustration. As the child shows more growth, the teacher can continue to help him find more acceptable classroom words for express-ing anger. Behavior-management systems often make it easy for teachers to gloss over the need to know each child.

■ *Knowledge of normal growth, development, and behavior*—Children who are behaving in ways that are normal for their age may be helped to learn more acceptable responses to be used at school. But such behavior will not be irritating to the knowledgeable teacher because he will realize that it is a normal part of working with this particular age group.

■ ***Willingness to accept discipline as an opportunity for teaching***—Discipline is not punishment. Teachers sometimes have to work hard at helping children control their behavior in ways that teach them new strategies for interacting successfully in groups or with individuals.

■ ***Avoidance of judgmental words***—Calling children "good" or "bad" does not help them learn alternative ways of behaving. More appropriate descriptions of behavior guide children without judging them.

■ ***Limited but cooperative rule making***—Being well-behaved in a classroom where there are long lists of rules is difficult for children because too many things are against the rules. As soon as children are old enough, they can begin to help teachers decide on rules that the group will follow.

CHILDREN WITH SPECIAL NEEDS

Many children with special needs require only guidance that is typical for their age, whereas others may require more support from the teacher. For many special-needs children, arranging the environment to facilitate their access to materials and equipment will greatly reduce their frustration and thus their inappropriate behavior, as well. Once children have equal access to materials and equipment, teachers can generally use the same guidance strategies they use with the children's peers.

Some children, however, may require more support, so teachers may need to use guidance strategies that are usually more appropriate for younger children. For example, consider a child with a physical disability who is in a wheelchair; she is chronologically and developmentally age four. Given this, her teacher should be able to employ the same problem-solving strategies in guidance that are applied to other children of the same age. If the child needs additional support, such as having just one or two options rather than a more open-ended approach, then the teacher can provide that support.

Guidance for children with disabilities may focus on teaching them social skills. In addition to making environmental arrangements, Lowenthal (1996) suggests several strategies: using group affection activities, such as modifying games and songs in which children touch or hug one another in affectionate ways; teaching typically developing peers to initiate play with special children by offering toys or extending invitations to play; and using teacher prompts to help children recognize elements in social situations that they might not pick up on their own. Obviously, the strategies selected must be individually appropriate for the child.

Brown, Althouse, and Anfin (1993) found that *guided dramatization* was an effective strategy in encouraging children with disabilities to interact in positive ways with other children. These authors guided the dramatization of a familiar story by teaching it to a child with disabilities through interactive reading, telling the story with a magnetic or flannelboard, and then asking the child to choose someone else to help tell the story. As the children dramatized the story, the teacher took photographs and used them in retelling the story again. The target child was photographed playing with the other children and asked to tell about the play. These authors found that this sequence helped the child with disabilities learn how to interact with others and that the child initiated play experiences with other children based on the story.

NAEYC CRITERIA
1.12

CELEBRATING DIVERSITY

Guidance always entails values. We all select what is important to us and what is supposedly correct behavior through the lens of our own culture and family. Teachers must always keep this in mind as they make decisions about which behaviors are acceptable or appropriate and which behaviors are not.

In addition, teachers must learn about the values and expectations that certain cultures have for the behavior of children and what children's families support within their cultural group. This learning is not supposed to result in teachers' feeling that they cannot make decisions about guidance. Rather, when teachers make decisions that conflict with children's cultural norms, they have an obligation to explain to the children (and their parents) why school behavior is different from home behavior. If parents understand the need for certain behaviors, they can help their children yet not feel that their own values and patterns are being ignored (Johns and Espinoza 1996).

Gender differences in expectations for behavior in educational settings are also an issue when thinking about diversity. Gordon and Browne (1996) have reported that teachers typically pay more attention to boys, give them more positive feedback, and give them more attention and praise for achievement. The same study found that aggression is tolerated more in boys, that disruptive talking is tolerated more in girls, that teachers use corporal punishment more with boys, and that teachers use more negative comments or disapproving gestures with girls.

All these findings should strengthen the resolve of teachers to pay equal attention to all children, to base standards of behavior on developmental and cultural information rather than on gender, and to discourage dependent helplessness and excessively conforming behavior in both boys and girls (Gordon and Browne 1996).

Parents and Guiding Behavior

● All guidance decisions must be made with knowledge about and sensitivity to the individual child's family and culture. Working with families in an open and caring relationship is a prerequisite to guidance that is appropriate for each child.

SUMMARY

● The term *discipline* usually means the way in which the teacher manages children's behavior. *Guidance* means the way the teacher plans to teach children how to control their own behavior, not simply to obey the person in authority. *Punishment* is the term for anything the teacher does to achieve children's compliance that does not help children learn to control their own behavior. *Corporal punishment* means any kind of physical punishment.

● Teachers plan for guidance by learning about children's developmental levels and needs and then planning a program that matches those levels and needs. Planning for the programs and activities, the materials and room arrangement, the classroom routines, and the daily schedule can help prevent behavior problems.

● Strategies for guiding behavior include teaching children the social skills they need to get along in a group, the verbal skills to tell others how they feel and what they need, the social knowledge of reading the behavior of others, and the dispositional skills to interact in positive ways with their peers and adults. Guiding group behavior requires some specific strategies, beginning with weighing the situation to determine if a response is required. If one is required, then the response should be private, developmentally appropriate, and supportive of the child's self-concept. Each teacher response should also reflect as much knowledge as he has about the child.

● Behavior-management systems, which are often adopted by schools, are designed to help teachers control children's behavior. Some of the best known of these programs are assertive discipline, the Glasser model, the Ginott model, and the Dreikurs model. Teachers often need staff development to implement these models.

● To provide guidance for a child with special needs, the teacher must assess the developmental level of the child and use strategies that are appropriate for that level regardless of the child's chronological age. Some children need adaptations in the classroom to participate fully in activities, and not providing those adaptations can lead to behavior problems. Others may need direct instruction in the social skills that help children interact in positive ways with their peers.

● All guidance decisions reflect the culture of the teacher and what she values personally. Thus, diversity in the classroom will force every teacher to examine her own values and learn to respect the values of others. This does not mean that the teacher must accept behavior in the classroom because parents accept that behavior at home. It does mean, however, that the teacher must learn about the cultures of all children, think about where any conflicts might arise, and try to solve any problems that result from such differences. Diversity also means that teachers have to think about gender differences and what is acceptable behavior for boys and girls.

REFLECTIONS

1. Describe how one or more of the following could lead to behavior problems in the classroom: an element of a program or activity, use of materials, room arrangement, class routines, and/or daily schedule.

2. What social skills can children learn to help them control their own behavior?

3. Should all misbehavior in the classroom receive an immediate response from the teacher? Why or why not?

4. Are the basic requirements of good behavior management the same for children with special needs as for any other children? Explain your answer using examples.

5. What cultural conflicts could occur over the behavior of children in the classroom? Again, use examples to explain your answer.

EXPLORATIONS AND ACTIVITIES

1. Observe a classroom of young children for at least an hour. Note every incident in which the teacher is involved in providing discipline of any sort. Note the strategies that the teacher uses to avoid or solve behavioral problems. What other strategies might have been used? Why do you think the teacher made the decisions she did?

2. Interview two teachers of young children. Ask each to describe her most common discipline problems and how she handles them. Compare your findings with those of your peers. What problems seem most common?

MyLabSchool is a collection of online tools for your success in this course, your licensure exams, and your teaching career. Visit **www.mylabschool.com** to access the following:

■ Online Study Guide
■ Video Cases from real classrooms
■ Help with your research papers using Research Navigator
■ Career Center with resources for:
  —Praxis and Licensure Preparation
  —Professional Portfolio Development
  —Job Search and Interview Techniques
  —Lesson Planning

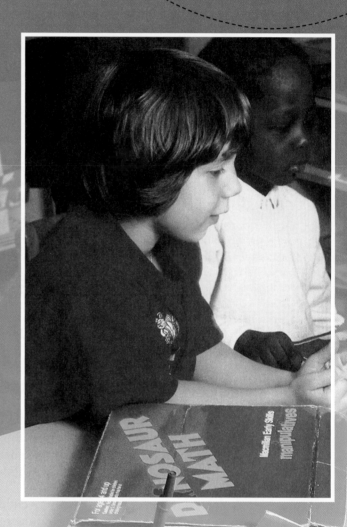

CHAPTER **7**

KEY TERMS you'll find in this chapter:

- Anecdotal records, 210
- Assessment, 202
- Formative assessment, 203
- High-stakes testing, 205
- No Child Left Behind (NCLB) Act, 206
- Portfolio, 219
- Readiness tests, 205
- Reliability, 205
- Rubric, 215
- Screening tests, 204
- Standardized tests, 205
- Summative assessment, 203
- Testing, 202
- Validity, 205

Assessment and Reporting

FOCUS QUESTIONS

- What are the differences between *assessment* and *testing?*
- Why and how should young children be tested?
- What strategies can be used to assess young children?
- How can assessment data be effectively organized?
- What strategies can teachers use for reporting assessment data to parents and others?
- Why and how should the program be assessed?
- What are strategies for assessing children with special needs?
- How can teachers ensure that assessment is culturally sensitive?

The local newspaper has just reported the test scores of children in area schools. Reading, mathematics, and writing scores are given by school and grade, with the percentages of increase and decrease since last year printed in bold type and the national averages highlighted. The almost-full-page newspaper article is accompanied by an interview with the superintendent of schools, who emphasizes that the district will focus all future staff development efforts on raising those scores before the next test.

The local TV stations have also reported the story about the test scores. One interviews an education professor from the university, who is critical of the newspaper article. As she points out, nowhere in the article is there any discussion about the match between the test and the local curriculum, between the norming samples and the population of the community, or the appropriateness of using standardized test scores as the only measure of progress in area schools. She also cites several critics of such "high-stakes" testing, who feel it is doing more harm than good in educating children (Andersen 1998; Kohn 1999; Ohanian 2000). They argue that such testing narrows the focus so that instructional programs are based on children's memorizing sets of facts, rather than understanding processes and developing concepts of how the world works.

You are really confused about these issues. What should be the role of testing in early childhood programs? How can children's growth be measured? How should educators respond to community pressure to prove that children are learning in school? These are difficult questions, and there are no easy answers. ■

Defining Assessment and Testing

Assessment and **testing** are not synonymous terms. Although testing is only one of several components of assessment, in recent years testing seems to have been misused and to have become the major determinant of the value of schools and the abilities of children.

Assessment is more than just testing, however; it is using a variety of strategies in an effort to uncover the understanding and determine the development of individual children. Teachers assess children's social, emotional, and physical development as well as their intellectual growth—just as a pediatrician assesses a child not only by weighing and measuring him and checking his visual acuity, his hearing, and his reflexes, but also by observing his ability to walk and his relationship to his parents. Similarly, programs are assessed by measuring not only the success of the children enrolled in them but also parents' satisfaction with their children's progress and teachers' feelings of accomplishment. Assessment is sometimes formal and sometimes informal.

In contrast to testing, assessment is ongoing. A test is a sample of behavior or knowledge taken at a specific time. Assessment covers a much longer timeframe and attempts to sample a much broader spectrum of behavior or knowledge.

Assessment is defined as collecting and evaluating information about the performance of an individual, the quality of a program, or the effectiveness of an activity. Testing may be one component of collecting data for assessment purposes, but it is only in the evaluating of data that assessment happens.

Webster's defines *assessment* as the action or instance of assessing. *Assess* comes from the French word *assidere,* meaning to sit beside or assist. Thinking of assessment as assisting or coaching creates a mindset about the purposes and uses of assessment that focuses on the positive results of good assessment.

Assessment is vital to good teaching; it is necessary to assess both the program and the progress of individual children. Good teachers would be involved in assessment even if there were no external requirements to do so; they want to know how well children are doing, and they want to know about the effectiveness of their programs. They even assess their assessment programs.

Good assessment not only helps teachers plan instruction but also empowers both children and teachers, as children become more aware of their accomplishments and teachers feel confident about their ability to guide children's learning. In addition, good assessment helps facilitate communication so that teachers and parents can talk about children and programs in meaningful ways.

Assessment alone does not improve children or programs—just as measuring a child's height and weight does not make the child grow. Only when assessment has a purpose and is used to help make decisions about curriculum, about individual children, and about programs can it help a child or a program grow.

Types of Assessment

Assessment can also be defined as formative and summative. **Formative assessment** is what teachers use most often on a daily basis. It is usually a quick check of what children are learning. Formative assessment is useful because it can help teachers adjust their instruction and make changes, if needed, for individual students. **Summative assessment,** on the other hand, occurs at the end of a teaching unit or topic. It is the final assessment for a given time period or topic. By the time summative assessment occurs, adjustments can no longer be made in instruction.

PRAXIS

Be able to explain formative and summative assessment and give an example of each

Teachers of young children will use formative assessment as they check on the progress of one or more children many times each day. Teachers will use summative assessment periodically to determine if children have met certain benchmarks at given times. For example, you might need to determine how many letter names each child knows at three or four specified times each year.

Types of Tests

Tests vary considerably in the purposes for which they were designed. The following definitions are based on the NAEYC's "Position Statement on Standardized Testing of Young Children 3 through 8 Years of Age" (1988):

Achievement test—A test that measures the extent to which a person has mastery over a certain body of information or possesses a certain skill after instruction has taken place

Criterion-referenced test—A test that evaluates a test taker in relation to a specified performance level (as distinguished from a test that compares the test taker's score to the performance of other people, which are norm-referenced tests)

Developmental test—An age-related, norm-referenced assessment of a child's skills and behaviors compared to those of children of the same chronological age; sometimes used incorrectly as screening tests

Norm-referenced test—A test that compares the test taker's performance to the performance of other people in a specified group

Readiness test—A test that assesses a child's level of preparedness for a specific academic or preacademic program

Reliability—The degree to which test scores are consistent, dependable, or repeatable; that is, the degree to which test scores can be attributed to actual differences in test takers' performance rather than to errors of measurement

Screening test—A test used to identify children who may be in need of special services; such a test focuses on the child's ability to acquire skills and may also be called a developmental screening test

Standardized test—A test composed of empirically selected items that is to be used in a specific way, is based on adequately defined norms, and is backed by data on reliability and validity

Validity—The degree to which a test measures what it is supposed to measure; also, the degree to which a certain inference from a test is appropriate or meaningful (p. 45)

Parents and Assessment

● Make assessment the focus of one parent meeting. Explain the differences between *assessment* and *testing*. Also provide parents with examples of various kinds of tests, and explain how each could best be used in a program for young children.

As a student, you have probably had experience with all these kinds of tests. For instance, you probably took achievement tests while you were in elementary school, or you might have taken one in order to be admitted to the teacher-education program you are in now. You might also have to take an examination in order to become a certified teacher in your state. Generally, achievement tests are norm referenced and standardized. You have also likely taken tests in your college classes. These tests are usually criterion referenced, as the teacher determines the correct answers, and, in theory, everyone could get a perfect score.

www.

www.ncrel.org/sdrs/areas/ issues/students/earlycld/ ea500.htm

Discusses appropriate assessment of young children

Testing Young Children

Young children are routinely given **screening tests.** Screening tests vary considerably, but most attempt to determine a child's ability to learn skills. Many of these tests ask children to identify objects, words, and numerals that are common in some environments. Developmental screening tests are designed to determine what children can do compared to other children their age. These tests often involve drawing geometric figures, bouncing balls, balancing on one foot, and repeating series of numerals or words.

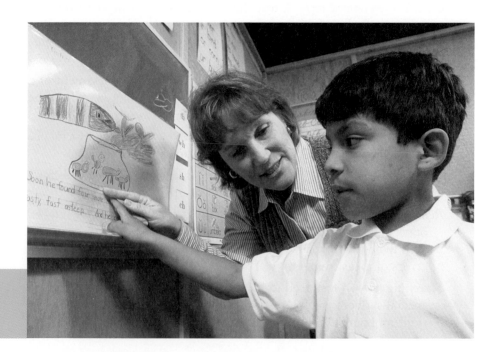

Having children read aloud is one way of assessing their reading skills.

Readiness tests ask young children to recognize letters and numerals, to find objects that go together, and to recognize objects that are not the same as other objects in a set. These tests are supposed to predict a child's success in coping with an instructional program.

Meisels (1987) argues that in most cases, screening tests lack **reliability** and **validity.** Further evidence of the problems of reliability and validity comes from a large-scale study conducted in Minnesota (Thurlow, O'Sullivan, and Ysseldyke 1986), in which every preschool child in the state was given a developmental screening test. Some districts found a problem with every child, and some found no problems at all. These results probably reflect the inadequacies of the tests themselves, the way in which they were administered, or the way in which the results were interpreted. In sum, the study makes clear one of the real dangers of using standardized tests, which is that decisions may be made on the basis of faulty information.

Standardized tests should be considered one of many avenues available for collecting information about a child, not the only avenue. Kamii and Kamii (1990) argue that standardized achievement tests encourage teachers to teach in ways that do not promote autonomous learning and that the tests do not tap children's thinking processes.

Martin (1988) disapproves of the use of standardized screening tests to homogenize the children in any program. She maintains that a flexible program "can accommodate a wide diversity in children's backgrounds, maturity, temperaments, interests, talents, abilities, and skills" (p. 489). Screening tests, she believes, are symptoms of the schools' refusal to accept differences.

www.fairtest.org/facts/ whatwron.htm

Questions and answers about what is wrong with standardized tests for all ages of learners

More recently, Meisels (2004) has been critical of the National Reporting System that is being used to assess Head Start children. He argues that there is no external validity for the subtests, that important aspects of both literacy and mathematics are not being adequately assessed, and that factors in the tests such as vocabulary and illustrations will influence the outcomes but are not related to what the tests are intended to measure. Moreover, he argues that testing every child is not justified. Others are wondering, as well, if it is appropriate to test four-year-olds (Jacobson 2004; Lewis 2003; Neisworth and Bagnato 2004).

A standardized test should be administered only if its administration can meet the criteria for good assessment, as defined by NAEYC (2003). These criteria include selecting a test only if it is ethical to use it, appropriate for the children to be tested, valid, and reliable. In addition, the test must be culturally and linguistically responsive and connected to specific, beneficial purposes. In fact, only the rare standardized test could meet these requirements.

There are some valid reasons for using standardized tests, such as to collect data for research studies that allow broad-based comparisons that can help make schools better places for children. Some tests may also help in diagnosing children who need special services. The responsibility for using tests in ways that benefit children lies with teachers and administrators.

High-Stakes Testing

You are probably familiar with the term **high-stakes testing** and know that it means tests on which major decisions are based. For example, in many states now, a student cannot graduate from high school without passing a state exam. You may also be experiencing high-stakes tests on a personal level because you probably have to pass a test in order to be certified to teach, regardless of your grades in classes or your performance in a field experience. There is the threat of high-stakes tests even for very young children, and early childhood educators must do all they can to make sure that young children are not tested inappropriately.

No Child Left Behind (NCLB) Act

www.ed.gov/nclb/landing.jhtml?src=pb

The government page for NCLB, with links to news releases, justifications, and so on

www.nea.org/esea/index.html

The National Education Association page on both NCLB and ESEA, including links to research and resources

Much has been written about the **No Child Left Behind (NCLB)** Act since it was signed into law in 2001. In particular, there have been many news reports about the difficulties of implementing the act and complaints about its unintended consequences.

The goals of NCLB are laudable: to help schools close the achievement gap between disadvantaged and/or minority students and their peers, to make sure that all teachers are qualified to teach, to make sure that all children in all schools are learning, and to give parents more choices in their children's education. Certainly, no one would argue against any of these goals. Everyone wants children to have the best possible teachers and to learn in schools that believe that all children can learn, regardless of their race or ethnicity, first language, or disability.

Many problems have been encountered, however, in implementing NCLB. One of the chief issues is that it requires testing each child (eventually, each child, each year, in each subject) and reporting these test scores by subgroup (e.g., minority students, English language learners, students with disabilities, etc.). First of all, these tests are expensive to give. The federal government is supposed to cover the costs of the exams, but many schools say that funding is inadequate and that states and districts are having to pay for the tests. And second, as explained in the previous section, many argue that such high-stakes testing narrows the curriculum so that teachers only teach to the test. In other words, children who might have learned all about, say, dinosaurs or rain forests will not have that opportunity unless these topics are to be tested. Some argue that children are actually learning less under NCLB because so much instructional time is devoted to testing. Schools are also having difficulty testing children with disabilities and children who are English language learners in ways that are appropriate.

> *The process of interacting with the children, not the content presented or placed around the children, is what counts.*
>
> —*David Weikart*

The provisions of NCLB are especially difficult for teachers of young children. Although the goals of NCLB and early childhood educators are not opposed, the means of assessing children's learning are not considered child centered or child friendly at all. Teachers with strong beliefs in developmentally appropriate practice (DAP) argue that a test of one or two skills (e.g., reading and math) will never be an accurate measure of a child's growth. Assessment should focus on all areas of development and employ the performance of tasks, not paper-and-pencil tests, to determine learning. This is not to say that DAP does not help children become skillful in reading and math; rather, DAP supports a curriculum that is broader in scope than just these areas.

Teachers of young children are also concerned about the expectation that all children will achieve the same standards at the same time. Anyone who knows children knows that is unrealistic. Today's teachers have to find a way to help all children learn using the best possible strategies and to focus on the individual needs of each child, regardless of the testing that is required.

The other responsibility of DAP teachers is to assess and record children's growth and learning in appropriate ways and to share these assessments with parents and others who make policy decisions. What is needed is more appropriate assessment of young children's learning and an understanding of the necessity for young children to grow and develop in all areas, not just two areas of academics.

Advocating for a more educated public in regard to educating young children does not mean abandoning the goals of all children learning under the tutelage of highly qualified and skilled teachers. On the contrary, it means demanding more in terms of the quality of teachers of young children and of support for the learning of all young children.

Strategies for Assessment

One of the hallmarks of the Reggio Emilia schools discussed in Chapter 2 is the incredible amount of time teachers spend documenting children's thinking and work. Most U.S. teachers do not have the time to provide that constant level of documentation. Nonetheless, *all* teachers need to assess the children in their programs—as well as the effectiveness of their programs—as part of good teaching.

Leonard (1997) states that observation helps teachers get to know children as individuals with unique personalities, provides a basis for making educational decisions, and generates the data needed to help parents see and understand their children's progress. And Helm, Beneke, and Steinheimer (1997) suggest that carefully documenting children's work has many advantages for teachers of young children. In addition to being able to respond to demands for accountability, teachers who document children's work in a variety of ways are able to plan for active learning experiences and meet special needs.

Figure 7.1 is a web diagram of the many types of successful documentation. As shown in the figure, teachers have many strategies from which to choose in making assessments of their children and their programs. In choosing which strategy or strategies to use, teachers must first decide what they need to know and how that information will be used. Not all strategies are equally useful, and not all are manageable in the time available to teachers.

The following sections will define and illustrate the various strategies available to early childhood teachers. Some of these strategies will require help from paraprofessionals and other professionals. For example, a specific tally cannot be recorded by the teacher who is trying to manage the behavior; rather, it must be done by an observer who is not intervening in the behavior.

Tallies

It is difficult to help a child change an inappropriate behavior without knowing exactly how often the behavior occurs. A *tally* provides a record of behaviors over a period of time.

www.

www.ncrel.org/sdrs/areas/ issues/methods/assment/ as800.htm

A discussion of the issue of equity in accommodating learners with special needs in school assessment

NAEYC CRITERIA
4.3, 4.5, 4.6, 4.9, 4.10

PRAXIS

Be able to explain the purposes of different assessment strategies

PRAXIS

Be able to explain how to avoid bias in assessment

FIGURE 7.1

Documenting Children's Work

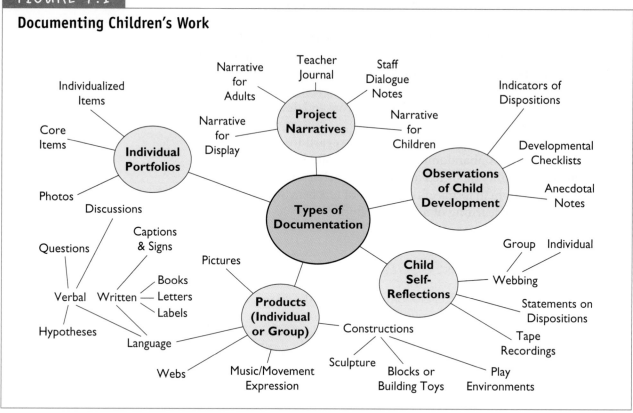

Source: J. H. Helm, S. Beneke, and K. Steinheimer, "Documenting Children's Learning," *Childhood Education* 73 (April 1997): 200–205. Reprinted by permission of Judy Harris Helm, Sallee Beneke, and Kathy Steinheimer, and the Association for Childhood Education International. Copyright © 2000 by the Association.

To mark each observed occurrence—for example, each incidence of aggressive behavior—the teacher would simply make one tally mark. The total tally count would provide some baseline data against which the child's improvement could later be judged. However, it would not provide information about the kind of aggression or the circumstances in which it occurs. A more specific tally would be more useful, perhaps including the time each incident occurred and a quick note describing the specific behavior (see Figure 7.2).

Running Narratives or Logs

A *running narrative* or *log* records the activities of the day (see Figure 7.3). It may help the teacher recall how often and when an activity has been offered and provide a general record for children and parents, who may enjoy recalling a certain day or activity.

Incident Records

An *incident record* documents the details of an isolated incident (see Figure 7.4). The amount of information provided by such a record is limited, but there are times when it is useful.

For example, suppose a child has never been able to choose a book independently and look at it for any length of time, but then one day, she does. An incident record would provide information about when and how

FIGURE 7.2

Specific Tally

Observer ___Linda Reynolds___ Date ___April 1___

Child Observed ___Taylor Thomas___

Time	Observation
8:30	Hit Sarah as she came into room
8:35	Pinched Jeremy as she sat down at puzzle table
8:42	Pushed Shawn away from puzzles
9:00	Pulled Trish's hair at water table
9:06	Grabbed a toy from Alex
9:30	Kicked Greg when he walked near her

this behavior occurred. Obviously, any time a behavior is observed for the first time, an incident record is a useful tool.

Narratives

A *narrative* can describe the behavior of one child or a group of children at a particular time, such as arrival time or snack time (see Figure 7.5). Although

FIGURE 7.3

Running Narrative

Observer ___Linda Reynolds___

April 1 All children were present today. Took a walk looking for signs of spring. Recorded signs on chartpaper when we returned. Each child contributed one thing to be recorded. Children chose their favorite song of the year ("Looby Lou"). We sang and danced it four times.

April 2 Tony and Liza were absent. It rained today, so we put out our rain gauge to measure how much. Wrote a class poem about the rain. Tara and Pete wanted to write their own poems. The class poem and Tara and Pete's poems are on the chart stand. We will read them again tomorrow.

April 3 Tony was absent again. Liza is back and feeling well. Favorite art activity today was easel painting. Ten children made paintings. Three made paper sculptures. The music teacher helped us learn a new song, "Round and Round the Village." This is a singing game, so we played and sang it several times.

April 4 Georgio brought three tadpoles to school, which his mother helped him catch in a pond near their house. Found a book in the library about frogs and toads. Watched a video about the growth of a frog from the egg to an adult frog. Drew pictures of tadpoles for our science journals.

FIGURE 7.4

Incident Record

Observer ___Linda Reynolds___   Date ___April 1___

Child Observed ___Nicole Byers___   Time ___9:30 A.M.___

Nicole selected a book from the library shelves. She took it to a beanbag chair and looked at it intensely for 10 minutes. During this time, she looked at the book all the way through two times. She turned to one page and pointed to each word as she told the story.

---

narratives are usually general in nature, they can provide useful information on which the teacher can base decisions about the program or individual children.

For example, in Figure 7.5, which is a narrative about arrival time, there is a lot of information about how the children come into the room and select activities. For the child who is typically late and hesitates to come into the classroom, the teacher should investigate that behavior or consider whether enough choices are available for the children.

Anecdotal Records

When teachers observe children's behavior and record their observations, they produce **anecdotal records.** Kept over a period of time, these records are likely to reveal patterns of behavior that will suggest strategies for helping an individual child become more competent or supporting the child's obvious growth. Irwin and Bushnell (1980) state that anecdotal records help teachers "test hunches about reasons for a child's behavior or learning style, . . . identify what conditions may be reinforcing behavior, and . . . gain

www.
www.prekinders.com/ anecdotal.htm

Good ideas for taking anecdotal records and making the process manageable

FIGURE 7.5

Narrative

Observer ___Linda Reynolds___   Date ___April 1___

Time ___Arrival Time: 8:30 A.M.___

Thomas, Nathan, and Cheryl arrived first and came into the room together. They hung up their coats and went to the blocks area. Theresa arrived next. She threw her coat on the floor and went to the easel and grabbed a smock. Freddie and Joe arrived next. They went to the blocks without hanging up their coats. Jason arrived next. He stepped into the room and stood barely inside the door for 5 minutes. Angelina and Edward walked past him to get into the room, but he did not move. They hung up their coats and went to the dramatic play center to get out the dolls and doll clothes. Jason took off his coat but held it in his arms while he walked over to Mrs. Jolie and asked her to help him hang it up. He then walked over to the blocks but only stood and watched. He made no effort to join the group playing.

feedback about what children have learned from a particular curriculum unit or presentation" (p. 23).

One key to making an anecdotal record is to record the information without interpretation—just the facts, please! For example, if the teacher observes Sally push Leon so hard that he falls backward into the sandbox, the teacher should record the act, not make a statement such as "Sally was aggressive." This may be the only incidence of pushing all year—Sally may be reacting to the fact that Leon pulled her hair. If Sally pushes several children and each incident is noted in the anecdotal record, then the teacher might interpret from the series of observations that Sally needs help in controlling her impulse to push people. A record stating that Sally was aggressive does not help the teacher focus on her behavior and find its causes. Any interpretation of behavior included in anecdotal records must be clearly labeled as such.

If possible, the teacher should record what happens just prior to an observation and also what happens after it. For example, if Leon pulls Sally's hair, that should be noted as part of the observation. What Sally does next should also be part of the recording. Knowing whether Sally runs away after pushing Leon, apologizes and helps him up, or sits down to play with him is valuable for the teacher in assessing Sally's behavior.

The bias of the observer is always an issue in an anecdotal record. Even though the observer may record an incident exactly as it happened, with no evaluative or interpretive comments, the choice of incidents to record, the frequency of recordings, and the lack of recordings may all reflect the bias of the observer.

Another key to making helpful observations is to observe children in many different situations and activities. Children who never initiate conversation inside the classroom may talk nonstop outdoors and single-handedly organize half the class for an activity.

WWW.
www.teachersnetwork.org/
NTNY/nychelp/need_to_know/
anecreport.htm
Very detailed instructions for writing an anecdotal record

NAEYC CRITERIA
4.19

Children have real understanding only of that which they invent themselves, and each time that we try to teach them something too quickly, we keep them from re-inventing it themselves.

—*Jean Piaget*

Observations should also focus on the total development of the child. Records of the child's physical, social, emotional, and intellectual development help the teacher put together a clear picture of the whole child. Katz (1984) suggests looking at preschoolers in terms of their range of affect, variations in play, curiosity, response to authority, friendship, interest, spontaneous affection, and enjoyment of life.

Various educators' guidelines for collecting anecdotal records (Bentzen 1985; Boehm and Weinberg 1987; Irwin and Bushnell 1980) are summarized here:

1. Record the incident as soon as possible after it occurs.
2. Include the setting, time, and activity.
3. Record the exact words of the participants when possible.
4. Record the actions and words of other people in the incident.
5. Make each record as objective, accurate, and complete as possible.

In addition, Boehm and Weinberg (1987, p. 17) recommend limiting discussion to one incident; separating interpretive comments from factual reporting; and considering supportive information in order to accumulate the most useful records.

Making anecdotal records is time consuming, which means this kind of information often stays in the teacher's head, rather than being put on paper. One technique for making note collecting easier is to prepare a looseleaf notebook with a page for each child. The teacher might carry a pad of sticky notes or computer labels in her pocket and jot down observations on individual notes; at the end of the day, these notes can be stuck on the appropriate child's page and the teacher won't have to recopy the information. Additional notes can be added as trends or patterns are observed (B. C. Hill and Ruptic 1994; Reardon 1991).

Teachers should make an effort to observe two or three children daily. Over time, they will have accomplished observations on every child. Sometimes, a teacher may choose one or two children and observe them for a week or two. Usually, these are children the teacher feels need special help because they have either behavior or learning problems.

Boyd-Batstone (2004) suggests that teachers use educational standards to guide their observations in anecdotal records. For example, the teacher could list the standards to be observed each day and document them using a set of abbreviations. The teacher should write the records in the past tense and provide specific examples whenever possible. Boyd-Batstone also suggests adding a specific task for the child to the observations as soon as possible. For example, a teacher might observe a child retell a story with puppets or a flannelboard and quickly note the accuracy with which the retelling was done. If elements were omitted, the task might be to ask the child to listen to that story again at the listening center and to listen for the omitted elements. If the retelling was accurate and complete, the task might be to introduce another story.

The goal is to document what the child can do at this time, not what he cannot do. Given this, anecdotal records are much more likely to capture the child's real progress than a standardized test. Including the task to be done can be helpful when planning instruction and can also be used to inform parents about what they might do at home to help the child.

Checklists and Rating Scales

Teachers can use *checklists* to make quick notes of what children actually do in the classroom. This information is valuable for determining which children are interested in which activities or which children have accomplished given tasks. Teachers can use the information obtained from checklists for evaluating learning areas and for reporting to parents.

Most checklists are constructed by teachers and used in a variety of activities, although some may be supplied by the district, state, or other administrators. Consider a checklist of children's physical skills. The skills to be observed would be listed across the top of the page and the children's names down the side of the page. If "Skipping" were one of the skills listed and a teacher observed a child skipping, he would enter the date beside the child's name. Other abilities are also relatively easy to record on a checklist: working puzzles, constructing patterns with beads or pattern blocks, cutting with the right or left hand, using counting as a problem-solving strategy, choosing a book and looking at it for five minutes, playing in a group for ten minutes, and so on.

Most teachers who use checklists find that it is most helpful to have a variety of such lists in the areas where the activities would be most likely to be observed. Table 7.1 identifies possible skills and abilities that can be noted on checklists.

TABLE 7.1 Skills and Abilities That Can Be Noted on Checklists

PHYSICAL DEVELOPMENT	SOCIAL–EMOTIONAL DEVELOPMENT	INTELLECTUAL DEVELOPMENT
■ Develop large muscles: run, hop, skip, gallop, balance, walk backward, throw and catch a ball ■ Develop small muscles: cut, paste, clap, button, zip, tie, stack ■ Manipulate tools ■ Copy simple shapes ■ Assemble puzzles ■ Draw, pretend write, write ■ Play games ■ Wash, use the toilet, dress without assistance ■ Visually follow a line of print from left to right and top to bottom and return ■ Distinguish sounds and symbols	■ Experience success at school ■ Interact with other children ■ Listen to and follow directions ■ Make choices ■ Initiate and complete activities ■ Accept responsibility ■ Express thoughts in a variety of ways ■ Show appreciation for and sensitivity to others ■ Explore and experiment ■ Practice social skills ■ Enjoy school ■ Maintain self-control ■ Talk ■ Play ■ Respond positively to adult authority ■ Share ■ Help clean up ■ Approach tasks positively and stay with tasks ■ Work independently ■ Cooperate ■ Respond to humor	■ Know and recite personal information: first and last name, age, address, birth-date, telephone number ■ Explain simple pictures ■ Show interest in print and desire to read and write ■ Differentiate between fantasy and reality ■ Speak in sentences of five or more words ■ Recognize colors ■ Recognize numbers ■ Count ■ Demonstrate one-to-one correspondence ■ Recite alphabet ■ Recognize upper- and lowercase letters ■ Write first name ■ Identify patterns and basic shapes ■ Recognize likenesses and differences ■ Measure ■ Ask questions ■ Brainstorm ■ Make lists ■ Classify objects and topics

FIGURE 7.6

Rating Scale

Observer ___Linda Reynolds___   Date ___April 1___

Child ___Ramon Martinez___

	Frequently	Sometimes	Not Yet
Uses language effectively		✔	
Solves problems in arithmetic with sums to 10	✔		
Participates in group discussions			✔
Participates in singing experiences		✔	

McAfee and Leong (1997) have identified the following advantages of using checklists:

1. Large amounts of information are recorded quickly.
2. Checklists are flexible and versatile. They are easily analyzed, interpreted, and quantified.
3. Other people, such as aides, can be trained to use checklists.
4. Checklists do not have to be completed in the day or week they are begun; they are ongoing.
5. Checklists keep track of a child's progress as well as achievement at a specific time. (p. 89)

Rating scales are similar to checklists except that the behaviors are marked in terms of frequency (always, sometimes, never) or quality (above average, average, or below average) (see Figure 7.6). Rating scales can also provide useful information for teachers as they plan learning experiences.

It is most appropriate to use rating scales to compare children's current behaviors to their previous behaviors. Teachers can get caught in the trap of comparing children to one another if they are not judicious in their use of rating scales.

Records of Conversations, Conferences, and Interviews

Records of conversations, conferences, and interviews with children can serve a variety of purposes. Notes from conversations can document a child's abilities with productive language (vocabulary, fluency, articulation of sounds), with concepts (explaining why fish do not sleep), and with processes (how a paper snowflake is cut out). Records of conferences and interviews are more formal in that the teacher designs a set of questions and records the child's responses. Figure 7.7 is an example of a reading–writing conference record. Any of these records can be useful for making instructional decisions for that child.

NAEYC CRITERIA
4.18

PRAXIS
Be able to explain how an assessment of a specific task can help guide instruction

NAEYC CRITERIA
4.15

FIGURE 7.7

Reading–Writing Conference Record

Teacher _____   Date _____

Child _____

What are you reading (or writing) today?

Are you having any problems?

Would you read your favorite part to me (or what you have written)?

Positive specific comments:

What are you going to learn next?

Asking questions in a conversation, conference, or interview is also a good way to gather information about how children feel about different activities and the things that interest them most. Often, these questions are intended to be open ended. For example, the teacher might ask, "What is your favorite thing to do in the classroom?" or "What is your favorite thing to do outdoors?" Some types of records are designed to gather information by asking children to mark responses to given questions.

Figure 7.8 shows an example of the type of form a teacher might complete during an open-ended interview with a child. Records such as these can help teachers make planning decisions. For instance, if the teacher determines that children are feeling uncomfortable about certain learning experiences, then those can be modified so that the children's attitudes about school might be improved. These records can also provide teachers with clues about experiences that would be of interest to the children and would therefore likely be the basis for successful learning experiences.

Rubrics

Many primary teachers have adopted rubrics as one method of evaluating children's work. A **rubric** is developed to specify the qualities of a given performance (e.g., a writing selection or an oral report) and used to determine how closely the performance meets those standards (Rickards and Cheek 1999).

In order to be effective, a rubric must be constructed carefully; it should be used to work with important goals. For example, a rubric to assess children's writing progress should specify major writing goals. If the standards of the first-grade writing program include writing stories that have a beginning, a middle, and an end, then the rubric should specify those elements and ask the teacher to determine how well each element was accomplished. Figure 7.9 is an example of such a rubric. Of course, when teachers specify elements in a rubric, they must make sure that the children

http://school.discovery.com/ schrockguide/assess.html

Many links to sites related to rubrics—from constructing them to understanding the purposes of them

http://edweb.sdsu.edu/ triton/july/rubrics/Rubric_ Guidelines.html

Clear steps for developing and using rubrics

FIGURE 7.8

Form for Open-Ended Interview

Teacher _____Linda Reynolds_____   Date _____April 1_____

Child _____Mary Ricard_____

1. Do you have a pet?

    A cat named Selena

2. What is your favorite toy?

    My Molly doll

3. What do you like to do best when you play outside?

    Hang on the monkey bars

4. Who do you like to play with?

    Cara, who lives next door

5. What do you like to do best here at school?

    Painting pictures

6. What is your favorite book or story?

    Color Zoo

have had a chance to learn each element as well as many opportunities to practice it.

One of the advantages of using rubrics is that children know in advance how their work will be evaluated, so there are no surprises. Rubrics can also

FIGURE 7.9

Rubric for Assessing Writing

Standard	3	2	1
There is a clear beginning to the story. The characters and setting are introduced	The beginning of the story includes the introduction of the characters and the setting in detail.	The beginning of the story includes the characters or the setting but not both.	The beginning of the story is not clear. No characters are introduced, and no setting is described.
There is a clear middle of the story. The problem is clear to the reader.	The middle of the story clearly reveals the problem of the story.	There is some reference to the problem, but it is not made clear.	There is no reference to the problem of the story.
There is a clear ending to the story. The solution to the problem is clear to the reader.	The ending of the story clearly reveals the solution to the problem.	The ending reveals a solution but not clearly.	The story does not reveal the solution to the problem.

be used to help parents understand how their child's work is being evaluated and what their child needs to do in order to improve.

Multiple websites offer teachers the opportunity to quickly put together a rubric by filling in the instructional elements and levels of success. These rubrics are only as useful as the quality of the entries provided by the teacher. Creating a good rubric requires careful thought—in particular, a good grasp of the goals of instruction and indicators that children are meeting those goals.

Parent Questionnaires

When Hill, Ruptic, and Norwick (1998) asked primary-grade teachers what assessment tools gave them the most information, one of the answers was *parent questionnaires*. Harp (2006) also recommends parent questionnaires as a useful tool for promoting cooperation between the parents and the school.

Parents can be asked what they have done to prepare their child for school, how their child feels about coming to school, how they would describe their child as a learner, and so on. The answers to these questions can help teachers communicate better with parents during conferences and plan activities that will involve them.

Self-Evaluations

Even very young children can begin to evaluate themselves. They can describe orally what they learned while they were involved in the activities of the day, or they can tell how they learned to do something. Older children can decide with the teacher which things they are learning are most important and record those in a booklet or on a checklist they have constructed.

> **PRAXIS**
>
> Be able to explain how young children can be involved in assessing their own progress

Primary children might be encouraged to complete short, written evaluations of selected pieces of their work to share with others. For example, they might complete the sentence "I think this is my best writing because _____" or "I want to share this art because _____."

Part of the process of *self-evaluation* should include what needs to come next, so as children think about what they have done well, they should be encouraged to think about what they need to learn, too. For instance, if a child has learned to print his first name, he should be acknowledged for that achievement and then asked if he wants to learn to print his last name (or perhaps the name of a friend or some other word of interest). If a child can read a given text successfully, then he might be encouraged to read a more difficult text or a text from a different genre. Self-evaluation should be linked to personal goal setting.

Is the language of assessment important in today's high-stakes testing world? Consider that question as you read the following An Expert Speaks box. In it, Dr. Ann Benjamin suggests that teachers learn about assessment and the language of assessment as well as develop their observational skills.

Organizing Assessment Data

Records alone do not constitute assessment; they must be evaluated by the teacher. If the teacher has collected various behavioral records over a period of weeks, he can then decide how much and in what ways a child's

AN **Expert** SPEAKS: Assessment in Early Childhood Education

Ann Benjamin, University of Massachusetts Lowell

Despite the call for developmentally appropriate assessment and evaluation practices in early childhood education (NAEYC 1988), policymakers and politicians have increasingly pushed for more standardized testing of children at younger and younger ages. Most teachers know intuitively that testing children under the age of seven or eight yields questionable results. Nonetheless, the "testing craze" ("Why the Testing Craze" 1999) is likely to continue, and teachers are well advised to prepare themselves to respond.

How do novice teachers equip themselves for a challenge that many veterans find daunting? Teachers who have successfully navigated their way through the complex world of assessment and evaluation offer the following advice:

1. Familiarize yourself with an array of assessment tools and techniques. There are many, and each type serves a different purpose (Airasian 2001; Harp 1996; Irwin and Bushnell 1980; Krechevsky 1998; Meisels et al. 1993). This will help you construct a rich understanding of learning and development, with test scores being only one component of a complex, multifaceted description of each child.

2. Learn the language of assessment and evaluation. Make sure you understand terms such as *objective* and *subjective, reliable,* and *valid.* Know the difference between formative and summative assessment. Become familiar with terms such as *portfolios, performance assessment, work samples, rubrics,* and *authentic assessment* (Airasian 2001; Brandt 1992; Woolfolk 2001).

3. Develop keen observation, recording, and reporting skills. Worthwhile assessment depends on the teacher's ability to observe children systematically across a variety of learning situations and to summarize her observations for parents and colleagues (Beaty 1986; Carlevale 1991; McNeely 1997; Nicolson and Shipstead 1994; Schweinhart 1993).

4. Use ongoing assessment to help plan the daily and weekly curriculum. Effective teachers know what children need to learn *before* they decide what to teach (Worthen 1996).

5. Involve children in the assessment process by designing age-appropriate self-evaluations and instruments that help children understand what they must do to produce quality work (Flagg 1998).

6. If you must grade children, insist that grading legends be clearly defined and linked to samples of children's actual work.

7. If you are required to test young children, prepare them to do their best. Involve their families by urging a good night's sleep, supportive attitudes, and a nutritional breakfast. Communicate honestly with students, telling them that the test is an opportunity to show what they have learned. Don't pretend that the results are not important.

Conferences are critical in communicating with parents; teachers must prepare carefully for conferences. Try to meet the parents before the conference so that your first meeting is not at the conference. Try to structure the conference so that you accomplish your goals in the allotted time. Encourage parents to plan their questions in advance. If you need a translator, make arrangements for one. As you speak to parents, try to put yourself in their place. Would you be glad you made the effort to attend the conference? Would you return for the next conference? Do parents leave the conference knowing what they can do to support their child's continued growth? Have you shared worthwhile suggestions for at-home activities? Finally, have you discovered what is special about the child? Do parents recognize that you appreciate their child's unique qualities? Have you shared with parents what is truly wondrous about their child? (Benjamin 1993, 1997).

When all is said and done, do parents tell you how the information you provided might help them make decisions on their child's behalf? Assessment succeeds only if the results help *each family* decide what is best for *their child's* educational future. Test scores alone will never accomplish that purpose.

behavior has changed. The records he has kept should provide evidence for his conclusions. And in order to be useful in documenting and reporting those conclusions, the records must be organized. One popular choice for organizing observations is the portfolio.

Portfolios

Paulson, Paulson, and Meyer (1991) define a **portfolio** as "a purposeful collection of student work that exhibits the student's efforts, progress, and achievements in one or more areas. The collection must include student participation in selecting contents, the criteria for selection, the criteria for judging merit, and evidence of student self-reflection" (p. 60).

Purpose

Portfolios are popular with teachers. But before teachers decide to use a portfolio system, they must decide the purpose the portfolio will serve: Will it be used to communicate with parents? Will it be used to determine the child's individual progress? Will it be used for teacher accountability? Will it be used for all these purposes?

In deciding purpose, teachers should understand that a portfolio alone is not an assessment; rather, it is a collection of materials that can be used to assess progress. Thus, a portfolio is not especially useful until the materials have been evaluated by the teacher or others. A collection of materials such as writing samples and artwork, for instance, is only that—a collection. It becomes an assessment tool when it has been used to determine a child's progress and needs.

Portfolios can be invaluable in communicating with parents. When a child receives a letter grade of A or C for an entire year's performance in a subject, parents have no way of knowing exactly what the child has learned or how much progress she has made since the beginning of the term. Flood and Lapp (1989) suggest a comparison portfolio strategy that is especially helpful in communicating a child's growth to parents. They suggest selecting writing samples, reading samples, and other pertinent information (such as the number of books read, how often reading is chosen as a free-choice activity, changes in attitudes, and so on) that will demonstrate the child's growth in an area.

Teachers should make sure that parents are aware of how pieces were selected for a portfolio: Are they the child's best work? work that demonstrates a particular competency? work that is in progress? Parents also should be invited to offer suggestions for portfolio entries or deletions.

Sometimes, portfolios are used to provide evidence for teacher accountability. For instance, items in portfolios can be used to document that given activities were provided for children. Teachers might also exchange three or four portfolios with peers in order to validate their own opinions about the instruction provided and the children's achievement.

If teachers choose to exchange portfolios, the selection of the portfolios for examination should be clearly understood. For example, if four were to be exchanged, one might be from a child showing outstanding performance, two from children showing average performance, and one from a child having difficulties of some kind. Teachers might even want to submit portfolios of selected children's pieces to their administrators in order to demonstrate effectiveness in fostering children's achievement.

Content

Portfolios can be valuable for documenting children's growth, for communicating with parents, and for validating the quality of instruction. However,

www.ncrel.org/sdrs/areas/ issues/students/earlycld/ es51143.htm

Definitions of portfolios, purposes of using them, and hints for managing them in the classroom

http://teacher.scholastic.com/ professional/assessment/ powerportfolios.htm

Getting started with portfolios, as well as how to store them and reasons to use them their usefulness depends on how and what materials are selected and how they are organized.

A variety of items can be included in a portfolio—drawings or paintings the child has made, photos of block constructions he has made, photos or videos of him climbing on outdoor equipment, notes about or videos of him throwing or catching a ball, records of books he has read (or listened to the teacher read), stories he has written or dictated, samples of his classification activities, and notes about his social growth.

Of course, portfolios may also contain teacher observations and notes. If, for example, a piece of writing is selected for inclusion in a child's portfolio, the teacher might add some observation about the selection—perhaps noting that the child worked on the piece over a period of four days but was reluctant to make any changes after a conference with the teacher. The same sort of comment might accompany art samples or other work. Work samples, when used along with other information collected by the teacher, clearly demonstrate the child's growth and the effectiveness of the program.

Organization

NAEYC CRITERIA
4.13

The most logical organization for a portfolio that will be used to determine a child's individual progress is to create a section of the portfolio to match each of the major program goals. For example, Meisels (1993, p. 36) suggests the categories of personal–social development, language and literacy, mathematical thinking, scientific thinking, social studies, art and music, and physical development.

The High/Scope program (Schweinhart 1993) recommends the following organizational categories:

- *Initiative*—Expressing choices, engaging in complex play
- *Creative representation*—Making, building, pretending
- *Social relations*—Relating to adults, making friends
- *Music and movement*—Exhibiting body coordination, imitating movements to a beat
- *Language and literacy*—Showing interest in reading, beginning reading, beginning writing
- *Logic and mathematics*—Sorting, counting objects, describing time sequences (p. 32)

Teachers of younger children might find different categories more appropriate for their students, whereas teachers of eight-year-olds might need more specific categories for mathematics, reading, and writing.

Once the major categories have been determined, one or two core items can be collected and dated in fall, winter, and spring. *Core items* are work samples that are common to all children. For example, all children in the first grade would be expected to complete some writing and reading. Other items can be added in each category that reflect the child's individual interests or activities.

Multiple Intelligence Categories Another strategy for organizing the information gathered about a child is to use Gardner's (1983) multiple intelligences as categorical headings and record information under them, perhaps one category per page. For example, behaviors related to language and print would be recorded under "Linguistic Behaviors" and mathematical experiences under "Logico-Mathematical." The primary advantages of this organizational system are that it reveals the child's strengths at a glance and indicates whether a balance of activities has been offered.

In addition to observing children's strengths in the intelligences, Krechevsky (1998) suggests that teachers observe children's working styles. For example, is the child easily engaged in activities? persistent in solving problems? planful? focused or easily distracted? Knowing how a child works can help the teacher plan activities for her and teach her valuable work strategies.

Developmental Areas Using the four areas of child development is another organizational strategy. The teacher's observations can be organized to reflect the child's physical development, social development, emotional development, and cognitive development. Observations that fit into more than one category should be duplicated so they can be included in the second category, as well. One advantage of this means of organization is that it enables the teacher to quickly determine which developmental areas are receiving a lot of attention and which are perhaps being ignored.

Overview of Portfolios

Whatever system is used to organize observations and assessments, a portfolio should include a table of contents or summary sheet listing the materials included and the dates they were collected. Two or three times a year, it will be helpful to summarize the data in the portfolio. Such a summary will help teachers determine where their information is too thin and to use what information they have more fully in planning learning experiences. Including some sort of summary will also help prevent the portfolio from becoming a jumble of materials over time.

Most teachers prefer to collect portfolio items in large, expandable folders or loose-leaf binders. However the materials are collected, they should be stored in a place that is easily accessible to both children and teachers. Often, children like to review what they have done already and add items that are especially significant to them. And teachers will certainly want to add to the portfolios on a regular basis.

A portfolio of work samples with careful summaries can be an accurate measure of a child's performance (Meisels et al. 1995). Because such a system is just as valid and provides much more information than an achievement test, it certainly seems reasonable to replace achievement testing with a well-developed portfolio system. Stone (1995) summarizes the differences between portfolio assessment and more traditional assessment in Table 7.2.

Portfolios are most useful when they are built into the instructional day and help teachers make good instructional decisions (Stone 1995). In schools and classrooms in which the use of portfolios for assessment is most successful, teachers and children work to describe good products. Then they think about how the portfolio entries demonstrate growth toward worthwhile goals. Finally, teachers, parents, and children use the portfolios to celebrate achievements, to set new goals, and to reflect on the process of learning together. Barclay and Breheny (1994) found that reporting to

TABLE 7.2 Portfolio Assessment versus Traditional Assessment

PORTFOLIO ASSESSMENT	TRADITIONAL ASSESSMENT
Uses multiple forms of assessment	Uses one form of assessment
Gives complete picture of child's learning	Gives narrow view of child's learning
Makes assessment within contexts	Makes assessment in contrived learning context (i.e., test)
Is child centered	Is curriculum centered
Is ongoing	Conducts one-time test on particular task
Supports the process of learning	Represents isolated task separate from the process of learning
Focuses on what children can do	Focuses on what children cannot do
Evaluates child's past achievements and potential	Evaluates by comparison to norms
Benefits children by supporting their growth	Labels, sorts, and ranks children
Provides teachers with information to extend child's learning	Provides little information teacher can use to help child
Provides opportunity for child to evaluate own learning	Uses only teacher evaluation

Source: S. Stone, *Understanding Portfolio Assessment: A Guide for Parents* (Wheaton, MD: Association for Childhood Education International, 1995). Reprinted by permission of S. Stone and the Association for Childhood Education International. Copyright © 1995 by the Association.

parents was much more effective when they kept portfolios of children's work to share at conference time.

Electronic Portfolios

Several websites are available that allow teachers to produce portfolios based on checklists and comments for each child and then make these available to parents. One of these sites is Creative Curriculum (www.creativecurriculum.net), where fifty objectives are grouped under the categories of social/emotional development, physical development, cognitive development, and language development. Each objective is explained through many examples so that both teachers and parents will know what the objective means. This site suggests that the checklists be completed three times a year.

Another site is Work Sampling Online, a system developed by Sam Meisels (1993), at www.worksamplingonline.com. At this site, the teacher can enter the data on each child in her class by entering a rating on many objectives grouped into the categories of personal and social development, language and literacy, mathematical thinking, scientific thinking, social studies, the arts, and physical development and health. This site also recommends entering the information on each child three times a year.

Another site is the Early Learning site, based on the assessment system developed by High/Scope, at www.earlylearner.net. The teacher is asked to complete questions three times each year that are grouped under the categories of initiative, social relations, creative presentation, music and movement, language and literacy, and logic and mathematics. Once the observations of each child are recorded, suggested activities for each area are displayed. If the teacher clicks on these activities, the site provides an explanation for these activities and what can be learned from each. It also provides suggestions for what to look for next in the child's development.

Each of these sites (1) features a place in the portfolio of each child where the teacher can make comments and provide explanations; (2) compiles the individual information into a group record and offers resources for the teacher, such as articles about children, curricula, and assessment; and (3) provides a forum through which teachers who are using the system can talk with one another and share their successes and any problems. Teachers can scan samples of artwork, photos of constructions, and photos of children involved in activities and post these on a website that is available to parents. The individual profiles of students on all the sites are available only by special password so that parents can see only the record of their child.

Electronic portfolios are relatively easy to construct and provide one more means for teachers to keep in touch with busy parents. However, all portfolio systems are only as good as the information recorded in them, and teachers will need to continue to engage in daily observations of their children, even if the portfolios are officially completed only three times a year.

In the following A Teacher Speaks box, Mary Giard describes her plan for assessment through the year. Would her plan work for you? Would you feel comfortable with the assessment program if you were the parent of a child in her classroom?

Reporting Assessment Data

Reporting to parents is an important part of the job of the early childhood teacher. Parents have a right to know about their children's performance and behavior in school. And while teachers have an obligation to be as honest as they can with parents, this honesty must be leavened with tact and sensitivity.

Nothing is as important to parents as their children; honesty does not have to be brutal or hurtful. Reports to parents usually take the form of report cards, conferences, narratives, telephone calls, casual conversations, newsletters, or videotapes.

Report Cards

Although many schools require report cards for children in kindergarten and the primary grades, report cards are frustrating to both parents and teachers of young children. Many parents and most educators question the information conveyed on report cards: What does a grade mean? Does an A in mathematics mean that the child knows a given set of concepts or that the child can complete a given number of computations correctly? Grades are notoriously unreliable and useless in conveying what young children have or have not learned (Culbertson, Doutt, and Jalongo 1999; Robinson 1997).

Many schools have done away with letter grades on report cards for kindergarten (and some for primary grades), but often letter grades have been replaced by checklists of skills mastered, such as "Speaks in complete sentences" and "Counts to 100." These checklists have some of the disadvantages of letter grades and leave the impression that the program consists of teaching isolated skills.

www.ncrel.org/sdrs/areas/
issues/students/earlycld/
ea5lk20.htm
Strategies and resources for
reporting assessment results
to parents and others

NAEYC CRITERIA
2.8, 2.9, 4.4

PRAXIS

Be able to describe four ways that
teachers can communicate assessment results to parents

A **Teacher** SPEAKS: *Assessment Practices for Primary-Age Children*

Mary Giard

Center for Teaching
and Learning
Edgecomb, Maine

"Miss G., you always ask us hard questions. Now we ask ourselves and each other hard questions, too."
—Ryan, age 7

- *History/Social Studies:* Log entries, list of things studied/researched, photos, and samples
- *Math:* Math log entries, examples of work done, list of demonstrated concepts understood by the individual, goals, and interests
- *Physical Education/Art/Music:* List of pieces studied, strengths, interests, goals, samples, tapes, and written responses

Ryan is right: I do ask hard questions so that all of us in the class community will learn to think, question, and reflect on the learning we do each day. Now my "bottom line" is this question to myself: Why am I doing what I am doing?

Public school often requires testing or assessment. It sometimes helps me learn about my children, but more often, the evaluation and assessment decisions made by my students and me are more meaningful. It is productive for us to determine what will best capture our strengths, interests, and goals.

We keep portfolios. They are not collections of papers that sit in a file cabinet. The items placed in our portfolios are documents that represent what we can do and where we want to direct our attention. Last year, my class put together a portfolio checklist of documents that were important for us to consider for inclusion:

- *Reading:* Monthly goals, copies of running records (and a piece of writing that described what the reader did to change and improve the use of strategies), a list of the books the child read independently, and photos or samples of book projects (play, poster, letter to the author, etc.)
- *Writing:* Monthly goals, monthly writing samples with attached self-assessments that described what the samples demonstrated in terms of the writer's growth and change, self-edit checklists, writing samples from prompts, rubrics, and any other materials the student selected
- *Science:* Samples from science and nature logs, photos, written explanations, and samples of experiments/results

Portfolios make it easy to organize student-led conferences held at the end of the year. Each child prepares a conference for his or her family. Other people may be included in the conferences (the Reading Recovery teacher, siblings, administrators, teachers from previous years, etc.). The portfolios and conferences represent the strong commitment to student involvement in the record-keeping and assessment procedures. The assessment model also keeps evaluation in sync with day-to-day learning and teaching.

I am busy maintaining records of children's academic, emotional, and social growth and change. My daily teaching plans come from what I observe the children doing as they work. Checklists do not work for me. They are more paperwork to transfer information. I now streamline my information to maintain a reasonable record-keeping system. Keeping folders or a notebook of running records helps me watch patterns and changes in students' reading behaviors over time. I also maintain notes on writing work, and I make conference notes as I work with individuals and groups. For work selected by students, I either concur with their choices or I pull other samples that I feel better represent their learning and work.

To be able to maintain the quality of teaching I want, my evaluation practices must be well thought out and simple. I observe the learners, evaluate their work, make teaching decisions, and reassess the growth. Assessment is ongoing, cyclical, and specific. To maintain that quality forces me to question my practices and get at the real issues.

A report card is not the best choice for reporting to parents. If teachers must use report cards, however, they should try to mediate the information for parents by enclosing written summaries of children's progress or at least comments that help parents understand the grades. Some schools have adapted their report cards so that they reflect more about what the child can do and depend less on letter grades. For example, rather than post a grade in reading, some parts of a developmental checklist might be on the report card, such as "Self-corrects errors that change meaning." A report card might also have spaces for the child, teacher, and parents to record their goals for the next grading period. Another strategy is to have a conference with the parents to discuss the child's progress and to review the report card.

Conferences

The most effective way of reporting to parents is face to face in a conference. A conference should not be conducted so that the parents sit passively while the teacher tells them about their child. Both parents and teachers (and sometimes children) should participate; each should learn from the other, and both should have the opportunity to share information.

Effective conferences require advance preparation. All the observational records, information gathered from checklists, information from inventories or interviews, and portfolios of work will need to be assembled and organized. Teachers must not withhold information from parents; all records should be open to them. Preparation should also include writing a summary of the child's progress in all areas of development and thinking about the implications of assessments for future planning for the child.

If you are new to parent conferences, you can gain experience by participating in a role-play of a conference with a colleague or your administrator. Seek advice from this person on how you could improve the communication during the conference. Following these guidelines can help a conference go well for all parties:

1. Be positive and personal. Parents want to know that you know their child, that you like their child even though he may have some difficulties, and that their child has good qualities.

www.geocities.com/smilecdg/ parentteacherconference.html
Tips for conducting parent–teacher conferences, purposes for them, and other useful links

www.teachervision.fen.com/ page/3730.html
Many links to parent–teacher conference ideas

www.teachersnetwork.org/ dcs/newteach/conferences
Preparing for successful parent–teacher conferences

NAEYC CRITERIA
4.23, 4.24

Teachers should follow these guidelines for appropriate assessment in planning instruction and communicating with parents:

1. Curriculum and assessment are integrated throughout the program; assessment is congruent with and relevant to the goals, objectives, and content of the program.

2. Assessment results in benefits to the child, such as needed adjustments in the curriculum or more individualized instruction and improvements in the program.

3. Children's development and learning in all domains—physical, social, emotional, and cognitive—and their dispositions and feelings are informally and routinely assessed by teachers' observing children's activities and interactions, listening to them as they talk, and using their constructive errors to understand their learning.

4. Assessment provides teachers with useful information to successfully fulfill their responsibilities: to support children's learning and development, to plan for individuals and groups, and to communicate with parents.

5. Assessment involves regular and periodic observation of the child in a wide variety of circumstances that are representative of the child's behavior in the program over time.

6. Assessment relies primarily on procedures that reflect the ongoing life of the classroom and typical activities of the children. Assessment avoids approaches that place children in artificial situations, impede the usual learning and developmental experiences in the classroom, or divert children from their natural learning processes.

7. Assessment relies on demonstrated performance during real, not contrived, activities, for example, real reading and writing activities rather than only skills testing (Engel 1990; Teale 1988).

8. Assessment utilizes an array of tools and a variety of processes, including, but not limited to, collections of representative work by children (artwork, stories they write, recordings of their reading), records of systematic observation by teachers, records of conversations and interviews with children, and teachers' summaries of children's progress as individuals and as groups (Chittenden and Courtney 1989; Goodman, Goodman, and Hood 1989).

2. Be ready to show examples of the child's work, and be ready to make suggestions for what the parents can do to support their child's learning. Even if the student is outstanding, you should offer suggestions for what the parents might provide as enrichment.

3. Don't be defensive. Parents may have questions about your classroom or your program, and you must answer them without being angry or acting insulted.

4. Show your caring. As you lay out all your information, don't forget to let the parents know that you care about their child.

5. Be a good listener. The use of active listening skills is critical. Also be sure to give parents enough time to ask questions and share with you what they have observed about their child.

9. Assessment recognizes individual diversity of learning and allows for differences in styles and rates of learning. Assessment takes into consideration children's ability in English, their stage of language acquisition, and whether they have been given the time and opportunity to develop proficiency in their native language as well as in English.

10. Assessment supports children's development and learning; it does not threaten children's psychological safety or feelings of self-esteem.

11. Assessment supports parents' relationships with their children and does not undermine parents' confidence in their children's or their own ability, nor does it devalue the language and culture of the family.

12. Assessment demonstrates children's overall strengths and progress, what children can do, not just their wrong answers and what they cannot do or do not know.

13. Assessment is an essential component of the teacher's role. Since teachers can make maximal use of assessment results, the teacher is the *primary* assessor.

14. Assessment is a collaborative process involving children and teachers, teachers and parents, school and community. Information from parents about each child's experiences at home is used in planning instruction and evaluating children's learning. Information obtained from assessment is shared with parents in language they can understand.

15. Assessment encourages children to participate in self-evaluation.

16. Assessment addresses what children can do independently and what they can demonstrate with assistance, because the latter shows the direction of their growth.

17. Information about each child's growth, development, and learning is systematically collected and recorded at regular intervals. Information such as samples of children's work, descriptions of their performance, and anecdotal records is used for planning instruction and communicating with parents.

18. A regular process exists for periodic information sharing between teachers and parents about children's growth and development and performance. The method of reporting to parents does not rely on letter or numerical grades but rather provides more meaningful, descriptive information in narrative form.

Source: From S. Bredekamp and T. Rosegrant, "Reaching Potentials through Transforming Curriculum, Assessment, and Teaching," in *Reaching Potentials: Transforming Early Childhood Curriculum and Assessment,* vol. 2, edited by S. Bredekamp and T. Rosegrant, 5–22 (p. 17) (Washington, DC: National Association for the Education of Young Children, 1995). Reprinted with permission from the National Association for the Education of Young Children.

6. Don't surprise parents. If you have concerns about a child, let the parents know in advance that you are going to discuss those concerns at the conference. If you want to invite another staff member to the conference to help you convey information about program choices, for example, let the parents know in advance that that person will be there.

7. Never dwell on the negative, and always suggest a solution to a problem. (Some items adapted from Million 2005.)

Effective follow-up to a conference will be helpful in planning the next conference and will increase the parents' trust. All agreements made during a conference should be summarized in writing, and copies should be made for both the teacher and the parents.

If the conference ends with an agreement that the teacher will perform certain tasks, then these tasks should be completed promptly and the information should be entered in the conference file. For example, if the parents request that the teacher observe their child for a specific behavior in the next two weeks and report to them, the teacher should make the observations, record them, and share them with the parents.

Student-Led Conferences

PRAXIS

Be able to explain how students can be involved in their own assessment

A relatively new approach to parent conferences is to have students lead them. Many teachers have invited students and parents to attend conferences together over the years, but only recently have teachers begun teaching children how to lead a conference, rather than simply observe one.

Teachers of first- and second-grade students have been successful in helping them select items from their portfolios to share with their parents. These teachers have also successfully coached the children about what they can tell their parents about their work and their goals. For example, a child showed her parents a piece of writing and explained what skill she mastered, as demonstrated in the writing, and what skill she will learn next.

Some parents may prefer more traditional conferences, and some schools have arranged for traditional conferences in the fall and student-led conferences in the spring. Teachers and schools that have tried student-led conferences agree that they help students take more responsibility for their work (Flannery 2004; Levine-Epstein 2003).

Narrative Reports

Another effective way of reporting to parents is through a narrative report. Narratives include basically the information that the teacher would share with parents in a conference. Statements in a narrative should be supported by evidence from the various records that the teacher has accumulated. One method of organizing the information is to focus on each area of development (intellectual, social, emotional, and physical). The narrative should also include what the teacher considers to be implications of the information and plans for the future.

A good narrative is a summary of the information from other records. For example, in summarizing a child's growth in social abilities, the narrative might read:

NAEYC CRITERIA

4.25

> Since the beginning of the year, Denise has gained in her ability to communicate her needs and wants with words most of the time. On three occasions, she has been observed asking a child for a toy that she wanted. She is also able to share classroom materials. She has been observed willingly sharing toy trucks and blocks with other children.

Note the objectivity of these remarks. They are specific observations, not judgments or generalizations. Statements such as "Jediah is unhappy" and "Samantha does not function at the level of her peers" have no place in a narrative report.

Telephone Calls

Generally, telephone calls are most useful for sharing with parents information about specific incidents. If, for example, Carly used words to express her frustration for the first time rather than hit someone, a telephone call to report that progress would be appropriate. Telephone calls should not be used to relay negative information about a child unless there is absolutely no alternative. Telephone calls should be brief and to the point and made at times that likely will be convenient for parents.

Casual Conversations

Sometimes, parents prefer to have casual conversations with the teacher when they are picking up or delivering their child. These conversations do not substitute for conferences, but teachers can help keep parents informed by reporting on progress or interesting anecdotes from the day. Again, these are not the times to report negative information. If a problem needs to be shared, a conference should be scheduled.

Newsletters

Although newsletters are not commonly listed as a means of reporting to parents, they can help keep parents informed about what is going on in the program. Some newsletters use reports that children write or dictate about field trips, visitors, and other events to provide interesting information to parents.

Newsletters need not be formal productions that require a lot of time. Kindergarten and primary children can write items to be included in newsletters. Even threes and fours can write items (these may need to be translated for the parents) or dictate items to be shared with families. A review of the week's events and a

Parents and Reporting

- Ask parents to help create newsletters that include items specifically of interest to them. Also ask parents to help create or edit videotapes of school activities.

list of plans for the next week will help parents know what their children are learning and doing. Many parents will engage their children in activities at home that relate to topics at school if they are kept informed through a newsletter.

Videotapes

Another general means by which teachers can keep parents informed about the school program is to make a videotape of a typical schoolday and encourage parents to check it out. After everyone has had a chance to view the video, the teacher should make a new one. The first video might provide general information about the program, and later videos might concentrate on specific topics: new themes, areas added to the classroom, classroom pets, story time, music and movement activities, and so on. The teacher should ensure that every child is included in class videos.

Evaluating Assessment and Reporting

It is hard to fathom why any educator would bother to institute a comprehensive program of assessment and then not share the information with others—

administrators, parents, and other teachers. It is also difficult to imagine attempting to report to parents about their children without having a strong, ongoing program of assessment.

In the process of collecting information and preparing for reporting, teachers can evaluate their assessment programs: Are some pieces of information missing? Are there areas in the child's development about which more information is needed? Are there more effective ways of gathering the needed information? Parents, too, will offer assessment information. For example, they may let the teacher know that the child is transferring the information being learned in school to other situations. Effective assessment and reporting are mutually supportive activities.

Program Assessment

When teachers assess an early childhood program, they are looking for evidence that the program is appropriate for the children enrolled and that it is effective in bringing about their growth. The following questions will help teachers assess their programs:

1. Would you like to be a child in your classroom?
2. Is there a balance of small-group, whole-group, and individual activities?
3. Do children spend more time in self-selected activities than in teacher-directed activities?
4. Do the children's interests influence activities and learning experiences?
5. Does every child find success and challenge every day?
6. Is there a balance of emphasis on intellectual, social, emotional, and physical growth?
7. Are skills taught in a meaningful context?
8. Can children withdraw from activities without penalty?
9. Are activities and experiences selected on the basis of their relationship to the goals of the program?
10. When planning activities, is the information gathered from assessments used to guide planning?
11. Do individual children show evidence of growth in all areas of development?
12. Are interactions with parents supportive of children's growth?

> The function of education is to teach one to think intensively and to think critically. Intelligence plus character—that is the goal of a true education.
>
> —*Martin Luther King, Jr.*

Answers to these questions will come from evaluating the schedule, the lesson plans, and the instructional materials and observations of interpersonal relationships in the classroom. A teacher who respects children's interests will not determine a list of topics to be studied before getting to know the children. (This is not to imply that a teacher cannot make tentative plans for topics he predicts will be of interest to the children.) Further, in a good program, materials will be readily available to help children learn a variety of facts and skills in a playful manner.

Finally, other evidence that the program is a good one can be found in the attitudes of the children. If they see themselves as a learners who seek support for their own learning, rather than waiting for the teacher to tell them everything to do, the program can be considered effective.

Parents and Assessment

● Adapt the twelve questions listed on page 230 so that they ask parents about their activities with their children. For example, adapt question 1 to ask: Would you like to be a child in your family? (Note that parents might not be able to answer question 10.)

CHILDREN WITH SPECIAL NEEDS

In planning assessment for children with special needs, teachers must think about performance strategies that focus on the strengths of these children rather than the limitations. Lowenthal (1996) suggests that assessment for young children with special needs should involve much more than simply standardized tests. She notes, however, that some standardized tests have adaptations for children with specific disabilities. Teachers of special-needs children should use whatever means are available to help make the best decisions about each child's progress and future needs. Sampling systems, play observations, anecdotal records, and portfolio assessment can be invaluable in highlighting children's abilities.

Every child who has been identified as having special needs will have an *individualized education plan* (*IEP*) or *individualized family service plan* (*IFSP*), depending on her age. Each child's IEP or IFSP is written by a team of specialists, including his classroom teacher and parents, who specify what goals are to be achieved and how. But it is often the task of the classroom teacher to monitor the child's progress toward achieving those goals. Ongoing monitoring may lead to revisions in the initial plan and/or the curriculum. Assessment and curriculum are closely related for children with disabilities (Wolery and Wilbert 1994).

Lowenthal (1997) states that children with special needs can benefit from assessments based on play behaviors, family interviews, and the multiple intelligences. Observations of play behaviors can indicate fine and gross motor development, social–emotional development, and intellectual development as children climb, take turns, and solve problems. Teachers should approach interviews with parents with the mindset that the parent is a partner who can share observations about the child's interests and behaviors at home.

Teachers' observations, conducted over time, can provide information about children's strengths in different kinds of knowing. One of the gifts of Gardner's (1983) multiple intelligences theory is that it prompts teachers to discover learning strengths that they otherwise might not have expected to find. Looking for strengths can only be positive for special-needs children.

NAEYC CRITERIA
3.1

NAEYC CRITERIA
4.28

Parents and Assessment

● Parents of children with special needs often require additional support in terms of providing information about assessment as it relates to their children or their placements. Invite specialists from the community to meet with parents and answer their questions about assessment.

Smith, and Heffner, and Algozzine (2003) recommend the use of portfolios with young children who are at risk for school failure. Often, standardized tests and other assessments are not sufficiently sensitive to capture the strengths of such children. A portfolio, however, can include videotapes of play behaviors, behaviors at group times, and other behaviors that might be missed or overlooked. A portfolio can also include teacher observations, student products, and parental observations.

CELEBRATING DIVERSITY

Good assessment for all students involves using strategies that help students recognize their progress toward clearly defined goals and standards. In order to be culturally responsive, assessment must allow for variations in language, cognitive and communicative styles, and beliefs and values. For example, children who know about clipping grocery store coupons from newspapers might be asked to demonstrate how to group the coupons, rather than recall nursery rhymes that might be unfamiliar to them, given cultural differences. Adapting activities in ways like this allows children to demonstrate what they do know without being penalized for what they do not know about things that are culturally foreign to them.

A portfolio can be a valuable tool for encouraging dialogue with parents and community members about what children are learning and how it can best be assessed. Creating a culturally responsive portfolio requires having a curriculum that is responsive to cultural differences and values. For example, what constitutes important learning for children may be defined differently in some communities than in others. To address these differences, parents and teachers can talk about the need to learn certain skills in school.

Parents also can help teachers understand how to help their children achieve certain goals or help the school modify the goals in light of cultural concerns. For example, suppose the school wants each child to attempt performing a new skill before having mastered it, whereas the cultural community advocates having the child observe the skill, practice it without an audience, and perform it only when he has decided that he is ready. In light of this cultural value, the school might need to think about curriculum and assessment differently. If each child is asked to cut on a line, create a poem, or the like, then classroom procedures should allow him to follow his own pattern of learning. Assessment would still evaluate the child's ability to perform the skill, but it would be initiated by the child. The work that is documented in a portfolio does not have to be the same for every child, nor does it have to be collected on the same schedule for every child.

Portfolio assessment focuses on issues that are specific to the child and therefore is more culturally sensitive than some other strategies for assessment. For example, portfolio entries can include work the child does in her first language. Moreover, input from the child's parents is valued, so they can offer suggestions that will be culturally appropriate for the child. Portfolio assessment gives every child the same chance to be successful at school (Farr and Trumbull 1997).

Here are some guidelines for conducting culturally and linguistically appropriate assessment:

- Determine how the child's family views language use. Do they want to maintain the first language while learning the second?
- Test administrators should be fluent in the child's first language.
- Conduct careful review of the assessment instrument to identify any mismatches with the child's cultural norms or language use.
- Select classroom materials that acknowledge diversity.
- Seek assistance from families and cultural guides to confirm your interpretations of the child's behavior during assessment.
- When assessment data are interpreted, a person qualified in the child's cultural or linguistic group should be involved (Santos 2004).

Teachers seeking information about cultural and linguistic appropriateness can consult the Early Childhood Research Institute on Culturally and Linguistically Appropriate Services at http://clas.uluc.edu.

SUMMARY

- *Assessment* and *testing* are not synonymous terms. Assessment is the collecting and evaluation of information. It is deciding, for instance, what a test score or an observation means for a particular child or a particular program. The primary purpose of assessment must be to help children by guiding instructional and programming decisions.

- Testing is one of several components of assessment. Several types of tests are commonly used in schools, including screening tests, achievement tests, and readiness tests. Teachers must be very cautious of making judgments about children based on single measures and must look at standardized test scores with a skeptical eye, since such scores for young children are typically unreliable.

- Young children should be tested only after the purpose of the test has been defined and the manner in which the results will be reported and used has been clarified. A test should only be given if the reasons for doing so outweigh any negative implications for the children. Concern over testing young children is one of the issues raised by the No Child Left Behind (NCLB) act, a federal law designed to make schools all over the country provide excellent teachers, a rigorous curriculum, and accountability. Accountability is measured by using standardized tests and reporting the scores to the federal government by subgroup.

- Strategies for assessment include keeping many kinds of records that will help teachers determine what children know and what might be the next step in instruction. These records include tallies; written narratives; records of particular incidents; anecdotal records; checklists and rating scales; notes from conversations, conferences, and interviews; rubrics; parent questionnaires; and self-evaluations by children.

- In order to be useful, assessment data must be organized in a such a way that they can be retrieved and shared. There are several ways of organizing the information; compiling a portfolio is a common strategy. Electronic portfolios are available that allow the teacher to enter information on a given child, make comments, plan the next instructional step, and give parents access to the records with a password.

- Assessment data are usually reported to parents, administrators, and others who make decisions about children. These reports can take the form of report cards, conferences, narrative reports, telephone calls, conversations, newsletters, and videotapes. Having a face-to-face conference is the first choice for reporting to parents.

- Children with special needs often have an individualized education plan (IEP) or individualized family service plan (IFSP) that specifies instructional needs and evaluation procedures. Portfolios are especially useful with special-needs children, as they focus on what children have learned and are able to do.

● Diverse learners can benefit from portfolio assessment that allows for including materials that are valuable to the child and his family, such as art, science, or construction examples. Portfolios can be composed of artifacts and/or photos; they do not necessarily have to be paper-and-pencil entries and so can be responsive to cultural expectations.

● Program assessment should be done on a regular basis as it is critical to determine what changes might be needed in order to meet the changing needs of children, to obtain information about the areas of development that might be strengthened, or to make adjustments to the curriculum.

REFLECTIONS

1. Assessment and testing are topics that cause anxiety for many teachers. If you are anxious about these topics, spend some time trying to determine the causes of your anxiety. Are you anxious because of your own experiences as a student? Are you worried about explaining assessment to parents? Are you worried that your assessments will cause children to feel less capable? When you know the source of your anxiety, then you can find resources (people or print) to help you.

2. Do you view assessment as integral to good teaching? If yes, describe that connection. If not, what do you see as the main purpose of assessment?

3. What should be the role of testing in an early childhood program? Explain your answer.

4. What information would you like to share with the parents of the children in your classroom? How would you like to present this information to parents? Do your preferences fit with the requirements of most schools? Why or why not?

5. Have the requirements of the No Child Left Behind act benefitted most young children? If yes, please explain how. If no, explain what you think should be done to improve schools for young children.

EXPLORATIONS AND ACTIVITIES

1. Interview three teachers of young children about the requirements of their programs for assessing children, and compare their responses. Are there some common elements? different elements? Would you want to teach in a program where the assessment requirements matched those of the first teacher you interviewed? the second? the third? For each, explain why or why not.

2. Observe a group of children for half an hour as they play or participate in activity time in a local preschool or kindergarten. Plan in advance how you will assess the behaviors that you observe (language, physical, social/emotional). How many observations would you need to make before feeling that you could adequately assess the children's ability or skill levels in these three developmental areas? Did you use any forms of assessment other than notes? If so, describe your choices.

mylabschool
Where the classroom comes to life!

MyLabSchool is a collection of online tools for your success in this course, your licensure exams, and your teaching career. Visit **www.mylabschool.com** to access the following:

- Online Study Guide
- Video Cases from real classrooms
- Help with your research papers using Research Navigator
- Career Center with resources for:
  —Praxis and Licensure Preparation
  —Professional Portfolio Development
  —Job Search and Interview Techniques
  —Lesson Planning

CHAPTER **8**

KEY TERMS you'll find in this chapter:

- Broken home, 240
- Deficit model, 239
- Home visits, 247
- Nonjudgmental attitude, 239
- Paraprofessionals, 256
- Parent involvement, 238
- Parent place, 249
- School handbook, 246
- Telecommunication, 252
- Volunteers, 253

Working with Parents and Paraprofessionals

FOCUS QUESTIONS

- Why is parent involvement important?

- How can teachers encourage parent participation?

- What are the best ways to communicate with parents?

- What are the appropriate roles and responsibilities of volunteers in the program?

- What are some strategies for working effectively with paraprofessionals?

- What specific issues might be involved in communicating with the parents of special-needs children?

- What are effective strategies for relating to families from diverse backgrounds?

Your observation this week was not what you had expected. You went to a school for children from ages three to five or six. Some of the children in this school had been identified as having special needs and were entitled to services provided by the school district. You expected to see teacher aides with these children, and your expectations were accurate in some instances—for example, interpreters were working with children who are deaf and aides were helping children in wheelchairs. What surprised you was the number of classrooms in which the teachers and aides were working together as a team. You knew that the teachers were ultimately responsible for all instruction in the classroom, but you also saw aides busy instructing small groups and tutoring individual children. Your only previous experience with teacher aides had been with some who supervised the playground and lunchroom.

You were also surprised at the number of parents who were volunteering. You knew that today most parents work outside the home, so you had thought that the days of "room mothers" and "room helpers" were over.

What does the teacher do to keep all these adults working together smoothly so that the children benefit from the extra hands, extra ears, and extra eyes? ∎

Parent Involvement

Research continues to support the importance of **parent involvement** in the success of children in school (Feuerstein 2000; R. Jones 2001; Machen, Wilson, and Notar 2005; Marcon 1999; McWayne et al. 2004). Even parents who participate infrequently in school activities can make a big difference in their children's academic lives compared to those who do not participate at all (Hampton and Mumford 1998). Henderson and Berla (1994) found that when parents are involved in their children's schooling, children achieve higher grades, have better school attendance, have more positive attitudes and behaviors, graduate from high school at a higher rate, and are more likely to enroll in higher education. There is no question that parent involvement pays off in better educational outcomes for children.

Realities of Parent–Teacher Relationships

There are good reasons for involving parents in the education of their children. In reviewing what we know about parent involvement programs, Epstein (1991) offers these conclusions:

- Parents and teachers are more similar than different. They have many goals in common and a need to share information.
- Programs must continue through the elementary and high school years, not stop after the early childhood years.
- Programs must include all families.
- Programs make the teacher's job easier.
- Program development takes time.

Parent–teacher relationships are not as simple as many articles lead us to believe. New teachers could mistakenly come to think that parent volunteers are common and that all parents will attend parent conferences if they are invited to do so. However, teachers of young children need to recognize that although parent involvement is very important, it is not always easy for the teacher, the school, or the parents to facilitate.

Pressures on parents today are tremendous due to changing family structures, economic conditions, and lack of support for the nuclear family. Many children live with single parents, in two-parent working families, or in blended families created by remarriages, and many live with relatives other than their parents or with people who are not related to them.

The plight of children in the United States continues to be serious. Nearly one child of every six is living below the poverty line ($14,824 for a family of three or $18,660 for a family of four). There are more poor children today than there were in the 1970s. For children falling into poverty since 2000, three out of every five children fell into extreme poverty, which is defined as a family income of one-half or less of the income levels designated as poverty levels. Even though the percentages are higher for Black and Hispanic children, there are actually more poor non-Hispanic White children. Many poor children live in suburbs and rural areas; child poverty is not confined to urban areas (Children's Defense Fund 2004).

In a statement on family income and child poverty, the Children's Defense Fund (2004) explains the impact on children:

Poor children are at least twice as likely as non-poor children to suffer stunted growth or lead poisoning, or to be kept back in school. Poor children score significantly lower on reading, math, and vocabulary tests when compared with otherwise-similar non-poor children. More than half of poor Americans (55 percent) experience serious deprivations during the year (defined as lack of food, utility shutoffs, crowded or substandard housing, or lack of a stove or refrigerator).

The enormous number of mothers in the workforce reflects economic conditions that make it ever more difficult for a family to survive economically. Many mothers work because they are the sole source of support for their children. These economic stresses in turn make it more difficult than ever before for parents to have choices about child care, to spend energy nurturing and educating their children rather than just trying to survive, and to become involved in the formal education of their children.

In addition to these pressures on the family, today's nuclear family does not have the support from the extended family that was available to past generations. Families often live long distances from other relatives and must depend on outsiders for child care and advice or support. Many parents are isolated; they have no one to help them cope with all the demands of caring for children and maintaining their daily lives.

PRAXIS

Be able to explain how a child's learning can be affected by his family or community

Implications for Teachers

One of the first rules for teachers who want to establish good relationships with all parents is to adopt a **nonjudgmental attitude** toward them. Parents who have been labeled "hard to reach"—usually those who have low incomes, are members of ethnic minorities, and have limited formal education—are often presumed to have little concern about education or to place little value on school. However, research indicates that this is not the case.

NAEYC CRITERIA
1.1, 1.2

Chavkin and Williams (1993) found that 90 percent of such parents were concerned about their children's education and wanted to be actively involved in it. Some believed that it was the teacher's duty to get parents involved; even so, these parents were interested in their children's school experiences.

There are many reasons parents do not get involved in school. Some may have had negative experiences in school, so that any contact with the school revives their own feelings of inadequacy; others may be overwhelmed with the pressures in their lives and unable to cope with one more demand; still others may not know what they can do to help their children in school. For some parents, it would be culturally inappropriate to be other than passive in their involvement with the school. In some cultures, teachers are highly respected figures of authority. For parents from such cultures to take an active role in school would be perceived as an infringement on the teacher's authority (Politis 2004).

> The art of education is one of enhancing lives. There is no art form more important nor any undertaking as delicate and complex.
>
> —*Elliot Eisner*

One of the responsibilities of teachers is to maintain relationships with the parents of the children in their care. Most teachers want parents to be involved, but some may have a narrow vision of what that involvement should look like. Especially with Hispanic parents, many schools operate on what Delgado-Gaitan (1991) calls a **deficit model:** "Deficit perspectives depict inactive parents in the schools as incompetent and unable to help their children because they have a different language, work long hours away from home, belong to different ethnic groups, or are just not interested" (p. 22). Her research says that this perception is simply not true. These parents often are very interested in their children's education and they do support it, but not always in ways recognized by the school.

New teachers must expect to be involved in major efforts to restructure family and school relationships. Expecting all families to meet middle-class standards for involvement in schools is unrealistic. It is also unrealistic to believe that only one model for family involvement is possible. Teachers who have such high but unattainable expectations may become frustrated and give up. A reasonable goal might be to get parents more involved this year than in previous years or to get more parents involved on a regular basis. Families and schools must learn new ways of interacting. Karr and Landerholm (1991) state the goal well: "Programs must meet the needs of the parents they serve rather than demand that the parents meet the needs of the program" (p. 6).

Teachers of young children must be especially sensitive to the needs of children from different family structures, and this sensitivity should be reflected in the language used to discuss families. The phrase **broken home,** for example, is inappropriate. A child's parents may be divorced and she may be living in a single-parent family, but there is nothing inherently wrong or deprived about such a family structure.

Similarly, teachers must avoid planning activities in which the child is to make gifts for parents or events that are labeled "father–son" or "mother–daughter." Activities involving gifts or family events should be presented as opportunities to share with someone special in a child's life—a foster mother, a grandparent, or any other person—rather than being specifically labeled for mothers and fathers. When using photographs of families, teachers should make sure that a variety of family structures is illustrated and that discussions are not limited to families made up of Mother, Father, and children.

Although it is not directly the responsibility of the teacher, it is important that all school employees treat parents with respect and consideration. There are many sad stories of the school secretary or other staff treating parents poorly when they come to school, such as when they enroll their children. If a problem with parental treatment is apparent, teachers should suggest that the school board of directors provide sensitivity workshops for all school employees.

Encouraging Parent Involvement

Strategies for Teachers and Schools

Getting parents involved in the classroom and in activities to help their children succeed in school is an important part of the work of a teacher, but it is not always easy to accomplish. Benson and Martin (2003) recommend seven principles for encouraging parent involvement that have worked in urban schools:

1. Focus on students' successes and achievements.
2. Send personalized information to parents—that is, specific information about their children that is directed to them.

www.education-world.com/ a_special/parent_involvement. shtml

A dozen activities to promote parent involvement

www.nwrel.org/scpd/sirs/3/ cu6.html

The importance of parent involvement in schools

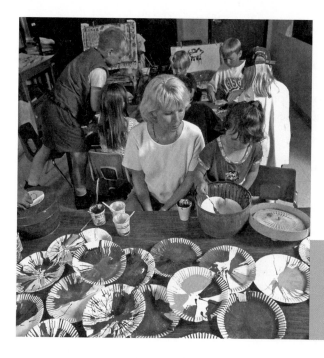

Parents can be a valuable addition to the classroom by supervising activities that require an adult at all times.

3. When possible, use extended family to support students.

4. Extend frequent invitations to parents.

5. Use school staff and parent volunteers in creative ways to organize programs.

6. Coordinate planning with administrators, parents, and teachers.

7. Think of other ways to make parents feel welcome in the classroom, such as serving refreshments, providing nametags, reimbursing parents for transportation and babysitting costs, meeting in accessible buildings such as community centers, planning events at different times and on different days, meeting in a room conducive to communication, using students as hosts/guides, and recognizing parents and staff for their efforts.

Schools that apply these seven principles have been successful in planning many activities, among them, the following:

PRAXIS

Be able to describe ways of creating a welcoming environment for parents

- Parent visitation/observation days
- Special events for families, such as ice-cream socials or "family fun" nights
- Curriculum fairs, where students display their projects
- Parent computer days, where parents can learn about technology
- Grandparents' day
- Coffee with the principal or director for an informal conversation
- "Summer fun" information fairs
- Parent homework or report cards, where parents report on activities at home (such as writing letters to relatives, working on badges for Scout or Campfire groups, taking music lessons, helping to prepare a meal, learning how to use a tool, taking language lessons or going to school to support native language and/or culture, and so on)

- Parent lending libraries, field trips, or workshops on topics suggested by parents
- Awards programs so that every child gets an award for something

Abrams (2002) reported on a school that had 100 percent of parents involved. She recommends the following strategies for enticing parents to become involved:

1. Offer incentives (coupons or prizes for food or books) for attendance.
2. Put on a show by having the children perform.
3. Provide rides to parents who need them.
4. Pay parents' PTA dues.
5. Call parents rather than send notes or e-mail.
6. Make parents feel safe at school.
7. Hold "parent nights."
8. Sponsor parent workshops.
9. Open a parent center.
10. Require attendance at parent–teacher conferences (i.e., withhold report cards until parents attend).
11. Keep in touch.

The suggestions from both Abrams (2002) and Benson and Martin (2003) can be implemented, but doing so will require planning, coordination, and support from administrators. The school and staff will need to make a concerted effort to get parents involved and to devote the resources necessary to achieve and maintain that involvement.

Kieff and Wellhousen (2000) suggest that as teachers plan any kind of meeting or activity for parents, they try to anticipate what barriers might make participation difficult for some parents. Figure 8.1 provides a list of possible modifications to overcome potential barriers.

Parent Roles

Parents may take on a variety of roles in the school. At one end of the continuum of parent involvement are parents who never participate in any school activities, although they are active in the sense of sending their children to school; one level higher are parents who participate in passive roles that only require them to listen. Further along the continuum are parents who participate by attending events at school and volunteering their time to help teachers in the classroom; even further along are those parents who get involved in decision making at the school or district level and who assist in teaching. Parents of children in cooperative schools usually are at this point. Some parents take total responsibility for their children's education and make the commitment to educate their children at home.

Many parents do not see how their involvement at school could possibly benefit their children. Teachers need to supply specific information about *why* parent involvement is important. For example, teachers often suggest that parents read to their children but do not share with the parents why reading will help the children become literate more easily. Parents who have specific information are much more likely to become involved.

FIGURE 8.1

Common Barriers and Possible Modifications Checklist

Barriers	Modifications
Time	☐ breakfast meetings ☐ weekend events ☐ one event scheduled over a number of days ☐ open invitations
Transportation	☐ school bus or van ☐ car pool arranged by teacher or parent volunteer ☐ buddy system among families
Child care	☐ school-provided child care ☐ child care provided by parent organization ☐ buddy system among families
Decorations/ celebrations	☐ artwork created by children in the art center ☐ artwork generated during a theme/project study
Curriculum	☐ opportunities for children to make multiple gifts and cards and to pick their recipients ☐ family members share expertise and culture ☐ bias-free curriculum
Food	☐ multiple menus available ☐ buffets ☐ picnics
Printed material	☐ translate copies ☐ make audiotapes ☐ make telephone calls ☐ use voice mail or e-mail
Special guest	☐ guest not specified by role ☐ a pal or friend ☐ open invitations to extended family members or a noncustodial parent
Expense	☐ support provided by community businesses underwriting the event or materials needed
Misunderstanding the role as parent volunteer in the classroom	☐ volunteer training sessions ☐ specific routines created ☐ recorded or printed instructions
Misunderstanding the parental role in home-extension learning activities	☐ specific routines created for home-extension learning activities ☐ parent workshops to explain activities ☐ demonstration tapes ☐ demonstrations during home visits
Discomfort in school situations	☐ alternative home visits or neighborhood meetings ☐ buddy systems among families ☐ small-group meetings

Source: Judith Kieff and Karyn Wellhousen, "Planning Family Involvement in Early Childhood Programs," *Young Children* 55 (May 2000): 18–25. Reprinted with permission from the National Association for the Education of Young Children.

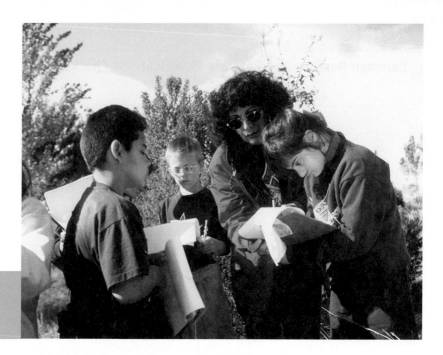

Field trips provide a great opportunity for getting parents involved in school activities.

Parents who choose not to be involved in their children's school cite as reasons health problems, economic differences between themselves and teachers, and work responsibilities. Some teachers, on the other hand, believe that parents are not more involved because of their unrealistic expectations of the school's role; an attitude that school is not important enough to warrant taking time from work; jealousy of teachers; teachers' lack of trust of parents; and a lack of activities to draw parents to school (Leitch and Tangri 1988).

Swick and McKnight (1989) found a cluster of characteristics in kindergarten teachers that strongly supported parent involvement, including belonging to a professional association and adhering to a developmentally oriented philosophy; they also found that administrative support for parent involvement was vital. Galinsky (1988) found that teachers who had more education and were parents themselves were more likely to have positive perceptions of parents. She explained that it is not being a parent per se that leads to positive perceptions but "the ability to put themselves in the parent's shoes and to be empathetic" (p. 8). If teachers feel that parental involvement is important, they will work to overcome the barriers that they perceive are keeping parents out of the school.

Every parent who wants to be involved should have the opportunity to do so. Teachers need to find out from parents how they would like to be involved. The most direct way of determining how parents feel and what they would like to do is to ask them—during a home visit or during a conference early in the year. Another way is to have them respond to a questionnaire. Figure 8.2 is an example of an interview form that teachers can use in determining the kind of involvement parents need or want.

PRAXIS

Be able to explain ways of supporting parents' or families' efforts to help their children in school

Activities for Involving Parents

Many activities can be arranged to involve both parents who choose to be active and those who choose more passive roles. A number of levels of participation are possible:

FIGURE 8.2

Parent Interview Form

Parent's Name _____   Date _____

Child's Name _____   Phone Number _____

1. How would you like to be involved in our school's activities?

   A. In the classroom:

- ☐ Helping with art activities?
- ☐ Helping with cooking activities?
- ☐ Helping with woodworking?
- ☐ Supervising water play?
- ☐ Supervising sand play?
- ☐ Reading to individual children or to small groups?
- ☐ Taking a small group on a nature walk?
- ☐ Helping children with the care of classroom pets?
- ☐ Driving or supervising on field trips?
- ☐ Making a classroom video?
- ☐ Other: _____

   B. At home:

- ☐ Typing a parent newsletter?
- ☐ Sewing a costume for the dramatic play area?
- ☐ Collecting and organizing teaching materials (such as prop boxes)?
- ☐ Calling parents to remind them of meetings?
- ☐ Bringing refreshments for a parent meeting?
- ☐ Repairing damaged or torn books for the classroom library?
- ☐ Making a classroom web page?
- ☐ Making tape recordings of stories or poems?
- ☐ Other: _____

2. What topics would you like us to cover in a program for parents?

- ☐ Literacy activities to do at home?
- ☐ Testing issues for young children?
- ☐ Family services available in the community?
- ☐ Places to take your child that are worthwhile and inexpensive?
- ☐ How to select appropriate toys or how to make toys?
- ☐ How to help my child with English when I am not a native speaker of that language?
- ☐ Other: _____

1. Family reading, family math, or family science nights are evenings when the children and their families are invited to school and participate in reading, math, or science activities that are developmentally appropriate and that help parents understand why such activities are provided in school.

2. Potluck dinners offer a way to celebrate holidays by inviting families to share social evenings together. If the children can make part of the meal to share, so much the better.

3. Parent education workshops can range from sessions in which outside speakers talk about child development, discipline, or some other topic of general interest to meetings of small groups who want to discuss specific issues such as sibling rivalry with other parents.

4. Formal organizations of parents such as Parent–Teacher Associations can provide programs for parents and teachers.

5. Committees of parents can discuss school issues, including curriculum decisions, school policies, and hiring of staff.

6. Parents can become members of teams involved in making recommendations for children with special needs.

7. Parents and teachers can attend workshops in which they make instructional materials for use in the classroom.

8. Chapman (1991) suggests that parents can help produce videotapes that focus on lessons and explain the "whys" of the lesson (why certain materials, teaching strategies, responses to wrong answers are used) or that teach other parents specific techniques for helping their children, such as how to motivate them.

Communicating with Parents

It is the teacher's responsibility to keep the lines of communication with parents open. Communication with parents can be divided into two categories: communication *about the program* and communication *about the individual child.* Parent conferences (discussed in the previous chapter), newsletters, and telephone calls are all avenues for communication, but they are used more to talk about an individual child than about the program. Home visits, parent visits to the school, school handbooks, letters and notes, and a teacher who is prepared with good written information about community resources will supplement the above-mentioned communication methods and keep parents informed about the school's program. Keller (2004) reports that teachers spend about two hours each week working on communication with parents.

Cattermole and Robinson (1985) asked parents what they considered the most effective forms of communication they received from school. Their first choice was information they received from their children—followed by school newsletters, report cards, parent–teacher conferences, visits to school, notes or phone calls from teachers, and formal meetings and informal contacts with friends.

School Handbooks

A **school handbook** is especially useful for sharing basic information about a program. A handbook should include the school calendar; the hours of each session; school policies such as procedures for getting refunds of tuition payments, celebrating birthdays at school, or handling sick children; a class list for each class; a list of the staff (with perhaps a short professional biography of each); and statements of the school's philosophy (Bundy 1991).

The school handbook might also list the goals and objectives for the children, emergency procedures, bus routes, and other information useful to parents.

Home Visits

Although not as common as they once were, **home visits** are still an important means of establishing solid parent–teacher relationships. Some parents are much more comfortable in their own homes than at school. However, teachers should be sensitive to the fact that some parents may find a home visit from the teacher uncomfortable or intrusive, for any number of reasons. The information gained about the child, the parents, and the home environment are well worth the investment of time and energy required to complete home visits.

If a home visit can be arranged before school starts, the child and teacher can get to know each other individually before having to relate to each other in a group setting. Parents will also appreciate meeting the teacher before school begins and having a chance to ask questions about the program and discuss expectations for their child.

Home visits can be effective if teachers plan and prepare for them. The following suggestions may help in planning visits:

1. Schedule the visit well in advance. Send a written reminder of the visit. Let the parents know how long you expect the visit to last. Arrive and leave on time.

2. Make sure that parents know the purpose of the visit. Assure parents that they do not need to make any special preparations for your visit.

3. Be a gracious guest. If the parent offers something to eat or drink, accept it politely. Respect the parents and the home.

4. Do not make snap judgments about the home environment. If the physical surroundings do not match your image of a home, do not conclude that the home is not a good environment for the child.

5. Be prepared to talk about the program and your plans for the children in an informal manner. Listen, ask questions, and listen some more.

Often, teachers like to take something when they visit—materials for making a nametag for the child, a camera for photographing the child, a photograph album of activities from the previous year, a puppet, a wooden puzzle, a book that can be returned to the classroom later, or paper and crayons for drawing. Taking something can provide openings for sharing information and opportunities for observations (Johnston and Mermin 1995).

It is also helpful for the teacher to take an information sheet for the parents that gives his name and phone number, a school calendar with holidays and special events marked, information about snacks if parents will be providing them, and a list of rules for celebrating birthdays and for bringing objects to share at school. The teacher might also take along a list of materials that he needs at school. Teachers in one school district hand out a list of "beautiful junk"—egg cartons, oatmeal boxes, assorted nuts and bolts, baby food jars, old paint brushes, wood scraps, bottle caps, used magazines, and the like—that most households accumulate and that even families of limited means can contribute.

NAEYC CRITERIA
1.4

NAEYC CRITERIA
1.5

PRAXIS
Be able to describe activities that recognize the family's role in teaching their child

During a home visit, the teacher may want to discuss the special needs and interests of the child, any allergies or health problems that the teacher needs to be aware of, and the expectations the parents have for the child in the program. If it seems appropriate, the teacher can also discuss how the parents would like to be involved in the program. Parents may also want to know about the teacher's background, training, and experience. She should be prepared to discuss the program, how decisions are made about what to study, and how she plans to deal with discipline problems.

If the teacher is unable to visit two or three parents at home, he might try inviting them to a special meeting at school, where he shares the information he would have shared in a home visit. Kieff (1990) found that parents of children labeled at risk by their school district preferred meeting in small groups with the teacher. These parents did not feel comfortable in large, formal parent meetings.

It is important that all parents understand how much they teach their children and how important they are in their children's education. Hohmann, Banet, and Weikart (1979) suggest that teachers help parents

> realize that . . . parenting is teaching, . . . they already know a lot about child development in general and about their own children in particular, and . . . teachers are not purveyors of knowledge but rather people who wish to support and extend the learning that's already going on at home. (p. 20)

If parents cannot or will not come to school and the teacher cannot visit them at home, the teacher might try inviting the family to meet at a park, library, or other public place. Meeting on neutral ground may help the parents feel more comfortable. If such a plan is impossible, then the teacher should try to contact the parents by phone or by letter to share the information. The teacher should make her contacts with them nonthreatening and nonjudgmental. It is vital that the teacher continue to reassure parents that she is interested in their child and will welcome their questions.

A real partnership between schools and families is possible only if both truly believe that the other has something valuable to bring to the relationship, that the common goal is the welfare of the child, and that there is a sense of shared responsibility (Workman and Gage 1997).

Parent Visits to School

Some parents can arrange to visit the school during school hours and should always be welcomed. Parents who come to observe the program and their children's participation in it should be invited to sit and watch or to join in activities, whichever they feel most comfortable doing. Every parent who comes to observe should be invited to schedule a conference so that any questions or concerns can be discussed. Teachers can use a checklist such as that shown in Figure 8.3 to prepare for conferences with parents.

One school sends a special invitation to each parent to attend school on a given day, beginning a few weeks before regularly scheduled conferences. The invitation indicates that if parents cannot come on the stated day, they can come any time. With a little persistence, teachers in this school get almost 100 percent of the parents to visit

The principal goal of education is to create men who are capable of doing new things, not simply of repeating what other generations have done.

—*Jean Piaget*

FIGURE 8.3

Parent–Teacher Conference Checklist

Parent's Name _____

Child's Name _____

☐ Arrange the time and place: _____.

☐ Gather all relevant information (e.g., assessments, samples of child's work, portfolio, anecdotal observations, checklists, and so on).

☐ Organize materials so they can be presented either by subject or by developmental area.

☐ Invite the parent to voice any changes observed since the last conference; make note of comments.

☐ Share information gathered with the parent.

☐ Ask for the parent's input about goals for the next learning period. (Perhaps set goals after each area of development is discussed.)

☐ Thank the parent for his or her interest and observations.

the school, and conferences are much more successful after parents have seen the program in action.

Parents can be invited to participate in holiday celebrations that the children have planned or invited to visit when the children are involved in a group activity so that they can observe their child's behavior in a group setting. Rather than having children put on performances, it is advisable to ask parents to visit when the children are involved in normal classroom activities, such as singing, playing musical instruments, or dramatizing stories. These activities do not require practice by the children but do allow the parent to feel good about their children's abilities.

The teacher might want to prepare an observation guide for parents so that they can see some of the important aspects of the program during their visit. Figure 8.4 is an example of such a guide, which can be adapted to fit the teacher's own needs.

Sometimes, parents who cannot attend school during the day can be invited for an evening visit. The children can come, too, and get involved in some of their usual school activities so that parents can learn more about what their children do at school.

A **parent place** in a corner of the classroom can help parents feel that they are important and needed. A table and a small bulletin board are all that is necessary to provide such a corner for parents. Parents can use the bulletin board to communicate with one another (notes about car pools, child care, and so on). The teacher can post photographs of parents working with the children or creating materials or games for the classroom, notices of special events of interest to families, lists of items that are needed in the classroom, and so on. The table can hold a small resource library for parents, providing copies of articles and books that parents might find helpful; pamphlets, magazines, and brochures such as those published by the National Association for the Education of Young Children (NAEYC) and

FIGURE 8.4

Observation Guide for Parents

Welcome to XYZ School!

We are always pleased to have parents visit our programs! This sheet may serve as a guideline for observing your child as he or she interacts with others in school. We encourage you to schedule an appointment with the teacher to discuss your observations. You may use any part of this form, or you may turn it over and write down some questions that you want to ask the teacher later. Please do whatever is most comfortable for you. Enjoy your visit!

Check or circle whatever items are appropriate.

Setting:
Indoors

Outdoors

Activity:
Choice time (individual)

Whole group

Small group directed by teacher

Social Interactions:
With other children

With adults

Materials, Equipment, or Activities Selected:
List here

Did your child use material or equipment as it was designed to be used? or did he or she use the material or equipment to make up a game?

Time Spent in Each Activity:
Estimate here

Types of Interactions:
Solitary activities (played alone)

Small-group activities (joined or formed a small group)

the Association for Childhood Education International (ACEI) on a variety of topics; and other materials. Some larger schools provide "parent rooms" where parents can meet other parents, wait to pick up their children, or find information about parenting. Epstein (1991) lists making room (literally) for parents as an important component of parent involvement programs.

When parents cannot visit school or stay long enough to observe, notes and photographs of their children engaged in activities help communicate

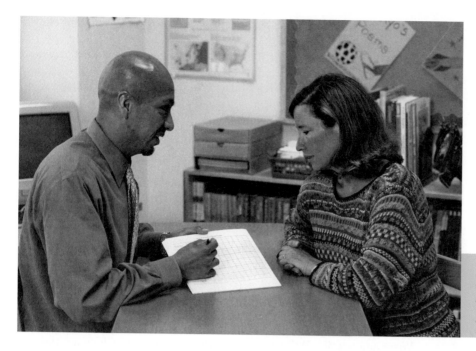

A place for parents to meet that is furnished with adult-sized furniture can help put parents at ease.

what is going on in class. A videotape of a day in the class that parents can borrow may also help to communicate with some parents. Greenwood (1995) reported very positive results when she created a video of children's activities that she circulated among parents. She made several videos during the year and also volunteered to make copies for parents if they sent blank tapes.

Letters and Notes

Parents appreciate letters that give them information about school programs and their children, in particular. Instead of newsletters, some teachers like to send form letters that may include suggestions for things the parents could do at home to complement what the children are learning in school. Adding a personal note about the child at the bottom of each parent's letter makes this practice even more effective. Brief notes that communicate the child's progress are an important way of letting parents know that the teacher is aware of their child and her accomplishments.

Notes should always be positive. A note saying that "Sebastian succeeded in tying his shoes today" or that "Nancy read a complete book independently" will help parents feel that the teacher is staying in touch with them. Most teachers keep a list of parents and jot down the date when they send each parent a note. When all parents have been contacted, the teachers start over. Some schools even have notepaper printed with captions such as "Good News" or "Happygram."

D'Angelo and Adler (1991) suggest the following guidelines for preparing effective written communication for parents:

- Keep sentences short. Try to keep sentences to ten or fewer words, and never allow them to include more than twenty words.
- Keep paragraphs short. Try to keep paragraphs to an average of six lines.
- Use easy words. Let the short, familiar words bear the main burden of getting your point across. Use big words or technical terms when only those words will express a message accurately.

- Get to the point. State the purpose of your message up front and omit irrelevant information.
- Write things in logical order. The newspaper formula of "who, what, where, when, why, and how" is helpful as an organizing device.
- Be definite. Don't hedge. Be careful with such words as *seems, may, perhaps, possibly, generally, usually,* and *apparently.* Give a clear picture of what you want to say.
- Be direct. Speak to each reader. Say "you should" or "please do" instead of "parents should."
- Use the active voice more often than the passive. Put the subject at the beginning of the sentence. For example, write "Please sign and return the consent slip if you want your child to go on the trip to the zoo," rather than "A consent slip must be signed by the parent in order for the child to attend the field trip to the zoo."
- Know your audience. Ask yourself, For whom is the material being written, and how well does the audience read? If you aren't sure, test your materials on a few people representative of the target audience. When in doubt, assume that there are at least some poor readers in your audience.
- Know yourself. Be yourself. Write as you would talk, and write to express— not to impress.
- Write and rewrite. Write a draft, then read it over. How long are the sentences? How many long words have you used? Have you used the passive voice a great deal? Are there unexplained technical words? Have you used jargon or abbreviations that your audience may not know? Can you say the same thing more clearly, more succinctly, or more interestingly? Ask someone else to read what you've written. Then rewrite it. (p. 354)*

In addition to these suggestions, make sure that your communications to the parents say something personal (if you are sending a form letter, add something personal), that they are positive, and that you think about the skill level of your audience.

Telecommunication

Some centers use **telecommunication** to make communication with parents quick and easy. Bauch (1990) reports that one center uses a computerized calling system to call parents and deliver messages about the program. These systems allow the calls to be placed at the times that are convenient for parents and in the language the parents prefer.

A similar use of current technology is to equip each teacher's room with voice mail or an answering machine on which the teacher records a short message like the following, which any parent can hear by calling:

> Today, we went to the zoo to look for patterns. We found patterns on the animals, in the enclosures, and in the pathways. You could help your child find patterns in your home. We printed patterns with junk items in art, and we read a patterned book, *Brown Bear, Brown Bear.* Your child has a copy of this book, and you could read it or let him or her read it to you. If you have a chance this weekend, encourage your child to look for patterns in numbers, such as the pattern of house or apartment numbers on your block.

---

*From Diane A. D'Angelo and C. Ralph Adler, "Chapter I: A Catalyst for Improving Parent Involvement," *Phi Delta Kappan* 72 (January 1991): 350–354. Reprinted with permission of the authors.

Providing a voice mail or answering system for each teacher allows parents to leave messages or ask questions about their child, helping them feel more connected. In addition to a summary of current activities, the outgoing message might also remind parents of upcoming meetings, programs, and so on. Some schools have found it useful to set up a hotline, which provides someone to help parents with questions about their children's homework or other activities.

Many schools now have websites with pages for individual classrooms, on which teachers can post photos of various activities or other information about daily classroom activities. Many of these sites are on intranet systems, which are open only to the school and its parents. Some schools are preparing electronic portfolios with postings of student work on a website that can be accessed with a personal identification number for security.

Whatever system is used, it should be accessible to parents beyond normal school hours. Many parents find it difficult to call the school during the day, and it is closed by the time they get home from work. Providing a message system, website, or hotline can help parents feel they are keeping in touch with the school.

In the following An Expert Speaks box, Dr. Michaela Wyman-Colombo suggests that teachers can help students by getting their parents involved. Do you believe that all parents can help their children?

Community Resources

Finally, many parents need information about resources available to them in the community. Teachers are not expected to be child psychologists or marriage counselors, but they can help by keeping on hand a supply of brochures that describe the services offered by various community agencies and provide contact and referral information.

Volunteers in the Classroom

Volunteers in the classroom are very important, especially as resources continue to shrink and schools cannot afford to hire enough adults to maintain adequate adult–child ratios. Volunteers can be parents or others from the community. Community volunteers can be recruited from colleges, service groups, senior citizen groups, church groups, and the like.

These volunteers often bring many skills and resources to share with children—talents in music, storytelling, woodworking, art, or other areas that can enhance the program. Many teachers are especially interested in recruiting older volunteers in order to promote the intergenerational contact that is so often missing in the lives of today's children.

Both community and parent volunteers must be screened and trained before working in the classroom. Some schools have volunteer coordinators who are responsible for interviewing prospective volunteers and determining their suitability for working with children. In other situations, teachers themselves interview volunteers. Whoever conducts the interviews should try to determine what the person has to offer the children, his expectations about volunteering, and his ability to communicate with and nurture children. If a volunteer seems unsuitable for working directly with the children,

www.inspiringteachers.com/
tips/parents/volunteers.html
Tips for using parent volunteers in the classroom

www.everythingesl.net/
inservices/bilingualparents.
php
Information about working with bilingual parents, with links to sites on rating schools and creating an atmosphere of success

AN **Expert** SPEAKS: *Involving All Parents*

Michaela Wyman-Colombo
University of Massachusetts Lowell

It's well accepted that parent involvement improves educational opportunities for children. Yet with the many responsibilities shouldered by teachers, trying to involve all parents sometimes seems like an overwhelming task. Thankfully, some parents involve themselves. They attend open houses and regularly participate in school activities and events. Typically, these parents know what to do and say, how to help their children with homework, and often read with their children using the same strategies you use in your classroom. Most often these parents share the culture and values of the school.

It may be more difficult to involve parents who are from diverse cultures and speak languages other than English. Yet ironically, parent/family involvement is even more important to the educational success of their children. Every day, culturally and linguistically diverse children cross from one world to another as they go from home to school. Yet teachers who reach out to culturally diverse parents can create bridges between children's two worlds.

We know that regardless of parents' culture, language, or socioeconomic standing, the single most influential factor in their school involvement is a teacher's belief that she can involve them. At times it may be difficult to believe in your ability to involve parents who do not respond as you would expect. Yet if a parent seems resistant or uncaring, remember that all parents want the best for their children, and try to understand the parents' cultural perspectives.

Parents may not know the expectations of the school. Parents from other cultures may actually consider it rude to visit a classroom and talk with the teacher about instruction. In their culture, the teacher is the expert and it is disrespectful to question her in the same way that middle-class American parents might. These parents will need ongoing invitations to visit your classroom. Once you've established a trusting relationship, you can begin to explain aspects of American school culture and your expectations for their involvement in educational activities.

Some parents have limited formal schooling. Others may have been professionals in their home countries but because of their limited English skills are now employed in low-paying jobs that require them to work long hours to support their families. Unlike middle-class parents, who may be able to leave work to visit the school, parents who are hourly workers generally do not have this luxury. Try to accommodate parents' work schedules by arranging conferences at various times and places. Parents may need to bring younger siblings, grandparents, or extended family members to these conferences. Expand your definition of parent participation and invite the entire family to meetings and school events. Create a warm and welcoming atmosphere.

Parents' lack of English ability sometimes may make them feel that they have little to offer their children. You can help by encouraging parents to read to their children in their home language. This will not interfere with children's English acquisition, and it will strengthen their literacy skills. If you send home book bags, include some native-language books. If books written in the home language are unavailable, encourage parents to create books with their children. Try to make materials available for this task. Explaining the relationship between storytelling and literacy will help illiterate parents become involved in their children's literacy.

When parents speak some English, be empathetic, speak slowly, and check for understanding. Sometimes your approach is more meaningful than your linguistic abilities. If parents speak no English, ask someone from the school or community to interpret. When working through an interpreter, always speak directly to the parent and allow the interpreter time to translate.

Involving culturally and linguistically diverse parents in their children's education requires time and commitment but is possible. By successfully involving these parents, you create cultural bridges that dramatically improve educational opportunities for all children.

he can be asked to perform tasks that do not involve the children, such as typing materials, mounting artwork, placing the children's work in their portfolios, and so on.

Training for volunteers should clearly describe the philosophy of the program, goals for the children, activities that are appropriate for volunteers, discipline in school, and school policies and procedures. Such training is important, as every person who works in the classroom models behavior for the children and teaches by example.

Volunteers should always feel that the work they do is of real benefit to the children. They must perceive that the tasks they are asked to do in the classroom are a value added to the regular program. For example, if volunteers are asked to correct papers, they may see that task as something the teacher would do anyway and believe that they are not really adding to the quality of the program. It would be more appropriate to ask volunteers to do tasks that the teacher simply could not do without their help. Any special experience that can be added because the volunteer is available to help will make it clear to the parent or community volunteer that she is needed to provide this experience for the children.

> **The great aim of education is not knowledge but action.**
>
> —*Herbert Spencer*

Here are some examples of appropriate activities for mature and well-trained volunteers:

1. Reading to children (individually or in small groups)
2. Supervising small groups in outdoor play
3. Taking a small group for a walk around the schoolgrounds (looking for signs of changing seasons, collecting natural materials, observing surface differences, and so on)
4. Supervising children in an area that could not be used without additional help (cooking, water, music, tumbling, sewing, and so on)
5. Playing board games with children or helping them learn to play checkers, chess, or other such games

It is important to take the time to help volunteers understand what they can do in the classroom and how to do it most easily. Although many parent and community volunteers are quite able to work with one child at a time, they may not have especially good group-management abilities.

Providing specific instructions will allow those who are not specially trained in working with groups of young children to feel more secure. If a volunteer were going to supervise the art area, for example, the instructions shown in Figure 8.5 would be helpful. A planning sheet such as the one shown in Figure 8.6 would guide a volunteer in supervising a cooking experience. Another approach is to develop a file of cards listing suggestions for different activities and to laminate the cards for durability.

Teachers should always take the time to thank volunteers for their help. Immediate positive verbal feedback is important. Written thank-you notes are also invaluable in helping volunteers feel appreciated. These need not be expensive—a small note that the teacher can send home with a child for his parent or mail to a community volunteer is appropriate.

More elaborate displays of appreciation for volunteers are often planned once or twice a year. Some schools like to have a tea, a luncheon, or a breakfast to honor those who have contributed volunteer time. If teachers can get publicity in the local paper for special contributions by volunteers, they should do so—public praise is always welcome. Articles in newsletters that go out to all the parents can note the work that volunteers are doing at home and at school.

FIGURE 8.5

Instructions for a Volunteer

Supervising the Art Area

➤ Children may choose to do art activities between 9:15 and 10:15.

➤ Choices available to the children: paint and easels, modeling clay, crayons and drawing paper, swatches of fabric for collage.

➤ Any child who chooses easel painting should wear a painting smock. The smocks are on the hooks beside the sink. Children should be encouraged to get their own smocks and to replace them when finished. Completed paintings are to be placed on the drying rack to the left of the sink. All children should be encouraged to clean up and put away the materials they used.

➤ We are emphasizing the concepts of texture. Please use texture words such as *rough, smooth, grainy, splintery, nubby, bumpy,* and so on when talking to the children about their work.

➤ Some children will need help labeling their work with their names. You can write their names and the date in one corner of their work. If they want you to write something about their work, please write exactly what they say.

Thank you so much for your help! We could not offer so many choices to the children without it!

Working with Paraprofessionals

www.nrcpara.org

The site of the National Resource Center for Paraprofessionals, with news about legislation and links to other information

http://ici.umn.edu/products/impact/152/over4.html

Links to effective training programs for paraprofessionals

Most classroom teachers are delighted to have **paraprofessionals,** or teacher aides, to work with in the classroom. Teacher aides can add immeasurably to the quality of the program; they can provide individual attention, increased supervision, scheduling flexibility, and assistance in instruction. (In most states, it is illegal for a teacher aide to *teach,* meaning that aides are not responsible for planning instruction and making instructional decisions.)

Paraprofessionals fill many different roles. For example, instructional aides teach under the supervision of the teacher; special-needs aides may be assigned to work with one child with special needs, such as an interpreter for a child with hearing impairment; some aides supervise the playground, cafeteria, or bus loading and unloading but do not teach; other aides perform clerical duties for teachers, such as making copies, but do not interact with children.

Clearly, the roles and responsibilities of paraprofessionals vary a great deal, and the training and supervision needs of the people in these roles also varies. Some will have completed programs of preparation to become paraprofessionals; others will have had no training at all. In most schools, paraprofessionals must have at least high school diplomas and be age eighteen or older.

After the teacher knows about the background and experience of the aide, she can make plans for training or orientation. Ashbaker and Morgan (2000/2001) recommend creating written job descriptions for teacher aides. Such descriptions can help in defining the roles of paraprofessionals, in

FIGURE 8.6

Planning Sheet for a Volunteer

Cooking Planning Sheet

Project ___Fruit Salad_____ Date ___3/25_____

Type: (Individual)   Small group

Purpose:

To help children learn about:

(new foods)   similarities and differences in color

other cultures   similarities and differences in size

texture changes   similarities and differences in weight

changes in smell   effects of heat

To develop:

(small muscle skills)   eye-hand coordination

other _____

Skills to be emphasized:

pouring   sorting   dipping   mixing   spreading

rolling   cracking   beating   juicing   grinding

slicing   grating   peeling   (cutting)   other _____

Ingredients needed:

___apple_____   ___walnut_____

___orange_____   _____

___banana_____   _____

___pineapple_____   _____

Procedure:

___1. Prepare stations for each step of the recipe._____

___2. Supervise children as needed as they complete each step__

___of the recipe._____

_____

_____

_____

_____

_____

promoting job satisfaction, and in guiding evaluation. Teachers can help children by encouraging schools and school boards to offer needed training for aides. Love and Levine (1992) found that training increased the effectiveness of teacher aides, which should not be surprising.

Working successfully with an aide requires some planning on the teacher's part and some ability to communicate well with adults. The following guidelines will help:

1. Take the time to discuss your philosophy, the program, what you consider appropriate discipline, and other pertinent information with the aide. Even if the aide has training and experience, it is important that you agree on how the class should be handled.

2. If the aide lacks training, provide it. This is not always easy because the aide may be paid by the hour and may not be willing to stay longer or come earlier without extra pay. Try to arrange for your aide to be paid for the time spent in training. Provide written information, explain why you do things the way you do, and then model the behaviors that you expect in the classroom. Take a few minutes for discussion each day.

3. Do not assign the aide all the "dirty" chores in the classroom. No one wants to clean the gerbil cage and the painting area all the time and never get a chance to do some of the more interesting classroom tasks, such as supervising a small group on a walk or in an art activity.

4. Make sure that paraprofessionals are included in professional development programs offered by the school.

5. Make sure that paraprofessionals have a mailbox in the school and that they are invited to participate in faculty meetings.

6. Paraprofessionals who are involved in teaching should also be involved in parent conferences with parents of the children with whom they work.

7. Ask the principal to provide training for supervision of paraprofessionals. Most teachers report that their only knowledge of how to supervise is "real life experience" (French 2001).

If the law states that aides are not to teach, what are they supposed to do? Generally, teacher aides can do almost everything that teachers do, with the exception of planning learning experiences and being responsible for assessment and reporting. However, aides can certainly contribute their observations of children or activities, which the teacher can communicate to parents and use in planning future activities.

Assignments for aides should be determined by their level of skill and experience. A teacher could not expect an aide with no experience to work with the whole class during music time, for example. Paraprofessionals can take on certain types of duties, including the following:

Instructional Duties

1. Reading to individual children or small groups or listening to children read
2. Providing individual help for children completing tasks
3. Providing small-group instruction that is planned by the teacher
4. Teaching children a song or a fingerplay
5. Working with a small group with manipulatives for mathematics or with materials for science investigations

Supervisory Duties

1. Supervising learning areas
2. Supervising outdoor play experiences (some states require one certified teacher on the playground during recess)
3. Supervising children on field trips
4. Supervising children as they move from one part of the building to another
5. Supervising children as they complete routines (hanging up coats, using the toilet, and so on)

Classroom Maintenance Duties

1. Preparing classroom displays and bulletin boards
2. Setting up and helping serve snacks
3. Helping to keep the classroom and materials clean and ready for use
4. Setting up and running audiovisual equipment
5. Gathering materials from the library or other resources

As the teacher and aide work together, the teacher should make sure to maintain good communication with the aide, discussing what needs to be done and the priorities for the day. The teacher should be sensitive to adults' need to be involved in making decisions and should plan to involve the aide in choosing tasks to be done. The teacher and the aide must also evaluate the process as they work together: Is the aide learning new skills so that different activities are now appropriate? Does the aide feel appreciated? Is the aide comfortable with the tasks that he does routinely? Do the teacher and the aide agree on most issues? Does the aide want to learn new techniques for working with the children? Are both the teacher and aide satisfied with the communication between them?

Working successfully with aides requires that teachers provide frequent positive feedback and praise for a job well done. Notes of appreciation to aides, notes to principals or administrators or in newsletters specifically commending aides, and any other special recognition that is deserved can make teacher–aide relationships more positive and assure that good work continues.

Margaret Egenhoefer, the subject of the next A Teacher Speaks box, works closely with her teaching assistant. Does this relationship seem to benefit the children in her classroom? Is working with a paraprofessional an opportunity for learning for both the teacher and the paraprofessional?

www.php.com
The Parents Helping Parents homepage, with many links to support groups and other information for parents of children with special needs

CHILDREN WITH SPECIAL NEEDS

Parents of children with special needs are by necessity more involved in their children's education than some parents because legal requirements specify that they be consulted and informed about decisions made about their children. Meetings to plan educational programs for children with special needs must include the parents. Communication with these parents may take the same forms it does with all other parents, but it may need to be more specific and more frequent. Teachers should check with their program administrators or principals about the legal requirements for communicating with parents of children with special needs.

Parents of children with special needs may themselves need support from the teacher. Spidel (1987) notes that the parent of a child who is exceptional often expects the child's teacher to do the following:

1. Understand his child's assets as well as his deficiencies.
2. Appreciate his child's accomplishments whenever and however they appear.
3. Help the parent (and the child) live without guilt or blame.
4. Tell his child how it really is. (The truth about himself may be difficult for a child who is learning disabled but not as difficult as the bewilderments and heartaches he experiences from half-truths and evasions.)

Shriver and Kramer (1993) found that most parents of students with special needs are satisfied with the services their children receive in the schools and with the teachers they have.

There is some concern in the early childhood profession about assigning teaching assistants to individual children. The presence of an assistant may encourage the teacher to feel that instruction for a given child is the responsibility of the assistant. Should that occur, it may result in the least-qualified staff teaching the student with the most complex learning problems (Giangreco et al. 2005).

A **Teacher** SPEAKS: The Relationship between Teachers and Teaching Assistants

Margaret Egenhoefer
Dixon Elementary School
New Berlin, Wisconsin

I teach kindergarten in a suburban school district. During the course of my twenty-year career, I have had the opportunity to work with various teaching assistants. I have strived to make this a beneficial experience for both the children and myself.

The most important point is to establish a good working relationship with your assistant. While it is not imperative that you become social acquaintances, a sincere yet professional rapport should be created for a positive experience. This will also make it easier to resolve any difficulties.

Before school starts, meet with your assistant—perhaps for lunch or a cup of coffee. Ask about family, past work experiences, hobbies, trips—just as you would when meeting a new colleague, neighbor, or friend. Share some of your personal background, including some of your strengths as a teacher. Use this time to show a sincere interest in her as a person and discover interests or strengths that your assistant might share in the classroom at some point.

It is important to set a framework. If your district doesn't have a job description for your assistant, then you need to create one. Include the amount of time she will be working with the children versus doing clerical duties, delegation of authority in the classroom, work schedule, evaluation system, and confidentiality expectations. It is also wise to share your educational philosophy and style of discipline.

It is essential to show your assistant respect in the classroom:

- Notice the good things and give sincere compliments, when they are deserved.
- Share important school memos about upcoming events, policies, school newsletters, and the like.
- Create a working space in the room for your assistant to keep notes, binders, books, and other school-job-related materials.
- Post her name next to yours on doors, bulletin boards, and so on.

- Introduce your assistant to parents via your newsletter, open house, or other means.
- Make sure your assistant is part of the class photo for the school memory book.
- Keep the lines of communication open—ask about her weekend, ask for an opinion about a classroom situation, and so forth.
- Share articles from professional journals or notices about upcoming conferences that might be of interest.
- Be realistic in your expectations. If your assistant doesn't understand a concept or method, model the technique in a nonthreatening manner.
- Let your assistant know your daily plans for the classroom in an informal planning session or in a written memo.

If a problem does arise, be honest and set time to talk things over. State the problem and listen to her response, but make sure your views are known, too. If the problem cannot be resolved, call in a third party, such as your principal. In the rare circumstance that an aide performs an undesirable behavior that is harmful to the children, make sure to document it as accurately and objectively as possible.

If your district requires a formal evaluation of your assistant, discuss the procedure with her. Be sure to provide reasons for your ratings and give your assistant a chance to respond.

I have been fortunate to have my present assistant for the past five years. The children see us as a unified team. It takes time and commitment to make our relationship work, but it is well worth the energy. It makes both of our jobs more satisfying. In turn, we feel that we are providing our students with the best teaching possible. And isn't that the point of education?

CELEBRATING DIVERSITY

Families can serve as resources for helping all children learn about and respect cultures that are different than their own. For example, all the children's families could be invited to contribute to the classroom some play items that are significant in their cultural traditions. Even families of limited means can contribute items such as empty food containers from traditional meals (Clark 1995). Having children bring in cultural items for sharing time is also useful in terms of celebrating diversity (Neuman and Roskos 1994). Families can become resources as food, songs, and stories from different cultures are studied.

It is very important for the school and its teachers to acknowledge children's cultures and help their families feel comfortable in the school. Both parents and children need to understand that speaking a language other than English is *not* unacceptable, so they need not feel embarrassed. Pena (2000) found that Hispanic parents were more likely to cite language barriers and the attitude of teachers and school administrators as reasons for their lack of involvement in schools. Community translators are often willing to help schools communicate with parents who do not speak English. Families respond well to activities such as potluck suppers, field days that include picnics or cookouts, and other activities that provide an atmosphere of acceptance and a chance to get to know other parents.

SUMMARY

- Parent involvement is important because of the difference it can make in a child's success in school. Students whose parents are involved in their education have higher grades, better attendance, and more positive attitudes about school. They are also more likely to graduate from high school, and to enroll in higher education than peers whose parents are not involved.

- Teachers and schools can encourage parent participation in many ways: by focusing on students' successes and achievements, sending personalized information to parents, helping families (not just parents) support students, extending frequent invitations to visit school or take part in activities, using school staff and volunteers to organize programs, and coordinating planning with administrators, parents, and other teachers. When parents do come to school, teachers should be sure to do things like serve refreshments, provide nametags, provide or pay for transportation and babysitting, meet in accessible locations, plan events at different times and on different days, meet in a place conducive to communication, use students as hosts/guides, and recognize parents for their efforts.

- The best ways to communicate with parents include parent conferences, school handbooks, home visits, parent visits to school, letters and notes, and technology such as recorded messages and webpages. Communicating with parents is the teacher's responsibility. Teachers must take time to plan and then assess the quality of their communications with parents.

- Volunteers who are well trained and experienced can assume responsibilities in several areas: supervising children in various learning areas and in outdoor play, reading to a child or small group, playing or teaching board games with children, and engaging in other activities that will enhance the children's experiences. Volunteers should not be used for clerical work or for tasks such as correcting papers.

- Working with a paraprofessional requires the teacher to take time to plan with the paraprofessional and to provide whatever training and experience are necessary. Paraprofessionals should not be assigned only the least pleasant tasks in the classroom, and they should be treated as professionals in terms of being invited to staff meetings and professional trainings sessions. Teachers should evaluate their work with paraprofessionals on a regular basis.

- Inviting all parents to school to share their cultures and traditions will encourage them to contribute to the classroom and be involved in the education of their children. Teachers have to plan carefully in order to help all parents feel welcome and valued at school. Providing translators and asking parents to informal gatherings where they can meet other parents are valuable strategies.

- Parents of children with special needs must be included when any decisions about the education of the child are made. Most are satisfied with the services their children receive in schools. Parents of children with special needs (like all parents) want their children to be happy and successful.

REFLECTIONS

1. Teachers often say that "The only parents who come to school are the ones who don't need to be there." What does this mean, and why does it happen? What can be done to change this pattern?

2. How can parents be encouraged to participate more in their children's school? What could you do, as one teacher, to help improve the relationships between the parents and the school?

3. If you have volunteers in your classroom (parents or others), what is your most important role in working with them? Why?

4. What kind of training would you recommend for paraprofessionals to make them most effective with the children? Would you want to do this training yourself, or would you prefer that the school train all paraprofessionals? Why?

5. What preparations could you make to ensure that parents from diverse backgrounds feel welcome and valued by your school and by you as an individual?

EXPLORATIONS AND ACTIVITIES

1. Attend a PTA or PTO meeting at your local school. Evaluate the meeting in terms of how a parent who does not speak English or does not read might feel while attending it. What changes might be made to make these parents feel more comfortable? If changes don't seem needed, what factors likely made the meeting comfortable for these parents?

2. Plan a parent meeting where you explain in an informal way what you are doing to encourage children's interest in literacy and encourage parents to involve their children in literacy events at home. Plan for those parents who cannot read English or who do not have books in their homes. You will want to assure them that they can, indeed, help their children become literate.

MyLabSchool is a collection of online tools for your success in this course, your licensure exams, and your teaching career. Visit **www.mylabschool.com** to access the following:

- Online Study Guide
- Video Cases from real classrooms
- Help with your research papers using Research Navigator
- Career Center with resources for:
    —Praxis and Licensure Preparation
    —Professional Portfolio Development
    —Job Search and Interview Techniques
    —Lesson Planning

PART II

The Curriculum Chapters

The chapters in this section of the book (9 through 15) are about the content that you will teach. There is a chapter for each of the content areas (e.g., math, science, and so on). That does not mean, however, that you should treat each area as a separate subject or make plans for lessons in one area without considering how lessons could help children develop concepts no matter what the subject might be.

Teachers are responsible for teaching content, and so you must know what is appropriate content for each of the subject-matter areas. That means knowing the standards for the curriculum in each area. That information is provided in every chapter, along with suggestions for developmentally appropriate activities and a complete Learning Plan, as well.

As you read through these chapters, also be thinking about how you can integrate the content across the curriculum based on ideas and concepts that will make sense to the children you teach. The theme of *spaces* is explored in each chapter in an Integrating the Curriculum box, which provides ideas for content-specific activities. The wonderful part of content-area teaching is that young children are interested and excited about all kinds of topics and ideas. Thus, our aim as teachers must be to keep that interest alive.

CHAPTER **9**

KEY TERMS *you'll find in this chapter:*

- Assistive technology, 290
- Communicative competence, 269
- Dialect, 294
- English language learners, 295
- Kidwatching, 283
- Language, 268
- Language delay, 290
- Linguistic model, 274
- Morpheme, 268
- Morphology, 268
- Phonology, 268
- Pragmatics, 269
- Semantics, 269
- Sociolinguistics, 271
- Syntax, 269

Celebrating the Magic of Language

FOCUS
QUESTIONS

- What is *language?*
- How is language learned?
- How can teachers create an effective language-learning environment and otherwise encourage children's language growth?
- How can teachers help children with special needs learn language most effectively?
- What strategies can teachers use to celebrate diversity in language use?

This week, your observation at a preschool focused on children's language. You observed a two-year-old, a three-year-old, and a five-year-old.

The two-year-old was a boy who was excited about dinosaurs and named several types of dinosaurs while showing you models of them. He also talked about dinosaur tracks; he rolled out a piece of Play Doh and pushed the feet of one of the dinosaur models into it to show you how tracks are made.

The three-year-old, a girl, was very quiet and did not initiate any conversation with you. You watched her play outdoors with the other children, but she never uttered a word; she just smiled and nodded when asked questions.

The five-year-old, another girl, was also quiet in the classroom, but when she was outdoors, she asked several children to play a game of tag with her and explained all of the rules to them. You noticed that she spoke Spanish and English and seemed quite competent in both languages.

When you returned to your classroom, you found that many of your peers had similar experiences. Now all of you have questions about the extraordinary variations found in children's language development. How do children learn language? What sort of program is best for helping them become more proficient users of language? Are published materials available to aid children in developing language abilities? What is the role of the teacher in planning for children's language development? ■

Defining Language

For the purposes of this chapter, **language** is defined as a system of communication used by humans. It is either produced orally or by sign, and it can be extended to its written form.

Characteristics of Language

Language also has characteristics that define it further. One characteristic is that language is rule governed. The rules of a given language are learned intuitively by those people who speak it; only speakers who make a scientific study of the language are likely to be able to verbalize these rules. An example of one of these rules is the placement of words denoting number, color, and size in descriptive phrases. For example, in describing *one big red balloon,* we would never say "red one big balloon."

Another characteristic of language is that it is arbitrary. There are no logical connections between the sounds that we use to label objects and the objects themselves. Social groups merely agree to use a particular combination of sounds to represent an object. Actually, very few words sound like what they represent, such as *buzz* or *hiss.* Words such as *table, chair, bottle,* and so on have no logical connections with their referents.

Language is also changing. New words are constantly entering our lexicon, and others are being discarded. Meanings, too, are changing. With a little thought, you could probably list thirty or forty words that have been added to the English language within the last five years and ten or so that have changed meaning. Even young children use words that were once uncommon (*download*), that did not exist a short time ago (*iPod*), or that have changed meanings recently (*Web, click*).

http://earthrenewal.org/secondlang.htm
A dictionary of language development terminology

Parents and Language

● Encourage parents to talk to their children and celebrate their language achievements. Suggest that parents keep journals of special words that their children enjoy.

www.answers.com/topic/semantics
A detailed explanation of semantics

Systems of Language

Every language is a set of systems: phonology, morphology, syntax, semantics, and pragmatics. **Phonology** is the system of sounds that make up the language; it includes the sounds that are used to make words, the rules for combining the sounds, and the stress and intonation patterns that help to communicate meaning. Different languages use different sounds and allow different combinations of sounds in words. In some languages, for instance, words can begin with the "ng" sound, but not in English. The task of the child is to learn to distinguish differences in sounds and intonation patterns that signal different meanings.

A second system of language is **morphology,** which deals with the meanings of sounds. A **morpheme** is the smallest unit of sound that carries meaning. Some words are morphemes; some are combinations of morphemes. *Tiger* is an example of a word that is a morpheme. The plural, *tigers,* is a combination of the free morpheme *tiger* and the bound morpheme *s*. The *s* is bound because it signals meaning but cannot carry meaning alone. Other morphemes signal changes of tense, person, and number rather than meaning. Mastering English morphology includes learning how to form possessives, plurals, and past and progressive verb tenses. For example, in English we say "one apple," but we must say "eight apples." Many other languages signal the number change with the number word only and do not require pluralization of the noun *apple*.

Syntax is a third system of language. In simple terms, the syntax of a language contains the rules for combining words into phrases and sentences and for transforming sentences into other sentences. Syntax provides information about word meanings based on their places in sentences. If you heard *A crad was zagging wickily,* you would know that the action described occurred in the past and that *wickily* described how the *crad* was *zagging*. You would also know that more than one *crad* existed because the article *a* signifies one of a set. Children mastering syntax learn how to construct negatives, questions, compound sentences, passives, imperatives, and eventually complex sentences that include embedded clauses.

Semantics is the fourth system of language. Learning semantics means acquiring vocabulary and meanings associated with words. Some words are probably learned by repeated association, such as *bottle*. The word and the object are presented to the child simultaneously, again and again. Other word usages reflect the child's growing ability to categorize. A very young child may begin by using *doggie* to refer to any four-legged animal but then learns more specific terms, such as *horse* and *cow*. A child's system of meanings is constantly developing and changing as a result of experience and maturation. Cognitive abilities are reflected in a child's speech. For example, a child will begin to use *gone* about the same time that he learns the concept of object permanence. Mastering the semantic system requires that a child learn word meanings and relationships between and among words.

In addition to learning all the other systems of language, the child must learn the rules for using language in social interactions. **Pragmatics** is the use of language to express intention and to get things done. Speakers must learn to adapt their language to achieve their communication goals in different situations and to do so in socially acceptable ways. Pragmatics includes the rules for appropriate language in church, on the playground, and at the dinner table. A speaker of any language would not be considered competent in its use until she had mastered the basic rules for language use in various social contexts. Children reflect their understanding of pragmatics when they learn to say *please* or when they speak more simply to a baby than they normally speak.

Table 9.1 provides a summary of the language development of children in the systems of phonology, semantics, grammar, and pragmatics. Note that the grammar system contains elements of morphology and syntax, which are discussed as separate systems in the previous paragraphs.

Communicative competence means the ability of a speaker to use language appropriately in a communication experience. Children may know more language than they are able to use at a given point in time, but how much they know and are able to use is constantly changing. Figure 9.1 illustrates the idea that linguistic competence (the language one knows) and

TABLE 9.1 Language Development Milestones

AGE	PHONOLOGY	SEMANTICS	GRAMMAR	PRAGMATICS
Birth–1 year	Has categorical speech perception Coos, then babbles Organizes speech sounds into phonemic categories of native language Babbles reflect sound and intonation patterns of native language	Prefers to listen to mother's voice and to native language Analyzes speech stream for words and syllable stress patterns Recognizes familiar words Uses preverbal gestures	Notices the structure of word sequences, distinguishing ABA from ABB patterns Develops sensitivity to clause and phrase boundaries	Establishes joint attention Engages in vocal exchanges and turn-taking games
1–2 years	Recognizes correct pronunciations of familiar words Uses systematic strategies to simplify word pronunciation	Says first words Vocabulary grows to several hundred words Sometimes underextends and overextends word meanings	Combines two words in telegraphic speech As three-word sentences appear, gradually adds grammatical morphemes	Engages in conversational turn-taking and topic maintenance
3–5 years	Phonological awareness increases Pronunciation improves greatly	Coins words to fill in for words not yet mastered Understands metaphors based on concrete, sensory comparisons	Gradually generalizes grammatical forms Continues to add grammatical morphemes in a regular order. Gradually produces complex grammatical structures	Masters additional conversational strategies, such as the turnabout Begins to grasp illocutionary intent Adjusts speech to listener's perspective and to social expectations Asks for clarification of ambiguous messages Produces chronological narratives
6–10 years	Phonological awareness extends to all phonemes in a word Masters syllable stress patterns signaling subtle differences in meaning	At school entry, has a vocabulary of about 10,000 words Grasps meanings of words on the basis of definitions Appreciates the multiple meanings of words, as indicated by metaphors and humor	Refines complex grammatical structures, such as the passive voice and infinitive phrases	Uses advanced conversational strategies, such as shading Continues to refine understanding of illocutionary intent Communicates clearly in demanding situations, such as on the telephone Produces classic narratives rich in orienting information and evaluations

Source: Adapted from Laura E. Berk, *Child Development,* 7th ed. (Boston: Allyn & Bacon, 2006), p. 388. Copyright © 2006 by Pearson Education. Reprinted by permission of the publisher.

270   **PART TWO** The Curriculum Chapters   www.ablongman.com/brewer6e

FIGURE 9.1

Linguistic and Communicative Competence

LC = Linguistic competence
CC = Communicative competence

Source: Celia Genishi and Anne Haas Dyson, Eds., *Language Assessment in the Early Years* (Norwood, NJ: Ablex, 1984). Reprinted with the permission of Ablex Publishing Corporation.

communicative competence (the language one can use in actual communication experiences) are not totally overlapping sets.

Sociolinguistics, the study of language in a social context, is closely related to pragmatics. Sociolinguists ask: "What are the key aspects of a communication encounter and how do they influence one another? How do we adapt the language to various social contexts? And how does the language style used affect the social context itself?" (Lindfors 1980, p. 6).

Anyone who has ever studied a foreign language should be familiar with the concept of knowing more language than can be used effectively. Early lessons in Spanish, for instance, will include learning words for foods, places, colors, numbers, and so on. The learner's ability to communicate, however, will be quite limited until he knows some of the systems of that language (for example, that adjectives follow nouns) and has experience in applying them. Similarly, a child learning a first language will know words that he cannot use effectively; competence will come with experience.

The learner's ability to communicate also will be quite limited until he knows some of the rules for putting together sentences and speaking in different situations. Children learning language may use phrases such as "Will you do me a favor?" or repeat patterns such as knock-knock jokes without fully understanding what a favor is or what makes a knock-knock joke funny.

Learning Language

The process of learning language often appears to be magic. No one seems to teach a child language, but he learns it, and learns it well, in a very short time. Most children have mastered the basic structures possible in their native language by the time they are four. In addition to using the basic

www.
www.utexas.edu/courses/ linguistics/resources/socioling
Examples of different dialects and links to many other linguistic terms

patterns of their language, they also have a vocabulary of around three thousand words.

Most children also know how to use what they have learned about language to get what they want. A child will whine or not whine, depending on how the adults in her life respond to whining, and she will change the tone and complexity of her language when she speaks to different audiences (e.g., a baby or an adult). Some children can even switch from one language to another effortlessly.

Two premises underlie this chapter and should be kept in mind as you read. One is the belief, articulated by Goodman et al. (1987), that language is not acquired externally but rather is part of a process of personal development and emerges in the context of social use (p. 38). This is not to say that language is not present in the child's environment but that learning language is a more complex process than simply adopting language that is outside oneself. Therefore, in this chapter, the term that will be used to describe the learning of language is *language development* rather than *language acquisition*. The other premise is that language, both oral and sign, is not developed in isolation; language is always related to cognitive development.

Learning to use language well is central to a child's success in many areas: If a child fails to learn language, then he will have no hope of being successful in learning to read and write, since they are both language processes. A child without language skills also will have more difficulty in getting along with other children because he will not be able to explain what he wants to do or how he wants to play. A skillful language user can often talk his way into a play group, whereas a less-skilled child will be left out. In addition, a child who can recognize and label his feelings can learn to explain them and perhaps control his frustrations more easily. Finally, a child who lacks the language skills to express what he knows about a given topic may be treated as less capable and offered experiences that are less cognitively challenging.

In sum, learning language must be a primary goal in every experience offered to children. Given the importance of language, this chapter should perhaps have been the first one in this book.

Sequence of Language Development

Language development follows a sequence, which is fairly predictable even though there are many individual variations. Most children move from differentiated crying (crying that sounds different in response to different stimuli: being pricked by a pin, feeling cold or wet, and so on) through cooing and babbling to expressive jargon and one-word sentences. Some children learn the names of objects before other words.

Nelson (1973) classifies children's language as *referential* or *expressive*. Common nouns are referential; social words are expressive.

Many children develop *idiomorphs* (not real words), which they apply to objects that they evidently find related. For example, when shown flowers or pictures of flowers, the child may make a sniffing sound. For a period of time, this sound will represent anything to be smelled.

Soon the child will develop longer utterances and learn to produce negatives and questions. Then the child's language will consist of some mature forms and some immature forms. By the time children are eight to ten years old, their language is mostly mature. At the same time, children's comprehension of language is developing rapidly.

Language development is not complete at the end of infancy; it continues throughout one's lifetime. Children continue to make rapid gains in vocabulary during the early childhood years. Three- and four-year-olds learn to construct questions and negatives. "Why he no go?" will change to "Why isn't he going?" and "Me no do it" becomes "I didn't do it." Children also begin to use and understand more complicated sentences, such as "The dog under the table is mine."

By the time a child begins kindergarten, she will have mastered most of the basic forms in her native language, although some immature forms, such as "gots" and "goed," will be present in her speech. Even children of eight and nine can be confused by such sentences as "The boy was bitten by the dog," because they respond to sentences as if the first noun named is doing the acting.

Older primary children are learning vocabulary and learning to use more complex sentence forms correctly. They are also becoming more aware of their audience. Very young children assume that their listeners share their context; older children can take the point of view of the listener and not assume a shared context. They gain skill in giving directions and relating stories in a sequence. They also gain abilities to use language that is not context bound and to discuss objects, events, and some abstract ideas, such as love.

Language play begins in infancy as children play with sounds and continues as young children create rhyming words or make up preposterous names or other silly words. The play of older children usually depends on changes in word forms or meanings. Children may create secret languages, such as Pig Latin, and a host of sayings for all types of situations, such as lying, cheating, name calling, begging, telling the truth, using table manners, and so on.

Older children and adults continue to learn language. People learn the vocabulary related to their professions and their hobbies, and they learn to use more formal speech when it is appropriate. Even the most literate person discovers new vocabulary words and new expressions as he listens and reads. Language development does not end as long as a person is mentally active and an environment for learning is available.

Theoretical Models of Language Learning

Three major models attempt to explain the development of children's language: the behaviorist model, the linguistic model, and the constructivist model (Berko-Gleason 1985; Butler 1974; King 1987). Each model will be examined briefly.

> We teach not what we know but who we are. We can't hide who we are and what we believe.
>
> —Mem Fox

Behaviorist Model

The **behaviorist model** of learning language describes the process as consistent with the rules of operant conditioning, based on a stimulus-response model. In the simplest terms, infants are presented with language, they imitate the language, they are rewarded for their imitations, and they continue to repeat what they have heard. Imitation does not have to be exact or immediate in order for children to make use of it in learning language.

Behaviorist explanations fail to account, however, for the fact that much of children's language is constructed in ways that have never been modeled

www.
http://maxpages.com/thena/ladiscussion

A discussion of language development theories as they apply to both first- and second-language learners

WWW.

http://home.cogeco.ca/ ~monicafitz/theories.htm

An explanation of the theories that explain how children learn language

by mature speakers. For example, a child may say, "Higher the swing!"—a construction not used by any other speaker in the child's experience.

Behaviorists also have difficulty explaining regressions in children's language. Typically, a young child will use the correct form of a past-tense verb, such as *went*. But as the child matures and generalizes the rules for constructing past-tense verbs, he replaces *went* with *goed*. Later, as the child learns that some words are exceptions to the general rules, *goed* is replaced by *went*.

The difficulty of modifying language through adult input is another problem for behaviorists. According to the stimulus-response model, the child should respond to adult correction of her language use. But as anyone who has attempted to correct a young child knows, this does not always happen. Literature on this subject contains many stories of adults' attempts to correct young children's language (McNeill 1966). The fact is, children do not change the forms of their language easily.

On the other hand, the behaviorist point of view does have some validity. Children obviously speak the languages of their homes. Any human child can learn any human language. No human language can be said to be more complex or more difficult than other languages. Children learn to produce the sounds needed in their native languages and to eliminate the sounds that are not required. Children also learn to repeat words and phrases that they hear around them, even when they do not know what they mean.

Linguistic Model

Another explanation for the development of language is the **linguistic,** or nativistic, **model.** Linguist Noam Chomsky (1965) was instrumental in developing this model. The theory holds that language is inherent in the child at birth and needs only to be triggered by social contact with speakers in order to emerge.

When the linguistic explanation for language acquisition was developed, the study of language was dominated by behaviorist thinking. Some theorists began to question whether children could learn language as quickly as they obviously did solely through interactions based on stimulus and response. These theorists reasoned that language must be part of children's human inheritance. Chomsky (1965) theorized that humans were equipped with a *language acquisition device*—a structure in the brain that made possible the learning of language.

Evidence in support of this theory is that humans are the only species to acquire language, which they use to communicate ideas and pass on to other generations knowledge they have gained. Linguistic theorists also point out that language development is almost universal among humans. Only humans who have experienced severe trauma or mental retardation are unable to use language; the vast majority of humans use language at some level of competence. Linguistic theorists have contributed to the field of language development by forcing researchers to examine their models and more carefully observe what children actually do in learning language.

Constructivist Model

A third approach to explaining language development is the **constructivist model.** This group of theorists—represented by Jean Piaget (1959), Jerome

Bruner (1983), and Lev Vygotsky (1962)—believes that children learn language quickly because the human brain seeks patterns and order in language, just as it constantly seeks patterns and order in the environment. For evidence, these theorists point to examples of language that is produced when there has been no previous model; to the uniqueness of language (the fact that except for clichés, we may never hear exactly the same sentence used in the same context more than once); and to the obvious reliance of the child on the rules of language, which are rarely taught but which are abstracted from examples presented to the child.

Learning language is not an effortless process. Children make a conscious effort to learn the names of things, feelings, and actions. The constructivist model views the learner as vital in the process of learning language. The learner is active in seeking and constructing meaning and in seeking communication with others (Bruner 1983; Jaggar and Smith-Burke 1985; Shuy 1987).

Learning to discriminate and correctly label a cat or a dog illustrates the active nature of language learning. If a child sees a dog and says "Doggie," the caregiver will likely respond, "Yes, it's a dog." If the child labels the animal "Kitty," the response will likely be, "No, it's a dog." The child is left on his own to determine the features of each animal that are distinctive, because it is difficult to describe the features verbally in a way that has any meaning for a very young child.

Children learning language produce hypotheses and test them with the speakers in their environments. They try different combinations of sounds and words in different situations. Constructivists believe that this problem-solving behavior is very important in learning language. They also believe that the errors in children's speech reflect new knowledge about language rules.

Constructivists also recognize the importance of social interactions in the development of language. Many of the words learned first, such as *bye-bye* and *hi*, have meaning only as parts of interactions with others. For constructivists, many factors affect language learning. These factors (social, maturational, biological, cognitive) interact and modify one another as a child learns language (Berko-Gleason 1985). Many constructivist researchers believe that infants control much of their interaction with adults in their environments by smiling, making sounds, and repeating adult sounds to continue the interactions.

Bruner (1983) describes the language acquisition support system that adults create for children who are learning language. The support system is *"scaffolding"* that provides a framework and supports the child until she has mastered language forms at a given level; the scaffolding is moved to a higher level when the child's language forms become more complex. For example, when a very young child in a highchair drops a cereal bowl to the floor, her parent says "Uh-oh." When the child has learned to say that phrase each time she drops something, the parent begins to say "Down" or "Gone" each time. As the child's language abilities increase, the parent begins to use longer sentences when something is dropped, such as "Please don't drop your cereal bowl on the floor."

Whitmore and Goodman (1995) point out that the *functions* of language—why we use it—precede the *forms*. For instance, children use sounds that are not recognizable as words to convey meanings such as "Turn the page," "Read," and "Pick me up."

TABLE 9.2 Comparison of Features across Models

FEATURE	BEHAVIORIST	LINGUISTIC	CONSTRUCTIVIST
Environment	X	X	X
Reward	X		
Imitation	X	x	x
Grammar		X	X
Social Interaction	x	X	X
Teaching	X		
Problem Solving		X	X

X = Dependent feature
x = Minor feature

Comparison of Models

PRAXIS

Be able to describe an environment that will encourage children's language development

Table 9.2 compares the primary features of the three major models of language learning. A large *X* means that the model depends on that feature, and a small *x* means that the feature plays only a minor role in learning language. As you can see, the greatest similarity among the three models is that they all place a great deal of emphasis on the language environment of the learner. All three focus on imitation as well, but linguistic and constructivist thinkers place less emphasis on imitation than do behaviorists.

Teaching Language

Creating an Effective Environment

Because almost all children learn language and can use it to satisfy their communication needs, observations of what parents and caregivers do naturally to encourage language development is helpful when planning for successful language learning. Parents and other caregivers teach language informally, focus on the intent or meaning of the child's utterances rather than on the form, expect success, recognize that language learning is holistic, and celebrate the child's unique, creative uses of language.

Use an Informal Approach

Adults and older children in an infant's environment do not teach language formally. What they do is talk to the child about the environment and happenings in the environment.

Long before an infant can produce language, speakers around the child will be talking to her: "Oh, are you thirsty? Here is a bottle of water" or "It's time for your bath now." They will also make attempts to talk about what is interesting to the child. If the baby is looking at something, the adult will attempt to determine what has caught the child's interest and talk about it. As the child grows and becomes mobile, the parent's or caregiver's language is more controlling, but it is still closely related to the context (for example, "Play here with your ball. Roll the ball on the floor.").

Parents do not plan language lessons each day. They just talk to their children as they make cookies, repair the sink, wash the car, cook dinner, and go through the daily household routines. Language is learned through meaningful interactions, not by talking about it or analyzing it.

In school settings, teachers can attempt to follow children's lead in conversations and talk about topics that are meaningful and interesting to them. Sometimes teachers are so determined to follow the given curriculum or their own agenda that they fail to respond to children's interests or to concentrate on topics that are actually important to children. It is not as easy to follow the child's lead at school as it is at home, where only one or two children are present, but teachers do need to think about children's needs and interests in communication experiences.

Focus on the Speaker's Intent

Learning language is a self-generated process. It is controlled by the learner and is not dependent on external rewards. Achieving communication with significant others seems to be reward enough to keep the child learning.

Parents and other adults seem to know this intuitively, because the majority of their responses to a child's language are focused on the child's intent, rather than on perfection of the utterance. Even parents who do correct their children's speech are much more likely to correct content than form. If the child runs into the house and shouts "Daddy gots a new car!" the adult is more likely to respond "No, Daddy has borrowed that car" than to instruct the child to say "Daddy *has* a new car." In fact, if Daddy does have a new car, the response is likely to be "Let's go see it!"

In the early childhood classroom, teachers can make a real effort to focus on what children are trying to say rather than the form they use. Teachers should concentrate on providing new objects and new experiences to help build the young child's vocabulary.

Efforts to correct grammatical structures are relatively useless with this age group. A study that compared teachers trained to repeat the child's incorrect utterance in correct form and those trained to extend the conversation based on the child's utterance showed that extension is more useful in helping children achieve language growth (Cazden 1965). If a child says "See red car," the teacher using extension would say "Yes, I see a red car and a blue car going down the street." These responses are much more closely related to what parents do in responding to the meaning rather than to the form of utterances.

In primary classrooms, teachers can help children learn the vocabulary of topics that interest them, provide opportunities to express their own ideas, and continue to focus on children's meanings. Strategies for encouraging language growth include the following:

- *Expansion* involves using the child's utterance but adding to it grammatically. If the child says "Red truck," the teacher might respond "The red truck is going fast."

- *Extension* has the teacher add meaning to the child's utterance but not necessarily change it grammatically. For example, if the child says "Red truck," the teacher might respond "I see a red truck, a blue truck, and a yellow truck."

- *Repetition* has the teacher take part of the child's utterance and repeat it. The child might say "Down" when going down the slide. The teacher might then say "Everyone is going down. Everyone is going down."

- *Parallel talk* is most often used in play when the teacher describes the child's actions. If the child says "Going fast" while riding a tricycle, the teacher might repeat "Going fast. Going very fast. Going faster."

- *Self-talk* is also used most frequently in play—for example, when the teacher is building with the blocks and says "I am going to need a larger block for this space. I will need a long block here."

- *Vertical structuring* involves the teacher responding to the child's utterance with a question that will encourage a longer response. For example, if the child says "I want to go" (pointing to where she wants to go), the teacher would ask "Where do you want to go?"

- *Fill-in* has the teacher using structured sentences and having the child fill in the last word or phrase. For example, if the child says "She hungry," the teacher might offer "Does she want something to _____?" and pause for the child to complete the thought. Fill-ins are often used with children during read-alouds, when the teacher pauses at the ends of the lines to allow the children to complete them (especially with a rhyming or repetitive text) (Kratcoski and Katz 1998).

In sum, you should note that *all* these strategies depend on the teacher using the child's utterance. Drilling children on the use of any element of language is not recommended.

Expect Success

If you went to the local hospital and interviewed parents of newborn infants about their expectations of whether their babies would learn to talk, you would probably get emphatically positive answers (along with strange looks for asking such a question!). Parents expect that their children will become mature speakers. When the baby makes errors, they know it is a normal part of the process in learning language. They do not expect that their child will be able to say "My bowl of cereal has fallen to the floor" when he drops his oatmeal off the highchair. They do know that their child's language will mature over time and that immature forms will be replaced by more mature and more complex forms.

In early childhood classrooms, teachers can also expect success as children are learning language. Teachers who view errors such as the use of irregular plurals (*mouses, feets*), adding *-ed* to form the past tense of verbs (*goed, runned*), and the use of incorrect verb forms as indicators of the child's growing mastery of the rules of English will treat those errors differently than teachers who view them as mistakes to be corrected.

Teachers will be better able to make this distinction if they understand what is typical of children's language development at various ages. Figure 9.2 presents benchmarks of oral language use for preschool through second grade.

In sum, language is learned through active exploration of the systems, not by direct imitation of models. Errors are indications of the active nature of language learning as well as growth and maturation.

FIGURE 9.2

Benchmarks for Children's Oral Language Development

Preschool

- Understands the overall sequence of events in stories
- Understands and follows oral directions
- Connects information and events to life experience when being read a story
- Knows that it is print that is read in stories
- Pays attention to separable and repeating sounds in language (e.g., Peter, Peter, Pumpkin Eater)
- Uses new vocabulary and grammatical construction in own speech
- Demonstrates understanding of literal meaning of stories by asking questions and making comments

Kindergarten

- Begins to track print when listening to a familiar text being read or when re-reading own writing
- Makes appropriate switches from oral to written language situations
- Connects information and events in text to life and life experiences to text
- Retells, re-enacts, or dramatizes stories of parts of stories

Grade 1

- Makes transition from emergent reading to "real" reading
- Shows evidence of expanding language repertory, including increasing use of standard, formal language registers
- Discusses features of stories and main ideas and prior knowledge of topics in informational text

Grade 2

- Reads and comprehends stories and informational text appropriate for grade level
- Participates in creative responses to texts such as discussions, dramatizations, oral presentations, and plays

Source: Every Child a Reader: Applying Reading Research in the Classroom, by E. H. Hiebert et al., 1988, Ann Arbor: University of Michigan, Center for Improvement of Early Reading.

Emphasize the Holistic Nature of Language Learning

Children learn language, language functions, and how to use language in social interactions all at the same time (Halliday 1982). Parents do not set out to teach language to their children by limiting their children's learning to one piece of the complex system of language. They help their children learn language by conversing with them in meaningful contexts and in social situations. They present language as a whole, within a context, and within a social milieu. Few parents would drill their children by asking them to learn a list of nouns, followed by a list of verbs, and then some adjectives. They would not expect their children to practice language outside a real context. The idea of a parent asking a child to go to his or her room and practice saying "I would like a drink of water" is ludicrous.

Teachers of young children can also preserve the holistic nature of language learning by not breaking language into bits and pieces for study in school. Words in isolation—or worse, *sounds* in isolation—have no meaning

Children's vocabulary and ability to use language changes and grows as they find new situations in which to practice.

that can be constructed. Children do not need to practice isolated elements of language; they do not learn the parts and then put them back together and use them.

Children do need to use language in a variety of situations and with a variety of speakers. They need to talk about topics of interest to them and to learn to adjust their language to meet the requirements of the speaking situation. Real talk provides young children a chance to practice their developing language.

Celebrate Unique and Creative Uses of Language

Goodman et al. (1987) describe a child learning language as always creative or inventive and at the same time pulled back into conformity. Children are always creating new words and phrases, but when they find that their words fail to communicate what they intended, they conform more to the usual social forms. This inventiveness in language is important. We could not create new terms when they were needed if we lost our capacity to be inventive language users.

Parents and others tend to celebrate some of the creative language of children. For example, many people have nicknames that were invented by younger siblings who could not pronounce their real names. Almost all families use special words that were either errors in pronunciation or words invented by their children.

In the classroom, teachers can celebrate children's unique expressions by recording them to share later or by posting them on a chart or bulletin board. Some of the expressions children use are very poetic. Teachers can also celebrate children's language by not changing it. If a child uses a dialect, these expressions can also be celebrated and recorded.

There are appropriate times and strategies for helping young children develop skill in speaking effectively in different contexts, but for very young children the focus should be on their unique ways of expressing that meaning. Children need to have their language accepted and valued.

Recognize Language Achievements

Children have made such amazing progress in mastering their native language before entering preschool that teachers sometimes fail to recognize how much they have accomplished. Children's linguistic competencies include the ability to select meaningful parts of a message, to recognize differences in linguistic contexts, and to use syntactic rules. If you say to a very young child "Your father has gone to the office to work," the child will respond "Daddy gone." Obviously, the child knows what is significant in the message.

Children adapt their language to listeners when they are very young. This is particularly noticeable in children from bilingual families, who sort out which language they should speak with which people. Children also use correct syntactical rules from the time they begin to use sentences of more than one word. They say "More milk" as opposed to "Milk more," for example.

Daniels (1994) found that children learning sign language along with spoken language were more advanced than their age peers in language development and that they had no trouble with *code switching* (knowing when to use sign versus oral language). In short, children are efficient users of language and able to use whatever is in their environment to communicate.

In summary, children learn language when they are in environments where language is used and when they interact with others. They learn best when meaning, rather than form, is stressed. Parents set the stage for successful language learning by using language in real-life situations, by dropping specific intentions to teach language, and by accepting approximations that gradually become closer to adult models. Parents also take delight in their child's progress and celebrate her imaginative and poetic uses of language.

Parents and Language

- Be sure that parents understand that so-called errors in their children's speech, such as adding *-ed* to verbs, are signs of language growth. Giving children opportunities to learn vocabulary in meaningful ways is the most useful strategy for helping them develop their language abilities.

Commercial Programs

Encouraging the development of language is always one of the primary goals of teachers of young children. Toward this goal, various commercial programs are available, often consisting of a teacher's guide, pictures of objects in various categories, and sometimes plastic models of objects. These materials may also be accompanied by audio recordings or computer programs designed to allow children to practice repeating words or phrases.

Commercial programs designed to teach children language are objectionable for several reasons. One, of course, is that these programs ignore the interactive and active nature of language learning. Another objection is that most programs are designed for small-group instruction, yet it would be rare to find a group in which all the children needed to learn the same words or phrases. A third objection to commercial language programs is that most of the actual production of language is done by the teacher, rather than by the children. Finally, most of these programs are expensive.

Using a commercial program is not the answer for promoting children's language growth. Setting up an environment that encourages language growth and that is responsive to children's language *is* the answer. Language is learned best when children use it for meaningful purposes.

In the best classrooms, children have many opportunities to talk with one another and with adults. Children playing with clay, sand, water, blocks, and other classroom materials are encouraged to talk about their experiences. As adults move around the play areas, they listen to the children's language, make observations, and expand on the children's language in meaningful interactions that are developmentally appropriate. If a three-year-old is playing with the sand, the adult might offer the language to describe what is taking place by remarking, for example, "You are making a tunnel in the sand." An eight-year-old playing with water and boats might be encouraged to use the vocabulary connected with boating: *deck, port, stern, aft, dock,* and so on.

Parents and Language

- Invite parents to observe the language that children use in the classroom and to talk with you about the differences they observe between classroom language and that used at home.

Wells (1986) reached several disturbing conclusions following an extensive longitudinal study of the language of children in Bristol, England. For *none* of the children studied was the language used in the classroom as linguistically rich as that used at home, which was self-motivated, spontaneous, unstructured, and supported by adults. Wells concluded that several factors made language development at school much more difficult than it was at home: a large number of students per teacher, a curriculum dominated by norm-referenced tests, and the fact that many teachers did not believe that talking was important for learning.

Standards for Language Development

The importance of children's language development to their success in and out of school cannot be overstated. This significance is reflected in the *Standards for the English Language Arts,* which were created and published by two professional associations of language educators: the International Reading Association (IRA) and the National Council of Teachers of English (NCTE). The purpose of these standards, as described by these sponsoring groups, "is to provide guidance in ensuring that all students are proficient language users so they may succeed in school, participate in society, find rewarding work, appreciate and contribute to our culture, and pursue their own goals and interests throughout their lives" (IRA/NCTE 1996).

Much of the content of the *Standards for the English Language Arts* addresses reading and writing skills, which are covered in Chapter 10 on literacy. The complete standards are presented and discussed in that chapter, as well (see page 313). But in this chapter on language development, it's important to point out that the IRA/NCTE standards are founded on the idea that children's literacy development begins before they enter school as they experience speech, print, and graphic representations of ideas. This is the concept of *emergent literacy,* which suggests that when children are encouraged to explore and experiment with language in a supportive environment, their early language behaviors lead to the development of conventional literacy (Teale and Sulzby 1989).

Observing Language Learners

Yetta Goodman (1985) coined the term **kidwatching** to describe how teachers should pay attention to children—to what they are thinking and saying and how they are responding—which is extremely important in assessing language development. Teachers have to learn how to observe children's language and how they use it. Teachers must also learn how to provide the environments that foster children's growth in language abilities and what specific activities can be most helpful to a given child at a given time (Goodman 1985).

The following guidelines will be helpful as teachers observe the language of young children:

1. Always observe a child's language in a variety of contexts before drawing any conclusions about her abilities. Some children who are almost nonverbal in school settings will be extremely verbal on the playground. Some children will not contribute to conversation even in small groups but can communicate effectively one to one with a child or an adult.

2. Look for competence in using language for a variety of purposes. For example, how does the child share information, get what is needed or wanted, or use imaginative language? Can the child communicate both with adults and with other children?

3. Look for effectiveness in communication, rather than for specific abilities, such as "The child speaks in complete sentences." Often, the most effective communication does not require the use of complete sentences. What teachers need to know is whether children can adapt their language to the requirements of different speaking situations.

4. Look for signs of growth in the child's knowledge of language systems. For example, are there changes in the child's use of inflectional endings and clauses?

5. Look for growth in vocabulary. As a child participates in the activities provided in the classroom, are labels for objects and actions becoming a part of his vocabulary?

Careful observation of children's language will provide insights that will help teachers plan activities and structure the environment to foster growth in language. The teacher who observes that a child does not know the language for expressing emotions, for example, will help by providing some of the labels for feelings when the child needs them. Other children may need more opportunities to recount incidents in sequential order. The teacher may guide by asking "What came first?" or "Then what happened?" and so on.

Plans and guidance that meet children's individual needs can be provided only on the basis of careful observation. Without knowledge of children's language, effective instruction is almost impossible.

Providing Activities That Encourage Language Growth

Almost everything that happens in the early childhood classroom will contribute to children's language development. If children are arguing over a toy, the teacher can help them use language that is appropriate for disagreeing and for solving the problem. If an adult visits the class, the children can

> **PRAXIS**
>
> Be able to describe the factors that influence language development

have opportunities for interaction with the visitor, who serves as another model of language use. If the children go on a field trip, they will have the opportunity to learn the vocabulary connected with what they are observing. Language development goes on all through the schoolday.

The activities described in the following sections are merely suggestive of the opportunities teachers have for helping children develop more competency as language users.

Conversation

Every child should have the opportunity to converse with an adult at least once a day. This means having a one-on-one conversation, not a group discussion. Of course, children should have other opportunities to talk to adults, as well, but they need their own times to talk when the teacher listens and responds to just them.

There are many ways to organize this talking time. The teacher can move around during activity time or outdoor play time and talk with individual children. Some teachers have found that moving to each child during rest time also works well (Soundy and Stout 2003). However you organize this time, keep a checklist of conversations so that you do not miss any child.

You might also make quick notes about the topics children introduce. You can use these notes to help you uncover the interests or concerns of a particular child. Weitzman and Greenbeerg (2002) suggest ways to extend a topic that a child introduces; these are summarized in Figure 9.3.

Literature

Language in children's books is very important. When an entire book contains only three hundred words, an author cannot waste words but must choose the best ones to convey the ideas. Martin (1986); Harste, Woodward, and Burke (1984); Blackburn (1985); and Isbell (2003) point out that everyone stores up all the words, phrases, and story elements they hear and that this language becomes theirs after a time. Books help children fill up their storehouses of beautiful words. Even simple stories can do this.

In *Whose Mouse Are You?* (Kraus 1970), when the little mouse is asked about his brother, he replies, "I have none." That is probably not the way most children would respond nor is it the language most children would hear at home, but it is elegant. Sometimes we choose books or stories just because the words sound so wonderful. The elephant's child says, "Good-by. I am going to the great, gray-green greasy Limpopo River all set about with fever trees to find out what the Crocodile has for dinner" ("The Elephant's Child," in Kipling 1965, p. 132). We read such language because we love to hear the sound of it. Children, too, love the sound of language, whether they understand the meaning of every word or not.

The language in books allows teachers to expand children's language in supportive and creative ways. Books with simplified vocabularies are somewhat useful for beginning readers, but for all other purposes, books should be chosen because they have beautiful language.

Narrative Stories Children's literature often serves as a focus for learning new vocabulary and new ways of expressing ideas and can provide the foundation for countless activities, including the following:

www.rif.org/educators/
articles/whentalk.mspx

An article that describes how becoming a skilled user of language is basic to learning to read

www.creativedrama.com

Suggestions for using creative drama to help children become more skilled users of language

NAEYC CRITERIA
1.13

NAEYC CRITERIA
2.25

There are only two lasting bequests we can hope to give our children. One of these is roots—the other, wings.

—*Henry Ward Beecher*

FIGURE 9.3

Six Ways to Extend the Topic

When you have a conversation with a child, you have lots of options for extending the topic.

Inform

- Give information about past or present.
- Relate present experience to past experience.
- Provide details.
- Compare/contrast two things.

Explain

- Give reasons for what is happening.
- Explain outcomes.
- Justify opinions or preferences.

Talk about Feelings and Opinions

- Talk about how feelings express sadness, anger, fear, frustration, excitement, happiness, friendliness, or delight.
- Talk about opinions and impressions.

Project

- Project into other people's (or into animals') lives, experiences, and feelings to help children think about others and understand that their experiences, lives, needs, and points of view are different than their own.
- Project into situations never experienced.

Talk about the Future

- Talk about/predict what will happen.
- Speculate about what might or could happen.
- Anticipate possible problems and possible solutions.
- Put potential problems into words and plan ahead to avoid them.
- Consider alternative ways of handling a situation. Help children learn to describe problems, think them through, and come up with solutions.

Pretend

- Talk about imaginary things.
- Play a pretend role.
- Create an imaginary "story" (based on real life or fantasy).

Source: Reprinted with permission from *Learning Language and Loving It: A Guide to Promoting Children's Social, Language, and Literacy Development in Early Childhood Settings,* Second Edition, pp. 278–279, by Elaine Weitzman and Janice Greenberg (Toronto: The Hanen Centre). Copyright © 2002 Hanen Early Language Program. May not be copied or otherwise reproduced without written permission from The Hanen Centre.

1. Compare the words used in different versions of familiar folk stories. For example, several words are used to label the woodcutter in versions of "Little Red Riding Hood." Children might discuss what they think is the best choice of words and what pictures the different words bring to mind.

2. Dramatize stories or rhymes. Actually speaking the words and performing the actions that go with them help children make vocabulary real and personal.

3. Have children retell stories in their own words and/or use puppets to recall stories.

4. Ask children to create new versions of stories by selecting words to fit the patterns in repetitive books. For example, in *Someday* (Zolotow 1965), the pattern is "Someday I'll _____." Children can think of what they will do "someday."

5. Encourage children to tell their own original stories and record them either in writing or on audiotape or videotape. Having children tell their own stories results in more complex language use and more detailed stories than is the case when children are asked to tell stories about a picture or wordless picture book (Hough, Nurss, and Wood 1987).

The following Learning Plan uses Kevin Henkes's (1991) book *Chrysanthemum* to develop children's vocabulary.

Storytelling   Telling stories can also aid in children's language development. Review Figure 9.2 to see how many language development benchmarks are tied to children's hearing and taking part in stories. Storytelling has the advantage of being a direct communication between the listener and the teller. Children listening to a story are required to be active listeners. If they tune out, the story will go on; there will be no instant replay. Storytelling also invites children to become active by participating in the story, repeating phrases or words or creating voices or gestures for the characters.

Storytelling is also flexible. If the audience gets restless, the storyteller can add more drama to the voices, shorten the story, end the story immediately, or whatever is required to make the session successful. Of course, this requires that the storyteller pay close attention to the audience and respond accordingly.

Stories told to children should contain language that they can understand from context so that the storyteller will not have to stop for explanations. Stories for children should also be about topics and situations that

---

LEARNING PLAN   Vocabulary Development for Grades 1—2

Objective: Children will learn new vocabulary words.

Materials: The book *Chrysanthemum* (Henkes 1991)

Procedure:

1. Show children the front cover of the book, and ask if they know the name of the flower pictured there. If they don't know, tell them that the name of the book is *Chrysanthemum* and that it is about a character named after this flower. Ask the children if they remember what it was like to go to school on the very first day. Tell them that this book is about a girl named *Chrysanthemum* and how she felt when she started to school. Tell them that Chrysanthemum's parents use some big words, and ask them to listen for those words as you read the story.

2. Read the book aloud, emphasizing the words the parents use.

3. Discuss the meaning of the story, and then get several children to retell parts of it to the group.

4. After discussing the book, ask the children if they heard any of the big words.

5. Find the words again in the story and reread them. Discuss the meanings of these words and how the parents might have learned them. Practice saying them together. Ask the children to share these words with their families when they get home.

6. Review the words one more time.

7. Put the book in the library area so that the children can look at again in choice time.

appeal to them; if the children are not interested in what the story is about, they will tune out and become restless.

The storyteller should invite participation in the tale, especially after the first telling. Possible activities include these:

1. Invite children to dramatize a story as you tell it. For example, "The Turnip," a Russian folktale, works very well (Morgan 1990).

2. Provide materials so that children can retell stories during activity periods. Make available flannelboard pieces, wooden characters, fingerpuppets, or puppets, depending on the age and experience of the children.

3. Encourage children to tell their own stories. Older children can write and produce their stories in many forms: a skit for TV, a scroll story, a flannelboard story, and so on.

4. Encourage children to join the storytelling by repeating certain phrases or sounds.

Poetry/Chants/Rhymes/Songs   Fingerplays and choral readings help children learn new vocabulary words and new sentence patterns that add to their repertoires. Teachers should plan activities such as the following:

1. Create new versions of song lyrics or rhymes by selecting words that fit the rhymes. For example, after learning *Alligator Pie* (Lee 1974), children can write or dictate new versions.

2. Dramatize rhymes or song lyrics. When children participate in drama, their actions indicate comprehension of the words. For example, the words of the various versions of "Bear Hunt" describe different actions; children can do the actions to demonstrate that they understand the words.

3. Dramatize concepts in science or social studies—such as the attraction and repelling of magnets or the arrival of a famous explorer—so that the language has real meaning for children.

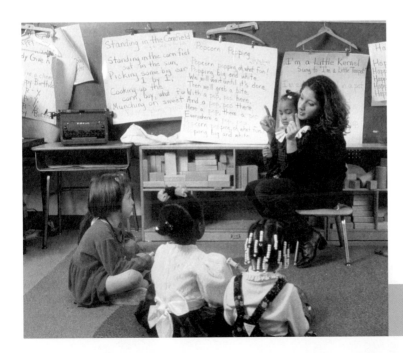

Rhyming and singing activities encourage language growth.

Sharing Time

NAEYC CRITERIA
2.27

Sharing time can have many positive benefits for language development, if managed appropriately. For instance, sharing time should be conducted in small groups so that children do not have to sit for long periods while each person has a turn. Objects should be displayed to the group, rather than passed around. Teachers should also help children learn how to begin and end presentations, and sessions should be structured so that children are not required to stand up or come to the front of the class in order to participate (Oken-Wright 1988).

Teachers should also control sharing time so that it does not turn into a session in which children show off their latest possessions. The following activities may help achieve that control:

1. Sharing can be organized so that children describe the details of the process for making objects they have created in class. For example, a child might share how a textile print or clay object was made. Cooking experiences and building with blocks are other activities that provide interesting topics for sharing.

2. Children can bring objects from home that are related to a theme or topic of study. For example, they might bring something square when the class is learning shape concepts.

3. Children can share personal experiences that are important to them. They might talk about a special trip or an exciting event that occurred at home, such as the birth of kittens.

4. Sharing time can be used as a brainstorming session for solving class problems and planning class activities.

Teachers must also consider children's ages in planning activities for sharing time. For instance, younger children might be asked to offer suggestions for classroom or playground safety, and older children might be asked to think about the room arrangement and how it might be altered for better traffic patterns. In planning themes and projects, older children might be asked to persuade others that a topic of study that interests them would be a good choice for the next class theme.

Classroom Centers and Activities

NAEYC CRITERIA
2.26

Classroom centers such as the blocks area, where several children work together, tend to encourage more language use than centers where the activities are more solitary. It follows that teachers who want to encourage children's language development and use will arrange learning areas so that children can talk to one another and will prompt children to work together.

Materials will also need to be interesting and novel enough that children will want to talk about them. Several research studies (Anen 1991; Dyson and Genishi 1991; Isbell and Raines 1991) have verified the commonsense knowledge that children who are encouraged to participate in active and interesting activities are more likely to use language and produce more language than children who are asked to complete skills activities. A classroom environment in which teachers and children use language for many purposes will contribute to the communicative competence of the children.

INTEGRATING the CURRICULUM

The theme to be developed in each of the content chapters in this edition is spaces. Spaces *was selected because it is a very broad theme; a wide variety of curriculum experiences can be related to it in ways that will help children make connections among the various areas of the curriculum. For young children, the curriculum is best conceptualized as a meaningful whole, not as separate content areas to be mastered. As children develop language, the theme of* spaces *can provide a useful link among many activities.*

Here are language-learning activities based on spaces:

- Place a variety of containers on a table. Help the children think about what objects might fit into the space created by each container. Make a list of their ideas. Bring in a variety of objects and have children attempt to fit them into the containers. Talk about the names of the objects.

- Provide children with a number of related objects (e.g., cooking utensils), and help them design a space to store them in the dramatic play "kitchen." Emphasize the vocabulary for the objects as children play with them.

- Ask each child to describe her favorite space in the classroom and to tell why it is her favorite. Each child could also be asked to describe her favorite space at home.

- Help children learn the vocabulary to describe spaces in the school neighborhood, such as parks, playgrounds, streets, intersections, and so on.

- Help children describe the characteristics of the spaces in the classroom, such as an art area that has a tile floor, storage shelves, a sink, easels, and so on.

- Help students describe spaces where animals live, pets live, people live, and so on.

- Describe a space and ask students to guess where it is located.

- Read aloud a description of a space, and ask children to explain whether they would like to be in that space.

- Help children describe a space that would be a good home for a given animal, such as a cave, a burrow, a pen, a barn, a pasture, a field, and so on.

- Help children describe spaces that are little versus big, huge versus tiny, and so on.

Language development also can be enhanced through thematic instruction (Bergeron et al. 1996). Themes that present real experiences and real materials to manipulate will certainly help children expand their vocabularies in meaningful ways.

CHILDREN WITH SPECIAL NEEDS

Most children learn to use language. For those few who cannot learn to use language in the usual ways, some specialized assistance may be required.

Children with disabilities may need special help in communicating effectively in the classroom. Many devices are available for assisting communication; some are very expensive and others are inexpensive. Parette,

www.
**www.epsbooks.com/
downloads/articles/
UnderstandingSpecific
Learn.pdf**

Understanding specific
language disabilities

Dunn, and Hoge (1995) describe some low-cost devices such as communication notebooks, communication vests, communication boards, communication aprons, and communication wallets. **Assistive technology** is becoming more commonplace for children with special needs. We can expect the technology in this field to continue to change, making such assistance more readily available.

Most schools offer programs for children with disabilities beginning at age three, and learning to communicate is a major goal of these programs. *Full-inclusion classrooms* (previously called *mainstreaming*) provide positive settings for promoting the language development of all children. Moreover, such classrooms provide the opportunity to include children with special needs in experiences that are not drill-and-practice sessions on words or phrases. For some children, teachers will need to ask for help from school language specialists to determine the most effective means of assisting the children in efforts to communicate.

Children with Language Delays

A **language delay** results in a child's using language that is noticeably deficient for his age (Dumtschin 1988). Sometimes, delays in language can be attributed directly to specific causes, including physical problems (such as loss of hearing or structural problems in the speech-producing organs) or disease (for example, cerebral palsy); mental retardation; or emotional problems (such as autism) (Cole and Cole 1989). Other delays in language have no apparent cause; the child seems normal in other areas, but his language is not typical for his age group.

General indicators of developmental language disorders include these characteristics:

- Absence of spoken words by age eighteen months
- Absence of two-word phrases with messages by age two years
- Inappropriate responses to questions

Children with language and hearing impairments may need help from aides in the classroom.

- Echoing of speech
- Poor intelligibility (unclear speech)
- Undeveloped play skills
- Poor understanding or use of adjectives and prepositions
- Problems with word finding
- Dependence on gestures to follow directions
- Need for frequent repetition of directions
- Poor social interactions with peers
- Poor school performance (Willig 1998)

One of the first steps in providing for the needs of a child with a language delay is to make a referral to diagnose or rule out any underlying cause for the delay. Some schools have speech and language therapists who can be consulted. If the center or school does not employ a therapist, the referral may be to a therapist in private practice. If no professional can be located, the National Association for Hearing and Speech Action can provide assistance.

If a cause for the delay can be identified, the therapist will make recommendations for activities or strategies that will be helpful to the teacher and parents. If no cause for the delay can be identified, the teacher will want to provide as much support for the child's language growth as possible.

Parents and Language

- Help parents find the assistance they need for their exceptional children: a speech therapist, a language specialist, communication devices, or other services.
- Help parents appreciate the value of helping children build broad vocabularies through real experiences.

A child's failing to talk on the normal schedule may lead to stress on the family and problems in peer relationships. When children are unable to communicate adequately with their peers, they may be excluded from their play groups and therefore have even less chance to learn to talk.

Research has shown that conversation between children and adults can be helpful in assisting children with language delays (Cross 1984; Lasky and Klopp 1982). As noted earlier, most adults respond to the meaning of a child's speech and continue conversations on topics introduced by the child. Children whose language is less mature than that of age peers may need even more conversation with adults that focuses on their meanings and intentions. Teachers need to be especially careful not to assume that children cannot understand normal conversation just because they cannot produce language typical of age-mates.

Restricting a child's language environment is not appropriate. Although children with specific language impairments may use the same language patterns as younger children, they have more communicative competence. In other words, they are able to use what language they have more effectively (Rollins et al. 1994).

Researchers have also found that children with language delays have more interactions with adults who are critical of their language production than do children who are making normal progress (Bondurant, Romeo, and Kretschmer 1983). Teachers should respond to children by supplying the correct labels for objects or actions without being negative. For example, if a child is looking at a book of zoo animals and mistakenly calls the tiger a lion, the teacher might respond, "This tiger is very large. Tigers and lions are both in the zoo."

Teachers should also be aware of their use of controlling language with children who have language delays. Girolametto, Hoaken, Weitzman, and von Lieshout (2000) found that children with language delays experienced more directive language from adults than did children whose language development was normal. Language that is controlling fails to help children develop positive interaction patterns or increase their vocabulary. For example, consider the message delivered by the command "Pick these up now!" versus that of the direction "Please help me pick up the large blocks and put them on the top shelf."

Children who are late talkers seem to benefit somewhat from intervention strategies (Robertson and Weismer 1999). However, a number of experts suggest that these children be observed carefully but not treated, as many catch up with their peers in language use by age three. Studies have not been able to show the long-term gains sought by intervention strategies (Tallal and Rice 1997).

Jones and Warren (1991) make several suggestions for working with children with language delays. First, the teacher should follow the child's lead, establishing dialogue and planning novel activities that reflect the child's interests. The teacher should also provide support for the child's language by commenting on the child's utterances but not necessarily expecting a response. Other strategies that teachers can use to help children develop their language are provided in Table 9.3. Children with language delays will benefit from the use of these techniques.

Finally, teachers also need to be aware of the amount of talking by adults and the amount of talking by children encouraged in classrooms. If children are constantly involved in teacher-directed activities, in which listening and following directions are the accepted behaviors, then little time will be left for active language production (Hough, Nurss, and Goodson 1984). Children need to talk to adults and to other children if their language is to improve. Most of the children's day should be structured so that language is an integral part of activities.

Teachers should make every effort to talk *to* children, not *at* them, and to accept children's language. All children need the same conditions in order to achieve maximum growth in language: an accepting environment, interesting things to talk about, and adults with whom to engage in meaningful conversations.

Ideas for the Classroom

Teachers who want to help all children develop their language abilities will encourage children to use language in classroom settings. This is especially true for those children whose language development is atypical. The following strategies may be useful in planning activities that enhance language development:

1. Encourage children to retell stories that you have read or told. A flannelboard may encourage older preschoolers to be more confident in their retellings.

2. Encourage children to use puppets to tell stories or to carry on conversations among puppet characters.

TABLE 9.3 Language Stimulation Techniques

TECHNIQUE	DESCRIPTION
Waiting	Adult uses a slow pace during conversation; adult actively listens to children when talking; adult does not dominate conversation.
Pausing	Adult pauses expectantly and frequently during interactions with children to encourage their turn-taking and active participation.
Confirming	Adult responds to all child utterances by confirming understanding of the child's intentions. Adult does not ignore child communicative bids.
Imitating	Adult imitates and repeats what child says more or less exactly. *Example:* Child: I did the puzzle. Adult: You did the puzzle.
Extending	Adult repeats what child says and adds a small amount of syntactic or semantic information. *Example:* Child: I did the puzzle. Adult: You did the puzzle well.
Labeling	Adult provides the labels for familiar and unfamiliar actions, objects, or abstractions (e.g., feelings).
Open questioning	Adult asks questions to which he or she does not know the answer; these include some what, where, and when questions (e.g., What are you going to do now?), as well as how and why questions.
Scripting	Adult provides a routine to the child for representing an activity (e.g., First you go up to the counter. Then you say, "I want a hamburger . . .") and engages the child in known routines (e.g., "Now it is time for circle time. What do we do first?").

Source: Laura M. Justice, "Creating Language-Rich Preschool Classroom Environments," *Teaching Exceptional Children* 37, 2 (2004): 36–44. Copyight © 2004 by the Council for Exceptional Children.

3. Involve children in learning fingerplays, song lyrics, chants, and choral readings.

4. Plan cooperative classroom activities in which children use language freely, such as card games or board games or building projects.

5. Be sure that children with language delays are not "talked down to" by anyone in the classroom and that their participation in activities is not limited.

CELEBRATING DIVERSITY

Language is one obvious and easily observable difference among the cultures of the children in any typical classroom. Suggestions for celebrating children's language in the classroom include the following:

1. Post signs and announcements in as many of the languages spoken in the class as possible.

2. Arrange for regular classroom use of books and recordings in the languages represented by students.

3. Encourage the parents of bilingual children to read to them frequently.

4. Share special words with children who speak other languages.

5. Share the feeling of accomplishment when children learn new vocabulary or forms in their native languages or new languages.

6. Buy good-quality books and computer programs that use the languages spoken by the children in the classroom.

Children Who Use Dialects

A **dialect** is a systematic variation of the common language spoken by a particular group. All of us speak dialects of some sort. There are regional dialects, social class dialects, and cultural/ethnic dialects. By definition, a dialect is rule governed and consistent.

Children who speak dialects are not merely making errors in their grammatical constructions; they are following the rules of their dialects. The most important thing for teachers to remember is that children who speak dialects are not less capable of learning language than other children, nor is the dialect less effective for communication than more standard English. When judgments are made about the correctness of children's speech, these judgments are usually social, not linguistic (Jaggar 1980).

DEVELOPMENTALLY APPROPRIATE PRACTICE

As you think about language development and developmentally appropriate practice, reflect on the following:

■ Many children learn to use language differently than middle-class White children. These differences are not just dialectal but reflect culturally appropriate uses of language in telling stories or entertaining groups. In a developmentally appropriate classroom, what goals and standards should be set for children's language use? For example, should all children be expected to achieve the middle-class model of language use? Why?

■ Language is best learned when it is used for a real purpose; thus, contrived activities to practice language skills are rarely effective. How should real language be used in activities for children of different ages—say, preschoolers versus primary-grade children?

■ The teacher must accept and respect the language of all children in a DAP classroom. How can the teacher demonstrate acceptance and respect for a student who speaks English as a second language?

■ The best environment for learning language includes the critical elements of DAP, such as choice, active involvement, age and individually appropriate expectations, and so on. How do these elements enhance learning language?

Dialects may differ in terms of vocabulary, syntax, and morphology. Vocabulary differences include all the various terms used to describe, for example, the parts of a car, the seed in a peach, or an ice cream drink. Vocabulary differences may also include some verb usages, such as the use of *carry* for *take* (as in "He will *carry* you to town"). Syntactical differences often include deleting some words. In some dialects, the correct form of "He is working today" is "He be working," which indicates that the subject is presently working. Morphological differences include dropping some inflectional endings so that possessives are formed differently ("That girl shoes") or tense or number are indicated differently ("He go there yesterday"). The differences in dialects and more standard speech are usually only minor, surface differences.

Teachers of young children who speak dialects that are different from the dialect of the majority should be especially sensitive to each child's use of language and be prepared to honor the child's ability to learn language. The child's dialect is certainly effective for communicating in her home or neighborhood. Exposure to literature and to models of other, more standard dialects may give the child alternative ways of expressing needs and thoughts over a period of time, but the teacher's goal should not be eradication of the dialect.

Ideas for the Classroom

Children who speak dialects need teachers who accept and respect their speech. The ideas that follow offer ways to help children develop their language skills in standard English while maintaining their dialect when it is appropriate:

1. Involve children in drama. They can dramatize stories and role-play various speaking situations.

2. Invite speakers to the classroom who are skilled in both the children's dialect and standard English.

3. Read children's books that use dialects.

4. Record the speech of several children saying essentially the same thing, and compare the words used.

5. Record what children say in standard spelling, but allow them to read what you have written in dialect.

6. Provide opportunities for children to talk to many different speakers.

English Language Learners

In the typical U.S. classroom today, many children do not speak English as their native language. To facilitate communication with these **English language learners,*** a number of approaches may be used.

Some schools offer special bilingual programs for students who do not speak English; other schools provide tutors whose goal is to help children learn English; and some schools expect classroom teachers to provide for English language learners in the regular classroom context. Because most teachers will have these children in their classrooms, they should be aware

www.ncela.gwu.edu
The Office of English Language Acquisition site. Provides information and suggestions for teachers and parents

http://coe.sdsu.edu/ people/jmora/MoraModules/ ELDPosition.htm

An excellent site with a discussion of bilingual programs and links to many other sites of interest to teachers working with bilingual children

---

*In some school systems, English language learners are referred to as having *limited English proficiency (LEP)* or as being *ESL (English-as-a-second-language) students.*

NAEYC CRITERIA
3.52, 3.53

of some of the research on second-language
learning and its implications for instruction.

The controversy about bilingual education continues to be played out in the popular
press, but bilingual programs offer benefits to
children that are often not apparent to the general public (Krashen 2000a). Dr. Jim Cummins
offers support for bilingual programs in the following An Expert Speaks box. Can you use his
statements to clarify your own feelings about
bilingual programs?

If at all possible, children whose native
language is not English should be enrolled in
a good bilingual program. However, with so
many languages represented in many U.S. schools, a bilingual program is
often not a possibility for the children.

To learn a second language successfully requires the same conditions
that foster learning a native tongue (Krashen 1981, 2000a). Specifically, the
English language learner needs someone with whom to talk as well as support for attempts at communication. Language is learned best within a social context in which success at communication is expected.

Because second-language learners use the strategies of simplification
and overgeneralization, which are also common in original-language development, they will benefit from encouragement rather than correction
during the early stages of learning English. For example, English language
learners may simplify all verbs to one tense and depend on context to help
communicate the real message.

Finally, second-language learners pick up more details in order to make
their communication more effective. They learn to say "I went there yesterday in the afternoon" rather than "I go there." For young children, this
process may take only a few months; for older children, it may take longer.

Tabors (1998) has identified a sequence for learning English by children
who are native speakers of other languages. At first, children will use only
their home languages. When they want to communicate with English speakers, they will enter a nonverbal but not a noncommunicative period. In this
stage, children may whine, point, mime, or cry in order to communicate.

The next stage is telegraphic and formulaic speaking in the target language.
Children learning a second language will use the same telegraphic speech used
by native speakers of that language when one or two words will capture the
meaning of a longer utterance. Formulaic speaking involves the use of common
catch words and phrases, such as "ok," "uh-oh," "bye-bye," "mine," and "I don't
know." Using these words and phrases can help children continue to play or
interact with others even though their language skills are minimal.

Finally, children achieve productive use of the new language. This stage will
be marked with errors because the children are no longer depending on memorized phrases but are beginning to combine elements into real utterances.

The following guidelines will help teachers of bilingual speakers be
more effective:

1. Get as much information as possible about the child's language background.
   Try to determine if the child is a talker or shy at home. Find out what languages the child's playmates speak.

AN **Expert** SPEAKS: *Bilingual Education*

Jim Cummins
University of Toronto

Few educational issues in North America have become as volatile or as ideologically loaded as the debate on the merits or otherwise of bilingual education. Organized campaigns against bilingual education have resulted in referenda in states such as California and Arizona that have placed major restrictions on the extent to which languages other than English can be used for instructional purposes. The public controversy about bilingual education contrasts with the considerable consensus among applied linguists regarding the outcomes of such programs. The research on bilingual education supports the following conclusions:

1. Bilingual programs for minority- and majority-language students have been successfully implemented in countries around the world. As documented in an enormous amount of international research, students educated for part of the day through a minority language do not suffer adverse consequences in the development of academic skills in the majority language. As one example, there are more than 300,000 English-background students in various forms of French–English bilingual programs in Canada.

2. The development of literacy in two languages entails linguistic and perhaps cognitive advantages for bilingual students. There are more than 150 research studies carried out since the early 1960s that report significant advantages for bilingual students on a variety of metalinguistic and cognitive tasks. Bilingual students get more practice in learning language (by definition), and this seems to sharpen their awareness of subtleties of linguistic meaning and form.

3. Significant positive relationships exist between the development of academic skills in L1 (first language) and L2 (second language). This is true even for languages that are dissimilar (e.g., Spanish and Basque, English and Chinese, Dutch and Turkish). These crosslingual relationships provide evidence for a common underlying proficiency that permits transfer of academic and conceptual knowledge across languages. This transfer of skills and knowledge explains why spending instructional time through a minority language entails no adverse consequences for the development of the majority language.

4. The most successful bilingual programs are those that aim to develop bilingualism and biliteracy. Most bilingual programs implemented in the United States have provided some first-language instruction as a short-term bridge to mainstream English-only programs. However, these short-term programs are less successful, in general, than programs that continue to promote both L1 and English literacy throughout elementary school. Particularly successful are dual-language programs that serve English-background students in the same classes as minority-language students, with each group acting as linguistic models for the other.

5. Bilingual education, by itself, is not a panacea for underachievement. Underachievement derives from many sources, and simply providing some first-language instruction will not, by itself, transform students' educational experience. Effective instruction will affirm student identities and build on the cultural and linguistic knowledge they bring to the classroom.

6. L1 loss among minority-language students is extremely common among second generation students and first generation students who arrive at an early age. Research shows that fewer than 20 percent of second generation students maintain fluency in their home language. This can cause communication problems within the family and represents a loss of linguistic resources for the nation. Furthermore, students who become fully bilingual report better relations with their families, greater self-esteem, and higher educational aspirations than those who lose their L1.

In short, there are compelling reasons why educators in both English-only and bilingual programs should be proactive in acknowledging the linguistic accomplishments of bilingual students and encouraging them to fully develop this personal and social resource.

2. Be careful about the conclusions you draw from the information you gather. Assuming a child who does not speak much does not know much about language can be very dangerous.

3. Compare the child's language only to other similar bilingual children.
4. Understand that second-language learners will make grammatical errors. There are common generalizations made by second-language learners that are not made by first-language speakers.
5. Be aware that second-language learners may lose some of their competence in their first language. For example, a child may move away from the environment in which the first language was used regularly and therefore lose some ability to use that language.
6. Know it is normal for second-language learners to use both languages to communicate. *Linguistic borrowing* describes what happens when a word from one language is inserted into a sentence of the other language. *Code switching* is switching back and forth between languages, but not necessarily single words. Both are normal for bilinguals.
7. Learn as much as possible about the cultures represented in the classroom. Make sure this information is both for traditional and contemporary lifestyles. Use this information in order to determine if any test used to evaluate bilingual speakers is biased. (Piper 1993, pp. 210–211)*

Burnett (1993) stresses that appropriate assessment of English language learners is crucial. He recommends setting up an assessment center that is more friendly than the usual testing office and conducting multiple assessments before decisions are made about any child. Peregoy and Boyle (2004) make several suggestions for how to begin to assess the language development of a child whose first language is not English: by engaging her in writing an autobiography (photos and drawings may be more prominent than writing), keeping a journal in her first language, keeping a dialogue journal (the teacher may need help in translating), and organizing themes such as *Our Family Roots,* in which all the children study the places from which their families came to the United States.

In summary, the best environment for second-language learning includes support, encouragement, meaningful purposes for communication, and an expectation that children will talk with others who speak the language to be learned. "For a learner to be free to learn another language, the learner must be able to trust others to respond to the messages communicated and not be laughed at or singled out. In addition, a learner must be active in seeking people to talk with" (Urzua 1980, p. 38).

Ideas for the Classroom

Teachers who want to help English language learners achieve competence in English will be thoughtful about the classroom environment and activities that make learning English as much like learning a first language as possible. The following suggestions may stimulate teachers' thinking:

1. Plan for activities that require children who speak English and children who are learning English to work together (Hester 1987). This is one of the best strategies for helping children learn English. In the early childhood classroom, it is not difficult to arrange for such cooperative experiences.
2. Encourage English language learners to share their native languages through songs, fingerplays, and books.

From *Language for All Our Children* by Piper, T., © 1993. Reprinted by permission of Prentice-Hall, Inc., Upper Saddle River, NJ.

3. Share (or find someone to share) with the class stories or poetry in another language and then in English.

4. Be careful not to separate non-English-speaking children or to exclude them from activities that you feel they will not understand. These children learn language by listening, watching, and following examples.

5. Writing and reading activities can be based on children's growing vocabulary in English. At first, children can make books of the words that they are learning. After only a few weeks, teachers will find that most children are learning too rapidly to use this technique.

6. Plan to help children learn English all through the day. Art, physical education, music, and math all offer children opportunities to learn new vocabulary and patterns of speech in English. Often, activities in these subjects are more relaxed for children, so using English to communicate during them may be less threatening than during other parts of the schoolday (Clancy and Hruska 2005; Szecsi and Giambo 2004/2005).

> **It is not enough to have a good mind; the main thing is to use it well.**
>
> —*René Descartes*

As described in the following box, A Teacher Speaks, Jennifer Rosholt helps children develop their language skills at the same time they are learning content. Can you visualize how children might learn language most effectively in your classroom?

Teachers should also help parents appreciate the importance of continuing use of the home language even after the child becomes fluent in English. Research indicates that children do better in acquiring English if the home language is maintained (Collier 1987).

In interviews with parents of English language learners, most reported that they appreciate the bilingual programs at their children's schools and many believed it was important to read in the children's native languages. However, some Hispanic parents were not interested in having the school teach their children to read in Spanish because the parents wanted to teach the children this at home. One group of Hispanic parents reported that writing the alphabet, sounding out words, and learning the sounds of letters were the most important skills to be taught in a school program. But a group of Khmer parents emphasized writing the alphabet, listening to stories, and learning simple words. All parents from both groups reported working with their children at home on letters and sound–letter relationships. None of these parents advocated giving up their native language in favor of English (Brewer 1998b).

SUMMARY

- *Language* is a system of communication used by humans that is produced either orally or by sign and that can be extended to its written form. All languages are rule governed, arbitrary, and changing. All languages are composed of systems of phonology (sounds), semantics (word meanings), morphology (rules for changing words), syntax (rules for how utterances can be structured), and pragmatics (how language can be used).

- Language is not acquired externally; rather, it is part of a process of personal development and emerges in the context of social use. In addition, language development is related to cognitive development. Language development follows a sequence, which is fairly predictable but allows for individual variations. Success in learning language is critical to children's success in school and in their social and emotional development. Three major theoretical models attempt to explain children's language development. The behaviorist model describes learning language according to stimulus-response theory. The linguistic model suggests that language

A **Teacher** SPEAKS: Teaching Content and Language Together

**Jennifer
Rosholt**
Stevenson
Elementary School
Seattle, Washington

My kindergarten/first-grade classroom welcomes students who come from many backgrounds and who speak many different languages at home. In our classroom, English is the bridge language. It bridges my students to each other and their learning while, at the same time, their first languages are honored and respected. Because my students are at all levels of understanding and use of English, I need to establish language objectives for each lesson as well as content objectives. I do not teach English instead of content. I teach both together in meaningful, interactive ways.

A kindergarten classroom is the perfect ESL (English-as-a-second-language) environment. It is *language rich* and involves many opportunities for social interaction. *Language rich* means a classroom filled with hands-on materials that students are using daily; pictures tagged with written words all around the room; and poems, songs, and books that are repetitive and fun. It encompasses all of the things that children touch and experience with infinite opportunities for them to talk and draw pictures about everything in their own way, at their own pace. Students are learning language by using language—speaking, listening, reading, and writing.

Our current study of insects in the classroom is one example of my ongoing instructional strategy of teaching content and language together. Students rotate among three different activities called *centers*. During this time, I bring together objectives in math, science, social skills, following directions, reading, writing, and English. I assess students' counting skills, numeral recognition skills,

and fine motor skills on paper as well as observe social skills and insect knowledge.

One center is an insect Lotto game. The students at this center each have a board with nine insect pictures. One student holds a stack of cards with matching pictures; that student shows one card at a time. Students look at their boards to see if they have matches. The game is played until all of the boards are filled. Students are cooperating, matching, recognizing insects, and using the newly introduced vocabulary (insect names, *please, thank you,* and so on).

At another center, students use clay and various materials to create insects. Each must have three body parts, six legs, and two antennae. Students are introduced to and have knowledge of these characteristics of insects prior to the centers. Students make their insects and draw pictures of them to show their work. They are demonstrating their knowledge about insects by using new vocabulary (body parts, legs, insect names, antennae), using fine motor skills to draw, and having the opportunity for creative expression.

At the last center, I interact with students. We each have a sheet of paper with pictures of some insects (ladybug, butterfly, caterpillar, grasshopper, bee, ant). Next to each picture is a box. Together, we clap out the name of the insect. Each clap corresponds to a single syllable. Students record the number of syllables in the box. They are becoming aware of the sounds in words, counting, and using new vocabulary words.

People who can speak more than one language experience many advantages. They enjoy a rich understanding of language as a concept. Their opportunities are broad. Children who walk into our class speaking little or no English bring many gifts to share with us. They want to learn what we offer to teach, and we must deliver this in the most effective and meaningful ways.

is inherent in children and emerges upon being triggered by social contact. The constructivist model asserts that language is learned by active construction on the part of the learner.

● Teachers can create an effective environment for language learning by taking an informal approach (no structured lessons), focusing on the speaker's intent (content is more important than form), expecting success, emphasizing the holistic nature of language learning (no lessons on isolated components of language), celebrating creativity in language, and recognizing the achievement of any child who has learned to communicate. In a class-

room setting, the best experiences for language are provided by meaningful interactions (not a commercial program), a teacher who observes children carefully, and activities that promote language growth (such as conversations, good books and stories, storytelling, sharing time, and interesting centers).

● Children with special needs might need the help of assisted communication devices to participate effectively in the classroom. In working with children with language delays, teachers should encourage their efforts and provide support without being controlling or critical.

● Diversity often means that the class has many children for whom English is not their first language. Teachers must support children in their first languages while helping them learn English. Learning English should be a goal all through the schoolday, not just during language lessons. Art, music, physical education, and other content-area activities can help children learn language if teachers plan for language goals along with content goals. Teachers also need to respect the language use of children who speak dialects and remember that doing so does not make them less able to learn language.

REFLECTIONS

1. Children who are learning language are engaged in an amazing process. What about this process is most interesting to you? What do the knowledge and theories about language development mean to you as a teacher of young children?
2. What elements in the school environment are most critical for aiding children in their language development? Why?
3. Teachers often tell the parents of English language learners to speak English at home. Is this good advice? Why or why not?
4. Suppose that a preschool class has twelve students, among whom nine languages are spoken. If you were the teacher of this class, what would be your plan to help the children communicate with you and their classmates? What would you celebrate about this challenge?
5. In planning experiences that will help children develop their language abilities, what guiding principles would you follow? Why?

EXPLORATIONS AND ACTIVITIES

1. Observe a small group of children playing together for half an hour, and try to record all the language that you hear. Then analyze your notes in terms of how the children use sentence structure, what kinds of vocabulary they use, and whether tone and gesture carry as much of the message as the words do. What implications should this information have for teachers? If possible, add something new to the play environment and record the children's language use again. Compare these findings to your previous findings.

2. Interview two or three people who began school speaking a language other than English. Ask them about their experiences in learning to speak English, how they felt about school, and how they felt about being unable to communicate for a period of time. Think about their answers in terms of how you could make the school experience more comfortable for students who are English language learners.

CHAPTER **10**

KEY TERMS *you'll find in this chapter:*

- **Emergent literacy,** 312
- **Environmental print,** 305
- **Guided reading,** 325
- **Journal writing,** 336
- **Listening,** 316
- **Literacy,** 304

- **Oral language,** 315
- **Phonemic awareness,** 319
- **Phonics,** 320
- **Print-rich environment,** 315

- **Read-aloud,** 317
- **Reading,** 305
- **Shared reading,** 325
- **Sight-word vocabulary,** 305
- **Writing,** 329

Developing Literacy

FOCUS QUESTIONS

- What is *literacy?*
- What teacher qualities support the development of literacy?
- What elements characterize a good literacy program?
- How do children learn to write?
- How can the literacy development of young children be assessed?
- How can teachers plan for the literacy development of children with special needs?
- How can teachers help diverse learners become literate?

Y ou and your classmates were anxious to observe this week. After reading so much about literacy, you wanted to see what kinds of literacy instruction were taking place in the schools.

Your visit was to a local school that deliberately selects students to maintain a ratio of about one-half English speakers, one-fourth Khmer speakers, and one-fourth Spanish speakers. Children begin in this program at age three and can continue through the fourth grade.

You spent most of your time in the classroom with three- and four-year-olds. You observed them listening to stories on tape (playing with puppets that are appropriate to the stories), listening to the teacher read (sometimes in all three languages), and playing with letters and word cards. The children also were encouraged to write using markers, whiteboards, paper, and other readily available writing materials. Their classroom contained many of the play areas common to preschools, such as a dramatic play area and a blocks area.

When you walked through the classrooms for older children, you saw many webs, word walls, word lists, and other indications that the children were focusing on word study. You also observed illustrations and other projects related to books. Second-graders were working on posters explaining the life cycles and characteristics of insects they had selected to learn about. The children were reading reference books, using the computer to check websites, and making their own observations of insects.

Back in your own class, you were not surprised to hear about so many variations in the observations of your classmates. Some observed in classrooms where no word study was apparent; others observed in classrooms where the literacy instruction was a scripted program. After all that you have read and heard about phonics and reading instruction, you are anxious to learn more about literacy instruction for young children. ∎

Defining Literacy

Historically, *literacy* has been defined in many ways. But in today's world, **literacy** means the ability to read and write well enough to solve one's problems, meet one's needs, learn new information, and find pleasure in the written word. This means that to be literate today requires a great deal more skill than ever before in history. Even in studies that claim people today read fewer books than those of years past, no one claims that people read *less*. Getting information from the Internet, newspapers, magazines, blogs, and so on often requires very skilled reading. Moreover, writing for effective communication in both business and personal modes is critical to success.

Instruction in reading has always been important to Americans. The Puritans of Massachusetts passed laws requiring parents to teach their children to read. Today's legislators, at both state and national levels, are similarly concerned with children's reading skill level. Some have passed legislation requiring the use of certain instructional strategies in reading programs in the public schools.

Teacher Qualities That Support Literacy

How well you teach children to read and write is very important. So is the clarity with which you can communicate to parents what you are doing to help their children become literate. To help all the children in your class develop literacy skills, you must be able to evaluate the volume of research on the processes of reading and writing and base your instructional decisions on your personal understanding of the development of literacy. The International Reading Association's *Standards for Reading Professionals* (IRA 2003) identify additional qualities of effective teachers of reading.

Evaluating the Research

Many, many studies are published every month about the various elements of learning to read and write. To be a responsible consumer of research, you must ask the following questions and evaluate the claims of the researcher:

1. Who wrote the article or conducted the study? What qualifications does this person have to conduct this research? If the research suggests classroom practice, what classroom experience has the researcher had?

2. What is the author's purpose in writing? Is it to convince you that one method is better than another? To buy a particular program for instruction? To share insights gained from observing children and teachers?

3. Was this work reviewed by a body of peers (i.e., other experts in the field)? If not, does this person make claims that need verification before taking action on them?

4. Who will benefit from following the recommendations in the article? Does the author have connections with, for example, a publisher that might bring monetary rewards or political power if the recommendations are followed?

5. How does the author view the reading process? Does he base the results of his study on reading lists of nonsense words or reading connected texts (stories or reports)? Are the children in the study comparable to the children you teach? Does the author claim that his work will lead to better test performance or more skilled readers and writers in the real world? Does he claim that following his suggestions will guarantee reading and writing success for all children? Does he recognize that children often learn to read at home, from other children, and from their daily experience (i.e., **environmental print,** such as milk, toothpaste labels, and doors labeled "Men" or "Women" or "Exit")?

Only after thinking about the answers to these questions can you decide the value of a given study for your own teaching situation.

Understanding How Literacy Develops

A great deal has been learned about the process of reading in the last few years. Researchers have been trying to develop a model that would explain the process of reading and could then be used to help children engage in that process.

Reading, by definition, means gaining meaning from print, not just pronouncing the words. As a reader tries to make sense of print, she predicts what the print will say, uses cues from the print to confirm or reject her prediction, and moves on if her prediction is confirmed. If it is rejected, she must recycle through the prediction-confirming or prediction-rejecting phase again, this time using more or different cues. At the same time, the reader is matching the meaning to what she knows about the topic. If what she knows matches, then she goes on; if it does not match, again she must reread (K. Goodman 1996; Y. Goodman and Burke 1980). Then the information is integrated into what the learner knows, and the cycle is repeated.

The true wonder of this process is that it happens so rapidly that good readers are not aware of doing it. Even beginning readers often apply several parts of the process simultaneously. What we know is that reading is not simply looking at the letters of the word, sounding them out, blending them, saying the word, and then repeating that process. Readers use *cueing systems* in the reading process, including the sound–letter relationship of the print itself, their background knowledge, their knowledge of language, cues from the illustrations (if the material is illustrated), and any number of other signals that are personal to them.

Cues That Readers Use

The print itself offers cues, as there are many words that we recognize instantaneously (our **sight-word vocabulary**). However, print cues sometimes

Parents and Literacy

● Plan a family literacy night, during which you use a "big book" demonstration to explain how you are helping the children learn to read. See Cairney and Munsie (1995) for ideas.

fail us. For instance, when we read the word *tear*, does it mean "water falling from our eyes" or "a rip in our clothing"?

Nonetheless, sound–letter relationships do provide information as we read. For example, if we are reading a text about big cats and come to a word that we do not recognize, the *p* at the beginning of the word would cue us that the word is not *tiger*. If we know that *mother* and other common words end with the sound represented by *-er*, that will also help us decode the word. We might also know the word *pan* and use that knowledge to determine the first part of the unknown word *panther*.

In addition to knowledge of sound–letter relationships, readers also use what they know about how language works. Language cues include *semantics*—knowledge of word meanings and the relationships between and among words. Meanings are rarely exact, but all language users have developed meanings for words. When several readers see the letters *c a t*, each may picture a different cat, but there will be enough shared meaning to communicate.

Another language cue is provided by the *syntax* of the sentence—the order in which the words and phrases are arranged. If, for example, the reader sees *the*, he will know that a noun will follow. Syntax is specific to a given language. In English, adjectives usually are placed before the nouns they modify, but in Spanish, adjectives are placed after the nouns.

Other cues include what we know about the world. If we read *A hurricane spawned a _____ when it came ashore*, we use our knowledge of weather to help us fill in *tornado*. We would not think that the word *spawned* had anything to do with laying eggs in this context.

Illustrations offer cues to readers if they correspond with the text and provide accurate information. Beginning and early readers often use pictures as cues to predict new and unknown words.

In summary, readers use a variety of cues to create meaning. Moreover, readers bring to the reading process a wealth of information about language, topics, story structure, and words represented by squiggles.

Cambourne's Model

www.personal.une.edu.au/
~lgrunwa2/une/KLAs/literacy/
teachingreading.html

Summarizes some of Cambourne's work on children learning to read

Brian Cambourne's work in defining the conditions under which literacy is learned most easily led to a model of learning that describes both the physical environment and the social or psychological environment. Based on his observations, he formulated the model shown in Figure 10.1.

In this model, Cambourne (1995) stresses the importance of *immersion* and *demonstration*. This means that the learner sees and hears those people who are important in her life using reading and writing. *Expectation* that the learner can become a successful user of print is vital, as students usually learn what is expected of them. According to the model, the learner takes *responsibility* for her own learning in that she chooses the pieces to be attended to in any experience, not the teacher. To illustrate this point, consider that a child will sit in her crib and practice sounds and sound combinations, but it would never work to send a toddler to her room to practice sounds.

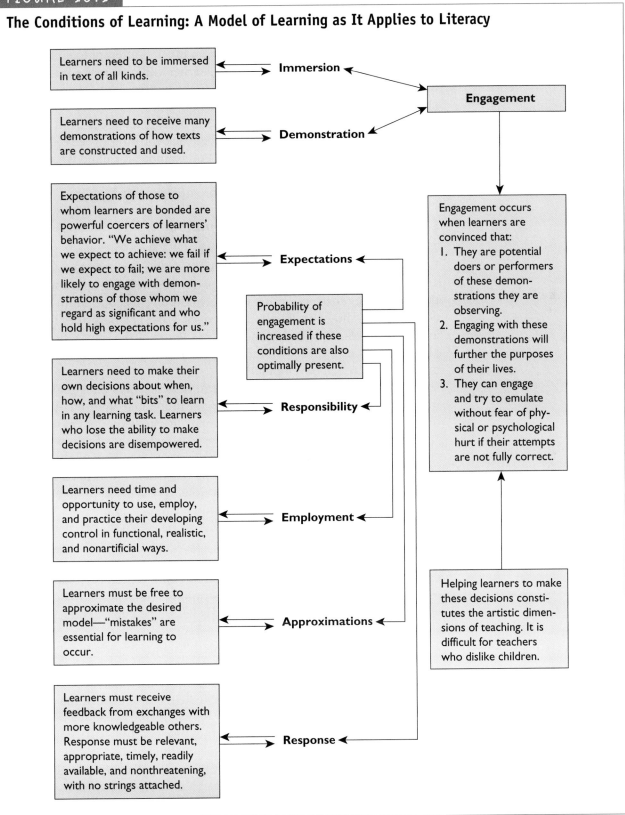

FIGURE 10.1

The Conditions of Learning: A Model of Learning as It Applies to Literacy

Learners need to be immersed in text of all kinds. → **Immersion**

Learners need to receive many demonstrations of how texts are constructed and used. → **Demonstration**

Engagement

Expectations of those to whom learners are bonded are powerful coercers of learners' behavior. "We achieve what we expect to achieve: we fail if we expect to fail; we are more likely to engage with demonstrations of those whom we regard as significant and who hold high expectations for us." → **Expectations**

Probability of engagement is increased if these conditions are also optimally present.

Engagement occurs when learners are convinced that:
1. They are potential doers or performers of these demonstrations they are observing.
2. Engaging with these demonstrations will further the purposes of their lives.
3. They can engage and try to emulate without fear of physical or psychological hurt if their attempts are not fully correct.

Learners need to make their own decisions about when, how, and what "bits" to learn in any learning task. Learners who lose the ability to make decisions are disempowered. → **Responsibility**

Learners need time and opportunity to use, employ, and practice their developing control in functional, realistic, and nonartificial ways. → **Employment**

Learners must be free to approximate the desired model—"mistakes" are essential for learning to occur. → **Approximations**

Helping learners to make these decisions constitutes the artistic dimensions of teaching. It is difficult for teachers who dislike children.

Learners must receive feedback from exchanges with more knowledgeable others. Response must be relevant, appropriate, timely, readily available, and nonthreatening, with no strings attached. → **Response**

Source: Figure 1 from Brian Cambourne. (1995, November). "Toward an Educationally Relevant Theory of Literacy Learning: Twenty Years of Inquiry." *The Reading Teacher 49*(3), 182–202. Reprinted with permission of Brian Cambourne and the International Reading Association. All rights reserved.

Employment means that the learner can actually use the information he is learning in real and meaningful activities—for instance, learning how to make cookies by reading the directions. *Approximations* in literacy learning are as necessary as they are in learning to speak. We would not expect a child to use the mature form of *cookie* on his first attempt to communicate the desire for a snack. Every literacy learner will also make mistakes, but these mistakes can be extremely useful to the teacher in uncovering what the child knows and can use about printed language.

Finally, the learner must receive a *response*, or feedback from his efforts. Do not confuse *feedback* with *praise;* feedback can simply be recognition of the meaning that the child attempted. For example, the child who writes *pst* on the supply list at school will get feedback if the teacher responds "Oh, yes, we do need paste. I'll get some from the supply closet."

Continuum of Literacy Development

The International Reading Association and the National Association for the Education of Young Children (IRA/NAEYC 1998) developed and published a joint position statement that defines developmentally appropriate practices in literacy instruction for young children. This continuum of literacy development, shown in Figure 10.2 (pages 310–311), describes five phases and grade levels. As stated in the note at the top of the figure, however, not all children at any grade will function at the same level in terms of literacy or any other area of development.

The information in Figure 10.2 can help teachers plan goals for their literacy programs and plan instruction for individual children. A preschool teacher of children who have not had many literacy experiences will need to begin with activities based on what the children know. For example, if a child has no experience in listening to books being read, then perhaps the teacher will need to tell him short and interesting stories. The next step might be to tell him stories using a flannelboard or a puppet. After the child has some experience with stories, then the teacher can begin to read to him from books. Once the child is engaged with book reading, the teacher can help him recognize how print works by demonstrating directionality and discussing the differences between the information that can be obtained from illustrations versus print. To begin such a child with drilling on letters and sounds before he knows about books and stories would make no sense.

> To the uneducated, an
> *A* **is just three sticks.**
>
> —*A. A. Milne*

Instruction for children with limited literacy experiences will require more individual story time, more story repetitions, and more talking about books individually and in small groups than might be required by more advantaged children. However, the results will be well worth the effort. Fox (1999) argues that a child who knows four nursery rhymes by heart by the age of four will probably learn to read without difficulty. Knowing these rhymes indicates the child has experience with words and sounds and pays attention to remembering them. If a child lacks that experience, then the teacher must supply it.

For every child, the goals must be to help her find satisfaction in literacy experiences and to encourage the disposition to continue learning. Any program that fails to achieve these goals is not appropriate for young children.

Standards for Reading Teachers

"What should new reading professionals know and be able to do?" That's the question that a committee from the International Reading Association set out to answer in revising the *Standards for Reading Professionals* (IRA 2003). They responded by creating a set of criteria for developing and evaluating teacher preparation programs. In revising the earlier 1998 document, the IRA shifted the focus of the criteria to *performance*—namely, the knowledge and skills that teachers-in-training develop as they complete their preparation programs. The reason for this was the change in the field of education to look more at learning outcomes than inputs.

www.**reading.org/downloads/ resources/545standards2003** The IRA's standards for reading teachers

The five standards are as follow:

1. Candidates have knowledge of the foundations of reading and writing processes and instruction.
2. Candidates use a wide range of instructional practices, approaches, methods, and curriculum materials to support reading and writing instruction.
3. Candidates use a variety of assessment tools and practices to plan and evaluate effective reading instruction.
4. Candidates create a literate environment that fosters reading and writing by integrating foundational knowledge, use of instructional practices, approaches and methods, curriculum materials, and the appropriate use of assessments.
5. Candidates view professional development as a career-long effort and responsibility. (IRA 2004)*

Note that the IRA does not intend for these standards to apply to seasoned teachers of reading, "who would be expected to demonstrate even higher performance levels" (IRA 2004). Regardless, seasoned teachers can use these standards as benchmarks against which to consider their own performance.

Program Elements That Support Literacy

In designing a program of instruction for young children, a range of important elements must be included. To begin, a successful program is founded on a set of goals that guide the content of the program as well as the methods used to deliver instruction. A successful program will also use as a framework the standards for literacy development. Providing a supportive classroom environment is also key to a program's success.

Other important program elements include an emphasis on oral language and listening, musical experiences that promote literacy development, story experiences that include reading aloud and storytelling, opportunities to learn about print, instruction that helps children attend to sound, and the presentation of selected text. All these program elements must be selected and implemented thoughtfully to help all children move along the continuum of literacy development.

---

*From IRA. (2004). *Standards for Reading Professionals–Revised 2003.* Professional Standards and Ethics Committee of the International Reading Association. Reprinted with permission.

FIGURE 10.2

Continuum of Children's Development in Early Reading and Writing

Note: This list is intended to be illustrative, not exhaustive. Children at any grade level will function at a variety of phases along the reading/writing continuum.

Phase 1: Awareness and Exploration (Goals for Preschool)

Children explore their environment and build the foundations for learning to read and write.

Children can

- enjoy listening to and discussing storybooks
- understand that print carries a message
- engage in reading and writing attempts
- identify labels and signs in their environment
- participate in rhyming games
- identify some letters and make some letter–sound matches
- use known letters or approximations of letters to represent written language (especially meaningful words like their name and phrases such as "I love you")

What teachers do

- share books with children, including Big Books, and model reading behaviors
- talk about letters by name and sounds
- establish a literacy-rich environment
- reread favorite stories
- engage children in language games
- promote literacy-related play activities
- encourage children to experiment with writing

What parents and family members can do

- talk with children, engage them in conversation, give names of things, show interest in what a child says
- read and reread stories with predictable texts to children
- encourage children to recount experiences and describe ideas and events that are important to them
- visit the library regularly
- provide opportunities for children to draw and print, using markers, crayons, and pencils

Phase 2: Experimental Reading and Writing (Goals for Kindergarten)

Children develop basic concepts of print and begin to engage in and experiment with reading and writing.

Kindergartners can

- enjoy being read to and themselves retell simple narrative stories or informational texts
- use descriptive language to explain and explore

- recognize letters and letter-sound matches
- show familiarity with rhyming and beginning sounds
- understand left-to-right and top-to-bottom orientation and familiar concepts of print
- match spoken words with written ones
- begin to write letters of the alphabet and some high-frequency words

What teachers do

- encourage children to talk about reading and writing experiences
- provide many opportunities for children to explore and identify sound–symbol relationships in meaningful contexts
- help children to segment spoken words into individual sounds and blend the sounds into whole words (for example, by slowly writing a word and saying its sound)
- frequently read interesting and conceptually rich stories to children
- provide daily opportunities for children to write
- help children build a sight vocabulary
- create a literacy-rich environment for children to engage independently in reading and writing

What parents and family members can do

- daily read and reread narrative and informational stories to children
- encourage children's attempts at reading and writing
- allow children to participate in activities that involve writing and reading (for example, cooking, making grocery lists)
- play games that involve specific directions (such as "Simon Says")
- have conversations with children during mealtimes and throughout the day

Phase 3: Early Reading and Writing (Goals for First Grade)

Children begin to read simple stories and can write about a topic that is meaningful to them.

First graders can

- read and retell familiar stories
- use strategies (rereading, predicting, questioning, contextualizing) when comprehension breaks down
- use reading and writing for various purposes on their own initiative
- orally read with reasonable fluency

FIGURE 10.2

Continued

- use letter–sound associations, word parts, and context to identify new words
- identify an increasing number of words by sight
- sound out and represent all substantial sounds in spelling a word
- write about topics that are personally meaningful
- attempt to use some punctuation and capitalization

What teachers do

- support the development of vocabulary by reading daily to the children, transcribing their language, and selecting materials that expand children's knowledge and language development
- model strategies and provide practice for identifying unknown words
- give children opportunities for independent reading and writing practice
- read, write, and discuss a range of different text types (poems, informational books)
- introduce new words and teach strategies for learning to spell new words
- demonstrate and model strategies to use when comprehension breaks down
- help children build lists of commonly used words from their writing

What parents and family members can do

- talk about favorite storybooks
- read to children and encourage them to read to you
- suggest that children write to friends and relatives
- bring to a parent-teacher conference evidence of what your child can do in writing and reading
- encourage children to share what they have learned about their writing and reading

Phase 4: Transitional Reading and Writing (Goals for Second Grade)

Children begin to read more fluently and write various text forms using simple and more complex sentences.

Second graders can

- read with greater fluency
- use strategies more efficiently (rereading, questioning, and so on) when comprehension breaks down
- use word identification strategies with greater facility to unlock unknown words
- identify an increasing number of words by sight
- write about a range of topics to suit different audiences
- use common letter patterns and critical features to spell words
- punctuate simple sentences correctly and proofread their own work
- spend time reading daily and use reading to research topics

What teachers do

- create a climate that fosters analytic, evaluative, and reflective thinking
- teach children to write in multiple forms (stories, information, poems)
- ensure that children read a range of texts for a variety of purposes
- teach revising, editing, and proofreading skills
- teach strategies for spelling new and difficult words
- model enjoyment of reading

What parents and family members can do

- continue to read to children and encourage them to read to you
- engage children in activities that require reading and writing
- become involved in school activities
- show children your interest in their learning by displaying their written work
- visit the library regularly
- support your child's specific hobby or interest with reading materials and references

Source: IRA and NAEYC. (1998). *Learning to Read and Write: Developmentally Appropriate Practices for Young Children.* A joint statement of the International Reading Association (IRA) and the National Association for the Education of Young Children (NAEYC). Newark, DE: International Reading Association; and Washington, DC: National Association for the Education of Young Children. Reprinted with permission.

Goals for Literacy Instruction

All literacy instruction must be founded on these basic goals:

1. To continue the oral language development of each child
2. To help each child learn how print is decoded

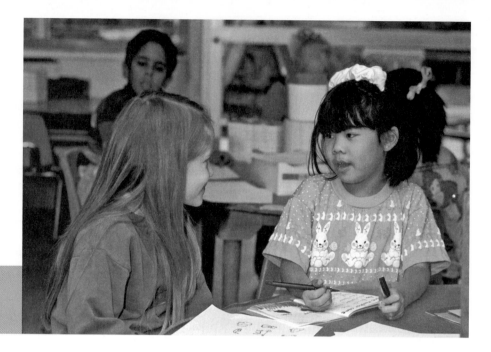

Talking, reading, and writing are all valuable components of literacy programs.

3. To ensure that each child feels that he can achieve success in literacy learning

4. To ensure that each child will have the disposition to continue learning about literacy

These goals will most likely be met in an interesting and safe environment where children can play and work together and where adults help children learn. None of these goals can be met by engaging children in isolated practice activities that are designed to teach specific skills.

Standards for Literacy Development

In 1996, after obtaining input from thousands of teachers, researchers, parents, and others, the International Reading Association (IRA) and the National Council of Teachers of English (NCTE) published *Standards for the English Language Arts*. The purpose of these standards, as described by these sponsoring groups, "is to provide guidance in ensuring that all students are proficient language users so they may succeed in school, participate in society, find rewarding work, appreciate and contribute to our culture, and pursue their own goals and interests throughout their lives" (IRA/NCTE 1996).

One of the assumptions underlying the IRA/NCTE standards is that children's literacy development begins before they enter school through their experiences with speech, print, and graphic representations of ideas. Given this, the standards are rooted in the concept of **emergent literacy,** which describes the early reading and writing behaviors of young children. According to this concept, when children are encouraged to explore and experiment with language in a supportive environment, these early behaviors lead to the development of conventional literacy (Teale and Sulzby 1989).

These are the ideas underlying the following twelve standards:

Standards for the English Language Arts

www.ncte.org/about/over/ standards/110846.htm

Online presentation of the IRA/NCTE *Standards for the English Language Arts*

1. Students read a wide range of print and non-print texts to build an understanding of texts, of themselves, and of the cultures of the United States and the world; to acquire new information; to respond to the needs and demands of society and the workplace; and for personal fulfillment. Among these texts are fiction and nonfiction, classic and contemporary works.

2. Students read a wide range of literature from many periods in many genres to build an understanding of the many dimensions (e.g., philosophical, ethical, aesthetic) of human experience.

3. Students apply a wide range of strategies to comprehend, interpret, evaluate, and appreciate texts. They draw on their prior experience, their interactions with other readers and writers, their knowledge of word meaning and of other texts, their word identification strategies, and their understanding of textual features (e.g., sound–letter correspondence, sentence structure, context, graphics).

4. Students adjust their use of spoken, written, and visual language (e.g., conventions, style, vocabulary) to communicate effectively with a variety of audiences and for different purposes.

5. Students employ a wide range of strategies as they write and use different writing process elements appropriately to communicate with different audiences for a variety of purposes.

6. Students apply knowledge of language structure, language conventions (e.g., spelling and punctuation), media techniques, figurative language, and genre to create, critique, and discuss print and non-print texts.

7. Students conduct research on issues and interests by generating ideas and questions, and by posing problems. They gather, evaluate, and synthesize data from a variety of sources (e.g., print and non-print texts, artifacts, people) to communicate their discoveries in ways that suit their purpose and audience.

8. Students use a variety of technological and information resources (e.g., libraries, databases, computer networks, video) to gather and synthesize information and to create and communicate knowledge.

9. Students develop an understanding of and respect for diversity in language use, patterns, and dialects across cultures, ethnic groups, geographic regions, and social roles.

10. Students whose first language is not English make use of their first language to develop competency in the English language arts and to develop understanding of content across the curriculum.

11. Students participate as knowledgeable, reflective, creative, and critical members of a variety of literacy communities.

12. Students use spoken, written, and visual language to accomplish their own purposes (e.g., for learning, enjoyment, persuasion, and the exchange of information). (IRA/NCTE 1996)*

In presenting the standards, the IRA/NCTE (1996) states, "We want to emphasize that they are not distinct and separable; they are, in fact, interrelated and should be considered as a whole." In addition, the standards "are not prescriptions for particular curriculum or instruction"; rather, they are to be used as a framework for planning.

Note, too, that these standards apply to students from kindergarten through grade twelve. Teachers are to tailor the standards and provide appropriate learning experiences based on the developmental levels of their

---

*From IRA and NCTE. (1996). *Standards for the English Language Arts*. Newark, DE: International Reading Association; and Urbana, IL: National Council of Teachers of English. Reprinted with permission.

students, at whatever grade. To help teachers tailor the standards effectively, the NCTE has published a series of books that provide age-appropriate ideas about activities, assessment, diversity, and more. The volume for early childhood teachers is called *Standards in Practice, Grades K–2* (Crafton 1996).

Providing a Supportive Classroom Environment

Classrooms that foster the development of literacy have several distinguishing characteristics: They are interesting and full of activity, they allow for participation in many different experiences, and they connect reading and writing to children's experiences. Classrooms where literacy emerges are also print rich: They contain a wide variety of reading, writing, and listening materials that are accessible to children.

In a stimulating, active environment, children will be encouraged to participate in a wide variety of experiences. Such a classroom will not be a quiet place! Children developing new concepts should want to talk about them, read about them, and write about them.

For example, as a science activity, children might observe hatching silkworms. This activity would require research about when silkworms hatch, when the mulberry leaves that they eat are available, what will happen to the silk if the larvae are allowed to mature, and how to hatch some eggs so that another generation of silkworms can be grown. This activity might also involve gathering food for the larvae and observing the metamorphosis of the larvae into silkworms. Children involved in such experiences will be constantly talking about their observations, reading from a variety of sources, listening to others read, and writing about their experiences and feelings. Activities that encourage thinking, talking, reading, and writing should be part of every schoolday.

> **Books are not written to teach lessons in safety or morality, but to arouse feelings, provide meaning for an individual, and to raise questions.**
>
> —*Marion Dane Bauer*

Several studies have found that adding selected materials to the play environment and guiding their use can encourage children to participate in more literacy activities in their play (Christie 1990; Morrow and Rand 1991; Neuman and Roskos 1993). Christie (1990) notes that giving children time to play is simply not enough. Teachers must also intervene to promote literacy activities, perhaps thinking about what literacy materials could be added to play areas, encouraging children to play in theme centers where literacy is a natural response to a theme, or modeling literacy behaviors in play areas.

For example, a teacher might set up an "office" or a "grocery store" or invite children to write labels for their block constructions. Theme areas that involve literacy experiences include a "doctor's office," a "shoe store," a "restaurant," a "home" (making lists, checking the TV guide, reading the newspaper, reading to babies, and so on), and a "post office."

Neuman and Roskos (1993) recommend using real literacy objects rather than pretend objects. An "office" might be equipped with real file folders and forms. The materials selected should be familiar to the children from their real-world experiences. Morrow and Rand (1991) suggest that literacy materials be kept in clearly marked places, that they be changed frequently to keep children's interest in them high, that teachers model the uses of materials as needed or suggest possible uses when appropriate, and that all levels of development be accepted for the most positive results.

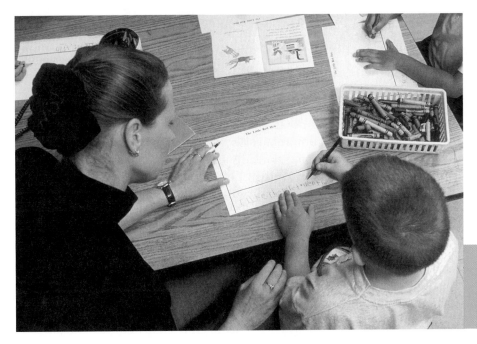

Literacy development is best fostered when children believe that they are capable learners of reading and writing.

Providing a **print-rich environment** and an attractive reading area can also support children's literacy development (Neuman 2004; Weigel Martin, and Bennett 2005). An environment is *print-rich* when it incorporates print into the play environment as much as possible. This means adding print to play, as described earlier and adding labels and signs that have meaning for children. These labels and signs need to be useful, not just decorative. For example, if the children name the class's pet rabbit, that name should be mounted on the cage. A record of what is fed to the rabbit should also be there, perhaps with a list of names to indicate whose turn it is to care for the rabbit as well as books about rabbits and their care.

An attractive reading area is a classroom library center that has a table and chairs, a sofa or a rocking chair, and some floor pillows. Of course, the primary focus should be the attractively displayed books, which are carefully selected and rotated frequently.

Children's development of literacy skills is ongoing. Thus, the environment needs to offer new and varied learning opportunities in safe and engaging ways.

Oral Language and Listening Skills

Because reading and writing are language activities, **oral language** development is critical for success in becoming literate. Teachers can engage children in oral language all through the day: as they check attendance, explain a new activity, work with individuals in a center, talk to small groups about an interesting change in the moldy orange the class has been observing, read stories with vocabulary that is slightly challenging, discuss the processes used to achieve an effect in art, label the movements of the children in dance, and so on.

Teachers must engage children in stimulating language experiences so that they have opportunities to learn new words and phrases. Several studies have found that children who show early difficulty with the development of vocabulary knowledge and grammatical skills are more likely to

NAEYC CRITERIA
2.38

PRAXIS

Be able to explain why a print-rich environment is important in developing literacy

www.

http://reading.indiana.edu/ ieo/digests/d107.html

A digest of the studies on the relationship between oral language and reading

www.

www.teachnet.com/lesson/ langarts/reading/vocabdev. html

A lesson plan for helping children develop vocabulary knowledge

PRAXIS

Be able to design and/or
evaluate lessons that promote
growth in oral language

experience literacy problems than children who gain language skills according to the typical schedule (Scarborough 1990; Snow et al. 1998). Language development needs to be more than simply vocabulary and phonemic awareness activities; it needs to be comprehensive (Storch and Whitehurst 2002).

Learning to be an active listener through many activities with stories, songs, fingerplays, and games is also an important literacy skill. **Listening** is the aural equivalent of comprehension when reading. When children learn to listen, they learn the same skills of checking for understanding, making connections, and visualizing the events being recounted that are required of readers when they comprehend text. Learning to listen means being engaged in predicting what will come next and learning to spot the language cues that signal a new event or the closing of the story. The ability to listen to stories, along with the desire to do so, are important motivators for becoming literate.

Music as a Literacy Activity

Music is important enough by itself to justify inclusion in the early childhood program. In addition, this enjoyable activity can also help young children develop literacy skills. Singing and remembering the lyrics to songs helps children learn to attend to and remember words. It also helps them learn about rhyming words and alliteration in a relaxed and pleasurable activity.

After children have learned the lyrics of a song, they can create song booklets. These booklets can then be used for learning about sound–letter relationships, spelling conventions, and punctuation, depending on what the children need to know and can understand. Children can also write new lyrics to familiar melodies or create picture books for favorite songs after seeing some published books of songs. A list of some song picture books is provided in Figure 10.3.

FIGURE 10.3

Examples of Song Picture Books

Bingo (Wells 1999)

Do Your Ears Hang Low? (Church 2002)

Down by the Station (Hillenbrand 1999)

Farmer in the Dell (Wallner 1998)

Fiddle-I-Fee (Hillenbrand 2002; Sweet 1992)

Frog Went a-Courting (Catalano 1998)

I Know an Old Lady Who Swallowed a Pie (Jackson 1997)

If You're Happy and You Know It (Cabrera 2005; Ormerod 2002)

If You're Happy and You Know It, Clap Your Hands (Carter 1997)

Itsy-Bitsy Spider (Wells 1998)

Knick-Knack Paddywhack (Zelinsky 2002)

Miss Mary Mack (Hoberman 1998)

Mockingbird (Ahlberg 1998)

Old MacDonald Had a Farm (Jones 1989; Schwartz 1999)

Over in the Meadow (Galdone 1986; Keats 1971; Wadsworth 2002)

Seals on the Bus (Hort 2000)

Skip to My Lou (Hoberman 1989/2003)

There Was an Old Lady Who Swallowed a Fly (Taback 1997)

This Land Is Your Land (Gutherie 1998).

This Old Man (Jones 1990)

What a Wonderful World (Weiss and Thiele 1995)

Wheels on the Bus (Zelinsky 1990)

Reading Aloud and Storytelling

Read-Alouds

Reading aloud to children—as individuals, in small groups, or as a whole class—is an absolutely essential part of literacy instruction. Not only do **read-alouds** provide children with a pleasurable experience, a positive emotional response to reading, and a means of getting "book" language in their heads, but it also offers distinct opportunities to become more literate. Reading aloud also produces these benefits:

1. The teacher can demonstrate the nature, pleasures, and rewards of reading, which will increase the children's interest in books and their motivation to read for themselves.

2. Children learn the ways in which language can be recorded.

3. Children realize that some of their own experiences and thoughts are like those that have been recorded by the authors they have read.

4. Children who listen to stories can compose narratives in their own heads and want to create and record their own texts.

5. Children refine their understanding of the elements of language: patterns, sounds, rhythms, and styles.

6. Listening to stories they already know allows children to confirm their predictions about how the episodes are arranged to make the story work. Listening to known stories also allows children to discover new levels of meaning in a story.

7. Children who have had extensive experience in listening to stories are better able to edit their own stories in their heads.

8. Children need to be challenged by reading material that is beyond their independent reading level.

9. Reading aloud a variety of different texts throughout the schoolday helps children understand that reading goes well beyond any lesson or school activity (adapted from Mooney 1990, pp. 21–24).

www.trelease-on-reading.com
www.literacyconnections.com/ReadingAloud.html
www.carolhurst.com/profsubjects/reading/readingaloud.html

All of these sites list recommended books for reading aloud; some provide tips for reading aloud

NAEYC CRITERIA
2.28

PRAXIS

Be able to describe the qualities of outstanding books for children and what it means to have a balanced collection of books in the classroom

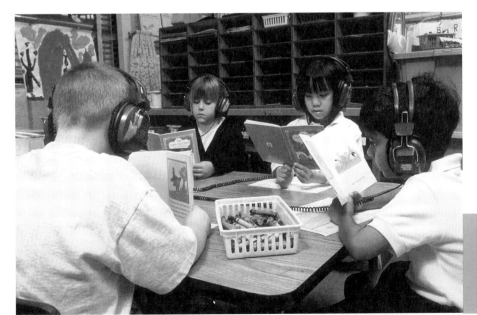

Listening to audiotapes in a classroom reading center is an efficient way for students to experience a story being read aloud.

FIGURE 10.4

Suggested Read-Aloud Books

For Threes and Fours

Goodnight Max (Wells 2000—Board Book)

Gossie & Gertie (Dunrea 2002)

Little Lamb (Harper 2003)

My Car (Barton 2001)

Ollie (Dunrea 2003)

Red Is a Dragon (Thong 2001)

Red-Eyed Tree Frog (Cowley 1999)

Wemberley's Ice-Cream Star (Henkes 2003—Board Book)

For Fours and Fives

Bunny Cakes (Wells 1997)

Goodnight, My Duckling (Tafuri 2005)

Mice Squeak, We Speak (dePaola 1997)

Mouse Mess (Riley 1997)

My House, Mi Casa (Emberley 1990)

Neighborhood Mother Goose (Crews 2004)

No, David! (Shannon 1998)

For Fives, Sixes, and Sevens

12 Ways to Get to 11 (Merriam 1993)

Bear Snores On (Wilson 2002)

Farmer Duck (Waddell 1991)

Muncha! Muncha! Muncha! (Fleming 2002)

The Color Box (Dodds 1992)

Tops and Bottoms (Stevens 1995)

What Do You Do with a Tail Like This? (Jenkins and Page 2003)

For Sevens and Eights

And the Dish Ran Away with the Spoon (Stevens and Crummel 2001)

Antics! (Hepworth 1992)

If a Bus Could Talk (Ringgold 1999)

Lizards, Frogs, and Polliwogs (Florian 2001)

Midnight Ride of Paul Revere (Longfellow/Bing 2001)

The Name Jar (Choi 2001)

Wild about Books (Sierra 2004)

With Love, Little Red Hen (Ada 2001)

Interactive reading aloud—in which children can ask questions, make comments, answer questions posed by the reader—is extremely valuable for young children but difficult to manage with large groups (Collins and Shaeffer 1997). Therefore, at least some read-aloud experiences need to be conducted with individuals or very small groups. Most teachers manage this kind of reading by using volunteers, teacher aides, or older children (Klesius and Griffith 1996).

Some suggested books for reading aloud are included in Figure 10.4.

Storytelling

For children with little experience in listening to stories being read aloud, *storytelling* can serve as a bridge to storybook reading. Storytelling can be adapted on the spot in terms of story length, vocabulary, and sentence structure. While storytelling, the teacher can maintain eye contact with the children at all times and observe them for signs of comprehension of the story and/or its vocabulary. Once children can listen to stories easily and with comprehension, the teacher can begin to tell a story while displaying some of the illustrations from a book and then move to more typical story-reading experiences.

Even if children are skilled listeners, storytelling should be a regular part of the program. It can achieve the same objectives as reading aloud but creates a more personal, immediate experience. Helping children tell

http://falcon.jmu.edu/ ~ramseyil/storyhandbook.htm

A handbook of storytelling, from why and how to do it to beginning stories their own stories is another good foundation for both reading and writing activities.

Learning about Print

As noted earlier, children need many opportunities each day to learn about print and how it is used, and these opportunities can be provided in many ways. For example, children can learn while observing the teacher as he reads a "big book" and passes his hand under each line of print as it is read or by collecting and classifying print that is found in various places, such as a grocery store or toy store or in a newspaper or catalog. Children also can learn about print as they observe the teacher record their own words and read them back, and they can learn about print as it regulates their daily schedule, announces important events, or communicates with them through records or signs.

Print is everywhere in U.S. society, and most children become aware of it and attend to it very early. It is not uncommon for a two-year-old to ask what print says. On those occasions when a child fails to notice print, the teacher can certainly bring it to his attention throughout the schoolday.

NAEYC CRITERIA
2.31

> *Education is not a race. A child who learns to read at age three has in no way "won" over a child who learns to read at age six or seven.*
>
> —*David Elkind*

Attending to Sound

Developing Phonemic Awareness

Phonemic awareness is the ability to "focus on and manipulate phonemes in written words" (Ehri and Nunes 2002, p. 111). Tasks to determine phonemic awareness include asking learners to isolate a sound ("Tell me the first sound in *paste*"); to identify a sound ("Tell me the sound that is the same in *bike, boy,* and *bell*"); to categorize a sound ("Which word does not belong—*bus, bun,* or *rug?*"); to blend sounds to create a word; to segment sounds in given words; and to delete sounds ("What is *smile* without the *s?*") Phonemic awareness falls under the umbrella of *phonological awareness,* which is the ability to recognize larger spoken units such as syllables, onsets, and rimes.

Several studies have concluded that phonemic awareness is highly correlated with success in beginning reading experiences (Hoffman et al. 1998; Lundberg, Frost, and Petersen 1988). Phonemic awareness is not a single skill but a cluster of skills that develops over time. For example, recognizing rhyming words is one level of phonemic awareness, being able to distinguish the beginning sound of a word from the rest of the word is another level, and completely segmenting the word is another. The skills that constitute phonemic awareness are developed as a result of children's experience with oral and written language.

Many common preschool and kindergarten activities help children become more aware of sounds in words—for instance, clapping the beats in the children's names, having the children complete the rhyming line of a nursery rhyme that the teacher starts, reading aloud books with rhyming words and a wide variety of alphabet books, making a list of words that begin with the same sound as a given word, and dictating sentences in which all the words begin with the same sound (Novick 1999/2000).

For a child who needs additional practice with sounds, the teacher might use an activity such as the Elkonin boxes (Elkonin 1973). The child is

www.kidsource.com/ kidsource/content2/phoemic. p.k12.4.html
A definition and explanation of the importance of phonemic awareness

NAEYC CRITERIA
2.35, 2.37

PRAXIS

Be able to define *phonemic awareness* and explain its importance in literacy development given a card with three boxes drawn on it along with some markers, such as pennies or plastic chips. He is instructed to place a marker in a box for each sound he hears in a given word. (The markers are for sounds, not letters.) A four-letter word such as *cake* would mean marking three boxes.

The National Reading Panel (2000) suggests in a report that skill in phonemic awareness is one of the best predictors of reading success. However, in their analysis of studies of phonemic awareness, they found that studies in which the children attached letters to sounds were more effective in aiding children's reading and spelling skills. In other words, these were studies of phonics instruction rather than phonemic awareness.

Cunningham and Cunningham (2002) state that children do need to develop phonemic awareness, but they also need to develop other skills if they are to learn to read successfully. These authors oppose spending large portions of class time on phonemic awareness programs without regard for what children know and can do. "Such single level instruction can only bore and even confuse those who already have or would learn phonemic awareness without it" (p. 93).

Most children develop phonemic awareness without specific instruction. They only need to take part in interesting language activities and have teachers who help them focus on the sounds of words from their oral language and how sounds are recorded in print.

Phonics Instruction

Phonemic awareness is often confused with phonics. To clarify, phonemic awareness is the child's awareness of sounds, not the relationship between sounds and the letters used to represent them. **Phonics** is learning how to decode the print symbols used to represent language sounds.

Much has been written in the professional and popular press recently about phonics instruction and its place in helping children learn to read. The debate is not about whether children should learn sound–letter relationships; everyone agrees that knowing such relationships is a critical skill. Instead, the debate is over when and how such instruction should take place. Advocates of the "phonics first" approach believe that children should master sound–letter relationships before actually reading meaningful material. Others argue that children should have rich experiences with meaningful literature, and when they have achieved a workable sight vocabulary, then they should learn sound–letter relationships to help them decode unfamiliar words.

Research on Phonics Instruction   After an analysis of studies examining the effectiveness of so-called systematic phonics instruction, the National Reading Panel (2000) found that phonics instruction was useful in helping children become more skilled readers. They found that kindergarten and first-grade learners benefited more from the instruction than did older children. Even so, the teacher need not follow a lock-step program for every child. She can keep records of the work done with individual children and make sure that every useful sound–letter relationship and the strategies for applying them have been covered over a period of time. Phonics can certainly be taught without a commercial program (Routman 2000).

In an extensive study of eight first-grade classrooms that met stringent criteria for whole-language instruction, Dahl et al. (1999) found that children were gaining skill in using phonics information through their reading. In sum:

www.readwritethink.org/ lessons/lesson_view. asp?id=157

A whole-to-part phonics lesson plan

PRAXIS

Be able to explain the importance of phonics instruction and to plan a lesson to teach a specific phonics skill

Findings demonstrated that whole language classrooms included a more complex and varied mix of phonics instructional events encompassing direct instruction, individualized instruction, and instruction embedded in ongoing reading and writing activities. . . . This was accomplished by teachers making informed instructional decisions based on the literacy development and progress of each student. (p. 338)

Many of the research studies that claim to prove that phonics instruction in a direct and systematic program results in higher reading achievement than alternate methods of reading instruction have been criticized by other researchers. For example, Taylor (1998) examined a study by Foorman et al. (1998) that supported direct phonics instruction for African American children and found that some of the results were based on a sample size of only five children (p. 46). Certainly, no valid generalization can be made from such a small sample.

Others have found problems with research studies sponsored by the National Institute of Health (Krashen 1999; McQuillan 1998; F. Smith 1999; Stahl, Duffy-Hester, and Stahl 1998). Many of these studies were conducted on children with special learning needs, so their findings cannot be generalized to all children. Other research was conducted by individuals aligned with specific programs of instruction that would obviously benefit from supportive findings. Another issue in some of the cited studies is that they call for systematic phonics instruction, which many teachers have interpreted to mean a program of instruction that is to be followed step by step.

Studies that used the reading of isolated words as the measure of success have drawn criticism because there is no research to connect the success of reading isolated words with real reading of connected text. Clay (1991), among others, cautions against using word lists as measures of reading competency.

None of this criticism is to say that phonics instruction is not important. Good teachers have always taught children phonics and will continue to do so. But like all other instruction, phonics instruction should be based on demonstrated needs of the child. If the child knows some letter–sound relationships, she does not need instruction in them but only in those she does not yet know.

Problems with Planning Phonics Instruction   Teachers of young children face several problems in planning phonics instruction. As already mentioned, teachers must assess daily in order to determine who needs instruction. A second problem occurs if teachers try to make every child pronounce a given sound in exactly the same way. Some sound differences are dialectal and will not hamper a child's reading unless the teacher believes it will. A third problem occurs when phonics instruction is considered the only means of helping children learn to read.

Some experts in the field are calling for *balanced instruction* that includes phonics. *Balanced* is a good descriptive term if it means that each child gets the amount of phonics that she needs but not if it means that every child gets exactly the same amount of instruction, needed or not. The following description of a first-grade class and the teacher's plan to meet the needs of all the students will help illustrate how appropriate phonics instruction is implemented.

An Example: A Typical First-Grade Class   There are twenty-two children in this class. Four of them are able readers of many texts. Three more can read many common words and indicate that they know many sound–letter relationships because they write them in their journals. Five of the children do not speak English as their first language. They are learning English rapidly as they play with their fellow students and engage in interesting activities, such as caring for a pet rabbit. These children learn the vocabulary of the activities in English with help from their teachers as well as their peers. Three other children have limited vocabularies, even though their home language is English. They, too, are learning new vocabulary and how to listen and respond to stories. The seven remaining children have just begun to find satisfaction in recognizing common sounds in the names of their classmates, to read the jobs chart, and to want to write stories on their own.

What will happen if all of these children are presented with phonics instruction, regardless of need? Some of them will become bored and conclude that school is not interesting; they will not learn much during school. Others will have no concept of letter–sound relationships in English and will be confused. These children will experience what Katz (1986) calls *learned stupidity:* that they are not capable of performing the tasks required of them in school.

So, how will the teacher of these children plan for their instruction? An entry from her plan book, shown in Figure 10.5, illustrates one option.

Appropriate Phonics Instruction In their article entitled "Everything You Wanted to Know about Phonics (but Were Afraid to Ask)," Stahl et al. (1998) provide seven principles for good phonics instruction. Namely, good phonics instruction should do the following:

1. Develop the alphabetic principle.
2. Develop phonological awareness.
3. Provide a thorough grounding in the letters.
4. Avoid teaching rules, using worksheets, dominating instruction, and boring learners.
5. Provide sufficient practice in reading words.
6. Lead to automatic word recognition.
7. Be one part of reading instruction (pp. 339–343).

Other reasonable suggestions for phonics instruction come from the Center for the Improvement of Early Reading Achievement (Hiebert et al. 1998), which has compiled a suggested list of phonics accomplishments for children from kindergarten to second grade:

- *Kindergarten:* Children should know many sound–letter relationships and begin to understand that the sequence of letters in a written word represents the sequence of sounds in a spoken word.
- *First grade:* Children should be able to decode phonetically regular one-syllable words in texts and monitor their own reading to self-correct if the word they have identified does not fit with the other cues provided in the sentence.
- *Second grade:* Children should be able to decode one-syllable words not yet known through sound–letter knowledge, through recognition

FIGURE 10.5

Literacy Activities from the Teacher's Plan Book

Whole group:
Read aloud One Duck Stuck (Root 1998). Take pleasure in the words and repeat some of them, encouraging the children to join in when they can.

Children who are reading exceptionally well:
Provide two children with two copies of the book, and encourage them to read it with one another. They could also write their own story following the same pattern established in the book. There is a moose stuck in the muck in the illustration on the final endpaper but not mentioned in the text; this might inspire the children to create a new story about the moose, either as small groups or individually. They could also read another book by the same author.

Children who are strong beginning readers:
Review the text with these children, and find all the rhyming words they can read (duck, muck, luck, stuck; fish, swish; moose, spruce; crickets, thickets). Call attention to the rhyming words that are not spelled with the same pattern (moose and spruce). Using several sets of words, help children apply the strategy of using a rhyming word they know to decode a new word. Make a book of rhyming words to use as a reference or to share with the class.

English language learners/Children with limited vocabulary:
Make sure that these children understand what all the words mean, including the invented words ("The crickets leap to the duck. Pleep, pleep."). Read the book in a shared reading experience, and encourage the children to join in when they can. Draw attention to the clues on the page for the number words (a numeral and the illustration). Let each child select a favorite page and help lead the others as that page is read again. Talk about the invented words that the author selected or created to describe the movements of the animals. Ask the children what words they would use to describe the movements of different animals. Enjoy the book one more time. Encourage the children to choose a word or words for their word banks.

Children making good progress:
Review the text with these children, and help them identify the repetitive patterns ("Help! Help! Who can help?" and "We can! We can!"). Use the /an/ from can and help the children create new words by changing the c to r, f, d, m, p, t, and v. If the children understand this activity, repeat it using another word from the text. If they do not know the /fr/, /sk/, or /tr/ sounds as onsets, then select words from the book with these onsets and ask the children to think of other words that begin with the same sounds. Help the children use their knowledge of these onsets to decode new words; write them on a whiteboard. Reread the book, stressing the patterns and words discussed. Encourage the children to write about their favorite parts of the book.

Source: Adapted from Katz 1986.

of phonograms, or by analogy to rhyming words and be able to decode multisyllabic words through phonic and structural analysis.

A Final Word on Phonics

Even the strongest advocates of the "phonics first" approach recognize that children need to develop a sight vocabulary because of the large number of common words in English that are not phonetically regular (Blachman 1991). Phonics advocates also recognize that children need interesting texts to read (Adams 1990). Lyon (1998) states that from the beginning, children need to be "playing with language through nursery rhymes, storybooks, and writing activities" and to have "as early as possible experiences that help them understand the purposes of reading, and the wonder and joy that can be derived from reading" (p. 12). Teachers must not be overwhelmed by the "phonics first" arguments without considering what they can do to help children enjoy reading experiences and develop a strong disposition to engage in literacy experiences.

Presenting Selected Text

As teachers encourage children's developing reading skills, they find ways of calling attention to the text and of presenting the text in ways that make it comprehensible. As mentioned before, teachers can emphasize text by running a hand under it as they read aloud from a "big book." Similarly, they can help children notice classroom print, such as the jobs board, attendance board, lunch count, announcements, menus, and so on.

In addition to providing these encounters with print, teachers will want to provide shared reading and guided reading for their classes, beginning in kindergarten. The texts selected for shared and guided reading should not necessarily be chosen for their literary qualities. Rather, they should be selected because the children will be able to read them independently in the near future. These texts should have repetitive language, rhyming patterns, limited vocabularies, and other features that will make learning to read them an achievable challenge for the children.

Shared Reading

Shared reading—an instructional strategy in which the teacher takes primary responsibility for the reading but involves the children actively in the process—is another important experience that supports the young child's developing literacy. Shared reading is often done with books in a large format ("big books") and print, which all the group can see. Although this approach certainly adds to the effectiveness, successful shared reading can be done with small groups and regular books.

In shared reading, the teacher introduces the book by reading the title, showing the children the front of the book, and asking them to predict what the story will be about. Once these predictions have been made and discussed, the teacher usually reads the name of the author and discusses other books by that individual (if appropriate). Then the teacher reads aloud the book, passing her hand or a pointer under the print as she reads it.

On the second and other repeated readings of the story, the children can be asked to join in the reading of repetitive phrases. The teacher might then call attention to some elements of the print, perhaps capital letters, punctuation, illustrations that do or do not match the print on the page, the author's use of a specific word, the style of the story (folktale, realistic, personal narrative, and so on), or other features that will be meaningful to the children. Often, the children themselves call attention to features of the print on successive repeated readings. They may notice rhyming patterns, spelling patterns, page numbers, or any number of other features (Clements and Warncke 1994; Stewart 1995).

Eventually, of course, the children will have memorized the story and be able to "read" it successfully. At that point, the teacher can suggest that the children write their own stories based on the pattern of the original, that they draw their own illustrations, that they write sequels, and so on, depending on the needs and abilities of the individual children. Some children may want to read the story independently, whereas others may want to play with the blocks and not do anything related to the story at the moment.

Offering a choice of responses is extremely important (Fallon and Allen 1994). Thus, assigning every child to create a caterpillar from an egg carton after having read *The Very Hungry Caterpillar* (Carle 1969) would not be appropriate; however, making the materials available if children want to make caterpillars would be appropriate.

Guided Reading

Guided reading is a teaching strategy often used with beginning independent readers. It is usually done with first- and second-grade students, although the strategy would be appropriate for some kindergartners, as well.

www.eduplace.com/rdg/res/ literacy/em_lit4.html
An explanation of shared reading

PRAXIS

Be able to describe the benefits of shared reading in literacy development

Parents and Literacy

● Send parents a newsletter that lists some of the children's favorite books, words to chants, and lyrics of songs that the children know by rote so that parents can enjoy reading or singing with their children. You should keep this newsletter short and make it reader friendly. Some teachers reproduce the covers of books, along with their titles, to help those parents who might not read themselves. Also encourage parents to tell family stories, and celebrate some of those in the newsletter (Buchoff 1995; Harding 1996).

www.mcps.K12.md.us/ curriculum/english/guided_ reading.html
Definition, procedures, and examples of guided reading

Guided reading requires that the teacher select a text for a specific group of readers and guide them through the reading of it. The group is usually no larger than six children. After selecting the text, the teacher decides on a reading strategy that will be emphasized in this lesson and where to stop reading before discussing the text with the children. Guided reading differs from shared reading in that the children have the primary responsibility for the reading.

Once the teacher has selected an appropriate text and called the group together, he asks the children to make predictions about the content of the story from the cover illustration. These predictions are recorded. Then he may introduce the story using some of the vocabulary that might be difficult for the readers but not quoting the sentences in the text exactly. Sometimes teachers use a "picture walk" in the introduction, which means that children turn the pages of the text looking at the illustrations and discussing what might be happening in the text. Next, the children read to the designated spot while the teacher observes their reading closely. The discussion at each stop will focus on strategies the readers used to figure out unknown words as well as the meaning of the passage.

Guided reading is an effective strategy, but the teacher must be skilled in selecting the appropriate text, planning strategy instruction, and leading the discussions. Fountas and Pinnell (1996) describe guided reading in great detail.

Commercial Programs for Literacy Instruction

Programs for reading instruction have existed for many years. Many of these programs are based on basal readers for which a publishing company produces a set of graded materials, including pieces of text, workbooks, skills pages, assessment schemes, and other materials that are intended to be used for reading instruction. These materials are accompanied by a detailed teacher's manual that specifies what the teacher is to do in detail.

Until recently, most of these materials did not contain a preschool program, so they did not have as much impact on early childhood programs as they did on elementary programs. Most of these programs now have materials for preschool, and many schools have adopted them as their primary instructional material.

Basal readers are intended to be a resource, but often they become the curriculum. Teachers whose districts have adopted a basal reader program must be aware of the philosophy of the series and know that they must take personal responsibility for literacy instruction regardless of what program has been adopted. Following a published program mindlessly will not result in good instruction.

Another type of instructional material is the *scripted program*, which is so prescriptive that the teacher is given no choice in presenting material. The teacher must follow the program exactly as it is written, including sticking to a rigid time schedule for activities and presenting the activities in an exact order. One such program is Success for All (Slavin 1996). This program presents research that supports program claims of reading achievement when compared to other types of reading instruction, but other researchers not affiliated with the program have not been able to replicate the research findings (Pogrow 2000).

Another approach intended to help teachers find balance and include all the elements of a literacy program is Four Blocks (Cunningham, Hall, and DeFee 1991). This program was designed to give teachers a framework for including guided reading, writing, word study, and independent reading during each instructional day. The time blocks are prescribed, but the content of each block is determined by the teacher based on what the children know and need to know. Four Blocks is not a published program or a basal reading program. The teacher must supply the materials for instruction and make the decisions about how and when to teach the elements of reading.

Helping All Children Feel Successful as Literacy Learners

The teacher who wants children to feel successful as literacy learners will provide many opportunities for them to choose their own literacy activities and will help individual children choose tasks that are appropriate. The key is to find the interest of each child and build literacy experiences around it. For example, if the child is interested in playing trucks in the sandbox but shows no interest in words or books, the teacher should choose some books about trucks, construction vehicles, and sand to share with that child and make available for browsing.

Another option is for the teacher to take dictation as the child tells what he has done that day with the blocks. The teacher should be sure to read the narrative back to the child so he can agree that it says what he said. Teachers should also include these dictated experiences in notes to the child's parents or in compilations of class activities.

A child's interest in words might be aroused by focusing on her name and the names of her classmates for activities, such as taking attendance and assigning classroom tasks. Art projects might be another way to stimulate interest, perhaps by having the teacher take dictation about the child's product or the process of creating it or by supplying books about art in the art center.

Whatever the child's interests, the instruction provided must be pleasant and successful. It must focus on the child's interests and help her begin to use literacy for her own needs. Many teachers have recognized that a child *was* paying attention to literacy upon catching her moving her name to the job she wanted to do on the classroom job chart!

It is also important that the teacher not treat reading and writing as the only important activities in which children are involved. Children need to be involved in play, art, music, and so forth, and the teacher must value these experiences for themselves, without always tacking on a reading or writing component to legitimize the experience. To do otherwise would send children the subtle message that only reading and writing are important.

The communication skills—speaking, reading, listening, and writing—should permeate all instruction in every subject. But each child's efforts in these areas should be natural—resulting from his own inclination and growing ability in each area. The artificial separation of learning into distinct instructional subjects must be avoided. When instruction is separated from experience, children develop the misconception that learning takes place only in school. Ideally, education is entering an era in which teachers will refocus on children's learning, rather than on defining education in terms of instruction.

If we honor children's attempts to read and write, they will continue to engage in these behaviors. That means keeping the children's work, paying close attention to their developing control of written language, encouraging role-play reading before children can actually read text, finding texts of interest as children move into independent reading activities, and helping children create their own texts frequently. Honoring children's efforts also means learning more about what each child knows about literacy every day and planning instruction for that child that will be satisfying and encouraging. Only by continuing to read and write will a child get better at reading and writing.

See the following box, An Expert Speaks, in which Dr. Mary Renck Jalongo speaks about the complexity of becoming literate. She reminds us of the difficulty in becoming literate and advises that those of us who learned

AN **Expert** SPEAKS: *Becoming Literate*

Mary Renck Jalongo
Indiana University of Philadelphia

Becoming literate is a complex task for young children. They pay attention to the language around them and can read environmental print, such as their favorite food labels or billboards. Most young children will attempt to write things that matter to them, such as printing their own names and those of their family members and pets. They usually pretend to write and read as fluently as adults do, for instance, scribbling rapidly to imitate the literate adult's handwriting or talking while looking at a newspaper. Young children often pretend to read a picture book by telling a story using the pictures as a prop. Their retellings incorporate words and phrases from the text of the book, and often they will memorize the entire text of a favorite book. But it isn't just having books around, as important as that is, that invites children into the world of literacy.

Language is a social instrument and is fundamentally interactive. In fact, it is the interaction that surrounds significant pieces of print—whether it is a grocery shopping list, a story on computer, or an e-mail message from family or friend—that urges children to invest the effort and concentration necessary to learn to read and write at a level that is acceptable to their dominant culture. What counts as being literate varies from one culture to the next, depending on what types and levels of literacy are required to participate fully in life and work and have a voice in community and society.

Many of the things that very young children are taught in the name of literacy are exceedingly difficult for them to understand. One kindergarten teacher's manual, for example, includes a lesson on helping five-year-olds to determine which syllable is emphasized in the words that they hear. In order to accomplish this task, the child would first need to understand what a syllable is and would also need to have sufficient audi-

tory discrimination to hear the emphasis. Yet in reality, many five-year-old children are baffled by this level of word analysis. They cannot always tell where the flow of speech that they hear is separated into words, much less syllables.

In helping children become literate, there are fundamental differences of opinion about how best to achieve success. Some experts make the part-to-whole argument in which young children first learn the alphabet, then connect letters with sounds, then begin building words, then progress to simple sentences, and finally are able to read paragraphs and books. In this skills-based approach, teachers tend to rely on direct instruction of skills and concentrate on giving students practice with these skills. In contrast, the whole-to-part approach argues that, under normal conditions of repeated exposure to favorite picture books, many young children learn to read. Using this literature-based approach, the emphasis is on oral language.

Best practices in early literacy combine the two approaches. This approach is called "balanced literacy" because it seeks to capitalize on the strengths of a literature-based approach such as child-initiated writing, self-selection of reading materials, and individualization, and, at the same time, utilize the strengths of direct instruction, such as systematic instruction in phonics and opportunities for guided practice in basic skills.

As you work with young children, it is important to keep their inexperience in mind and to build on their assets in oral language. It is also important to maintain a balanced literacy program capable of optimizing the potential of every child in the diverse groups of learners found in early childhood programs.

to read and write many years ago should remember the difficulty and celebrate what children know when they come to us.

Learning to Write

In the past, teachers and parents assumed that children would learn to write after they learned to read and that this learning would take place primarily in a school setting. That view of writing dominated the instructional literature for years. Then in 1971, Carol Chomsky made a radical departure from the traditional view when she advocated that nonreaders should be writing and that reading instruction should begin with writing. Since that time, there has been a flurry of research activity focusing on young children and their writing. The resulting information has greatly expanded the view of writing—what it is, how it develops, and how best to teach it.

The more traditional view defined **writing** in terms that were mostly limited to handwriting. Children were expected to copy letters until they could reproduce close approximations of the teacher's model. Then they were expected to copy sentences. Teachers often gave children exercises in a handwriting text to copy or began the schoolday by writing a poem or a quotation on the board for the children to copy. Children's attempts at writing on their own were basically ignored or perhaps even punished—certainly not encouraged (Atkins 1984). In light of the research conducted since the 1970s, however, writing is generally defined more broadly today to include children's efforts at making marks on paper—beginning with scribbles.

We now recognize that children construct their understanding of written language in a developmental sequence that is observable and very similar in all children. The stages of writing development have been described by Temple et al. (1993), Clay (1975), and Ferreiro and Teberosky (1982). These stages are outlined in the following sections.

Development of Writing

Scribbling Stage

Writing begins with *scribbling*, as illustrated in Figure 10.6. A scribble may seem to be only random marks on a paper. But in this example, note that the child (who is three years, six months old) has begun to make some lines (the up-and-down marks at the top) that are more like writing and has contained the major part of the scribble in a box. This scribble indicates increasing control of the writing instrument and increasing knowledge of letter shapes. This child says he has written *Milk, hotdogs, and mustard.*

Parents and teachers of scribblers should provide them with a variety of materials, such as paint, books, paper, and crayons. Parents and teachers should label the children's scribbling as "writing" and model writing just as they model reading for their children. Parents can model writing in everyday

www.
www.ncte.org/prog/writing/
research/113328.htm
An NCTE position statement
on writing in the early grades

www.
www.readwritethink.org/
lessons/lesson_view.
asp?id=45
A lesson plan for Draw a Story:
Stepping from Pictures to
Writing

FIGURE 10.6

Scribbling

situations, for instance, saying "We are almost out of milk. We should write it on our grocery list," or "I am writing a letter to Aunt Sue. Would you like to write something to her?" or "I am going to leave a note for Daddy so he will know where we are," and so on. Parents should also read aloud and encourage children to talk to one another and to adults.

Linear Repetitive Stage

The next stage in writing development is the *linear repetitive stage*. In this stage, children discover that writing is usually horizontal and that letters appear in a string across a page. Children in this stage think that a word referring to something large has a longer string of forms than a word referring to something small (Ferreiro and Teberosky 1982; Schickedanz 1988). In other words, children look for concrete connections between words and their referents.

Figure 10.7 is an example of linear repetitive writing. Given a form, the child completed it with linear scribbles. Such examples of writing provide opportunities to observe children's knowledge of print as they use it in different ways. Figure 10.8 shows how the child (three years, six months old) made shapes in a linear pattern. The longer (bottom) scribble translates to *mustard*, and the shorter (top) scribble is *milk*.

Children in the linear repetitive stage need the same support that scribblers need from parents and teachers. Adults might also begin watching for the emergence of letter forms.

Random-Letter Stage

The next stage is the *random-letter stage*, in which children learn which forms are acceptable as letters and use them in some random order to record words or sentences. Children produce strings of letters that have no relation to the sounds of the words they are attempting to record. They may also include some forms that are not recognizable as letters because their repertoire of letters is so limited.

The five-year-old child who created Figure 10.9 wrote *This is a ghost.* But the five-year-old who created Figure 10.10, when asked what it said, responded, "I don't know what it says. I can't read." Perhaps he was merely making a list of letters that he knows or experimenting with letter shapes and had no intention of saying anything with this writing. If this child does

FIGURE 10.7

Linear Repetitive Writing

FIGURE 10.8

Linear Repetitive Writing

FIGURE 10.9

Random-Letter Writing

FIGURE 10.10

Random-Letter Writing

not write to communicate a message at least occasionally, his teacher should stress to him the communicative nature of print. An example would be to attach a note on the cracker basket at snack time that says "2 Ritz crackers, 1 Vanilla wafer." Such a purposeful use of print can be applied all through the day.

Figure 10.11 is an example of a common feature in children's early writing: using a set of letters that they know (often the letters of their name) by writing them again and again and saying that they carry a message. This child wrote *Once upon a time two little girls liked to play outside. I like to play outside, I said. Let's go see your snowman, said sister. The end.*

FIGURE 10.11

Random-Letter Writing

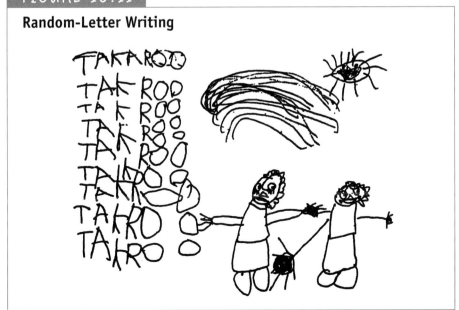

Teachers and parents should encourage children's attempts to write. Children need the adults around them to respond to the intent of their writing, not to correct their form. If the people around them honor their attempts to write and treat their writing as important, children's writing skills will grow. Just as we know that a child who is saying "goed" is actually making progress in learning language, we know that a child who has discovered letters and understands that they stand for thoughts has made progress in learning about written language.

Letter-Name, or Phonetic, Writing

The next stage of development is that of *early phonetic writing,* in which children begin to make the connection between letters and sounds. The beginning of this stage is often described as *letter-name writing* because children write the letters whose names and sounds are the same. For example, they write the word *you* with the letter *u.* They begin to represent words with graphemes that reflect exactly what they hear.

Figure 10.12 is an example of early phonetic writing. In this sample, the child (five years old) has used dots to mark the spaces between words, which is a common feature in beginning writing. These words say *Sweater, socks, hats, jacket.*

Figure 10.13 is an example of *late phonetic writing,* when the child has mastered many print conventions, such as the spaces between words, but spells many words phonetically. With a little practice, one can read phonetic writing. This sample says *The turtle drinks a bowl of water. A turtle has to stay by a tree. My turtle was born at my grandma's. It was as big as a quarter. A turtle is born in an egg. Turtles carry their home on their back.*

NAEYC CRITERIA
2.36

FIGURE 10.12

Early Phonetic Writing

FIGURE 10.13

Late Phonetic Writing

Transitional Spelling

As children learn more about the written language system, they begin to learn the conventions of written language. They begin to spell some words in conventional ways, even though their spelling up to this point has been phonetic. A good example is the word *love*. Because children are exposed to this word so often, they begin to spell it in its conventional form very early. *The* is another common example. This stage of spelling is called *transitional* to indicate that children are moving from phonetic spelling to more standard or conventional spelling.

Figure 10.14 is an example of transitional spelling. Much of the writing is correct by conventional standards. Note the spelling of *they* (*thay*) using a pattern that works with other English words, such as *day, pray,* and so on. This child will learn that *they* is an exception to the usual pattern. In the line that begins *The smoning,* the child probably meant to put the *s* on *the* (for *this*) but put it with *moning* (*morning*). Teachers should ask children to read back their writing so that they learn to catch these errors themselves. Children's writing is less automatic than that of adults, so their thinking gets ahead of their production.

Teachers and parents can foster independence in writing at this stage by asking children how they think words are spelled, by supplying needed information, and by encouraging children to help one another in the writing process. Instruction in spelling as an isolated subject is not necessary at this point. Children will learn to spell conventionally the words they need for writing. In Figure 10.14, much of the writing is correct. Teachers should focus on how much children know at this stage, rather than correcting spellings they do not yet know.

Conventional Spelling

Finally, children achieve mostly *conventional spelling*. Just as children move slowly from babbling to adult speech, they need time to learn the conventions of written language. Adult speech is not mastered without considerable time and effort from the learner and support from sensitive adults. Children deserve the same support as they move from scribbling to mature writing.

Figure 10.15 is an example of conventional spelling, written by a child in the summer after first grade. Note that this child spells all the words conventionally and has also mastered apostrophes. She makes a line to indicate a substitution for a word that she marked out. The spacing makes the line "I like to sail with my mom and get a tan" a little more difficult to read, but generally the spacing is appropriate.

FIGURE 10.14

Transitional Spelling

One deay I promist
Emily M. that I would
play with her. And the
day befor that I promist
Grace I word play with
her. The smoning thay came
up to me!

FIGURE 10.15

Conventional Spelling

I Live on the beach,
that's where I Like
to find SeaGlass
at the beach.
I Like to swim,
Shells, I collect
Sail with my like to
Mom and get
a tan. collect

Conventions of Written Language

Children must learn other elements of written language that are not related to representing sounds with specific letters or combinations of letters. One of these elements is *directionality:* the convention that in English, writing begins on the left and moves to the right. Other conventions include the use of space around words and the use of abbreviations. Children must also learn to arrange words on a page and in a book. Children may temporarily ignore what they know about directionality if they cannot fit a word on a page or line. Through experience, they learn to carry words over to the next page or to put extra words on the backs of pages.

Graves and Stuart (1985) observed that the space around words was negative space and that learning what to do with it was a difficult concept for young children. Some children attempted to fill up negative space by placing periods between the words. They recognized spaces but tried to make them positive rather than negative.

In order to make all these discoveries about written language, children need experience exploring writing, opportunities to make hypotheses about how print works, and feedback that verifies their guesses. Teachers and parents who recognize that children are exploring the flexibility of written language and constructing an understanding of what is possible will be able to foster growth in children's writing. They will offer many opportunities for writing, will recognize most mistakes as explorations of the written language system, and will be able to celebrate the growth that they can observe in the children's understanding.

The Learning Plan that follows addresses the use of two writing conventions: capitalization and punctuation of sentences. This plan is intended for first-graders.

LEARNING PLAN | A Learning Plan on Writing: First Grade

Students: A small group of not more than six children who often fail to capitalize the first word in a sentence or fail to punctuate a sentence

Materials: At least one book per child and a piece of text that has no capital letters and no punctuation marks but is otherwise readable

Procedure:

1. Ask each child to look at one of the books and locate a sentence in it. (This assumes the children have had enough reading experience to know the meaning of *sentence.*)
2. Ask each child to point to the letter at the beginning of the sentence.
3. Ask one person what she notices about this letter. When she says it is "a capital letter," ask all the others if they also have a capital letter at the beginning of the sentence.
4. Ask what is at the end of the sentence. (A punctuation mark.)
5. Ask the children why the author used a capital letter at the beginning and a punctuation mark at the end of each sentence. (Children's explanations should include "To make it easier for the reader to know where the sentence begins and ends"; if not, supply that yourself.) Show the children a piece of text with no capitals and no punctuation marks and discuss how difficult it is to read without these indicators.
6. Remind children that when they write, they will really help the reader if they always use a capital letter at the beginning and a punctuation mark at the end of each sentence.

Assessment: Over the next few days, pay special attention to capital letters and punctuation marks in children's writing in journals and in any other writing.

The Writing Process with Young Children

Much has been written in recent years about the writing process and means of implementing it across the curriculum so that elementary children can achieve competence in writing. The work of Graves (1994) and Calkins (1986) has been helpful to teachers of older elementary children who want to create an environment that promotes writing skills and to take the time necessary to implement the process. The whole point of emphasizing the process of writing is to help teachers move away from giving children isolated bits and pieces of instruction in the conventions of printed language and toward helping children learn those conventions while engaging in relevant and meaningful writing activities.

Helping younger children write meaningfully requires providing the necessary tools (paper, writing instruments) and helping children appreciate the usefulness of writing. Even very young children should be encouraged to keep journals in which they can record their experiences and feelings. Young children may begin by drawing pictures and talking about them. As they participate in classroom activities, they may begin to use letters or words and phrases to aid in expressing their ideas. Gradually, the amount of writing will increase. Teachers of young children should be aware that not all children will choose to write in journals. Children are to be encouraged but not forced to write in their journals regularly.

Figure 10.16 shows three samples of writing taken from a first-grade child at one-month intervals. Note the progress this child has made with only two months of school experience as a writer. Green (1998) kept a record of children's writing by asking three- and four-year-olds to sign in each day. She recorded the changes in how they wrote their names from September to April and classified them into the following categories: *controlled scribbles, controlled scribbles and mock letters, one or two letters of name, full first name letters out of order,* and *full first name letters in order.* For the four-year-olds, she added the categories *first and part of last* and *first and last, complete.*

PRAXIS

Be able to plan a unit that incorporates the writing process for young children

NAEYC CRITERIA
2.33

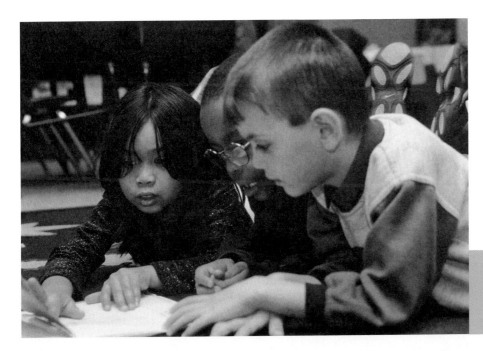

These children are sharing their writing and working collaboratively in developing their literacy abilities.

FIGURE 10.16

First-Grader's Writing at One-Month Intervals

9-10-93
BOT

First Month

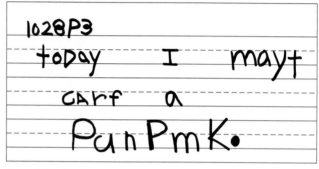

1028P3
today   I   mayt
carf   a
PunPmK.

Second Month

I Like School
School is fun
We get   to   go
outseid   wen   the
Bell   rings   We
have   to   go   inseid ⊃

Third Month

Green learned much about the children's development as writers from this activity and had opportunities to observe their discoveries about print, such as spacing, letter reversals, and so on. Teachers need to find their own systems for observing children's writing carefully.

Journal Writing

Providing journals and a time for writing in them is a strategy that will be successful for some four-year-olds and most five-year-olds. **Journal writing** may begin with drawing pictures and eventually move to writing messages and then to recording ideas. A journal in which the entries are dated and the teacher has sometimes recorded what the child has "read" from her writing will serve as an excellent record of the child's progress in writing.

When milestones are reached, copies of significant pages can be made and sent home to parents. Some primary-grade children may want parts of their journals to remain private, and teachers should respect their wishes.

In the following A Teacher Speaks box, Sandy Bjorklund describes how she structures her day to include time for literacy activities. How could you use her plan to manage literacy instruction?

Assessing the Development of Literacy

The IRA/NAEYC (1998) position statement on reading and writing makes this assertion about assessing literacy:

> Sound assessment should be anchored in real-life writing and reading tasks and continuously chronicle a wide range of children's literacy activities in different situations. Good assessment is essential to help teachers tailor appropriate instruction to young children and to know when and how much intensive instruction on any particular skill or strategy might be needed. . . .
>
> Teachers need to regularly and systematically use multiple indicators—observations of children's oral language, evaluation of children's work, and performance at authentic reading and writing tasks—to assess and monitor children's progress in reading and writing development, plan and adapt instruction, and communicate with parents. (pp. 206, 210)

As a teacher, you will not be able to plan activities that will support a given child's development of literacy without knowing what he understands about reading and writing now. In her book *An Observation Survey of Early Literacy Achievement*, Clay (2002) describes in detail several strategies for observing the literacy development of a child. Three of these techniques are critical for teachers of young children: (1) observing the child's writing, (2) determining his knowledge of books and print, and (3) observing his reading behaviors. Observing a child's oral language is a fourth critical assessment in planning literacy instruction.

Observing Oral Language

The success of literacy instruction is often dependent on the child's oral language ability. If the child does not understand the language of instruction (*first, beginning, last, page, bottom,* and so on), then instruction will not likely be successful. Phonics instruction assumes that once the child has sounded out a word, he will know what the word means. However, it does no good for the reader to sound out words if he does not know what they mean.

The assessment of oral language must be a basic consideration in planning literacy experiences. Much of oral language can be assessed through careful observation of the child's use of language in the classroom. In addition to keeping anecdotal records, teachers who want to use a more systematic assessment can use the Teacher Rating of Oral Language and Literacy, or TROLL (Dickinson, McCabe, and Sprague 2003). This easy-to-use observation guide will help teachers plan for individual instruction.

Observing Writing

As a child writes, the teacher needs to observe the process the child follows on a regular basis and keep samples of her products on at least a biweekly

A **Teacher** SPEAKS: Reading in the Literacy Classroom

Sandy Bjorklund

Madison Camelview School
Phoenix, Arizona

I teach 26 second-graders in an urban school. My classroom includes about 40 percent non- or limited-English speakers and 80 percent subsidized lunch students. Student abilities in reading range from emergent to fluent, and many of my students lack language experience. I strive to make every minute count!

The formal literacy time in my classroom occurs over a two-and-a-half-hour block. My goal is to immerse my students in literacy (reading and writing) during this time. In order to do this, I plan each day based on assessments of individual student needs. Ongoing daily assessments include such things as running records, samples of student writing, observations made during rove time, and monitoring notes. Monitoring notes can be formal (i.e., when taken during a reading group) or informal. I use these notes, along with student draft books, for parent conferences and progress reports.

Learners are grouped in both reading and writing based on individual strengths and their next teaching point. Groups change often—in some cases, daily—to meet the learners' needs. Short, focused teaching is used during these times with the whole group, small groups, and individuals.

In order for me to have the opportunity to work with learners individually or in small groups, students need to be able to work independently. To achieve this, each student is given a daily plan. This plan provides the literacy activities students should be working on when not working with me. The plan sheet changes over the course of the year, but children are expected to write, read from independent book boxes, practice spelling, and work on handwriting. After these four parts of the plan are completed, they can choose language activities around the room from their plan, such as listening center, exploring books, alphabet games and puzzles, whiteboards, buddy reading, word-building activities, and chalkboard.

My plan of the day is built to include a number of short pieces of instruction interspersed within literacy time. I call this the "Yo-Yo" method of instruction, as I constantly pull the kids back to the whole group for short instructional objectives. The rest of the literacy block is divided as follows:

- *Write to . . .* (10–15 minutes): I model some piece of the writing process. This might be shared writing with the students helping me compose the piece, depending on my focused teaching objective.
- *Students work on their daily plans* (35 minutes): I pull two small groups for reading and/or writing instruction and move between meeting with the groups and working with individuals.
- *Read to whole group* (20 minutes): I read to the children from a book that meets a focused objective. Often this objective is linked to the writing process, and thus we read like writers, discussing what good writers do.
- *Students work on their daily plans* (20 minutes): I work with one small group and rove among individual students.
- *Skills instruction with whole group* (15 minutes): This lesson may cover phonics, word study, or the mechanics of writing. The lesson is always based on teacher observation/assessment and is always taken from whole to part in order to show the skill in the context of meaning.
- *Students work on their daily plans* (20 minutes): I rove and support students in checking that they have accomplished their plans for the day.
- *Status of class* (10 minutes): Students open their draft books on their desks with their daily plans visible. I check to make sure they have met the expectations for that day and guide students in what they will do the next day.
- *Share published works* (10 minutes): Students may choose to share any work they have published before giving it to the intended audience.

This is an overview of the literacy time block in my classroom. It did not happen quickly but evolved as my understanding grew. I suggest that a new teacher begin slowly and stay focused on a smaller piece of the process until it is working successfully.

basis. Observing the process will provide information about how many letters the child can use in writing, what she knows about the directionality of print, how she solves problems such as spelling unknown words, and how she works at writing. (Is it with pleasure, or does it seem to be a struggle?)

Observing the products of writing can produce information about what the child knows about letters, sound–letter relationships, and punctuation and other conventions of writing (Button, Johnson, and Furgerson 1996). Such observations can help in judging the zone of proximal development for that child. For example, if a child spells *friend* as *frend*, then a little assistance will enable her to spell the word in the conventional way. If, however, the child spells *friend* as *frd*, then it seems likely that she is hearing the beginning and ending sounds of words and recording them accurately, but trying to teach the conventional spelling of *friend* would probably not be useful at this time (Taylor 1996).

Determining Knowledge of Books and Print

In observing how children handle books and what they know about print, the teacher may ask each child individually to show her the parts of the book (such as the front and back), where to start reading, what to do when finished reading one page, and where the top of the page is. The teacher might also ask the child to point to an uppercase letter, to point out a certain word, and so on.

PRAXIS

Be able to describe the value of books in helping children decode sentences and recognize word families

The teacher may also observe the children's behavior with books as they choose them from the classroom library shelves. Observing younger children will reveal if they know how to hold a book, which way is right side up, or how to turn the pages. Observing older children will provide information about how they determine which book to read and what they are interested in (Harp 2006).

In addition, the teacher will want to know how many letters children can recognize, whether they can distinguish lowercase and capital letters, what concept they have of *word,* and so on. Much of this information can be gained from careful observations of the children's writing. If more information is needed, then the Concepts about Print test described in *An Observation Survey* (Clay 2002) can be administered.

Observing Reading

Many effective techniques are available for observing children's reading behaviors. For instance, keeping running records or miscue inventories is an excellent means of learning what children know and can do as readers. Each of these records is taken as the child reads aloud a selected text. For younger children, this text is often their own writing. As the child reads, the teacher marks exactly what the child does and says.

Clay (2002) has developed a set of conventions for marking such records so that they can be shared with others. Goodman and Marek (1996) have also developed a system for recording and analyzing reading behaviors. Please consult these sources for details on marking and analyzing reading behaviors.

Listening carefully to a child read can reveal what kinds of errors she makes, how often the child corrects her own errors, and other reading behaviors such as finger pointing and reading word for word. Each of these recording systems also includes checking the child's comprehension of the text. The value of such records is that over time, the child's growth as a reader can be documented and appropriate instruction can be planned.

INTEGRATING the CURRICULUM

Continuing our theme of spaces, *here are some suggestions for literacy experiences:*

- Have each child draw a favorite space and write a description of it.

- Have the children pay close attention to how the author and illustrator use space in a picture book. How are the words arranged on the page? Are there any empty spaces? If so, why are they there?

- With the children, examine the fonts in several picture books. Then compare them. How do these fonts and the spaces they use add to the message of the words? What do large letters that take up a lot of space mean? Is the author indicating that these words are being shouted?

- Try to read aloud a short piece of text with no spaces. Discuss how the spaces between the words help the reader.

- Make one list of the criteria for a good reading space and another of the criteria for a good writing space. Are they the same? Do all the children agree on what is a good space?

- How can the space in the class reading area be made more comfortable? More attractive? What would the children like to see there?

- Compare the sizes of several of the children's favorite books. Does the space each book takes up (its size) connect somehow to its content?

- As a class, make a list of descriptive words that could be used to describe happy spaces.

- As a class, make a list of spaces outside where print can be found.

- Find and talk together about spaces that have rules for using them posted (such as swimming pools, skating rinks, recreation areas).

- With the children, make a list of rules for using classroom spaces and then post it.

- Talk about spaces in the neighborhood where it's common to find people reading and writing. Make a list of these places, and if possible, visit each one to check the predictions and note what kind of reading and writing are being done there.

- If a child has no space at home to keep her books, try to find a source for small bookshelves. Students in a woodworking class at a local high school might be interested. People find spaces for what they believe is important, and children need to feel that books are important.

CHILDREN WITH SPECIAL NEEDS

www.ldonline.org/ld_indepth/ teaching_techniques/ strategies.html

Tips for teaching children with special needs

Certain children may need special help in becoming successful users of printed language. Although some schools place all students with disabilities in very structured, direct instruction programs, more and more special educators are finding that these students respond to the principles of developmentally appropriate practice just like their classmates do. Special-needs students need choices, chances to follow their own interests, and opportunities for success as much as any other children.

One approach that may be helpful in teaching children with special needs is for the teacher to spend extra time with them in techniques such as assisted reading. Giving these children more specific strategy instruction in the context of authentic reading experiences may also prove beneficial (Sears, Carpenter, and Burstein 1994). Teachers must also use observational strategies to discover children's understanding of the reading and writing processes before attempting to help them learn successive steps.

Children with physical disabilities, such as sight or hearing loss, may need special materials to make their encounters with print successful. Teachers may need to provide materials printed in braille or very large print for children with vision limitations. Teachers may need to learn to sign or to have an interpreter present to take dictation from children who use sign rather than spoken language. Children who cannot hold ordinary writing instruments may need an adult or older child to act as a scribe for them; children who have difficulty with controlling pens or pencils can learn to use typewriters or computers to communicate.

Some children may require more specialized equipment in order to engage in literacy activities with other learners and become literate. Langone, Malone, and Kinsley (1999) state that assistive technology is not only beneficial in helping children become as independent as possible but that it is mandated by law when appropriate. Such assistive technology devices as portable keyboards, touch screens, speech synthesizers, and voice recognition devices can help children with disabilities participate in all classroom activities—from composing stories to completing research on topics of their choice.

Beyond these special materials and devices, children with sight or hearing challenges need teachers who assume that they will be successful, who determine what they know (even though it may take some outside help to do so), and who support their learning. It is important to remember that these children need to read and write about what is meaningful to them and to learn what they want to learn at the time, not what the teacher may have planned.

Ruiz (1995) documented the stages that her child who was deaf went through in learning to write. One of the outcomes of this study was to verify that children do not need a perfect, overlearned mastery of sound–letter relationships in order to be successful readers and writers. Ruiz's daughter learned to read and write with very little sound knowledge at all but in stages that roughly parallel those of hearing children.

Children who have not achieved the oral language skills typical of their age group may need more opportunities to learn and practice oral language forms. When words are introduced in print, some children may need more background experiences in order to develop meanings for these words. Teachers should arrange for children who have language delays to interact with other children as much as possible and to talk with adults, as well.

CELEBRATING DIVERSITY

Most classrooms have some students who are bilingual or who represent various cultural and ethnic groups. Helping these children continue to develop as readers and writers is an extremely important task. Recall

www.
www.ericdigests.org/
1992-4/diverse.htm
Research on teaching
diverse populations

Cambourne's (1995) condition of expectation and the concept of engagement, as discussed earlier in this chapter. Teachers must expect that all children are users of literacy in some way and try to discover what they know about print and how print is used in their homes.

Teachers must also consider how to engage children and take steps to see that the classroom activities are appropriate and meaningful for all children, not just those from mainstream cultural groups or whose first language is English. As Schmidt (1995) states, "Schools may actually interfere with children's literacy learning if educators do not work to understand the diverse backgrounds of the children in their classrooms. Schools must take the first steps toward connecting with the children's cultures" (p. 411).

Activities that are arranged around meaningful themes may help children who are English language learners become more skilled as readers and writers and speakers of English (Ernst and Richard 1995; Twiss 1996). For example, as children study houses, they can draw pictures of the houses they live in now and the houses they lived in before in their native countries. Sharing these children's pictures with the class provides opportunities for meaningful oral experiences and writing and reading experiences, whether in English or in students' native languages.

Learning to use what children know—such as how to recite street rhymes or classify grocery coupons—can help children feel that the literacy of their households is important and valued. Families can be encouraged to keep their own albums of literacy activities, perhaps using some materials provided by the school (Clements and Warncke 1994). Teachers can also use sharing time to help children present objects and events that are important to them and their families.

As noted earlier, teachers of children who speak dialects need to value the children's language and encourage them to develop their dialectal abilities while providing models of standard English when appropriate. For example, a child may communicate more effectively in his dialect on the playground but need a model of standard English when he has the opportunity to interview a guest speaker. Teachers who value children's language will not correct the use of dialects but will acknowledge them as an acceptable form of communication.

When taking dictation from a child who speaks a dialect, the teacher should record the words in conventional spelling but not change the syntactical structure of the child's utterances. As a child reads from charts or books, the teacher should not correct the child who reads the text "My mother is going to work" as "My mama be going to work." The child has demonstrated an understanding of the printed text, and that is much more important than an absolutely perfect rendering of the text at this point.

According to Sanacore (2004), many African American children have a cultural background that does not match the what the school expects of them. If teachers modify their instruction so that it is more interactive and includes more physical movement, it can make a difference in the achievement of some students. Respecting the child's dialect also may help her become more willing to learn another oral form, standard English.

English language learners need many opportunities to interact with English-speaking children and adults. The worst possible approach is to isolate such children from the other children in order to give them special help in learning English. Children who play and talk with other children who speak English will learn the language quickly.

Teachers should allow children to use their native languages when necessary for communication. In past years, schools often limited children's use of native languages in order to force them to speak English more quickly (Watts-Taffe and Truscott 2000). This approach does not facilitate more rapid learning of English; rather, it does much harm to children's self-concepts and feelings of acceptance and actually hinders language development. The goal is not to eliminate children's first language but to help them achieve competence as speakers of a second language.

Ideally, all children would learn to read in their first languages and then be taught to extend their skills in English (Snow et al. 1998). Obviously, this is not always possible; even so, teachers can help children learn English and can use the children's native languages as much as possible in the classroom. Signs, posters, announcements, and other print can be posted in more than one language. Lenters (2004) offers the guidelines in Figure 10.17 for successful reading instruction for young second-language learners.

Freeman and Freeman (1999) urge teachers to be very careful when planning step-by-step instruction in literacy for bilingual speakers. They state, "Never have we seen so much emphasis placed on testing students and putting them into leveled groups. This word-recognition approach specifically targets poor and minority students" (p. 247). Such programs may lead to more failure for these children.

The concerned teacher will also learn enough about a child's native language to recognize where she might have particular difficulties with English. For example, some sounds used in English, such as the *sh* at the beginning of *sheep*, are rare in Spanish; there are differences in syntactical patterns between the two languages, as well. Chapter 9 mentioned the differences in placement of adjectives in Spanish sentences; Spanish also allows redundancy. A Spanish-speaking child might say "My mother, she," which is acceptable in Spanish. Some languages, such as Chinese, are not alphabetical; for Chinese children, teachers can provide experiences with sound–letter relationships in meaningful contexts. As a child begins to learn words in English, the teacher will record those words in print for the child and will make sure that the child has many opportunities to write and explore English (Brewer 1998b).

Rubin and Carlan (2005) suggest that teachers of bilingual children use their writing in order to assess what they understand about English and how it is written. Children who are bilingual make progress in writing in stages that are very similar to those of monolingual children; thus, their writing can reveal a great deal about what they understand.

Finally, using literature that represents the cultures of the children in the school in an authentic manner is an extremely effective means of celebrating diversity. Teachers should try to find books printed in the languages of the children and use them for read-alouds, perhaps bringing in parents or volunteers. All children need to be able to find positive images of themselves in books and other print media. Finding just the right book or story can help a child see the importance of his culture and its literacy. For young learners especially, Opitz (1999) suggests that teachers attend to the supports in the texts of culturally appropriate books as well as to their cultural content. *Supports* are defined as rhyming texts, texts with repetition, familiar events or sequences, and illustrations that readers can use.

FIGURE 10.17

Guidelines for Reading Instruction for Young Second-Language Learners

Oral Language

- Develop the child's oral vocabulary to the point of basic communicative competence before attempting reading instruction.
- Continue to work on vocabulary training with the child well beyond the point of basic communicative competence to ensure adequate vocabulary for increasingly more difficult text.
- Provide opportunity for second-language children to converse in the classroom, being careful not to place undue emphasis on accurate speech.

Reading Materials

- Remember that the child must know 90% to 95% of the vocabulary in the text before that text is used for reading instructional purposes.
- Use graded readers with second-language readers to ensure that text difficulty keeps pace with vocabulary development. But be sure to supplement with authentic literature first in read-alouds, then shared reading, and finally independent reading to ensure second-language readers are exposed to text that reflects natural speech.
- Encourage and provide opportunity for rereading of text.

Phonemic Awareness

- Extend phonemic awareness training to include phonics instruction, using materials that teach sound–symbol correspondences in a multisensory and systematic manner.

Comprehension

- Use a language experience approach to provide meaningful materials the child is able to read.
- Pay attention to cultural biases in text and illustrations presented to young second-language learners.
- Fill in the missing cultural information when materials must be used that are culturally unfamiliar to the learner.
- When possible, use translations alongside English texts to enhance comprehension and support first-language reading skills. Parents and older siblings may be enlisted for this process.
- Allow students to respond to text in their first language.

First-Language Reading Support

- Form strong home-school connections with the families of second-language learners.
- Value the child's first language.
- Find any means possible to ensure that the child receives reading instruction in his or her first language.

Source: Figure (p. 332) from Kimberly Lenters, "No Half Measures: Reading Instruction for Young Second-Language Learners," *The Reading Teacher* 58, 4 (December/January 2004): 328–336. Reprinted with permission of the International Reading Association. All rights reserved.

- *Literacy* is broadly defined as the ability to read and write well enough to meet one's personal needs, solve problems, learn information, and find pleasure in the written word. Literacy is best conceptualized as a continuum beginning at birth and having no end point. Children come to school not as blank slates but as knowledgeable about print in some way and at some level. Being able to help children become more literate is a critical teaching skill.

- Teachers who support literacy development evaluate and become responsible consumers of research, understand how literacy develops, know the cueing systems and their importance in helping children become literate, and plan classrooms where learning to be more literate is supported by the environment.

- A successful literacy program includes a range of elements. It is based on a set of goals that are the foundation for all instruction, and it uses the standards for literacy development as a framework for planning. Providing a supportive classroom environment is also key to a program's success. Other important elements are an emphasis on oral language and listening, musical experiences that promote literacy, story reading and storytelling that engage children, opportunities to learn about print, instruction that helps children attend to sound, and the presentation of appropriate texts to learners.

- Children learn to write (compose) in a process that is observable and predictable, although there are individual variations in any learning. The development of writing moves through observable stages: scribbling, linear repetitive writing, random-letter writing, letter-name or phonetic writing, transitional spelling, and conventional spelling. Through experiences with print and writing, children also learn the conventions of written language.

- Assessing literacy requires close observation of the child's behavior as a speaker, a reader, and a writer. More formal assessment may be required for individual children, such as the Teacher Rating of Oral Language and Literacy (TROLL). Observing writing requires that teachers collect samples of children's writing and talk to children about their work.

- Children with special needs may need additional help in becoming literate. Sometimes this help is provided by a special education teacher, but often it is the classroom teacher who must provide extra instruction, such as more assisted reading. Children with physical disabilities may require adaptations including special materials and assistive devices.

- All children's oral language skills and knowledge of print must be assessed individually before instruction is offered. Such assessment is especially important for English language learners, who need opportunities to learn English while also learning to read and write in English. Most researchers believe it would be beneficial if each child could learn to read in his native language, but that will not happen in most schools. Therefore, the teacher must try to learn what the child knows about literacy in either his native language or in English and build on that knowledge to help the child become a successful learner.

REFLECTIONS

1. So much has been written about literacy in the popular press, in scholarly journals, and in "how to do it" books and magazines that it is difficult to believe that any student could come to this chapter without already having some ideas and perhaps strong feelings about what is good for children in terms of literacy. Think about the suggestions in this chapter for helping children develop literacy, and list the three or four that make the most sense to you. Can you defend these ideas with research? Experience? If

not, how can you apply these ideas as a teacher of young children? Or can you?

2. Children's books are an integral part of a good literacy program. Is choosing the very best books for children important to your program, or are any books valuable so long as you can get children to read them or listen to them read? Explain your answer.

3. Create a plan for assessing the literacy development of a class of four-year-olds. Outline your plan for the first weeks of school and then for the entire schoolyear. Does your plan reveal how you feel about literacy instruction? How should your assessment plan relate to your teaching ideas?

4. What would you say to a parent (or school administrator) who does not want any children's writing that contains unconventional spelling? Is the use of conventional spelling more important than the act of composition? How can you balance the demand for perfection and your knowledge of children's development?

5. Phonics instruction is at the center of much controversy in educational circles. Most teachers agree that children need some phonics instruction, but they generally do not agree on the details of how and when and how much. How would you plan a phonics lesson for a group of five-year-old children whose background includes few literacy experiences? Many literacy experiences? Who are already reading?

EXPLORATIONS AND ACTIVITIES

1. Observe a first-grade class for at least an hour, and note what literacy activities and experiences are provided for the children. Also, note the time spent in whole-group instruction, small-group instruction, and individual instruction. Evaluate the quality of the instruction for a very skilled first-grader and a not-so-skilled first-grader. Was the instruction better for one learner than the other? If so, how could you have adapted the instruction to better meet the needs of both groups?

2. Examine the materials used for literacy instruction in a preschool program, a kindergarten, or the primary grades. Do these materials seem appropriate for all the children in the program? Do teachers use these materials as a resource or as the actual program? Would you be comfortable using these materials? If so, explain how they fit your philosophy of literacy development. If not, explain why not and what would need to change for you to be comfortable.

mylabschool
Where the classroom comes to life!

MyLabSchool is a collection of online tools for your success in this course, your licensure exams, and your teaching career. Visit **www.mylabschool.com** to access the following:

■ Online Study Guide
■ Video Cases from real classrooms
■ Help with your research papers using Research Navigator
■ Career Center with resources for:
    —Praxis and Licensure Preparation
    —Professional Portfolio Development
    —Job Search and Interview Techniques
    —Lesson Planning

CHAPTER **11**

KEY TERMS *you'll find in this chapter:*

- **Algorithm**, 355
- **Communication**, 371
- **Content strands**, 354
- **Functions**, 367
- **Logico-mathematical learning**, 350
- **Manipulatives**, 372
- **Mathematics**, 350
- **Patterns**, 366
- **Problem solving**, 369
- **Process strands**, 355
- **Reflective abstraction**, 352
- **Representation**, 372
- **Simple abstraction**, 351
- **Strand model**, 354

Manipulation and Discovery through Mathematics

FOCUS QUESTIONS

- What is *mathematics* for young children?
- How do children learn mathematics?
- How should teachers teach mathematics, based on the strand model and national standards?
- How should teachers select appropriate materials for mathematics instruction?
- How can mathematics be integrated with other subjects in the curriculum?
- How can teachers assess children's mathematical understanding?
- What adaptations will teachers of mathematics need to consider for children with special needs?
- How can diversity be recognized in the mathematics classroom?

When you were assigned to observe mathematics instruction this week, you thought you would see young children working the simple addition problems you remembered from your own childhood. You visited a kindergarten classroom and observed the children playing. The teacher helped you see the geometry they were learning in block play and in playing with pattern blocks, the patterns they were creating in art, the measuring they were doing as they compared the sizes of three pumpkins, the counting they were doing as they prepared and ate their snack, and the computations they did to solve the problems of how many more sunny days they had recorded than cloudy ones and how many children wanted a rabbit for a pet versus how many wanted a gerbil. You were impressed; these children were really mathematical thinkers.

During your discussion of your observations, many of your peers shared your observations of mathematics embedded in the curriculum, but others had observed children engaged in completing worksheets as part of a formal math curriculum. These children were able to add and subtract numbers totaling ten or less, and a few were able to regroup and work with numbers larger than ten.

When you heard these reports, you were anxious about mathematics instruction. What is the best way to help children learn about math? What kind of experiences are most valuable for young learners? You know that math is a major part of the state tests and wonder what kind of instruction will help children be successful on those tests. ■

Defining Mathematics

This chapter and the next, on mathematics and science, are titled "Manipulation and Discovery" because young children learn mathematics and science from their manipulation of objects and their discovery of relationships and patterns in their environments.

Mathematics means much more than just *arithmetic*. Perhaps when you were a child, math meant practicing arithmetic: working addition, subtraction, and multiplication problems on reams of ditto sheets. If you think of math for young children as limited to such simple equations as 1 + 1 = 2, observe young children for a few minutes while they play. You will become aware of both their interest in mathematics and the scope of mathematics itself: "You got a bigger cookie than me!" "I am taller than you." "I have more clay than you." "I gots five pennies."

Many topics that seem relevant to mathematics activities are also relevant to science activities. As children learn to classify and group and as they think about functions and relationships, they are learning both math and science. In fact, it is often difficult to separate math and science in the early childhood classroom.

The dictionary defines **mathematics** as "the science of numbers and their operations, interrelations, combinations, generalizations, and abstractions, and of space configurations and their structure, measurement, transformations, and generalizations." But for young children, mathematics is a way of viewing the world and their experiences in it. It is a way of solving real problems. It is an understanding of number, operations on number, functions and relations, probability, and measurement. It is much more than the pages of simple equations that you may remember working as a child.

Children are mathematical thinkers outside school. The challenge is to keep that interest, enthusiasm, and curiosity alive in the school setting.

Learning Mathematics

Piaget (1970) describes three ways that human beings learn. They learn from these sources:

1. *The physical world*—Concepts such as *hot, cold, rough, smooth,* and so on
2. *The social world*—Socially transmitted information such as *language, religion, superstition,* and so on
3. *The construction of mental relationships*—Concepts such as counting, seriation, numeration, conservation, and so on

Piaget calls the construction of mental relationships **logico-mathematical learning.** This type of learning will be our focus in this chapter (DeVries and Kohlberg 1987a; Elkind 1998; Kamii and DeClark 1985; Kamii and Joseph 1989; Piaget 1970).

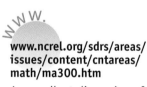

www.ncrel.org/sdrs/areas/ issues/content/cntareas/ math/ma300.htm

An excellent discussion of a critical issue: providing hands-on, minds-on, and authentic learning experiences in mathematics

Logico-mathematical thinking requires the learner to create categories and hierarchies of objects without regard to their physical properties. For example, if you hold three yellow, wooden pencils in your hand, you will observe that they are made of wood and that they are inflexible. Those are physical facts. You cannot decide those characteristics. However, that there is a set of three pencils is a mental construct. They are physically separate objects, but their forming a set of three is a mental relationship.

Think about the concept of *threeness*. It is not dependent on the physical properties of the objects to which you are applying it. You could have three houses, three whales, three mustard seeds, three amoebas, and so on. In sum, the physical characteristics of the objects (including size, shape, color, texture, and temperature) do not determine that there are three; your placing them in a relationship is what makes that determination.

As learners, children abstract certain information from their experiences. For example, children learning color names learn to ignore other properties of objects and to focus on the property of color. Piaget (1970) calls this **simple abstraction** (also known as *empirical abstraction*). Although theorists do not agree on exactly how simple abstraction is accomplished, most believe that children abstract the concept of *color* from repeated experiences with objects that someone labels as *blue, red, yellow,* and other color names. It is sophisticated learning for the child to be able to label as "blue" all the many tints and hues of color that we call blue. Children also make abstractions about the rules that govern language use from repeated experience with language.

However, logico-mathematical concepts cannot be abstracted from experience. If, for example, a child plays with three dolls, he must reflect on the relationship he has created among the dolls; he cannot merely abstract the concept *three* because there are three dolls. We know this is true because we can think about millions, billions, and trillions even though we have

The object of education is to prepare the young to educate themselves throughout their lives.

—*Robert M. Hutchins*

Working with manipulatives helps children construct basic mathematical concepts.

probably never had any experience with sets of this magnitude. We are able to think in these terms because we understand the hierarchical nature of the number system; that is, we understand that millions, billions, and trillions are made up of thousands, hundreds, tens, and ones.

Piaget (1970) explains that we construct ideas by means of logico-mathematical learning by a process called **reflective abstraction.** This process works as follows: The learner manipulates objects and then reflects on the results. This reflection leads to reorganizing her mental constructs. Once this reorganization has taken place, it is impossible for the learner to think in exactly the same way again.

To illustrate the process of reflective abstraction, consider an example from mathematics. Most young children lack number conservation skills. Suppose a young child is presented with two identical sets of objects, such as plastic chips. In one of the sets, the chips are arranged in a row so closely that they almost touch one another; in the other set, the chips are arranged so that there are large spaces between them. Observing these two sets of chips, the young child will believe that the set that occupies the most space contains the most chips. After experience with manipulating sets and reflecting on the number of items in sets arranged in various physical configurations, the child will learn that the physical arrangement has no bearing on the number of objects in the set. This observation will produce a mental reorganization, so the child will never again think that physical configuration influences number.

Even very young children can recognize the difference between numbers of items in small sets—for instance, two cookies compared to five cookies. Piaget (1970) calls these *perceptual numbers*. But with numbers larger than eight or so, perceptions are no longer reliable and a system of numbers must be constructed. This system must be based on the relationship among numbers: that 1 is included in 2, 2 in 3, and so on.

When a child has created this system, he can begin to understand operations on numbers, such as addition, subtraction, multiplication, and division. Children can be taught that 2 + 3 = 5, but *"they cannot be taught directly the relationships underlying this addition"* (Kamii and DeClark 1985, p. 14; italics in original). These relationships must be constructed by the learner, based on his observations.

When we count objects, we have to order them so that each is counted only once. Creating that order is a mental operation. When we order objects from largest to smallest, for instance, we create a relationship among the objects. Concepts of *size*, *time*, and *geometry* must also be constructed by the learner.

Applied to mathematics, Vygotsky's (1978) view would prompt teachers to think about what children might be on the verge of discovering and to provide the materials and assistance that would enhance making those discoveries. Vygotsky's view would not support a step-by-step curriculum that fails to take into account the individual achievement of each child.

Teaching Mathematics

Think once again about your own experiences with math and math teachers. Most students have been in the situation of having a math teacher who truly understood geometry or calculus but could not teach students what he knew.

If math could be taught directly from one person to another, then students could learn what was in the teacher's head. Obviously, that is not the case.

If we accept the thesis that mathematical concepts must be constructed by each learner, based on observations with real-life materials and situations, then what are the responsibilities of the teacher? One responsibility is to supply the language for the concepts that the child is constructing. A child can discover the concept *five* but must have the label "five" supplied. Teachers should use the language that mathematicians use, even with young children. It is no more difficult for children to learn the correct terminology than it is to learn some other terms. Moreover, using the correct terminology from the start will eliminate the need to change terminology in the future (Monroe and Panchyshyn 1994/1995; Tracy 1994).

Another of the teacher's responsibilities is to arrange the environment so that the materials that best represent a concept are available for manipulation and to provide time for manipulation. When children are involved physically, the teacher must also involve them mentally by engaging them in reflective thinking; this can be accomplished through asking questions about what the children observe and then guiding their observations.

We can conclude, then, that mathematics instruction must be based on the hands-on manipulation of objects by learners and that symbols should be introduced after concepts are well in place.

Standards for Mathematics Education

In planning instruction, teachers of young children should also take into account the standards established for this age group. The *National Council of Teachers of Mathematics Standards* (NCTM 2000) for preschool through second grade (Pre-K–2) include five content standards and five process standards:

www.nctm.org/standards/
principles.htm

An explanation of the principles for school mathematics instruction: equity, curriculum, teaching, learning, and assessment

Content Standards	Process Standards
1. Number and operations	1. Problem solving
2. Geometry and spatial sense	2. Reasoning and proof
3. Measurement	3. Communication
4. Patterns, functions, and algebra	4. Connections
5. Data analysis, statistics, and probability	5. Representation

However, it is not possible to separate these standards for content and process in designing mathematics experiences for young children. The standards are interconnected and interwoven throughout the curriculum. For example:

Children recognize patterns of all sorts in the world around them and gradually begin to use patterns as a strategy for solving problems. Both number and geometry are used in measurement, for example, as children answer questions such as "How heavy?" "How big?" and "How tall?" The ability to gather, organize, represent, and use data to answer questions is likely to involve all of the process standards. Skills are acquired in ways that make sense to children. Teachers must continually attend to maintaining a balance

Parents and Mathematics

● Ask parents to observe their children's use of mathematics at home and to keep weekly records of what they see. By doing so, parents will become more aware of how mathematics is used in their children's lives and thus more able to help children make connections between math at school and math at home.

*The National Council of
Teachers of Mathematics (NCTM)
position statement (2000) declares, "All students, regardless
of their personal characteristics, backgrounds, or physical challenges, must
have opportunities to study—and support to learn—mathematics." The joint
position statement from the NAEYC and NCTM (2002) on mathematics
instruction for young children makes the following statement about
instruction in mathematics:*

> In high-quality mathematics education for 3- to 6-year-old children,
> teachers and other key professionals should:
>
> ■ Enhance children's natural interest in mathematics and their dispo-
> sition to use it to make sense of their physical and social worlds
>
> ■ Build on children's varying experiences, including their family, lin-
> guistic, and cultural backgrounds; their individual approaches to
> learning; and their informal knowledge
>
> ■ Base mathematics curriculum and teaching practices on current
> knowledge of young children's cognitive, linguistic, physical, and
> social-emotional development
>
> ■ Use curriculum and teaching practices that strengthen children's
> problem-solving and reasoning processes as well as representing,
> communicating, and connecting mathematical ideas
>
> ■ Ensure that the curriculum is coherent and compatible with known
> relationships and sequences of important mathematical ideas
>
> ■ Provide for children's deep and sustained interaction with key
> mathematical ideas
>
> ■ Integrate mathematics with other activities and other activities
> with mathematics
>
> ■ Provide ample time, materials, and teacher support for children
> to engage in play, a context in which they explore and manipulate
> mathematical ideas with keen interest
>
> ■ Actively introduce mathematical concepts, methods, and language
> through a range of appropriate experiences and teaching strategies
>
> ■ Support children's learning by thoughtfully and continually assess-
> ing all children's mathematical knowledge, skills, and strategies.

Source: National Council of Teachers of Mathematics, "Early Childhood Mathematics Education:
Promoting Good Beginnings." Available online: www.naeyc.org/about/positions/psmath.asp

www.

**http://mathforum.org/
library/levels/elem1**

Suggestions for activities for
prekindergarten through second grade and links to other
resources

between emphasis on conceptual and procedural [skill] aspects of mathematics.
Children whose skills and strategies are based on understanding of fundamental mathematical concepts are more likely to retain and be able to expand their
knowledge and understanding in later years. (NCTM 2000, p. 3)

The Strand Model

The **strand model** is one way of conceptualizing the important elements of
mathematics instruction (see Figure 11.1). Each of the **content strands**—

Algebra (Patterns and Functions), Geometry, Measurement, and Data Analysis and Probability—is represented on the model; Number and Operations are at the center because they are used to solve problems in all the strands. The **process strands**—Problem Solving, Communication, Connections, Reasoning and Proof, and Representation—surround the content strands because good instruction embeds the content within the framework created by the process strands.

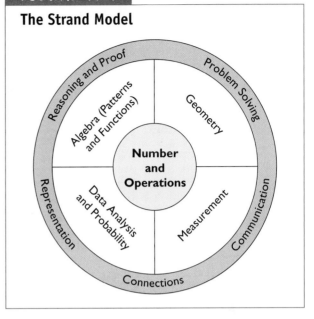

FIGURE 11.1

The Strand Model

In an early childhood program, these strands must be interpreted in ways that are developmentally appropriate. For example, one teacher (Meriwether 1997) made menu cards that indicated how many crackers or slices of fruit each child could have for a snack. When yogurt appeared on the snack tray, the children had to learn how to indicate a serving of what they called "wet stuff." They had always measured milk and juice by the glassful, so they decided to measure "wet stuff" by the container. Different kinds of crackers offered opportunities to talk about shapes and the relationships between them. For instance, a square of graham cracker can be broken into two rectangles, and a sandwich can be cut into triangles, rectangles, or squares. Children making menu cards for the group also discovered the concept of *zero* and thought it was a fine joke to mark that each person could take zero of something.

These experiences covered the geometry strand, the number strand, the measurement strand, and the reasoning strand while being embedded in problem solving. And when the children learned to write the menu cards, they were learning representation and communicating their understandings.

Depending on the children's understandings and the strategies they have developed for solving problems, the teacher can introduce mathematical symbols and **algorithms** that will make sense to the learners. Problem solving is not a set of standard procedures that children memorize and apply in given situations. Most real-world problems are not clearly defined; they do not lend themselves to solution by memorized strategies.

As children gain skill in computing by using objects, they gradually shift to paper and pencil to record their thinking. For example, a second-grade class wanted to solve the problem of how many cars would be needed to take all the second-graders on a school field trip. There were seventy-three second-graders, and each car would hold five children. The work of three children is shown in Figure 11.2. As you can see, two of them counted by fives; the other started with seventy-three tally marks, circled five marks at a time, and then counted the circles. Also notice that two of the children added wheels to their boxes to make their representations more concrete.

It is not necessary to restrict young children to solving problems using the conventional algorithms. If the strategies they use make sense and are accurate, they do not need to change them. Allowing such diversity of strategies also provides opportunities for discussions and for learning that problems can be solved in more than one way.

Thinking about each strand can help teachers plan balanced programs of mathematics. Effective mathematics teaching requires understanding

FIGURE 11.2

Three Students' Approaches to Problem Solving

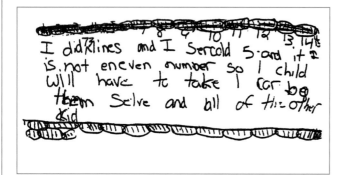

http://users.stargate.net/
~cokids/teacher2.htm1

Covers many subject matter
areas; scroll down to find links
to math activities and games
as well as serious theory pages

NAEYC CRITERIA

2.39, 2.40

PRAXIS

Be able to describe developmentally appropriate practice in
providing instruction in whole-
number operations

what students know and need to learn and then challenging and supporting them to learn it well. The following sections provide specific examples of mathematics instruction in a developmentally appropriate classroom.

The Content Strands

Number and Operations   As noted earlier, number and operations are at the center of the strand model, and like problem solving, they are part of every strand of mathematical thinking. Young children can use basic arithmetic concepts in solving problems. Arithmetic includes the concepts of one-to-one correspondence, counting, number, place value, operations on whole numbers, and fractions.

Children's concept of number develops fairly rapidly between the ages of about three and six. In their investigation of children's concepts of the magnitude of the first nine numbers in the counting string, Murray and Mayer (1988) found that most three-year-olds recognized 1 as a small number and other numbers as large but did not make other discriminations. Four-year-olds were able to discriminate between small and medium-sized numbers and small and large numbers, but they had trouble comparing medium-sized and large numbers. Five-year-olds could categorize all the numbers correctly.

Number can be explored without computation in many ways. Threes and fours can make books of numbers that relate to them: their measurements, ages, shoe sizes, clothing sizes, birthdates, number of teeth, and so on. Fives and sixes can explore how numbers are used in or on buildings. The teacher might ask the children to talk about what they learn from how the rooms are numbered, how the seats in an auditorium are numbered, or how the houses on a street are numbered. The teacher might also have children look for as many other uses of numbers as they can find (Turkel and Newman 1988). Sevens and eights can continue to look for numbers in the environment and explore larger numbers.

Developing a sense of numbers and their relationships to one another (numbers can be less than, more than, or part of other numbers) is basic to being able to carry out operations on whole numbers (Van de Walle 1988). Primary children should have many opportunities to explore numbers and their relationships to one another before they are introduced to formal addition and subtraction exercises.

One-to-One Correspondence   One-to-one correspondence is the concept that one object can be related to another object. Thousands of pages of workbook exercises have been filled with pictures of rows of dogs and rows of bones, with directions to the child to draw a line from one dog to one bone. Worksheets like these are supposed to help children recognize that if there is a bone for each dog, then the sets are equivalent.

In fact, these practice sheets are not very effective in helping children understand one-to-one correspondence because children need to create their own sets and construct their own understanding of equivalency. Providing them with sets that someone else has constructed does not allow them to develop the concept. For those of us who are no longer preoperational thinkers, it seems obvious that equivalency of sets can be established by counting. But for preoperational children who do not conserve number, counting is not a reliable strategy.

Some teachers have tried to teach children one-to-one correspondence by having them physically attach one element of each set to an element in another set. Even these physical connections are not as effective in helping children develop the concept as are repeated experiences in creating sets of their own.

What children must do is create sets and then think about the relationships that exist between the sets. Children create sets that help them understand one-to-one correspondence when they place one chair at the table for each person, put one brush in each jar of paint, pass out one sheet of paper for each person, or give each person a carton of milk. Teachers can help guide children's reflections by asking them if they had too few, enough, or too many chairs, brushes, papers, or cartons of milk. One-to-one correspondence also figures in seriation tasks, as children relate items in one series to items in another.

Counting   If you asked the next three or four people that you met on the street what young children should learn first about mathematics, it's likely they would all say "counting." Some program goals include counting to 10 as appropriate objectives for fours and counting to 100 as an appropriate objective for fives or sixes.

Counting can be either rote counting or rational counting. *Rote counting* is naming the numbers in order without making any connection between

PRAXIS

Be able to describe your state's standards for whole-number operations, geometry, number sense, and estimation numbers and sets of real-life objects. *Rational counting* is the ability to order and enumerate objects in sets. Rote counting is often encouraged by parents and teachers, but when children learn to count by rote it is *social knowledge* (that is, things children learn merely because they are told to do so by an adult) and not really related to mathematical understanding.

Learning to count proceeds in stages: The child knows that each object must have a distinct tag (counting word); the child knows that the list of tags must have a particular order; and the child makes the connection between counting and number. Teachers of young children can appreciate these stages, just as they appreciate stages in learning to walk or to write (Price 1989). Two-year-olds have a concept of counting and often attach number words to objects, even though it is almost impossible for them to count correctly. Researchers (Bullock and Gelman 1977; Gelman and Tucker 1975) have found that very young children can attach number tags to objects in ascending order (1, 5, 7) long before they can count accurately.

Counting is, of course, a useful problem-solving strategy. It is best if the child discovers the strategy rather than has it imposed by the teacher or parent. For example, rather than say, "Count the plates and get a napkin from the cupboard for each one," a parent or teacher might say, "Make sure that we have enough napkins for each plate." Discovery of counting as a problem-solving strategy takes some time, but it is worth it to the child.

Teachers will find many opportunities for helping children develop the concept of counting. Threes and fours are likely to be able to count only a limited number of objects correctly; therefore, counting activities should be individualized to match each child's abilities. Threes and fours can count these items:

- Pieces of paper needed for art
- Place settings needed in the housekeeping center
- Blocks used to build a structure
- Chairs or mats needed for the group
- Dolls in the doll center
- Trucks and cars

Most counting experiences for fives and sixes will involve larger numbers, such as the number of papers needed for the whole class, and will involve recording and comparing different numbers. Fives and sixes can become involved in these activities:

- Counting the pieces of equipment taken outdoors and recording the number of items so that everything can be put away later
- Keeping score in a game
- Counting the number of children absent each day and comparing the records over a month
- Counting the number of pieces of paper needed for a class project and multiplying to find how many would be needed for two projects
- Counting by twos, fives, and tens

Sevens and eights can continue to count, record, and compare numbers that have meaning for them in their daily lives and also learn to count by threes and fours.

See Figure 11.3 for an overview of children's knowledge and skills in number and operation, as well as appropriate teaching strategies for this content strand.

Place Value   Children obviously need to know that 12 and 21 do not represent the same number. Traditionally, place value has been included in the first-grade curriculum and again in the second-grade curriculum before children begin working on two-digit addition problems that require regrouping.

FIGURE 11.3

Children's Skills/Knowledge and Teaching Strategies in Early Mathematics: Number and Operations

Examples of Typical Knowledge and Skills		Sample Teaching Strategies
Age 3 ⟶ Age 6		
Counts a collection of 1–4 items and begins to understand that the last counting word tells "how many."	Counts and produces (counts out) collections up to 100 using groups of 10.	Models counting of small collections and guides children's counting in everyday situations, emphasizing that we use one counting word for each object: ❤ ❤ ❤ "one . . . two . . . three . . ." Models counting by 10s while making groups of 10s (e.g., 10, 20, 30 . . . or 14, 24, 34 . . .)
Quickly "sees" and labels collections of 1–3 with a number.	Quickly "sees" and labels with the correct number "patterned" collections (e.g., dominoes) and unpatterned collections of up to about 6 items.	Gives children a brief glimpse (a couple of seconds) of a small collection of items and asks how many there are.
Adds and subtracts nonverbally when numbers are very low. For example, when one ball and then another are put into the box, expects the box to contain two balls.	Adds or subtracts using counting-based strategies such as counting on (adding 3 to 5, says *"five, six, seven, eight"*), when numbers and totals do not go beyond 10.	Tells real-life stories involving numbers and a problem. Asks "how many" questions (e.g., *How many are left? How many are there now? How many did they start with? How many were added?*) Shows children the use of objects, fingers, counting on, guessing, and checking to solve problems.
Age 7 ⟶ Age 8		
Uses addition and subtraction to solve problems. Begins more formal instruction in multiplication and division if based on real problems.		Provides opportunities to count by 3s and 4s. Supports counting large collections by grouping into 10s. Encourages keeping score in games. Requests voting on various choices. Poses solving such problems as "If the class goes to the zoo, how many parents will be needed to have an adult for every four children?" Or "How many pieces of paper do we need if every class member needs three?"

Source: Adapted from a joint paper by the NAEYC and NCTM, "Learning Paths and Teaching Strategies in Early Mathematics," which appeared in *Young Children,* 58, 1 (January 2003): 41–43.
Reprinted with permission from the National Association for the Education of Young Children and the National Council of Teachers of Mathematics. Full position statement available online: www.naeyc.org/about/positions/pdf/psmath.pdf.

Doing math problems in pairs and groups helps children learn to articulate how they "worked through" a problem.

Kamii and DeClark (1985) and Kamii and Joseph (1989) recommend that place value not be taught at all in first grade but that it be included in second grade when children use it to solve two-digit addition problems. They cite extensive research and classroom observations in which less than half the children below fourth grade understood that the 1 in 16 represents 10.

In traditional mathematics texts, children are taught to write the answers to two-digit problems beginning with the ones column. Kamii believes that this is also social knowledge (as defined earlier). Real understanding of place value is not achieved until children are solid conservers and can understand the part-whole relationships involved in place value. Building an understanding of tens requires extensive experience in doing arithmetic; teachers cannot foster that understanding simply by supplying materials bundled into tens to help the child see the tens and ones in a problem.

Operations on Whole Numbers Threes and fours can begin to develop the concepts necessary for addition, subtraction, multiplication, and division, even though these problems are not presented to them symbolically or formally. Children can observe many meaningful examples of operations on whole numbers at home and in school settings:

www.ericdigests.org/2001-3/
pre.htm

An explanation of standards, along with suggestions for questioning techniques and helping all children meet the standards

www.pbs.org/teachersource/
math/k2-appliedmathematics.
hmtl

Suggested strategies for mathematics instruction, with a focus on math as sense making

- They see that when objects from two separate sets are combined, one larger set is created. While playing in the blocks center, children may put the blocks from two piles together and create one larger pile. They may pick up the crayons from each place at the table and put them together.

- They observe subtraction when they see a set reduced as elements are taken away. If a plate of crackers for snack time is passed around, children see the number reduced as each child takes a portion. After they spend some pennies, they know that they have fewer.

- They observe multiplication when the teacher counts materials by sets or when they count groups such as place settings rather than individual pieces.

- They observe division when materials must be shared in equal portions. Often, it is a child's responsibility to determine how to divide food or play materials so that everyone has an equal share.

Instruction in addition and subtraction should not be attempted formally for fives and sixes until the children have achieved reversibility in thinking and understand subtraction as the inverse of addition. Instruction in multiplication and division should continue informally as they are needed to solve real problems; these operations can be presented as repeated addition or repeated subtraction.

Fives and sixes can improve their arithmetic understanding by observing adults recording equations for arithmetic operations, recording the equations themselves, counting the sets of shoes worn by the children in the class, or passing out cards for a game by sets of two. Sevens and eights will continue the use of addition and subtraction to solve problems. Teachers can begin more formal instruction in multiplication and division with children of these ages.

Each child should have numerous experiences working both multiplication and division problems with manipulative materials before she is asked to use the symbols. Children should not be asked to work problems without access to manipulative materials with which the problems can be solved. As addition, subtraction, and multiplication facts become familiar to children, they may not use the manipulatives on every problem, but they should always be available. Every child should view a problem involving operations as something to be worked out, not as something that will be unsolvable if she forgets a fact.

Arithmetic is basic, but it should always be a tool for solving problems, not simply an end in itself. Achieving expertise in computation should be secondary to achieving the thinking and reasoning skills that are possible through all the strands of mathematics.

Fractions   As in other areas of mathematics, the symbols for fractions should not be introduced until the concept is fully understood. Teachers of young children can use fractional terms (*one-half, one-fourth*) when they are relevant to children's experiences: one-half of a graham cracker, one-half cup of water, one-fourth of the paper, and so on. But the symbol ½ should not be introduced until second or third grade. Fractions can indicate either how many of a set of equal-sized parts are being considered or a number. For children who are just developing a stable concept of whole numbers, formal fractions will be difficult.

Manipulatives for helping children learn about fractions include pattern blocks, fraction tiles, and teacher-made materials such as cardboard circles, squares, and rectangles cut into various fractional parts. Even for second- and third-graders, work with fractions should involve oral problem solving with manipulatives. Goals of instruction in fractions should include helping children know what halves, thirds, and fourths mean; know the difference between unit fractions (elements of a set) and nonunit fractions (parts of one whole); and recognize equivalent fractions.

In the following An Expert Speaks box, Dr. Susan Sperry Smith talks about a school where second-graders are required to take timed math tests every week. If you were a new teacher and required to use a timed test every

AN **Expert** SPEAKS: *Let's Face the Facts*

Susan Sperry Smith

Cardinal Stritch University

Imagine that you are a new teacher who has just been hired to teach second grade. When interviewed, you impressed the principal with your knowledge and enthusiasm for reform mathematics. You enjoy helping young children solve problems and gain skills by thinking about what they are doing. During the first week of school, a veteran teacher reminds you that the school policy is that grades one through four give timed tests every Friday. The timed math tests begin in first grade with one-digit addition and continue in second grade with more difficult addition and subtraction facts (e.g., 14 − 6). In grade three they give tests on multiplication, and in grade four they test on division facts. There are about thirty written facts to complete in three minutes in grades one and two. There are one hundred multiplication/division facts to complete in five minutes in grades three and four. What are you going to do?

Now imagine that you are a parent of a second-grade child who attends this school. Your son works so hard to learn these facts and do the right thing, but he cannot perform under these time constraints. The teacher puts large red slash marks on any problem that is missed or wrong and then puts a big red percentage on the top of the paper. Your son cannot achieve the 95 percent needed to pass these tests. Both of you dread Fridays. You know that efficiency is important and systematic practice will help achieve it, but at what cost to your child's self-esteem and self-confidence?

As a teacher you can talk with your colleagues about what you learned in your college courses. Children follow a developmental sequence as they approach a problem. If you build on what they already know, they will learn their facts much more quickly. The rate at which young children accomplish the goal of efficiency varies greatly. Some researchers found that emphasizing speed for speed's sake actually can hinder student progress (Isaacs and Carroll 1999).

It *is* important to practice once a week. For motivation you may wish to give each child a sturdy chart where he can color in each fact as it is mastered. Make a cardboard rectangle with the type of fact listed in the left-hand column and the actual facts written in squares across the grid. For example, the top line would say "The number +1" . . . 0 + 1, 1 + 1, 1 + 2, etc. Use the order that has been researched by several authors (S. S. Smith 2001). Each child will need triangle flashcards with the types of problems he is working on. A triangle flashcard uses a fact family where the sum is in the top corner and each addend occupies a corner. To practice addition, cover up the top corner. To practice subtraction, cover up one of the bottom corners.

Individual testing is needed. Perhaps you can use peer tutors from the upper grades, or you can quiz several children each day during your free moments. A general rule of thumb is that when a child gets a fact correct within a few seconds five times in a row, he can color it on his chart. How do you know that he really knows it? With a young child, you can watch his or her face. If he frowns and starts to count on his fingers or pauses to think, it isn't committed to memory. It is important to test both orally and in the written form. To give a written quiz, just draw triangles on a worksheet and leave one corner of each triangle blank for the child to fill in.

Early childhood passes so quickly. We can make a difference in the way children feel about mathematics.

---

week, even though you believed this to be an inappropriate strategy, how would you approach this problem?

Geometry and Spatial Sense   The second strand of mathematics is geometry and spatial sense. Geometry involves more than Euclidean shapes. It includes topology (the connectedness of objects) and concepts of how shapes and forms are related to each other. The sequence of development of geometric concepts includes recognition of familiar shapes such as spoons, recognition of figures as open or closed, and recognition of Euclidean shapes such as squares and triangles (Copeland 1984).

Very young children have difficulty recognizing the differences between shapes such as squares and rectangles. The emphasis for young children

PRAXIS

Be able to describe developmentally appropriate practice in geometry instruction and to design a lesson to teach basic geometric shapes

NAEYC CRITERIA

2.42

should be on experiences that help them develop the concept of *space* and the relationships of objects in space. Some examples of activities to encourage geometric understanding follow.

Threes and fours can use two- and three-dimensional objects of various shapes in their play and discover the properties of these shapes. At this age, children do not necessarily need to learn the names of shapes. They can build with blocks and begin to discover how space can be enclosed with lines and that objects can be inside or outside these lines.

Fives and sixes can do activities such as playing with blocks; playing with pattern blocks and exploring these shapes and their relationships; constructing a square from four smaller squares; and discovering that a regular hexagon can be divided into two regular trapezoids.

At any age, the emphasis should be on manipulation and on reflecting on what has been constructed, rather than on learning labels. Some children will be interested in labels and will want to know them, but drill-and-practice is not appropriate for children of this age.

Teachers can encourage sevens and eights in the following kinds of tasks:

- Continuing to explore both two-dimensional and three-dimensional shapes
- Exploring area and volume of different shapes—Children can fill hollow three-dimensional shapes such as cylinders, cubes, rectangular prisms, and spheres with sand or water and determine how they could compute the volume of each.
- Exploring spaces on a geoboard and constructing various shapes and repeating or rearranging them
- Using geometry and measurement in planning room arrangements that will fit everything, use space to the best advantage, and allow for the best movement patterns
- Applying their growing knowledge of geometry to problems in arranging the furniture in their rooms at home

Figure 11.4 summarizes children's skills and knowledge in geometry and spatial sense and recommends appropriate teaching strategies, as well.

Measurement Measurement is the third strand in the model. Measurement experiences for young children must be based on their ability to conserve length and area. Many children are interested in measuring, and some measurements are meaningful to them. For instance, children are usually quite interested in their own heights, weights, ages, and so on.

Threes and fours can take part in activities such as the following:

- Exploring measurement through materials such as balance scales
- Finding a block of the proper length to fill a given space
- Measuring each other for new shoes or new clothes

> ## Parents and Mathematics
> - Ask parents to help their children look for geometric patterns and shapes. They should find as many shapes as possible in their houses or apartments and record their findings.

> **NAEYC CRITERIA**
> 2.41

> **NAEYC CRITERIA**
> 2.43, 2.44

FIGURE 11.4

Children's Skills/Knowledge and Teaching Strategies in Early Mathematics: Geometry and Spatial Sense

Examples of Typical Knowledge and Skills		Sample Teaching Strategies

Age 3 ———————→ Age 6

Begins to match and name 2-D and 3-D shapes, first only with same size and orientation, then shapes that differ in size and orientation (e.g., a large triangle sitting on its point with a small one sitting on its side).	Recognizes and names a variety of 2-D and 3-D shapes (e.g., quadrilaterals, rhombi, hexagons, spheres, cubes) in any orientation. Describes basic features of shapes (e.g., number of sides or angles).	Introduces and labels a wide variety of shapes (e.g., skinny triangles, flat rectangles, prisms) that are in a variety of positions (e.g., a square or a triangle standing on a corner, a cylinder "standing up" or horizontal. Involves children in constructing shapes and talking about their features.
Uses shapes, separately, to create a picture. 	Makes a picture by combining shapes. 	Encourages children to make pictures or models of familiar objects using shape blocks, paper shapes, or other materials. Encourages children to make and talk about models with blocks and toys.
Describes object locations with spatial words such as *under* and *behind* and builds simple but meaningful "maps" with toys such as houses, cars, and trees.	Builds, draws, or follows simple maps of familiar places, such as the classroom or playground.	Challenges children to mark a path from a table to the wastebasket with masking tape, then draw a map of the path, adding pictures of objects appearing along the path, such as a table or easel.

Age 7 ———————→ Age 8

Recognizes most plane and 3-D shapes. Begins to explore volume and area and to use geometry to solve problems.	Makes available frames for building shapes from pattern blocks. Finds ways to determine the area of the classroom. Compares the volumes of many different-shaped containers that hold the same amount.

Source: Adapted from a joint paper by the NAEYC and NCTM, "Learning Paths and Teaching Strategies in Early Mathematics," which appeared in *Young Children,* 58, 1 (January 2003): 41–43. Reprinted with permission from the National Association for the Education of Young Children and the National Council of Teachers of Mathematics. Full position statement available online: www.naeyc.org/about/positions/pds/psmath.pdf

- Using different-sized containers in the sand and water areas—Children can use one container to fill another and thereby develop concepts of *larger* and *more.*
- Using blocks to build walls or towers with lengths and heights equal to those of other objects

Fives and sixes still do not have stable understandings of linear measures, but they can begin to use nonstandard and some standard measures to measure objects of interest to them. Children of this age are still usually most interested in measuring themselves. The following kinds of measurement are appropriate:

- Measuring their heights with strips of paper or yarn and hanging the strips on the wall for comparison

- Measuring their tables with their hands or some other personal item such as their shoes

- Measuring the classroom by counting how many steps it takes to cross it

- Determining the number of pieces of paper that are required to cover their tables—If each group is given a different size of paper to use, the children can begin to recognize the need for standard measures.

- Measuring the cloth needed to cover the doll bed

- Using containers in the sand and water that are standard measuring cups or metric measures—The children can count how many cups are required to fill a quart or half-gallon milk carton.

- Measuring ingredients required in cooking experiences—Remember that a container that holds one-quarter cup is still one cup to the pre-operational child; therefore, a real understanding of fractions usually will not be gained from cooking experiences.

- Estimating the sizes of objects using strings—The children can cut strings that they think will fit around their heads or their waists and then try them out to check their predictions. They can use this same technique for estimating the girth of their Halloween pumpkins, a watermelon, or their teacher.

- Measuring the heights of their block constructions or determining how many tiles their constructions cover on the floor

Sevens and eights can continue to use nonstandard linear measurements. Some children may be able to make the transition to standard measures, especially when a task does not require repeated measures. Here are some appropriate measurement tasks for this age group:

- Choosing the appropriate measuring device for measuring a piece of paper for a book cover or a piece of wood for something they are building in the woodworking area

- Accurately measuring given quantities of liquid, such as cups, pints, quarts, liters, and so on

- Using units (squares of paper or wooden blocks) to measure surface areas and making comparisons with arithmetical computations

As always, the emphasis should be on meaningful measurement tasks; the transition to standard measurements should be based on individual development.

Time   Time is a component of measurement that is often emphasized in programs for young children. However, children do not have the ability to quantify and integrate durations of time until about age ten (Levin, Wilkening, and Dembo 1984). Preschoolers are certainly aware of time, as they hear adults talk about time for a snack, time for outdoor play, time to get ready to go home, and so on, but they believe that they can influence the passage of time.

**www.pbs.org/teachersource/
prek2/issues/303issue.
shtm#math**
Select "Math and Science" on the home page to find many ideas for a preschool curriculum in math and science

NAEYC CRITERIA
2.45, 2.46

Teaching young children to tell time is not an appropriate goal. Preschoolers can be shown the clock face when it is time for certain events in their day, but they should not be expected to tell time. For a preschooler, a digital clock is easier to read than an analog clock because he only needs to recognize the numerals. A dial requires that the child translate the numbers 1, 2, 3, and so on to 5, 10, and 15 to indicate minutes, while also remembering that the numbers stand for the hour. Being able to read the time from a digital clock does not mean that the child understands time; it just means he can recognize the numerals and read them in two parts.

Fives and sixes may attach more meaning to the passage of time, but learning to read time is still only appropriate for individual children who are ready for the information. Some sevens and eights will begin to make the transition to a stable view of time and will need to learn to tell time. For other children, time still will not be a stable concept and they will need to know only the times that are important in their daily schedules.

Money   The money system is another component of measurement that is often included in curriculum plans. Remember that for young children, *bigger* means "more." It is difficult for a young child to understand that a dime is worth more than a nickel when a nickel is physically larger than a dime. Money should be a topic in the curriculum only if children have a real use for the knowledge. Preschool children certainly do not have a concept of how much money is needed to buy objects. Some preschoolers think that if you need more money, you need only write a check or go to a cash machine.

Preschoolers can begin to explore the ideas of money as they play "grocery store," "shoe store," or "riding on the bus." Teachers may make play money available for the children. Some fives and sixes may need more knowledge of money if they receive a small allowance and save money for special purchases.

Sevens and eights can begin to use computations that involve money and change if the problems are real. For example, they might learn about change if some of them buy lunch at school: What amount of money did each student bring to buy lunch? Is it enough? Will there be change? If there is change, how much will it be? Can anyone buy an extra carton of milk today? How much more must the teacher pay for lunch?

Figure 11.5 summarizes young children's measurement skills and knowledge and suggests appropriate teaching strategies for this content strand.

Algebra (Patterns and Functions)   The fifth strand of mathematics is algebraic patterns and functions. **Patterns** are visual, auditory, spatial, numerical, or combinations of these. The base 10 system is organized in patterns of ones, tens, hundreds, and so on, and patterns are evident in all the strands of mathematics.

Promoting recognition of patterns is extremely important in helping young children develop mathematical concepts (Burton 1982; Ditchburn 1982; Taylor-Cox, 2003). Recognizing and creating patterns helps children learn to order, predict, and estimate. Children can make patterns with beads, blocks, tiles, pattern blocks, pieces of paper, shoes, their bodies, leaves, flowers, seeds, and numerous other materials. Children can be helped to recognize patterns on the calendar, in blocks, in games, and in art materials.

www.journal.naeyc.org/btj/
200301

Math games, books with math content, math terms, and links to math resources

NAEYC CRITERIA
2.47, 2.48

FIGURE 11.5

Children's Skills/Knowledge and Teaching Strategies in Early Mathematics: Measurement

Examples of Typical Knowledge and Skills		Sample Teaching Strategies
Age 3 ⟶ **Age 6**		
Recognizes and labels measurable attributes of objects (*I need a long string; Is this heavy?*). Begins to compare and sort according to these attributes (more/less, heavy/light; *This block is too short to be the bridge*).	Tries out various processes and units for measurement and begins to notice different results of one method or another (for example, what happens when we *don't* use a standard unit). Makes use of nonstandard measuring tools or uses conventional tools such as a cup or ruler in nonstandard ways (e.g., *It's three rulers long*).	Uses comparing words to model and discuss meaning (*This book feels heavier than that block. I wonder if this block tower is taller than the desk*). Uses and creates situations that draw children's attention to the problem of measuring something with two different units (e.g., marking garden rows "four shoes" apart, first using a teacher's shoe and then a child's shoe).
Age 7 ⟶ **Age 8**		
Some develop an understanding of standard measures. Uses measurement to solve problems.		Finds areas created on geoboards and areas that are equivalent in area but not the same shape. Prompts children to find the best way to measure a given object and share their reasoning. Invites guest speakers who use various kinds of measurement in their work: lab technicians, carpenters, mechanics, paper hangers, greenhouse managers, chemists, and so on.

Source: Adapted from a joint paper by the NAEYC and NCTM, "Learning Paths and Teaching Strategies in Early Mathematics," which appeared in *Young Children,* 58, 1 (January 2003): 41–43. Reprinted with permission from the National Association for the Education of Young Children and the National Council of Teachers of Mathematics. Full position statement available online: www.naeyc.org/about/positions/pdf/psmath.pdf.

Functions are the patterns created when certain actions are performed on objects or numbers. When a piece of paper is folded once, the result is two sections of paper; when it is folded twice, the result is four sections; and so on. When preschoolers can begin to observe how many sections are created when they fold pieces of paper or that there are two shoes for every one person, that is functional thinking. Some ideas for encouraging functional thinking in threes and fours include having children observe the number of shoes per person when they take off their shoes for a movement experience; observe the number of crayons or pencils per person; and fold paper and observe the number of sections created.

Fives and sixes can record their findings about activities in function tables. For example, if every person has two shoes, a function table of this information would look like this:

People	Shoes
1	2
2	4
3	6
4	8

The children should be encouraged to find patterns among numbers in the table. Function tables could be created for a variety of activities.

Sevens and eights can work on creating more involved function tables. A child might create a table of a mathematical operation, such as multiplying by 4, and let a partner determine the function illustrated. Tables could be created for addition, subtraction, multiplication, or division problems from the children's experiences. (Note that this is *not* a suggestion to teach children mathematical operations formally.)

Guess the Function

2	8
3	12
4	16

For an overview of children's skills and knowledge in patterns/algebra, see Figure 11.6. Appropriate teaching strategies are recommended, as well.

Data Analysis and Probability   The final content strand in the model is data analysis and probability. Data analysis is an appropriate topic in the early childhood classroom when it is defined as comparing and analyzing information. Many activities in the classroom involve relationships that can be compared and analyzed.

FIGURE 11.6

Children's Skills/Knowledge and Teaching Strategies in Early Mathematics: Patterns, Functions, and Algebra

Examples of Typical Knowledge and Skills		Sample Teaching Strategies
Age 3 ⟶ Age 6		
Notices and copies simple repeating patterns, such as a wall of blocks with long, short, long, short, long, short, long. . . .	Notices and discusses patterns in arithmetic (e.g., adding 1 to any number results in the next "counting number").	Encourages, models, and discusses patterns (e.g., *What's missing? Why do you think that is a pattern? I need a blue next*). Engages children in finding color and shape patterns in the environment, number patterns on calendars and charts (e.g., with the numerals 1–100), patterns in arithmetic (e.g., recognizing that when zero is added to a number, the sum is always that number).
Age 7 ⟶ Age 8		
Extends patterns of various kinds.		Encourages using the commutative and associative properties to solve problems (e.g., *If you know 25 + 35, then you know 35 + 25*).
Creates patterns of various kinds.		
Understands commutative and associative properties of numbers in operations.		Asks children to create patterns for their peers to solve.
Understands equality and balance.		Explores numerical equality when other properties of sets are not equal.

Source: Adapted from a joint paper by the NAEYC and NCTM, "Learning Paths and Teaching Strategies in Early Mathematics," which appeared in *Young Children,* 58, 1 (January 2003): 41–43. Reprinted with permission from the National Association for the Education of Young Children and the National Council of Teachers of Mathematics. Full position statement available online: www.naeyc.org/about/positions/pdf/psmath.pdf.

Fives and sixes can carry out these kinds of tasks:

- Creating graphs of information, such as their choices at snack time
- Graphing how many children walk, ride the bus, or come by private car to school
- Graphing how many children have on certain types of shoes
- Voting for their favorite books and recording the results with tally marks
- Collecting and analyzing data on such topics as birthdates (Curcio and Folkson 1996)

Sevens and eights can work with information that is important to them by completing these kinds of activities:

- Graphing how many children eat the school lunch and how many bring their lunch each day for a month—Children can then try to determine why the choices were made. (Were there more children eating the school lunch when hamburgers were served as opposed to meat loaf?)
- Surveying the school to determine the students' favorite play equipment
- Tallying the number of books checked out of the class library, comparing the information for several weeks, and trying to determine the reasons for any variations

www.tsbvi.edu/math/ early-childhood.htm

Links to help, activities, and examples of materials for blind and visually impaired children

In the process of solving these problems, children use computation and logical thinking as well as statistics.

Children do not develop a firm concept of probability until they are in the concrete operational stage of thinking. However, sevens and eights can begin some interesting activities with probability involving small numbers. For example, they might flip a coin for a given number of times and record the numbers of heads and tails. Or they might draw colored cubes from a bag containing ten cubes: seven red and three blue. As each draw is completed, the child tallies the color of the cube and then returns the cube to the bag. After ten draws, the child predicts how many cubes of each color are actually in the bag. Drawing, tallying, and predicting can be repeated several times.

Figure 11.7 provides an overview of children's data analysis/probability skills and knowledge and also suggests appropriate teaching strategies. The sample Learning Plan on page 370 also addresses children's ability to display and analyze data. The object of this plan is to have children think logically about mathematics and to explain what might have happened to influence the numbers on a graph.

The Process Strands

Refer again to Figure 11.1 (on page 355) and note the outer ring, which makes up the *process strands:* Problem Solving, Reasoning and Proof, Communication, Connections, and Representation. The process strands surround the content strands because good instruction embeds the content within the framework created by these processes.

Problem Solving As discussed earlier in this chapter, **problem solving** provides a context for mathematical activities and thinking throughout the

FIGURE 11.7

Children's Skills/Knowledge and Teaching Strategies in Early Mathematics: Data Analysis, Statistics, and Probability

Examples of Typical Knowledge and Skills		Sample Teaching Strategies
Age 3 ────────▶ Age 6		
Sorts objects and counts and compares the groups formed.

Helps to make simple graphs (e.g., a pictograph formed as each child places her own photo in the row indicating her preferred treat—pretzels or crackers). | Organizes and displays data through simple numerical representations such as bar graphs and counts the number in each group. | Invites children to sort and organize collected materials by color, size, shape, etc. Asks them to compare groups to find which group has the most.

Uses "not" language to help children analyze their data (e.g., *All of these things are real and these things are NOT real*).

Works with children to make simple numerical summaries such as tables and bar graphs, comparing parts of the data. |
| **Age 7 ────────▶ Age 8** | | |
| Develops a concept of probability.

Interprets various kinds of simple graphs by reasoning about the "why" of each graph, not just the numbers. | | Involves children in taking surveys of class members for various reasons, such as parental occupations, and reasoning about them.

Has children predict what will happen when a die is thrown 10 times. |

Source: Adapted from a joint paper by the NAEYC and NCTM, "Learning Paths and Teaching Strategies in Early Mathematics," which appeared in *Young Children,* 58, 1 (January 2003): 41–43. Reprinted with permission from the National Association for the Education of Young Children and the National Council of Teachers of Mathematics. Full position statement available online: www.naeyc.org/about/positions/pdf/psmath.pdf.

LEARNING PLAN Displaying and Analyzing Data: Grade Two

Objective: Children will be able to present logical reasons for why the number of students eating in the school cafeteria varies each day.

Materials:

A large sheet of paper taped to the classroom wall
Markers
Copies of the lunch menu each day

Procedure:

1. For two weeks, the children will determine the number of lunches purchased each day in the cafeteria. (Send a child to collect the information from the cafeteria. This task will probably require at least five students across two weeks.)
2. As a class, create a bar graph to represent the information collected.

3. When the graph is finished, compare the numbers. Determine which days have the most students eating in the cafeteria and which days have the fewest, Are these days the same days each week? Discuss the possible effects that days of the week might have on the numbers (e.g., families being out of lunch makings at home on Fridays or Mondays, activities in the community that occupy parents so they cannot make lunches, and so on).
4. Now match the menus to the days of the week. Do more children eat when, say, the menu is hamburgers versus fish sticks? Discuss the possible effects that different foods might have on the numbers.
5. Close by discussing any other possible explanations that the children might have thought about during the previous discussions.

day. Thus, the additional process strands are related to problem solving and to the content of the other strands.

Reasoning and Proof   The Reasoning and Proof strand calls for teachers to help children recognize and value the habits of thinking clearly and checking new ideas against what they already know, making and investigating mathematical conjectures, developing and evaluating mathematical arguments, and selecting and using various types of reasoning and methods of proof (Whitenack and Yackel 2002).

For example, a child observing a classmate creating a pattern might ask for an explanation of the pattern or might suggest a different explanation for the pattern. In the earlier example of the children solving the number-of-children-per-car problem, they discussed their methods of solving the problem, explained their reasoning, and offered proof that they were correct.

Teachers can also help children develop the language of logic (e.g., *not, and, or, all, some, if/then,* and *because*) through the many different experiences of a schoolday. For instance, the teacher might say, "*If* you choose one toy now, *then* you can choose another later."

When children sort and classify, they can be asked to explain the reasoning behind their categorization. Almost everything in the classroom can be sorted when it is stored at the end of activities time: toys, crayons, markers, tools, and so on. Children can also sort collections (shells, buttons, keys, and so on) and then be challenged to sort them another way.

For sixes, sevens, and eights, O'Brien and Moss (2004) recommend playing games such as "I am thinking of a person," in which the players ask questions until they figure out the answer. The game could also be about an animal, a tree, or so on. The teacher might also list categories on the board and ask children to determine what category she is thinking about by asking questions.

Communication   Children have to learn to organize their mathematical thinking in order to communicate it to others. For young children, such **communication** may be in the forms of drawings, gestures, and body movements. And then gradually, children will be introduced to the conventions of using mathematical symbols. For example, if preschool or kindergarten children create a graph of the kinds of shoes worn by the class members, the graph could be constructed using pictures of the shoes. Older children could construct a comparable graph using colored squares and then finally using the numerals and bars of a typical bar graph.

NAEYC CRITERIA
2.49

The process of making a model of mathematical information should begin with real objects and then gradually move to mathematical symbols. The goal is to help children learn to think about how they can communicate their mathematical findings and knowledge to others. At the conclusion of any math activity, the teacher should help the children find ways to communicate their learning with one another and with those outside the classroom.

Connections   The Connections strand is included to help teachers focus on the logical connections among mathematics and the other subject areas in the curriculum. For example, in reading, children learn the concepts of number and seriation through page numbers, chapter numbers, and the use of ordinal numbers to signify the order of events in a story. In physical education, children learn about measurement when they compare the distances they can throw or the number of times they can bounce a ball. In music, children learn about patterns and the values of the notes used to represent music in its written form.

Teachers who are aware of these connections can help children realize them, as well, by recording some of the information from other subject areas using mathematical symbols the children already know. For example, if the book the children are reading does not have page numbers, the teacher might help the children determine why this convention was not followed and how page numbers could be added.

> He knows enough who
> knows how to learn.
>
> —*Henry Adams*

NAEYC CRITERIA
2.50

Representation **Representation** is the skill of finding ways to illustrate one's understanding in communication, reasoning, and problem solving so that the information can be preserved, referred to, remembered, and discussed. Obviously, as children gain skill in representation, their communication about math concepts will be more accurate and they will make more use of traditional mathematical symbols. Children need to develop a repertoire of basic representation skills—such as model building, making drawings and graphs of various types, and creating symbols—as they move toward the more conventional forms of representation.

Process Skill Instruction

All the process skills are intended to be used in a natural, integrated fashion in the early childhood classroom. Teachers are not expected to plan lessons on, say, representation or communication. Rather, they should aim to help children use their growing skills and understanding in ways that promote the view of mathematics as a natural, comfortable way of looking at and describing the world around them. In order to meet the goals of mathematical instruction, teachers must be alert to the variety of mathematical learning that is possible in many ordinary experiences throughout every day.

Materials for Mathematics Instruction

Many excellent materials for helping children make discoveries about mathematical concepts are available today. Both commercial and teacher-made materials can be useful in good math programs.

Manipulatives

Commercial materials such as Unifix cubes, pattern blocks, geoblocks, and base 10 blocks are basic for a sound program based on the use of **manipulatives.** Teacher-made manipulatives might include bean sticks, boxes of junk to be sorted and classified, glass beads on strings in sets from one to ten, geoboards, and so on. Most of these materials can also be purchased if not made by the teachers.

When creating manipulative materials, teachers should ensure that mathematical concepts are presented accurately and that the materials do not distract from the concept to be learned. One does not bring in an elephant to teach the concept *gray.*

Materials that help children develop concepts in mathematics must be carefully selected.

www.
www.indiana.edu/~reading/ieo/bibs/childmat.html
Resources from the ERIC digests and the Web for connecting math and literature

Some materials—such as Cuisenaire rods, Dienes blocks, and Montessori rods—are not good choices for helping young children develop the concept of number. Remember that most of these children do not yet conserve number or length. When given a Cuisenaire rod that is supposed to represent 5 because it is five times as long as the 1 rod, most preconservers will say that this rod is one (and it is one rod). According to Piaget (1952a):

> Cuisenaire rods . . . are open to the most totally opposed methods of using them, some of them genuinely operative if the child is allowed to discover for himself the various operations made possible by spontaneous manipulations of the rods, but the others essentially intuitive or figurative when they are limited to external demonstrations and to explanations of the configurations laid out by the teacher. (p. 73)

Better representations of number are provided by individual objects, such as Unifix cubes, chips, and beans. Once when observing a group of gifted kindergartners, the author saw a child build a square pyramid with Cuisenaire rods. To determine how many units had been used to construct the structure, she still counted each of the different-sized rods as one unit, even after several explanations by the teacher about how to count each rod.

Other materials may also be ineffective in helping children develop concepts. For children who do not yet conserve length, a counting line is not the best strategy for promoting understanding of addition and subtraction. It is also important to be careful when choosing materials for representing fractional parts of a whole. Objects that cannot be divided accurately are not appropriate for developing fractional concepts. Pattern blocks and fraction tiles are better representations of fractions than apples and pies, which cannot be cut accurately into fractional pieces.

Some teachers continue to use worksheets and workbooks rather than manipulatives. They may believe that manipulatives are too expensive, that manipulatives take up too much time, or that parents expect to see paper-and-pencil evidence of children's work (Stone 1987). Some manipulatives are expensive, but materials of good quality will last indefinitely, and many manipulatives can be constructed by teachers for very little cost. Using manipulatives does take time, but covering the topics without achieving understanding is not efficient teaching. Taking the time initially to make sure that children understand will save time eventually because the same topics will not have to be taught again and again.

Calculators and Computers

Most young children have had some experience with calculators (Pagni 1987). Many households have one or more calculators that children have observed being used, and many young children have their own calculators.

It is reasonable for children to use calculators to solve arithmetic problems and to check their own and their peers' solutions to problems. But a calculator cannot substitute for real experience as a way of developing the concept of number or appropriate counting strategies. Thinking about the problem and how it can be solved should be the focus of instruction. Teachers should not be so concerned about developing children's basic skills, however, that they do not use calculators. Calculators can be useful in computation.

Young children should be allowed to explore calculators. They may enjoy pushing the buttons and watching the numbers change. Older children can begin using calculators to solve equations and learn the importance of entering the numbers correctly. By the time children are seven or eight, they can use calculators in computation and for exploring functions and relationships among numbers.

Many young children may also be familiar with computers and the variety of tasks they can do. Some computer software can enhance a good manipulatives-based math program. Children who have had real experience with geoblocks and geoboards can extend their experiences with a program called Logo, especially if they are able to manipulate the turtle. Yelland (1995) found that children using Logo worked in a collaborative environment to solve problems and that doing so enhanced their reasoning and logic skills.

Other programs are being developed almost daily. Many are simply drill-and-practice on arithmetic problems, but more and more programs ask children to interact with different situations and to think logically about outcomes. Teachers should evaluate software carefully and choose programs that allow children to think, rather than simply practice algorithms.

Integrating Mathematics into the Curriculum

In fact, mathematical experiences are available to children all through the schoolday. Children can learn to think mathematically during snack time (described earlier in the chapter), through play activities, through literacy experiences, and through children's literature.

Mathematics and Play

Children can play games with cards, dominoes, or dice that help them think about math. (In some communities, such gaming materials might be un-

INTEGRATING the CURRICULUM

Continuing our theme of spaces, *consider these suggestions for mathematical experiences:*

- Measure the spaces in school: the classroom, the playground, a learning center, and so on.

- Compare the spaces created in block play. Can they make a circle?

- Create spaces using geoboards or children holding a rope. How many children does it take to create a circle?

- Plan and create an obstacle course that incorporates spaces that must be gone over, through, and under.

- Construct a structure that includes spaces inside it. How can the number or shapes of inside spaces be changed without changing the outside?

- Create as many spaces of equal area as you can.

- Given a set of blocks, have two children construct spaces, and then compare what they built with identical numbers and sizes of blocks.

- Outline the spaces in learning areas, and count the number of blocks it takes to form a perimeter around each space.

- Build a space from the large blocks to serve as a reading area or some functional area in the classroom.

- Determine how much space there is for each child in the classroom.

- Discuss the space needed for storage, and determine the most efficient space to store classroom materials.

- Have children measure their rooms, and then compare their personal spaces at home. Consider issues such as whether they have to share a room with a sibling or siblings.

acceptable, and teachers will need to be creative in selecting other materials that encourage the same kinds of thinking.)

In teaching mathematics using games, teachers should note that there are several goals of such play (DeVries et al. 2002). Moreover, those goals overlap with goals from other areas of the curriculum. Goals of math games are as follows:

1. To play according to the rules established for the game
2. To understand that numbers can be represented in different ways—for instance, as numerals, dots, or symbols
3. To count in various ways
4. To compare quantities of, for instance, objects, spaces, or symbols
5. To take others' perspectives, both cognitive and social
6. To think about strategies for game playing
7. To invent new rules and adapt to new rules invented by others (pp. 195–197)

Children in all types of play group, sort, classify, and seriate objects. They construct sets of blocks, beads, crayons, and other materials. Attendance records and weather charts provide many opportunities for thinking mathematically. As children play "grocery store" or participate in cooking activities, they can weigh, measure, and count in meaningful situations. Almost any topic of study lends itself to helping children develop mathematical concepts in addition to other knowledge. For example, if the class is studying shells or leaves, then classification, seriation, graphing, counting, and measuring will be integral parts of the study.

> **Education should help students think creatively, see beyond themselves, and relate learning to life's realities.**
>
> —*Ernest Boyer*

Andrews (1995) suggests that teachers can find activities that meet the NCTM standards in play activities with water, blocks, and art. Finding these activities, however, requires teachers to think much more broadly about mathematics than might have been the case several years ago.

For example, young children learn very little about the calendar as it is typically taught in most programs (e.g., days of the week: "Today is _____; Yesterday was _____; Tomorrow will be _____"; date of the month: repeats similar sequence; months of the year: repeat months in order). Schwartz (1994) suggests that the calendar can be useful if it is used to record or plan for events. She suggests beginning with a daily plan (a schedule) and then adding a weekly plan and a multiple-week plan when doing so is necessary and will make sense to the children. For instance, a weekly plan would be needed to schedule for a field trip or classroom visitor, and keeping records of sprouting plants or hatching eggs would require a multiple-week plan. Teachers should try to think of how the children can really use the information from a calendar, rather than simply having them repeat words about concepts that mean nothing to them.

Instruction in mathematics should focus on providing experiences and activities for young children and asking questions to guide children's reflections. Children should be encouraged to think of mathematics as real problems to solve, not simply as calculations to complete. Burns and Richardson (1981) have identified the problem of teaching arithmetic first:

> We teach the abstract processes of arithmetic first and then hope that children will learn to use these processes to solve problems. . . . The emphasis on problems must come first; it's the starting place for developing arithmetic understanding and for establishing the need for computation. (p. 39)

Figure 11.8 identifies some of the mathematical concepts that are common in children's play experiences.

Mathematics and Literacy

Teachers can help children use reading and writing in mathematics to record their questions, their discoveries, and their solutions to problems. Many teachers (especially those in the primary grades) provide each child with a notebook in which to write his questions and solutions. The teacher responds to the child's work in the notebook, writes questions, and presents new problems to be solved. Children are also encouraged to read one another's notebooks and to discuss their solutions and discoveries.

FIGURE 11.8

Children's Mathematical Activities during Play

Number and Operations*

- Counting
- Recognizing quantities by sight without actually counting objects
- Reading numbers
- Putting objects together or taking objects apart
- Adding or taking away numbers

Algebra*

- Patterning or arranging objects in a regular and rule-governed manner

Geometry*

- Drawing or verbally describing shapes or using shape words
- Exploring symmetrical relationships (for example, drawing a picture of a butterfly in which one of the wings is a mirror image of the other or using legos to construct a building in which the towers on the left and right sides are identical to one another in terms of number, size, and shape)
- Telling or representing position (*where*) and direction (*which way*)

Measurement*

- Comparing magnitudes (for example, whose is bigger) by directly matching objects
- Comparing quantities (for example, who has more) by counting objects
- Estimating magnitude or quantities without directly measuring or counting objects

Data Analysis and Probability*

- Sorting objects by color, shape, size, or type

*Content standards for school mathematics recommended by the National Council of Teachers of Mathematics

Source: Kyoung-Hye Seo, "What Children's Play Tells Us about Teaching Mathematics," *Young Children,* 58, 1 (January 2003): 31. Reprinted with permission from the National Association for the Education of Young Children.

In describing the reading and writing experiences of her class, Richards (1990) noted that children made books of ways they had solved problems and that their writing about mathematics was quite varied. They wrote summaries, descriptions, definitions, reports, instructions, notes, evaluations, explanations, and personal responses to math.

Scott, Williams, and Hyslip (1992) suggest that mathematics is best conceptualized as communication and reasoning, not as a series of mysterious rules and symbols. They found that second-graders responded well to journal-writing experiences in the math curriculum, including stories, pictures, and diagrams to explain their understandings. Brown (1997) encouraged first-graders to keep journals of mathematics experiences both inside and outside school, noting when they used math in some way.

Whitin (1997) kept a clipboard that was designated as the data-collection board. Children used it to take surveys of anything that interested them, and they learned to write or draw the conclusions they reached in ways that others could interpret.

**www.gse.buffalo.edu/org/
buildingblocks/about.htm**

Ideas for instructional materials that were created through
a project funded by the
National Science Foundation

**http://falcon.jmu.edu/
~ramseyil/mathpict.htm**

The paper "Children's Literature in Mathematics," with
links to other sources and
good suggestions

www.songsforteaching.com

A variety of mathematics
songs, including lyrics and
sound clips

**www.ldonline.org/ld_indepth/
math_skills/coopmath.html**

Strategies for using cooperative learning to teach
mathematics to students with
learning disabilities

Mathematics and Literature

Literature can also contribute to the instructional program in mathematics. The most obvious types of literature to use are counting books and rhymes. Many excellent counting books are available. In addition, problems in classification, ordering, and the basic operations can be introduced through literature (see Figure 11.9). As described by Whitin (1994), "Books portray mathematics not as a sea of symbols and potentially frustrating mental tasks that have no meaning for children but as a tool for making decisions and solving problems" (p. 10).

In selecting books that support the development of math concepts for young children, teachers should remember that the authors of children's books are not math teachers—nor do they need to be. Well-written books grow from their authors' appreciation of mathematical concepts as they appear in the real world. Teachers should avoid using books that are basically math workbooks in disguise. Children do not want to find practice problems in their literature.

Assessment of Mathematics

When assessing their knowledge of mathematics, it is not enough to find out what children can *do*—it is important to know what children *understand*. Historically, educators assumed that if children could do things such as counting and adding, they understood what they were doing. Research has proven otherwise.

Richardson (1988) found that children who could count often had no concept of number and that some who could do place-value problems in their workbooks could not use place-value information to solve real problems. Labinowicz (1980) reported similar findings: Only about half the children who could work out equations such as 5 + 4 could work out the same problem logically when presented with real objects to add.

In a later work, Labinowicz (1985) reported that children who had completed drills of number combinations could not automatically recall the correct answers. In interviews about how they solved problems, many children reported that they had taught themselves other ways of thinking about the number combinations in order to make sense of the problems.

The most effective type of assessment presents the child with a problem and has the teacher observe carefully the strategies the child uses in solving that problem. For example, to assess counting abilities, the child should be presented with real objects to count; the number of objects should be larger than the teacher estimates the child can count. To check a child's understanding of place value, the teacher should try to determine how she organizes objects in a large set for counting and question her about her strategies to try to reveal her thinking processes.

Problems in creating patterns, in classification, and in basic operations should be presented with manipulative materials that the child can use to

Parents and Mathematics

● Share examples of problem-solving strategies (similar to those shown in Figure 11.2, page 356) in a newsletter to parents with the goal of helping them understand that their children learn standard algorithms at given times. Stress that in school math focuses on understanding, not memorization.

FIGURE 11.9

Books with Mathematical Content

Counting

Arlene Alda's 1 2 3: What Do You See? (Alda 1998)

City by Numbers (Johnson 1998)

Counting Wildflowers (McMillan 1986)

Count with Maisy (Cousins 1997)

Grandfather Counts (Cheng 2000)

The Handmade Counting Book (Rankin 1998)

More, Fewer, Less (Hoban 1998)

1 is for One (Wheatley 1996)

One Less Fish (Toft and Sheather 1998)

12 Ways to Get to 11 (Merriam 1993)

Two Ways to Count to 10 (Dee 1988)

Multiplication

Bunches and Bunches of Bunnies (Mathews 1990)

Counting by Kangaroos (Hulme 1995)

Two of Everything (Hong 1993)

Division

The Doorbell Rang (Hutchins 1986)

One Hundred Angry Ants (Pinczes 1993)

A Remainder of One (Pinczes 1995)

Reasoning

Who Sank the Boat? (Allen 1982)

Fractions

Eating Fractions (McMillan 1991)

Give Me Half! (Murphy 1996)

Gator Pie (Mathews 1979)

An Inchworm and a Half (Pinczes 2001)

Geometry

Cubes, Cones, Cylinders and Spheres (Hoban 2000)

The Hole Story (Merriam 1995)

Round Is a Mooncake (Thong 2000)

Shapes, Shapes, Shapes (Hoban 1986)

So Many Circles, So Many Squares (Hoban 1998)

Money

Alexander, Who Used to Be Rich Last Sunday (Viorst 1978)

Bunny Money (Wells 1997)

Measurement

Biggest, Strongest, Fastest (Jenkins 1995)

How Big Is a Foot (Myller 1990)

If You Hopped Like a Frog (Schwartz 1999)

Is It Larger, Is It Smaller? (Hoban 1997)

King Bidgood's in the Bathtub (Wood 1985)

Measuring Penny (Leedy 1998)

Twelve Snails to One Lizard (Hightower 1997)

More Complex Problems

Arithme-Tickle (Lewis 2002)

Bats on Parade (Appelt 1999)

Chimp Math (Nagda 2002)

How Much Is a Million (Schwartz 1993)

The King's Chessboard (Birch 1993)

Math Curse (Scieszka 1995)

Math for All Seasons (Tang 2002)

One Grain of Rice (Demi 1997)

Sea Squares (Hulme 1991)

Ten Monkey Jamboree (Ochiltree 2001)

Tiger Math (Nagda 2000)

Window (Baker 1991)

Note: Full bibliographical information is provided in the "Children's Books" section of the References (pages 525–528).

find solutions. Paper-and-pencil tests may help determine what a child can do, but only by giving a child real problems to work can a teacher uncover what she understands (Sgroi et al. 1995).

Teachers will need to assess children's abilities to conserve number and length in order to plan experiences. If children cannot conserve, it does not mean that the teacher must wait until they can before offering them mathematics instruction. Problems and tasks must be evaluated in terms of the kinds of thinking required to solve them; appropriate experiences can be selected based on children's levels of thinking. Children learn a great deal

FIGURE 11.10

Assessment Principles for Early Childhood Mathematics

1. **Benefiting children**   The primary purposes of mathematical assessment are to benefit children and identify their strengths and specfic needs.

2. **Observing and listening**   Observing and listening are essential skills for the early childhood teacher.

3. **Using multiple sources of evidence**   To best assess mathematical understanding, teachers should use multiple sources of evidence collected on a systematic basis.

4. **Assessing learning and development**   Teachers have a responsibility to assess their own teaching effectiveness as well as children's learning and development in mathematics.

Source: Adapted from Juanita Copley, *The Young Child and Mathematics* (Washington, DC: National Association for the Education of Young Children, 2000), p. 23. Reprinted with permission from the National Association for the Education of Young Children.

about mathematics before they can conserve number and length (McClintic 1988).

Teachers should not limit themselves to assessing children's computation abilities or problem-solving skills. Teachers should also assess how children feel as learners of mathematics, how children view mathematics, and what abilities children have to apply mathematical thinking to everyday problems.

Micklo (1997) suggests that using a math portfolio in the primary grades can help teachers assess children's mathematical understandings and provide information about individuals' strengths and needs that letter grades cannot. Using portfolios will also help teachers reflect on the activities and experiences provided for the children in terms of their developmental appropriateness and their contribution to mathematical understanding.

Copley (2000) summarizes the principles for assessment in early childhood mathematics in Figure 11.10. Another view of assessment is provided in the following A Teacher Speaks box. The featured teacher, Karen Yourd, thinks of assessment as an everyday, ongoing process to be done throughout the schoolday. Is this another important principle underlying assessment in mathematics?

CHILDREN WITH SPECIAL NEEDS

In mathematics, as in any other curriculum area, the teacher must take responsibility for making sure that children with disabilities have access to the materials they need to help them understand the concepts, as well as the time they need to explore those materials.

Some materials may have to be modified, such as making tactile materials and providing braille numerals for students with visual challenges. Adaptations can make it possible for children with motor problems to roll dice or spin spinners—for instance, providing cups for the dice and easy-to-grasp handles on the spinners. Adaptations also may be needed for com-

www.
www.ed.gov/pubs/
EarlyMath/activities1.html
www.edu.gov.on.ca/eng/
document/brochure/
earlymath
Both sites have suggestions
for parents who want to
help their young children
with math

A **Teacher** SPEAKS: A Kindergarten Teacher's Approach to Mathematics Assessment

Karen Yourd

Bon Meade Elementary School
Moon Township, Pennsylvania

Mathematics filters into almost every aspect of the day in my kindergarten classroom. The children become mathematicians magically, without even being aware that it is happening. Positional and directional words are used daily in many situations. Sorting and patterning activities are part of play, calendar, and snack times. Adding and subtracting take place long before the children can put words to their actions. The mathematical activity adds excitement to the classroom and provides many opportunities for me to assess the learning of each student.

Assessment is an ongoing process, a collection of data that are then used for planning and instruction. Anecdotal records can provide useful information for planning instruction. One strategy for collecting these records is to use computer labels on which notes are recorded. When a label is full, it is transferred to a file for that child.

Another technique is to keep a growth-over-time piece for each child. The tasks completed should be fairly consistent so that growth can be demonstrated. Begin with a piece of paper divided into quadrants; write a direction in each square. Read the directions to the children. The four directions might include "Write your name," "Draw a picture of yourself," "Draw a picture of your house," and "Draw five things." As the year progresses, the last direction might change to "Show a set with one more/less than 5," "Write the numeral 5," or "Write an addition equation."

I call another activity *silent sorting*. I send two children with black shoes to one corner, two children with white shoes to another, and two children with sandals to another. Then each child in the remainder of the group tries to find where she belongs. The criteria for the sorting can be any number of factors.

Graphing is a skill that can be introduced to young children and that they generally enjoy. The most basic form of graphing is to use the children themselves, lined up according to some given criteria, such as height. Then objects can be used, like the children's shoes, if determining the most popular shoe color, or fruit, if determining the children's fruit preferences. The next step is to transfer the results to a paper or chart graph. Results should always be discussed and observations noted. Self-stick notes are wonderful for attaching children's observations directly onto the chart. Eventually, individual charts can be made. Children especially like manipulatives that are edible, such as cereal or candy. I use this type of activity to assess sorting skills, reasoning skills, and counting ability as well as the ability to create and interpret a graph.

Whatever the task, it is important that children explain how they came up with their answers. Their explanations provide insight into the approaches and ways of thinking they use to solve problems. Information from observations, tasks, daily activities, and explanations all help determine a child's strengths and what can be done to help her grow in mathematical thinking.

puters and calculators so that children can manipulate them easily. For example, some computers can produce very large print or can read aloud materials on screen.

CELEBRATING DIVERSITY

Most cultures employ the same concepts of number, counting, and the like that are employed in the United States. Thus, children who do not speak English as their first language often do well in math because they know the concepts and have only to learn new labels for the numerals and operations.

Teachers can take advantage of the knowledge these children have when planning working groups that will solve problems involving mathematics. These children should also be encouraged to write their own story problems in their native languages and to share what they know about math with their classmates. For example, a child could tell about the money used in his home country, and it could be compared to the money used in the United States. Counting words from the various languages represented in the class could be used for counting experiences or for labeling sets. Most teachers are aware that children like to learn how to count in other languages.

Teaching the history of mathematical learning in other cultures may not be appropriate for young children. It would be appropriate, however, for the teacher to mention contributions to mathematical knowledge made by cultures other than European Americans.

SUMMARY

- Mathematics is learned as children manipulate objects and create relationships between and among objects. Children cannot abstract the concept of number directly from their experiences because they do not have experiences with very large numbers. Rather, children construct their understanding of number from their experiences with materials and activities.

- The National Council of Teachers of Mathematics (NCTM) has defined the content strands of mathematics as Algebra, Geometry, Measurement, Data Analysis, and Probability. Each of these strands relies on Number and Operations for solving problems. The content strands are embedded within a framework of process strands: Problem Solving, Communication, Connections, Reasoning and Proof, and Representation. The purpose of the strand model is to help teachers think about the organization of instruction in mathematics so that the emphasis is on problem solving and thinking, rather than simply computation.

- Materials for math instruction should be selected carefully. They should allow creating an accurate model of the concept being learned, be durable enough to be handled by young children, and be available in a large enough quantity to make individual exploration possible.

- Mathematics can be integrated across the curriculum. Many mathematical ideas can be explored during play, both in games and other activities. Children can also read and write about problems and how they solved them, and they can explore math through children's literature, which offers many books with mathematical content.

- Assessing mathematics should be considered an everyday, ongoing process of understanding what children understand, as opposed to a system of testing what children can do. Many children can understand how to answer problems even though they do not understand the meaning of what they are doing. The most useful assessment involves observing children while they solve real problems.

- Teachers may have to adapt materials for children with special needs so that everyone can manipulate them. Teachers should also make sure that every child has access to manipulative materials when they are needed.

- Since all cultures use mathematics, English language learners who are studying mathematics do not face the same language barriers they might encounter in other areas of study. Children of all cultures will have experiences with mathematics, such as how money is used, how time is measured, and how families solve problems. Sharing the mathematical knowledge gained at home will help children understand the value of different ways of solving problems.

- Mathematics is much more than arithmetic; it is a way of thinking about the world and the objects in the world and how these objects are related. From the beginning of their explorations of the world, children are interested in big/little, fast/slow, more/less, and other mathematical concepts. Mathematics is understanding number, operations on number, functions and relations, probability, and measurement.

1. Many adults claim that they are "not good at math." Why do you think they say that? What do they mean when they say that? Will students who are taught to understand math by constructing their own understanding of it ever say that?

2. How can you use the strand model that underlies the standards of the National Council of Teachers of Mathematics to help you plan a curriculum for your class?

3. Explain why assessment of mathematics understanding requires more than simply asking children to compute the numbers in a problem. What does effective assessment require?

4. Is mathematics a language? If so, then do people everywhere speak this same language? What do English language learners have to learn when they know mathematical concepts in their own language?

5. Is it reasonable to integrate mathematics with other subjects in prekindergarten through second grade? Why or why not?

EXPLORATIONS AND ACTIVITIES

1. Make a plan for teaching children to add numbers with sums ten or less. How would you begin? In planning, what would you want to know about the children's knowledge of addition? Would all children be ready to have the same instruction at the same time? How will you manage different groups if you need to offer different instruction? What real-life experiences could you provide to build children's understanding?

2. Examine the curriculum materials that the teachers in your local primary-grade school are using for mathematics instruction. Do they seem to respect the differences that should be expected in the mathematical understanding of young children? Do they suggest ways of integrating mathematics into content-area classroom activities? Do they suggest that having experiences involving mathematics is important long before formal instruction? Are there other criteria that you want to use to evaluate these materials? If so, make a list of the other questions you would ask.

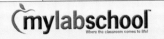

MyLabSchool is a collection of online tools for your success in this course, your licensure exams, and your teaching career. Visit **www.mylabschool.com** to access the following:

- Online Study Guide
- Video Cases from real classrooms
- Help with your research papers using Research Navigator
- Career Center with resources for:
  —Praxis and Licensure Preparation
  —Professional Portfolio Development
  —Job Search and Interview Techniques
  —Lesson Planning

CHAPTER **12**

KEY TERMS you'll find in this chapter:

- Classifying, 388
- Communicating, 389
- Comparing, 389
- Experimenting, 389
- Measuring, 389
- Observing, 388
- Physical knowledge, 387
- Science, 386
- Scientific process, 388

Manipulation and Discovery through Science

FOCUS QUESTIONS

- What is *science* for young children?

- How do children learn science?

- How should teachers plan for science experiences in the early childhood program?

- How can science be integrated into the early childhood curriculum?

- What adaptations, if any, are needed for children with special needs?

- How can the science program reflect the diversity of learners?

Your observation task this morning in the child-care center was to look for children engaged in scientific learning. You chose to observe a group of three- and four-year-olds for the first hour and a group of seven-year-olds for the second hour. In observing the younger children, you expected to see play and language learning, but you did not expect to see much "science." After all, threes and fours cannot really be expected to do experiments, can they?

Once you reviewed your notes, however, you found that children were engaged in many activities that could be labeled "science." Some children compared the textures of sand in different containers; other children tried to sink little wooden barges in water. You also found that many of the children's expressed interests were related to science. You overheard two children asking the teacher what had happened to the orange they had brought for snack several days ago—it was covered with mold. You noticed that the teacher did not throw the orange away but left it out for the children to see and smell.

In the second hour, you watched as seven-year-old children were instructed to take out their science books. They were provided with the materials to complete an experiment described in their textbooks: They were to observe the results of mixing unknown powders with water. At the end of the experiment, the teacher guided the children's discussion of their observations. Then they read the discussion in the text about dissolving.

After observing these two classrooms, you are left with the question: What is science? Is science the informal learning that was taking place in the class of younger children, or is it the more formal guided learning in which the older children were participating? ■

Defining Science

www.

www.project2061.org/ publications/earlychild/ online/context/elkind.htm

Information from David Elkind, one of the leaders in early childhood education, about instruction in science and math and the requirements for teaching science successfully

In general terms, **science** is the process of observing, thinking, and reflecting on actions and events. Kilmer and Hofman (1995) define *science* more specifically as the "knowledge about specific phenomena, . . . the processes used to collect and evaluate information, . . . and as a recently added aspect, [*technology* when defined as] the application of science to problems of human adaptation to the environment" (p. 43).

Children engaged in scientific thinking are constructing a framework of relationships within which factual information can be organized into meaningful and useful concepts. Science is an attitude exemplified by curiosity and interest in the world. Science is problem solving. Science is not just learning facts and memorizing formulas. Kilmer and Hofman (1995) use the criteria listed in Table 12.1 to define *science*, identifying both what it is and is not.

Science in early childhood education is encouraging children to explore their environments and reflect on their observations and discoveries. Ideally, science is not a time set aside from other experiences; it is part of an ongoing integrated approach in which children think and construct basic understandings about the world. Broadly speaking, a child at the easel follows the basic scientific process when he hypothesizes (predicts that the paint is ready to apply to paper), collects data (paints), revises the prediction (determines that the paint is too runny or too thick), and draws conclusions about how paint reacts under given conditions. He may also discover the interactions of primary colors and explore those interactions very scientifically.

Many teachers report that they feel less prepared to teach science than any other subject-matter area (Wenner 1993). Perhaps such feelings are a result of teachers' misconceptions that science requires complicated materials and is a hard subject to master. This view of science is changing as more teachers at all grade levels are encouraged to think about science as exploring and inquiring rather than learning specific facts.

Learning Science

Manipulation, Observation, and Discovery

www.

www.childdevelopmentinfo. com/learning/science_at_ home.htm

Explains how science is all around us and how children learn science throughout the day

Just as children learn mathematics through manipulation and discovery, they learn science by manipulation, observation of the results of their

TABLE 12.1 Criteria for Defining Science

FOR CHILDREN 3 THROUGH 8, DEVELOPMENTALLY APPROPRIATE SCIENCING...	
Is	**Is Not**
Actively participating	Memorizing a lot of facts
Handling materials	Watching the teacher do most of the demonstrating and handling of objects
Controlling their own actions	
Investigating familiar phenomena	Studying content with no link to their knowledge or experience
Reflecting on teachers' open-ended questions	Being restricted by closed, single-right-answer questioning or being told what to expect
Observing the results of their own actions	Lacking opportunities to observe the results of their own actions
Experiencing both planned and spontaneous opportunities	Experiencing science only as teacher-planned activities
Investigating and working individually or in small groups	Participating in science activities only in a large group
Investigating the range of basic concepts	Learning about only one or two concepts
Exploring a variety of content from life, earth, and physical sciences	Learning only limited content
Having their knowledge and skills assessed in multiple ways	Having their knowledge and skills assessed only by written tests

Source: S. J. Kilmer and H. Hofman, "Transforming Science Curriculum," in *Reaching Potentials: Transforming Early Childhood Curriculum and Assessment,* vol. 2, edited by S. Bredekamp and T. Rosegrant, 43–63 (p. 62) (Washington, DC: National Association for the Education of Young Children, 1995). Reprinted with permission from the National Association for the Education of Young Children.

manipulations, and discovery of relationships and effects. The role of experience in science is primary—science cannot be done without touching, tasting, feeling, smelling, pushing, pulling, rotating, mixing, comparing, and so on (McIntyre 1984).

Learning in the area of science involves primarily *physical knowledge* and *logico-mathematical knowledge*. When children explore the properties of materials, they are gaining knowledge from the materials themselves, which is **physical knowledge.** When they create relationships among materials, as in classifying leaves, their learning is logico-mathematical. As Chaille and Britain (1991) explain:

> Constructivism is based on the idea that children are actively engaged—naturally and without the aid of direct instruction—in building theories about the world and the way it works. From a constructivist perspective, children are natural scientists and, given the opportunity, will engage on their own in experimentation and problem solving. (p. 23)

Based on the work of Lev Vygotsky, a constructivist approach to teaching science would include the following elements:

- Active engagement with phenomena
    Students ask questions
    Students mindfully interact with concrete materials

- Use and application of knowledge
    - Teachers and students use prior knowledge
    - Students identify and use multiple resources
    - Students plan and carry out investigations
    - Students apply concepts and skills in new situations
    - Students are given time for reflection
- Multiple representations
    - Teachers use varied evaluation techniques
    - Students create and revise products or artifacts to represent understanding
    - Students use language as a tool to express knowledge
- Use of learning communities
- Authentic tasks (Krajcik, Czerniak, and Berger 1999, pp. 37–38)

If a teacher believes that children must construct their own knowledge, then she will not make the mistake of *telling* them about concepts in science. Even so, believing that children must construct their own understanding does not free the teacher of the obligation to help children learn science. The teacher's role, then, is to plan appropriate activities, select appropriate materials, present challenges, provide time for experiences, and ask questions to guide children's thinking. Teaching science requires thoughtful planning and reflection.

The Scientific Process

PRAXIS

Be able to explain how learning about the scientific process can help promote children's curiosity and thinking skills

The **scientific process** is a cycle of forming hypotheses, collecting data, confirming or rejecting the hypotheses, making generalizations, and then repeating the cycle. The basic skills used in the scientific process include observing, classifying and comparing, measuring, communicating, experimenting, relating, inferring, and applying. Because inferring and applying require more abstract thinking, young children should not be expected to be competent in these skills in a formal sense.

Each of these skills, as it applies to an early childhood science program, is discussed in the following sections. Keep in mind, however, that these skills are important in learning generally. They do not apply *only* to learning science.

Parents and Science

- Help parents understand the nature of scientific learning by including reports of science investigations (such as freezing and melting) in the parent newsletter.
- Encourage parents to do science with their children during everyday experiences, such as taking a walk to look for patterns and shapes (or shades of color, plants, animals, and so on).

Observing

Looking and **observing** are not the same thing. Teachers need to provide guidance in observation techniques. Children can be encouraged to look carefully for specific actions or information. For example, children can be encouraged to observe the behavior of a bird on the ground—does it walk or hop? Observation is certainly not limited to visual input; it should involve all the senses—seeing, hearing, smelling, tasting, and feeling.

Classifying

Classifying is a basic process skill used in organizing information. In order to classify objects or information, children must be able to compare and contrast the properties of objects or information. Very young children begin to classify by function, color, and shape. Older children can classify on the basis of specific characteristics or properties, but multiplicative classifications, in which objects fit into multiple categories, are difficult for children in the early childhood years.

Children must be able to think in concrete operational terms before they can think of objects as belonging to several categories at once, and most children are not concrete thinkers in the early childhood years. Teachers can encourage children to classify objects and to explain how objects have been grouped. Children can classify blocks by shape, group the materials that are stored in the art area, or sort buttons, leaves, shells, or other collections.

> We are now at a point where we must educate our children in what no one knew yesterday, and prepare our schools for what no one knows yet.
>
> —*Margaret Mead*

Comparing

Comparing is the process of examining objects and events in terms of similarities and differences. It usually involves quantifying, counting, measuring, and closely observing. Comparing is important as children observe, for example, the behavior of a mouse and a guinea pig and then determine what is alike and different about them. Another example would be having children compare the petals on a daisy with those of a rose.

Measuring

Measuring is a basic process skill necessary for collecting data. Measurement does not refer only to using standardized measures. Children can measure the hamster's food by scoops, cut a piece of string the height of their bean plant, compare the sizes of seeds or rocks, or use a beaker to collect snow and observe the amount of water produced when the snow melts.

Communicating

Communicating is another basic process skill. Children can be encouraged to share their observations and their data collections through a variety of means. They can talk about their findings, make pictorial records, produce charts and graphs, or write narratives in order to share information, data, and conclusions. The communication process is important, as children begin to understand how knowledge is created in the field of science.

Experimenting

Experimentation is not a new process for young children. They have been **experimenting** since they first picked up a rattle or threw a cereal bowl off the high chair tray. In the scientific process, experimenting means controlling one or more variables and manipulating conditions.

Teachers can help children think of their play activities as experiments by skillful questioning and encouraging children to reflect on their actions and the results of their actions. When children try to balance one block on a tower of blocks, drop food coloring into glasses of water, or plant several seeds in different soils, they can be guided to think of these activities as experiments.

Relating, Inferring, and Applying

Young children will use the process skills of relating, inferring, and applying only in very informal ways:

- *Relating* is the process of drawing abstractions from concrete evidence. For example, children who observe water freezing may not be able to relate that observation to the abstract idea that given liquids become solids at given temperatures.

- *Inferring* is the ability to determine cause-and-effect relationships or explanations for phenomena when the processes are not directly observable. Examples of such unobservable phenomena include electricity and magnetism.

- *Applying* is using information from experiences to invent, create, solve new problems, and determine probabilities. Children can be involved in applying scientific knowledge but not in a formal, analytical sense. For example, if children can observe the behavior of water when it is dropped on waxed paper, blown across waxed paper with a straw, or left outside on a winter night, they can apply some of these observations to other liquids and make predictions about what will happen to them under the same conditions. It is unreasonable, however, to expect children to analyze results and apply them without having provided concrete experiences to think about.

You will notice that the steps in the scientific process outlined in Figure 12.1 are not always linear. As a learner observes some phenomena, she may decide to compare her observations to the observations of others, she may decide to set up an experiment that will allow her to measure the results of adding more water to a solution, she may communicate her findings to others at this point, or she may decide to repeat the experiment but to vary it by adding salt water, and so on. Experimenting will require more observations,

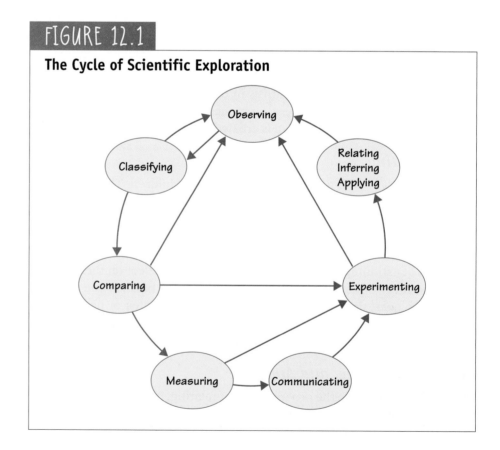

FIGURE 12.1

The Cycle of Scientific Exploration

A **Teacher** SPEAKS: Engaging First-Graders in Science

Pamela Pottle

Happy Valley
Elementary School
*Bellingham,
Washington*

According to Webster's *Beginning Dictionary, science* is "Knowledge about things in nature and the universe. Science is based on facts that are learned from experiments and careful study." The first-grade students in my classroom, like many young children, have extensive background knowledge about topics that are of interest to them, such as nature and animals. Young learners are naturally curious, willing to explore, and excited to share what they have discovered. As a teacher of science, I need to ensure how and what children learn about earth science, life science, and physical science is made as concrete as possible.

Several roles come to mind when I think about teaching science. My primary role is to provide a model for how the scientific process works. This process can be modeled through reading, writing, talking, building, and drawing. My goal is to provide my students with opportunities to become scientists themselves.

During our recent study of a wetland located near the school, I identified the process skills of observing, communicating, collecting, and interpreting data in addition to possible inferences my first-graders could make based on their learning experience as the desired outcomes of this area of study. Initially, I had the students draw pictures of what they believed a wetland was. This was an assessment sample that helped me see what knowledge my students possessed about wetlands. These illustrations were also posted to create a bulletin board entitled

"Is this a wetland?" As the students explored and learned more about wetlands, they replaced their first-impression drawings with realistic drawings reflecting their observations of wetlands.

In order to build opportunities for conversations about the wetlands, I posed this question to my students: *What habitat differences can you find within a wetland?* We took our clipboards on our walk along established trails in order to record our observations. As we discovered a habitat difference, we stopped and discussed what we noticed and wondered about it. Young learners are very skilled at collecting information. My job is to guide them toward interpreting what they have learned to ensure that science is more than just observing and communicating.

We then brought our findings from the walk back to the classroom. I worked with the students to come to some conclusions as to what we noticed about differences in habitats. Having conversations about the differences in habitats led to another question: *How might this habitat support life for certain animals?* I allowed students to explore and create paper models of the animals that might be found in this habitat. At the conclusion of this unit, my students had learned what a wetland actually was and what kinds of life could survive in it.

When I teach science, I try to consider how to make the real world accessible to my first-graders' senses. I must take an abstract concept and provide opportunities to see, touch, smell, feel, hear, and do. This allows my students to represent their learning through charts, graphs, illustrations, diagrams, and maps. Once my students have created a picture in their minds, they begin to use the scientific process in a meaningful way.

which may lead to more comparisons or more measurements, which may lead to more observations, so the cycle is usually recursive, not linear.

In the above A Teacher Speaks, Pamela Pottle writes about engaging her first-grade students in science experiences and involving them in the scientific process. Her description shows this process is much more available to children than you might have predicted.

Teaching Science

As you think about providing instruction in science for young children, you should consider some basic issues, such as safety, as well as some basic

www.prichardcommittee.org/ pubs/primaryschool-ch.2.pdf

A discussion of developmentally appropriate practice in science, with an interesting chart of less effective/more effective strategies for instruction

> **Teaching is the art of assisting discovery.**
>
> —*Mark Van Doren*

scientific concepts and attitudes. In addition, you should think about how to present activities and experiences so that they help children build concepts and how to plan content using the standards for science instruction.

Ensuring Safety

It is the responsibility of the teacher to examine the environment for any hazards to young children. As children mature and become more skillful, safety rules may change. Here are some general safety rules:

1. Equipment should be sturdy and in good repair. Although glass may be the best choice for some activities (such as making an aquarium), most materials provided for the children should be unbreakable. Metal materials should not have torn places or rough edges. Tubs and bins should not be cracked or torn.

2. Use of all heat sources should be well supervised. All electric outlets should have safety covers; electric cords should be taped against walls.

3. Plants in the classroom should be nonpoisonous.

4. Tubs and pools of water should be closely supervised.

5. Tools such as knives and hammers should be in good condition, and their use should be supervised carefully.

Once the environment has been made safe, teachers need to think about rules to help children safely explore materials, objects, animals, and plants. These general guidelines will help ensure safe explorations:

1. No material should be tasted or eaten unless the children know that it is edible or safe to taste. If, for example, the teacher provides powder for the children to explore, children must be taught not to taste the powder without instruction to do so. Children should be taught never to taste any unfamiliar substance.

2. Plants also should not be tasted or eaten unless the children know what they are or an adult says they are safe to eat. For instance, children should never eat leaves, berries, or roots unless they know they are safe. Children should be aware of safety precautions even when eating commercially obtained foods.

3. Children should be taught how to smell any unfamiliar substance. A child who plunges his face into a container could irritate his eyes or nose. Teachers can demonstrate how to hold and sniff any substance without danger of inhaling the substance or burning membranes.

4. Children should be taught not to touch or handle unknown animals. Every child should know not to touch wild animals and how to hold any pet or classroom animal without hurting or frightening it.

The art is in teaching children to be properly cautious without dimming their enthusiasm. Teachers should make sure that children understand the necessity for these precautions while encouraging safe explorations and discoveries.

Teaching Basic Concepts and Encouraging Positive Attitudes

In teaching children about science, teachers should encourage the development of these concepts and attitudes:

- *Conservation*—Children should begin learning early about the importance of conserving the world's limited resources. Most of this teaching can be done through modeling. For example, teachers should arrange for children to wash vegetables in a pan of water rather than under running water. By recycling all paper used in the classroom, teachers will help children learn not to waste paper. Lights should be turned off when they are not needed. Food should be used only to eat; use junk for printing, rather than potatoes or other vegetables. Collages can be made with inedible weeds rather than edible seeds (Holt 1989).

- *Respect for life*—Teachers can help children learn to respect life and not destroy it. For example, insects and spiders can be captured and released outdoors, rather than killed. Care should be taken that proper food and habitats are provided for any animal visitor to the classroom.

- *Respect for the environment*—Children can become aware of pollution, including litter. They can be taught not to litter and to recycle the materials used in the classroom.

Teachers should also encourage children to enjoy science. For the most part, children delight in their scientific discoveries. They may be cautious about touching a toad for the first time, but once they have, they will not be able to wait to share that experience with their families. Teachers of young children may need to relearn some attitudes about science themselves in order to enjoy and guide children's explorations.

Science should be nonbiased. Many adults feel that science is more appropriate for boys than for girls. In fact, all children should be encouraged to participate in a variety of activities and their interests should be respected, regardless of their sex or socioeconomic status. Children involved in a science-based curriculum gain observation skills and classification skills. They may also be encouraged to pursue careers in science. This encouragement is especially important for girls and children from ethnic and cultural minorities, who continue to be underrepresented in the science professions.

www.

www.newhorizons.org/trans/ woo.htm

Rationale for good science instruction beginning with pre-K children

Planning the Sequence of Activities

Kamii and DeVries (1993) have outlined some principles to follow in planning activities through which children can develop physical and logico-mathematical understanding. They suggest that teachers consider various levels of acting on objects when selecting activities:

- *Acting on objects to see how they react*—Young children engage in actions such as rolling, squeezing, and pushing objects. Teachers can ask children what will happen if they squeeze an object and so on.

- *Acting on objects to produce desired effects*—Children also act on objects not simply to explore them but intentionally to make things happen. They may pour the milk from their cup onto the highchair tray so they

PRAXIS

Be able to explain how a planned sequence of activities can help children develop concepts such as cause and effect can splash it. The teacher might ask children to blow on a spool to move it across the floor and so on.

- *Becoming aware of how an effect is produced*—Many children can produce effects without knowing how they achieved the results. The teacher might ask a child to tell someone else how an effect was achieved. If the child is unable to do so, the teacher will know that the request was inappropriate for the child's level of development.

- *Explaining causes*—Most young children cannot explain the causes of many effects that they observe and should not be asked to give explanations.

Introducing the Activity

- *Principle I*—The teacher should introduce the activity in a way that maximizes children's initiative. An activity can be introduced by putting out material to which children will naturally gravitate; by presenting the material and telling them "See what you can think of to do with these things"; or by proposing a specific problem to be solved with the materials.

- *Principle II*—The teacher should begin with parallel play. Because teachers want children to do things with materials, they must make sure that each child has her own materials. (If, however, several children want to play together, they should of course be encouraged to help one another with questions, comparisons, and so on.)

During the Activity

NAEYC CRITERIA
2.56

- *Principle I*—The teacher should figure out what the child is thinking and respond sparingly in his terms. Figuring out what the child is thinking is sometimes quite difficult. The teacher may get clues from the child's actions or from his questions. The direction to "respond sparingly" may force the teacher to drop his own agenda and follow the child's, at least for the time being. Teachers can help children with practical problems to facilitate experimentation and observation, offer materials to encourage comparisons, or model new comparisons.

- *Principle II*—The teacher should encourage children to interact with other children.

- *Principle III*—The teacher should offer the child activities that increase her physical knowledge and that exercise her current social, moral, and motor abilities.

After the Activity

Teachers should encourage children to reflect on activities briefly after they have been completed. This can be accomplished through questions about what they did, the results of what they did, what they noticed, what other children did, the problems they encountered, and so on. The point is not to get all children to arrive at one right answer but to allow children to think about what they did.

Standards for Science Education

The *National Science Education (NSE) Standards,* published in 1996 by the National Research Council, are intended to "present a vision of a scientifically literate populace" (National Academies Press 2006). As such, they should be considered a framework that will help guide the planning of the science curriculum.

The standards do not, however, dictate a specific curriculum. They identify areas of science content that "can be organized and presented with many different emphases and perspectives in many different curricula" (National Academic Press 2006). Even so, the publisher of the standards recommends using them as a whole "because each content standard subsumes the knowledge and skills of other standards. . . . Although material can be added to the content standards, using only a subset of the standards will leave gaps in the scientific literacy expected of students" (National Academies Press 2006).

The *NSE Standards* identify these eight categories of content for students in kindergarten through grade four:

- Unifying concepts and processes
- Science as inquiry
- Physical science
- Life science
- Earth and space science
- Science and technology
- Science in personal and social perspectives
- History and nature of science (NRC 1996)*

Each content area will be addressed in the following sections.

Unifying Concepts and Processes

This content standard is included for all grade levels because it represents underlying concepts that are essential for students' developing knowledge of science. The specific concepts covered by this standard are as follows:

- Systems, order, and organization
- Evidence, models, and explanation
- Constancy, change, and measurement
- Evolution and equilibrium
- Form and function (NRC 1996)

Teachers should provide activities that are developmentally appropriate for their students, whatever their grade level. Young children, for example, tend to see objects as separate entities. Teachers should therefore provide activities that will help them recognize objects as parts of larger systems. Teachers should also provide activities that will help children understand the concepts involved in measurement and the changes that can occur in volume, mass, and space (National Academic Press 2006).

Clearly, many of the concepts addressed in this content standard overlap with those addressed in beginning mathematics instruction (see Chapter 11).

---

*From *National Science Education Standards,* © 1996 by the National Academy of Sciences. Reprinted by permission of the National Academies Press, Washington, DC.

www.
**http://newton/nap.edu/
html/nses**
The *NSE Standards* online

Science as Inquiry

As described by the publisher of the *NSE Standards,* "From the earliest grades, students should experience science in a form that engages them in the active construction of ideas and explanations that enhance their opportunities to develop the abilities of doing science" (National Academic Press 2006). This second standard recommends instruction in these areas for children in kindergarten through grade four:

- Abilities necessary to do scientific inquiry
- Understanding about scientific inquiry (NRC 1996)

For young children, scientific inquiry should involve asking a simple question, investigating and thus answering that question, and then sharing the results with others. Activities might include investigating the differences among types of animals or trees, for example. Children also enjoy conducting simple experiments "to see what happens." These experiments should employ basic scientific equipment and processes and produce concrete results. By third or fourth grade, most children can grasp the concept of conducting a fair test, which is one in which a single variable is changed.

Physical Science

The value of children learning about physical science comes not from memorizing specific concepts and facts but from having opportunities "to act on objects and see how objects react—to build the foundation for physics and chemistry" (Kamii and DeVries 1993, p. 12). For young children, activities in physics should meet these criteria:

1. Children must be able to produce the movement by their own action.
2. Children must be able to vary their action.
3. The reaction of the object must be observable.
4. The reaction of the object must be immediate. (Marxen 1995, p. 213)

The *NSE Standards* for content knowledge in physical science include the following:

**http://ksnn.larc.nasa.gov/
educator.html**

Explanations of "why" for some science activities and links to many sites with activities and information

- Properties of objects and materials
- Position and motion of objects
- Light, heat, electricity, and magnetism (NRC 1996)

Threes and Fours   Physical science experiences, like all school experiences for very young children, must be based on play experiences and everyday classroom activities. Some possibilities include the following:

- Manipulating modeling clay and observing its properties—Can it be rolled? stretched? pushed? Children can compare the properties of Silly Putty and Play Doh to those of clay.
- Using pull toys with removable wheels to discover the difference between moving toys with wheels and moving toys without them
- Painting with tempera paints—Children can observe how paint drips and runs, what consistencies paints have, and how colors mix.

- Playing with water—Teachers should provide a variety of containers, tubes, funnels, and so on for explorations with water (Bird 1983).

- Playing with blocks—Children learn about gravity, balance, and support as they build structures.

- Blowing activities with straws—Children can explore wind and air pressure (blowing) as forces to move different objects.

- Rolling balls toward targets from various distances and angles (Kamii and DeVries 1978)

- Using rollers and boards for moving materials, balancing themselves, and so on (Kamii and DeVries 1978)

- Observing light and shadows—Very young children often believe that shadows are parts of the objects that cast them. Activities need not include technical explanations of shadows.

Fives and Sixes Teachers of fives and sixes can begin to introduce some activities to help the children develop specific concepts and can extend their experiences through reading and writing tasks. Children might share some of what they learn orally as a way of evaluating their daily activities in addition to recording some of their discoveries in their journals. The following activities are appropriate for this age group:

NAEYC CRITERIA
2.55

- Playing with water—Children can explore floating and sinking with a variety of materials. They can sort the materials into categories and then try to modify the materials that float so that they sink and vice versa. Modifications might include adding materials or making boats out of different materials.

- Moving objects across water by blowing on them through straws—Children can have races (Kamii and DeVries 1978).

- Blowing bubbles—Children can mix and compare bubble solutions and record the best mixtures. They can also experiment by dipping

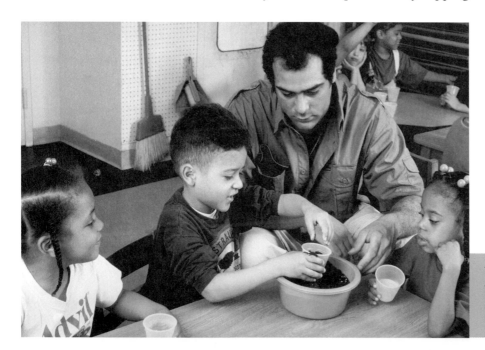

This teacher is using an engaging, hands-on experiment to explain the concept of solids and liquids to these first graders.

different shapes into bubble solutions and record their findings (shapes of bubbles, which bubbles last longer, which shapes produce the most bubbles, and so on).

- Finding gears, levers, and planes in the environment—Children can take apart old appliances to examine their parts.
- Learning about clamps, vises, and levers at the woodworking table (Schiller and Townsend 1985)
- Creating elevators during block play; using pulleys
- Experimenting with different weights in different positions on balance scales or teeter-totters
- Experimenting with sound using different materials and different ways of vibrating the materials
- Controlling the variables for some physical changes in matter—Is there a way to make ice or snow melt faster or water evaporate more quickly?
- Making paper airplanes and paper helicopters—Do different folds in the paper produce different results?
- Cooking—Children can observe changes in matter (melting, hardening, expanding, shrinking, and so on).

Sevens and Eights The physical science exploration of sevens and eights can be extended by reading and writing tasks associated with keeping careful records and recording discoveries:

- Playing with water—Experiences should be extended to exploring the properties of water and beginning activities that focus on water cycles. Children can record the results of rate-of-flow experiments on sand in the sandbox or changes in evaporation rates of water and other liquids.
- Dissolving and heating substances—Children can observe different reactions of matter by finding substances that dissolve in water or testing the effects of heat and cold on different materials.
- Changing states of matter (solid, liquid, vapor)—Children can observe matter in these states, record their observations, and form hypotheses about the causes of the changes.
- Inventing machines—Children can invent machines using gears, levers, inclined planes, or pulleys. Kuehn (1988) suggests that humorous inventions (balloon poppers, dog feeders, and so on) are appropriate because the children learn invention strategies without having to produce serious machines.
- Exploring magnets—Children can explore magnets by creating structures with magnetic building pieces and testing which materials will or will not be attracted by magnets. They can also explore magnetic forces using different materials: Will iron filings be attracted through paper? plastic? wood? thin metal? (Harlan 1980).
- Studying sources of light and shadows—Children can measure the shadows of the same object at different times of day and record the results. Children can also create shadow plays or make silhouettes from shadows of children.

NAEYC CRITERIA
2.54

- Cooking experiences—More complex activities are appropriate, during which children can explore the reactions of different combinations of ingredients, temperatures, or other conditions of cooking. An example is separating biscuit dough into two portions, adding baking powder to one portion only, and then cooking and comparing the two portions.

Life Science

The *NSE Standards* for life science include these goals for content knowledge:

- The characteristics of organisms
- The life cycles of organisms
- Organisms and environments (NRC 1996)

In a constructivist classroom, the teacher's role in helping children connect with nature will not be exactly the same as it is in teaching earth science or physical science. In those areas, the teacher may provide the children with materials and time so they can experiment in order to find answers to their questions. But as Chaille and Britain (1991) remind us, such experimentation is not possible with most questions about the natural world. Children cannot be allowed to experiment in ways that may harm other creatures, even if doing so will answer their questions.

Therefore, to help children learn about the natural world, the teacher will assist them in active observation, model respect for all living creatures, and serve as a resource person in answering questions. Wilson (1995) suggests bringing nature into the classroom. Adding materials in learning centers and taking children outdoors as often as possible (but with a focus on the beauty and wonder of nature, not in naming every plant and animal) are two ways of helping children gain appreciation for the natural world.

Threes and Fours Science experiences for three- and four-year-olds should be playful. Teachers should be alert to the discoveries that children are making as they play and should be ready to guide the children's thinking as they participate in the following kinds of activities:

- Observing animals—Small animals that can be held are ideal, such as rabbits, guinea pigs, and snakes. Teachers may want animals to visit for short periods of time rather than be permanent residents. Fish, birds, insects, spiders, and reptiles are also interesting to children.
- Observing simple ant farms or beehives—Some schools have specially prepared beehives that attach to windows so that children can observe the bees safely from inside the room.
- Observing spiderwebs, bird nests, and other animal homes
- Providing some care for classroom pets, such as feeding the fish or filling the rabbit's water container
- Collecting and observing tadpoles from the local pond
- Observing the life cycles of butterflies or moths
- Examining the different textures found in natural items such as tree bark

www.kidsource.com/kidsource/ content2/Doing.Science.with. child.html
Suggestions for interesting activities, especially for science, that can be found at home and in the community

PRAXIS

Be able to explain how a life science experience can help children develop the concept of structure and function

This kindergartner is practicing a skill that is important in the life sciences: observing a living being!

■ Sprouting sweet potatoes, pineapple and carrot tops, grapefruit or orange seeds, and so on—With care (and a little luck), the children may actually be able to eat the results of their work.

Fives and Sixes   Science experiences for five- and six-year-olds should continue to be based primarily on play experiences. Teachers will want to record or encourage children to record their discoveries on charts and in reports. Many print materials can be provided to extend children's interests in science topics, and more planned experiences are appropriate as children mature. Activities for fives and sixes can include the following:

■ Making a collection of seeds to sort—Most seeds sold commercially are treated with substances that are poisonous when ingested, so if the class uses commercially prepared seeds, the teacher should ensure that children do not put them in their mouths and that they wash their hands carefully after handling the seeds.

■ Conducting an ongoing study of animals—During the course of the year, many different animals can be introduced into the classroom: hamsters, goldfish, lizards, gerbils, crayfish, turtles, garter snakes, and land snails. With some guidance (and some good library re- sources), children can help construct habitats for these animals, study their life cycles, and focus reading and writing experiences around these visitors. Teachers are cautioned not to use a human family analogy when studying animals. The animals should be referred to as "male" and "female" rather than as "Mommy" and "Daddy." If a family analogy is used and the male gerbil eats the offspring, the teacher will have some explaining to do about what daddies do! The important concepts that children should learn are that it takes a male and female of the same species to produce offspring, that the amount of care animals provide for their young varies, and that each animal needs food, water, and protection in order to survive.

- Starting and maintaining a class garden—If creating one is possible, a garden plot outdoors is ideal. If weather and space limit outside gardening options, an inside garden can be planted in tubs or old wading pools. Children can help prepare the garden with pebbles or sand for drainage, soil for planting, and organic material for fertilizer. Children can learn about appropriate plants, plant seeds, and sprouts and care for the plants. They can also cook and eat the products of a garden.

- Conducting an intensive study of the life cycles of selected insects or amphibians—To learn about life cycles, children might study silk-worms, butterflies, moths, frogs, or other creatures. The life cycles must be readily observable in the classroom so that children can record changes and keep scientific records of the stages.

- Hatching eggs—Many classrooms hatch eggs in the spring. Ideally, eggs should be hatched by a mother hen at school, but an incubator is the next best choice. Hatching eggs can stimulate many reading and writing projects. Children can describe the development of the embryo or care of the eggs. Teachers should keep in mind that no hatching experiences should be undertaken without planning for what will be done with the baby animals after they have been hatched. It is not appropriate to teach children that life is expendable.

- Making collections of natural materials for sorting and classifying, such as leaves, pinecones, and seashells—What to choose depends on the environment and the children's experiences. Print materials such as posters, books, and magazines can be added to displays of natural materials, and experiences can be extended from these collections.

- Building a bug—After they have observed insects, ask children to choose material (clay, paper, cardboard, wire, pipe cleaners, and so on) to build an insect of their choice. Provide a field guide of insects to help them. Keep in mind that "the goal is not for the child to create a scientifically accurate rendering of the insect, but to construct the insect as he or she sees it, to internalize how it fits together, which features are important, and how the parts relate to the whole" (Danoff-Burg 2002, pp. 44–45).

- Extending play experiences—Ross (2000) suggests activities built on children's play experience, such as a disassembly line, a windy day party, a digging experience, and playing with roly-polies.

Sevens and Eights Experiences for sevens and eights should continue to be based on their interests and their home and school environments. More of their experiences should involve experimenting and employing the scientific process. Activities for children of this age include the following:

- Studying plants—Children might learn the names and purposes of parts of plants

Parents and Science

- Prepare a set of activities based on kitchen science (things to do with common kitchen materials) or backyard science (things to do in the backyard or park) that can be sent home with children periodically.

and seeds and experiment with different conditions for sprouting seeds and growing plants while controlling environmental elements (light, soil conditions, amount of water, and so on). The teacher could introduce children to some plants that are not green (fungi, mushrooms) and plants that reproduce without seeds (ferns).

■ Studying the characteristics of different animals and performing classifications based on these characteristics—Rule and Barrera (1999) found that examining collections in object boxes helped children understand the characteristics used to classify each set of items. For example, the class collected several boxes of bird-related materials. One was a collection of tools that students could compare to bird beaks, another was a set of cards of bird pictures and objects related to their food, and another was a collection of bird shapes or representations (toys, baskets, and so on) that could be matched to a set of descriptive adjectives.

■ Studying birds in the local environment—Activities might focus on adaptations in feet, bills, wings, and so on to meet environmental demands and on the place of birds in ecosystems.

Earth/Space Science

The *NSE Standards* for content knowledge in earth/space science include the following:

■ Properties of earth materials
■ Objects in the sky
■ Changes in the earth and sky (NRC 1996)

Threes and Fours As in other areas of science, basic concepts of scientific thinking about earth and space are developed while young children play. For threes and fours, such concepts are developed when they play with different mixtures of sand and water and different textures and colors of sand; observe rain, snow, or other precipitation; or watch snow melt or water freeze or evaporate.

Fives and Sixes Earth/space science experiences for fives and sixes might include these activities:

■ Classifying rocks by size, shape, color, density, and hardness—Children can experiment with rocks by scratching them with nails, using eye droppers to drop vinegar on their surfaces, weighing rocks of approximately equal size, chipping rocks with a rock pick (if safety goggles are supplied), or comparing polished and unpolished rocks of the same kind. The teacher can read *Everybody Needs a Rock* (Baylor 1974).

■ Making simple maps of the school property that show all the different surface coverings (grass, asphalt, gravel, and so on)

■ Examining the different compositions of soil collected in the children's yards or from different places on the schoolgrounds—Are there differences in color, smell, and texture? What happens when water is added? Children can put each sample through a screen and compare what they find or plant seeds in each sample and record the results.

- Recording weather daily over the course of the year—What is the most common type of weather in any given month? Some children may be able to start taking some weather measurements with a large thermometer, a wind sock, and a rain gauge.
- Observing the change of seasons by noting the weather, plants, and animals in the local environment during each season
- Exploring the wind with kites, pinwheels, bubbles, and their own bodies

Sevens and Eights The following activities are appropriate for seven- and eight-year-old children:

- Learning about air and air pressure through experiments such as blowing up balloons, creating bubbles in water, or moving materials with air
- Observing the weather—A simple weather station allows children to take their own measurements and record them. Weather studies can be extended into a study of light, air, wind, and clouds (Huffman 1996).
- Becoming familiar with the relationship of the earth, the moon, and the sun—Children might make models or observe the position of the moon in the sky for one complete phase.
- Learning about land features in the region—Children might observe land features such as ponds, lakes, mountains, rivers, and deserts and study the characteristics of these features as habitats for people and animals.
- Comparing temperatures in full sun and in the shade, holding other conditions constant
- Placing different materials in the sun and measuring their temperatures to begin understanding the differential heat absorption rates of different materials

DEVELOPMENTALLY APPROPRIATE PRACTICE

Think about what you have read and what you have experienced in regard to science instruction as you reflect on these questions:

- What elements of a science program are essential for DAP? Why?

- In comparison to traditional science programs, will developmentally appropriate programs produce more people who are scientifically literate? Why or why not?

- Why are some teachers more successful at traditional science instruction than others? Is it motivation? Intelligence? Experience? Are any of the reasons for that success relevant to developmentally appropriate practice? If so, how?

- Should learning scientific facts ever be part of a developmentally appropriate program? If so, for what age group?

- Learning about gardening—Invite a guest whose hobby is gardening to talk about plants and gardening techniques suitable for the area.
- Learning from speakers—Write invitations and thank-you letters to speakers. Write reports as a group or as individuals using the information learned.

Science and Technology

NAEYC CRITERIA
2.60, 2.61, 2.62

For young children, a reasonable goal in the content area of technology is to help children learn to distinguish what is natural from what is hummanmade. Sorting materials of various kinds into these two groups will help children begin to develop this concept. For the youngest children, the materials should be obvious, such as leaves or stones versus plastic objects. As children gain more experience, the materials can require finer classifications—for example, "should buttons made from shell or wood be classified as natural or humanmade?"

Science in Personal and Social Perspectives

Young children can begin to understand the relationship between science and society in terms of their own health—for instance, when they relate their experience of seeing the doctor and having medicine prescribed for a given problem or when they think about eating healthy food in order to have better health. Children can also pay attention to the changing environment in terms of the seasons or as a neighborhood loses trees to a construction project.

Children can observe changes in the seasons where they live but cannot be expected to understand the scientific explanation for these changes. They can, however, relate what they must do personally as the seasons change, such as wear different clothing (if that is true in their environment) or perform different outdoor activities.

History and Nature of Science

I touch the future. I teach.

—*Christa McAuliffe*

Young children will begin to understand that it is *people* who study science and make contributions to knowledge if various community members whose work is focused on science come to the classroom. For example, if the children live near a river, the teacher could invite someone who studies water quality to bring examples of clean and dirty water and to show ways to help keep the river water clean. Another local person could come to class to demonstrate what happens to plants when they have ideal growing conditions. Although these experiences are not science that children can touch or taste, they can help children develop the concept that people do the work of science.

Whatever the content that teachers choose to present, Barclay, Benelli, and Schoon (1999) suggest that teachers use questions and comments to promote scientific thinking, as illustrated in Figure 12.2.

In the next An Expert Speaks box, Dr. Gergory Potter makes a plea for recognizing science as an important component of the curriculum. When so much emphasis is put on test scores in reading and math, does science have an important place in the curriculum for young children?

FIGURE 12.2

Questions and Comments to Promote Scientific Thinking

- What do you think will happen if . . . ?
- I don't know, either. Let's see if we can find out.
- This looks interesting. What are you trying to do?
- Tell me about _____.
- What can you do to make that happen?
- Let's see who can _____.
- What did you mix together? What happened?
- Put together all the things you think belong together.
- Tell me how you put your group of objects together.
- Tell us something about the _____'s size and shape.
- What did you do first? What did you do next? When did this happen? What happened afterward?
- Does _____ look the same today as it did yesterday?
- How are these alike? How are they different?
- How does it feel/look/smell/sound/taste (if safe)?
- Where have you seen something like this before?
- How did you do that?
- I wonder how _____ works?
- It *does* look like magic. How do you suppose that magic works?
- What else can you think of that works like/does that?
- What can you change to try to make _____ work/happen?
- What have you found out?
- How can you use what you learned?
- Draw a picture of what you see.

Source: K. Barclay, C. Benelli, and S. Schoon, "Making the Connection! Science and Literacy," *Childhood Education* 75 (Spring 1999): 145–149. Reprinted by permission of Kathy Barclay, Cecelia Benelli, and Susan Schoon, and the Association for Childhood Education International. Copyright © 2000 by the Association.

Integrating Science into the Curriculum

Science is so interesting to children that it can be used as a unifying force in planning the curriculum (French 2004). Children can investigate various topics, read about them, write about them, present their ideas to others, and explore how these topics relate to their social community. For example, building a curriculum around the theme of *growing* might involve the children in a study of animals and their life cycles, plants and their growth, and the growth of the children themselves. As they observe, measure, and report their observations, they will meet the goals in many areas of learning.

www.

www.pbs.org/teachersource/ prek2/issues/502issue.shtm

An exemplary preschool science program

NAEYC CRITERIA
2.58, 2.59

AN **Expert** SPEAKS: Science Education

Gregory Potter

University of the Pacific

Science education is an often neglected portion of the curriculum in elementary school, particularly during the primary grades. If science is taught, it is often reduced to a compilation of facts that are not meaningful to a young child. This shortchanges both the students and their teachers. If teachers would take a meaningful learning approach to science, they would be able to tap into children's natural curiosity about their surrounding world. One way to accomplish this would be by integrating science and literacy.

Studies with literacy have shown that if reading can be related to a child's everyday life, it becomes more meaningful for the child, as he understands its practical use and is eager to gain a skill he sees adults use daily (Y. Goodman 1986; Purcell-Gates 1996; Roskos and Neuman 1994; Strickland 1990). Teachers already use ideas such as mock post offices and student book creations to make literacy more meaningful. Teachers could also use science, such as the recording of data from simple experiments, to emphasize literacy as a useful tool in yet another area.

Using the natural world to teach science would make young students aware that typical student questions such as "Why is the sky blue?" are the types of questions "real" scientists ask. If more meaningful science were incorporated into the curriculum, students would view science as a way to satisfy their curiosity and answer their questions about the natural world. Thus, rather than viewing science as a difficult, unfriendly subject consisting of a sterile, impractical collection of facts, students might have a more positive attitude toward it.

The teachers are the primary gatekeepers of early childhood education. In order to achieve a meaningful learning approach, teachers must be willing to include science in their curriculum. While early childhood educators have many choices in their curricula, two constants remain: literacy and math education. It would seem ideal if early childhood educators could be persuaded to integrate science into either their math or literacy curricula. For instance, the literacy program could gain meaning through the integration of science, and the children would be exposed to a vital topic that will continue to impact their lives through high school and beyond.

Conezio and French (2003) identify the following benefits of placing science at the center of the curriculum:

1. Science responds to children's need to learn about the world around them.
2. Children's everyday experience is the foundation for science.
3. Open-ended science activities involve children at a wide range of developmental levels.
4. Hands-on science activities let teachers observe and respond to children's individual strengths and needs.
5. The scientific approach of "trial and error" welcomes error—interprets it as valuable information, not as failure.
6. Science strongly supports language and literacy.
7. Science helps English-language learners to participate in the classroom and learn English.
8. The problem-solving skills of science easily generalize to social situations.
9. Science demonstrations help children become comfortable in large-group conversations.
10. Science connects easily to other areas, including center-based play, math, artistic expression, and social studies. (pp. 8–9).

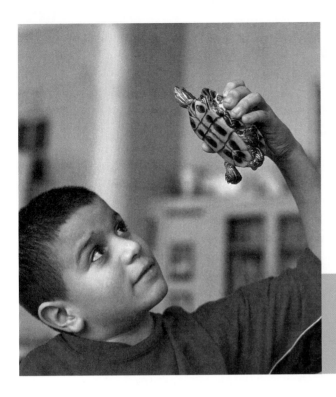

Children are interested in the world around them and this interest can be the focus of instruction in science.

Science and Literacy

Science activities are excellent sources of many literacy experiences. Moore, Hart, and Daisey (2004) found that children enrolled in an after-school program were motivated to engage in literacy activities when the tasks were related to science topics.

For example, in a study of the life cycle of chickens (or birds), the children can compute the cost of the eggs, record the number of days before the eggs hatch, and make sure that the temperature is kept at the correct setting in the incubator. As the chicks hatch, the children can record their appearance (in drawings), how much food they eat each day (in a chart), and how they change as they grow (in journals with words and drawings). In addition, the teacher can make available books about the hatching of chicks, read about chicks and hatching them, and help the children create posters to recall the sequence of events in hatching the eggs. When the chicks are old enough, the children can write a letter to the farm where the chicks will go to live, explaining why they studied the hatching of chicks and what they learned. They can also create a book to recall the experience in sequence and write or dictate the contents. They can illustrate the book with drawings and/or photographs of the chicks in various stages.

Children can also be encouraged to write about science in ways other than recording experiments. Again, having children keep science journals allows them to record their findings and discoveries with pictures and text. For example, children might write narratives explaining how an orange molded or how a carrot dried up when left out long enough. Feely (1993) suggests that children can write procedural texts (how to do something) and explanations (how something works) and draw accompanying flowcharts.

INTEGRATING the CURRICULUM

To continue with our theme of spaces, *here are some science activities for young children:*

■ Explore the spaces in a container filled with pea gravel, and compare them with the spaces in a same-sized container filled with larger stones. Have children fill the containers with water, and then measure the amount that each holds.

■ Observe powders as they are dissolved in liquids. For each powder, does the amount of space filled by the liquid change?

■ Observe an ant farm, in which the spaces underground are visible.

■ Experiment with balloons and air. Help the children understand that all spaces are filled with something.

■ Freeze water and observe that it takes up more space when frozen than when liquid.

■ Determine the space needs of different animals. What animals can share a space?

■ What inventions or technologies have made the spaces where humans live more comfortable? less comfortable?

■ Find out what fills the space inside a human body.

■ Observe the changing phases of the moon. Some older children might be able to use models of the earth, moon, and sun to explain these phases. Younger children can observe and draw the phases.

■ Observe the sizes of various materials before and after different processes are applied. For example, a carrot is smaller after it dries, batter for bread is smaller before it is cooked, and so on.

Children can also create word webs, concept webs, and KWL charts. (A *KWL chart* lists what children Know about a topic, What they want to learn, and, when the study is completed, what they Learned [Ogle 1989].) A popular form of structured poetry, called a *cinquain*, is also useful in encouraging children to express what they know in a poetic form. See the Learning Plan that follows for teaching children to write cinquains in science.

In addition, teachers can make use of the variety of children's information books that are available. In fact, it is difficult to imagine a scientific topic that children would study for which no such books could be found. Books can be used to introduce a topic, to expand children's knowledge of it, and to aid children in consolidating their knowledge. For example, to interest children in spiders, the teacher could read *Spiders Spin Webs* (Winer 1998). As the study continued, the teacher might want to read *Spectacular Spiders* (Glaser 1998), and reading *Spiders Near and Far* (Dewey 1992) might be useful to help children recall what they know. (Winer's book contains lists of books and websites about spiders that can be accessed through the publisher's web page.)

Objective: Each child will be able to complete a cinquain that is scientifically accurate about a science topic of her choice.

Materials:

Samples of cinquains
Whiteboard or large chartpaper
Markers

Procedure:

1. Read cinquains to the children over several days, until they have heard at least five or six examples.
2. Read another cinquain and discuss its structure:
   First line—Two syllables announcing the topic (Note that there is no title.)
   Second line—Two adjectives that describe the topic
   Third line—Three action words that are associated with the topic (-*ing* words)
   Fourth line—Four words that express a feeling about the topic
   Fifth line—A synonym for the topic word

3. After this discussion, create a cinquain as a whole group. As children contribute ideas, record them on the whiteboard or chartpaper. Be prepared to erase and edit as the children make suggestions. A sample cinquain is as follows:
   Tadpole
   Soft, translucent
   Swimming, growing, changing
   Can live in water
   Baby frog
4. Ask children in small groups to create cinquains. (Everyone in the group should participate in creating one cinquain. If some children are unclear about what to do, repeat this step.)
5. Ask children to write individual cinquains.

Accommodations: Help individual children by taking dictation and providing other examples as needed.

Evaluation: Determine if the science in the cinquain is accurate. If children have misconceptions, plan an experience to correct them.

Read-alouds of books with science content can be interesting and informative, and many good information books are available. Each year, a committee from the National Science Teachers Association selects outstanding science trade books and publishes the list in the journal *Science and Children*. These books are judged for content, illustration, and presentation for the intended audience. They are listed by category, and the *NSE standards* that could be addressed when using each book in the classroom are indicated. The books are also labeled to indicate the grade levels for which they would be appropriate.

Language is important when learning science. Owens (1999) suggests that children need to have experiences to talk about, to trust that adults will not laugh at their incomplete ideas, and "blocks of time to devote to wondering about their world without adult constraints concerning subject matter, curricular areas of study, or the mastery of factual content" (p. 7). In other words, children need interesting things to do, the time to talk about them with their peers and with adults who value their ideas, and the freedom to follow their own interests without adults telling them what to do. Children will learn science in such an environment!

Parents and Science

- Some teachers have been successful in using a "science backpack" that children take home on a rotating basis. The backpack contains a letter explaining the purpose of the activity, an information book and perhaps a narrative story that are related to the activity, and all the materials necessary for completing the activity (Kokoski and Downing-Leffler 1995; Patton and Kokoski 1996).

CHILDREN WITH SPECIAL NEEDS

Science instruction for children with special needs can best be accomplished by a team effort, with the classroom teacher and special education teacher working together. Some children may need additional experiences to help them develop the vocabulary of science, and some may need help in learning to work in groups to explore materials and report on findings.

In any case, it is the collaboration between teachers that should determine what is needed and how to achieve the goals. Steele (2004) presents a summary of suggestions for teaching children with special needs in Table 12.2.

In addition to working with the special education teacher, the classroom teacher can use a variety of formats when presenting information. For example, if you want all children to learn about frogs, you might begin with a KWL chart to find out what the children already know and what questions they may have. In order to answer their questions, you could provide tadpoles to be observed, present videos for viewing, collect books about frogs for reading and some on tape or CD for listening, and bookmark some websites about frogs.

Adapting materials may be needed to help certain children participate in the experiences presented. For instance, teachers might do any of the following:

- Help children with visual impairments sort and classify objects using tactile cues.
- Help children with hearing impairments experience sound through tactile means. For example, children can feel the vibrations of tuning forks, guitar strings, and rubber bands stretched across cigar boxes.

TABLE 12.2 Suggestions for Teaching Science to Students with Special Needs

- Use a team approach (elementary and special education teachers) to combine expertise in science and individualized instruction.
- Present material in a variety of ways (visual, auditory, kinesthetic, and tactile).
- Use cooperative learning activities including children with and without disabilities working together.
- Focus instruction on a few broad themes.
- Break down material into small segments for each lesson.
- Create lessons involving student participation and activity.
- Teach and prompt the use of learning strategies such as mnemonics.
- Clarify language in science lessons by teaching vocabulary words and using study guides and outlines.
- Use a variety of evaluation techniques (tests, projects, reports, activities, portfolios).

Source: Marcee Steele, "Teaching Science to Students with Learning Problems in the Elementary Classroom," *Preventing School Failure* 49, 1 (Fall 2004): 19. Reprinted with permission of the Helen Dwight Reid Educational Foundation. Published by Heldref Publications, 1319 Eighteenth St., NW, Washington, DC 20036-1802. Copyright © 2004.

- Arrange materials so that children with physical disabilities can work with these easily and as independently as possible.

Children who are gifted deserve a more challenging science curriculum. Given these children's verbal facility, teachers may be tempted to move them past manipulative learning experiences and allow them to approach science through reading. Doing so would be a mistake. Like all children, gifted children need to investigate, report, solve problems, and communicate their understandings. They can choose their own topics for exploration and/or go further in exploring topics that interest them. But they still need a science curriculum that encourages them to use their abilities to think and solve problems, not one that asks them simply to remember facts from reading.

CELEBRATING DIVERSITY

Teachers should be sure to include the contributions of various cultures when they discuss inventions and materials that make everyone's lives safer and more pleasant. When visitors are invited to the classroom to demonstrate or talk about science, they should not all be White males. Children need to know that people from both genders and all ethnic and cultural groups have contributed to the world's storehouse of scientific knowledge.

In addition, teachers should make sure they know enough about the cultures of students in their classrooms that they do not engage the students in activities that will be offensive. For example, people from some cultures will find playing with cornmeal on a sand table offensive. Others will be disturbed by studies of plants or animals that have symbolic meanings in their particular cultures. The key is to understand the various communities of the children well enough to avoid offending them.

www.wcer.wisc.edu/ncisla/
whatwedo/index.html
This center is promoting better science and math instruction based on research and support for teachers who want to implement instruction based on their research.

SUMMARY

- *Science* for young children is instruction that is focused on actively exploring interesting phenomena in their environment and helping them develop the skills of observing, investigating, and sharing information.

- Science is learned by manipulation, the observation of manipulation, and the discovery of relationships and effects. Experience is primary in learning science. The content of science is not learned by the passive avenues of listening and reading but by actively constructing understanding.

- Planning for science instruction requires teachers to think about what topics children can understand through active exploration, to choose activities and experiences that will help children develop accurate concepts, to ask appropriate

questions to guide children's explorations, and to think about how to help children record what they have learned. Appropriate science activities for young children include those that encourage them to explore actively through touch, taste, smell, sound, and sight. This means that carefully observing the growth and development of animals such as butterflies and chicks is appropriate, while studying electricity is not. Activities should also help children develop concepts that are meaningful to them. Young children can understand the concepts of growth and change in animals, but they cannot understand the notion of space more than simply knowing that the sun, moon, and stars appear in the sky.

- Science can be integrated into many of children's daily classroom experiences—particularly literacy experiences. Books are available that can supplement the activities for any topic an early childhood teacher could select. Moreover, children can record their observations in various ways such as writing, drawing, and photographing. Children can perform movements to help them understand how various insects and animals move, and children can use the problem-solving skills learned in scientific explorations to solve other types of problems.

● Children with special needs can succeed in learning science through cooperative learning activities, having opportunities to learn concepts in a variety of ways, organizing experiences around broad themes, and adapting activities to meet their individual needs.

● Science instruction that highlights the contributions of all cultures to scientific knowledge and that recognizes the meanings of various materials in different cultures can help all students celebrate their cultural backgrounds.

REFLECTIONS

1. Many elementary and early childhood teachers admit that they are afraid of teaching science. Now that you have read this chapter, do you feel confident that you can teach science effectively? Why or why not? If you didn't like science as a student, how can you plan to avoid the kinds of instruction that made you dislike it?

2. Describe what you believe is an effective science program for four- and five-year-olds. Be able to defend your plan.

3. Suppose that your second-grade science textbook contains a unit on electricity. What will you do with such a unit? What if you are required to teach it?

4. What would you tell a parent who wants her child to be learning "facts" in science, such as the distance to the nearest star?

5. What criteria will you use for choosing good activities for science instruction for young children?

EXPLORATIONS AND ACTIVITIES

1. Design a lesson that will help children develop specific concepts about a collection of stones, a collection of seashells, or other similar materials. Be specific about the concepts you want to develop and how you will assess children's understanding when you have completed the lesson.

2. A few years ago, sinking-and-floating activities were very common in early childhood science programs. In these activities, children were provided with a large container of water and a collection of materials from around the classroom or from home to try out to determine if they would sink or float. The goal was to help children discover the properties of materials that sink versus float in water. Some teachers realized that children were developing inaccurate concepts because of the materials provided for them to explore. How would you select materials for this experience to make sure that these concepts were developed accurately?

mylabschool
Where the classroom comes to life!

MyLabSchool is a collection of online tools for your success in this course, your licensure exams, and your teaching career. Visit **www.mylabschool.com** to access the following:

- Online Study Guide
- Video Cases from real classrooms
- Help with your research papers using Research Navigator
- Career Center with resources for:
  —Praxis and Licensure Preparation
  —Professional Portfolio Development
  —Job Search and Interview Techniques
  —Lesson Planning

CHAPTER 13

KEY TERMS you'll find in this chapter:

- **Craft activities,** 427
- **Creativity,** 416
- **Dance education,** 437
- **Drama,** 438
- **Drawing realism,** 421
- **Guided listening,** 434
- **Movement experiences,** 436
- **Music,** 428
- **Preschematic stage,** 420
- **Schematic stage,** 420
- **Scribbling,** 420
- **Specialists,** 441
- **Visual arts,** 419

Encouraging the Creative Arts

FOCUS QUESTIONS

- How are the arts important in an early childhood curriculum?

- What are appropriate experiences in the visual arts?

- What are appropriate experiences in music?

- What are appropriate experiences in movement and dance?

- What are appropriate experiences in drama?

- How can classroom teachers work effectively with arts specialists?

- How can arts experiences be assessed?

- How can the arts be integrated into the curriculum?

- How can arts experiences be provided for children with special needs?

- How can diversity be celebrated with the arts?

Today you visited a first-grade/second-grade combination class with the objective of observing arts instruction. You wanted to know how the classroom teacher incorporated the arts into the daily program and what the specialists at the school did in their classes.

Your observations were very interesting. You saw children painting at easels, cutting paper for illustrating a story they had written, and creating clay objects that were going to be fired and given as gifts. A little later, as the children gathered for story time, they participated in singing several songs. The teacher had the lyrics to these songs printed on large charts, and one child used a pointer to point to the words as they were sung. After reading a story, the teacher encouraged three or four children to spend some time planning what they could do to act out the story on another day.

The teacher worked with the specialists on the staff to select experiences that would enhance topics of study in the classroom. The specialists planned experiences for their time with the children in conjunction with the classroom teachers.

When you met with your peers to debrief your observations, you found that instruction in the arts varied a great deal. For example, in one school, there was no art at all because the specialist was responsible for four schools, and each school got only one nine-week period of art per year. Some teachers had been observed teaching children art lessons in perspective following a model in a children's book. In yet another school, the entire curriculum rotated around art experiences.

You have many questions about instruction in the arts and the place of the arts in an early childhood curriculum. Should the classroom teacher plan for art activities, or should the art specialist be responsible for all art instruction? How can participation in the arts be evaluated? When there is so much emphasis on test scores, can a teacher afford the time for the arts? ■

The Importance of Arts Experiences

The arts are vital to a good early childhood program. Who can imagine a program for young children in which there is no music? no painting? no movement or dance? no drama? Children sing and dance and draw as part of their daily lives, whether they are in school or at home. If children are natural participants in the arts, then obviously the arts are important in any program for young children.

The Consortium of National Arts Education Associations (1996), a policy-making group comprised of many other arts organizations, explains the importance of arts education as follows:

- The arts are worth studying simply because of what they are. Their impact cannot be denied. Throughout history, all the arts have served to connect our imaginations with the deepest questions of human existence. . . .
- The arts are used to achieve a multitude of human purposes: to present issues and ideas, to teach or persuade, to entertain, to decorate or please. Becoming literate in the arts helps students understand and do these things better.
- The arts are integral to every person's daily life. Our personal, social, economic, and cultural environments are shaped by the arts at every turn. . . .
- The arts offer unique sources of enjoyment and refreshment for the imagination. They explore relationships between ideas and objects and serve as links between thought and action. Their continuing gift is to help us see and grasp life in new ways.
- The arts help students develop the attitudes, characteristics, and intellectual skills required to participate effectively in today's society and economy. The arts teach self-discipline, reinforce self-esteem, and foster the thinking skills and creativity so valued in the workplace. They teach the importance of teamwork and cooperation. They demonstrate the direct connection between study, hard work, and high levels of achievement.

An early childhood program would be much the poorer without music, art, movement and dance, and drama.

Definitions of **creativity** vary considerably. For the purposes of this chapter, *creativity* is defined as "the proactive, purposeful impulse to extend beyond the present, characterized by originality, imagination, and fantasy" (Edwards 1990, p. 8). To foster creativity, the teacher of young children must help them express themselves and avoid teaching them that their interpretations of their world are not "correct" or "good."

Young children are willing to draw and sing and dance without self-consciousness. They do not worry that the colors they use are not the colors of the things they are representing in real life. Nor do they worry that what they have drawn does not look like what they say it is. They believe in themselves and their abilities. The challenge is to maintain their belief in themselves while working in a group setting.

The arts can serve as an integrating force that helps children make connections with their experiences. The arts help young children put together what they know about topics in science, social studies, health, math, literature, and so on. The arts are also important for personalizing education. "There is an increasing awareness among educators that the development of instructional approaches that integrate the student's affect and unique personal experiences with course content can increase student motivation, participation, and learning" (Edwards 1990, p. 5).

As noted in Chapter 2, probably the most discussed early childhood programs in the world in recent years are the preschools of Reggio Emilia in northern Italy. Arts are the major focus of the school experience in these programs, and the curriculum is project based. Projects generally grow out of children's play and interests, although some are initiated by teachers in response to observed needs of the children. Children express what they are learning and observing in their environment through the arts. For example, children might be encouraged to create images of themselves using many different media. These images and the discussions about them might lead to explorations of body movements. The environment is also visually stimulating in ways that encourage pondering, wondering, and remembering.

The goal of these preschools is to enhance children's creative and intellectual development, and the arts are believed to be central to that development (New 1990). Gandini (1993) states that teachers in Reggio Emilia view art as only one of the child's means of expression: "Children's expression through many media is not a separate part of the curriculum but is inseparable from the whole cognitive/symbolic expression in the process of learning" (p. 8).

Even though many people and organizations have made statements about the importance of the arts, they are still neglected in many school systems. Moreover, the arts are the first area to be cut whenever schools have budget problems. Engel (1995) suggests that the difficulty of assessing art skills and performance is one of the reasons the arts are not especially valued in schools.

> **Every child is an artist. The problem is how to remain an artist once he grows up.**
>
> —*Pablo Picasso*

Parents and the Arts

- Plan a session to help parents look at and respond to their children's art products in positive terms. Make sure parents do not feel they have to be artists to be involved with the arts.

In the following An Expert Speaks box, Dr. Susan Wright talks about the importance of the arts in meaning making. Think about how you will explain to parents and administrators the importance of the arts in the early childhood curriculum given the current educational focus on testing.

Goals of Arts Education

As one of the groups represented in the Consortium of National Arts Education Associations, the Music Educators National Conference (MENC)—along

AN **Expert** SPEAKS: *Art in the Curriculum*

Susan Wright
Queensland University of Technology

There are several approaches to the arts in U.S. schools. First, in the Nurture the Natural approach (see McArdle 2001), arts practice is based on the belief that the child is the center of the program and that most learning should occur through free, playful, spontaneous, and unstructured experiences. Art is valued because it provides opportunities for the child's self-expression of thoughts and feelings, and although it is deemed appropriate for adults to observe children's processes of expression and to gently discuss a child's artwork in order to grasp a deeper understanding and appreciation of the child, to *teach* the child in the arts would be seen as inappropriate, as it could potentially stifle his or her creativity and sense of self. The teacher's role is one of simply providing developmentally appropriate materials and then essentially standing back and letting children's creativity unfold. However, the program can have a tendency to become laissez-faire, and anything that the child creates is considered beautiful, charming, spontaneous, and unique. The negative aspect of this is that children do not learn how to discern and strive for quality within their own arts experiences and are not given any guidance to go beyond their current level of competence.

Second, in the Polish the Product approach (Gardner 1997b; Wright 1997), it is believed that the development of technique and skill is more important than free expression and that creativity and self-expression cannot develop if children don't have adequate mastery of the discipline (i.e., music, dance, drama, art). The ease of full-group instruction can lead to mass-production art activities, such as stencils (e.g., twenty-five identical colored-in green apples), templates (e.g., egg carton caterpillars), and gimmicks (e.g., painting with feather dusters). Music, dance, and drama can become focused almost exclusively on events such as an end-of-year performance, where it is expected that the teachers and children present a product that is as polished as possible. The message to children can be that the works produced by children are not as valued as those provided by adults and that children should look to adults for artistic inspiration rather than find it from within.

Finally, an approach that takes the best from those presented above is the Free the Discipline approach, which brings together both the child's freedom of expression and creativity and his or her artistic mastery and refinement of the discipline. In other words, arts education should integrate both Nature and Polish. What a child is born with should be more than simply nurtured, it should be cultivated. Clearly, children cannot learn without assistance in any of the disciplines, including the arts. Just how much and what type of assistance is the key to good early childhood arts education.

> **NAEYC CRITERIA**
> **2.80**

Through the arts, children participate in meaning-making through visual–spatial imagery and the use of the body, and they turn action into representation using the unique symbol systems of the arts—still and moving 2-D and 3-D images; movement, gesture, dance, and dramatization; and the use of the voice, musical instruments, words, and sound effects (Wright 2003). In a Free the Discipline approach, adults assist young children to develop the "grammars" of the arts and the ability to not only create but also "read" or interpret a range of texts—visual, aural, bodily-kinesthetic, spatial, intrapersonal.

with many other organizations of teachers, administrators, and school districts—published a position paper in January 1999 called "The Value and Quality of Arts Education: A Statement of Principles." That paper identified these seven principles as providing the foundation for arts education:

1. Every student in the nation should have an education in the arts.
2. To ensure a basic education in the arts for all students, the arts should be recognized as serious, core academic subjects.
3. As education policy makers make decisions, they should incorporate the multiple lessons of recent research concerning the value and impact of arts education.
4. Qualified arts teachers and sequential curriculum must be recognized as the basis and core for substantive arts education for all students.

5. Arts education programs should be grounded in rigorous instruction, provide meaningful assessment of academic progress and performance, and take their place within a structure of direct accountability to school officials, parents, and the community.

6. Community resources that provide exposure to the arts, enrichment, and entertainment through the arts all offer valuable support and enhancement to an in-school arts education.

7. We offer our unified support to those programs, policies, and practitioners that reflect these principles. (MENC 1999)

Standards for Arts Education

In 1994, the Consortium of National Arts Education Associations published the *National Standards for Arts Education,* which outline basic arts learning outcomes for students in grades kindergarten through twelve. This consortium, which was directed by the National Committee for Standards in the Arts and funded by the Music Educators National Conference/National Association for Music Education (MENC/NAME), was responding to what many Americans thought was a deficiency in arts education in U.S. public schools.

The authors of the standards argued that having arts education standards is important for two reasons:

1. To help define what a good arts education should provide in terms of knowledge and skills as well their application in producing and enjoying art

2. To give school districts and states across the nation guidelines for what a good arts education should include (Consortium 1994)

Regarding this second point, the authors emphasized that the standards are intended to identify student learning outcomes. Specifically, the standards "do not provide a course of study, but they can help weak arts instruction and programs improve and help make good programs even better" (Consortium 1994). As is true of other content-area standards, the intent in creating these standards is to provide a framework for curriculum planning, thus allowing individual teachers and programs flexibility and choice in teaching the arts.

In fact, there are separate sets of standards for the visual arts, music, dance, and drama and for children at different grade levels. The specific standards for young children (kindergarten through grade four) will be presented in their relevant sections throughout this chapter.

Visual Arts

The term **visual arts** usually refers to graphic arts, such as using crayons, chalk, and paint and creating sculpture or collage. From the constructivist point of view, as children grow and develop, their representations with graphic materials change in predictable and unvarying stages. Every child moves through the same sequence of stages, but every child moves through them at an individual rate. As teachers observe these stages, they can make inferences about the child's cognitive development and thinking processes. The following are brief descriptions of the stages in drawing.

www.

http://artsedge.kennedy-center.org/teach/standards

The *National Standards for Arts Education* online

www.

www.learner.org/channel/workshops/artsinevery classroom/abtpops/stvak4.html

How children learn the visual arts

Stages in Development

Many art educators have tried to describe the stages in the development of children's drawing. Lowenfeld and Brittain (1982) have identified these stages as scribbling, preschematic, schematic, and drawing realism.

The first stage, **scribbling,** usually begins at about thirteen months of age. Before that age, children put the crayons or pencils in their mouths. At about thirteen months, children begin to mark with crayons and pencils. The first scribbles are generally zigzags, not distinct shapes. Kellogg (1970) has examined children's scribbles and concluded that they usually fall into distinct patterns, which can be identified by an educated observer. By around three years of age, children begin to include distinct shapes, mostly circles, in their scribbling. Figure 13.1 is an example of scribbling.

At about four years of age, children begin to make attempts to represent objects that are familiar in their environment. This stage is the **preschematic** stage. Children in this stage typically draw human figures with very large heads and legs coming out of heads. Kellogg (1970) points out that these first drawings of humans derive from the circles and lines that children have created in their scribbles. Children may also draw other objects that are part of their experience, such as animals, using basically the same forms. Colors used in children's drawings are not realistic, and figures tend to be placed randomly on a page. Figure 13.2 is an example of a drawing by a child in the preschematic stage.

At about seven years old, children move into the **schematic stage,** in which they develop definite forms representing their environment. Children will repeat basically the same forms, again and again—drawing people or trees or birds with the same forms or symbols. Figures or objects are often arranged on a baseline, rather than placed at random on the page; however, the baseline itself may be placed randomly or at an angle to the edge of the paper. Children in this stage often represent objects in space from a point of view that is much different from the adult point of view. Children may use an "X-ray" perspective so that viewers can see the inside and outside of a house at the same time. They may also draw objects from different views in

FIGURE 13.1
Scribbling

FIGURE 13.2
Preschematic Drawing

FIGURE 13.3

Schematic Drawing

one picture. The drawings in Figure 13.3 are representative of the schematic stage.

At around nine, children enter the stage of **drawing realism.** They begin to make their drawings much smaller and include much more detail; they are also no longer eager to share their work with adults. Some children in early childhood classrooms may be making the transition into this stage. The drawing in Figure 13.4 is typical of the drawing realism stage. Observe how the horse's legs are drawn not touching the ground and the several attempts to get the stirrup just right. The horse was also colored brown in the original drawing.

Another approach to describing children's art development is that of Engel (1995, 1996), who believes that teachers can view children's drawings from two perspectives: one, a descriptive perspective and the other, a

FIGURE 13.4

Realistic Drawing

developmental perspective. In looking at children's drawings from a descriptive perspective, teachers should keep the following questions in mind:

1. *Materials, context: What is it made of? And, if the information is available, when and under what circumstances was it made? . . .*
2. *Basic elements, techniques: What can the observer see? . . .*
3. *Character of communication: What does it represent? . . .*
4. *Aspects of organization, meaning: How is the picture organized? . . .*
5. *Function, intent: What is it about? . . .*
6. *Sources, origins: Where does the idea come from? . . .* (1995, pp. 31–34)

In viewing children's drawings from a developmental perspective, teachers should consider the descriptors outlined in Table 13.1, which presents a developmental continuum.

How young children draw does not seem to reflect training. Brittain (1969) reported his experience in trying to teach nursery school children to draw squares. After many experiences with squares, the children began to draw them at around four years of age. As Brittain put it, children accomplish the task of drawing a square at about the same time with or without instruction.

Even though instruction may not result in changes in children's drawing, children can learn the vocabulary of art. Dixon and Tarr (1988) demonstrated that children could be taught to recognize elements of art. In a unit on lines, the children moved to music to create lines with their bodies; looked at examples of lines in art; and used lines in their own art with straws, strips of paper, and markers. After these experiences, the children could identify lines as elements of art. Schirrmacher (1986) recommends that teachers point out the elements of color, line, mass or volume, pattern, shape or form, space, and texture when discussing art with young children.

Aylward et al. (1993) found that preschoolers were able to classify works of art by style after a course of study that specifically introduced abstract art and artists. In addition, the teachers observed that the children were more involved in their own art projects during and after this study.

Epstein (2001) recommends that teachers ask children questions about their own art experiences that will help them think more about the content of art. For example, she suggests that when a group of children has finished an art experience, they should be asked why their products are so different when they all used the same materials. They also could be asked to think about why some artists want to make large pictures and some want to make small pictures.

Davis and Gardner (1993) suggest that teachers respond to children's art not by asking them to tell about their pictures and then writing on them (usually just labeling the components) but by demonstrating their own perceptions. For example, the teacher might say "Look at the action in this line; this figure is indeed scribbling around on this page" or "This is a nicely balanced drawing; see how you have placed these large figures over here; it makes your drawing very strong" (p. 202). Such statements help children realize that the symbols of art can indeed communicate and that the symbols need not be accompanied by words in order to be valuable.

Goals of Visual Arts Experiences

The expected outcomes of art instruction are much more process oriented than product oriented. In other words, goals are likely to be general—for

TABLE 13.1 Developmental Continuum of Children's Drawing

PRESCHOOL (AGES 2–5)	EARLY PRIMARY (AGES 4–6)	MIDDLE PRIMARY (AGES 5–8)	LATE PRIMARY (AGES 7–10)
■ scribbles, loops, zigzags, wavy lines, jabs, arcs—often partially off the paper at first ■ chance forms or shapes ■ trying out different effects ■ meaning in the act itself, not in results or product ■ experimenting with leaving a mark, with colors and motions to leave a sign or have an effect ■ reflecting motion of hand/arm ■ separate lines, circlelike shapes, combined straight and curved lines ■ other basic forms, controlled marks, first schematic formulae, mandalalike shapes *Sources:* physical act of moving a hand and arm, basic concepts such as the circle, exploration of possibilities of line	■ shapes combined, becoming schemas; intentional image repetition of schemas; development of preferred schemas ■ beginnings of representation, often of people; letterlike forms; basic forms represented consistently—houses, flowers, boats, people; animals in profile ■ meaning (subject matter) increasingly readable ■ repertory or symbolic forms repeated, practiced, and new elements added ■ beginnings of individual style (e.g., typical way of drawing a house) ■ figures isolated, no context or baseline; each discrete (no overlapping of whole or of parts); size and details according to perceived importance or interest (e.g., long arms) ■ several figures on the page; beginning representing of events or narratives; schematic figures placed in a larger concept, for example, knowing an elephant is a four-legged animal with a trunk, the child uses a well-established routine or schema, for drawing animals—cats, dogs, and so forth—and adds a trunk *Sources:* child's concepts and knowledge about the world, which take precedence over direct perception (as in the elephant example above)	■ elaboration and variation of schematic figures and experimentation; repetition of imagery, practicing "set pictures" (always drawn the same way), such as racing cars ■ details often traditional or formulaic, such as windows with tie-back curtains, chimneys with smoke coming out at an angle, girls defined by skirts and long hair ■ narrative, illustrative, inventive; baselines often multiple; "see-through" houses; most figures in own space, without overlapping *Sources:* copying conventional renderings by other children, imagination, book illustrations, TV, cartoons, and so on	■ increased differentiation—of kinds of animals, flowers, buildings, and so on; practiced drawing of favorite subjects—battle scenes, princesses, characters from TV, comics, books; pictures often telling detailed stories ■ interest in drawing from nature ■ figures sometimes in profile, with limbs bent, props added to indicate roles (e.g., cowboy hat and rope); increasing demand for looking real ■ color more naturalistic; scenery, overlapping, shadows, beginning perspective, and shading; more realistic use of scale; distance, elevations, and perspective added ■ backgrounds: landscapes, seascapes, sky, under-ground, under the sea; figures more logically interrelated; elevations, consistent viewpoints given ■ action: eye still seeing one relationship at a time, the mind having to put them together on the page to solve problems; fine control of line *Sources:* observation, imagination, book knowledge, copying, and so forth

Source: B. S. Engel, *Considering Children's Art: Why and How to Value Their Works* (Washington, DC: National Association for the Education of Young Children, 1995), p. 35. Reprinted with permission from the National Association for the Education of Young Children.

instance, "Involving children in art experiences" and "Helping children become aware of the elements of art"—and are unlikely to include having each child complete a certain product. Other important goals of visual arts experiences in the early childhood classroom include the following:

1. Encouraging children to explore a wide variety of materials

2. Providing activities that give sensory pleasure to the participants

3. Allowing children to make discoveries about color, shape, and texture

4. Helping children gain control of fine muscles and practice eye–hand coordination

5. Helping children feel comfortable with their ability to express themselves through art

6. Introducing children to the work of the world's artists

Clearly, these goals are very broad; they do not focus on specific skills, such as mastering perspective. The purpose of art in the early childhood years is to help children express what they know and feel and to begin to recognize how others express themselves through art. One teacher summed up this approach by saying, "I never thought of children's art as something to decorate the hallways. My main task is to keep children thinking, experimenting, trying, changing, and moving things—going beyond what's obvious to seeing and expressing relationships" (Dighe, Calomiris, and Van Zutphen 1998, p. 4.).

Standards for Visual Arts Education

http://artsedge.kennedy-center.org/teach/standards/standards_k4.cfm

The K–4 visual arts content standards online

As mentioned earlier in this chapter, the Consortium of National Arts Education Associations published the *National Standards for Arts Education* in 1994 in an effort to define what a good arts education should provide and to give schools and programs a framework on which to build in curriculum planning. In the section of the standards devoted to the visual arts for kindergarten through grade four (K–4), the authors provide this rationale:

These standards provide a framework for helping students learn the characteristics of the visual arts by using a wide range of subject matter, symbols, meaningful images, and visual expressions, to reflect their ideas, feelings, and

Visual arts activities provide unique opportunities for children to explore their own thoughts and feelings.

emotions; and to evaluate the merits of their efforts. The standards address these objectives in ways that promote acquisition of and fluency in new ways of thinking, working, communicating, reasoning, and investigating. They emphasize student acquisition of the most important and enduring ideas, concepts, issues, dilemmas, and knowledge offered by the visual arts. They develop new techniques, approaches, and habits for applying knowledge and skills in the visual arts to the world beyond school. (Consortium 1994)*

Here are the K–4 visual arts content standards:

Visual Arts Content Standards

1. Understanding and applying media, techniques, and processes
2. Using knowledge of structures and functions
3. Choosing and evaluating a range of subject matter, symbols, and ideas
4. Understanding the visual arts in relation to history and cultures
5. Reflecting upon and assessing the characteristics and merits of their work and the work of others
6. Making connections between visual arts and other disciplines (Consortium 1994)*

For each of these content standards, achievement standards are also provided that describe the skills or behaviors that demonstrate successful learning outcomes. For instance, for the first content standard about "media, techniques, and processes," the achievement standards are as follows:

Students know the differences between materials, techniques, and processes
Students describe how different materials, techniques, and processes cause different responses
Students use different media, techniques, and processes to communicate ideas, experiences, and stories
Students use art materials and tools in a safe and responsible manner (Consortium 1994)*

Using the content and achievement standards together, teachers can plan developmentally appropriate activities and observe students to assess their level of success in each area.

Suggested Visual Arts Experiences

Colbert and Taunton (1992) suggest that children need many opportunities to create, look at, and talk about art; they also need to become aware of art in their everyday lives. The activities described in the following sections will help achieve these objectives.

Graphic Art Children can draw with pencils, crayons, chalk, and markers. A variety of papers of different colors, surface textures, and shapes can add interest to drawing activities. Patterns, dittos, and coloring books carry the message that the child cannot produce acceptable representations for herself; these should therefore be avoided. If the goal is for a child to learn to control the marker or chalk in order to fill in spaces, the child can fill in her own spaces, achieve the goal, and maintain a feeling of competence by drawing her own shapes and figures.

Painting   Young children can paint with tempera at easels or on tables, or they can fingerpaint. Children painting at easels have freedom to move their arms and can use more muscles than they can sitting at tables, where the muscular movements tend to be confined to the hands. When painting at easels, children can learn to control the paint drips, explore the results of using paints of different thicknesses, and stand back to look at their work from eye level more easily than when painting at tables. Fingerpaint invites children to explore texture and to risk the messiness. Children can be encouraged to use the sides of their hands and their palms as well as their fingers in the paint.

Teachers may want to offer other paint experiences, such as rolling paint from a roll-on bottle; spatter painting; blowing paint with a straw; dropping paint on paper; using objects other than a brush to apply paint (sponges, crumpled paper, aluminum foil, and so on); or rolling a small ball or marbles in paint and then on paper placed on the bottom of a box.

Printing   Printing can range from quite simple experiences, such as dipping a sponge or a piece of junk into paint and then pressing it onto paper, to complex projects, such as preparing a print form, rolling ink on it with a brayer, and then printing with it. Most kindergarten and primary children can make simple prints. Younger children tend to smear the paint when they try to press objects on paper. In addition to junk prints, kindergartners and primary children can make prints by gluing yarn, fabric scraps, or pieces of natural material onto cardboard or cylinders and then printing with these. Or they can combine media by doing a crayon rubbing and then printing over it.

Sculpture   Children enjoy sculpting with a variety of media; modeling clay is most commonly used. Clay should be available to children regularly. Clay experiences can be varied by using potter's clay that will harden; then children can paint their creations. Other variations include mixing clay with collage materials so that objects are embedded in the clay to achieve three-dimensional creations.

Paper is also a popular medium for sculpting—it can be folded, torn, crumpled, or glued into three-dimensional forms. Cardboard tubes and small boxes are useful, too.

Wood sculpture is also popular; children can glue wood scraps to create extraordinary shapes and designs. (Cabinet shops will often save wood scraps for teachers. Hardwood scraps usually have interesting shapes.)

Collage   Collages can be made with tissue paper; natural materials, such as bark and seeds; fabrics; and a variety of found materials. Collage gives children opportunities to develop an appreciation for texture and appealing arrangements of objects that are not possible

Parents and the Arts

- Send home supplies for arts activities that can be done by families—for example, clay that can be molded, dried, and painted; some cut paper strips for paper sculptures (glue only the ends of the strips to a base sheet, twist strips over and under other strips, fold them, and so on).

with other media. Another advantage of collage is the use of glue. Paste and glue offer unique sensory experiences, and children will want to explore the stickiness, adhesive qualities, and spreadability of different adhesives.

Sewing and Weaving   Very young children can sew on styrofoam trays with holes punched in them or on net stretched in a frame. Kindergartners can sew on burlap with yarn. If children have trouble tying knots, the ends of the yarn can be taped on the back of the burlap with masking tape. Older children can sew with a variety of fabrics, either to create soft sculptures or to decorate the fabrics. Primary children can produce simple projects on circular or straw looms. They can also weave paper or fabric strips into interesting designs.

Combining Techniques   Teachers will think of many other experiences that are appropriate for young children and many ways to combine basic techniques. For example, children might paint on fabric; dye fabric; create simple batiks using crayons and dye on fabric; create puppets using paper, clay, or fabrics; use yarn to create a string design on cardboard and then print with the cardboard; fingerpaint on a table top and then make a print of the design by covering it with paper and rubbing lightly; create a crayon resist by drawing with wax crayons and painting over the drawing with tempera; or color with crayons, cover the colors with black crayon, and then scratch a design through the black crayon.

The list of ideas is almost endless. Keep in mind, however, that as Wachowiak (1977) notes, children often do not enjoy or appreciate a new process or media until they become involved in it.

Viewing and Talking about Art   Schiller (1995) describes her experiences with bringing examples of fine art into her preschool classroom. Although she received very little response from the children at first, over time they began to discuss the artworks during group times and to choose their favorite pieces. Adding appropriate artworks that relate to topics of interest to the children is the key to getting them to talk about and look at art more closely.

Viewing and talking about the works of various artists is another good approach. See the following Learning Plan for first- and second-grade children, in which they learn about the different styles of well-known artists.

Art versus Craft Activities

Art and craft activities are not the same. *Art,* as it is being defined in this chapter, is an opportunity for children to explore media with no external product goals. Although children may indeed create products as part of an art experience, they have control of their products, and the process of creating is more important than the products that result.

Craft activities, on the other hand, generally require that children produce something, and most of the products will be very similar or even exactly the same. Some craft activities, such as making pencil holders for gifts, are acceptable if children have a choice about whether to participate. Such craft activities can be made more appropriate for children if the materials and designs for decorating the cans are selected by the children rather than dictated by the teacher. The planning, decision making, and self-expression

NAEYC CRITERIA
2.79

Exploring Artists and Their Styles: First- and Second-Graders

Objectives: Children will be able to describe the particular style of an artist and create art that illustrates the style.

Materials: A collection of prints of the art of Kandinsky (available as posters on the Web, or get your librarian to help you). Choose several that are not too dense, such as *Farbstudie Quadrate, Farbstudie, Color Study–1913, Squares and Concentric Circles, Houses in Munich, Structure Joyeuse,* and *Accent in Rose*. Make sure that the art center is well stocked with paint, paper, brushes, and so on.

Procedure:

1. Show the children the first print that you have selected. Discuss how the painting was made (what was painted first and so on). Discuss the use of line and color.
2. Repeat this discussion with other selections until the children know several of the pieces and can discuss them in terms of line, color, and composition.
3. Encourage the children to try some of Kandinsky's styles the next time they paint. Remember to stress applying his styles, not making exact copies of his pieces.
4. Continue until all the children who wish to do so have had a chance to paint in Kandinsky's styles.
5. Leave all the paintings you have discussed on display in the classroom (at the children's eye level).

Accommodations: If a child does not choose to paint in a Kandinsky style, allow him to paint what he wishes, but discuss the style with him and make sure he can describe the style.

Assessment: Observe children's paintings and have children describe Kandinsky's style orally.

Extended Activity: Hosting an art show of the children's paintings would be ideal. Mount and hang the paintings on a bulletin board or a wall. If the parents are invited to visit, each child could explain to his own parents what he incorporated of Kandinsky's style. Taking the children to a museum to see Kandinsky's work in the originals would also be ideal but not probable in many schools.

---

that are so important in art are rarely found in craft experiences, in which the outcome is predetermined.

Many activities presented to young children as art are neither art nor craft. When children are given patterns for making owls or spiders at Halloween or flowers in the spring, what they learn from these cut-and-paste activities is to follow the teacher's directions, to wait until they are told what to do with materials, and to make their products look exactly like the teacher's model. Such activities meet none of the goals of art. Justifying these experiences with the claim that they teach children to follow directions is questionable—children can learn to follow directions in other activities. The negative learning and frustration that often accompany these projects outweigh any advantages in learning to follow directions.

Both art and craft activities have important places in an integrated curriculum. When provided with needed materials, children can paint a mural of snow activities, build a birdhouse or bird feeder, or illustrate a class book on a topic they have studied (Dever and Jared 1996).

Certainly, it is not difficult for teachers to think of art and craft activities that might accompany certain topics of study. However, teachers must stay focused on allowing children to choose the activities they want to do and to express themselves as they participate in art and craft activities that enhance instruction in other areas.

www.

www.amc-music.com/child_development.htm

Various reports supporting music as a part of children's education

Music

Music, like the visual arts, is a basic way of learning, experiencing, and communicating. All children deserve a rich musical environment in which to learn to sing, to play music, to move, and to listen. Music is also a valuable tool for helping children gain content knowledge and make sense of their experiences.

Music is a pervasive influence in our lives. We hear music when we worship, exercise, relax, drive, and attend baptisms, weddings, and funerals (Merrion and Vincent 1988). Planned musical experiences should not be delayed until children can participate in group singing or until they can keep an accurate beat. Because research indicates that children respond to music very early, McDonald (1979) suggests that "the starting time for learning about music is the same as the starting time for any learning. Music is one facet in the total education of the child. It must emerge with the nature and needs of the child, from birth onward" (p. 4).

Goals of a Music Program

The Music Educators National Conference/National Association for Music Education (MENC/NAME 1994) has established the following guidelines for "Curriculum and Scheduling" for young children:

1. Music is integrated into the curriculum throughout the day.
2. The children's learning experiences include singing, playing instruments, listening to music, creating music, and moving to music.
3. At least 12 percent of the contact time with children in every prekindergarten and kindergarten is devoted to experiences with music.

> **The purpose of education is to awaken joy in creative expression and knowledge.**
>
> *—Albert Einstein*

In addition, in a position paper entitled *The School Music Program: A New Vision,* the MENC/NAME suggests that music experiences should be grounded in the following beliefs:

1. All children have musical potential.
2. Children bring their own unique interests and abilities to the music learning environment.
3. Very young children are capable of developing critical thinking skills through musical ideas.
4. Children come to early-childhood music experiences from diverse backgrounds.
5. Children should experience exemplary musical sounds, activities, and materials.
6. Children should not be encumbered with the need to meet performance goals.
7. Children's play is their work.
8. Children learn best in pleasant physical and social environments.
9. Diverse learning environments are needed to serve the developmental needs of many individual children.
10. Children need effective adult models. (MENC 1994)

These beliefs underlie the standards for music education, the subject of the following section.

For very young children, music need not necessarily be a group experience, although very short group experiences may be successful. More frequently, music is an individual or small-group activity. As children go

www.bestchildrensmusic.com
Lists of musical books, easily accessible music, research articles on music education, and links to other music education sites

www.menc.org
The National Association for Music Education page, with links to a forum and resources for music education

about the day's activities, they and their teachers can sing and chant about what they are doing. A wide variety of songs and rhythms should be used, and children should be guided to move rhythmically to the beat and melodic direction they hear. Teachers can also provide safe toys with musical sounds the children can control (MENC 1994).

Also, music need not be limited to actual songs—it is *sound* that brings pleasure and helps children express feelings or thoughts. A child crooning a lullaby while rocking a doll or splashing rhythmically in water is making music a part of everyday experience.

Standards for Music Education

www.

http://artsedge.kennedy-center.org/teach/standards/standards_k4.cfm

The K–4 music content standards online

The *National Standards for Arts Education,* published in 1994, also provide specific music education standards for students in kindergarten through grade four (K–4). The authors of the standards offer this rationale for music education at this level:

> Performing, creating, and responding to music are the fundamental music processes in which humans engage. Students, particularly in grades K-4, learn by doing. Singing, playing instruments, moving to music, and creating music enable them to acquire musical skills and knowledge that can be developed in no other way. Learning to read and notate music gives them a skill with which to explore music independently and with others. Listening to, analyzing, and evaluating music are important building blocks of musical learning. Further, to participate fully in a diverse, global society, students must understand their own historical and cultural heritage and those of others within their communities and beyond. Because music is a basic expression of human culture, every student should have access to a balanced, comprehensive, and sequential program of study in music. (Consortium 1994)*

Here are the nine music education content standards for grades K–4:

Music Content Standards

1. Singing, alone and with others, a varied repertoire of music
2. Performing on instruments, alone and with others, a varied repertoire of music
3. Improvising melodies, variations, and accompaniments
4. Composing and arranging music within specified guidelines
5. Reading and notating music
6. Listening to, analyzing, and describing music
7. Evaluating music and music performances
8. Understanding relationships between music, the other arts, and disciplines outside the arts
9. Understanding music in relation to history and culture (Consortium 1994)*

For each content standard, several achievement standards are also provided; they describe the student skills or behaviors that demonstrate successful learning outcomes. For instance, for the first content standard about singing, the achievement standards are as follows:

---

*From *National Standards for Arts Education.* Copyright © 1994 by Music Educators National Conference (MENC). Used by permission.

Students sing independently, on pitch and in rhythm, with appropriate timbre, diction, and posture, and maintain a steady tempo

Students sing expressively, with appropriate dynamics, phrasing, and interpretation

Students sing from memory a varied repertoire of songs representing genres and styles from diverse cultures

Students sing ostinatos, partner songs, and rounds

Students sing in groups, blending vocal timbres, matching dynamic levels, and responding to the cues of a conductor (Consortium 1994)*

Teachers can use the content and achievement standards together to plan developmentally appropriate activities and observe students' performance.

Singing

Learning to sing is a developmental process. Young children need a supportive and encouraging environment for singing. Their ability to sing is closely related to their growing abilities in other areas of development. From research, we know that most children can sing by age two, that songs with a limited range are easier for children to sing, that play contributes to the development of singing, and that young children often enjoy listening to favorite songs again and again (McDonald 1979). Primary children increase their repertoire of songs and can often learn to sing in parts, such as singing a round. Singing, like other skills, is learned through singing, and all children should be considered singers (Neely 2002).

Selecting Songs

In choosing songs for children, teachers must consider the pitch range, the intervals, and the subject of the song. The range must be one in which most children are comfortable singing, which includes approximately the A below middle C to the G or A above middle C. As children mature, the range can be increased; children in the primary grades who are comfortable singing can be introduced to songs with greater ranges. Songs with descending intervals and few wide skips in the melody are more easily sung by young children. Songs should also be repetitious, both in melody and rhythmic patterns. Children enjoy a wide variety of songs about animals, themselves, or their friends, and some nonsense rhymes and jingles (McDonald and Simons 1989).

Gilbert (1981) lists the following points to consider when choosing songs to teach:

1. The song should *appeal to the children.* It may be the tune itself or the rhythm that is attractive; whatever it is, if children like the song and can remember it easily, they will enjoy singing it.
2. The song should *not be too long* and, in general, the younger the child the greater the need for repetition and for a predictable pattern within each verse.
3. Songs with a *chorus* encourage even shy children to join in.
4. Songs which lend themselves to *movement* often have greater potential with young children.

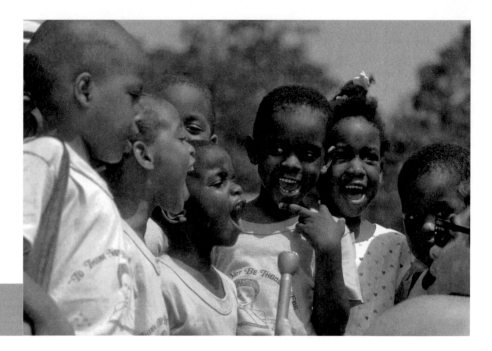

Singing is one of the pleasures of being with a group.

5. Avoid tunes with very *high notes* or *difficult leaps.*
6. Choose songs with words that the children *understand.* Sometimes it is necessary to explain a particular word; at other times it is better to substitute another word or phrase. Always try out new words to see how they "sing." (p. 16)

A surprising number of songs fit the criteria described above. Some examples include "Go Tell Aunt Rhody," "Twinkle, Twinkle Little Star," "Where Is Thumpkin?" "Baa, Baa Black Sheep," and many other nursery songs. Older children will enjoy folk songs ("Michael Row Your Boat Ashore" and "This Land Is Your Land"), humorous songs (such as the songs from *Mary Poppins*), and songs from other cultures. Teachers will know that songs are good choices if the children sing them spontaneously or ask to sing them in group music times.

Not only is singing a delightful experience, but children who are learning songs and creating words to melodies are also learning phonemic awareness and phonics skills (Smith 2000). If you make charts of the songs they know or make song booklets, the children can match the words they know to the words in print.

Presenting Songs

Teachers who are not confident of their singing voices can begin by learning a few simple folk songs and singing them with individual children or small groups before singing with the whole group (Jalongo and Collins 1985). What children need most is a teacher who loves music and shares that interest and enthusiasm; young children are appreciative of the teacher's singing and are not music critics. Jalongo (1996) believes that "teachers who have limited musical backgrounds can do as well in teaching music as do teachers with extensive musical backgrounds, but only if nonmusicians are conscientious and enthusiastic about following a daily musical curriculum featuring high-quality music" (p. 6).

Teachers who play the piano or feel comfortable about their own singing voices usually introduce songs by playing or singing them several times for the children and then encouraging children to sing along with them. Teachers who cannot play the songs can use recordings to introduce music quite successfully.

After presenting the whole song several times, the teacher may want to sing a line if the children are having difficulty learning it, but each experience should end with the children singing the whole song through again. This routine will need to be repeated several times over a period of days before the children will be comfortable with a new song (Persellin 2003).

Musical experiences can be opportunities for problem solving, as children invent new words to songs or new ways of moving to music. Singing games such as "Hokey Pokey" and "Punchinella" lend themselves naturally to problem solving, as children must create their own movements. Children can also create new words to familiar songs. They might substitute any five-letter name in "B-I-N-G-O" and make up a verse about that person. Problem solving is encouraged when children are free to explore and play and when their efforts are supported (Hildebrandt 1998).

Chants such as "The Bear Hunt" are also valuable in the music program, as children learn the rhythms and patterns of language. Many chants lend themselves to instrumentation or body percussion sounds; children can add claps, snaps, or clicks to the rhythm of the chant. Buchoff (1994) suggests that many poems and jump-rope rhymes are appropriate for classroom use. After the children have learned a chant, they can add physical accompaniments, such as clapping, snapping their fingers, tapping their fingers or toes, and so on. Putting the words to a chant on a poster or in a booklet or newsletter can also help children share the chant with their peers and parents.

Playing Instruments

Today's approach to playing instruments with young children focuses on their exploration of sound and rhythm. Even very young children like to produce sounds by banging on pots and pans. Such interest usually continues, and they are eager to explore sound with drums, bells, xylophones, and shakers.

Even though the focus is on exploration, the teacher can help individuals or small groups with instruction in how to hold an instrument or how to strike it to get a more satisfactory sound. As children become able to keep a beat, they can invent simple accompaniments to familiar songs. Primary children can begin to learn to play simple instruments such as recorders.

Studies of children's use of musical instruments and the implications for teachers can be summarized as follows:

1. Children should have many opportunities for free exploration with instruments before any structured activities are attempted.

2. Teachers should attend to children's interests and needs when providing any instruction on how to play an instrument.

Parents and the Arts

- Teachers can help parents encourage the musical development of their children by making the music accessible to parents, helping parents understand that the music needs to be beautiful for optimal effect, and ensuring that parents feel comfortable sharing music with their children as they grow.

3. Children need to express rhythm through physical movement before instruments are introduced.

4. Exploration with instruments can help children learn about pitch, timbre, rhythm, and melody.

Teaching should focus on helping children achieve the technical skills needed to express creative ideas (McDonald and Simons 1989).

Listening Experiences

Children can be encouraged to listen to a variety of music. **Guided listening** experiences for younger children should be very short. As children mature, the pieces of music selected for listening can be longer and the children can be expected to hear more complex patterns. Teachers should select classical music, folk music, and music from a variety of cultures and ethnic groups. Listening experiences are most effective if the children are comfortable, both physically and psychologically, and if new experiences are based on the children's previous experiences. Children also need guidance in what to listen for, such as repeated phrases or passages that create moods or images.

Listening experiences can be created through games and other everyday experiences. Children can be encouraged to listen to environmental sounds, both inside and outside the room. Games can include guessing what produced a given sound, clapping back a pattern produced on a drum by the teacher or another student, or recognizing voices (as in "Doggie, Doggie, Who Has the Bone?").

Older preschoolers and primary children can benefit from listening to short, live performances. Often, local symphony orchestras or high school groups prepare special programs for young children. Some of these programs introduce the instruments of the orchestra and help children listen for their sounds; others present musical stories that children will enjoy.

Suthers (1993) found that introducing children to musical selections in advance of a program greatly enhanced their ability to listen to and appreciate the performance of an orchestra. To achieve this, teachers were provided with teaching kits consisting of plans for musical activities and recordings of the music to be played.

Whether to use music in the background when children are engaged in other activities is a question that teachers will have to answer for themselves. Some teachers argue that children ignore background music; this makes it difficult for them to learn to listen to music attentively. Others argue that providing carefully selected background music at quiet times of the day can be a way of exposing children to music when there might otherwise be no time to do so. No one advocates playing music that adds to the noise level when the children are engaged in noisy activities.

Many teachers choose to make records and tapes available for children to use at listening stations during the activity times of each day. Such stations allow children who wish to listen to music the opportunity to do so without disturbing other children.

Approaches to Music Instruction

Three approaches to musical instruction for young children will be described briefly in the following sections: Dalcroze Eurhythmics, the Kodály method, and the Orff approach.

Dalcroze Eurhythmics

Emile Jaques-Dalcroze (1865–1950), a Swiss composer and teacher, developed an approach to teaching music based on the belief that rhythm was the fundamental force in music and that children should develop an awareness of music through body movement. Jaques-Dalcroze believed that sequence was important in teaching children music and that the simplest of rhythmic experiences should be first, followed by more difficult and complicated activities, followed by instrumental study. This method—called *eurhythmics*—emphasizes the importance of an immediate physical response to music and of having children dramatize music with their bodies.

Findlay's *Rhythm and Movement: Applications of Dalcroze Eurhythmics* (1971) is a good source for teachers; it contains a brief explanation of the child's need for a rhythmic response and a wealth of ideas and activities that any teacher of young children will find interesting and helpful. Dalcroze training for teachers is also available at many universities across the United States.

www.dalcrozeusa.org
The home page of the Dalcroze association, with information about Dalcroze and his techniques

The Kodály Method

Zoltán Kodály (1882–1967), a Hungarian composer, was a contemporary of Jaques-Dalcroze. He believed that the most important instrument in a child's music education was her own voice. Kodály relied heavily on children's games, nursery songs, and folk music in helping children learn to sing. He believed that accompaniments to songs should be simple and that a child should learn to "appreciate music as a pure, unadulterated melody emanating from himself, this appreciation being achieved through ear-training exercises" (Bayless and Ramsey 1991, p. 218).

The Kodály method is not complicated. Most teachers can implement the program without special training or special equipment.

http://home.earthlink.net/~debrajet/Kodaly.html
Information about Kodály and his techniques

The Orff Approach

Carl Orff (1895–1982), a German composer, developed his method from work with young dance students in his school. Orff is most commonly associated with the pitched instruments that bear his name. (Most catalogs of musical instruments for children include the Orff instruments.)

The Orff program involves structuring a musical environment and then helping children improvise within the environment. Important elements of the Orff method include rhythm, body percussion (stamping, slapping the thighs, clapping, and finger snapping), dramatic movement, melody, and the use of instruments (both percussion instruments and pitched instruments). Orff advocated that activities progress from speech to rhythmic activities to song and then to playing musical instruments.

Although Orff instruments are fairly expensive, many schools use them. Orff training is available to teachers who are interested in learning the approach (McDonald and Simons 1989).

Crinklaw-Kiser (1996) found that the Orff–Schulwerk approach to music is very compatible with a developmentally appropriate curriculum. (The word *schulwerk* in the title means "schoolwork.") This approach begins with what children like to do—sing, clap, dance, and so on. Starting with the rhythm of a song, first the words are added, and then activities are added to expand on that knowledge, such as word cards, charts, booklets, and so on.

www.keyofz.com/keyofz/langley/orff.html
Information about Orff and his techniques

Movement and Dance

Movement to music begins very early—children often sway and nod to music they hear. Emile Jaques-Dalcroze, discussed earlier, believed that movement was the best way to help children learn to love and appreciate music. He believed that training in moving in response to music should begin in the first year of life.

Fundamental motor abilities are learned and mastered during the preschool years; it therefore makes sense to focus on the *process* of movement instruction during this time, rather than on the *product*. Most children have mastered the basic movements by the time they enter first grade, but as Malina (1982) notes, "The quality of performance continues to improve as the fundamental patterns are refined and integrated into more complex movement sequences" (p. 215). Seven- and eight-year-olds continue to gain skill and control in motor development. They can add a beat to music, keep a beat with an instrument while singing, and learn simple folk dances.

Movement Experiences

Movement experiences should be planned to include both creative and more structured movements. Creative movement activities are those in which children interpret instructions in their own ways; their movements may not necessarily match the beat of the music. Examples of creative movement activities are having children move in a given direction and then change direction when the music changes; use movements that are heavy or light; move fast or slow; and so on. More structured movement experiences include asking children to learn to keep a beat and move to a beat.

A typical structured movement experience is clapping to simple rhythms. Teachers often have children clap the syllables in their own and their classmates' names. Teachers might also ask children to walk to a drumbeat or walk to the beat of music played on the piano or a recording. As children gain more control and are able to keep the beat more accurately, they may be asked to learn simple dance steps.

Sullivan (1982) recommends another simple movement exercise, "Clap, Clap, Clap Your Hands." With the children sitting down, the teacher plays:

C   C   G   F   E   C   C   D   E D   low G
Clap, clap, clap your hands. Clap your hands to-geth-er.

C   C   G   F   E   E   E   D   D D   C
Clap, clap, clap your hands. Clap your hands to-geth-er.

Children can be encouraged to think of other movements, such as tapping their knees, tapping their elbows, shaking their hands, shaking their heads, and so on.

Primary children can be encouraged to keep the beat and explore movement through such exercises as "Copycat." The children find their own space. The leader improvises a movement on the count of one, and the children imitate the movement on the count of two. A drum may be used to help keep the beat.

In another exercise, the children stand in a long line across the room and are numbered off by threes. Together, they walk forward for eight counts, backward for eight counts, and then turn in their original spot for eight counts. When this pattern has been mastered, the "1s" perform the routine alone, followed by the "2s" and then the "3s." The whole pattern is repeated several times (Findlay 1971).

Dance Education

Dance education is important in helping children learn to express themselves through movement. According to Koff (2000), "Dance education can be described as the sequential development through the exploration of time, space, and energy in order to express oneself" (p. 28). Dance training, on the other hand, prepares children to perform as dancers. Dance education, then, is a movement program that can help children learn and can balance their need for movement against the more sedentary activities of most schooldays.

Dance education can be integrated into the curriculum as students learn story elements and the parallel dance elements or the understanding of culture through the medium of dance. Dance provides children with the opportunity to learn nonverbal communication skills, which can help many of them solidify their understandings of the other communication skills that get so much attention in the typical curriculum.

Standards for Dance Education

A set of dance education standards was also included as part of the *National Standards for Arts Education*, published in 1994 by the Consortium of National Arts Education Associations. For students in kindergarten through grade four (K–4), the authors offer this philosophy of dance education:

http://artsedge.kennedy-center.org/teach/standards/standards_k4.cfm

The K–4 dance content standards online

> Children in grades K-4 love to move and learn through engagement of the whole self. They need to become literate in the language of dance in order to use this natural facility as a means of communication and self-expression, and as a way of responding to the expression of others. Dancing and creating dances provide them with skills and knowledge necessary for all future learning in dance and give them a way to celebrate their humanity. (Consortium 1994)*

There are seven dance education content standards for grades K–4:

Dance Content Standards

1. Identifying and demonstrating movement elements and skills in performing dance
2. Understanding choreographic principles, processes and structures
3. Understanding dance as a way to create and communicate meaning
4. Applying and demonstrating critical and creating thinking skills in dance
5. Demonstrating and understanding dance in various cultures and historical periods
6. Making connections between dance and healthful living
7. Making connections between dance and other disciplines (Consortium 1994)*

As with the visual arts and music standards, several achievement standards are provided for each dance education standard. For instance, for the

---

*From *National Standards for Arts Education*. Copyright © 1994 by Music Educators National Conference (MENC). Used by permission.

third content standard, "Understanding dance as a way to create and communicate meaning," these are the achievement standards:

> Students observe and discuss how dance is different from other forms of human movement (such as sports, everyday gestures)
> Students take an active role in a class discussion about interpretations of and reactions to a dance
> Students present their own dances to peers and discuss their meanings with competence and confidence (Consortium 1994)*

Teachers can observe students' skills and behaviors, as described by these achievement standards, to determine students' success in the arts education content areas.

Drama

www.

www.illinoisearlylearning.org/ tipsheets/drama.htm

Ideas for involving young children in drama

Drama in the early childhood classroom is defined as experiences in which children play, pretend, role-play, or create characters or ideas. McGregor, Tate, and Robinson (1987) state that the essential characteristic of drama is acting out. In acting out,

> there is an agreement to suspend the normal social roles with each other in identifying with the new imagined roles. There is an agreement to make a different use of the environment. In this case a desk becomes a dining table laden with food, a chalk box becomes a cigar box, and so on. This different use of the environment includes a shift in the conventions of time. Events may be telescoped to give them greater or less significance. The usual conventions of space and time may be suspended during acting out. (p. 12)

Parents and the Arts

● Encourage parents who are interested to participate with their children in creative dramatics or other arts experiences.

Drama in early childhood education is not the production of plays in which children memorize lines and act given roles. Such productions are often appropriate for older children but are not appropriate for the early childhood years. Creative drama usually refers to spontaneous productions in which children create or recreate stories, moods, or incidents without learning lines or practicing their roles.

Drama in the classroom can contribute to the general goals of early childhood programs, fostering the development of skills such as these:

1. Critical-thinking and problem-solving skills
2. An ability to work cooperatively with others
3. An increased ability to understand the perspectives of others
4. An ability to communicate more effectively
5. The integration of ideas from many sources into a meaningful whole

Of course, drama experiences provide another avenue for self-expression and developing creativity that is as important as their contributions to other curriculum goals.

---

*From *National Standards for Arts Education.* Copyright © 1994 by Music Educators National Conference (MENC). Used by permission.

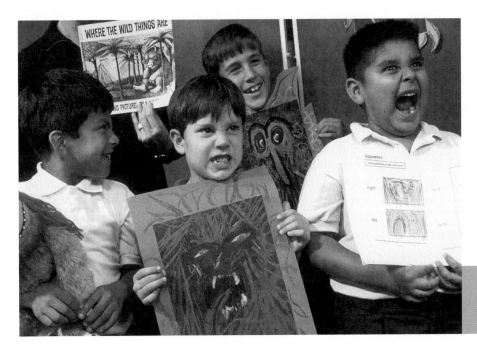

Children's literature provides an excellent foundation for drama activities.

Encouraging Drama

Most experiences with drama occur spontaneously in children's play or in response to music, songs, stories, or other experiences. Teachers will want to encourage and support these dramatic activities, but they may also plan for specific experiences in drama. Teachers can encourage children's play and help them add or extend dramatic elements. For example, a teacher observing children choosing roles for dramatic play might help a child think of a role or imagine how someone might act in a given role or provide a prop or costume to help the child conceptualize the role more fully.

Most teachers of young children have observed that drama, like other creative arts experiences, is a natural response that arises in a supportive classroom environment with teacher encouragement. Children returning from a trip to the zoo often assume the roles of the people or animals they encountered there. After hearing a story, children will often act out the roles of some of the characters. Even very young children will imitate voices or pretend to be as sad or as scared as one of the characters in a story.

Planned drama experiences may be incorporated into movement, music, and literature experiences. If the children are exploring movement patterns, they might be asked to move in a way that represents a given character or mood—to tiptoe quickly to represent the movement of mice, for example. Children might also use drama to demonstrate their understanding of the lyrics of songs they are learning. (If they are asked to glide and they flap their arms, the teacher can assume that they do not understand the term *glide*.) After listening to a story, children often want to retell it through dramatic representations. If, after listening to *Where the Wild Things Are* (Sendak 1963), they can act out Max's anger, the power of the "wild things," and Max's relief when he returns to his very own room, there will be no need to ask them comprehension questions. Roser (2001) notes that drama is an underused response to reading or hearing a story read. Often, teachers turn first to writing and art, but drama can play an important role in helping children clarify their understanding of a text by acting it out.

Other planned drama experiences can extend children's concept knowledge. Fox (1987, pp. 59–60) describes a dramatic activity that she calls "Caterpillars and Butterflies." (If the class were studying insects or caterpillars, these activities would not only add interest but would also give the teacher a chance to observe the children's understanding of concepts.) Fox suggests that children begin by observing how real caterpillars move. After these observations, the children crawl around, imitating the movements of the caterpillars (perhaps to music). After hearing the teacher read *The Very Hungry Caterpillar* (Carle 1969), some children can form a tight circle to create an orange, and others can crawl through the orange (eating a hole in the orange). Then the children can think about what happens to the caterpillar after it has eaten all the food. They can curl themselves into cocoons and then pretend to nibble out and spread their butterfly wings. It is helpful if the children can observe the movements of a real butterfly or watch a film of a butterfly in slow motion before they imitate the butterfly movements. Children might also create butterfly wings with scarves or tissue paper and use them in their movements.

> **The arts are an even better barometer of what is happening in our world than the stock market or the debates in Congress.**
>
> —*Hendrik Willem Van Loon*

Dyer and Schiller (1993) suggest that dramatic performances be approached as problem-solving opportunities instead of the usual memorize-and-rehearse activities. Children should be allowed to figure out how to present to an audience different elements of a story or different interpretations of an event. When this problem-solving experience is part of preparing for a performance, the results will be children's intellectual growth as well as greater audience interest.

Cline and Ingerson (1996) provide the following tips for successful drama experiences:

- Keep story lines and sessions short.
- Focus initially on action instead of dialogue.
- Use many characters (even inanimate objects can be played). Create new ones if you need to.
- Encourage children to be specific ("If Humpty is fat, how can he move to show it?").
- Always keep a distinct physical boundary between the stage and the house (audience), even if it is just a line of tape on the floor. . . .
- Rotate players and audience frequently. . . .
- Narrate the stories during rehearsals and performances until the children become more proficient. . . .
- Interject comments or questions (side coaching). . . .
- Respect and encourage children's decisions. . . .
- Do not introduce the story with a movie, video, or play. These performances irrevocably become the "right" way and short-circuit the children's creativity. (p. 8)

Standards for Drama Education

www.

http://artsedge.kennedy-center.org/teach/standards/standards_k4.cfm

The K–4 theater content standards online

Drama, or theater, is the fourth area addressed by the *National Standards for Arts Education*. The authors of the standards provide this rationale for theater education for students in kindergarten through grade four (K–4):

Theatre, the imagined and enacted world of human beings, is one of the primary ways children learn about life—about actions and consequences, about customs and beliefs, about others and themselves. They learn through their social pretend play and from hours of viewing television and film. For instance, children use pretend play as a means of making sense of the world; they create situations to play and assume roles; they interact with peers and arrange environments to bring their stories to life; they direct one another to bring order to their drama, and they respond to one another's dramas. In other words, children arrive at school with rudimentary skills as playwrights, actors, designers, directors, and audience members; theatre education should build on this solid foundation. These standards assume that theatre education will start with and have a strong emphasis on improvisation, which is the basis of social pretend play. (Consortium 1994)*

The theater education content standards for grades K–4 are as follows:

Theater Content Standards

1. Script writing by planning and recording improvisations based on personal experience and heritage, imagination, literature, and history
2. Acting by assuming roles and interacting in improvisations
3. Designing by visualizing and arranging environments for classroom dramatizations
4. Directing by planning classroom dramatizations
5. Researching by finding information to support classroom dramatizations
6. Comparing and connecting art forms by describing theatre, dramatic media (such as film, television, and electronic media), and other art forms
7. Analyzing and explaining personal preferences and constructing meanings from classroom dramatizations and from theatre, film, television, and electronic media productions
8. Understanding context by recognizing the role of theatre, film, television, and electronic media in daily life (Consortium 1994)*

As with the other arts areas, several achievement standards are provided for each content standard. For the sixth content standard about "comparing and connecting art forms," the achievement standards include the following:

> Students describe visual, aural, oral, and kinetic elements in theatre, dramatic media, dance, music, and visual arts
> Students compare how ideas and emotions are expressed in theatre, dramatic media, dance, music, and visual arts
> Students select movement, music, or visual elements to enhance the mood of a classroom dramatization (Consortium 1994)*

By using the content and achievement standards together, teachers can plan developmentally appropriate activities and observe students' performance.

Roles of Specialists

Teachers who are privileged to teach in schools that have **specialists** in art, music, or physical education on staff should not hesitate to call on these people. They can be excellent resources. However, specialists do not relieve classroom teachers of the responsibility for teaching art, music, or movement.

---

*From *National Standards for Arts Education*. Copyright © 1994 by Music Educators National Conference (MENC). Used by permission.

The best situation is for specialists and classroom teachers to work together to achieve mutual goals. Because art, music, and movement are integral to most content-area instruction, the classroom teacher's role is to inform the specialist of the concepts that she is seeking to help the children develop; the specialist's role is to advise the teacher of activities that would be appropriate for those concepts. For example, if the focus in the classroom is on small animals, an art specialist might suggest having children create torn-paper collages of animals or tempera paintings of animals.

An art specialist can help the classroom teacher not only by suggesting appropriate activities but also by helping the teacher recognize the language of art that is important for the children to learn and by helping the teacher develop other concepts. The art specialist is also a good resource person for the teacher who wants to present the works of other artists to young children. Exposure to fine art can serve as a stimulus to creative experiences and can increase awareness of aesthetic elements (Bowker and Sawyer 1988). The art specialist can also aid the classroom teacher in helping children learn to look at and talk about art. Unless the teacher and art specialist provide opportunities for this kind of art appreciation, it may never occur (Cole and Schaefer 1990).

Similarly, the music specialist can help the classroom teacher incorporate music into daily classroom activities. He can help the teacher select songs that are appropriate for the group and provide guidance in choosing movement experiences or instruments appropriate for the specific theme the teacher is using. For a theme of *small animals,* the music specialist might help the children learn songs about the small animals in the classroom; listen to animal sounds; distinguish pitch in animal sounds; and produce rhythm patterns to represent various animals.

The physical education specialist can also provide assistance for the classroom teacher of young children. The specialist can help select appropriate movement experiences and provide opportunities for motor activities that can contribute to children's learning in other areas. To extend the theme of *small animals,* the physical education specialist might help children reproduce the movement patterns of the animals in the classroom. These movements could further the objectives of the physical education program by promoting body control and integrating patterns of motor abilities.

The classroom teacher can take advantage of the expertise of specialists by keeping them informed about topics of interest in the classroom and needs that have been observed. Each specialist has much to offer that will expand children's experiences and further the collaborative development of the best program possible for each child.

Assessing Experiences in the Arts

Assessment of children's performance in the arts must be individualized. One cannot give a grade to a child's drawing, but one can note whether the child chooses to participate in drawing activities and keep samples of the child's drawings in order to document the child's development. In assessing music, the teacher must also observe individual children as they participate in activities, become able to sing in tune, and keep the rhythm of a piece of music. Drama and movement activities must also be observed on an individual basis. It is important to know that children are

It is hard to conceive of a developmentally appropriate program that fails to include the creative arts. For young children, the arts provide many opportunities to explore materials and techniques, to make choices, to express themselves, and to gain social and cognitive skills. Think about the arts in these terms:

■ *Allowing each child to choose her own activity and within that activity, to choose how to complete the activity*—For example, a child might choose to paint at the easel and then choose which colors to use, how to place the elements of the composition on the paper, and how long to work on the painting.

■ *Providing intellectual challenge*—A child can continue to learn new techniques and continue to explore new media. The arts are never learned in the sense of learning facts; every experience with the arts is new and challenging.

■ *Providing opportunities for growth in all domains*—While participating in the arts, children gain physical skill (control of body and fine motor skills), grow intellectually (making decisions, planning, organizing), gain social competence (work with others, have responsibility for materials, share space and materials), and develop emotionally (expressing feelings, gaining empathy for the feelings of others, and so on).

learning to modulate their voices and control their body movements, but there is no need to compare one child to another. Assessment in the arts requires the development of a portfolio for work samples and anecdotal records of progress. A child's performance is always compared to his own earlier work, not to the work of other children. The goal is for children to learn through the arts and to enjoy their arts experiences without fear that they will be criticized or made to feel less than adequate for their work.

Integrating the Arts into the Curriculum

Although the goals and objectives of a creative arts program are important enough to stand alone, the arts also contribute to other curriculum areas in powerful ways. Children learning concepts in science, math, health, and social studies can express their understandings through art, music, movement, and drama. The following sections provide a few examples of the many possible ways the arts can be integrated into different themes or subject-matter areas.

Science

Shadows Children can attempt to make their shadows move in certain ways, to move without touching other shadows, to create a shadow play, and to select music to accompany a shadow play.

NAEYC CRITERIA
2.77

PRAXIS

Be able to explain how the arts can be integrated into the curriculum

www.
www.ericdigests.org/2003-4/gifted-students.html

Ways to integrate arts into the curriculum for gifted students

INTEGRATING the CURRICULUM

Continuing our theme of spaces, *here are some suggestions for art experiences:*

- Explore the idea of spaces in drawing, painting, and sculpture. Determine how artists in these media provide the viewer with an image of space.

- Explore the spaces needed for dancing and movement.

- Label the spaces created in dances (circles, squares, and so on).

- View paintings created with geometric shapes and color. Create images by using shapes.

- Look at the spaces in musical notation, and determine the effect they have on the music that is produced.

- Explore the changes in sound that result when certain spaces are altered, as in different sizes of drums, different lengths of strings, different sizes of blocks of wood, and so on.

- Try out the use of space in drama by having characters stand closer or farther away and observing the types of communication that result.

- Explore how space can be used to help tell a story, as in different settings or changes in settings.

- Experiment with different ways to manage space in drawing and painting by using line (light, heavy, cross-hatching, and so on) and color (washes, stripes, light or dark color, no color).

www.

http://ceep.crc.uiuc.edu/
eccearchive/digests/1995/
edward95.html

The article "Encouraging Creativity in the Early Childhood Classroom"

Birds   Children can imitate the movements of birds; listen to bird songs and learn to recognize a few distinctive calls; create drawings, paintings, or sculptures of birds; create a bird nest from natural materials; note color patterns of birds and chart common colors; and become familiar with John James Audubon's famous paintings of birds.

Sea Creatures   Children can recreate the movements of sea creatures; sort seashells by color, pattern, and/or shape; look at paintings or drawings of seashells or sea creatures; and listen to the recorded sounds of sea creatures (whales, dolphins).

Literacy

Children can learn to read the words to familiar songs and create songs to accompany familiar stories. For example, Ringgenberg (2003) suggests singing the words to the book *I Went Walking* (Williams 1989) to the tune of "Frère Jacques." Children can also select musical accompaniment for books, such as jazz for *Ben's Trumpet* (Isadora 1979) and fiddle music for *Barn Dance* (Martin and Archambault 1989). Another option is to find picture books of songs, such as *Fiddle-I-fee* (Hillenbrand 2002), *Over in the Meadow* (Langstaff 1957), and *Mary Wore Her Red Dress and Henry Wore His Green Sneakers* (Peek 1985). Creating picture books for favorite songs, acting out stories, using puppets for retelling stories, using reader's theater with scripts adapted to children's own needs, creating movements that represent characters in stories, and writing and illustrating original stories are also possible literary activities.

Mathematics

Have the children count the beats in marching music; compare the patterns of marching and skipping; create a pattern with drum beats or hand claps; combine two patterns to make a more complex pattern; learn to recognize the intervals in notes on the scales as equal distances; or create a song or rhyme to help remember algorithms.

Social Studies

Children can find art/artists to represent the various ethnic groups in the classroom and compare them; create art in the styles of different cultural groups; play examples of music from different cultural groups; learn simple dances from several different cultural groups; and invite performers from several different cultural groups to play instruments used in their traditional music.

See the following A Teacher Speaks box, in which Carol Schroeder talks about using art to help her class develop the concept of *community*. Think of other concepts that could be enhanced by integrating the arts into content-area lessons and experiences.

PRAXIS

Be able to develop a unit that integrates the arts into social studies

PRAXIS

Be able to defend integration of the arts in the curriculum

CHILDREN WITH SPECIAL NEEDS

Many experiences in the arts can be modified or adapted to make participation by children with special needs possible. Children with developmental delays may not be ready for group work or for some of the cognitive tasks in the arts program. Teachers will have to determine which experiences are developmentally appropriate for individual children and provide alternative experiences when necessary.

Because most art activities are planned for individuals, most children can participate in art at their own levels without adaptations; work surfaces or materials may have to be adapted for children with orthopedic disabilities. Examples of adaptations include providing work surfaces that are accessible for children in wheelchairs and providing sturdy materials that are easy to grasp so that children can draw and paint. Some children who do not have much control of their arms and hands might benefit from creating computer art; a computer program allows them to control color and so on. Children with visual impairments can paint, fingerpaint, create collages, and sculpt.

Teachers may need to seek expert advice about planning activities for children with specific types of hearing impairments. Some children are able to hear or feel many sounds—especially percussion or rhythmic elements. Gfeller (1989) makes these recommendations for adapting activities for children with hearing impairments:

1. Children who use hearing aids may hear better if background noises can be minimized.

2. If children use sign language, incorporate signing into singing activities.

www.

www.kinderart.com/special
Art ideas for children and adults with disabilities

www.

**http://childparenting.
about.com/library/bILD.
htm**

Ideas for parents (but teachers can use them) for engaging children with special needs in arts activities

www.

www.vsarts.org
Information about arts education for persons with disabilities

A **Teacher** SPEAKS: Integrating Art and Social Studies

Carol Schroeder

Town Center Elementary
Plainsboro, New Jersey

My second-grade class is heterogeneously grouped and quite culturally diverse. Some students have recently immigrated to the United States; others have always lived in the United States, and their families are very much involved in the traditions and customs of their own cultural community as well as the U.S. community. While teaching a unit on communities as part of our social studies curriculum, I find that integrating works of art into discussions and activities allows the students to observe and discuss how various communities from different time periods and cultures are alike and different.

I have adapted an integrated fine arts program called Art Tells a Story about Communities (Fitzpatrick and Parrish 1995) into my unit on communities. By looking at five paintings that depict various aspects of community life, the students make predictions about what they see in the paintings and the artists' motivations to paint the scene, answer questions asked by their peers and me, and observe and discuss five attributes common to all communities. I introduce each concept through one painting. Then I provide a variety of read-alouds, literature-based activities, role-playing simulations, art projects, and guest speakers to enhance and build on the community focus we originally discussed and observed in each of the paintings.

Each student completes an independent self-study of the painting by answering questions, writing his own questions, and making predictions about the people, places, things, and activities he sees in the painting. Finally, the class discusses their ideas about the painting as a group. After we have discussed their ideas, I give them some information about the artist, the style of the painting, and the story behind the painting. The students' favorite part of the discussion is sharing the title they would give the painting. I cover up the real title before we look at the painting, and after they have shared their predictions I reveal the title that the artist gave the painting.

We look at Norman Rockwell's *Norman Rockwell Visits a Family Doctor* to focus on community helpers and Grandma Moses's *Sugaring Off* to develop the concept of people in communities working together. We use Diego Rivera's *Piñata* to explore the concept of communities celebrating together and *Snap the Whip* by Winslow Homer to focus on the concept of communities playing together. Finally, we use *View of Paris with Furtive Pedestrians* by Jean Dubuffet to explore the idea that communities have important places. Art activities such as making books and posters are included in the study of each concept about communities.

The majority of primary students learn most effectively with visual aids. By studying community concepts through works of art, the students are able to make visual connections to the features that all communities share. The paintings motivate them to make comparisons to what they see and experience in their own U.S. community as well as communities they are familiar with from around the world. It allows them to see how communities of the past functioned similarly to present-day communities and how people help communities grow and change for the good of their citizens. Integrating the fine arts into a social studies unit is a great way to bring new ideas, points of view, and experiences to the students in your classroom.

3. Use visual aids to help children recognize patterns and other musical information that they may not be able to hear.

4. Placement in the group should make lip reading or watching or feeling instruments possible.

5. Using quality sound equipment that does not distort the sound helps children with some residual hearing.

6. Some children can hear better in the lower frequencies; therefore, instruments with lower pitches should be selected.

7. Rhythmic and percussive elements should be emphasized.

Children with delays in motor development may require instruments that do not have to be grasped, such as bells on a strap that can be fastened around the child's wrist or ankle; stands that hold instruments so that the child can play them are also helpful. During group movement sessions, children can be encouraged to move their heads, arms, legs, or whatever body parts they can control; they need not feel left out just because they cannot manage whole-body movements.

Singing may be difficult for some children with speech disabilities, and teachers may need to use more chants and rhythmic speech experiences with them. The teacher may need to consult with a speech specialist to determine the best course of instruction for such children. Madsen (2004) found that using picture books of songs helped nonverbal children learn the songs and feel more comfortable about the words.

Music also contributes to other skills and abilities. For example, children may gain cognitive skills and social abilities in the course of learning music (Ockelford, Welch, and Zimmerman 2002).

Brown (1991) suggests that signing can be added to many drama activities. She recommends that teachers use the following techniques for adapting drama for children with special needs:

1. Use pictures to visually represent new vocabulary and concepts.
2. Break the drama lesson up into a series of short segments.
3. Use repetition to reinforce new language and concepts.
4. Allow children to imitate as a starting point.
5. Sequence the activities, building from the simple to more complex.
6. Begin the activities with warm ups and end with a closing.
7. Introduce techniques to maintain focus and control. (pp. 173–174)

Brown (1991) goes on to suggest that having children sing during drama is a good way to involve those individuals who cannot physically participate in activities:

> While some children become frogs hopping from log to lily pad, other children may carry out the action with a puppet-frog and environment created from

Experiencing music is something that can be enjoyed by all students.

signs and gestures. Give children in wheelchairs a special role by using the chair as an integral part of the activity. Wheelchairs make great spaceships and train engines. Children with limited movement can be given the role of the tree in the middle that the other children's hand/leaves fall from, or the Indian chief who must call back braves from a hunt. (p. 178)

Structured drama experiences can help children build social competence. Learning how to pretend and how to participate in pretend activities is very important in the social and intellectual growth of children with special needs (Peter 2003).

As with all children, exposing children with special needs to the arts is a matter of thinking about what they can do, providing materials that are appropriate for them, and providing guidance in helping each child achieve his own goals. Table 13.2 presents a summary of suggested adaptations of activities in the arts for children with special needs.

CELEBRATING DIVERSITY

NAEYC CRITERIA
2.78

Parents and the Arts

● Encourage parents who are engaged in the arts—whether vocationally or avocationally—to share their art with the children.

The creative arts offer teachers invaluable opportunities for celebrating the diversity of their classrooms and communities. When choosing examples of fine art to share with children, teachers should make sure that the pieces represent many cultures. Moreover, pieces should include traditional styles from various cultures, which may not be used by contemporary artists but will help children appreciate the various ways humans have represented forms that were important to them. For example, the traditional carvings of the Maori people of New Zealand represented the animals and plants around them; these patterns became stylized and were used in carvings and on fabric. The traditional art of the American Indians of the Pacific Northwest represented the animals that were important in the stories of the tribes.

In addition to the visual arts, many cultural groups have rich histories of music, drama, and dance. Find videos or photographs of such arts. Learn some traditional songs and dances with the help of local members of the culture, if possible.

Creative arts also offer children with language differences opportunities to be successful. Difficulties with a dialect or learning a second language will not affect a child's ability to create a painting or sculpture. Cultural and ethnic differences can be honored in musical and dance experiences and in sharing art from many cultures.

The arts provide excellent avenues for children to work together and appreciate the strengths of learners from many cultural backgrounds. Teachers can also gain an understanding of what children know in the content areas through the arts and can use the achievement in the arts as a form of alternative assessment. Ivey (1999) says it well when he states,

Democracy offers the promise of equal participation to hundreds of cultural traditions that shape our landscape—Native American, Asian, European, Black, and Hispanic—and this promise translates into an endless process of

TABLE 13.2 Intervention Examples Using the MOST Approach

Disability	Creative Activity	M = MATERIALS MODIFYING MATERIALS	O = OBJECTIVES EMBEDDING OBJECTIVES	S = SPACE ADAPTING THE ENVIRONMENT	T = TIME PROVIDING ADEQUATE TIME
Visual impairment	Pretend play	Use paint or colored tape to outline the edges of the furniture in the area to increase the child's ability to focus. Include bright-colored materials, large pictures, and large print	The child will increase his or her social skills through participation in pretend activities with peers.	Keep the space consistent. Acquaint the child with the area in advance.	Build in time for the child to interact with peers. Use a peer-buddy system to promote engagement.
Hearing impairment	Music "Row, Row, Row Your Boat"	Incorporates the use of sign language into songs. Use songs that incorporate motions.	The child will use sign language to communicate with others during daily activities.	Seat the child close to the teacher during music activities.	Review the words (motions) to the song prior to singing.
Autism	Visual arts "Sponge paint"— dipping shaped sponges into paint and creating pictures on construction paper.	Provide plastic gloves for the child to wear during the activity (to manage an oversensitivity to textures. Make and display a chart showing step-by-step directions for the activity.	The child will use visual cues to assist in the completion of daily activities.	Arrange the furniture so the child can work alongside or with a peer during the activity.	Follow a flexible schedule so the child has enough time to complete the activity.
Physical (e.g., cerebral palsy)	Movement "The Freeze"— children move to music, wave streamers, and stop when the music stops.	Attach a strap or piece of Velcro to the streamer to make it easier to hold.	The child will increase the use of the right arm and hand through participation in fine motor activities. The child will use a walker to provide needed support for movement during daily classroom activities.	Create adequate space for the child to move using a walker.	Increase the time when the music plays to support the child's participation.

Source: Linda C. Mitchell, "Making the Most of Creativity in Activities for Young Children with Disabilities," *Young Children* 59, 4 (July 2004): 46–49. Reprinted with permission from the National Association for the Education of Young Children.

negotiation and accommodation. Art represents a place in which borrowing, blending, and sharing can really work.

Bilingual and limited English speakers have more opportunities to express their understandings through the arts when their language is not yet sufficient to express them in English (Goldberg 2001). English language learners do not face a language barrier when they participate in musical activities, such as playing instruments or clapping a beat. Music is one of the avenues of success for diverse learners (Madsen 2004). It is difficult to think of any part of the curriculum in which cultural diversity can be celebrated more easily than in the arts.

SUMMARY

- The arts are important in the curriculum in several ways: for what they add to the experience of the children, for the fostering of creativity, for developing problem-solving abilities, for enhancing cognitive development, and for helping children develop content-area concepts.

- Development in the visual arts is easily observed through the products of children's work. Visual arts experiences should help children develop the concepts of color, shape, and texture; help them become familiar with basic art materials; and help them understand that art is found in all human cultures and all time periods of human history.

- Music is a basic way of learning, experiencing, and communicating about the world. Music should be integrated throughout the schoolday, as children sing, play instruments, and listen to music. Three well-known approaches to music education are Dalcroze eurhythmics, the Kodály method, and the Orff approach.

- Movement and dance experiences offer children other ways to express themselves and to learn to recognize patterns and structure in music as they move in response to it. Young children can learn to move their bodies in controlled ways and to respond to the moods of different pieces of music.

- Drama for young children does not mean the production of plays with costumes and memorized scripts. Rather, it means having children act out stories and play various roles in play settings. Drama can encourage critical thinking and problem solving, and it can help children learn how to

work cooperatively with and take the perspectives of others. Drama experiences can also enhance children's ability to communicate.

- Arts specialists can help classroom teachers achieve goals in the arts as well as help extend content-area learning through activities related to children's interests and projects.

- Assessment of arts experiences must be individualized. Teachers need to carefully observe children as they work in the arts and compare their work only to their own previous work. It is important to know that children are learning in the arts, but products in the arts curriculum should not be graded.

- The arts can contribute to learning in the other subject-matter areas as children record what they know by drawing and painting, building structures, role-playing, singing and dancing, developing counting skills, recognizing patterns, and so on.

- To benefit from arts experiences, children with special needs may require some adaptations in materials and equipment or in the arts experiences themselves. The arts can allow children to express themselves when their other means of expression are limited.

- Children from all racial and ethnic groups will be able to find their own cultures represented in arts experiences. English language learners can participate in arts experiences without facing a language barrier, since no language is required to participate in painting, sculpting, or dancing. Diversity in the arts is easy to celebrate!

REFLECTIONS

1. The arts are important enough to stand alone as a necessary element of the curriculum for an early childhood program, but they also add value to other

parts of the curriculum. Explain how the arts contribute to children's development physically, socially/emotionally, and intellectually.

2. Explain how music can provide children with aesthetic experiences and help them develop specific literacy concepts at the same time.

3. Explain the value of integrating arts experiences into the curriculum in terms of children's interest, engagement, and achievement.

4. Assessment in the arts can be difficult because people do not always agree on what is "good" art. Children's ability in the arts may also vary widely, making it difficult to judge the products of their efforts. Describe how you plan to assess art experiences in your classroom.

5. Suppose that you are planning to display a collection of the paintings of four-year-olds. Write an explanation to include with it that explains the importance of the experience of painting and what children learn as they engage in painting. (Since paintings by four-year-olds are often just brown splotches by the time the children finish with them, parents may not be aware of the underlying processes.)

EXPLORATIONS AND ACTIVITIES

1. If you feel that you are not as personally skilled in the arts as you would like to be, what are some ways that you can be an effective teacher of the arts? For example, look at the selections of records available in children's music that would help you teach songs to the children, or examine some of the websites on art that would be useful in helping you find art and information about artists that would be appropriate for sharing with the children. Also, find what resources are available in the community that could help you develop an outstanding arts program.

2. Select a content area for first- or second-graders and plan arts experiences that would enhance the development of the children's concepts related to that topic. For example, a study of leaves could easily incorporate movements of leaves as they fall from the trees, musical experiences that involve the rustling of leaves or the crunching of leaves underfoot, painting, printing with leaves, and collages emphasizing various shapes and colors of leaves.

Where the classroom comes to life!

MyLabSchool is a collection of online tools for your success in this course, your licensure exams, and your teaching career. Visit **www.mylabschool.com** to access the following:

- Online Study Guide
- Video Cases from real classrooms
- Help with your research papers using Research Navigator
- Career Center with resources for:
  —Praxis and Licensure Preparation
  —Professional Portfolio Development
  —Job Search and Interview Techniques
  —Lesson Planning

CHAPTER **14**

KEY TERMS you'll find in this chapter:

- Body of knowledge, 457
- Conflict resolution, 458
- Constructivist model, 455
- Decision making, 459
- Eclectic approach, 461
- Expanding curriculum, 458
- Holiday celebrations, 472
- Social development, 457
- Social skills, 457
- Social studies, 454
- Themes, 470

Living Together: The Social Studies

FOCUS QUESTIONS

- What is *social studies?*
- How do young children learn social studies?
- What should teachers focus on in social studies instruction for young children?
- How can teachers integrate social studies into the curriculum for young children?
- How should holidays be celebrated in the classroom?
- How can teachers plan appropriately for children with special needs?
- How can teachers celebrate diversity in the social studies curriculum?

Your instructor began this week's class by asking you and your classmates what you remembered about social studies as part of your own school experience. Almost all of the responses were negative. Some students recalled reading chapters in a textbook and answering the questions at the ends of the chapters. Others told about memorizing lists of names, dates, and places. (Some were *still* memorizing historical facts.) A few of your classmates had learned to like history by reading biographies and historical novels. Others admitted being somewhat embarrassed by their lack of knowledge about geography and historical events.

You wondered what social studies instruction was like in today's schools. And what you found when you observed in a first-grade classroom really surprised you: The children were investigating problems in their school and neighborhood and learning how to solve those problems. For instance, the class you visited was concerned that the schoolyard was always littered with paper and trash. With the teacher's guidance, the children determined the source of the litter, wrote letters to the offending neighbors, petitioned the principal to place more trash receptacles on the playground, and started an antilitter campaign in their school. They presented their antilitter skit to all the classes in the school and put up antilitter posters and slogans near all the school exits. The teacher told you that these activities had developed over several weeks and that the children had decided that the next problem they would address was the lack of play equipment on the playground.

Back in your own class, your classmates had much to report about the social studies instruction they had observed. Some had found children studying heroes and heroines, and others had found children memorizing the famous speeches of various Americans. In some schools, the social studies curriculum was organized around holidays, and in others, social studies was based on the notion of learning to live together in harmony. At this point, you and your classmates are thoroughly confused about what instruction in social studies should involve. ■

Defining Social Studies

www.socialstudies.org/ standards/execsummary

The document in which the NCSS defines *social studies*

As a content area, social studies is perhaps more difficult to define than, say, mathematics or science. Social studies is not a single discipline, such as history or geography, yet it is usually taught as a single class called "social studies," at least through the primary grades (NCSS 1997). Just what and how that class teaches "social studies," however, can vary considerably from classroom to classroom, as will be discussed later in this chapter.

In 1992, the National Council for the Social Studies (NCSS), which is the primary organization that social studies teachers belong to, provided this definition of **social studies:**

> Social studies is the integrated study of the social sciences and humanities to promote civic competence. Within the school program, social studies provides coordinated, systematic study drawing upon such disciplines as anthropology, archaeology, economics, geography, history, law, philosophy, political science, psychology, religion, and sociology, as well as appropriate content from the humanities, mathematics, and natural sciences. The primary purpose of social studies is to help young people develop the ability to make informed and reasoned decisions for the public good as citizens of a culturally diverse, democratic society in an interdependent world.

While this definition covers a lot of ground, two main characteristics stand out to distinguish social studies:

1. The focus of social studies is multidisciplinary and integrative, addressing many subjects and fields of interest.
2. The purpose of social studies is to produce informed and reasonable citizens (NCSS 1997).

We will come back to these characteristics at various points throughout the chapter in examining both the learning and teaching of social studies for young children.

Learning Social Studies

How do children become informed and reasonable citizens? As described by the NCSS (1997), "Knowledge is constructed by learners as they attempt to fit new information, experiences, feelings, and relationships into their existing or emerging intellectual, aesthetic, and emotional constructs." Thus, as they do in any other area of learning, children construct their understanding of concepts in the social studies over a period of time.

A Constructivist View

This is the belief that underlies the **constructivist model** of education. The following figures provide a graphic illustration of these changes in understanding.

Figure 14.1 is a map drawn by a four-year-old. A visiting grandmother had volunteered to drive the child to school and asked her mother to draw a map of the route, but the child wanted to draw the map herself. As shown in the figure, her concept of *map* is that it is something with many lines and squiggles. The small circle outside the larger circle may be the child's home.

Figure 14.2 is a map drawn the next year by the same child, who now needed to be driven to kindergarten. Note that it has many fewer lines and scribbles and that some are quite identifiable. For instance, her house is the square with the four small squares inside it (windows). The long lines that encircle the house are roads; they are connected to the circular lines at the top of the page by a narrow rectangular box divided by lines indicating a railroad crossing. The small rectangle (at the left side) indicates a four-way-stop intersection.

The third map, Figure 14.3, was drawn by the same child in the summer between kindergarten and first grade to give directions to her primary

FIGURE 14.1

A Four-Year-Old's Map

FIGURE 14.2

A Five-Year-Old's Map

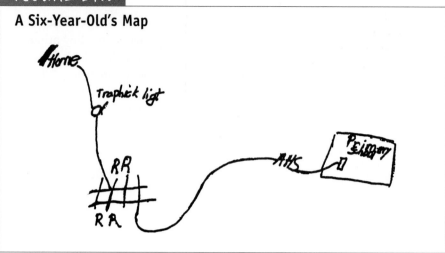

FIGURE 14.3

A Six-Year-Old's Map

school. This map looks much more like a map that you would draw to help a friend find your house. It contains only the necessary information, not every cross street and building. It shows a traffic light (where one should go straight) and a railroad crossing (which is carefully marked). And the street actually did make a wide curve before the schools. The *AHS* stands for the high school building that must be passed before coming to the primary school. The door on the school designates the entrance where parents were supposed to drop off their children.

What can we conclude about the child who has drawn these maps? In sum, she has developed concepts through many experiences, and those concepts have been refined over time with more experiences. The initial concept of *map* might have come from observing her parents using a street or highway map, from watching adult friends draw maps as part of giving directions to different locations, and from hearing her parents talk about directions to various locations. With more experience and some instruction, the child's concept of *map* was expanded beyond road maps to include many kinds of maps and refined to a more sophisticated understanding. Knowledge about maps cannot be mastered through lessons, however; it must be developed over time.

Similarly, other important concepts in the social studies must be learned through the same developmental stages. A child might be taught that George Washington was the first U.S. president, but it will take time to fully develop the concept of *president* and what it meant to be the *first president*.

Teaching Social Studies

Multiple Views of the Social Studies Curriculum

Although most experts today would agree with the NCSS's definition of *social studies*, provided earlier, they would likely not agree on how to teach social studies to young children. Several approaches can be found in the literature and in schools. In addition to the constructivist view, which was described in the previous section on learning, the primary views on teaching social studies are as follows:

- That social studies is a body of knowledge to be mastered
- That social studies should focus primarily on the social development of children
- That experiences in social studies should be organized according to an expanding curriculum model
- That decision making should be the focus of the social studies curriculum

Finally, there is an eclectic approach, which combines elements of the others.

A Body of Knowledge to Be Mastered

When social studies is treated as a **body of knowledge,** the curriculum might include asking children to identify a given set of holidays—such as Columbus Day, Presidents' Day, and Independence Day—and to tell why we celebrate them. Children might also be asked to name the state in which they live, the country in which the state is located, and the continents of the world. Another goal might be to identify the people in the community who promote the welfare and safety of children and adults. Economics goals might include explaining why people work and what people buy with the money they earn. Geographic goals might include naming the cardinal directions, defining a *map* and a *globe,* locating the North and South Poles and the equator on a globe, and providing examples of a continent, mountain, river, lake, and ocean.

Under this type of curriculum, first-grade children might be asked to name the current president, identify the White House and the Statue of Liberty, recite the Pledge of Allegiance, and identify famous Americans (e.g., the Wright Brothers, Elizabeth Cady Stanton, Daniel Inouye, Cesar Chavez, Clara Barton, Roberto Clemente, Sacagawea, Jonas Salk, Rosa Parks, and so on). In second grade, students might be asked to read globes and maps, apply their knowledge of cardinal directions to maps and globes, list some of the rights and responsibilities that citizens have, explain what buyers and sellers are and give examples of goods and services bought and sold in their community, locate the continents and major oceans on a globe, locate major mountain ranges on a map, locate the five major rivers of the world on a map, and describe ways that people have achieved great distinction.

This content-oriented approach to social studies is usually quite familiar to teachers because of their own experiences in learning social studies. Factual content is also more easily tested, which makes this approach popular for purposes of accountability.

Social Development

The social studies curriculum offers many opportunities for children to develop **social skills.** For example, learning to take turns when talking about a topic in a group, learning to abide by a group decision without undue complaining, and learning that not everyone has the same perspective are basic elements of social studies instruction.

The children need modeling and direct instruction in order to continue their **social development.** Teachers should model respect for all children and all cultures in terms of how books are selected for the library corner, how parents are invited and accepted into the classroom, and how responses

> **PRAXIS**
>
> Be able to design lessons to help children develop concepts of history, geography, and economics

> **NAEYC CRITERIA**
> **2.63**

are given to the children. As the children make group decisions, the teacher may need to use discussion and role-play to help them understand how to handle disappointment when the group's choice is contrary to theirs.

Teachers will also need to help children learn that other people have other perspectives. Holiday celebrations, in which the children can share how their families celebrate, should be planned along with other activities that help children understand cultural differences and similarities.

Katz and McClellan (1997) offer suggestions for helping children gain social skills in three areas that seem particularly significant in social studies:

1. *Helping children participate appropriately in discussions:* Teachers should help individual children learn to be more patient with their peers and to judge what might interest their peers by making specific suggestions or through puppet play.

2. *Helping children learn to negotiate and compromise:* Teachers should offer language models and direct instruction in these skills.

3. *Helping children assert their own preferences more gracefully:* Teachers should offer children appropriate language examples. For example, a child may need to learn to state his reasons for his choices or to soften his rejections of other children's ideas.

Another area of social development that is critical to good social studies instruction is **conflict resolution.** The goals of conflict resolution overlap several of the knowledge, skill, and attitude goals just listed. Drew (1987) identifies the major concepts of conflict resolution as "accepting self and others, communicating effectively, resolving conflicts, and understanding intercultural differences" (p. 1). Teachers who focus on conflict resolution will help children learn alternate responses to social situations, learn about other people, and learn how to communicate their feelings and expectations in ways that lead to peaceful solutions to problems.

Kreidler (1994) advises teachers to consider children's developmental levels when planning conflict resolution activities. For example, problem solving and point of view may be difficult concepts for young children to grasp, but they can work on concrete examples. Children also need to learn about cause and effect as part of conflict resolution. For example, if a child concludes that hitting is the solution when someone takes the toy she is playing with, then she must learn the consequences for hitting another person. Children also need help in expanding the choices that are available to them for solving conflicts.

Luke and Myers (1994/1995) and Kreidler (1994) suggest that using carefully selected literature, in which the characters solve their problems in a positive manner, is an effective means of teaching children about conflict resolution. Proponents of teaching conflict resolution skills hope that more people will learn to apply them and that eventually even nations will use these techniques to solve problems, rather than resorting to violence or war.

The Expanding Curriculum

The **expanding curriculum** was developed from the ideas of Lucy Sprague Mitchell (1878–1967). The expanding curriculum typically begins in kindergarten or first grade with a focus on the individual; the focus then moves to the individual in a group, a community, a state, a nation, and finally, the world.

Mitchell believed that children learn social studies by participating in real experiences. She described how children learn geography, for example, from field trips during which they can examine the real features of the region around them (Mitchell 1928). Mitchell believed that in order to learn, children must have experiences, see relationships, and make connections and generalizations. She expected teachers not merely to supply information but to arrange activities that would enable children to gain information through experience.

The curriculum at Bank Street College of Education (n.d.) is an example of an expanding curriculum. Such a social studies curriculum for three-year-olds would include as content the transition from home to school. It would focus on children's home lives and at the same time encourage children to become curious and interested in their school and classroom. The teacher would help children learn how they and their families are both different from and alike others. The teacher would also help children learn how their classroom fits into the school by learning about other classrooms as well as gyms, cafeterias, and offices in the school.

In an expanded curriculum, four- and five-year-olds would learn about the connections among their homes, their school, and the broader neighborhood. They would explore how their families live, work, and spend leisure time and study the interdependence of their families and area. The teacher might focus on the types of stores that sell food in the neighborhood and how they relate to families' preferences for specific foods. The teacher might also engage children in comparing skin colors, hair textures, holidays celebrated, and family structures represented in the classroom.

Five- and six-year-olds would continue to study the relationships among their families, the school, and the world of work that surrounds both the home and family. Children might study how the neighborhood functions in terms of the various workers that are employed by the city or town. A study of firefighters, for instance, could lead to a dramatic reenactment of the firefighters answering a call to a fire, to constructing a replica of the fire station with blocks, and to other activities connected to the work of firefighters. Other neighborhood places of work could also be explored and studied. The study of a local grocery store might lead to a visit to a farm to study where the food sold at the store comes from or how the grocer obtains the food products sold there. Since the local store would reflect the diversity of the neighborhood in terms of the kinds of food available, children could be encouraged to reflect on the importance of diversity in their neighborhood and how their own families fit into it.

Decision Making

In 1960, Shirley Engle published an article called "Decision Making: The Heart of Social Studies Instruction" (Engle 2003), in which he stated that social studies should not be taught as an accumulation of facts but as a process of effective **decision making.** Engle felt that *social studies* and the *social sciences* have different purposes: The social sciences are concerned with research and knowledge for its own sake, whereas social studies is concerned with the

The best school, after all, for the world of childhood, is not the school where children know the most answers, but the school where children ask the most questions.

—*Joe Coe*

education of citizens. Engle believed that good citizenship is marked by the quality of the decisions made, both individually and in groups.

Although Engle never wrote about social studies for young children, his focus on decision making is prominent in the social studies guidelines of many states as well as those of the National Council for the Social Studies. According to the NCSS (1997), children learn "to connect knowledge, skills, and values to civic action as they engage in social inquiry." To help children achieve this, teachers can do the following:

PRAXIS

Be able to plan a lesson to promote character education

- **Knowledge:** Provide children with information from a variety of sources and fields. Doing so reinforces the universal nature of social studies and encourages children to be individual thinkers and decision makers. The knowledge that comes through social inquiry provides the foundation for civic action.

- **Skills:** Help children learn and apply these skills, not in isolation but as a network of abilities:

    How to acquire information and manipulate data

    How to develop and present ideas, opinions, and stories

    How to construct new knowledge

    How to participate in groups

- **Values:** Teach children the values that underlie their society and that are generally considered to contribute to the common good of all people—for instance, *equality, justice, liberty,* and *freedom.* Understanding the complexities of having choices in a democratic society is particularly important.

- **Civic Action:** Once children have the recommended knowledge, skills, and values, they are ready to take civic action, whether as individuals or members of groups. Help them make this connection between what they believe and what they do.

Decision making for young children could include helping them solve problems related to their classroom environment or their personal behaviors and choices. Helping children gather and then interpret information would be important in a decision-making curriculum.

For example, in an election year, first- or second-graders might interview their parents and other adults in their environments about their plans for voting. People who plan to vote could be asked how they decide whom to vote for. People who do not plan to vote could be asked the reasons for their decisions. As the class compiles the information they have gathered, they will have opportunities to summarize their data and generalize their information to other issues and decision-making opportunities in their community. In their own classroom, they might investigate the popularity of different activities or centers and decide if they should be expanded or replaced. Thus, in the process of making decisions, children learn how to gather information and consider the implications of what they decide.

An Eclectic Approach

Proponents of all the approaches discussed believe that social studies is important because world conditions are changing and citizens must be prepared to participate effectively in government and society. Education as a cornerstone for participation in democracy is not a new idea.

The focus of American schools following the Revolutionary War was on educating citizens to participate in the new democratic government. Thomas Jefferson (1743–1826) stated, "If a nation expects to be ignorant and free, in a state of civilization, it expects what never was and never will be" (qtd. in Butts 1960). To be successful, a representative democracy requires a citizenry capable of examining the issues and making decisions that will benefit the nation.

John Dewey (1859–1952) also emphasized the importance of learning to live in a democratic society. He believed that classrooms should be democratic and that children should learn to participate in the decision-making process as part of their school experience (Dewey 1916). His thinking was considered to be radical in his time because schools of that era were so authoritarian.

What approach do most teachers follow? Most teachers choose to combine several of the approaches described to develop what they consider the best social studies curriculum for young children, creating an **eclectic approach** to social studies education. For instance, most teachers want children to know some facts, but they want the facts to be meaningful. It is not useful for children to memorize the names of the continents if they have no concept of *continent* or even of *country*. Likewise, it is not useful for children to memorize the names of the presidents unless the concept of *leadership* is in place.

NAEYC CRITERIA
2.64, 2.65

Social studies can be the core around which other curriculum experiences are arranged (see later in this chapter). But before that can happen, teachers have to think about their own beliefs about teaching and learning social studies and then choose topics and themes that will make sense to their students and that will be useful for further learning. In planning the curriculum, teachers also must consider the developmental levels of the learners, their experience with various concepts and ideas, and their personal interests. Teachers who listen to children will note that they are very interested in the world around them—both its physical qualities and the experiences of the people who live in it. Children *want* to know about their families, their neighborhoods, and their communities. Given all this, the most reasonable approach to organizing the curriculum for young learners is an expanding curriculum that is implemented by teachers who carefully consider how children learn the concepts of social studies and who believe in the value of helping children make good decisions. Such a curriculum fits the standards of the NCSS, which will be discussed in a later section.

Current Expectations

In recent years, the teaching of social studies has been widely criticized in the popular press. Critics have pointed to the lack of factual knowledge and skills exhibited by students, especially high school graduates, who lack geographic knowledge and often cannot even locate North America on a map. Critics also find that very few Americans have what they consider an adequate knowledge of U.S. history.

In response to this criticism, the current focus of social studies in many states is on learning history and facts. Proponents argue that other approaches have failed to teach students the basic knowledge needed to be an informed

> The political climate in any society has an impact on children's development. The laws that are passed affect all children and families.
>
> —*Carol Seefeldt and Nita Barbour*

American citizen. To some degree, they are right; young children can learn much more than some social studies programs have offered. On the other hand, memorizing facts without understanding the concepts that underlie them is not an acceptable approach in early childhood education.

In the rush to produce higher achievement, many new standards have been created. However, some of the new standards have failed to take into account what is known about child development and how children can learn in meaningful ways (Seefeldt 1995b).

The NCSS has identified the key features that should underlie social studies teaching and learning, summing them up in the statement that "social studies teaching and learning are powerful when they are meaningful, integrative, value-based, challenging, and active" (NCSS 1992). What does each of these qualities represent?

www.socialstudies.org/
positions/powerful

The NCSS position statement, that supports "powerful" teaching and learning of social studies

- *Meaningful*—Teachers present content that is worth learning, useful in and out of school, and appropriate in terms of its depth and breadth. The motivation for teaching and learning comes from interest and appreciation, not accountability and grading.

- *Integrative*—Teachers present a broad range of content using a variety of resources and activities. The approach is multidisciplinary and involves the use of themes and the identification of overarching concepts. Students gain new perspectives by connecting the past and present to the future. They become motivated to act on what they believe.

- *Value-based*—Teachers' presentation of topics includes the related ethical issues and controversies, particularly in terms of how they pertain to what is considered the common good in society. Students gather and analyze information, evaluate competing arguments, and learn to respect well-supported positions.

- *Challenging*—Teachers encourage students to function as a "learning community," which means participating assertively but respectfully and productively. Teachers present multiple perspectives for students to consider and evaluate. Students learn the skills needed to be competent citizens.

- *Active*—Students actively construct new understanding by relating it to what they already know about the topic, and they participate in a range of activities with determination and purpose. Teachers continually plan and then adapt their planning to acknowledge "teachable moments" and otherwise match students' needs and interests (NCSS 1992).

In the next An Expert Speaks box, Dr. Carol Seefeldt argues that social studies is an essential part of the experience for young learners. Do you agree with her argument? What would you say to someone who suggests that there is no time for social studies in the early childhood classroom?

Standards for Social Studies Education

www.socialstudies.org/
standards/teachers/vol1

The *NCSS National Standards for Social Studies Teachers*

The *National Standards for Social Studies Teachers* were developed by a task force of the National Council for the Social Studies (NCSS) and approved by the NCSS Board of Directors in April 1997. In describing the context in which the standards were created, the authors wrote:

AN **Expert** SPEAKS: The Social Studies

Carol Seefeldt
University of Maryland

Under great pressure to prepare young children for later academic success, far too many teachers claim they have no time for the social studies. "In our school we alternate between social studies and science every other semester," said a teacher. Others claim, "The curriculum is already overcrowded, and with the focus on reading and math there's just no time for frills like social studies."

Yet the study of the social sciences is critical. If our democracy is not only to persist, but to continue to change and improve, the development of the knowledge, skills, and attitudes required of citizens of a democratic society must begin in the early childhood classroom. Teachers who claim they have no time for social studies do not understand the true meaning of the social studies.

Here, children begin developing an understanding of an essential, if difficult, principle of democracy, that of giving up some of their needs, wants, and freedom for the good of the group. In the classroom, young children automatically give up some of their individuality. Once in a group setting, children face the hard reality of having to share. They must learn to share the attention of the adults who care for and teach them, as well as materials, play yard equipment, toys, and easels. Their wants—to continue to build with blocks, for example—are balanced by the needs of the group—to stop their work to eat lunch.

Within the democracy of the classroom, choice making is encouraged. Children choose which center they want to begin working in, what they will do once in the center, whether to work by themselves or with others, and when they are finished and ready to move to another center. Choice making extends to developing initial abilities to vote. At first children vote between two choices, such as do you want to play Duck, Duck, Goose or Cross over the Bridge? Progressing from these initial voting experiences, by age five or so, children can vote and then accept the will of the majority.

Children's here-and-now world is rich in learning resources. Think of the transportation, communication, and other social systems and institutions in children's worlds. Beginning with the center or classroom, children can study people and their jobs, where water comes from, where the trash goes, and myriad other social, economic, and scientific entities. Three-year-olds studying babies made graphs of foods they ate and that babies ate, weighed and measured themselves and a baby, tried on baby clothes, dictated and drew stories—meeting every academic standard yet developed for young children and many more. Second and third graders, using *Journey North* (www.learner.org/jnorth), studied the migration of monarch butterflies. Tracking the migration of the butterflies, children planted milkweed seeds, watched butterflies lay a single egg on each plant, tagged butterflies, and, through the Internet, kept track of their flight north.

No time for the social studies? Think again. The social studies, which enable young people to develop the ability to make informed and reasoned decisions for the public good as citizens of a culturally diverse, democratic society in an interdependent world (NCSS 1998), are integral to and integrated within the total curriculum. To say there is no time for the study of an interdependent world, beginning during the earliest years and building throughout a lifetime, is ludicrous. Rethink the basics. Begin with the social studies, and the academics fall into their proper places, becoming necessary tools for children to learn ever more about the world in which they live and their role in improving that world.

[The standards] pay attention to the specific contributions of history, the social sciences, humanities, fine arts, the natural sciences, and other disciplines, while simultaneously providing an umbrella for the integrative potential of these several disciplines. This characteristic is the nature and strength of social studies: recognizing the importance of the disciplines and their specific perspectives in understanding topics, issues, and problems, but also recognizing that topics, issues, and problems transcend the boundaries of single disciplines and demand the power of integration within and across them. (NCSS 1997)

The standards consist of the following ten themes, which can be tailored to be developmentally appropriate for students from the early grades through high school:

Thematic Standards

- Culture and Cultural Diversity
- Time, Continuity, and Change
- People, Places, and Environments
- Individual Development and Identity
- Individuals, Groups, and Institutions
- Power, Authority, and Governance
- Production, Distribution, and Consumption
- Science, Technology, and Society
- Global Connections
- Civic Ideals and Practices (NCSS 1997)

www.education-world.com/
standards/national/soc_sci/
index.shtml

More information on the standards of related disciplines, such as history and geography

The NCSS recommends that in designing a curriculum, teachers and other planners should first establish their program framework using these thematic standards as a guide. Then they should develop grade-level content strands and courses that meet the developmental levels of their students by referring, as appropriate, to the standards from history, geography, civics, economics, and other disciplines. By taking this approach, teachers can provide integrated social studies instruction while also addressing topics or themes in specific disciplines.

The complete *NCSS National Standards for Social Studies Teachers* document (NCSS 1997) outlines in more detail how to use the standards as a framework in curriculum planning. In addition, the document provides student performance expectations and examples of classroom activities.

Planning Social Studies Experiences

Threes and Fours

Appropriate experiences in the social studies, like any experiences for children who are three and four, cannot be separated from play. Just as in math and science, teachers will want to provide not only play materials that help children learn some social studies concepts but also time to use them. In developing topics for organizing the curriculum, teachers should make sure that social studies concepts are included when they are appropriate. The following descriptions may suggest other possibilities:

- Toys related to methods of transportation can be included in play areas. Trucks, cars, buses, trains, airplanes, and helicopters can be added to the blocks area, and boats and barges can be added to the water play area. The teacher can help children focus on the concept of the necessity of transporting goods and people.

- Children can take short walks in their neighborhood and identify different types of structures (houses, businesses, churches, and so on).

- Children can be led to observe changes in their immediate environments, such as changes in the room, on the playground, or in the school building.

- Children can be encouraged to create structures with blocks that represent what they know of their neighborhood or community. They might construct a fire station if they live near one or if the school is near one, an airport (if it is part of their experience), a gas station, a harbor, or other structures.

NAEYC CRITERIA
2.66

- Children can work together to move toys or materials that need to be moved or to clean up the materials and play areas.

- Teachers can keep a large scrapbook with records of important events in the children's experiences. Reviewing it with the children will teach them that we can keep records of events and that these records help us to recall the events accurately.

- Teachers can develop multicultural and gender-neutral prop boxes that help children explore similarities and differences in people. Boutte, Van Scoy, and Hendley (1996) recommend gathering the props needed to recreate a shoe store, bakery, hair salon, department store, grocery store, and restaurant. Making available materials that reflect a wide variety of cultural and ethnic differences will provide opportunities for discussion and active participation in learning about people. Prop boxes can be enhanced by adding music, literature, foods, art, cultural artifacts, and items for special needs.

Fives and Sixes

Social studies for the school beginner should continue to be based on play experiences and meaningful activities. The teacher will want to plan some experiences that help children develop specific concepts, but this does not imply that lessons in the social studies should be isolated from other experiences. Here are some suggested activities:

- Children can continue to learn about change by observing any changes in their neighborhood or community (such as buildings being constructed or torn down). The children can record their observations in their journals, or the teacher can help them record their observations on experience charts. Photographs of the sequence of the changes can help children keep records. Children can also learn about change in themselves by bringing in baby pictures or baby clothes and comparing them with their current looks and clothing.

- Children can celebrate the diversity of family structures in which they live. The teacher can find pictures to represent the family structures in the class, and the children can write or dictate lists of common features and positive attributes of families.

- Children can begin to explore racial and ethnic differences by examining differences in skin color, hair texture, and eye shape. After selecting paint chips or mixing paint to match their individual skin colors, they can create a chart illustrating the range of colors in the class. They can create another chart of hair textures and eye colors. With guidance from the teacher, kindergarten children can discuss the advantages of physical characteristics under different environmental conditions—for example, dark skin provides more protection from the sun (Derman-Sparks and ABC Task Force 1989).

- Children can begin to categorize objects or goods as "wants" or "needs." They can develop the concept that people are paid for their work and that the money is used to acquire goods.

NAEYC CRITERIA
2.68

www.

**www.csun.edu/~hcedu013/
plans.html**

Select "Social Studies" for
many interesting lesson ideas

www.

**http://teacherweb.com/NY/
Arlington/OverlookLibrary/
links5.stm**

Many links to lesson ideas for
social studies

www.

**www.pbs.org/teachersource/
social_studies/prek-familylife.
html**

Lesson ideas on a variety of
social studies topics

■ Children can create three-dimensional maps of their classroom and their neighborhood. Photographs can be attached to models of buildings or other structures in the neighborhood. These maps can be created with blocks, milk cartons, cereal boxes, and so on.

■ Children can trace the route taken by the milk that is served every day in the classroom from the dairy farm to the dairy, the distributor, the delivery truck, and the cafeteria. They can make books of their observations and learn about the animals that provide milk and the people who process and deliver it.

■ Children can create lists or pictures of items that can and cannot be bought with money. The items can then be reclassified as "wants" and "needs."

■ Children can compare the rules at school with those at home in terms of who makes the rules, why the rules are needed, and how the rules can be changed.

■ Children can create personal timelines by recording the important events of their lives, such as moving, having a new baby in the family, going to preschool, and so on. The timelines can be illustrated with drawings or photographs to indicate changes.

■ Children can learn about the people who work at their school, including their names and what they do (see the following Learning Plan).

LEARNING PLAN   Social Studies for Kindergarteners (five-day lesson)

Objective: Children will be able to name the principal, the secretary, and the custodian of the school and to describe their jobs.

Materials: Chartpaper, markers

Procedure:

1. Schedule the visits with the principal, the secretary, and the custodian in advance.
2. On the first day, ask the children if they know the names of the some of the people who work at the school. Record the names on a chart. Let children tell what they know about the work of the people named. Record two or three statements, if they are correct.
3. On the second day, ask children to create three or four questions to ask the principal about the work that a principal does. Record these questions and have the children take them along when they visit the principal. Ask one child at a time to ask one of the questions. Take notes of the answers. When you get back to the classroom, record what the principal said on the chart with the questions. Read the answers to the children and make sure that is what they heard. Review the two or three most important components of the principal's work.

4. On the third day, repeat the procedure during a visit to the secretary. Have different children ask the questions.
5. On the fourth day, repeat the procedure during a visit to the custodian. Again, different children should ask the questions.
6. On the fifth day, ask children to describe the most important work done by the principal, the secretary, and the custodian and to name the individuals who do these jobs at their school. Record children's answers on the chart so that they can be reviewed at a later time.

Accommodations: Make available play materials so that children can create a "school" with the blocks and small figures or costumes to help them role-play the positions that they have learned about. Observe the play and note which children need additional information about the individuals and their work.

Assessment: Observe children as they participate in the discussion or in play activities. Indicate whether they demonstrate that they know the information or talk with you informally about what they learned.

Sevens and Eights

Sevens and eights can do more with maps and learn more about economics and politics than younger children; however, they still need real experiences. Teachers should not expect sevens and eights to learn from textbooks alone or to be able to handle abstract concepts that are not part of their experience. Activities for this age group include the following:

■ Children can map their school and perhaps their neighborhood by constructing three-dimensional maps and then transferring the information to a two-dimensional form. They can create legends for the two-dimensional maps.

NAEYC CRITERIA
2.69

■ Children can learn about elections and voting. They can visit a polling place and see how the records are kept and how the ballots are marked. They can invite people who are running for local office to visit and explain why they want to be elected. They might interview several different people to determine how people make decisions about voting or why they do or do not vote. They can participate in classroom and school elections and make classroom decisions by voting.

■ Children can survey others in school to find out what kinds of jobs their parents hold. This information can be presented on charts and graphs. (The teacher can use the work done by parents as a source of topics—for example, factory production or service industries.) If some parents are unemployed, receiving aid, on strike, or laid off from their jobs, teachers can help children learn some of the reasons for these conditions in their neighborhoods.

■ The class can survey the community to determine local natural resources and how they are used. They can determine who in the community makes decisions about resources and interview those people about their long-term goals. The teacher can help children obtain information on conserving natural resources from books, speakers, films, and so on. Children can make lists of what they can do to conserve resources.

■ Children can determine who is responsible for all the services provided in the community and create Venn diagrams of government and private responsibilities.

■ Current events can provide learning experiences for this age group if they are related to the children's interests and experience. Interesting pictures or stories from newspapers can be posted on a bulletin board as a catalyst to spark discussion or further explorations.

■ Children can compare the tools they use in school to those used by children in the past and learn about the inventors of the tools that are new.

■ Students can create timelines to record the important events and people they learn about. For example, after reading *Minty: A Story of Young Harriet Tubman* (Schroeder 1996), they could place a picture of Harriet Tubman on the timeline to indicate that she lived after the Pilgrims and after Charlotte Haines, a Revolutionary War character (*Charlotte,* Lunn 1998), but before Rosa Parks (*If a Bus Could Talk: The Story of Rosa Parks,* Ringgold 1999) and Ruby Bridges (*The Story of Ruby Bridges,* Coles 1995).

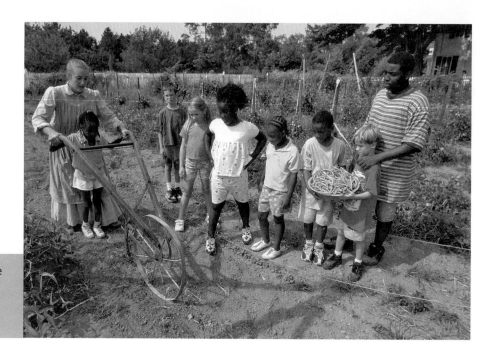

Understanding the past is made easier when children have hands-on experiences with objects from the past.

Integrating Social Studies into the Curriculum

www.journal.naeyc.org/btj/ 200509/mindes.asp

An article that argues that children are "born" into social studies and that an integrated approach to instruction makes the most sense

Children's books with social studies content can be used to introduce new topics, to extend children's knowledge, and to add interest for certain children. For example, if the topic were homes, relevant books would include *Building a House* (Barton 1990), *How a House Is Built* (Gibbons 1990), *The House I Live In* (Seltzer 1992), and *Home* (Rosen 1992). The teacher would use each book in a way that would be appropriate for her students. For instance, the text is long in Seltzer's book, but it could be read one page at a time, and the poems in *Home* vary in difficulty. There are books on any topic that could be introduced in social studies.

One valuable source of information about new books is the bibliography of notable social studies trade books for young people that is published each year in the journal of the NCSS *Social Education*. (The list is also available at www.ncss.org.) These books can be used for read-alouds, for shared reading experiences, or for independent reading, depending on the abilities of the children.

These books could also be used to prompt children to write stories about their own families. Children could write reports on their families, contribute to a class book on families, or make invitations asking families to come to the school for a special event. Children could also choose books to share with their families, which would give them another opportunity to read or have someone read to them.

Many other opportunities are possible for meaningful literacy experiences as children explore social studies topics of interest. For example, if children are studying the work of their parents or of school personnel, they could write reports of their findings from their surveys, read more about some of the occupations that especially interest them, write entries for an ABC book of

A teacher who is attempting to teach without inspiring the pupil with a desire to learn is hammering on cold iron.

—*Horace Mann*

jobs, write letters inviting speakers to class and thank-you notes to speakers who have shared information, and so on. The children might also create charts, reports, books of various kinds, narrative stories, and poetry. For example, if the children have been exploring the cultures of the children in their class, they could create journals in which they record their responses to foods they have tried, pictures of articles of clothing, or their personal responses to something they learned. The class might create a "big book" with photographs and reports they have dictated, which could be reviewed often.

INTEGRATING the CURRICULUM

Continuing our theme of spaces, *here are some suggestions for social studies experiences:*

- Survey the spaces in the neighborhood that are private versus public.

- Determine who has control of public spaces and how decisions are made about their use.

- Measure the spaces in the school that are used for various functions, and graph the results (e.g., administration, cafeteria, playground, classrooms, halls, etc.).

- Explore the definition of *neighborhood* in terms of spaces. How do we know the boundaries of a neighborhood?

- What are the reasons for having city boundaries? Country boundaries? State boundaries?

- What are the reasons for having public spaces to be used for recreation, such as parks, ballfields, tennis courts, and so on? Are these spaces important? Who should pay for them?

- Create a map of the classroom. What spaces can be shown on the map? What spaces cannot be shown?

- Build a three-dimensional model of the neighborhood from milk cartons, cereal boxes, and so on. Can all the spaces be represented?

- Interview the person in charge of public spaces in the neighborhood. Ask about problems in those spaces, plans for those spaces, and how people can help care for those spaces.

- Plan the ideal public park. What spaces would be included?

- Make a graph of the favorite spaces of the members of the class. Are these private spaces or public spaces?

- Build a "neighborhood" with blocks. What spaces are needed? roads? sidewalks? stores? playgrounds? houses? schools? churches? places for children? places for older people?

- Select a space in a park or another outdoor location that can be visited several times during the year. Make periodic visits and observe changes in this space over the year. Note seasonal changes, different wildlife that visit the space, people who visit the space, changes in plant life, and so on. Record your observations on a large sheet of chartpaper, and review them before and after each visit.

There are many ways of recording and summarizing what children learn. Such documentation allows children to present and reflect on what they learn. It is also useful to teachers in reporting to parents and administrators the concepts that children are developing and their growing literacy abilities and understandings in the social studies. Literacy activities can help teachers meet their goals of having all children develop pride in their own cultural heritages, appreciate the contributions of people of diverse backgrounds to the larger society and culture, and demonstrate respect for the cultures of diverse groups.

Social Studies Themes

As with other subject-matter areas, a thematic approach to social studies offers opportunities for children to do meaningful tasks that can help them acquire important knowledge, skills, and attitudes. As noted earlier in this chapter, the NCSS Standards represent a thematic approach to social studies (see page 000).

A list of possible **themes** that would be useful for developing social studies concepts would be nearly endless. Teachers could focus on the family; justice; change; the neighborhood; the city; celebrations; historical places in the community; parks; interdependence; workplaces; bread—and this is by no means an exhaustive list. Suggestions for developing four such topics are described in the following lists.

Immigration

- Read aloud the following books about immigration:*

  American Wei (Pomeranc 1998)

  Anushka's Voyage (Tarbescu 1998)

  The Butterfly Seeds (Watson 1995)

  Coming to America: A Muslim Family's Story (Wolf 2004)

  The Dream Jar (Pryor 1996)

  From Far Away (Askar 1995)

  Lights for Gita (Gilmore 1995)

  A Picnic in October (Bunting 1999)

  The Silence in the Mountains (Rosenberg 1999)

  The Tangerine Tree (Hanson 1995)

  A Very Important Day (Herold 1995)

  When I First Came to This Land (Ziefert 1998)

  When Jessie Came across the Sea (Hest 1997)

- After finishing each book, talk about people's reasons for immigration. Record these reasons on a chart.

- Have children interview their parents and grandparents to learn their immigration stories. Compile the stories to create a book of family stories.

_____

*Full bibliographic information is provided in the References (pages 529–548).

www.journal.naeyc.org/btj/
200509
Several links to articles and bibliographies that will be useful in supporting teaching

Parents and Social Studies

- Keep parents informed about social studies activities by including information about them in the class newsletter. Solicit parental involvement by making a list of needed materials, asking for volunteers for field trips, and suggesting the sharing of skills such as cooking or sewing costumes.

PRAXIS

Be able to design an activity to promote cultural education

NAEYC CRITERIA

2.72

- If possible, ask families to come to school to share family treasures they brought with them when they came to the United States. And if appropriate, ask them to tell about what they left behind.
- Ask several recent immigrants to come to class to share their experiences. What do they expect from their new lives in the United States?

Transportation

- Have the children think of as many ways of transporting people and goods as possible. Make a list of these kinds of transportation, and then categorize them as land, air, and sea vehicles.
- List all the possible ways children get from home to school. Make a graph that shows how many students get to school in each way.
- If possible, take the class on a trip on a train or subway. Find out how traveling by train or subway (as opposed to traveling by personal car) benefits the community.
- If possible, visit a port to observe the unloading of a ship. Find out what kinds of goods are transported by ship. Also find out where these goods go after being unloaded from the ship. Most ships are loaded with containers that go directly to trains or trucks.
- Visit a local supermarket and determine how foods have been shipped to the market and from where. Locate the points of origin on a map or globe.

Communication

- Have the children interview family members to determine how many ways they communicate with others. Make a graph of the results for the class.
- Determine how many languages are spoken in the homes of the children in the class. Together, learn how to say the word *school* in each of these languages.
- Ask a person who signs to demonstrate sign language and teach the children some common signs. As a class, learn how to sign a short poem or song.
- Create a timeline that shows the ways people have communicated throughout history. Have the children add drawings or cutout pictures of the various types of communication.
- Make a list of all the reasons people need to communicate at school.
- Visit local businesses that are involved with communication: TV stations, radio stations, the newspaper office, the telephone company, and so on. Ask people about the jobs they do at these businesses.
- Make a list of the rules for communication in the classroom. Make another list of the rules for communication at home. Make a third list of the rules for communication in public places. Discuss how and why these three sets of rules vary.
- Write to a pen pal in another part of the world using e-mail or regular mail. Find out if communication is equally accessible to all people everywhere.
- Research inventions and inventors related to communication. Talk about how people's lives would be different without these inventions.

My Neighborhood

■ As a class, walk around the school neighborhood and record the different kinds of buildings: houses, stores, churches, apartment houses, and so on.

■ Determine the method used for numbering the buildings in your neighborhood. What information is provided in a street address?

■ Determine what services families need that are in your neighborhood: grocers, dry cleaners, laundries, shoe repair shops, medical facilities, banks, and so on.

■ What recreation facilities are available in your neighborhood? Look for parks, playgrounds, tennis courts, basketball courts, gyms, and so on.

■ Determine the types of houses in the neighborhood. How many are one-family houses? two-family houses? multifamily houses?

■ Determine how many types of vehicles are parked on one block in the neighborhood.

■ Find out what kinds of jobs are available in the neighborhood.

■ Identify one problem in the neighborhood that the class could help solve: litter in the streets (petition for more trash receptacles); dirty sidewalks (send letters to merchants, asking them to help you beautify the neighborhood by cleaning the sidewalks); lack of plants (ask merchants to provide flowers and containers; the class will plant and water them); and so on.

In the following A Teacher Speaks, Emilie Rodger describes how she uses the theme of *family* in her primary classroom and incorporates many areas of instruction with social studies. Do you agree that using a theme can help children build a solid understanding of concepts? Why or why not?

Celebrating Holidays

In some programs for young children, instruction in social studies centers on holidays. Some schools move from one holiday to another without much in between, justifying the emphasis on holidays as important to the cultural heritage of the children. Such a rationale is logical only if the children share the culture in which the holiday originated. It is acceptable to celebrate holidays appropriately with young children, but social studies should certainly be more than completing worksheets about Lincoln's birthday.

Planning appropriate **holiday celebrations** seems to be a difficult task in some school settings. Holiday planning should be approached with the same careful considerations for developmental appropriateness of various activities and determination of goals that are applied in other curriculum areas. Bisson (1997) suggests that teachers follow these guidelines in planning for holidays:

■ Talk about some holidays rather than celebrate each one. For example, the class might talk briefly about Presidents' Day, but it will have little

Parents and Social Studies

● Invite parents to school to ask them how they feel about celebrating holidays in the classroom. In your invitation, make sure that you describe the cultural diversity of your school so that parents can think about how others might feel about holidays.

A **Teacher** SPEAKS: *Promoting the Home–School Connection*

Emilie Rodger

Sedona Elementary School
Sedona, Arizona

Social studies—or the study of societies and their interdependence on one another—by definition means learning about our place and the places of others in the world. In order for young children to make sense of this concept, we must start with that which is most important to youngsters: their families. They know their families, and they know they belong to their families.

As a teacher, I further promote the home–school connection in all other topics, as well, so that we—the children and I—may embark on our family discovery adventures together. I've used several methods of making the connections:

1. *Sending a family survey letter home to the parents and asking them to complete it together, if at all possible*—This survey letter includes questions relating to family names, number of people in the family, pets, occupations, interests, hobbies, and special traits of individuals in the family. Students are asked to return the surveys and share their information with the class. Translations of the letters are sent in the languages needed.

2. *Having children construct a bulletin board of the classroom "family," which is made up of individual students' families*—This bulletin board includes any information the students desire to share about themselves and their families using any chosen media: poetry, artwork, songs, chants, pictures, and the like. Children's literature is used as a springboard for discussions about family configurations, dynam-

ics, and traditions. Students develop skits about their roles in their families and/or their classrooms. Parents, grandparents, and other available family members are invited to the classroom to share stories about their cultures or occupations. Many discussions occur about how families are the same and different, again illuminating the common bond of humanity.

3. *Encouraging students to keep journals*—These journals are used to record interviews with various family members, comments about what families do together, any traditions they have shared, as well as ideas the children would like to incorporate into the classroom community.

This unit or topic extends for approximately one month, culminating in a presentation to families about the discoveries students have made about themselves and each other. The presentation often includes songs, artwork, portfolios, and/or collages depicting each student in the middle of a sheet of paper surrounded by the meaningful people, objects, or hobbies in her life. The success of this unit is due to young children's self-absorption and their need to make sense of the world around them. This unit on families is a simple, exciting, challenging way to incorporate and involve all youngsters in an awareness of the external world.

This unit is the central thread in the cultural tapestry woven throughout the year, as the children learn about themselves. Having this knowledge increases their self-esteem, and as their self-esteem increases, they learn and care about other cultures, their relation to them, and their interdependence on each other. The result is an understanding and clear awareness of the importance of each unique individual in the human family.

meaning for young children. Perhaps invite a family to tell about a holiday they celebrate that is not selected for a school celebration.

- As much as possible, fit holiday celebrations into regular routines. Do holiday art projects as part of "choice time," or invite families to join the children in singing holiday songs they have learned. An elaborate production that involves practice and pressure is not an appropriate response to a holiday.

- Avoid basing classroom themes on holidays. A holiday should not be the focus of the curriculum for an extended period of time.

Achieving DAP in social studies instruction, in which topics are fairly abstract, may seem more complicated than in math or science instruction, in which real things can be manipulated and observed. Teachers of young children will be especially challenged in planning appropriate social studies activities. In deciding what is developmentally appropriate, teachers should consider the following:

- Can children understand the concepts to be learned? If the concepts depend on being able to understand historical times or places far from children's experience, then children will be unlikely to understand them.

- Are the concepts related to children's real-life experiences? Learning about a harbor may not be appropriate for children who live far inland.

- Can meaningful activities in which children are involved be planned around the concept? Field trips, resource people, and real objects to explore may bring concepts to life for young children; completing dittoed worksheets and coloring pages, however, will not promote concept development.

- Can the concept be integrated into other areas of the curriculum? For example, can the concept be developed through activities in which children sing songs, learn dances, read stories, and create art?

- Do the activities honor the diversity of the children and their families?

- Will stereotypes be reduced rather than increased through participation in social studies activities?

- Avoid materials and activities that scare the children, such as certain costumes and masks. Instead, have children create their own masks and costumes from dress-up clothes.

- Offer activities that calm the children and focus them on a process. For example, creating a center for making holiday cards and adding holiday colors to sand and water play will help children be creative without also feeling pressure. A variety of open-ended materials can be made available so the children can choose and create what is satisfying to them.

- Offer a choice of holiday-related activities or other activities that meet curriculum goals but are not holiday related.

Also consider these suggestions for holiday planning:

- Evaluate what the children will learn if the holiday is acknowledged in the curriculum. Each holiday should be evaluated in terms of the curriculum goals of the program (Dimidjian 1989; Timberlake 1978).

- Determine what the children think the holiday means and what they know about it.

- Remember that the children should have the most important role in deciding how the holiday should be celebrated. Involve them in planning and implementing the celebration. Is the celebration something they can really do themselves, or is it so elaborate that an adult must do it for them?

■ Keep in mind that some commercial holiday materials are stereotypical. Thanksgiving might be a good time to help children understand why stereotypical images of American Indians are not appropriate and to help them learn what can be done to combat these stereotypes, such as writing letters of complaint to the company or refusing to buy such materials. Holiday celebrations should help children gain knowledge, show respect for others, and develop a deeper understanding of the similarities and differences among people.

The following suggestions for specific holiday celebrations are based on ideas in two books: *Anti-Bias Curriculum: Tools for Empowering Young Children* (Derman-Sparks and ABC Task Force 1989) and *Celebrate! An Anti-Bias Guide to Enjoying Holidays in Early Childhood Programs* (Bisson 1997).

Thanksgiving

■ The children can focus on the harvest aspects of the holiday by visiting a farm, harvesting their own garden, or finding evidence of harvest in the community.

■ The teacher can help the children find information about other harvest festivals and how they are celebrated.

■ The teacher can help the children relate the eating of a meal to the celebration of the harvest.

■ The teacher should supply *accurate* information about contemporary American Indians using books, pictures, and guest speakers. The teacher can help children critique greeting cards and TV specials for images of American Indians and the authenticity of the portrayals of the first Thanksgiving. In the words of author and American Indian rights activist Michael Dorris, "It must be communicated to educators that no information about Native peoples is truly preferable to a reiteration of the same old stereotypes, particularly in the early years" (cited in Derman-Sparks and ABC Task Force 1989, p. 88).

■ The children can help cook some foods typical of Thanksgiving celebrations, such as cornbread, squash, and cranberries.

Halloween

■ The teacher can help children recognize the harvest aspects of Halloween (scarecrows, pumpkins, and so on).

■ Children can learn to recognize the similarities between jack-o'-lanterns and other cultures' representations of human figures with food. They can create some "vegetable people" from squash, turnips, or ears of corn. The vegetable people can be washed and eaten after the activity.

■ Children can explore costumes for different purposes (theater, other entertainment). Younger children can be encouraged to explore the concept of being the same person even though they look different in costumes.

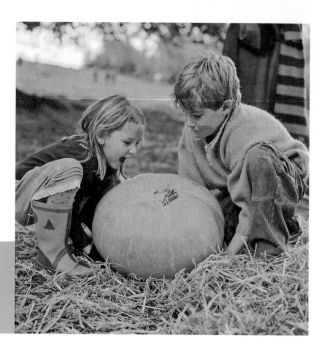

Holiday celebrations can be more meaningful if children are involved in the planning.

- A maker of masks can be invited to share his collection and help the children understand some of the cultural uses of masks or show slides of different masks from around the world. Involve the children in mask making. In order to avoid having them associate the color black with scary things, children can be encouraged to make masks that are scary but not black and others that are black but not scary.

- Teachers can help children explore scary feelings. Children can create paintings, songs, or dances that help them express their feelings. They can find scary things in books such as *Where the Wild Things Are* (Sendak 1963) and *There's a Nightmare in My Closet* (Mayer 1968) and talk about how the characters responded to being scared.

- Children in communities that still maintain the tradition of going from house to house at Halloween can explore how that tradition is carried on in other celebrations. Teachers can help children understand the trick in *trick or treat* by sharing "trickster" stories from the southwestern American Indian tradition and inviting children to plan some tricks.

- Older children can trace the origins of symbols used in Halloween celebrations.

Mother's Day and Father's Day

- Celebrate Family Day instead, hosting a program or open house to which children's families are invited.

- Have the children make cards or gifts for anyone in their families.

- Invite grandparents and other elderly relatives to the classroom to tell stories about when they were young children.

Valentine's Day

- Focus activities on the idea of friendship.

- Have materials available so each child can make a card for one special friend at home or at school.

- Involve parents and children in planning a friendship celebration that does not involve commercial valentines or decorations.

Martin Luther King Day

- List and discuss things that are fair and unfair—say, on the playground or in the lunchroom.
- Read a short book about the life of Dr. King.
- Talk about King's efforts to change unfair laws using peaceful means.
- Be sure to plan what you will tell the children about Dr. King's death so as not to frighten or upset them.

CHILDREN WITH SPECIAL NEEDS

A sensitive teacher will recognize that experiences in the social studies can be easily adapted for individual learners. For example, suppose the children are learning about their own community and will be engaged in visiting neighborhood stores, parks, and so on; mapping the community; graphing the kinds of work people in the community do; inviting visitors from the community to share their work; and so on. For children with special needs, these activities can easily be adapted. For some children, visiting one neighborhood store and reporting on it will be challenging, while for others, visiting and comparing three or more stores will be appropriate. When inviting visitors to the classroom, make sure that people with disabilities are included and that their contributions to the community are highlighted. Social studies includes the study of *all* people, so children with special needs can be accommodated and develop the same important concepts as other members of the class. Adapting the experiences and activities provided for these children should not result in their learning less or contributing less to the class than other children.

CELEBRATING DIVERSITY

Of all the content areas, social studies is the one in which diversity can be most easily celebrated in the classroom. All children want to learn about their families and neighborhoods, and examining these topics will offer an opportunity for exploring the commonalities in and differences among them. The study of any community should include its diversity and express appreciation for all its members.

Teachers should remember, as well, that there are many ways that communities can be diverse: by race or ethnicity, by age, by interests, by skills, by religion, and so on. All communities have diversity that can be explored and celebrated.

By asking families to contribute to the study of their native cultures (e.g., clothing, food, games, and other traditions), teachers can avoid the stereotyping that often results when knowledge of cultures comes only from books and videos. Having family members share the information guarantees that it will be accurate and authentic.

NAEYC CRITERIA
2.73

Art projects can provide great opportunities for children to explore other cultures.

Parents and Social Studies

● After parents visit the classroom or contribute significant items from their cultures, be sure to acknowledge them in newsletters, on bulletin boards, and in displays.

As different families share, the information can be charted and compared. Children should learn that all families have both common and unique features—even families that might appear to be exactly the same or entirely different. Whatever the topic in social studies, the diversity of people can be celebrated.

SUMMARY

● According to the NCSS (1997), the two defining characteristics of *social studies* are (1) that it is multi-disciplinary and integrative, addressing many subjects and fields of interest, and (2) that its purpose is to produce informed and reasonable citizens.

● According to the constructivist view, children learn social studies by constructing their understanding of social studies concepts over a period of time and according to their own level of development. The maps constructed by the same child at ages four, five, and six, for example, will become increasingly sophisticated, reflecting the child's increasing experience with and knowledge of the topic.

● Teachers can take any of several approaches to planning social studies instruction—for instance, viewing social studies as a body of knowledge, as being focused on social development, as following an expanded curriculum model, and as being focused on decision making. Many teachers take an eclectic approach, combining elements of several approaches. The NCSS (1992, 1997) advocates teaching children the knowledge, skills, and values they need to engage in civil action and describes social studies teaching and learning as "powerful" when they are "meaningful, integrative, value based, challenging, and active." The NCSS stan-

dards consist of ten themes, which are to provide a framework for the social studies curriculum.

● Many aspects of social studies can be integrated into the curriculum through reading, writing, music, and games. For example, children can read or listen to the teacher read books with social studies content, learn to write reports and journals about their learning, and sing songs or learn dances and games from various time periods or cultures. The use of themes is an especially effective way to integrate social studies with the other content areas.

● Holidays should not be the focus of the curriculum in early childhood social studies. Holiday celebrations should be planned by the children and be very low key. The holidays and concepts being celebrated should be meaningful and sensible to the children. Children do not need more frenzy than is provided in the commercial world at each holiday season.

● The social studies curriculum is the ideal place for including children with special needs, as it is a study of people and their lives. Special-needs children can be involved in activities when appropriate adaptations are made, and visitors to the classroom should include people with special needs. Recognizing the contributions of citizens with special needs is very important and can easily be included in the social studies curriculum.

● Celebrating diversity is also easily accomplished in the social studies program. Any activity that involves a study of people in the neighborhood, the work of individuals, and so on provides an excellent opportunity to learn about and honor differences and similarities—in individuals, in families, or in neighborhoods. Families can be active in the social studies curriculum by helping children learn about their home cultures and lives.

REFLECTIONS

1. Many people disagree about what is the best approach to teaching social studies. Now that you have read this chapter and thought about social studies as a content area, what do think is the best approach? What should children learn in social studies? Why?

2. When integrating social studies into the curriculum, how can you be sure to achieve the true goals of social studies?

3. In some programs, holiday celebrations take over the curriculum for days and even weeks. How much time should be allotted to holiday celebrations? What should be the purpose of holiday celebrations? Think about how you would justify your decisions about holidays to administrators and parents.

4. Social studies is very important in the lives of young children. After all, what is more important than learning to live together peacefully, to respect oneself and others, and to know how to resolve conflicts in an appropriate manner? How could you integrate goals like these into the curriculum and then assess children's fulfillment of them?

5. Social studies is often perceived as a collection of activities. If that is your perception, how can you adapt it to ensure that social studies becomes an important content area with clear goals in a program for young children?

EXPLORATIONS AND ACTIVITIES

1. Interview three to five teachers of young children to ask how they treat holidays in their program. Interview three to five parents of young children to ask how they would like the school to treat holidays in the programs their children attend. Summarize the responses. Do teachers and parents agree? If so, do they support your ideas of appropriate holiday celebrations? If not, can you use the comments to help you plan communication between parents and teachers around the celebration of holidays in school programs?

2. In many programs for primary children (grades one and two), social studies is being either eliminated or deemphasized as more time is devoted to instruction aimed at increasing reading scores. How could you make a case to the school board or administration that the social studies is a vital and worthy part of the curriculum for young children?

MyLabSchool is a collection of online tools for your success in this course, your licensure exams, and your teaching career. Visit **www.mylabschool.com** to access the following:

■ Online Study Guide
■ Video Cases from real classrooms
■ Help with your research papers using Research Navigator
■ Career Center with resources for:
　—Praxis and Licensure Preparation
　—Professional Portfolio Development
　—Job Search and Interview Techniques
　—Lesson Planning

CHAPTER **15**

KEY TERMS *you'll find in this chapter:*

- **Food pyramid,** 497
- **Fundamental motor skills,** 482
- **Health education,** 490
- **Latchkey children,** 502
- **Medical procedures,** 492
- **Nutrition education,** 494
- **Physical development,** 484
- **Physical education,** 483
- **Physical fitness,** 483
- **Safety education,** 498

Promoting Wellness
Physical Education and Health, Nutrition, and Safety Education

FOCUS
QUESTIONS

● What are appropriate goals and activities for physical education for young children?

● What are appropriate goals and activities for health, nutrition, and safety education for young children?

● How can teachers integrate physical education and health, nutrition, and safety education into the curriculum?

● How can teachers help children with special needs be actively involved in activities that encourage motor development?

● How can teachers celebrate diversity through activities designed to help children live safe and healthy lives?

Your assignment this week—to observe for instruction in health and wellness, motor development, nutrition, and safety—seemed so broad. You thought you were not likely to see all these areas addressed in any one day, but in the kindergarten you visited, you did see some aspects related to all these topics.

For example, as the children played outdoors, you saw the teacher encouraging children to participate in activities such as jumping over ropes on the ground. When the children had their snack, you noticed that the teacher talked about the value of eating vegetables and that the snack was a tray of cut-up vegetables from which children could select one or two to try. You knew the class was going to make vegetable soup the next day. During the circle time, a police officer visited the class and the children participated in a bicycle safety program.

As you talked to the teacher, you realized that not all these topics would be included every day but that safety, nutrition, and health were integrated into the regular curriculum as much as possible. Motor development was the focus of outdoor play planned by the teacher or physical education planned by a specialist. The children had physical education at least three days a week with the specialist. Both teachers planned jointly for these activity periods.

You are glad that you saw so much focus on physical development because you believe that physical development should not be ignored any more than social or intellectual development. However, your peers' observations ran the gamut. In some schools, no specialist was available for physical education, some schools did not require physical education, and some schools had eliminated recess in order to get more time for academic topics. Some schools had a safety or nutrition lesson once a week, but there was no effort to integrate these lessons into the curriculum.

You have many questions about what kind of physical education is appropriate for primary children and how to integrate health and safety into an appropriate curriculum. ■

Physical Education

NAEYC CRITERIA
2.81

In this era when physical fitness is of such concern to many adults, the media continue to report that U.S. children are neither as fit as they once were nor as fit as they should be. Many more children than ever before are obese, have limited capacity to perform physical tasks, or have hypertension and cardiovascular disease.

The solution to this problem lies in educating children to make more healthful choices in their lives—choices that include active exercise and a healthy diet. The list of fitness facts in this chapter emphasizes the need to develop the habit of healthy exercise in young children.

Encouraging Motor Development

Young children need the opportunity to develop **fundamental motor skills.** Motor fitness is defined in terms of these qualities:

1. *Agility*—The ability to change the movement direction of the entire body in space, both rapidly and accurately
2. *Balance*—The maintenance of equilibrium while either stationary or moving
3. *Coordination*—The ability to perform motor skills smoothly and accurately
4. *Power*—The ability to transfer energy into force at a fast rate
5. *Reaction time*—The time elapsed between stimulation and the beginning of a reaction to that stimulation
6. *Speed*—The ability to perform a movement in a short period of time (Corbin and Lindsey 1996)

Motor fitness can be achieved through regular opportunities to run, jump, hop, slide, gallop, and skip. Controlling these movements, as in running to the beat of a drum or changing the lead foot when they hear a signal while they are galloping, can help children gain motor control and can be accomplished with nothing but some space and a whistle or drum.

There are many good reasons children should participate in vigorous physical activity each day. Such activity helps to prevent chronic disease and obesity and helps in optimizing growth and development. Of course, physical activity helps children develop motor skills, which are useful all through life. Cognitive functioning also can be improved through physical activity, and such activity does not detract from academic achievement. Finally, physical activity encourages wellness of the body as a whole (Corbin and Pangrazi 2004). It is obvious that full inclusion of all students would be a hallmark of good programs and that no physical activities would be used as punishments.

Teachers know that motor development is important and can contribute to children's development in other areas. The psychomotor domain is stimulated by activities that require thought and deliberate movement, such as bouncing a ball, hitting a target with a ball, or hitting a ball with a bat. This area of development includes fundamental motor skills such as walking and running, which are necessary for participation in games and sports throughout life.

Seefeldt (1984) notes that "the rudimentary skills which make up the components of our games and sports can be learned by children in an enriched environment before they are six years of age" (p. 35). He goes on to state that opportunities both for practice and motivation are at their highest levels in the early childhood years.

Although physical fitness for young children is more difficult to define than fitness for older populations (Seefeldt 1984), with a minimal level of **physical fitness,** young children will be able to perform physical tasks such as walking and running. Fitness is also defined by cardiorespiratory function, relative leanness, abdominal endurance, lower-back flexibility, and upper-body strength and endurance (Gober and Franks 1988; Leppo 1993; Ross and Pate 1987).

Children younger than age ten have been included in national studies of children's fitness only recently; however, standards now exist, beginning with six-year-olds. Standards for the different levels of fitness—presidential, national, and health fitness—are available on the Web (see marginal notation).

Teachers must not overlook **physical education** activities in their efforts to balance a program, so that every area of a child's development is fostered. Physical education activities can contribute to a child's social and intellectual development as well as to her physical development.

For example, through sports and games, children learn to interact with others in positive ways. They may learn the importance of interdependence and the feeling of belonging that being part of a team can offer. A child's self-concept may be enhanced as she becomes physically skillful. Children gain intellectual skill by creating games and movements, expressing themselves as they negotiate in games, and solving problems related to physical goals. Working puzzles, cutting, and pushing buttons to operate teaching equipment all require not only thinking but physical skills, as well.

Children need both physical skills and cognitive abilities to feel good about themselves. Emphasizing only cognitive abilities may strengthen a child in one area while undermining her ability in another. Weiller and Richardson (1993) state the case well: "Regular, appropriate physical activity

www.presidentschallenge.org
Standards for physical fitness, along with information on modifying these standards for children with disabilities

is the responsibility of all educators. It is crucial that children acquire appropriate skills, develop a sound fitness level, and feel positive about their movement abilities" (p. 137).

Goals of Physical Development Programs

PRAXIS

Be able to describe developmentally appropriate practice in physical education

In a document developed by the Council for Physical Education for Children (COPEC), which is an organization within the National Association for Sport and Physical Education (NASPE), Corbin and Pangrazi (2004) provide physical activity guidelines for teachers, administrators, parents, and others who see the value of promoting such activity among children. *Physical activity* is broadly defined to include not only exercise and sports but also dance and movement activities. These authors provide four guidelines:

1. Children should accumulate at least 60 minutes, and up to several hours, of age-appropriate physical activity on all, or most days of the week. This daily accumulation should include moderate and vigorous physical activity with the majority of the time being spent in activity that is intermittent in nature.
2. Children should participate in several bouts of physical activity lasting 15 minutes or more each day.
3. Children should participate each day in a variety of age-appropriate physical activities designed to achieve optimal health, wellness, fitness, and performance benefits.
4. Extended periods (periods of two hours or more) of inactivity are discouraged for children, especially during the daytime hours. (Corbin and Pangrazi 2004)

These guidelines are for grades Kindergarten through twelve and do not mention prekindergarten. Preschool children certainly do need to participate in physical activity every day, and planning for vigorous physical activity is very important. Many children will participate in active play without any more planning than giving them time and a playground, but observations have revealed that a percentage of children will stand around and talk on the playground rather than do anything. It is for these children that the teacher has to do careful planning to get them moving and participating.

The goals of **physical development** programs for young children include having children participate in a variety of activities that will foster motor development; helping children develop gross motor skills; helping children develop a positive attitude toward active movement experiences; and helping children develop fine motor skills. These goals, like goals in other areas of curriculum, are broad and can best be met by a balance of planned and spontaneous activities.

Activities designed for specialized skill development should never overshadow, replace, or serve as the primary purpose of general physical education (Gallahue 1981). However, teachers must make a concerted effort to involve children in active physical experiences. One study (Miller 1978) found that children in free-play situations often spent the time playing quietly and spent very little time in vigorous physical activities. Participation in vigorous activity can be increased through planned activities, teacher modeling and participation, and careful observation of children to ensure their involvement.

www.

www.pbs.org/teachersource/ prek2/issues/202issue.shtm

An explanation of the importance of physical movement in children's development

www.

www.cem.msu.edu/~leej/ development-motor.html

Summaries of typical motor development of children ages three to five

A developmentally appropriate program of physical education is based on three principles: "(1) motor skill development is sequential and age-related; (2) children progress through similar sequences of motor development; and (3) the rates at which children progress through sequences of motor development varies" (Grineski 1992, p. 33). Table 15.1 provides an overview of the gross motor development of young children.

Gabbard (1995) agrees that children need to participate in age-appropriate activities and adds that gender should not determine participation in activities, that activities should be noncompetitive, and that equipment should match the size, confidence, and skill of the children. Primary-age children should be involved in activities designed to help them develop movement awareness and basic motor skills. As in any other area of

TABLE 15.1 Gross Motor Development in Early and Middle Childhood

AGE	GROSS MOTOR SKILLS
2–3 years	Walks more rhythmically; hurried walk changes to run.
	Jumps, hops, throws, and catches with rigid upper body.
	Pushes riding toy with feet; little steering.
3–4 years	Walks up stairs, alternating feet, and down stairs, leading with one foot.
	Jumps and hops, flexing upper body.
	Throws and catches with slight involvement of upper body; still catches by trapping ball against chest.
	Pedals and steers tricycle.
4–5 years	Walks down stairs, alternating feet; runs more smoothly.
	Gallops and skips with one foot.
	Throws ball with increased body rotation and transfer of weight on feet; catches ball with hands.
	Rides tricycle rapidly, steers smoothly.
5–6 years	Increases running speed to 12 feet per second.
	Gallops more smoothly; engages in true skipping and sideways stepping.
	Displays mature, whole-body throwing and catching patterns; increases throwing speed.
	Rides bicycle with training wheels.
7–12 years	Increases running speed to more than 18 feet per second.
	Displays continuous, fluid skipping and sideways stepping.
	Increases vertical jump from 4 to 12 inches and broad jump from 3 to over 5 feet; accurately jumps and hops from square to square.
	Increases throwing and kicking accuracy, distance, and speed.
	Involves the whole body in batting a ball; batting increases in speed and accuracy.
	Dribbling changes from awkward slapping of the ball to continuous, relaxed, even stroking.

Source: Laura E. Berk, *Child Development,* 7th ed. Boston: Allyn & Bacon, 2006, p. 175. Copyright © 2006 by Pearson Education. Reprinted by permission of the publisher.

the curriculum, the teacher has to observe the children carefully in order to know when to increase the difficulty of the task and when to provide more time for development of individual skills.

Standards for Physical Education

The *National Standards for Physical Education,* designed for children in grades kindergarten through twelve, were created by the National Association for Sport and Physical Education (NASPE 2004). These standards "reflect current thinking on what students should know and be able to do as a result of a quality physical education program." The philosophy underlying the standards is as follows:

> Physical activity is critical to the development and maintenance of good health. The goal of physical education is to develop physically educated individuals who have the knowledge, skills, and confidence to enjoy a lifetime of healthful physical activity. (NASPE 2004)*

According to the *National Standards for Physical Education,*

A physically educated person:

Standard 1: Demonstrates competency in motor skills and movement patterns needed to perform a variety of physical activities.

Standard 2: Demonstrates understanding of movement concepts, principles, strategies, and tactics as they apply to the learning and performance of physical activities.

Standard 3: Participates regularly in physical activity.

Standard 4: Achieves and maintains a health-enhancing level of physical fitness.

Standard 5: Exhibits responsible personal and social behavior that respects self and others in physical activity settings.

Standard 6: Values physical activity for health, enjoyment, challenge, self-expression, and/or social interaction. (NASPE 2004)*

NASPE offers these three purposes for the standards:

1. To provide the framework for a quality physical education program
2. To provide guidance for developing state and local standards
3. To increase the professional stature of physical education (NASPE 2004)*

A significant benefit of having national standards, as stated by the NASPE, is in establishing physical education as a valuable content area in the curriculum. Namely, the national standards

> demonstrate that physical education has academic standing equal to other subject areas. They describe achievement, show that knowledge and skills matter, and confirm that mere willing participation is not the same as education. In short, national physical education standards bring accountability and rigor to the profession. (NASPE 2004)*

---

*From *Moving into the Future: National Standards for Physical Education,* 2nd ed. (2004). Reprinted with permission from the National Association for Sport and Physical Education (NASPE), 1900 Association Dr., Reston, VA 20191-1599.

Physical Education Activities

Planned Activities

Physical education programs should include experiences with movement and games and activities that help to foster skill development. In each of these areas, activities must be matched to children's developmental levels and to the needs of individuals. Some children will be able to jump from a standing position or catch a ball while others will still be learning to walk backward or to go down steps by alternating feet.

When planning for individual differences, teachers can accommodate a wide variety of skill levels in the way that directions are given. For example, rather than ask all children to do headstands, teachers could ask all children to "Find a way to balance using three parts of your body" (Petersen 1992, p. 37). As you read the following ideas for planned experiences, keep in mind that all activities must be evaluated in terms of their appropriateness for individual children.

Movement   In planning movement activities, emphasize the exploration of space and how the human body can move in space. Many movement activities can be enhanced with the addition of music or rhythmic accompaniment.

Jumping   Lay two ropes on the ground about ten inches apart, and allow children to practice a standing broad jump over them; as children's skills increase, move the ropes farther apart. Place hula hoops in a pattern across the floor or on flat ground so that children can jump from one to another. Position a sturdy bench or box so that children can jump off it safely. Encourage children to explore how they can turn while jumping or how they can stretch their bodies or make them as small as possible while jumping.

> To insure good health: Eat lightly, breathe deeply, live moderately, cultivate cheerfulness, and maintain an interest in life.
>
> —*William London*

WWW.
http://northonline.sccd.ctc.edu/eceprog/games.html
Cooperative games and activities for young children

WWW.
www.aahperd.org/NASPE/template.cfm?template=toddlers.html
Guidelines for physical education programs for toddlers

Physical fitness activities foster motor development, physical skill development, and self-esteem in young children.

Climbing on Apparatus Encourage children to think of different ways to hang, move, stretch, or curl and to find different ways to get on and off the apparatus safely. To determine how high children should be allowed to climb, Readdick and Park (1998) suggest following this rule of thumb: Allow about one foot of height for each year of age until about age five. After that, the children's competence and the teacher's own comfort level should guide decisions about height.

Following an Obstacle Course Build an obstacle course with materials in the classroom. For example, create a path to follow that requires children to crawl under a table, climb over a sturdy bench, jump through a series of hula hoops placed on the floor, and crawl through a tunnel created with a quilt and chairs. Invite children to move over, around, under, and through obstacles in as many ways as possible.

Rolling and Tumbling If you have a grassy slope that children can roll down, use it. If not, encourage children to roll and find ways to turn their bodies on mats.

Using a Parachute Preschool children will enjoy stretching a parachute and moving it up and down. They will also enjoy getting under it. Older, more coordinated children will enjoy games in which they bounce objects on the parachute, take turns running under it, and use it in stretching and rhythmic activities.

Games Games such as circle games, in which only one person is "It," often require all other participants to sit or stand and wait for most of the play period. Better choices are games that involve the whole group. Teachers can invent games of Tag with multiple "Its" for kindergarten and primary children.

Staley and Portman (2000) note that the research clearly demonstrates the need for making sure that children are engaged in vigorous activity at least thirty minutes a day (although it does not have to be all at one time). Games as part of the curriculum must therefore get everyone moving and have very little waiting and watching time.

For preschool children, one game that keeps everyone moving is Soap Bubbles, in which all the children move within a marked space without touching anyone else. If children touch, they "burst" and must make themselves as small as possible. (Children who have been touched can move outside the space and continue moving.) The game begins with a very large space, but the teacher moves the space markers so that there is less and less space until most children have been touched. This game can be accompanied by music (Pangrazi and Dauer 1992).

Many games for primary children involve an entire group in movement activities. One example is Back-to-Back, for which there must be an uneven number of children. Children pair off and stand back-to-back; the child left over claps her hands and calls out a movement ("run," "hop," "skip," "slide," "gallop," or "jump"). Following the command, each child must move forward a certain distance and then turn and find a new partner; the one left over becomes the leader for the next round.

Parents and Wellness

- Get parents involved in their children's physical development by sending home descriptions of activities that the whole family can enjoy together—for example, bowling with a ball and empty soda containers.

In a similar game called Stop and Start, the children are spaced far enough apart to move freely. The leader calls out a movement, such as "skip." All the children move until the leader signals them to stop. Any child who moves after that must wait on the sidelines for one round.

Recess Some schools do not have recess scheduled, and so children do not have physical activity every day. Dr. Judith Kieff defends recess in the following An Expert Speaks piece. Do you agree that children should be active every day? If your school does not, what can you do to help the children get the active physical movement that they need?

AN **Expert** SPEAKS: The Immediate and Long-Term Benefits of Recess

Judith Kieff, University of New Orleans

Young children think and learn differently than older children and adults. Therefore, best practice for programs serving young children will include specific teaching and learning strategies designed to fit their unique learning styles and abilities and promote optimal development. Recess is one such strategy. Traditionally, recess is a fifteen- to twenty-minute break from formal classroom instruction that provides opportunities for young children to freely engage in activities that simultaneously promote health, cognitive and social development, and emotional well-being. Therefore, recess can be seen as a strategy that has both immediate and long-term benefits related to school success.

The immediate benefits of recess include the opportunity for children to escape the formality of classroom instruction and do what children do naturally: run, climb, hop, dance, walk, talk, and bounce freely in the outdoor environment. These may not seem like remarkable activities, but the combination of whole-body movement with fresh air and sunshine provides children with a mental break from sustained periods of concentration and focus, thus allowing their brains time to process information. Children return to the classroom with a renewed sense of focus and mental energy. Another immediate effect of recess is the feeling of pleasure and control that comes from having choices in activities and interacting with peers and adults in an informal setting. The resulting sense of value and well-being can sustain a child's persistence when he or she is later faced with challenging academic tasks.

The long-term benefits of recess result from the multiple opportunities it provides for sustained play and social interactions. Play is a primary vehicle for the development of physical and logico-mathematical knowledge, social competency, and perceptual-motor skills during childhood. Play offers children the opportunity to explore and discover facts about their environment, practice and consolidate previously learned academic skills, and apply language and communication skills in authentic contexts. Sociodramatic play episodes often provide children with negotiating and problem-solving challenges. While children are playing, they are freed from the stress of "being wrong," so they often function at their highest cognitive level. The cumulative effect of functioning at a high level of play during recess will ultimately benefit children's academic achievement.

Certainly, to be effective, recess must take place on well-maintained playgrounds where equipment is safe, abundant, and age appropriate. Recess should be supervised by multiple staff members who are both well acquainted with the children they supervise and trained not only to interact with children, but also to foster children's positive interactions with one another. When these high standards are met, recess becomes a time- and cost-effective strategy that promotes long-term academic gains.

Policymakers, administrators, and sometimes even parents may call for the limitation or abolishment of recess on the grounds that children need more time to work at structured academic tasks. Unfortunately, they do not understand the young child's unique style of learning. Early childhood professionals are charged with the responsibility of advocating for and demonstrating the effectiveness of strategies that support the optimal learning environment for children. Recess is one such strategy.

Skill Activities

Throwing and Catching   Very young children should practice throwing with relatively large, soft balls. Balls about six inches in diameter are easiest to catch. Threes and fours can begin to catch with their arms extended. A yarn ball or a Nerf ball is good for these children.

Children can be encouraged to throw a ball as high as possible, to roll it on the ground, and to stop the ball with their feet or other body parts while it is rolling. Children can also toss the ball with two hands, with one hand, and play catch with a partner. Tossing bean bags or tossing and rolling small balls at a target (a bowling pin or an empty bleach bottle) are also appropriate activities.

Kicking and Batting   Primary children can begin to learn to kick a ball. To learn how, they should begin with a stationary ball and be encouraged to tap the ball with their feet, to tap it so that it goes to a partner, and to kick the ball to a target area. Batting a ball should also begin with the ball stationary, perhaps on a cone. Children should be encouraged to think of as many ways to hit the ball as possible.

Benelli and Yongue (1995) suggest making a bat from a two-liter plastic bottle and a wooden dowel. The handles of most bats are too large for small hands and the hitting surfaces are too small.

Health, Nutrition, and Safety Education

Helping children develop their physical abilities and encouraging them to be physically active is certainly important. It is also important to help children learn to make good choices in health practices, nutrition, and safety. Young children, of course, do not make these choices without guidance from parents and teachers, but they can begin to develop healthy habits.

Health Education

Historically, health care was an important goal of early preschool programs. In today's world of more personal responsibility for health, education for healthful choices continues to be important; however, it tends to be overlooked in many programs (Bruhn and Nader 1982). Because children and young adults do not perceive themselves as vulnerable to illness (Gochman and Saucier 1982), health educators have recommended that programs in **health education** be developed and implemented for children as young as two or three (Kingsbury and Hall 1988).

Standards for Health Education

In responding to the question *"Why National Health Education Standards?"* the American Association for Health Education (AAHE) states, "In this era of education reform, *National Health Education Standards* are critical to the healthy development of children and youth." Thus, the stated goals of these standards are twofold: "improved educational achievement for students and improved health in the United States" (AAHE 2005–2006).

Here are the eight *National Health Education Standards*, which are intended for students in prekindergarten through grade twelve (PreK–12):

National Health Education Standards

1. Students will comprehend concepts related to health promotion and disease prevention to enhance health.
2. Students will analyze the influence of family, peers, culture, media, technology and other factors on health behaviors.
3. Students will demonstrate the ability to access valid information and products and services to enhance health.
4. Students will demonstrate the ability to use interpersonal communication skills to enhance health and avoid or reduce health risks.
5. Students will demonstrate the ability to use decision-making skills to enhance health.
6. Students will demonstrate the ability to use goal setting skills to enhance health.
7. Students will demonstrate the ability to practice health-enhancing behaviors and avoid or reduce risks.
8. Students will demonstrate the ability to advocate for personal, family and community health. (AAHE 2005–2006)*

www.aahperd.org/AAHE/
template.cfm?template=
natl_health_education_
standards.html

The *National Health Education Standards* online

For each standard, the AAHE also provides specific grade-level performance indicators, which are behaviors and skills that demonstrate achievement of the standard. For instance, for the grade level Pre-K–2, these performance indicators are given for the first standard, which addresses "concepts related to health promotion and disease prevention":

1. Identify that healthy behaviors impact personal health.
2. Recognize that there are multiple dimensions of health.
3. Describe ways to prevent communicable diseases.
4. List ways to prevent common childhood injuries.
5. Describe why it is important to seek health care. (AAHE 2005–2006)*

Separate clusters of performance indicators also are given for grades three through five, six through eight, and nine through twelve.

As is true of the standards for the other content areas, the *National Health Education Standards* are intended to be used as a framework for curriculum planning, instruction, and assessment. In addition, the standards are intended to serve as a guide for teacher preparation and continuing education (AAHE 2005–2006).

Personal Routines

Health education is not a lesson to be taught on a schedule. It must be integrated throughout the day and made a part of many activities. Children learn about good health habits in many ways: observing parents and teachers (especially those who take time to explain why they are making the decisions they make); listening to stories; and making regular visits to the doctor and dentist. For example, as children wash their hands after using the toilet and before eating, the teacher can mention the importance of cleanliness in staying healthy; as children brush their teeth after eating, the teacher may demonstrate how to hold the brush and point out that brushing down over the teeth is best.

Brushing teeth also can be encouraged if the children can reach their own toothbrushes and the sink so that they can be independent about the

---

*From pre-publication document of *National Health Education Standards, PreK–12.* American Cancer Society. December 2005–April 2006.

task. A visit by a dental hygienist to demonstrate the correct procedures
for brushing and flossing will remind children to brush on a regular basis.
The children might also visit a dentist's office and get a chance to sit in the
chair and look at the tools and equipment. A flashlight and a chair will
probably be all the children need to play "dentist" after such a visit. When a
child loses a tooth, the teacher is given a perfect opportunity for discussing
and reading about teeth—how they grow and the importance of caring for
them.

A significant portion of health education in early childhood programs
will be taught as daily routines are established. Children will learn to wash
their hands after using the toilet or blowing their noses or before eating and
to brush their teeth after eating. As they participate in these routines, they
can be taught the reasons these behaviors are important. Although young
children are not able to understand the causal relationships between germs
and disease, they can understand that regular hygiene routines contribute
to their staying well and feeling healthy.

Teachers also must be aware of sanitary procedures that will help
prevent illness. Teachers of infants and toddlers must be careful to wash
their hands thoroughly after diapering or assisting children at the toilet. Often teachers of young children must help them blow their noses or
clean their faces after a sneeze. Teachers should scrub their hands after
every such incident. Teachers must also model the importance of washing their hands carefully before either serving or cooking food. Changing
tables and tables where food is served should be scrubbed and disinfected
regularly.

Medical Procedures

The health education program should also include helping children become more comfortable and accepting of **medical procedures,** health care
professionals, and hospitals. Parents should be involved in planning these
particular activities, as they can provide specific information about their
children's experiences and possible fears.

www.

**www.cincinnatichildrens.org/
health**

Links to many articles about
and resources for health
information

Many activities in the classroom—such as playing with puppets, listening to stories, playing with toy medical equipment (or real equipment, if that is possible and appropriate), and meeting health care professionals—can help children understand and feel more positive about medical care. Field trips to the offices of health care professionals and to hospitals can also be arranged. These trips must be planned carefully, but most hospitals have programs for educating even very young children about being in the hospital.

Children can learn some simple first aid procedures. One program uses puppets to dramatize stories in which first aid is required (Marchand and McDermott 1986). Children learn first aid procedures and why they are necessary. They also learn to select the most appropriate procedure from the alternatives available and how to use the telephone to get help in an emergency.

www.headstartinfo.org/
infocenter/guides/
healthsafetynutrition.htm
Information for health, safety, and nutrition education, plus links to many other resources

NAEYC CRITERIA
2.90

Substance Abuse and HIV/AIDS

Two relatively new facets of health education for young children are substance abuse programs and programs to educate children about HIV (human immunodeficiency virus) and AIDS (acquired immune deficiency syndrome). In many public schools, such programs are now required. With so much about drugs and HIV/AIDS on television and in the conversations of adults, teachers in preschool settings must be able to answer children's questions and understand their fears. Early childhood educators are in a unique position to contribute to preventing drug abuse and educating the public about HIV and AIDS, because both problems affect many children's lives directly and because early childhood educators can work with parents in ways that have positive results over long periods of time.

In a longitudinal study that followed a group of children from the time they were five until they were eighteen, Shedler and Block (1990) found that young adults who were frequent users of drugs were relatively maladjusted as children of seven years old. The frequent users were described at age seven as

> not getting along well with other children, not showing concern for moral issues (e.g., reciprocity, fairness), having bodily symptoms from stress, tending to be indecisive and vacillating, not planful or likely to think ahead, not trustworthy or dependable, not able to admit to negative feelings, not self-reliant or confident, preferring nonverbal methods of communication, not developing genuine and close relationships, not proud of their accomplishments, not vital or energetic or lively, not curious and open to new experience, not able to recoup after stress, afraid of being deprived, appearing to feel unworthy and "bad," not likely to identify with admired adults, inappropriate in emotive behavior, and easily victimized and scapegoated by other children. (p. 618)

Based on these findings, Shedler and Block (1990) recommend that resources for prevention of drug abuse be focused on intervening in the development of the personality syndrome that underlies drug use, rather than on campaigns such as "Just Say No." The research highlights the importance of positive experiences for children at home and at school that will develop stronger self-concepts, more skill in social interactions, and more prosocial behaviors.

Even young children know about HIV/AIDS and may fear that they or people close to them will become infected. Children see programs, news stories, and commercials on television aimed at educating the public about HIV and AIDS, but they rarely understand what they see and hear. Teachers who feel the need to provide information about HIV and AIDS must consider the children's cognitive development and needs when making decisions about what to say.

Teachers of young children can be prepared to answer children's questions in positive ways. For example, they can say that HIV is the virus that causes the disease called AIDS but that children who do not have the virus or the disease are not likely to catch it and that children cannot get it from touching a person who has it. Most children asking such questions are seeking reassurance that they are safe; they do not need a lesson on adult sexual behavior or drug use. Parents also may need guidance in what to say when children ask them questions. Primary-grade children are likely to encounter some sort of planned instruction that is aimed at making children aware of the dangers of HIV/AIDS. The goals of most programs for primary children are limited to having the children understand that they cannot contract HIV or AIDS by being with or touching someone who has it.

When making a decision about what to tell children when one of their classmates is HIV positive or has AIDS, teachers will have to exercise their own judgment, based on knowledge of the children and how much they have heard from parents. If the children know that a child is ill and ask questions, the teacher should answer as honestly as possible while helping children feel safe from the disease.

Even though young children do not need to know much about HIV and AIDS, teachers *do* need to know. In particular, teachers must be able to sort out the facts from the myths about HIV and AIDS. Because many teachers will have children who have HIV/AIDS in class or will know of parents who do, they will be faced with providing information to other parents. Thus, teachers need accurate, up-to-date information. They also need to work together to determine the best alternatives for teaching children about HIV/AIDS and the best information to provide to parents.

www.projectinform.org
Information about HIV and AIDS

Nutrition Education

Food is not only basic to life, but it is also closely related to people's social and cultural lives. Food is an integral part of family, religious, and cultural celebrations. Many aspects of food are culturally determined: what people think is appropriate to eat; how they eat it (with fingers, pieces of bread, chopsticks, or forks); with whom they eat (with men, with women and children, or in family groups); and when they eat during the day.

How food is used socially is also culturally determined. Many people offer guests something to eat or drink as soon as they are in their homes, and food is often central to social gatherings. For years, business was conducted over lunch—now people even have "power breakfasts"! Teaching children to make healthy choices in the food they select is certainly a worthwhile goal and one that will affect their lives through adulthood.

> **Health is a state of complete physical, mental and social well-being, not merely the absence of disease or infirmity.**
>
> —*World Health Organization*

Nutrition education is important because children commonly have problems related to nutrition. Although children do not often have control over what they are offered to eat, they do make choices from the food offered to them. The choices provided for them in a school setting should be

Preparing a snack can contribute to children's knowledge of healthy eating habits.

nutritious and should help them learn about food and nutrition. Physical problems related to nutrition include tooth decay, obesity, iron deficiency anemia, and hypersensitivity to foods. Teachers need to focus on providing nutritious snacks; controlling the amounts of sugar, salt, and fiber in children's school diets; and establishing good food habits.

Appropriate goals for nutrition education with young children would include helping children learn to eat a variety of foods; increasing children's awareness of their reasons for selecting certain foods; and helping children develop positive attitudes about food.

Notice that these broad goals do not include teaching children to recite the names of the food groups on cue. Primary children might find it meaningful to classify foods according to their contributions to a healthy diet, but Herr and Morse (1982) believe that classifying foods into the six groups specified by the new U.S. Department of Agriculture food pyramid requires more skill in generalization than should be expected from young children. They recommend that foods be categorized into ten groups: milk, meat, dried peas and beans, eggs, fruits, vegetables, breads, pastas, cereals/grains/seeds, and nuts.

Snack and Meal Times

The goals of teaching children sound eating habits can be achieved in the classroom by offering nutritious snacks and meals and through food preparation experiences. Teachers are responsible for the quality of food that children are offered; children can then choose if and how much they are going to eat. The following foods are appropriate for snacks:

Raw Vegetables

Celery	Cauliflower florets
Peas in pod	Turnip sticks
Cucumber wedges	Jicama sticks
Tomato slices	Broccoli florets

Fresh Fruits

Apple wedges	Pineapple cubes
Orange segments	Pear or peach slices
Banana slices	Kiwi
Strawberries	Papaya
Blueberries	Mango

Other Snacks

Unsweetened fruit juice	Cottage cheese
Dried fruit	Peanut butter
Milk	Muffins
Milkshakes made from milk and fruit	Dry cereals (unsweetened)
Lowfat yogurt	Whole-grain crackers
Cheese	

In programs in which children are offered lunch or both breakfast and lunch, teachers should follow the guidelines of the U.S. Department of Agriculture (USDA 2004) or the guidelines in the accreditation standards of the National Association for the Education of Young Children (NAEYC 1998) describing the nutritional and caloric requirements for children.

Teachers of children younger than three will want to be especially careful not to offer children food they cannot chew easily, such as raw carrots or peanuts, or bite-sized pieces of food that they can swallow without chewing. Foods such as raisins and popcorn can easily cause choking. Unless the children can be supervised carefully while they eat, other foods are better choices.

Teachers and parents must work together in order to achieve the goals of nutrition education. If parents know what teachers are trying to do with nutrition information, they can help reinforce the ideas. For example, teachers who work in schools where children bring their own snacks to school can ask parents to cooperate in sending only nutritious snacks for the children. A letter explaining the importance of reducing the sugar in children's diets (Rogers and Morris 1986) and a list of suggested snacks will aid parents in choosing snack foods that are appropriate.

One strategy for helping children learn to eat a variety of foods is to offer new foods at snack time. Colker (2005) recommends that snacktime be handled by setting up a cooking center and allowing children to have their snacks as they choose. For example, the teacher might put out a sign in the center each day to explain the snack. If it is "ants on a log," the celery, the peanut butter (not the whole jar but a more manageable amount in a container), and the raisins will be available. The sign will say "Ants on a log"—2 pieces, Juice—1 cup, and Water—as much as is wanted." Using this approach, the children will learn to wash their hands before making and eating the snack and to clean up the tables when they are finished so others will have a clean place to eat. Teachers will have to observe, however, so that some children do not have a snack more than once and that others do not ignore it altogether because they are so busy.

Teachers might also think about how to add discussions of food when not all the children are together for the snack. A food-related discussion could be added in a few minutes once a week or to the short morning or

NAEYC CRITERIA
2.88, 2.89

before-going-home group times. Such a discussion might cover sources of food, foods that are related, forms of food (apples of different colors), or food or food preparation vocabulary.

To encourage children's eating of new foods, make colorful vegetable mixes, include the children in preparing the food, model good nutritional behaviors, and invite parents to help you model such behaviors at home. Also try foods in many forms, and present new foods more than once so children can have more opportunities to taste them.

In this era, when childhood obesity is becoming a major threat to children's health and leading to life-long health problems, learning to eat nutritional foods is more important than ever. In one study, Lino et al. (2002) found that 72 percent of the children had a diet that needed improvement and that 9 percent had a poor diet.

The new **food pyramid,** created by the USDA, is available online (see marginal note). At this website, one can fill in her age, gender, and activity level and then compute a personal food pyramid. Teachers could print out a personal pyramid for each child and send it home as well as discuss it at school. Although teachers cannot control what children eat outside school, they can certainly ask that children eat only healthy foods at school and teach them why doing so is important.

www. www.mypyramid.gov
The new food pyramid, with games and activities for children

To help older children learn to appreciate new foods, involve them in cooking experiences as part of their social studies or science studies, ask parents or volunteers to share special cultural or ethnic dishes, and taste foods that are mentioned in stories that they read or hear. For example, if the teacher reads the Paddington books aloud to the class, he could have children taste marmalade and could explain its place in a healthy diet.

> ## Parents and Wellness
> - If school snacks are supplied by parents, ask them to send nutritious foods. Be on the lookout for simple, healthy snack ideas that you can share with parents.
> - If food allergies in some children make certain snack foods dangerous, contact parents and seek their cooperation. They can help reinforce the idea of not sharing foods or simply not sending foods to school that are dangerous for some children.

Fuhr and Barclay (1998) suggest that teaching units on various kinds of food can also help children learn to appreciate new foods and to gain experience with trying them. These authors developed units on bread, fruit, protein, potatoes, milk, and vegetable soup that included reading, art, music, and cooking activities.

Cooking Experiences

Many teachers involve children in preparing foods for snacks or meals to be eaten at school. Even very young children can spread peanut butter or cheese on their crackers, sprinkle topping on their toast, or make simple sandwiches. Older children can peel vegetables, cut fruit, squeeze oranges to make juice, make English muffin pizzas with cheese and pizza sauce, and cut up apples for applesauce. Kindergarten and primary children can read and follow simple recipes for a variety of foods.

Teachers should follow these basic guidelines for cooking experiences:

1. Cook only nutritious foods.
2. Let the children do the cooking. Watching while the teacher measures the ingredients and then getting to stir does not give children a feeling of being involved. In planning a cooking experience, consider the maturity

www. http://dmoz.org/Home/
Cooking/For_Children
All kinds of recipes for cooking with children, many with photos

and skills of the children. Can they do what is required—measure, cut, mix, and so on? How many children can participate in the activity? Experiences should be planned for individuals or very small groups.

3. Plan for the children's safety, particularly if an experience involves heat or cutting. Make sure children are carefully supervised when using sources of heat. Tape electrical cords of appliances to the wall so that children cannot trip over them and pull appliances off the table; position appliances so that spills land on the table rather than on the floor. Make sure that children understand how to use cutting tools and sources of heat safely.

4. Be attentive to cleanliness. Are the children's hands and the utensils clean? In some areas of the United States, hepatitis has been a problem and teachers have been asked not to cook at school. Check local policies before cooking in the classroom.

Teachers will, of course, want to anticipate the learning outcomes that will be possible from cooking experiences. Children will be able to relate content from other subject-matter areas to cooking experiences. The following are only a few examples of the possibilities:

- *Science*—Observing changes in matter such as melting, congealing, shrinking (greens before and after cooking), expanding (rice before and after cooking), and transformation of water into steam
- *Language*—Learning cooking vocabulary, such as *boil, simmer, roll, knead, dice, shred,* and *grate,* as well as the names of foods and utensils
- *Mathematics*—Comparing quantities, measuring
- *Social studies*—Working cooperatively, learning about people involved in food production, preparing or tasting ethnic or cultural foods, and learning about food customs
- *Literacy*—Reading recipes or charts, connecting food experiences to stories (for example, making blueberry muffins after reading *Blueberries for Sal* [McCloskey 1948]), writing shopping lists, writing recipes, collecting and illustrating booklets of favorite recipes

See the Learning Plan for a project that involves completing a class cookbook. Many opportunities for discussing food and nutrition will be presented while completing this project.

Safety Education

Teachers of young children need to address questions of fire safety, traffic safety, water safety, poison safety, and personal safety. The teacher is responsible for checking the classroom and the play yard for any safety hazards, planning for emergencies, teaching children safe behaviors and what to do in an emergency, and supervising children closely. Pickle (1989) demonstrated that even preschoolers can benefit from instruction in **safety education;** primary children can also benefit from such instruction.

Fire Safety

Most elementary schools have a fire safety program that includes visits from local firefighters, poster contests about fire prevention, instructions about

Creating a Class Cookbook: First Grade

Objective:

- Each child will be able to write and illustrate a recipe to contribute to a class cookbook.
- Each child will be able to share her recipe orally with the class or a small group.

Materials:

Paper
Crayons and markers
Cookbook with photos (enlarged)

Procedure:

1. Explain that the class is going to make a cookbook of their favorite foods, and that each person will make a page for the book. Place the materials in the writing center, and allow children time to finish their recipes over two to three days.
2. Show the children a cookbook with photos or a recipe from the Web with photos. Explain that many cooks like to see how the food will look when it has been completed.
3. Ask each child to draw a picture of her favorite food and then write the directions for preparing the food.
4. Collect the pages as children finish their recipes. If children want to share their pages, provide time to do so.
5. Bind the pages into a class book that will be kept in the classroom library.

Accommodations: For children who have difficulty writing, take dictation to provide the recipe after they draw the picture.

Assessment:

- Note the levels of composition and spelling in each child's entry. Note words that each child could learn soon in conventional spelling. Discuss any indicators of growth in a child's writing ability with the child and make a copy of the writing for her parents.

---

what to do if there is a fire, and regular fire drills. A fire safety program should help children recognize the danger of fire and learn to treat fire with caution; prepare children to respond appropriately during a fire through regular fire drills; and teach children how to call the fire department.

Every classroom should have a written plan of action in case of fire that specifies the duties and responsibilities of each person (who will check the restroom, who will be responsible for children who are disabled, who will carry the class list, and so on), the exits to be used, and the point of assembly outside. Every class should practice fire drills on a regular basis. In some drills, selected exits should be blocked; drills should be planned to occur at unpredictable times such as meal or nap times. Near each exit, the teacher should post a map showing all exits and routes for evacuating the building and a class list to be used to account for the children after the building has been evacuated. Finally, teachers should provide parents with information about the fire drill procedures at school and encourage parents to plan regular fire drills at home.

Asking a local firefighter to visit the classroom can help promote children's awareness of fire safety. Most fire departments have an educational specialist who is responsible for teaching children fire prevention and fire safety. These people are usually talented in communicating with young children; they can teach children the "stop, drop, and roll" technique and demonstrate the pieces of equipment used by firefighters. Some firefighters encourage children to touch or try on equipment so that it does not frighten them when they see it on a firefighter. If children do try on firefighting gear, the firefighter can talk to the children about how different they look when they wear it. It is important that children recognize and not be afraid of

www.nfpa.org/riskwatch/kids.html

A fire safety webpage for children—readers and nonreaders

firefighters in full gear in case they should ever have to be rescued from a fire. Teachers should preview any presentation to ensure that it is appropriate for their children.

All children should be taught that in the case of a fire, they should leave the building or house first and then call the fire department. In the dramatic play area, a toy telephone and a large poster with the numbers to be dialed can help children practice dialing "0" or "911" to call the fire department in an emergency.

Traffic Safety

www.

www.nysgtsc.state.ny.us/
kids.htm

A traffic safety webpage for children

Teachers must share with parents the responsibilities for teaching children about traffic safety. The most frequent accidents involving children are those in which the child darts into the street, usually in the middle of the block. Goals of a traffic safety program include teaching children to stop before entering a street; teaching children how to cross a street safely; and teaching children to interpret traffic signals.

With repetition and the cooperation of parents, teachers can impress on children the importance of stopping at every curb. If there are no curbs on local streets, children should be taught to identify the boundary of the street and to stop there every time.

> Cheerfulness, sir, is the principle ingredient in the composition of health.
>
> —Arthur Murphy

Children need direct experience in looking and listening for traffic and then walking—not running—across the street. Often, very young children do not know what to look and listen for when they approach a street. With guidance from teachers and parents, they can learn to look and listen for approaching traffic and to cross carefully after the traffic has cleared. Children also must learn to make sure that drivers of stopped vehicles have seen them before crossing in front of the vehicles. Children may also need help understanding directions from crossing guards at school crossings. It may be prudent to teach children younger than four not to cross the street at all unless an adult tells them it is safe to do so.

Street crossings can be simulated in the dramatic play area so children can practice stopping, looking and listening for traffic, and walking carefully across the street. An area outdoors can be marked as a street, especially where children are riding wheel toys, and with guidance the children can practice crossing these "streets" carefully. The teacher might also mark some streets on the floor inside with masking tape and have the children role-play pedestrians and drivers of vehicles as they practice traffic safety. Teachers can make or purchase replicas of traffic signals for the blocks center and help the children set up their own streets, complete with signals, and practice safety procedures.

The third goal, teaching children to interpret traffic signals, can be furthered by constructing paper traffic signals or wiring a simple signal to a battery. Games such as Mother, May I? help children learn to move when the signal is green and stop when the signal is yellow or red. Teachers can invent other games based on Follow the Leader or Tag in which children must respond to traffic signals.

With help from a police officer and volunteers, the children can be taken to an intersection and helped to cross the street with the signals provided. At intersections in some communities, children must learn to read symbols or the word WALK, rather than traffic signals. Pictures or posters of these words and symbols will teach the children to interpret them.

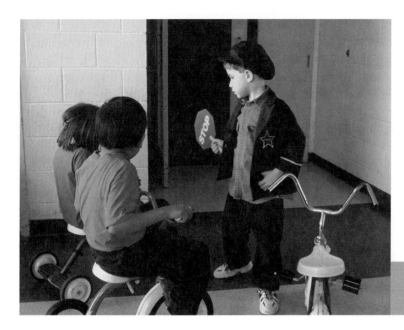

Traffic safety can be practiced indoors in safe play areas.

Involve parents by explaining what you are trying to teach in traffic safety and seek their help in reinforcing the same rules when they are with their children. Both parents and teachers must model safe traffic behavior if children are to learn it.

Water Safety

Discussions of water play in this book have stressed that such play should be carefully supervised. Water play is enjoyable and important for meeting program goals, and teachers should not hesitate to include water play in their programs—but it must be supervised. In some areas where backyard swimming pools are popular, drowning has become the leading cause of death for young children. Children should never be left unsupervised when near swimming pools, lakes, or ponds. Even children in wading pools must have constant supervision.

No child should ever be allowed to swim alone, even if she is a capable swimmer. Swimming lessons do not make a child immune to danger, and supervision should not be relaxed simply because a child has had swimming lessons. The American Academy of Pediatrics (AAP 2000) recommends that only children four and older be given swimming lessons. The AAP's view is that the risk of contracting infectious disease or swallowing dangerous amounts of water during swimming lessons is too great for children younger than four.

Poison Safety

Teachers have a responsibility to make sure that school environments are poison free. Anything poisonous, including ornamental plants, should be removed. Cleaning compounds and other hazardous materials must be stored in locked cabinets, out of children's reach. All such materials must be carefully marked with poison symbols and never stored in old food containers.

www.
**www.nfpa.org/riskwatch/
topwater.html**
Teacher tools and parent information on water safety

Parents and Safety
- Keep parents informed about the safety lessons conducted at school so they can reinforce those lessons with their children at home.

Children must learn that they are never to eat any unknown substance or anything that is not food. Children younger than three or four cannot be expected to remember not to put objects in their mouths. Teachers of children this young need to take extra precautions to remove any dangerous items and to supervise the children closely.

Children should be taught to recognize the symbol for poison and to avoid containers that show it. Teachers should keep in mind that many household chemicals, such as automatic dishwasher detergent, are very dangerous if ingested yet are not marked with the poison symbol. Children must learn to recognize these dangerous items.

Personal Safety

Periodically, horror stories in the news remind us that the world is not always a safe place for children. Children must learn some rules of personal safety. In many police departments, officers are specially trained to communicate to children the importance of not talking to, accepting rides with, or taking treats from strangers. Many young children do not know what the word *stranger* means—they must be given practice in distinguishing strangers from people they know.

Identifying strangers might be made into a game, using pictures of familiar people and unfamiliar people so that children develop the concept that an unknown person is a stranger. Children might also role-play what to do if approached by a stranger offering treats or rides. Parents might be alerted to the dangers of having their child's name displayed on clothing or backpacks, which makes children identifiable; young children will be confused if a stranger knows their name.

Teaching children about "safe touching" from people they know is also very important. In many communities, groups present puppet plays that help children understand the difference between "good touching" and "bad touching." Films and videos can also help teachers convey these messages to children, and children might role-play how to tell the appropriate person if they have been touched inappropriately.

Many primary-grade children are **latchkey children,** meaning that they stay alone after school until their parents return from work. Many communities offer special programs for helping these children learn rules for safety and for feeling more secure while they are alone. In the best of worlds, young children would not be left alone, but if they are, they need some guidance in answering the telephone and the door and in practicing fire safety and first aid. Efforts to keep children safe must involve the parents, the school, and the community.

The Internet poses a new source of danger for children, who may stumble on or be drawn into inappropriate chatrooms and websites. As discussed in Chapter 4 (page 126), children should be taught some basic guidelines about Web safety—for instance, that they should never give out their real names, their parents' names, or their home addresses or phone numbers. The Web offers much to explore but also potential danger to children who fail to take these simple precautions.

Parents and Safety

- Hatkoff (1994) suggests that parents should be informed about what community resources are available to help their children. Teachers and schools can help provide this information by sponsoring programs such as Kids on the Block, a national program that helps first- through eighth-graders learn self-protection strategies.

Integrating Physical Education and Health, Nutrition, and Safety Education into the Curriculum

Many health and safety concepts can best be taught by establishing healthy routines, modeling healthy choices for the children, and incorporating discussions about health or safety procedures into the normal activities of the day. Children will learn nutrition lessons at snack and meal times by what is served and through conversations with the teacher. Traffic safety can be reviewed every time children go on a walk, although instruction should not be limited to these reviews.

Some safety lessons can also be incorporated into other experiences. For example, if the focus in literacy is on reading environmental print, then poison signs and traffic signs can be incorporated into the experience. However, some safety instruction should be included in the curriculum even if it cannot be integrated with other classroom experiences. Teachers may choose to present short lessons on safety once a week or so throughout the year; this approach is more effective than focusing on a safety theme and concentrating all the instruction in a one- or two-week period.

Parents and Wellness

- Involve parents who work as health care professionals by asking them to share their work with the class.

INTEGRATING the CURRICULUM

Continuing our theme of spaces, *here are some suggestions for wellness experiences:*

- With the help of the children, build an obstacle course that has several different kinds of spaces.

- Explore the spaces that can be created on the playground by rearranging moveable pieces of equipment.

- Determine how much horizontal space each child can jump over by placing ropes at wider and wider distances and allowing each child to jump over them.

- Determine how much space is needed between children to move and dance freely without bumping into anyone else.

- Have a dental hygienist show the children how food can collect in the spaces between their teeth and how to clean these spaces.

- Make a list of safe spaces for performing various activities: jumping and running on the playground or outside, cutting and pasting in a quiet place with no running, using electrical appliances in a place that is supervised by an adult, swimming only where and when there is an adult to supervise, and so on.

- Compare the spaces filled by some foods when they are uncooked and cooked (popcorn, rice, spinach, apples, and so on).

- Use hula hoops or ropes to define spaces in which children are to move.

Physical education and nutrition education are easier to integrate into the classroom routine than safety education. If, for example, the current topic is *animals,* children can imitate animal movements, learn what animals need to eat to be healthy, compare human food to animal food, and so on. If the topic is focused on the *neighborhood,* children can determine how food is obtained and distributed in the neighborhood and identify facilities for physical activities (parks, jogging trails, exercise stations, courts for basketball or volleyball, and so on).

Science activities can include growing food and observing changes in foods as they cook. Social studies experiences can include visiting producers or distributors of food; learning about what manners are considered appropriate in different cultures (in some cultures, people eat with their fingers; in other cultures, people do so only with certain foods or at specific times, such as at picnics); and learning about who prepares food in different cultures (men, women, or both).

Goldberg (1994) has described a health program that addresses the special needs of children with asthma and food allergies. The entire class learned about the medical procedures used in treating asthma and allergies through activities in the dramatic play area, which was equipped with masks and other medical supplies. Goldberg recommends that teachers contact local health care professionals to collaborate with them in planning medically oriented dramatic play. Involving health care professionals in planning programs will help ensure that both parents and children understand the medical needs of others and live more comfortably with any conditions of their own, as well. This is particularly important in classes and schools in which students or staff may have life-threatening conditions.

Physical education and nutrition education can easily be integrated into literacy experiences. In addition to tasting foods mentioned in stories, children can create ABC books or reference books of healthy foods, learn to read recipes, find foods mentioned in stories, write stories about special times when food is served in their homes, and find food words used in conversation (for example, "That's peachy," "He's a ham," "That car is a lemon"). Children also can create movements to tell stories, describe movements after they do them, write about how exercise makes them feel, keep records of their exercise, and find examples of movements and exercise in the books they hear and read.

CHILDREN WITH SPECIAL NEEDS

Children with special needs can participate in outdoor play and physical education activities with some adaptations in equipment and in activities. The teacher must consider the developmental level of the individual child and the child's abilities when planning for physical experiences.

Children with mental retardation can participate in most outdoor activities, but they may need more encouragement and more praise than other children. Teachers may have to help children with retardation establish motor patterns by moving them into positions or by modeling behaviors again and again. These children may also make less rapid progress, and teachers should be aware that children may have to repeat activities many times before mastering them.

Children with visual disabilities can participate in many climbing, swinging, and sliding experiences without adaptations. For skill activities for these children, the teacher will need to be attentive to lighting conditions and equipment choices. For example, Pangrazi and Dauer (1981) recommend that when teaching a child with visual limitations to catch a ball, the area should be well lighted and a yellow ball should be used. In certain games, children with visual limitations can get help from other children; the teacher can make sure that tactile information is provided to help children identify home base, boundary lines, and so on.

Auditory disabilities rarely prevent children from participating fully in physical activities. Such children should be placed in front of the teacher so they can read lips and have the best opportunity for hearing directions. Children with auditory disabilities may need interpreters in order to follow the directions in games and may need visual signals to supplement some auditory signals. For example, if children were playing Stop and Start, described earlier, the teacher could wave a flag when the group was to stop moving.

Teachers who want to involve children with orthopedic disabilities in programs of physical education should first consult with the child's physician or case manager to determine the level of activity recommended. A physical education specialist can help the teacher make the adaptations that will benefit each child. Some will need modified equipment—for example, a bat with straps that enable the child to hold it. Others will need to use larger or softer balls or to participate in activities that involve upper-body strength if their legs are immobile. Every child needs to interact as much as possible with other children, and physical education should not be inaccessible to children with disabilities.

Pangrazi and Dauer (1992) recommend that teachers think about modifications for youngsters lacking strength and endurance by lowering or enlarging goals, softening balls, reducing the distance balls must be thrown, and using lighter balls and bats. If coordination is a problem, teachers should have children begin with stationary objects when learning to strike an object; throw for velocity without concern for accuracy when learning to throw; and use soft, lightweight objects for catching, such as beach balls and balloons. For children who lack ability in balance, teachers might increase the width on balance beams; suggest learning to balance with as many body parts touching the floor as possible; provide assistance with balance, such as a cane or chair; and think about play surfaces so that children are not playing on slick floors with slick shoes.

In the following A Teacher Speaks box, Ellen Bissaillon urges teachers to think about the whole child, including physical development, when planning experiences. Perhaps you can use her suggestions for adding physical activity to your lesson ideas.

www.
www.pecentral.org/ adapted/adaptedmenu.html
Information on adapted physical education, including articles and links to other resources

CELEBRATING DIVERSITY

To involve families in physical education, health, nutrition, and safety programs, teachers can invite them to participate in field days or other such outings in which adults and children can join in a variety of games and activities. Some of these might be traditional games of skill from the cultures represented in the classroom or games from earlier historical periods, such as rolling a hoop.

A **Teacher** SPEAKS: *Doing It All*

Ellen Bissaillon

Perley Elementary School

Georgetown, Massachusetts

Today's teachers are expected to do it all. When evaluating your favorite teachers, you may realize they did do it all by educating the whole child, not just his brain. When reflecting back on a day of school, notice if you nourished a student's spirit, mind, and body. Take the number 4 as an example. See and say "4" on a flashcard, and the mind is being addressed. Have a student hold up four fingers, do four jumps, or balance on one leg four seconds, and the body is at work. Ask the child what is special about the number 4 to evoke an emotion, and his spirit is being addressed. Encourage creative answers: "There are four people in my family." "My mom comes home at 4:00." "I wish I had four fish."

Educating the whole person by engaging his spirit, mind, and body takes a bit of creativity on the teacher's part. When planning a lesson, reinforce the knowledge part with a physical manipulative that is interesting to do. Start out trying the integrated approach with just one concept a day, and over time new strategies will pop into your head. The practice of educating the whole person is far from new, but in today's high-stakes, paper-and-pencil-testing atmosphere, it is sometimes overlooked. People agree that it is not healthy for a child to sit for hours in front of a television, yet we expect students to sit calmly in school to learn. There are times sitting still is necessary, but build in some movement breaks and the mind will be more ready to concentrate.

When a colleague brings a class to the physical education teacher, a typical comment from the classroom teacher is "Run them; they need it!" If your students don't have a physical education period in their day, schedule some form of movement into a lesson. Sing songs with body movements. Practice flexibility by putting your bodies into the shape of a letter. Carry things from one place to another to use muscles. Do small-space physical activities that require students to track with their eyes and cross the midline.

For the final two weeks of school, a teacher used the *camp* theme and took her students on a "nature hike" each morning. The hikes were meant to be outside, but a week of rain did not put a damper on things. The teacher had her students put on their hats, walk the "paths" (hallways), and climb the "mountains" (stairs). The teacher related back to me that the children enjoyed using their imaginations and were ready to focus on their morning activity upon returning to the classroom.

The next time you send home a notice that says "Read twenty minutes a day with your child," think about adding a suggestion to visit a local hiking trail. There are playgrounds in every town, but not everyone knows about them. Walking around a museum is great exercise for the whole person. Healthy habits start as thoughts but require the whole body.

Families can also be wonderful resources for sharing foods that they enjoy or that are served at special times in their cultures. Teachers should help children understand that people from many cultures eat essentially the same things on a daily basis but that their special foods may vary. Having tasting parties with foods from different cultures may help make this clear. For instance, a study of breads from around the world might help children understand how all cultures have some special foods, even though they have many other foods in common, such as fruits and vegetables.

SUMMARY

- Appropriate goals for motor development include introducing children to a wide variety of physical movements (such as running, jumping, throwing, kicking, and so on) and helping them not only learn these basic skills but also enjoy participating in active movement experiences. Children should view active physical activities as opportunities for enjoyment, challenge, self-expression, and social interaction. Movement goals for young children do not include mastery of specific games or sports. Many activities can be planned for encouraging motor development, both indoors and out. Children can walk, run, hop, skip, crawl, climb, throw, catch, kick, and so on if provided with the space and materials appropriate for their individual needs. Inappropriate activities are those that focus on competition and rewarding individual skills, rather than helping all children develop skills.

● The goals of health, nutrition, and safety are focused on helping children develop concepts and attitudes that will encourage lifelong healthy behaviors. Many of these goals can be met by involving young children in experiences that promote healthful living and by helping them develop concepts of what is healthy and safe.

● Many activities in physical education such as climbing, walking on beams, and completing obstacle courses can be integrated into the daily curriculum. Instruction in health, nutrition, and safety is rarely effective unless it is integrated into children's daily lives. Some direct instruction, especially in safety, may be required and can be accomplished through puppets, role-play, and other active teaching strategies. However, most lessons in these areas are learned as children wash their hands, brush their teeth, eat nutritious food at school, learn to use tools with care, and so on.

● Children with special needs may require adaptations in materials and activities before they can be fully engaged in physical activities. All children should be encouraged to achieve skills in motor activities in line with their abilities; therefore, all children will need some adaptations. Children with special needs must not sit on the sidelines as passive observers. If they cannot walk or run, perhaps they can throw or catch. Making adaptations with the help of a specialist can help ensure that every child will be engaged in positive ways.

● To celebrate diversity, children and families can share foods with the class that are part of their traditional diets and customs. Likewise, they can teach the class to play traditional games and activities that will help all children be physically active.

REFLECTIONS

1. How is motor development important to the development of the whole child?
2. Some concepts, and especially safety concepts, must be taught directly, not discovered through experience. How does this affect children's retention and application of these concepts?
3. As content areas, physical education, as well as health, nutrition, and safety education, should be integrated into the curriculum. Select a concept from each of these areas that you believe is important, and describe how it could be developed in the course of teaching other content areas.
4. Some schools are so concerned about students' test scores that they are canceling recess and devoting more time to academic studies. If you could talk to the school board of one of these schools, what would you say about this policy?
5. If you taught in a school where parents supplied snacks for their children, how would you explain to them the importance of providing healthy snacks? If parents supplied snacks that were not healthy, how would you handle the situation?

EXPLORATIONS AND ACTIVITIES

1. Plan a role-play experience or a puppet play that will help children develop concepts of safety (e.g., traffic, fire, water). What characteristics of this experience do you believe are most useful in helping children develop safety concepts? Would a

demonstration—such as from a firefighter for how to respond to a fire—be more effective than a dramatic experience? How can you evaluate the effectiveness of your safety instruction?

2. Some children are reluctant to participate in vigorous physical activity during outside play experiences. Create a plan for getting these few children engaged so that they benefit from the outdoor play in ways that meet the standards for physical education.

---

mylabschool
Where the classroom comes to life!

MyLabSchool is a collection of online tools for your success in this course, your licensure exams, and your teaching career. Visit **www.mylabschool.com** to access the following:

- Online Study Guide
- Video Cases from real classrooms
- Help with your research papers using Research Navigator
- Career Center with resources for:
    —Praxis and Licensure Preparation
    —Professional Portfolio Development
    —Job Search and Interview Techniques
    —Lesson Planning

Glossary

Adaptive equipment   Equipment used by people with disabilities, such as wheelchairs, walkers, and so on.

Algorithm   The general rule or procedure for solving a specific kind of math problem; for instance, adding multidigit numbers often involves moving (or "carrying") the tens or hundreds value to the next column.

Anecdotal records   Informal records of the teacher's observations of children's behavior; these records are likely to reveal patterns of behavior over time.

Antibias curriculum   A curriculum aimed at eliminating bias of all types by teaching children to respect people regardless of their sex, age, race/ethnicity, and other traits.

Arrival time   The period just before the start of the schoolday, when children are arriving at the classroom; providing activities during this period can help occupy children who arrive early and avoid behavior problems before the official start of the day.

Assessment   Use of a comprehensive evaluation system to determine the quality of a program or the progress of a child.

Assistive technology   Devices such as portable keyboards and speech synthesizers that allow children with disabilities to communicate.

Autonomy   The ability to make decisions for oneself; autonomy is essential to effective guidance because asking children to obey without understanding why does not help them learn to make good decisions about their behavior.

Behaviorist model   A method of education based on the theory that learning is a behavior that can be manipulated by a system of rewards and punishments or by operant conditioning.

Behavior-management systems   Approaches to managing children's behavior that are rooted in various theories of child development and discipline.

Body of knowledge   What is known in any field of study; in social studies, this would include knowing the major holidays, the names of the states, the directions on a map or globe, and so forth.

Broken home   A phrase often used to describe families who are divorced; it is a negative phrase and does not describe the home or the family in any useful way.

Child care   Care for children in a group, usually for the entire working day; the term *day care* was used previously.

Classifying   Sorting materials or objects into pre-specified categories or into categories that one can explain.

Cognitive development   Development of the ability to think and reason.

Communicating   In science, sharing one's observations and data collections with others through a variety of means.

Communication   In mathematics, being able to organize and express to others the solutions to problems, how problems were solved, and so on.

Communicative competence   The ability of a speaker to use language appropriately to achieve his needs.

Comparing   Examining objects and events in terms of their similarities and differences.

Complex unit   A play material that has several different purposes and that can be used by several children at once.

Conflict resolution   The set of skills needed to manage difficult social situations, including recognizing alternate responses, understanding others' viewpoints, and communicating one's own feelings and expectations in positive ways.

Constructivist model   A method of instruction that recognizes the importance of the learner in the learning process; learners have to build their own understandings, especially of math and science concepts.

Content strands   In the model of the National Council of Teachers of Mathematics (NCTM), the content strands define the subjects that will be taught: Number and Operations; Geometry and Spatial Sense; Measurement; Patterns, Functions, and Algebra; and Data Analysis, Statistics, and Probability.

Corporal punishment   Physical punishment, such as spanking, pinching, and slapping.

Craft activities   Activities in which the focus is on the product, suggesting that the work that results is more important than the process used to create it.

Creativity   Purposeful behaviors and ideas that extend beyond the present and are original and imaginative.

Curriculum   A written plan for learning experiences.

Daily class schedule   A plan for daily classroom activities that provides routine, structure, and balance yet is flexible enough to accommodate individual and group needs.

Dance education   Planned activities that help children learn to express themselves through movement.

Decision making A focus in social studies education that involves helping children solve problems and make decisions related to the classroom environment or their own behaviors and choices.

Deficit model A point of view that regards parents in terms of what they do not know or do and that ignores the strengths of the family.

Departure time The end of the schoolday, when materials are being distributed, coats are being put on, and children are getting ready to leave; having a routine for these tasks can help avoid behavior problems at this time of day.

Developmentally appropriate practice (DAP) Teaching that is age and individually appropriate for each child in a program.

Dialect A systematic variation of the common language that is spoken by a particular group; the variation can be in word order, meaning, or pronunciation; by definition, a dialect is rule governed and consistent.

Direct instruction Instruction in which the teacher presents information directly to the children.

Directed play Play in which the teacher instructs the children in how to accomplish a specific task.

Discipline Guidance aimed at helping children gain self-control of their behavior.

Dispositional learning Learning to be more empathetic, to try different techniques, and to avoid negative behaviors (such as sulking, whining, and having tantrums) in discipline situations; modeling these skills is an effective way of helping children learn them.

Drama Experiences in which children play, pretend, role-play, and create characters and ideas.

Drawing realism The fourth stage in children's art development, which is marked by creating smaller drawings, adding more detail, and being less willing to share their art.

Early childhood The period from birth to age eight.

Eclectic approach An approach to social studies instruction that combines parts of several different approaches—for example, teaching children the names of the states as well as what underlies the concept of a *state* or a country such as the *United States*.

Ecological systems theory A theoretical point of view that explains a child's development through a dynamic system of relationships, including the family and the culture of the child.

Egocentric thought patterns Thought patterns in which the child fails to consider the viewpoints of others.

Emergent literacy The concept that children start to learn about printed language in infancy and develop their skills gradually, rather than at one point in time; children's early literacy behaviors lay the foundation for their development.

Emerging curriculum An approach to curriculum development in which the teacher follows the lead of the children.

English language learners The most common term for describing children who do not speak English as their first language; in some school systems, these children are described as being *limited English proficiency (LEP)* or as *ESL (English-as-a-second-language) students*.

Environmental print Print that occurs in the everyday environment, such as stop signs and product labels.

Expanding curriculum A social studies curriculum that begins with a focus on the individual in kindergarten or first grade and moves on in subsequent grades to address the family, the community, the state, the nation, and the world.

Experimenting Controlling one or more variables and manipulating the conditions; the purposes are to determine if the results obtained match those that were expected and if those results can be repeated.

Exploratory play Play in which children have no objective other than exploration.

Food pyramid A model that specifies the amounts and kinds of food needed for a healthy diet; the current model was created by the U.S. Department of Agriculture and is called *My Pyramid*.

Formative assessment Assessment that is conducted on a regular basis as children work through a project; this feedback allows instruction to be adapted if children are not making progress.

Free play Play in which children have many choices of materials and how to use them.

Functions The patterns created when certain actions are performed on objects or numbers.

Fundamental motor skills Basic motor skills, such as running, jumping, hopping, throwing, and so on.

Games of construction Games in which children build mechanical constructions or solve problems by using materials symbolically.

Games with rules Games in which children play according to rules they have created or rules that are generally agreed on for the given game.

Guidance An approach to behavior management that helps children gain self-esteem, learn to be cooperative, and gradually learn the skills necessary for taking responsibility for their own behavior.

Guided listening An instructional strategy in which the teacher selects a piece of music for a specific group of children and then guides them through their initial hearing of it.

Guided play   Play in which the teacher has selected materials from which the children may choose in order to discover specific concepts.

Guided reading   An instructional strategy in which the teacher selects a text for a specific group of readers and then guides them through their initial reading of it.

Head Start   A federal program initiated in 1965 that provides educational, social, medical, dental, nutrition, and mental health services to low-income preschool children.

Health education   Activities integrated throughout the schoolday that help children learn good health habits, such as daily personal routines.

High-stakes testing   Testing for which the results are used to make major decisions about children and their futures (e.g., to pass to another grade, to graduate from high school, and so on).

Holiday celebrations   In social studies education, choosing and celebrating holidays that are relevant to children's lives and the goals of the curriculum.

Home visits   Planned visits to children's homes by a school staff member such as a teacher, counselor, or principal.

Illicit play   Play that is discouraged and perhaps forbidden by the teacher, such as gun play, sex play, and "superhero" play.

Incidental learning   Learning opportunities that present themselves in the course of a day through the child's play or interaction with people and materials.

Instructional materials   The materials provided to help children develop specific skills and learn specific concepts.

Instrumental play   Play that the teacher plans and encourages to teach specific concepts or ideas to children.

Integrated curriculum   A curriculum in which the content is integrated across subject areas; learning goals in the subject areas are met by organizing the curriculum around a topic or theme.

Journal writing   An instructional strategy in which children record messages and ideas in personal notebooks through drawing and writing.

Kidwatching   A term coined by Goodman (1985) to describe how teachers should observe children's language, thinking, and responses; doing so is very important in assessing language development.

Kindergarten   A class or school for children who are usually from four to six years old; kindergarten precedes first grade.

Language delay   A delay in a child's language development that results in her skills not matching what is typical of age peers.

Language   A system of communication used by humans; it is either produced orally or by sign and can be written.

Latchkey children   A term used to describe children who are home alone after school until a parent or caregiver returns from work.

Learning areas   Places designated in the classroom where certain activities take place and related materials are stored; also called *learning centers*.

Learning environment   A space, indoors or out, that is planned to facilitate instruction.

Learning plan   A comprehensive plan of learning experiences for children.

Least restrictive environment (LRI)   The educational setting that is least restrictive for an individual with given characteristics; the setting that provides the best educational opportunity for a child who is disabled.

Linguistic model   An approach to language development that suggests that language is inherent in the child at birth and needs only to be triggered by social contact with speakers to emerge.

Listening   Being engaged in hearing and comprehending oral language and other sounds.

Literacy   The ability to read and write well enough to function in day-to-day life.

Logico-mathematical learning   Learning that requires children to create and reflect on relationships between and among objects; unlike social learning (such as language), logico-mathematical learning involves replacing previously learned concepts.

Mainstreaming   A placement approach in which children with disabling conditions are included in regular classrooms; now more frequently referred to as *inclusion*.

Mandated goals   Goals set by the school director or written into the school curriculum that both the teacher and children are expected to meet.

Manipulatives   Materials such as cubes, blocks, beads, and the like that children can physically handle while learning mathematical concepts.

Mastery learning   The concept that children can master the tasks presented to them at school but that some of them will need more time and more activities or guidance to do so.

Mathematics   The science of numbers and space configurations; for children, it provides a way of viewing the world and their experiences in it.

Maturationist theory   A theoretical point of view suggesting that when given optimal conditions, a child will develop according to his own schedule.

Measuring   Collecting and quantifying information; it is not restricted to using standard measures.

Medical procedures   The common procedures that children undergo when visiting a doctor, such as getting a shot, wearing a splint on a limb, being weighed and measured, and the like.

Metaknowledge   Knowledge of what one knows.

Montessori model   A model of education that focuses on the individuality of each child and that emphasizes that children are different from adults in terms of how they develop and think.

Morpheme   The smallest unit of sound that carries meaning; some words are morphemes (e.g., *tiger*) and some are combinations of morphemes (e.g., *tigers = tiger + s*).

Morphology   The system of language that involves the meanings of sounds; included are the prefixes and suffixes that change the meanings of words (for instance, adding an *s* to form a plural).

Movement experiences   Planned activities in which children respond to music through various types of movement, such as clapping or tapping, walking or skipping to a beat, moving slowly or quickly, and so on.

Multicultural education   An approach to education that encourages children to understand and respect all people and cultures.

Multiple intelligences theory   A theoretical point of view that suggests learners have particular strengths in one or more areas, such as verbal skill, physical skill, or musical skill.

Music   Vocal, instrumental, and mechanical sounds that are characterized by rhythm, melody, and harmony.

No Child Left Behind (NCLB) Act   Legislation passed in 2001 that requires states to administer content-area tests to students at various grade levels and to use those test scores as the basis for determining effectiveness of individual schools.

Nonjudgmental attitude   An attitude of acceptance; a refusal on the part of the teacher to criticize parents.

Nutrition education   Planned activities about various kinds of food and how to make nutritious choices to ensure good health.

Observing   Examining objects in an attempt to notice specific qualities or behaviors; it involves all the senses, not just sight.

Open-ended materials   Play materials that allow multiple outcomes and unique uses in each situation, such as blocks, sand, and water.

Operant conditioning   Rewards that are offered to a subject for moving closer to a desired behavior.

Oral language   Communicating by expressing information through speech.

Paraprofessionals   Paid assistants in the classroom, who are sometimes referred to as *teacher aides*.

Parent involvement   Parents' interest and participation in their children's schooling; it has been shown to result in higher grades, improved attendance, more positive attitudes and behaviors, a higher graduation rate, and an increased likelihood of enrolling in higher education.

Parent place   A special area of the classroom or a room in the school that is set aside for parents for the purpose of making them feel important and needed.

Patterns   Discernible combinations or arrangements of numbers, sounds, words, color, and so on.

Phonemic awareness   The ability to understand language separate from meaning and manipulate its component sounds; it involves a cluster of skills that develop over time.

Phonics   A method of instruction that involves teaching readers how to decode the print symbols used to represent language sounds.

Phonology   The system of language that involves the sounds of the language; included are rules for combining sounds and how to adjust stress and intonation to communicate meaning.

Physical development   The process of ongoing physical growth and maturation; the acquisition of motor skills is generally sequential and age related.

Physical education   A content area that involves studying movement, increasing skills in movement, and learning to play games; some teachers have special certification for teaching physical education.

Physical fitness   For young children, physical fitness is defined by cardiorespiratory function, relative leanness, abdominal endurance, lower-back flexibility, and upper-body strength and endurance.

Physical knowledge   Knowledge gained by exploring objects and identifying their properties (such as *hard, soft, square, able to roll*, and so on).

Play   An active behavior that is personally motivated, is often nonliteral, has no extrinsic goals or rules, and for which the individual supplies the meaning.

Portfolio   A collection of artifacts and anecdotes that document a student's efforts and achievements; the student is involved in selecting and evaluating these materials.

Practice play   Play in which children explore the nature of objects or materials with no other play goals.

Pragmatics   The system of language that determines the use of language in social interactions; speakers must learn acceptable ways to adapt their language to achieve communication goals in different situations.

Preschematic stage   The second stage in children's art development, which is marked by attempts to represent familiar objects in the environment.

Print-rich environment   An environment in which functional print is prevalent, such that learners notice it, use it, and add to it.

Problem solving   The basic feature of mathematics instruction, given that the purpose of learning math is to solve problems; this term should not be confused with the term *word problem*.

Process strands   In the model of the National Council of Teachers of Mathematics (NCTM), the process strands represent how mathematical content knowledge is used: Problem Solving; Reasoning and Proof; Communication; Connections; and Representation.

Progressive education movement   A model that rejects methods involving memorization and recitation and provides more active and engaging experiences for learners.

Pullout programs   Special lessons and activities that involve removing children from the classroom at certain times of day—for instance, speech therapy.

Punishment   Removing children's privileges or physically reprimanding them with the intent of changing their behavior.

Read-aloud   A critical reading instructional strategy in which the teacher reads aloud a carefully selected text to a whole class, small group, or individual.

Readiness tests   Tests designed to predict children's preparedness for specific instructional programs.

Reading   Gaining information from print.

Reflective abstraction   Learning a concept by manipulating objects and examining the results.

Reliability   The degree to which the scores generated by a test are consistent, repeatable, and thus dependable.

Representation   Related to communication in mathematics, representation is the skill of finding ways to record one's information so that it can be retrieved, discussed, used again, and so on.

Room arrangement   The arrangement of furniture and materials to meet the needs of the children and the teacher.

Rubric   A scoring plan that indicates the tasks or qualities that underlie successful completion of a given activity (say, writing a story) as well as the weight or value of each task or quality.

Rule-governed play   Play in which children have objectives, such as finding the solution to a problem or determining cause and effect.

Safety education   Planned activities that help children learn how to protect themselves and what to do in an emergency; topics include fire safety, traffic safety, water safety, poison safety, and personal safety.

Schematic stage   The third stage in children's art development, which is marked by using specific forms and shapes to represent elements of the environment.

School handbook   A booklet prepared by the school for the parents that describes the school's philosophy and goals and provides practical information such as a calendar, phone numbers to call, and so on.

Science   The process of observing, thinking, and reflecting on actions and events; for children, science involves constructing a framework of relationships within which factual information can be organized into meaningful and useful concepts.

Scientific process   The cycle or steps of investigating various properties and reactions: forming hypotheses, collecting data; confirming or rejecting hypotheses; making generalizations; and repeating the cycle.

Screening tests   Tests designed to determine whether children are eligible for particular programs or need special attention.

Scribbling   In the visual arts, the beginning stage in development; also the first stage in the development of writing.

Semantics   The system of language that governs the meanings of words; context is very important in determining meaning.

Shared reading   An instructional strategy in which the teacher takes primary responsibility for the reading but actively involves the children in the process.

Sight-word vocabulary   The set of words that a given reader can recognize on sight and without having to do any other decoding.

Simple abstraction   Learning a concept from repeated experience with objects.

Simple unit   A play material that has one obvious use and that only one child can use at a time.

Social development   The process of acquiring social skills and understanding the nature of social interactions and relationships.

Social knowledge   The ability to put incidents into perspective and to gain a basic understanding of the concept of justice.

Social learning theory   A theoretical point of view that describes the importance of social learning and the use of modeling as an important method for assisting learning.

Social play   Play in which children are involved to various degrees with other people.

Social skills   The set of behavioral skills that a child needs to interact with others in positive ways while being assertive about meeting his own needs.

Social skills   The skills needed to interact effectively with others, especially in a group—for instance, taking turns when talking, abiding by group decisions, asserting preferences gracefully, and recognizing individual differences.

Social studies   The integrated study of the social sciences and humanities; for young children, the purpose is to help them learn how to make decisions as informed citizens in a diverse, democratic society.

Sociodramatic play   Play in which children assume roles and act out episodes, such as putting a baby to bed.

Sociolinguistics   The study of language in a social context; this study is closely related to pragmatics.

Specialists   Those teachers who are certified to teach art, music, or physical education to children.

Standardized tests   Tests for which individuals' scores are interpreted against the scores of a norm group that has taken the test and that is considered representative of the population.

State standards   Standards implemented at the state level that specify, in more or less detail, what is to be taught at each grade level in each subject.

Stimulus-response theory   The theory that when a stimulus is offered and a reward or punishment is given in response, a certain behavior will be repeated or extinguished over time; this is one of the key mechanisms for learning from the behaviorist point of view.

Strand Model   A way of conceptualizing the important elements of mathematics instruction using content strands (actual math topics) and process strands (ways of using math knowledge).

Summative assessment   Assessment that is conducted at the end of a project or unit; the final assessment, after which instruction can no longer be adjusted to provide a different outcome.

Super unit   A play material that has three or more purposes and that can be used by several children at once.

Symbolic play   Play in which children use items to represent other items—say, using blocks to build a corral and dominoes to represent the animals in it.

Syntax   The system of language that provides the rules for combining words into phrases and sentences and for transforming sentences into other sentences.

Teaching strategies   Methods of presenting instruction, such as demonstrations, lectures, and simulations.

Telecommunication   Communication that is facilitated by electronic means, such as computerized calling and voice mail systems, answering machines, and websites; its use in school makes communication with parents quick and easy.

Testing   The administration of various kinds of tests (such as standardized, readiness, screening, achievement, and so on) to measure certain outcomes.

Theme   A topic of study that can be addressed across the content areas; it should be worthy of study and relevant and of interest to learners.

"Time out"   Removing a child from the group and isolating her, perhaps by sitting on a chair; the intent is to provide an opportunity for the child to gain control of her behavior and then return to the group when ready.

Traffic patterns   The paths where children and teachers walk in the classroom, which are often determined by the arrangement of furniture.

Transitions   The periods of time needed between activities, which may involve movement from one area to another; these are the most likely times for behavior problems and other disruptions.

Validity   The degree to which a test measures what it is intended to measure.

Verbal skills   The set of language skills that a child needs to solve problem situations, such as being able to negotiate with others and express one's own needs without being rude or sullen.

Vertical space   Wall space and space on the sides of file cabinets, bookshelves, and so on; this space is often overlooked and thus underused in classrooms.

Visual arts   The graphic arts, such as drawing, painting, and printing as well as producing sculpture and collage.

Volunteers   Parents and community members who help in the classroom without being paid.

Withitness   The teacher's ability to know what is going on in the classroom and on the playground at all times.

Writing   Communicating by recording information in print.

Zone of proximal development (ZPD)   The gap between what a child can do independently and what he cannot do even with assistance.

Resources for Further Reading

Chapter 1

Bandura, Albert. *Social Learning Theory.* Saddle River, NJ: Prentice Hall, 1976.
Bandura explains his theory of how children learn from modeling the behaviors of those around them.

Bronfenbrenner, Urie. *The Ecology of Human Development: Experiments by Nature and Design.* Cambridge, MA: Harvard University Press, 2005.
Bronfenbrenner explains his theory of human development within the layers of human society.

Gardner, Howard. *Frames of Mind: The Theory of Multiple Intelligences.* New York: Basic Books, 1983.
This is the first of the books about multiple intelligences; although more information was added to later books, Gardner's descriptions of the intelligences are very thorough in this book.

Ilg, Frances L., and Louise Bates Ames. *The Gesell Institute's Child from Birth to Ten.* New York: HarperCollins, 1985.
This book describes typical child development at given ages; each age is described in detail.

McClellan, Diane, and Lilian Katz. *Fostering Children's Social Competence: The Teacher's Role.* Washington, DC: National Association for the Education of Young Children, 1997.
The authors describe the importance of social competence and how teachers can discuss children's interactions in ways that help them become more socially competent.

Piaget, Jean. *The Language and Thought of the Child.* London: Routledge & Kegan Paul, 1959.
This book discusses how language and thought develop and explains the relationship between them.

Piaget, Jean, and Barbel Inhelder. *The Psychology of the Child.* New York: Basic Books, 1969.
The subtitle of this book says it is the definitive summary of the work of the world's most renowned psychologist. Even though Piaget was a philosopher, not a psychologist, this book is a good summary of his thoughts about child development.

Vygotsky, Lev. *Mind in Society: The Development of Higher Psychological Processes.* Cambridge, MA: Harvard University Press, 1978.
This is the classic book that describes how learning takes place in a sociocultural context.

Vygotsky, Lev. *Thought and Language.* Cambridge, MA: MIT Press, 1986.
Vygotsky explains how language and thought develop in a social context and how one influences the other.

Winsler, Adam, and Laura Berk. *Scaffolding Children's Learning: Vygotsky and Early Childhood Education.* Washington, DC: National Association for the Education of Young Children, 1995.
These authors explain what Vygotsky's theories mean to teachers of young children and how best to plan instruction based on them.

Zigler, Edward and Marilou Hyson. *The Emotional Development of Young Children: Building an Emotion-Centered Curriculum.* New York: Teachers College Press, 2003.
The authors discuss children's emotional development and how teachers can foster it.

Chapter 2

Bergen, Doris, and Juliet Coscia. *Brain Research and Childhood Education: Implications for Educators.* Olney, MD: Association for Childhood Education International, 2001.
This book is an examination of current brain research and identifies what early childhood educators can use from that research to plan and organize instruction.

Helm, Judy, and Sallee Beneke. *The Power of Projects: Meeting Contemporary Challenges in Early Childhood Classrooms—Strategies and Solutions.* Washington, DC: National Association for the Education of Young Children and Teachers College Press, 2003.
These authors offer suggestions to teachers for planning and implementing projects that will help move students toward literacy, for helping children who are learning a second language, and for meeting the standards.

Helm, Judy, and Lilian Katz. *Young Investigators: The Project Approach in the Early Years.* New York: Teachers College Press, 2001.
This book explains how to select and implement projects appropriate for children; it also provides suggestions for meeting the standards while organizing the curriculum and planning challenging projects.

Hildebrandt, Carolyn, Rebecca Edmiaston, Rheta DeVries, and Christina Sales. *Developing Constructivist Early Childhood Curriculum: Practical Principles and Activities.* New York: Teachers College Press, 2002.
These authors address the theories supporting constructivist programs; they also give practical advice for planning specific activities and offer good examples of how to extend children's reasoning and thinking.

Jones, Elizabeth, Kathleen Evans, and Kay Rencken. *The Lively Kindergarten: Emergent Curriculum in Action*. Washington, DC: National Association for the Education of Young Children, 2001.
Based on their own extensive experience in developing child-centered programs, these authors explain how to manage instruction that comes from the children, the teacher, and their interactions.

Wortham, Sue. *Childhood 1892–2002*. Olney, MD: Association for Childhood Education International, 2002.
This resource book begins with a discussion of the formation of the International Kindergarten Union in 1892 and traces the history of early childhood education through over a century of change.

Wurm, Julianne P. *Working in the Reggio Way: A Beginner's Guide for American Teachers*. St. Paul, MN: Redleaf Press, 2005.
This book offers useful guidance for any teacher who would like to implement the positive strategies of the Reggio Emilia schools; it includes suggestions for studying individual children and how to implement interactive activities for individuals or small groups.

Chapter 3

Bronson, Martha. *The Right Stuff for Children Birth to 8: Selecting Play Materials to Support Development*. Washington, DC: National Association for the Education of Young Children, 1995.
Selecting learning materials that will support the curriculum is an important task for the early childhood teacher; this book will help teachers determine what they need and what is important for the children.

Curtis, Deb, and Margie Carter. *Designs for Living and Learning: Transforming Early Childhood Environments*. St. Paul, MN: Redleaf Press, 2003.
The wonderful photographs in this book will help teachers think about how they can arrange their own classrooms in appealing ways.

Hirsch, Elizabeth. *The Block Book*. Washington, DC: National Association for the Education of Young Children, 1996.
This book points out how blocks can be used to contribute to children's learning in many ways; it also provides practical suggestions for storing and organizing blocks to bring maximum benefit to the children.

Isbell, Rebecca, and Betty Exelby. *Early Learning Environments that Work*. Beltsville, MD: Gryphon House, 2001.
Based on the notion that the classroom environment can have powerful effects on children's learning, these authors provide suggestions for environmental planning that will help teachers reach their learning goals.

Rivkin, Mary. *The Great Outdoors: Restoring Children's Right to Play Outside*. Washington, DC: National Association for the Education of Young Children, 1995.
An argument for the outdoor play of children, a description of exciting playgrounds, and practical suggestions on safety, accessibility, and curriculum.

Wellhousen, Karyn, and Judy Kieff. *A Constructivist Approach to Block Play in Early Childhood*. Albany, NY: Delmar, 2000.
The authors provide a constructivist rationale for and describe the learning that takes place in block play.

Chapter 4

ABC Task Force and Lucille Derman-Sparks. *Anti-Bias Curriculum: Tools for Empowering Young Children*. Washington, DC: National Association for the Education of Young Children, 1989.
This classic work defines the antibias curriculum and suggests ways that teachers of young children can help them learn to be respectful and proactive in combating bias.

Alvarado, Cecelia, et al. *In Our Own Way: How Anti-Bias Work Shapes Our Lives*. St. Paul, MN: Redleaf Press, 1999.
Teachers share their own experiences in implementing an antibias curriculum with young children.

Bredekamp, Sue, and Teresa Rosegrant. *Reaching Potentials: Appropriate Curriculum and Assessment for Young Children*. Washington, DC: National Association for the Education of Young Children, 1992 (Vol.1) and 1995 (Vol. 2).
These two volumes discuss all the subject areas and how they can be taught in ways most appropriate for young children.

Byrnes, Deborah, and Gary Kiger, eds. *Common Bonds: Anti-Bias Teaching in a Diverse Society*. Olney, MD: Association for Childhood Education International, 1996.
This book describes the ways teachers can help young children find and honor the common bonds between all humans.

Chen, Jie-Oi. *Project Spectrum: Early Learning Activities*. New York: Teachers College Press, 1998.
The activities in this book have been carefully selected to illustrate teaching for the multiple intelligences.

McIntyre, Ellen, Ann Roseberry, and Norma Gonzales, eds. *Classroom Diversity: Connecting Curriculum to Student's Lives*. Portsmouth, NH: Heinemann, 2001.
These authors suggest how to think about what children know and how that knowledge can be used to plan the curriculum.

Vance, Emily, and Patricia Weaver. *Class Meetings: Young Children Solving Problems Together*. Washington, DC: National Association for the Education of Young Children, 2002.

This book describes how teachers helped children learn to use class meetings to solve problems in the classroom.

York, Stacey. *Roots and Wings Revised: Affirming Culture in Early Childhood Education.* St. Paul, MN: Redleaf Press, 2003.

York offers classroom activities and suggestions to help teachers make sure that every child will be valued and helped to grow.

Chapter 5

Bergen, Doris, ed. *Play as a Medium for Learning and Development.* Olney, MD: Association for Childhood Education International, 1998.

This is a collection of articles and essays by many well-known experts in early childhood education; the topics range from methods of studying play to using computers in the play environment.

Garvey, Catherine. *Play: The Developing Child.* Cambridge, MA: Harvard University Press, 1990.

Garvey explores children's development and the play experiences that lead to further development; this book provides a basic explanation of children's need to play.

Jones, Elizabeth, and Gretchen Reynolds. *The Play's the Thing: Teachers' Roles in Children's Play.* New York: Teachers College Press, 1992.

Jones and Reynolds describe what teachers can do to foster and support children's play.

Jones, Elizabeth, and Renatta M. Cooper. *Playing to Get Smart.* New York: Teachers College Press, 2005.

Jones and Cooper describe why children need to play to be "smart" in fun and humorous ways.

Koralek, Derry, ed. *Spotlight on Young Children and Play.* Washington, DC: National Association for the Education of Young Children, 2004.

These articles from *Young Children* focus on the many dimensions of play: as a tool for learning, as a source of enjoyment, as a strategy for academic learning, and so on. Outdoor play and making adaptations for children with special needs are covered, as well.

Koste, V. Glasgow. *Dramatic Play in Childhood: Rehearsal for Life.* Portsmouth, NH: Heinemann, 1995.

Koste, who has many years of experience in working with children and dramatic play, shares techniques and strategies that help children express themselves and their understandings through play.

Paley, Vivian G. *A Child's Work: The Importance of Fantasy Play.* Chicago: University of Chicago Press, 2004.

Paley declares that fantasy play is increasingly important for children and that teachers cannot educate young children to achieve their full potential without it.

Play: Readings from Childhood Education. Olney, MD: Association for Childhood Education International, 1996.

These articles from *Childhood Education*—all of which are about play and its benefits—were selected for this collection because they were initially well received and represent some of the best thinking on this topic from early childhood professionals.

Rogers, Cosby, and Janet Sawyers. *Helping Young Children Develop through Play: A Practical Guide for Parents, Caregivers, and Teachers.* Washington, DC: National Association for the Education of Young Children, 1988.

This book offers detailed and practical suggestions on how to foster play with young children; it also includes an easy-to-read overview of the importance of play in children's lives.

Rogers, Cosby, and Janet Sawyers. *Play in the Lives of Children.* Washington, DC: National Association for the Education of Young Children, 1988.

These authors believe that play provides the best opportunity for children to reach their full potential and urge teachers and parents to support that play.

Sluss, Dorothy S. *Supporting Play, Birth through Age 8.* Clifton Park, NY: Delmar, 2005.

This book contains many ideas for children's play activities along with suggestions for assessing that play; it also provides current research on the positive effects of play on children's development.

Wellhousen, Karyn. *Outdoor Play Everyday, Innovative Play Concepts for Early Childhood.* Albany, NY: Delmar, 2002.

Wellhousen discusses the importance of play, how to attend to the play of special-needs students, and how to assess play; she also gives many suggestions for improving play and playgrounds for young children.

Chapter 6

Bickart, Toni S., Judy R. Jablon, and Diane T. Dodge. *Building the Primary Classroom: A Complete Guide to Teaching and Learning.* Portsmouth, NH: Heinemann, 1999.

These authors discuss how to create a positive classroom environment that is appropriate for all children; they also discuss how discipline problems are reduced in such an environment.

Gartrell, Dan. *The Power of Guidance: Teaching Social-Emotional Skills in Early Childhood Classrooms.* Clifton Park, NY: Delmar, 2004.

Gartrell focuses on how to help children develop the social and emotional skills needed to interact in the classroom in positive ways. These behaviors must be learned; they do not just happen.

Kaiser, Barbara, and Judy Rasminsky. *Challenging Behavior in Young Children: Understanding,*

Preventing, and Responding Effectively. Boston: Allyn & Bacon, 2003.

Managing children's challenging behavior is a concern for all teachers of young children; these authors offer practical advice for dealing with such behavior.

Miller, Darla F. *Positive Child Guidance.* Clifton Park, NY: Delmar, 2004.

Miller believes that teachers need to plan for teaching appropriate behavior as carefully as they plan for teaching content.

Rogovin, Paula. *Why Can't You Behave? The Teacher's Guide to Creative Classroom Management, K–3.* Portsmouth, NH: Heinemann, 2004.

Rogovin makes useful suggestions for how to combine curriculum planning and classroom management to help children learn content and manage their own behavior.

Stone, Jeannette. *A Guide to Discipline.* Washington, DC: National Association for the Education of Young Children, 1978.

Although this book is older, its content is timely; children still need to have teachers who can help them learn needed skills in positive ways.

Chapter 7

Atkins-Burnett, Sally, and Samuel Meisels. *Developmental Screening in Early Childhood.* Washington, DC: National Association for the Education of Young Children, 2005.

The authors explain the purposes of developmental screening and provide guidelines for how it should be conducted.

Bridges, Lois. *Assessment: Continuous Learning.* Portland, ME: Stenhouse, 1996.

According to Bridges, every learning event is an opportunity for assessment, and teachers' knowing what students know is critical for appropriate planning; this book provides many forms for practical use by classroom teachers as well as a sound perspective on assessment.

Charlton, Beth C. *Informal Assessment Strategies: Asking Questions, Observing Students, Planning Lessons.* Portland, ME: Stenhouse, 2005.

Assessment involves much more than testing. This author wants teachers to think about how to evaluate what children are learning and to use that information to inform planning for individual children.

Koralek, Derry. *Spotlight on Young Children and Assessment.* Washington, DC: National Association for the Education of Young Children, 2004.

This collection of articles from *Young Children* focuses on how to plan and implement positive assessment.

McAfee, Oralie, Deborah Leong, and Elena Bodrova. *Basics of Assessment: A Primer for Early Childhood Professionals.* Washington, DC: National Association for the Education of Young Children, 2004.

This small volume has clear descriptions of what teachers of young children need to know about assessment and how to assess children to obtain meaningful information.

Project Zero. *Making Learning Visible: Children as Individual and Group Learners.* Burlington, VT: Reggio Children, 2001.

This book discusses ways of documenting children's work so that what they are learning is clear to them and to others.

Project Zero. *Making Teaching Visible: Documenting Group Learning as Professional Development.* Burlington, VT: Reggio Children, 2003.

This volume traces the experiences of teachers as they learned to think about children's learning and to rethink their own ideas about the teaching/learning process.

Schipper, Beth, and Joanne Rossi. *Portfolios in the Classroom: Tools for Learning and Instruction.* Portland, ME: Stenhouse, 1997.

For teachers who want to begin using portfolios, this book offers excellent information about planning them. The authors also explain how portfolios have such positive effects on children as learners.

Shea, Mary, Rosemary Murray, and Rebecca Harlin. *Drowning in Data?* Portsmouth, NH: Heinemann, 2005.

These authors have many suggestions for helping teachers manage all the data that are necessary in this era of testing and accountability. In particular, they recommend a specific portfolio organizational strategy to deal with all the information.

Schuster, John, Kelly Maxwell, Mary Hammeter, and Melinda Ault. *Assessment of Practices in Early Elementary Classrooms.* Washington, DC: National Association for the Education of Young Children, 2001.

These authors describe appropriate practices for assessment in the primary grades and offer suggestions that will help teachers plan for assessment that is not damaging to children.

Walker, Catherine, and Edgar Schmidt. *Smart Tests: Teacher-Made Tests That Help Students Learn.* Portland, ME: Stenhouse, 2004.

These authors want teachers to use evaluation tools that help children learn and that help children better demonstrate what they have already learned.

Chapter 8

Dudley-Manning, Curt. *A Family Affair: When School Troubles Come Home.* Portsmouth, NH: Heinemann, 2000.

A child struggling in school can affect the entire family. In this publication, Dudley-Manning helps teachers understand how to help the parents of struggling children.

Epstein, Joyce, Mavis Sanders, Beth Simon, Karen Salinas, Natalie Jansorn, and Francis Van Voorhis. *School, Family and Community Partnerships: Your Handbook for Action.* Thousand Oaks, CA: Corwin Press, 2002.
This handbook offers solid advice for helping teachers plan and implement strong parent involvement programs.

Eulina, Maria, and P. de Carvalho. *Rethinking Family-School Relations: A Critique of Parental Involvement in Schooling.* Mahwah, NJ: Erlbaum, 2000.
These authors look at parent involvement from a critical standpoint and make suggestions for effective parent involvement.

Morgan, Jill, and Betty Y. Ashbaker. *A Teacher's Guide to Working with Paraeducators and Other Classroom Aides.* Reston, VA: Association for Supervision and Curriculum Development, 2001.
Answers are provided to questions about how to lead classroom instructional teams and provide on-the-job training for paraprofessionals.

Vukelich, Carol. *Teachers and Parents: Together for Children's Benefit.* Olney, MD: Association for Childhood Education International, 1993.
This collection of articles focuses on helping teachers work with parents in positive ways.

Chapter 9

Gibbons, Pauline. *Scaffolding Language, Scaffolding Learners: Teaching Second Language Learners in the Mainstream Classroom.* Portsmouth, NH: Heinemann, 2002.
This book suggests ways for teachers to support second-language learners—for instance, by providing appropriate contexts for learning language, by supporting reading and writing in the child's first language, and by promoting an integrated curriculum.

Hart, Betty, and Todd R. Risley. *The Social World of Children Learning to Talk.* Baltimore: Paul H. Brooks, 1999.
These authors describe learning language as a social dance. After studying three-year-olds to determine the nature of their language use in interacting with their parents, the authors concluded that there are significant differences between families and that these differences affect children's language learning.

Koralek, Derry, ed. *Spotlight on Young Children and Language.* Washington, DC: National Association for the Education of Young Children, 2003.
The topics covered in this collection of articles on learning language range from fostering language use at school and at home, to helping children who are linguistically and culturally diverse learn language, to helping children learn to use language for many purposes.

Krashen, Stephen D. *Explorations in Language Acquisition and Use.* Portsmouth, NH: Heineman, 2003.
Krashen is well known for his work on language acquisition in both first and second languages. In this short book, he discusses the principles of language acquisition and how learning language by problem solving is critical for successful learning.

Luongo-Orlando, Katherine. *A Project Approach to Language Learning: Linking Literary Genres and Themes in Elementary Classrooms.* Portland, ME: Stenhouse, 2001.
In each chapter in this book, the author focuses on a different genre and details how to develop a theme that highlights language; she also gives suggestions for authentic types of assessment.

Roskos, Kathleen, Patton O. Tabors, and Lisa A. Lenhart. *Oral Language and Early Literacy in Preschool: Talking, Reading, and Writing.* Newark, DE: International Reading Association, 2004.
These authors describe typical language development and provide practical suggestions for making usual classroom experiences rich with language. They focus on sound and on providing children a strong language base for learning to read.

Weitzman, Elaine, and Janice Greenberg. *Learning Language and Loving It: A Guide to Promoting Children's Social and Language Development in Early Childhood Settings.* Washington, DC: National Association for the Education of Young Children, 2002.
This is a step-by-step guide to promoting the language development of children, including those who have delayed language or social skills.

Chapter 10

Bowman, Barbara. *Love to Read: Essays in Developing and Enhancing Early Literacy Skills of African American Children.* Washington, DC: National Black Child Development Institute, 2002.
These essays cover the current achievement of Black children in literacy and focus on how teachers and parents can promote children's mastery of literacy.

Duncan, Marilyn. *The Kindergarten Book: A Guide to Literacy Instruction.* Katonah, NY: Richard C. Owen, 2005.
This detailed book is about helping children learn to read; it includes information on setting up the classroom, managing time, and assessing young learners.

Matteson, David M., and Deborah K. Freeman. *Assessing and Teaching Beginning Writers: Every Picture Tells a Story.* Katonah, NY: Richard C. Owen, 2005.
This book uses illustrations to help explain children's movement on the literacy continuum and provides assessment ideas and how to record children's growth.

Meier, Daniel. *The Young Child's Memory for Words*. New York: Teachers College Press, 2004.
Meier presents teaching strategies and practical guidelines that are appropriate for all children but especially multilingual and multicultural children; he also addresses how to support English language learners as they become literate.

Neuman, Susan, Carol Copple, and Sue Bredekamp. "Taking Stock of What You Do to Promote Literacy." In *Learning to Read and Write: Developmentally Appropriate Practices for Young Children*. Washington, DC: National Association for Young Children, 2000.
Using this excellent checklist will help teachers evaluate their classrooms and instruction for best literacy practices.

Owocki, Gretchen. *Literacy through Play*. Portsmouth, NH: Heinemann, 1999.
This book provides good information about play and playful ways of developing literacy.

Roskos, Kathleen, Patton O. Tabors, and Lisa A. Lenhart. *Oral Language and Early Literacy in Preschool: Talking, Reading, and Writing*. Newark, DE: International Reading Association, 2004.
This short book has numerous checklists, assessment ideas, and lesson plan ideas as well as an explanation about why preschool teachers need to talk, read, and write with young learners.

Schickedanz, Judith A. "A Framework and Suggested Guidelines for Prekindergarten Content Standards." *Reading Teacher* 58 (September 2004): 96–97.
This article presents a list of content standards that were compiled from a number of states' standards for the prekindergarten curriculum.

Schickedanz, Judith A., and Renee M. Casbergue. *Writing in Preschool: Learning to Orchestrate Meaning and Marks*. Newark, DE: International Reading Association, 2004.
These authors give a detailed description of the process of learning to write, along with samples of children's writing and suggested responses to give to children as they produce pieces of writing.

Strickland, Dorothy S., and Judith Schickedanz. *Learning about Print in Preschool: Working with Letters, Words, and Beginning Links with Phonemic Awareness*. Newark, DE: International Reading Association, 2004.
The authors suggest materials and ideas for helping children develop the concepts of letters and words and to begin to understand the sounds represented by letters.

Vukelich, Carol, and James Christie. *Building a Foundation for Preschool Literacy: Effective Instruction for Children's Reading and Writing Development*. Newark, DE: International Reading Association, 2004.
In this book, the authors provide ideas for lesson plans, room arrangements, and activities that will help children build a foundation for reading and writing.

Chapter 11

Andrews, Angela, and Paul Trafton. *Little Kids–Powerful Problem Solvers: Math Stories from a Kindergarten Classroom*. Portsmouth, NH: Heinemann, 2002.
These authors describe how children developed answers to problems such as how to build a pyramid with paper cups and then found out how many cups it would take to build a larger pyramid. This book is encouraging for teachers because it describes children learning math without having an actual math program.

Charlesworth, Rosalind. *Experiences in Math for Young Children*. Clifton Park, NY: Delmar, 2005.
This book focuses on the sequence in which children develop mathematical concepts and discusses how mathematics can be integrated into music, movement, language, science, and the visual arts.

Copley, Juanita V. *Showcasing Mathematics for the Young Child: Activities for Three-, Four-, and Five-Year-Olds*. Reston, VA: National Council of Teachers of Mathematics, 2004.
This book presents a strong description of how children grow in mathematical understanding; it also gives many suggestions for learning experiences based on the content and process strands of the NCTM model for mathematics instruction.

Copley, Juanita V. *The Young Child and Mathematics*. Washington, DC: National Association for the Education of Young Children, 2000.
Just as teachers are encouraged to create a print-rich environment, they should create a mathematics-rich environment. Copley suggests many activities for doing so and explains how to talk to children as they explore mathematical ideas.

Gallenstein, Nancy L. *Creative Construction of Mathematics and Science Concepts in Early Childhood*. Olney, MD: Association for Childhood Education International, 2003.
This author discusses how children learn math and science; describes the learning cycle of engagement, exploration, explanation, expansion, and evaluation as it applies to math and science; presents concept mapping; and summarizes the critical-thinking models for young children.

Kamii, Constance. *Number in Preschool and Kindergarten: Educational Implications of Piaget's Theory*. Washington, DC: National Association for the Education of Young Children, 1982.
This little book provides a wonderful explanation of how children learn mathematics and what that should mean in planning instruction.

Kamii, Constance, and Linda L. Joseph. *Young Children Continue to Reinvent Arithmetic: Implications of*

Piaget's Theory. New York: Teachers College Press, 2003.

Kamii and Joseph explain how children must construct their own understanding of mathematics; they cannot learn it from being told how to compute. Having tried the activities in a second-grade classroom, the authors report on children's thinking as they worked through problems.

Koralek, Derry, ed. *Spotlight on Young Children and Math.* Washington, DC: National Association for the Education of Young Children, 2003.

In this excellent resource, teachers are encouraged to foster children's problem solving and mathematical thinking across the curriculum.

Chapter 12

Chalufor, Ingrid, and Karen Worth. *Exploring Water with Young Children.* St. Paul, MN: Redleaf Press, 2005.

Water activities are intrinsically interesting to young children. These authors help teachers see how to apply that interest in helping children learn important science concepts while playing with water.

Chalufor, Ingrid, and Karen Worth. *Building Structures with Young Children.* St. Paul, MN: Redleaf Press, 2004.

Children are also naturally interested in building with blocks. These authors suggest using that interest and extending children's block experiences to meet the science standards.

Chalufor, Ingrid, and Karen Worth. *Discovering Nature with Young Children.* St. Paul, MN: Redleaf Press, 2003.

Children are innately curious about the world around them. This book describes how teachers can use the natural world to help young children develop essential lifelong reasoning skills and specific science skills.

Koralek, Derry, and Laura J. Colker, eds. *Spotlight on Young Children and Science.* Washington, DC: National Association for the Education of Young Children, 2003.

These articles from *Young Children* focus on science instruction and include descriptions of projects; ideas are also provided for relating science to other curriculum areas and documenting children's learning in science.

Ling, Karen K. *Exploring Science in Early Childhood Education.* Clifton Park, NY: Delmar, 2005.

Ling makes suggestions for teaching science so that children develop the necessary concepts and skills. These suggestions are presented in developmental sequence and are aligned with the standards for science instruction.

Martin, David J. *Constructing Early Childhood Science.* Clifton Park, NY: Delmar, 2001.

Martin gives suggestions for hands-on, engaging activities that will help children construct their understanding of scientific concepts. In each chapter, he also includes suggestions for teaching children from different cultural backgrounds and for using technology.

Martin, Ralph, Colleen Sexton, and Teresa Franklin. *Teaching Science for All Children: Inquiry Lessons for Constructing Understanding.* Boston: Allyn & Bacon, 2005.

This book has great suggestions for lessons, activities, and teaching materials that will help children develop their own understanding of science.

Worth, Karen, and Sharon Grollman. *Worms, Shadows, and Whirlpools: Science in the Early Childhood Classroom.* Portsmouth, NH: Heineman, 2003.

After explaining inquiry as a method of teaching, the authors offer suggestions for activities in life science, physical science, and earth and space science. All the descriptions of activities also include ideas for documenting children's learning.

Chapter 13

Althouse, Rosemary, Margaret H. Johnson, and Sharon T. Mitchell. *The Colors of Learning: Integrating the Visual Arts into the Early Childhood Curriculum.* Washington, DC: National Association for the Education of Young Children, 2002.

This book discusses how to create an environment for teaching art and how to integrate art into other subject areas.

Booth, David. *Story Drama: Creating Stories through Role Playing, Improvising, and Reading Aloud.* Portland, ME: Stenhouse, 2005.

Booth explains how to enhance children's development of literacy through storytelling and drama.

Booth, David, and Masayuki Hachiya. *The Arts Go to School.* Portland, ME: Stenhouse, 2004.

The arts make a powerful contribution to children's learning in other subject-matter areas, and these authors describe how to accomplish that growth.

Burton, Leon H., and Takeo Kudo. *SoundPlay: Understanding Music through Creative Movement.* Reston, VA: National Association for the Music Education, 2000.

This book contains lessons and a CD for creative movement experiences.

Engel, Brenda S. *Considering Children's Art: Why and How to Value Their Works.* Washington, DC: National Association for the Education of Young Children, 1995.

For the untrained artist, this book provides useful information about how to look at and talk about children's art with children and with others.

Koralek, Derry, ed. *Spotlight on Young Children and the Creative Arts.* Washington, DC: National Association for the Education of Young Children, 2005.

In this collection of articles from *Young Children,* the topics include art, music, and movement and how the arts can contribute to the curriculum for young children.

Lasky, Lila, and Rose Mukerji-Bergeson. *Art: Basics for Young Children*. Washington, DC: National Association for the Education of Young Children, 1993.
This basic book describes setting set up an art center, planning appropriate art activities, and storing art materials; it also argues for the value of art in the curriculum.

Mayesky, Mary. *Creative Activities for Young Children*. Clifton Park, NY: Delmar, 2006.
Mayesky offers many ideas for activities that promote children's creativity through art and all through the day.

Schirrmacher, Robert. *Art and Creative Development for Young Children*. Clifton Park, NY: Delmar, 2006.
This author offers teachers many ideas for incorporating art into the curriculum. Especially useful are the ideas for diverse populations and children with special needs.

Thompson, Susan C. *Children as Illustrators: Making Meaning through Art and Language*. Washington, DC: National Association for the Education of Young Children, 2005.
Dozens of ideas are presented for combining art with writing and reading to benefit the understanding of young readers and writers.

Zakkal, Jennifer. *Dance as a Way of Knowing*. Portland, ME: Stenhouse, 1997.
The author provides model lessons to help teachers plan dance experiences that will extend the curriculum and encourage children to express what they know.

Chapter 14

Arezzo, Diane, Kate Hendrix, Ronald Slaby, and Wendy Roedell. *Early Violence Prevention: Tools for Teachers of Young Children*. Washington, DC: National Association for the Education of Young Children, 1995.
The authors discuss ways of helping children become assertive and nonviolent problem solvers.

Bisson, Julie. *Celebrate: An Anti-Bias Guide to Enjoying Holidays in Early Childhood Programs*. St. Paul, MN: Redleaf Press, 1997.
Bisson offers developmentally appropriate holiday ideas that encourage meaningful participation and help overcome the hype that surrounds many holidays.

Levin, Diane. *Teaching Young Children in Violent Times*. Washington, DC: National Association for the Education of Young Children, 2003.
Levin suggests ways to help children learn peaceable alternatives to the violent behaviors they see in the media and to learn how to deal with the violent news they are exposed to on a daily basis.

Seefeldt, Carol. *Social Studies for the Preschool-Primary Child*. Upper Saddle River, NJ: Prentice Hall, 2004.
Seefeldt defines what social studies is, explains how to plan for social studies experiences, and suggests ways to develop an appropriate social studies curriculum.

Vance, Emily, and Patricia Weaver. *Class Meetings: Young Children Solving Problems Together*. Washington, DC: National Association for the Education of Young Children, 2002.
As described by these authors, holding class meetings for working out conflicts and problems can contribute to the goals of the social studies program, as children gain the skills needed to become good citizens.

Chapter 15

Council on Physical Education for Children (COPEC). *Appropriate Practices in Movement Program for Young Children, Ages 3–5*. 2000. Available online: www.aahperd.org/NASPE/peappropriatepractice/Appropriate%20Practices%20for%20Young%20Children.pdf. (One copy of this booklet can be downloaded for free.)
A booklet that describes appropriate practices in movement programs for young children. Examples are contrasted with inappropriate practices.

National Association for Sport and Physical Education. *Active Start: A Statement of Physical Activity Guidelines for Children Birth to Five Years*. Available online: www.aahperd.org/NASPE. (Click on "Publications" and then "Online store.") Available in Spanish and English.
Using these guidelines will help teachers plan programs that will make children become more physically active.

Sanders, Stephen W. *Active for Life: Developmentally Appropriate Movement Programs for Young Children*. Washington, DC: National Association for the Education of Young Children, 2002.
The author describes a program for movement experiences that is developmentally appropriate and manageable in the classroom.

Schneider, Lynne, and Marianne Torbert. *Follow Me Too: A Handbook of Movement Activities for Three- to Five-Year-Olds*. Washington, DC: National Association for the Education of Young Children, 1993.
Even though this book is a little older than other recommended texts, it has many good ideas for helping teachers plan appropriate movement experiences.

Children's Books

Ada, Alma Flor. *With Love, Little Red Hen.* Illustrated by Leslie Tryon. New York: Atheneum, 2001.

Ahlberg, Allan. *Mockingbird.* Illustrated by Paul Howard. Cambridge, MA: Candlewick Press, 1998.

Alda, Arlene. *Arlene Alda's 1 2 3: What Do You See?* Berkeley, CA: Ten Speed Press/Tricycle, 1998.

Allen, Pamela. *Who Sank the Boat?* New York: Coward-McCann, 1982.

Appelt, K. *Bats on Parade.* New York: Morrow, 1999.

Askar, Saoussan. *From Far Away.* Illustrated by Michael Martchenko. Loganville, GA: Annick Press, 1995.

Baker, J. *Window.* New York: Greenwillow, 1991.

Barton, Byron. *Building a House.* New York: HarperTrophy, 1990.

Barton, Byron. *My Car.* New York: Greenwillow, 2001.

Baylor, Byrd. *The Desert Is Theirs.* New York: Charles Scribner and Sons, 1970.

Baylor, Byrd. *Everybody Needs a Rock.* New York: Atheneum, 1974.

Baylor, Byrd. *Your Own Best Secret Place.* New York: Atheneum, 1979.

Best, Cari. *Three Cheers for Catherine the Great!* New York: DK Publishing, 1999.

Birch, David. *The King's Chessboard.* Illustrated by Devis Grebu. New York: Puffin, 1993.

Brown, Margaret Wise. *The Indoor Noisy Book.* Illus. by Leonard Weisgard. New York: HarperCollins, 1994.

Brown, Margaret Wise. *The Noisy Book.* Illus. by Leonard Weisgard. New York: HarperCollins, 1993.

Bunting, Eve. *A Picnic in October.* Illustrated by Nancy Carpenter. San Diego: Harcourt Brace, 1999.

Bunting, Eve. *Secret Place.* New York: Clarion, 1996.

Cabrera, Jane. *If You're Happy and You Know It!* New York: Holiday House, 2005.

Carle, Eric. *The Very Hungry Caterpillar.* New York: Scholastic, 1969.

Carter, David A. *If You're Happy and You Know It, Clap Your Hands!* New York: Scholastic, 1997.

Catalano, Dominic. *Frog Went A-Courting.* Honesdale, PA: Boyds Mills Press, 1998.

Cheng, Andrea. *Grandfather Counts.* Illustrated by Ange Zhang. New York: Lee and Low, 2003.

Choi, Yangsook. *The Name Jar.* New York: Knopf, 2001.

Church, Caroline J. *Do Your Ears Hang Low?* New York: Scholastic, 2002.

Coles, Robert. *The Story of Ruby Bridges.* Illustrated by George Ford. New York: Scholastic, 1995.

Cousins, Lucy. *Count with Maisy.* Cambridge, MA: Candlewick, 1997.

Cowley, Joy. *Red-Eyed Tree Frog.* Illustrated by Nick Bishop. New York: Scholastic, 1999.

Crews, Nina. *The Neighborhood Mother Goose.* New York: Greenwillow, 2004.

Dee, R. *Two Ways to Count to Ten.* New York: Henry Holt, 1988.

Demi. *One Grain of Rice.* New York: Scholastic, 1997.

dePaola, Tomie. *The Cloud Book.* New York: Scholastic, 1975.

dePaola, Tomie. *Mice Squeak, We Speak.* New York: Putnam, 1997.

Dewey, Jennifer O. *Spiders Near and Far.* New York: Dutton, 1992.

Dodds, Dayle Ann. *The Color Box.* Illustrated by Giles Laroche. Boston: Little Brown, 1992.

Dragonwagon, Crescent. *This Is the Bread I Baked for Ned.* New York: Macmillan, 1989.

Dunrea, Olivier. *Gossie & Gertie.* Boston: Houghton Mifflin, 2002.

Dunrea, Olivier. *Ollie.* Boston: Houghton Mifflin, 2003.

Emberley, Rebecca. *My House, Mi Casa.* Boston: Little, Brown, 1990.

Fleming, Candace. *Muncha! Muncha! Muncha!* Illustrated by G. Brian Karas. New York: Atheneum, 2002.

Florian, Douglas. *Lizards, Frogs, and Polliwogs.* San Diego: Harcourt, 2001.

Galdone, Paul. *The Gingerbread Boy.* Boston: Houghton Mifflin, 1985.

Galdone, Paul. *Over in the Meadow.* New York: Simon & Schuster, 1986.

Gibbons, Gail. *How a House Is Built.* New York: Holiday House, 1990.

Gilmore, Rachna. *Lights for Gita.* Illustrated by Alice Priestley. Gardiner, ME: Tilbury House, 1995.

Glaser, L. *Spectacular Spiders.* Illustrated by Gay W. Holland. Brookfield, CT: Millbrook, 1998.

Guthrie, Woody. *This Land Is Your Land.* Illustrated by Kathy Jakobsen. Boston: Little, Brown, 1998.

Hanson, Regina. *The Tangerine Tree.* Illustrated by Harvey Stevenson. New York: Clarion, 1995.

Harper, Piers. *Little Lamb.* New York: Scholastic, 2003.

Hausherr, Rosemarie. *Celebrating Families.* New York: Scholastic, 1997.

Henkes, Kevin. *Chrysanthemum.* New York: Greenwillow, 1991.

Henkes, Kevin. *Wemberley's Ice-Cream Star.* New York: Greenwillow, 2003.

Hepworth, Cathi. *Antics!* New York: Putnam, 1992.

Herold, Maggie R. *A Very Important Day.* Illustrated by Catherine Stock. New York: William Morrow, 1995.

Hest, Amy. *When Jessie Came across the Sea.* Illustrated by P. J. Lynch. Cambridge, MA: Candlewick, 1997.

Hightower, Susan. *Twelve Snails to One Lizard: A Tale of Mischief and Measurement.* Illustrated by Matt Novak. New York: Simon and Schuster, 1997.

Hill, Elizabeth. *Evan's Corner.* New York: Puffin, 1993.

Hillenbrand, Will. *Down by the Station.* San Diego: Harcourt, 1999.

Hillenbrand, Will. *Fiddle-I-Fee.* San Diego: Harcourt, 2002.

Hoban, Tana. *Cubes, Cones, Cylinders and Spheres.* New York: Greenwillow, 2000.

Hoban, Tana. *Is it Larger? Is it Smaller?* New York: Harper Trophy, 1997.

Hoban, Tanya. *More, Fewer, Less.* New York: Greenwillow, 1998.

Hoban, Tanya. *Shapes, Shapes, Shapes.* New York: Greenwillow, 1986.

Hoban, Tanya. *So Many Circles, So Many Squares.* New York: Greenwillow, 1998.

Hoberman, Mary Ann. *A House Is a House for Me.* Illustrated by Betty Fraser. New York: Viking, 1978.

Hoberman, Mary Ann. *Miss Mary Mack.* Boston: Little, Brown, 1998.

Hoberman, Mary Ann. *Right Outside My Window.* Illustrated by Nicholas Wilton. New York: Mondo, 2002.

Hoberman, Mary Ann. *Skip to My Lou.* Illustrated by Nadine Westcott. Boston: Little, Brown, 1989.

Hong, Lily Toy. *Two of Everything.* New York: Albert Whitman, 1993.

Hort, Lenny. *The Seals on the Bus.* Illustrated by G. Brian Karas. New York: Holt, 2000.

Howard, Elizabeth F. *Aunt Flossie's Hats (and Crab Cakes Later).* New York: Clarion, 1991.

Hulme, Joy N. *Counting by Kangaroos: A Multiplication Concept Book.* Illustrated by Betsy Scheld. New York: W. H. Freeman, 1995.

Hulme, Joy N. *Sea Squares.* Illustrated by Carol Schwartz. New York: Hyperion, 1991.

Hutchins, Pat. *The Doorbell Rang.* New York: Greenwillow, 1986.

Isadora, Rachel. *Ben's Trumpet.* New York: Greenwillow, 1979.

Jackson, Alison. *I Know an Old Lady Who Swallowed a Pie.* Illustrated by Judith Byron Schachner. New York: Dutton, 1997.

Jenkins, Steve. *Biggest, Strongest, Fastest.* New York: Tichnor & Fields, 1995.

Jenkins, Steve, and Robin Page. *What Do You Do with a Tail Like This?* Boston: Houghton Mifflin, 2003.

Johnson, Stephen T. *City by Numbers.* New York: Viking, 1998.

Jones, Carol. *Old MacDonald Had a Farm.* Boston: Houghton Mifflin, 1989.

Jones, Carol. *This Old Man.* Boston: Houghton Mifflin, 1990.

Keats, Ezra Jack. *Over in the Meadow.* New York: Scholastic, 1971.

Kipling, Rudyard. *Just So Stories.* New York: Grosset and Dunlap, 1965.

Kraus, Robert. *Whose Mouse Are You?* New York: Macmillan, 1970.

Langstaff, John. *Over in the Meadow.* Illustrated by Feodor Rojankorsky. New York: Harcourt, 1957.

Lee, Dennis. *Alligator Pie.* Toronto: Macmillan of Canada, 1974.

Leedy, Loreen. *Measuring Penny.* New York: Henry Holt, 1998.

Leonard, M. *Food Is Fun!* New York: HarperFestival, 2000.

Lewis, C. S. *The Lion, the Witch, and the Wardrobe.* New York: Macmillan, 1951.

Lewis, J. Patrick. *Arithme-Tickle.* Illustrated by Frank Remkiewicz. San Diego: Silver Whistle, 2002.

Longfellow, Henry Wadsworth. *The Midnight Ride of Paul Revere.* Illustrated by Christopher Bing. Brooklyn, NY: Handprint, 2001.

Lunn, Janet. *Charlotte.* Illustrated by Brian Deines. Toronto: Tundra Books, 1998.

Martin, Jr., Bill, and John Archambault. *Barn Dance.* Illustrated by Ted Rand. New York: Henry Holt, 1989.

Mathews, Louise. *Bunches and Bunches of Bunnies.* New York: Scholastic, 1990.

Mathews, Louise. *Gator Pie.* New York: Dodd Mead, 1979.

Mayer, Mercer. *There's a Nightmare in My Closet.* New York: Dial Books, 1968.

McCloskey, Robert. *Blueberries for Sal.* New York: Viking, 1948.

McMillan, Bruce. *Counting Wildflowers.* New York: William Morrow, 1986.

McMillan, Bruce. *Eating Fractions.* New York: Scholastic, 1991.

Merriam, Eve. *The Hole Story.* New York: Simon and Schuster, 1995.

Merriam, Eve. *12 Ways to Get to 11.* Illustrated by Bernie Karlin. New York: Simon and Schuster, 1993.

Morgan, Pierr. *The Turnip.* New York: Macmillan, 1990.

Morris, Ann. *Bread, Bread, Bread.* New York: Scholastic, 1989.

Morris, Ann. *Loving.* New York: Lothrop, Lee & Shepard, 1990.

Murphy, Stuart J. *Give Me Half!* Illustrated by G. Brian Karas. New York: Scholastic, 1996.

Myller, R. *How Big Is a Foot?* New York: Dell, 1990.

Nagda, Ann Whitehead, and Cindy Bickel. *Chimp Math: Learning about Time from a Baby Chimpanzee.* New York: Henry Holt, 2002.

Nagda, Ann Whitehead, and Cindy Bickel. *Tiger Math: Learning to Graph from a Baby Tiger.* New York: Henry Holt, 2000.

Oberman, Sheldon. *The Always Prayer Shawl.* Honesdale, PA: Boyds Mills Press, 1994.

Ochiltree, Dianne. *Ten Monkey Jamboree.* Illustrated by Anne-Sophie Lanquetin. New York: McElderry, 2001.

Ormerod, Jan. *If You're Happy and You Know It!* Illustrated by Lindsey Gardiner. New York: Oxford University Press, 2002.

Paul, A. *Eight Hands Round.* New York: HarperCollins, 1991.

Peek, Merle. *Mary Wore Her Red Dress and Henry Wore His Green Sneakers.* New York: Clarion, 1985.

Pinczes, Elinor J. *An Inchworm and a Half.* Illustrated by Randall Enos. Boston: Houghton Mifflin, 2003.

Pinczes, Elinor J. *One Hundred Angry Ants.* Illustrated by Bonnie MacKain. New York: Scholastic, 1993.

Pinczes, Elinor J. *A Remainder of One.* Illustrated by Bonnie MacKain. Boston: Houghton Mifflin, 1995.

Pomeranc, Marion Hess. *American Wei.* Illustrated by Dyanne Disalvo-Ryan. New York: Albert Whitman, 1998.

Pryor, Bonnie. *The Dream Jar.* Illustrated by Mark Graham. New York: William Morrow, 1996.

Rankin, Laura. *The Handmade Counting Book.* New York: Dial, 1998.

Riley, Linnea. *Mouse Mess.* New York: Scholastic, 1997.

Ringgold, Faith. *If a Bus Could Talk: The Story of Rosa Parks.* New York: Simon and Schuster, 1999.

Rosen, Michael, ed. *Home: A Collaboration of Thirty Distinguished Authors and Illustrators of Children's Books to Aid the Homeless.* New York: HarperCollins, 1992.

Rosenberg, Liz. *The Silence in the Mountains.* Illustrated by Chris K. Soentpiet. New York: Orchard Books, 1999.

Schroeder, Alan. *Minty: A Story of Young Harriet Tubman.* Illustrated by Jerry Pinkney. New York: Dial, 1996.

Schwartz, Amy. *Old MacDonald.* New York: Scholastic, 1999.

Schwartz, David. *How Much Is a Million?* New York: Mulberry, 1993.

Schwartz, David. *If You Hopped Like a Frog.* New York: Scholastic, 1999.

Scieszka, Jon. *Math Curse.* New York: Viking, 1995.

Seltzer, Isadore. *The House I Live In: At Home in America.* New York: Macmillan, 1992.

Sendak, Maurice. *Where the Wild Things Are.* New York: Harper and Row, 1963.

Shannon, David. *No, David!* New York: Scholastic, 1998.

Sierra, Judy. *Wild about Books.* Illustrated by Marc Brown. New York: Knopf, 2004.

Stevens, Janet. *Tops and Bottoms.* San Diego: Harcourt, 1995.

Stevens, Janet, and Susan S. Crummel. *And the Dish Ran Away with the Spoon.* San Diego: Harcourt, 2001.

Sweet, Melissa. *Fiddle-I-Fee.* Boston: Little, Brown, 1992.

Taback, Simms. *There Was an Old Lady Who Swallowed a Fly.* New York: Viking, 1999.

Tafuri, Nancy. *Goodnight, My Duckling.* New York: Scholastic, 2005.

Tang, Greg. *Math for All Seasons.* Illustrated by Harry Briggs. New York: Scholastic, 2002.

Tarbescu, Edith. *Anushka's Voyage.* Illustrated by Lydia Dabcovich. New York: Clarion, 1998.

Thong, Roseanne. *Red Is a Dragon: A Book of Colors.* Illustrated by Grace Lin. San Francisco: Chronicle, 2001.

Thong, Roseanne. *Round Is a Mooncake: A Book of Shapes.* Illustrated by Grace Lin. San Francisco: Chronicle Books, 2000.

Titherington, Jeanne. *A Place for Ben.* New York: Harper Trophy, 1999.

Toft, K., and A. Sheather. *One Less Fish.* Watertown, MA: Charlesbridge, 1998.

Viorst, Judith. *Alexander, Who Used to Be Rich Last Sunday.* New York: Atheneum, 1978.

Waddell, Martin. *Farmer Duck.* Illustrated by Helen Oxenbury. Cambridge, MA: Candlewick, 1991.

Wadsworth, Olive A. *Over in the Meadow.* Illustrated by Anna Vojtech. New York: North-South, 2002.

Wallner, Alexandria. *The Farmer in the Dell.* New York: Holiday House, 1998.

Watson, Mary. *The Butterfly Seeds.* New York: Morrow/Tambourine, 1995.

Weiss, George, and Bob Thiele. *What a Wonderful World.* Illustrated by Ashley Bryan. New York: Atheneum, 1995.

Wells, Rosemary. *Bingo.* New York: Scholastic, 1999.

Wells, Rosemary. *Bunny Cakes.* New York: Dial, 1997.

Wells, Rosemary. *Bunny Money.* New York: Dial, 1997.

Wells, Rosemary. *Goodnight Max.* New York: Viking, 2000.

Wells, Rosemary, *The Itsy-Bitsy Spider.* New York: Scholastic, 1998.

Wheatley, Nadia. *1 Is for One.* Illustrated by Darius Detwiler. Greenvale, NY: Mondo, 1996.

Williams, Sue. *I Went Walking.* Illustrated by Julie Vivas. San Diego: Harcourt, 1989.

Williams, Vera. *A Chair for My Mother.* New York: Greenwillow, 1982.

Wilson, Karma. *Bear Snores On.* Illustrated by Jane Chapman. New York: McElderry, 2002.

Winer, Yvonne. *Spiders Spin Webs.* Illustrated by Karen Lloyd-Jones. Watertown, MA: Charlesbridge, 1998.

Wolf, Bernard. *Coming to America: A Muslim Family's Story.* New York: Lee and Low, 2003.

Wood, Audrey. *King Bidgood's in the Bathtub.* New York: Harcourt Brace Jovanovich, 1985.

Zelinsky, Paul. *Knick-Knack Paddywhack.* New York: Dutton, 2002.

Zelinsky, Paul. *Wheels on the Bus.* New York: Dutton, 1990.

Ziefert, Harriet. *When I First Came to This Land.* Illustrated by Simms Taback. New York: Putnam, 1998.

Zolotow, Charlotte. *Someday.* New York: Harper and Row, 1965.

References

Note: See the separate list of Children's Books on pages 523–525.

Abrams, Dolores. "This School Gets 100% Parent Involvement—You Can Too!" *Pro Principal* 14 (July 2002): 5.

Adams, Marilyn J. Beginning to Read: Thinking and Learning about Print. Cambridge, MA: MIT Press, 1990.

Airasian, P. W. Classroom Assessment: Concepts and Applications. Boston: McGraw-Hill, 2001.

Alger, Harriet A. "Transitions: Alternatives to Manipulative Management Techniques." *Young Children* 39 (September 1984): 16–26.

Alliance for Childhood. *Fool's Gold: A Critical Look at Computers and Childhood.* 2000. Available online: www.allianceforchildhood.net/htm.

Almy, Millie. "A Child's Right to Play." *Childhood Education* 60 (May–June 1984): 350.

Ambron, Sueann R. *Child Development.* 2nd ed. New York: Holt, Rinehart and Winston, 1978.

American Academy of Pediatrics. *Safe Swimming for Your Young Child.* Washington, DC: AAP, 1988. (This leaflet is one in a series called "TIPP: The Injury Prevention Program.")

American Association for Health Education (AAHE). *National Health Education Standards.* Cited from prepublication document of *National Health Education Standards, PreK–12.* Reston, VA: Author, 2005–2006. Available online: www.aahperd.org/AAHE/template.cfm?template=natl_health_education_standards.html.

American Montessori Society. *Standards and Criteria for AMS School Accreditation.* ERIC Document Reproduction Service 2523040. New York: AMS, 1984.

Andersen, Susan R. "The Trouble with Testing." *Young Children* 53 (July 1998): 25–29.

Anderson, M. P. "ACT against Violence." *Young Children* 56 (July 2001): 60–61.

Andrews, Angela G. "The Role of Self-Directed Discovery Time in the Development of Mathematics Concepts." *Teaching Children Mathematics* 2 (October 1995): 116–120.

Anen, Judith. *Enhancing the Curriculum through the Addition of Rich and Diverse Language Development Activities.* ERIC Document Reproduction Service 329944. 1991.

Antler, Joyce. *Lucy Sprague Mitchell: The Making of a Modern Woman.* New Haven, CT: Yale University Press, 1987.

Ashbaker, Betty, and Jill Morgan. "Paraeducators: A Powerful Human Resource." *Streamlined Seminar* (Winter 2000/ 2001): 19. ERIC Document Reproduction Service 453573. 2000/2001.

Association for Supervision and Curriculum Development. *Developmental Characteristics of Children and Youth.* Alexandria, VA: ASCD, 1975.

Atkins, Cammie. "Writing: Doing Something Constructive." *Young Children* 40 (November 1984): 3–7.

Aylward, Kim, Scott Hartley, Tiffany Field, Jean Greer, and Nitza Vega-Lahr. "An Art Appreciation Curriculum for Preschool Children." *Early Child Development and Care* 96 (September 1993): 35–48.

Baker, Katherine Read. *Let's Play Outdoors.* Washington, DC: National Association for the Education of Young Children, 1966.

Bandura, Albert. "Social Cognitive Theory: An Agentic Perspective." *Annual Review of Psychology* 52 (2001): 1–26.

Bandura, Albert. *Social Learning Theory.* Englewood Cliffs, NJ: Prentice-Hall, 1977.

Bank Street College of Education. *Curriculum.* "Social Studies in the Lower School." n.d. Available online: www.bankstreed.edu/sfe/socialstudies–lower.html.

Banks, James A., and Cherry A. Banks, eds. *Multicultural Education: Issues and Perspectives.* 3rd ed. Boston: Allyn & Bacon, 1997.

Barbour, Ann C. "The Impact of Playground Design on the Play Behaviors of Children with Differing Levels of Physical Competence." *Early Childhood Research Quarterly* 14 (January 1999): 75–98.

Barbour, Nita, Tupper Dooly Webster, and Stephen Drosdeck. "Sand: A Resource for the Language Arts." *Young Children* 42 (January 1987): 20–25.

Barclay, Kathy, Cecelia Benelli, and Susan Schoon. "Making the Connection! Science and Literacy." *Childhood Education* 75 (Spring 1999): 146–152.

Barclay, Kathy H., and Camille Breheny. "Letting the Children Take Over More of Their Own Learning: Collaboration Research in the Kindergarten Classroom." *Young Children* 49 (September 1994): 33–39.

Barnett, Lynn A. "Research Note: Young Children's Resolution of Distress through Play." *Journal of Child Psychology and Psychiatry and Allied Disciplines* 25 (1984): 477–483.

Bauch, Jerold P. "The TransParent School: A Partnership for Parent Involvement." *Educational Horizons* 68 (Summer 1990): 187–189.

Bayless, Kathleen M., and Marjorie E. Ramsey. *Music: A Way of Life for the Young Child.* 4th ed. Columbus, OH: Merrill, 1991.

Beaty, J. J. *Observing Development of the Young Child.* Columbus, OH: Merrill, 1986.

Becker, H. J. *Findings from the Teaching, Learning and Computing Survey: Is Larry Cuban Right?* Revision of paper written for January 2000 Technology and Leadership Conference of the Council of Chief State School Officers, Washington, DC, July 2000.

Benelli, Cecelia, and Bill Yongue. "Supporting Young Children's Motor Skill Development." *Childhood Education* 71 (Summer 1995): 217–220.

Benjamin, Ann C. "I Wish the Teacher Would Tell Me What Is Really Special about My Child." Paper presented at the annual conference of the Essex County AEYC, September 1997.

Benjamin, Ann C. "Observations in Early Childhood Classrooms: Advice from the Field." *Young Children* 49 (September 1994): 14–20.

Benson, Forrest, and Sean Martin. "Organizing Successful Parent Involvement in Urban Schools." *Child Study Journal* 33 (March 2003): 187–193.

Bentzen, Warren. *Seeing Young Children: A Guide to Observing and Recording Behavior.* New York: Delmar, 1985.

Bereiter, Carl, and Siegfried Engelmann. *Teaching Disadvantaged Children in the Preschool.* Englewood Cliffs, NJ: Prentice-Hall, 1966.

Bergen, Doris. "Should Teachers Permit or Discourage Violent Play Themes?" *Childhood Education* 70 (Annual Theme 1994): 300–301.

Bergen, Doris. "Using a Schema for Play and Learning." In *Play as a Medium for Learning and Development*, edited by D. Bergen, 169–180. Portsmouth, NH: Heinemann, 1988.

Bergeron, Bette S., Sarah Wermuth, Melissa Rhodes, and Elizabeth A. Rudenga. "Language Development and Thematic Instruction: Supporting Young Learners at Risk." *Childhood Education* 72 (Spring 1996): 141–145.

Berk, Laura E. *Child Development.* 6th ed. Boston: Allyn & Bacon, 2006.

Berk, Laura E. *Infants, Children, and Adolescents.* Boston: Allyn & Bacon, 1996.

Berk, Laura E. "Vygotsky's Theory: The Importance of Make-Believe Play." *Young Children* 50 (November 1994): 30–39.

Berk, Laura E., and Adam Winsler. *Scaffolding Children's Learning: Vygotsky and Early Childhood Education.* Washington, DC: National Association for the Education of Young Children, 1995.

Berko-Gleason, Jean, ed. *The Development of Language.* Columbus, OH: Merrill, 1985.

Betz, Carl. "Beyond Time-Out: Tips from a Teacher." *Young Children* 49 (March 1994): 10–14.

Bigler, R. S., and L. S. Liben. "Cognitive Mechanisms in Children's Gender Stereotyping: Theoretical and Educational Implications of a Cognitive-Based Intervention." *Child Development* 63 (1992): 1351–1363.

Bigler, R. S., and L. S. Liben. "The Role of Attitudes and Interventions in Gender-Schematic Processing." *Child Development* 61 (1990): 1440–1452.

Bird, John. *Science from Water Play.* London: Macdonald Educational, 1983.

Bisson, Julie. *Celebrate! An Anti-Bias Guide to Enjoying Holidays in Early Childhood Programs.* St. Paul, MN: Redleaf Press, 1997.

Bjorkland, Gail. *Planning for Play: A Developmental Approach.* Columbus, OH: Merrill, 1978.

Blachman, Benita A. *Getting Ready to Read: Learning How Print Maps to Speech.* Timonium, MD: York Press/U.S. Department of Health and Human Services, Public Health Service, National Institutes of Health, 1991.

Blackburn, Ellen. "Stories Never End." In *Breaking Ground: Teachers Relate Reading and Writing in the Elementary School*, edited by J. Hansen, T. Newkirk, and D. Graves. Portsmouth, NH: Heinemann, 1985.

Blair, Umbreit, and C. Kwang-Sun. "Analysis of Multiple Variables Related to a Young Child's Aggressive Behavior." *Journal of Positive Behavior Interventions* 2 (Winter 2000): 33–40.

Bloom, Benjamin S. *Stability and Change in Human Characteristics.* New York: John Wiley and Sons, 1964.

Bloom, Benjamin S., ed. *Taxonomy of Educational Objectives: The Classification of Educational Goals. Handbook I: Cognitive Domain.* New York: David McKay, 1956.

Bodrova, Elena, and Deborah J. Leong. *Tools of the Mind: The Vygotskian Approach to Early Childhood Education.* Englewood Cliffs, NJ: Prentice-Hall, 1996.

Boehm, Ann E., and Richard A. Weinberg. *The Classroom Observer: Developing Observation Skills in Early Childhood Settings.* 2nd ed. New York: Teachers College Press, 1987.

Bondurant, J. L., D. J. Romeo, and R. Kretschmer. "Language Behaviors of Mothers of Children with Normal and Delayed Language." *Language, Speech and Hearing Services in Schools* 14 (1983): 233–242.

Bottini, Michael, and Sue Grossman. "Center-Based Teaching and Children's Learning: The Effects of Learning Centers on Young Children's Growth and Development." *Childhood Education* 81 (May 2005): 274–277.

Boutte, Gloria S., Irma Van Scoy, and Susan Hendley. "Multicultural and Nonsexist Prop Boxes." *Young Children* 52 (November 1996): 34–39.

Bowker, Jeanette E., and Janet K. Sawyer. "Influence of Exposure on Preschoolers' Art Preferences." *Early Childhood Research Quarterly* 3 (1988): 107–115.

Boyd, Brenda J. "Teacher Response to Superhero Play: To Ban or Not to Ban?" *Childhood Education* 74 (January 1997): 23–27.

Boyd-Batstone, Paul. "Focused Anecdotal Records Assessment: A Tool for Standards-Based, Authentic Assessment." *Reading Teacher* 28 (November 2004): 230–239.

Brandt, Ron. "Educators Need to Know about the Human Brain." *Phi Delta Kappan* 81 (March 1999): 235–238.

Brandt, R. "On Performance Assessment: A Conversation with Grant Wiggins." *Educational Leadership* 49 (1992): 35–37.

Brannon, Diane. "Full- or Half-Day Kindergarten: What Parents Pick-and Why." *Education Digest* 70 (April 2005): 57–62.

Bredekamp, Sue, ed. *Developmentally Appropriate Practice in Early Childhood Programs Serving Children from Birth through Age 8.* Washington, DC: National Association for the Education of Young Children, 1987.

Bredekamp, Sue. "Reflections on Reggio Emilia." *Young Children* 49 (November 1993): 13–17.

Bredekamp, Sue. "Twenty-Five Years of Educating Young Children: The High/Scope Approach to Preschool Education." *Young Children* 51 (May 1996): 57–61.

Bredekamp, Sue, and Carol Copple, eds. *Developmentally Appropriate Practice in Early Childhood Programs.* Rev.

ed. Washington, DC: National Association for the Education of Young Children, 1997.

Bredekamp, Sue, and Teresa Rosegrant. *Reaching Potentials: Appropriate Curriculum and Assessment for Young Children,* vol. 1. Washington, DC: National Association for the Education of Young Children, 1992.

Bredekamp, Sue, and Teresa Rosegrant. "Reaching Potentials through Transforming Curriculum, Assessment, and Teaching." In *Reaching Potentials: Transforming Early Childhood Curriculum and Assessment,* vol. 2, edited by S. Bredekamp and T. Rosegrant, 15–22. Washington, DC: National Association for the Education of Young Children, 1995.

Brewer, Jo Ann. "Literacy Development of Young Children in a Preschool Setting." In *Facilitating Preschool Literacy,* edited by R. Campbell, 119–130. Newark, DE: International Reading Association, 1998a.

Brewer, Jo Ann. "A Study of the Literacy Preferences of Parents of Three Language Groups." Unpublished manuscript, 1998b.

Brittain, W. L. "Some Exploratory Studies of the Art of Preschool Children." *Studies in Art Education* 10 (1969): 14–24.

Bromer, Billi L. "Who's in the House Corner? Including Young Children with Disabilities in Pretend Play." *Dimensions of Early Childhood* 27 (February 1999): 17–23.

Bronfenbrenner, Urie, and G. W. Evans. "Developmental Science in the 21st Century: Emerging Theoretical Models, Research Designs, and Empirical Findings." *Social Development* 9 (2000): 115–125.

Brown, Mac H., Rosemary Althouse, and Carol Anfin. "Guided Dramatization: Fostering Social Development in Children with Disabilities." *Young Children* 48 (January 1993): 68–71.

Brown, Nancy, Nancy Curry, and Ethel Tittnich. "How Groups of Children Deal with Common Stress through Play." In *Play: The Child Strives toward Self-Realization,* edited by G. Engstrom, 26–38. Washington, DC: National Association for the Education of Young Children, 1971.

Brown, Sue. "First Graders Write to Discover Mathematic's Relevancy." *Young Children* 52 (May 1997): 51–53.

Brown, Victoria. "Integrating Drama and Sign Language: A Multisensory Approach to Learning for Children with Special Needs." In *Early Childhood Creative Arts: Proceedings of the International Early Childhood Creative Arts Conference,* edited by L. Overby. Reston, VA: American Alliance for Health, Physical Education, Recreation and Dance, 1991.

Bruer, John T. "In Search of Brain-Based Education." *Phi Delta Kappan* 80 (September 1999): 649–657.

Bruhn, John G., and Philip R. Nader. "The School as a Setting for Health Education, Health Promotion, and Health Care." *Family and Community Health* 4 (1982): 57–59.

Bruner, Jerome. *Child's Talk: Learning to Use Language.* New York: W. W. Norton, 1983.

Bruner, Jerome. *The Process of Education.* New York: Vintage Books, 1960.

Bruns, Deborah A., and Robert M. Corso. *Working with Culturally and Linguistically Diverse Families.* ERIC Digest, 2001. Available online: http://ceep.crc.edu/eecearchive/digests/2001/bruns01.html (Retrieved August 5, 2005).

Buchoff, Rita. "Family Stories." *Reading Teacher* 49 (November 1995): 230–233.

Buchoff, Rita. "Joyful Voices: Facilitating Language Growth through Rhythmic Response to Chants." *Young Children* 49 (May 1994): 26–30.

Bullock, Merry, and Rochel Gelman. "Numerical Reasoning in Young Children: The Ordering Principle." *Child Development* 48 (June 1977): 427–434.

Bundy, Blakely Fetridge. "Fostering Communication between Parents and Preschools." *Young Children* 46 (January 1991): 12–17.

Burnett, Gary. *The Assessment and Placement of Language Minority Students.* ERIC Document Reproduction Service 357131. 1993.

Burns, Marilyn, and Kathy Richardson. "Making Sense Out of Word Problems." *Learning* 10 (January 1981): 39–44.

Burriss, Larry L. "Safety in the Cybervillage: Some Guidelines for Teachers and Parents." *Childhood Education* 79 (May 2003): 318–319.

Burton, Grace M. "Patterning: Powerful Play." *School Science and Mathematics* 82 (June 1982): 39–44.

Butler, Lester G. "Language Acquisition of Young Children: Major Theories and Sequences." *Elementary English* 51 (1974): 1120–1123.

Button, Kathryn, Margaret J. Johnson, and Paige Fergerson. "Interactive Writing in a Primary Classroom." *Reading Teacher* 49 (March 1996): 446–454.

Butts, R. Freeman. "Search for Freedom—The Story of American Education." *National Education Association Journal* (March 1960): 33–48.

Byrum, Donna, and Virginia L. Pierce. "Bringing Children to Literacy through Theme Cycles." In *Bringing Children to Literacy: Classrooms at Work,* edited by Bill Harp, 105–122. Norwood, MA: Christopher Gordon, 1993.

Cadwell, Louise Boyd. *Bringing Reggio Emilia Home: An Innovative Approach to Early Childhood Education.* New York: Teachers College Press, 1997.

Cairney, Trevor H., and Lynne Munsie. "Parent Participation in Literacy Learning." *Reading Teacher* 48 (February 1995): 392–403.

Calkins, Lucy. *The Art of Teaching Writing.* Portsmouth, NH: Heinemann, 1986.

Cambourne, Brian. "Conditions for Literacy Learning." *Reading Teacher* 53 (February 1999): 126–127.

Cambourne, Brian. "Toward an Educationally Relevant Theory of Literacy Learning: Twenty Years of Inquiry." *Reading Teacher* 49 (November 1995): 182–202.

Canter, Lee. *Assertive Discipline.* Seal Beach, CA: Canter and Associates, 1976.

Canter, Lee. "Assertive Discipline and the Search for the Perfect Classroom." *Young Children* 43 (January 1988): 24.

Caples, Sara E. "Some Guidelines for Preschool Design." *Young Children* 51 (May 1996): 14–21.

Carlevale, J. M. *Observing, Recording, Interpreting Child Behavior.* West Greenwich, RI: Consortium Publishing, 1991.

Carlsson-Paige, Nancy, and Diane E. Levin. "Can Teachers Resolve the War-Play Dilemma?" *Young Children* 50 (July 1995): 62–63.

Cattermole, Juleen, and Norman Robinson. "Effective Home/School Communication—From the Parents' Perspective." *Phi Delta Kappan* 67 (September 1985): 48–50.

Cazden, Courtney. "Environmental Assistance to the Child's Acquisition of Grammar." Doctoral dissertation, Harvard University, 1965.

Ceglowski, Deborah. "Understanding and Building upon Children's Perceptions of Play Activities in Early Childhood Programs." *Early Childhood Education Journal* 25 (February 1997): 107–112.

Chaille, Christine, and Lori Britain. *The Young Child as Scientist: A Constructivist Approach to Early Childhood Science Education.* New York: HarperCollins, 1991.

Chaille, Christine, and Steven B. Silvern. "Understanding through Play." *Childhood Education* 72 (Annual Theme 1996): 274–277.

Chapman, Warren. "The Illinois Experience: State Grants to Improve Schools through Parent Involvement." *Phi Delta Kappan* 72 (January 1991): 355–358.

Charles, C. M., and Karen Blaine Barr. *Building Classroom Discipline.* 3rd ed. New York: Longman, 1989.

Chavkin, N. F., and D. L. Williams. "Minority Parents and the Elementary School: Attitudes and Practices." In *Families and Schools in a Pluralistic Society*, edited by N. F. Charkin, 73–119. Albany, NY: SUNY Press, 1993.

Children's Defense Fund. *Family Income and Jobs.* 2004. Available online: www.childrensdefense.org/family income/childpoverty (Retrieved June 29, 2005).

Chomsky, Noam. *Aspects of a Theory of Syntax.* Cambridge, MA: MIT Press, 1965.

Christie, James F. "Dramatic Play: A Context for Meaningful Engagements." *Reading Teacher* 43 (April 1990): 542–545.

Christie, James F., E. Peter Johnson, and Roger B. Peckover. "The Effects of Play Period Duration on Children's Play Patterns." *Journal of Research in Childhood Education* 3 (1988): 123–131.

Christie, James F., and Francis Wardle. "How Much Time Is Needed for Play?" *Young Children* 47 (March 1992): 28–32.

Clancy, Mary E., and Barbara L. Hruska. "Developing Language Objectives for English Language Learners in Physical Education Lessons." *Journal of Physical Education, Recreation & Dance* 76 (April 2005): 30–35.

Clark, Patricia. "Culturally Appropriate Practices in Early Childhood Education: Families as the Resource." *Contemporary Education* 66 (Spring 1995): 154–157.

Clark, Patricia. "Recent Research on All-Day Kindergarten." ERIC Document Reproduction Service 453982. 2001.

Clay, Marie M. *Becoming Literate: The Construction of Inner Control.* Portsmouth, NH: Heinemann, 1991.

Clay, Marie M. *An Observation Survey of Early Literacy Achievement.* Portsmouth, NH: Heinemann, 1993a.

Clay, Marie M. *Reading Recovery: A Guidebook for Teachers in Training.* Portsmouth, NH: Heinemann, 1993b.

Clay, Marie M. *What Did I Write? Beginning Writing Behavior.* Portsmouth, NH: Heinemann, 1975.

Clements, Douglas H., Bonnie K. Nastasi, and Sudha Swaminathan. "Young Children and Computers: Crossroads and Directions from Research." *Young Children* 48 (January 1993): 56–64.

Clements, Douglas H., and Julie Samara. "The Role of Technology in Early Childhood Learning." *Teaching Children Mathematics* 5 (2002): 340–343.

Clements, Douglas H., and Julie Sarama. "Young Children and Technology: What Does the Research Say?" *Young Children* 58 (November 2003): 34–40.

Clements, Nancy E., and Edna W. Warncke. "Helping Literacy Emerge at School for Less-Advantaged Children." *Young Children* 49 (March 1994): 22–26.

Clewett, Ann S. "Guidance and Discipline: Teaching Young Children Appropriate Behavior." *Young Children* 43 (May 1988): 26–31.

Cline, Dusty B., and David Ingerson. "The Mystery of Humpty's Fall: Primary-School Children as Playmakers." *Young Children* 51 (September 1996): 4–10.

Cline, R. K. J. *Focus on Families: A Reference Handbook.* Santa Barbara, CA: ABC-CLIO, 1990.

Colbert, C., and M. Taunton. "Developmentally Appropriate Practices for the Visual Arts Education of Young Children." National Art Education Association Briefing Paper. Reston VA: National Art Education Association, 1992.

Cole, J. D. "Prevention of Violence and Antisocial Behavior." In *Preventing Childhood Disorders, Substance Abuse, and Delinquency*, edited by R. D. Peters and R. J. McMahon, 1–18. Thousand Oaks, CA: Sage, 1996.

Cole, Elizabeth, and Claire Schaefer. "Can Young Children Be Art Critics?" *Young Children* 45 (January 1990): 33–38.

Cole, Martha L., and Jack T. Cole. *Effective Intervention with the Language Impaired Child.* 2nd ed. Rockville, MD: Aspen, 1989.

Colker, Laura J. *The Cooking Book: Fostering Young Children's Learning and Delight.* Washington, DC: National Association for the Education of Young Children, 2005.

Collier, Robert G. "Reading, Thinking, and Play: A Child's Search for Meaning." In *Claremont Reading Conference 47th Yearbook*, edited by Malcolm P. Douglas. Claremont, CA: Claremont Reading Conference, 1983.

Collier, Virginia. "Age and Rate of Acquisition of Second Language for Academic Purposes." *TESOL Quarterly* 21 (April 1987): 617–641.

Collins, N. L. D., and M. B. Shaeffer. "Look, Listen, and Learn to Read. *Young Children* 52 (May 1997): 65–68.

Comenius, John Amos. *A Reformation of Schools.* 1642. Reprint, London: Scolar Press, 1969.

Conezio, Kathleen, and Lucia French. "Capitalizing on Children's Fascination with the Everyday World to Foster Language and Literacy Development." In *Spotlight on Young Children and Science* (pp. 4–15). Washington, DC: National Association for the Education of Young Children, 2003.

Consortium of National Arts Education Associations. *National Standards for Arts Education.* 1994.

Available online: http://artsedge.kennedy-center.org/teach/standards.

Consortium of National Arts Education Associations. *Summary Statement*. March 1996. Available online: www.menc.org/publication/books/summary/html.

Cooper, Carolyn S., and Mary A. McEvoy. "Group Friendship Activities: An Easy Way to Develop the Social Skills of Young Children." *Teaching Exceptional Children* 28 (March 1996): 67–69.

Cooper, Jaclyn L., and Martha T. Dever. "Sociodramatic Play as a Vehicle for Curriculum Integration in First Grade." *Young Children* 56 (May 2001): 58–63.

Coopersmith, Stanley. *The Antecedents of Self-Esteem*. San Francisco: W. H. Freeman, 1967.

Copeland, Richard W. *How Children Learn Mathematics: Teaching Implications of Piaget's Research*. 4th ed. New York: Macmillan, 1984.

Corbin, C., and R. Lindsey. *Concepts of Physical Education with Laboratories*. Madison, WI: W. C. Brown/Benchmark. Cited in Marjorie L. Leppo, Diane Davis, and Bruce Crim, "The Basics of Exercising the Mind and Body." *Childhood Education* 76 (1996): 142–147.

Corbin, Charles R., and Robert P. Pangrazi. *Physical Activity for Children: A Statement of Guidelines for Children Ages 5–12*, 2nd ed. Reston, VA: National Association for Sport and Physical Education, 2004. Available online: www.aahperd.org/naspe/template.cfm?template=ns_children.html

Crafton, Linda K. *Standards in Practice, Grades K–2*. Urbana, IL: National Council of Teachers of English, 1996.

Crinklaw-Kiser, Donna. "Integrating Music with Whole Language through the Orff-Schulwerk Process." *Young Children* 51 (July 1996): 15–21.

Cross, T. G. "Habilitating the Language-Impaired Child: Ideas from Studies of Parent–Child Interaction." *Topics in Language Disorders* 4 (1984): 1–14.

Crosser, Sandra. "Managing the Early Childhood Classroom." *Young Children* 47 (January 1992): 23–29.

Cryan, John R. "The Banning of Corporal Punishment." *Childhood Education* 63 (February 1987): 146–153.

Cuban, L. "So Much High-Tech Money Invested, So Little Use and Change in Practice: How Come?" Paper prepared for Council of Chief State School Officers Annual Technology Leadership Conference, Washington, DC, January, 2000.

Culbertson, Linda Doutt, and Mary Renck Jalongo. "'But What's Wrong with Letter Grades?' Responding to Parents' Questions about Alternative Assessment." *Childhood Education* 75 (Spring 1999): 130–135.

Cunningham, Patricia M. *Phonics They Use: Words for Reading and Writing*. New York: Addison-Wesley, 2000.

Cunningham, Patricia M., and James W. Cunningham. "What We Know about How to Teach Phonics." In *What Research Has to Say about Reading Instruction*, edited by Alan E. Farstrup and S. Jay Samuels, 87–109. Newark, DE: International Reading Association, 2002.

Cunningham, Patricia M., D. P. Hall, and M. DeFee. "Nonability Grouped, Multilevel Instruction: A Year in

a First Grade Classroom." *Reading Teacher* 44 (1991): 566–571.

Curcio, Frances R., and Susan Folkson. "Exploring Data: Kindergarten Children Do It Their Way." *Teaching Children Mathematics* 2 (February 1996): 382–385.

D'Angelo, Diane A., and C. Ralph Adler. "Chapter I: A Catalyst for Improving Parent Involvement." *Phi Delta Kappan* 72 (January 1991): 350–354.

Dahl, Karin L., Patricia L. Scharer, Lora L. Lawson, and Patricia R. Grogan. "Phonics Instruction and Student Achievement in Whole Language First-Grade Classrooms. *Reading Research Quarterly* 34 (July/August/September 1999): 312–341.

Daniels, Marilyn. "The Effect of Sign Language on Hearing Children's Language Development." *Communication Education* 43 (October 1994): 291–298.

Danoff-Burg, James A. "Be a Bee and Other Approaches to Introducing Young Children to Entomology." *Young Children* 57 (September 2002): 42–47.

Davidson, Jane, and June L. Wright. "The Potential of the Microcomputer in the Early Childhood Classroom." In *Young Children: Active Learners in a Technological Age*, edited by June L. Wright and Daniel D. Shade, 77–91. Washington, DC: National Association for the Education of Young Children, 1994.

Davis, Jessica, and Howard Gardner. "The Arts and Early Childhood Education: A Cognitive Developmental Portrait of the Young Child as Artist." In *Handbook of Research on the Education of Young Children*, edited by B. Spodek, 191–206. New York: Macmillan, 1993.

Day, Mary Carol, and Ronald K. Parker. *The Preschool in Action: Exploring Early Childhood Programs*. 2nd ed. Boston: Allyn & Bacon, 1977.

del Gaudio Weiss, Andrea. *Differential Impact of Type of Kindergarten Experience on Academic Achievement and Cost-Benefit through Grade 4: An Examination of Four Cohorts in a Large Urban School District*. School District of Philadelphia. 2002. Available online: www.phila.K12.pa.us/offices/res-eval/reports.html#2 (Retrieved August 23, 2005).

Delgado-Gaitan, Concha. "Involving Parents in Schools: A Process of Empowerment." *American Journal of Education* 100 (November 1991): 20–46.

Derman-Sparks, Louise. "Markers of Multicultural/Antibias Education." *Young Children* 54 (September 1999): 43.

Derman-Sparks, Louise, and the ABC Task Force. *Anti-Bias Curriculum: Tools for Empowering Young Children*. Washington, DC: National Association for the Education of Young Children, 1989.

Dever, Martha T., and Elizabeth J. Jared. "Remember to Include Art and Crafts in Your Integrated Curriculum." *Young Children* 51 (March 1996): 69–73.

DeVries, M. W., and A. J. Sameroff. "Culture and Temperament: Influences on Infant Temperament in Three East African Societies." *American Journal of Orthopsychiatry* 54 (1984): 83–96.

DeVries, Rheta, and Lawrence Kohlberg. *Constructivist Early Education: Overview and Comparison with Other Programs*. Washington, DC: National Association for the Education of Young Children, 1987a.

DeVries, Rheta, and Lawrence Kohlberg. *Programs of Early Education: The Constructivist View.* New York: Longman, 1987b.

DeVries, Rheta, Betty Zan, Carolyn Hildebrandt, Rebecca Edmiaston, and Christina Sales. *Developing Constructivist Early Childhood Curriculum.* New York: Teachers College Press, 2002.

Dewey, John. *The Child and the Curriculum.* Chicago: University of Chicago Press, 1902.

Dewey, John. *Democracy and Education.* New York: Free Press, 1916.

Dewey, John. *The School and Society.* New York: McClure, Phillips, 1900.

Dickinson, David K., Allyssa McCabe, and Kim Sprague. "Teacher Rating of Oral Language and Literacy (TROLL): Individualizing Early Literacy Instruction with a Standards-Based Rating Tool." *Reading Teacher* 56 (March 2003): 554–564.

Dighe, Judith, Zoy Calomiris, and Carmen Van Zutphen, "Nurturing the Language of Art in Children." *Young Children* 53 (January 1998): 4–9.

Dimidjian, Victoria Jean. "Holidays, Holy Days, and Wholly Dazed." *Young Children* 44 (September 1989): 70–75.

Dinkmeyer, D., and R. Dreikurs. *Encouraging Children to Learn.* Eric Document Reproduction Service 447391. 2000.

Ditchburn, Susan J. *Patterning Mathematical Understanding in Early Childhood.* ERIC Document Reproduction Service 218008. 1982.

Dixon, Glen T., and Patricia Tarr. "Extending Art Experiences in the Preschool Curriculum." *International Journal of Early Childhood* 20 (June 1988): 27–34.

Drew, Naomi. *Learning the Skills of Peacemaking: An Activity Guide for Elementary-Age Children on Communicating, Cooperating, Resolving Conflict.* Rolling Hills Estates, CA: Jalmar Press, 1987.

Dumtschin, Joyce Ury. "Recognize Language Development and Delay in Early Childhood." *Young Children* 43 (1988): 16–24.

Dyck, James A. "The Case for the L-Shaped Classroom. *Principal* 74 (November 1994): 41–45.

Dyer, Suzanne M., and Wendy Schiller. "'Not Wilting Flowers Again!' Problem Finding and Problem Solving in Movement and Performance." *Early Child Development and Care* 90 (May 1993): 47–54.

Dyson, Anne Haas, and Celia Genishi. *Visions of Children as Language Users: Research on Language and Language Education in Early Childhood.* Technical Report No. 49. ERIC Document Reproduction Service 335678. 1991.

Echevarria, Jana, MaryEllen Vogt, and Deborah J. Short. *Making Content Comprehensible for English Learners: The SIOP Model.* Boston: Allyn & Bacon, 2003.

Edwards, Carolyn, Lella Gandini, and George Forman, Eds. *The Hundred Languages of Children: The Reggio Emilia Approach to Early Childhood Education.* Norwood, NJ: Ablex, 1993.

Edwards, Linda C. *Affective Development and the Creative Arts: A Process Approach to Early Childhood Education.* Columbus, OH: Merrill, 1990.

Eheart, B., and R. Leavitt. "Supporting Toddler Play." *Young Children* 40 (March 1985): 18–22.

Ehri, Linnea C., and Simone R. Nunes. "The Role of Phonemic Awareness in Learning to Read." In *What Research Has to Say About Reading Instruction,* edited by A. E. Farstrup and S. Jay Samuels, 110–139. Newark, DE: International Reading Association, 2002.

Elias, Cynthia, and Laura E. Berk. "Self-Regulation in Young Children: Is There a Role for Sociodramatic Play?" *Early Childhood Research Quarterly* 17 (April 2002): 216–239.

Elicker, J., and S. Mathur. "What Do They Do All Day? Comprehensive Evaluation of a Full-day Kindergarten." *Early Childhood Research Quarterly* 12 (January 1997): 459–480.

Elkind, David. "Child Development and Early Childhood Education: Where Do We Stand Today?" In *Curriculum Planning for Young Children,* edited by Janet Brown, 4–11. Washington, DC: National Association for the Education of Young Children, 1982.

Elkind, David. *Educating Young Children in Math, Science, and Technology.* ERIC Document Reproduction Service 416993. 1998.

Elkind, David, and G. J. Whitehurst. "Forum: Young Einsteins: Much Too Early, Much Too Late." *Education Matters.* Summer 2001. Available online: www.ed matters.org.

Elkonin, D. B. "Reading in the USSR." In *Comparative Reading,* edited by J. Downing, 551–579. New York: Macmillan, 1973.

Ellis, M. "The Complexity of Objects and Peers." In *Play and Learning,* edited by Brian Sutton-Smith. New York: Gardner Press, 1979.

Engel, Brenda. *Considering Children's Art: Why and How to Value Their Works.* Washington, DC: National Association for the Education of Young Children, 1995.

Engel, Brenda. "Learning to Look: Appreciating Child Art." *Young Children* 51 (March 1996): 74–79.

Englemann, Sigfried. "How Sound Is High/Scope Research?" *Educational Leadership* 56 (June 1999): 83–84.

Epstein, Ann S. "Thinking about Art: Encouraging Art Appreciation in Early Childhood Settings." *Young Children* 56 (May 2001): 38–43.

Epstein, Joyce L. "Paths to Partnership: What We Can Learn from Federal, State, District, and School Initiatives." *Phi Delta Kappan* 72 (January 1991): 344–349.

Erikson, Erik. *Childhood and Society.* 2nd ed. New York: Norton, 1963.

Ernst, Gisela, and Kerri J. Richard. "Reading and Writing Pathways to Conversation in the ESL Classroom." *Reading Teacher* 48 (December/January 1995): 320–326.

Fallon, Irmie, and JoBeth Allen. "Where the Deer and the Cantaloupe Play." *Reading Teacher* 47 (April 1994): 546–551.

Fantuzzo, John, Yumiko Sekino, and Heather Cohen. "An Examination of the Contributions of Interactive Peer Play to Salient Classroom Competencies for Urban Head Start Children." *Psychology in the Schools* 41 (March 2004): 323–336.

Farr, Beverly P., and Elise Trumbull. *Assessment Alternatives for Diverse Classrooms*. Norwood, MA: Christopher Gordon, 1997.

Farver, Jo Ann. "Aggressive Behavior in Preschoolers' Social Networks: Do Birds of a Feather Flock Together?" *Early Childhood Research Quarterly* 11 (March 1996): 333–350.

Farver, Jo Ann, and Yoohim L. Shin. "Social Pretend Play in Korean- and Anglo-American Preschoolers." *Child Development* 68 (1997): 544–556.

Feely, Jenny. "Writing in Science." In *Science and Language Links*, edited by Johanna Scott, 27–37. Portsmouth, NH: Heinemann, 1993.

Ferreiro, Emilia, and Ana Teberosky. *Literacy before Schooling*. Portsmouth, NH: Heinemann, 1982.

Feuerstein, Abe. "School Characteristics and Parent Involvement: Influences on Participation in Children's Schools." *Journal of Educational Research* 94 (September/ October 2000): 29–41.

Findlay, Elsa. *Rhythm and Movement: Applications of Dalcroze Eurhythmics*. Evanston, IL: Summy-Birchard, 1971.

Finn, Jeremy, and Gina M. Pannozzo. "Classroom Organization and Student Behavior in Kindergarten." *Journal of Educational Research* 98 (February 2004): 79–92.

Fitzpatrik, Shannon, and Genelle Parrish. *An Integrated Fine Arts Program: Art Tells a Story about . . . Communities*. Huntington Beach, CA: Creative Teaching Press, 1995.

Flagg, A. *Rubrics, Checklists, and Other Assessments*. New York: Scholastic, 1998.

Flannery, Mary Ellen. "Turning the Tables." *NEA Today* 23 (November 2004): 36–37.

Flood, James, and Diane Lapp. "Reporting Reading Progress: A Comparison Portfolio for Parents." *Reading Teacher* 42 (March 1989): 508–514.

Foorman, Barbara R., David J. Francis, Jack M. Fletcher, and Christopher Schatschneider. "The Role of Instruction in Learning to Read: Preventing Reading Failure in At-Risk Children." *Journal of Educational Psychology* 90 (January 1998): 37–55.

Ford, Sylvia A. "The Facilitator's Role in Children's Play." *Young Children* 48 (September 1993): 66–69.

Forman, George E., and David S. Kuschner. *The Child's Construction of Knowledge: Piaget for Teaching Children*. Washington, DC: National Association for the Education of Young Children, 1983.

Fountas, Irene C., and Gay Su Pinnell. *Guided Reading: Good First Teaching for All Children*. Portsmouth, NH: Heinemann, 1996.

Fowlkes, Mary Anne. "Gifts from Childhood's Godmother—Patty Smith Hill." *Childhood Education* 61 (September/October 1984): 45–49.

Fox, Mem. *Teaching Drama to Young Children*. Portsmouth, NH: Heinemann, 1987.

Fox, Mem. "Writing Picture Books for Young Children." Speech at National Association for the Education of Young Children National Conference, New Orleans, LA, November 10, 1999.

Frank, Lawrence K. "Play Is Valid." *Childhood Education* 44 (March 1968): 433–440.

Freeman, David, and Yvonne S. Freeman. "The California Reading Initiative: A Formula for Failure for Bilingual Students?" *Language Arts* 76 (January 1999): 241–248.

French, Lucia. "Science as the Center of a Coherent, Integrated Early Childhood Curriculum." *Early Childhood Research Quarterly* 19 (January 2004): 138–149.

French, Nancy K. "Supervising Paraprofessionals: A Survey of Teacher Practices." *Journal of Special Education* 35 (Spring 2001): 41–53.

Froebel, Friedrich. *The Education of Man*. Translated by W. N. Hailmann. New York: D. Appleton, 1826.

Frost, Joe L., and Joan B. Kissinger. *The Young Child and the Educative Process*. New York: Holt, Rinehart and Winston, 1976.

Frost, Joe L., and Susan C. Wortham. "The Evolution of American Playgrounds." *Young Children* 43 (July 1988): 19–28.

Fuhr, Janet E., and Kathy H. Barclay. "The Importance of Appropriate Nutrition and Nutrition Education." *Young Children* 53 (January 1998): 74–79.

Fusaro, J. A. "The Effect of a Full-Day Kindergarten on Student Achievement: A Meta-Analysis." *Child Study Journal* 27 (1997): 269–277.

Gabbard, Carl. *Playground Apparatus Experiences and Muscular Endurance among Children 4–6*. ERIC Document Reproduction Service 288190. College Station, TX: Texas A&M University, 1979.

Gabbard, Carl. "P. E. for Preschoolers: The Right Way." *Principal* (May 1995): 21–24.

Galinsky, Ellen. "Parents and Teacher-Caregivers: Sources of Tension, Sources of Support." *Young Children* 43 (March 1988): 4–12.

Gallagher, Kathleen C. "Brain Research and Early Childhood Development: A Primer for Developmentally Appropriate Practice." *Young Children* 60 (July 2005): 12–20.

Gallahue, David L. *Fundamental Movement Experiences for Children: A Developmental Skill Theme Approach*. ERIC Document Reproduction Service 211459. 1981.

Gandini, Lella. "Fundamentals of the Reggio Emilia Approach to Early Childhood Education." *Young Children* 49 (November 1993): 4–8.

Gardner, Howard. "The First Seven . . . and the Eighth." *Educational Leadership* 55 (January 1997a): 8–14.

Gardner, Howard. *Frames of Mind: The Theory of Multiple Intelligences*. New York: HarperCollins, 1983.

Gardner, H. "The Key in the Key Slot: Creativity in a Chinese Key." *Journal of Cognitive Education* 6 (1997b): 15–26.

Gardner, Howard. "The Understanding Pathway." *Educational Leadership* 57 (March 1999): 12–15.

Garrison, C. G. *Permanent Play Materials for Young Children*. New York: Scribner's, 1926.

Gartrell, Dan. "Assertive Discipline: Unhealthy for Children and Other Living Things." *Young Children* 42 (January 1987a): 10–11.

Gartrell, Dan. "Misbehavior or Mistaken Behavior?" *Young Children* 50 (July 1995): 27–34.

Gartrell, Dan. "Punishment or Guidance?" *Young Children* 42 (March 1987b): 55–61.

Gartrell, Daniel. "Replacing Time-Out: Part I—Using Guidance to Build an Encouraging Classroom." *Young Children* 56 (November 2001): 8–16.

Gartrell, Daniel. "Replacing Time-Out: Part II—Using Guidance to Maintain an Encouraging Classroom." *Young Children* 57 (March 2002): 36–43.

Garvey, Catherine. *Play*. Cambridge, MA: Harvard University Press, 1977.

Geist, Eugene, and Angela C. Baum. "'Yeah, Buts' That Keep Teachers from Embracing an Active Curriculum: Overcoming the Resistance." *Young Children* 60 (July 2003): 28–34.

Gelman, Rochel, and Marsha F. Tucker. "Further Investigations of the Young Child's Conception of Number." *Child Development* 46 (March 1975): 167–175.

Gerson, Bev. "Implementing the Reggio Emilia Curriculum at Salem State Preschool." Presentation at Salem State College, Salem, MA, April 3, 2000.

Gfeller, Kate. "Integrating the Handicapped Child into Music Activities." In *Musical Growth and Development: Birth through Six*, edited by Dorothy T. McDonald and Gene M. Simons, 113–140. New York: Schirmer Books, 1989.

Giangreco, Michael, Susan Yuan, Barbara McKenzie, Patricia Cameron, and Janice Fialka. "Be Careful What You Wish for: Five Reasons to Be Concerned about the Assignment of Individual Paraprofessionals." *Teaching Exceptional Children* 37 (May 2005): 26–34.

Gilbert, Jean. *Musical Starting Points with Young Children*. London, England: Ward Lock Educational, 1981.

Giles, Jessica, and Gail D. Heyman. "Young Children's Beliefs about the Relationship between Gender and Aggressive Behavior." *Child Development* 78 (January/February 2005): 107–121.

Ginott, Haim G. *Teacher and Child*. New York: Macmillan, 1972.

Girolametto, Luigi, Lisa Hoaken, Elaine Weitzman, and Riet van Lieshout. "Patterns of Adult–Child Linguistic Interaction in Integrated Day Care Groups." *Language, Speech, and Hearing Services in Schools* 31 (April 2000): 155–168.

Glasser, William. "A New Look at School Failure and School Success." *Phi Delta Kappan* 78 (April 1997): 597–602.

Glasser, William. "School Violence from the Perspective of William Glasser." *Professional School Counseling* 4 (December 2000): 77–81.

Gober, Billy E., and B. Don Franks. "Physical and Fitness Education of Young Children." *Journal of Physical Education, Recreation, and Dance* 59 (September 1988): 57–61.

Gochman, David S., and T. F. Saucier. "Perceived Vulnerability in Children and Adolescents." *Health Education Quarterly* 9 (1982): 46–59.

Goffin, Stacie G., and Catherine S. Wilson. *Curriculum Models and Early Childhood Education: Appraising the Relationship*. Columbus, OH: Merrill, 2001.

Goldberg, Ellie. "Including Children with Chronic Health Conditions: Nebulizers in the Classroom." *Young Children* 49 (January 1994): 34–37.

Goldberg, Merryl. *Arts and Learning: An Integrated Approach to Teaching and Learning in Multicultural and Multilingual Settings*. New York: Longman, 2001.

Goodman, Kenneth. *On Reading: A Common-Sense Look at the Nature of Language and the Science of Reading*. Portsmouth, NH: Heinemann, 1996.

Goodman, Kenneth, E. Brooks Smith, Robert Meredith, and Yetta Goodman. *Language and Thinking in School*. 3rd ed. New York: Richard C. Owen, 1987.

Goodman, Yetta. "Children Coming to Know Literacy." In *Emergent Literacy: Writing and Reading*, edited by W. H. Teale and E. Sulzby, 1–14, Norwood, NJ: Ablex Publishing Company, 1986.

Goodman, Yetta. "Kidwatching: Observing Children in the Classroom." In *Observing the Language Learner*, edited by Angela Jaggar and M. Trika Smith-Burke. Newark, DE: International Reading Association/National Council of Teachers of English, 1985.

Goodman, Yetta, and Carolyn Burke. *Reading Strategies: Focus on Comprehension*. Katonah, NY: Richard C. Owen, 1980.

Goodman, Yetta, and A. M. Marek. *Retrospective Miscue Analysis: Revaluing Readers and Reading*. Katonah, NY: Richard C. Owens, 1996.

Gordon, Ann, and Kathryn W. Browne. *Guiding Young Children in a Diverse Society*. Boston: Allyn & Bacon, 1996.

Gowen, Jean W. "The Early Development of Symbolic Play." *Young Children* 50 (March 1995): 75–84.

Grangaard, E. M. *Color and Light Effects on Learning*. ERIC Document Reproduction Service 382381. 1995.

Graves, Donald. *A Fresh Look at Writing*. Portsmouth, NH: Heinemann, 1994.

Graves, Donald. Presentation at a conference of the International Reading Association, Atlanta, Georgia, May 1990.

Graves, Donald, and Virginia Stuart. *Write from the Start*. New York: New American Library, 1985.

Green, Connie R. "This Is My Name." *Childhood Education* 74 (Summer 1998): 226–231.

Greenwood, Deborah. "Home-School Communication via Video." *Young Children* 50 (September 1995): 66.

Grubb, Norton. "Young Children Face the State Issues and Options for Early Childhood Programs." *American Journal of Education* 97 (August 1989): 358–397.

Halliday, M. A. K. "Three Aspects of Children's Language Development: Learning Language, Learning through Language, Learning about Language." In *Oral and Written Language Development Research: Impact on the Schools*, edited by Y. Goodman, M. Haussler, and D. Strickland. Urbana, IL: National Council of Teachers of English, 1982.

Hampton, Fredrick M., and Dawne A. Mumford. "Parent Involvement in Inner-City Schools." *Urban Education* 33 (September 1998): 410–428.

Harding, Nadine. "Family Journals: The Bridge from School to Home and Back Again." *Young Children* 51 (January 1996): 27–30.

Hardman, Michael L., et al. *Human Exceptionality: Society, School, and Family*. 4th ed. Boston: Allyn & Bacon, 1993.

Harlan, Jean. *Science Experiences for the Early Childhood Years*. 2nd ed. Columbus, OH: Merrill, 1980.

Harms, Thelma. "Evaluating Settings for Learning." *Young Children* 25 (May 1970): 304–309.

Harp, B. *Handbook of Literacy Assessment and Evaluation*. Norwood, MA: Christopher-Gordon, 1996.

Harp, Bill. *The Handbook of Literacy Assessment and Evaluation*. Norwood, MA: Christopher-Gordon, 2006.

Harp, Bill, and Jo Ann Brewer. *Reading and Writing: Teaching for the Connections*. Fort Worth, TX: Harcourt Brace, 1996.

Harste, J., V. Woodward, and C. Burke. *Language Stories and Literacy Lessons*. Portsmouth, NH: Heinemann, 1984.

Hartup, W. *Having Friends, Making Friends, and Keeping Friends: Relationships as Educational Contexts*. ERIC Document Reproduction Service ED34584. 1992.

Hathaway, Warren. "Effects of School Lighting on Physical Development and School Performance." *Education Canada* 33 (April 1993): 34–41.

Hatkoff, Amy. "Safety and Children: How Schools Can Help." *Childhood Education* 70 (Annual Theme 1994): 283–288.

Haugland, Susan W. "What Role Should Technology Play in Young Children's Learning? Part 1." *Young Children* 54 (June 1999): 26–31.

Haugland, Susan W. "What Role Should Technology Play in Young Children's Learning? Part II. Early Childhood Classrooms in the 21st Century: Using Computers to Maximize Learning." *Young Children* 54 (July 2000): 12–18.

Healy, J. M. *Endangered Minds*. New York: Simon & Schuster, 2000.

Healy, Jane M. "Young Children Don't Need Computers." *Principal* 82 (May/June 2003): 64.

Heath, Harriet E. "Dealing with Difficult Behaviors—Teachers Plan with Parents." *Young Children* 49 (July 1994): 20–24.

Hektner, Joel M., Gerald J. August, and George M. Realmuto. "Patterns and Temporal Changes in Peer Affiliation among Aggressive and Nonaggressive Children Participating in a Summer School Program." *Journal of Clinical Child Psychology* 29 (2000): 603–615.

Helm, Judy Harris, Sallee Beneke, and Kathy Steinheimer. "Documenting Young Children's Learning." *Childhood Education* 73 (April 1997): 200–205.

Henderson, Anne T., and Nancy Berla. *A New Generation of Evidence: The Family is Critical to Student Achievement*. Washington, DC. ERIC Document Reproduction Service 375968. 1994.

Herlein, Woodie S. "Teaching Tips for Learning Centers: Providing a Safe and Educational Outdoor Environment." *NHSA Journal* (Summer/Fall 1995): 41–45.

Herr, Judith, and Winifred Morse. "Food for Thought: Nutrition Education for Young Children." *Young Children* 39 (November 1982): 3–11.

Hester, Hilary. "Peer Interaction in Learning English as a Second Language." *Theory into Practice* 26 (1987): 208–217.

Heyman, Mark. *Places and Spaces: Environmental Psychology in Education*. Fastback no. 112. Bloomington, IN: Phi Delta Kappa Educational Foundation, 1978.

Hiebert, Elfrieda H., et al. *Every Child a Reader: Applying Reading Research in the Classroom*. Ann Arbor: Center for the Improvement of Early Reading Achievement, University of Michigan School of Education, 1998.

Hildebrandt, Carolyn. "Creativity in Music and Early Childhood." *Young Children* 53 (November 1998): 68–74.

Hill, Bonnie C., and Cynthia Ruptic. *Practical Aspects of Authentic Assessment: Putting the Pieces Together*. Norwood, MA: Christopher Gordon, 1994.

Hill, Bonnie C., Cynthia Ruptic, and Lisa Norwick. *Classroom Based Assessment*. Norwood, MA: Christopher Gordon, 1998.

Hill, Carol B. *Creating a Learning Climate for the Early Childhood Years*. Fastback no. 292. Bloomington, IN: Phi Delta Kappa Educational Foundation, 1989.

Hill, David. "Order in the Classroom." *Teacher Magazine* (April 1990): 70–77.

Hill, Patty Smith. "The Home and the School as Centers of Child Life." *Progressive Education* 5 (July/August/September 1982): 211–216.

Hill, Patty Smith. "The Function of the Kindergarten." *Young Children* 42 (July 1987): 12–19. (Originally published in 1926)

Hill, Patty Smith. *Kindergarten*. ERIC Document Reproduction Service ED346995. 1992.

Hirsch, Elisabeth S., ed. *The Block Book*. Rev. ed. Washington, DC: National Association for the Education of Young Children, 1984.

Hitz, Randy. "Assertive Discipline: A Response to Lee Canter." *Young Children* 43 (January 1988): 25–26.

Hoffman, James, Patricia M. Cunningham, James W. Cunningham, and Hallie Yopp. *Phonemic Awareness and the Teaching of Reading*. Newark, DE: International Reading Association, 1998.

Hohmann, Mary, Bernard Banet, and David P. Weikart. *Young Children in Action*. Ypsilanti, MI: High/Scope Press, 1979.

Hohmann, Mary, and David P. Weikart. *Educating Young Children: Active Learning Practices for Preschool and Child Care Programs*. Ypsilanti, MI: High/Scope Educational Research Foundation, 1995.

Holt, Bess-Gene. *Science with Young Children*. Rev. ed. Washington, DC: National Association for the Education of Young Children, 1989.

Honig, Alice Sterling. "Compliance, Control, and Discipline." *Young Children* 40 (January 1985): 50–58.

Hough, D., and S. Bryde. "The Effects of Full-Day Kindergarten on Student Achievement and Affect." Paper presented at annual conference of American Educational Research Association, New York. ERIC Document Reproduction Service 395691. 1996.

Hough, Ruth A., Joanne R. Nurss, and M. S. Goodson. "Children in Day Care: An Observational Study." *Child Study Journal* 14 (1984): 31–46.

Hough, Ruth A., Joanne R. Nurss, and Dolores Wood. "Tell Me a Story: Making Opportunities for Elaborated Language in Early Childhood Classrooms." *Young Children* 43 (1987): 6–12.

Hubbard, Ruth S. "Creating a Classroom Where Children Can Think." *Young Children* 53 (September 1998): 26–31.

Huber, Linda K. "Making the Most of Multicultural Materials." *Early Childhood Today* 19 (November/December 2004): 3.

Huffman, Amy B. "Beyond the Weather Chart: Weathering New Experiences." *Young Children* 51 (July 1996): 34–37.

Hunt, J. McVicker. *Intelligence and Experience.* New York: Ronald Press, 1961.

Ilg, Frances L., and Louise B. Ames. *The Gesell Institute's Child Behavior.* New York: Dell, 1955.

International Reading Association. *Standards for Reading Professionals–Revised 2003.* Newark, DE: 2004. Available online: www.reading.org/resources/issues/reports/professional_standards.html.

International Reading Association (IRA)/National Association of Educators of Young Children. Joint Position Statement. "Learning to Read and Write: Developmentally Appropriate Practices for Young Children." *Reading Teacher* 52 (October 1998): 193–215.

International Reading Association (IRA)/National Council of Teachers of English (NCTE). *Standards for the English Language Arts.* Newark, DE: IRA; Urbana, IL: NCTE. 1996. Available online: www.ncte.org/about/over/standards/110846.htm.

Irwin, D. Michelle, and M. Margaret Bushnell. *Observational Strategies for Child Study.* New York: Holt, Rinehart and Winston, 1980.

Isaacs, A. C., and W. M. Carroll. "Strategies for Basic-Fact Instruction." *Teaching Children Mathematics* 5 (1999): 505–508.

Isbell, Rebecca. "Telling and Retelling Stories: Learning Language and Literacy." In *Spotlight on Young Children and Language,* edited by Derry Koralek, 18–22. Washington, DC: National Association for the Education of Young Children, 2003.

Isbell, Rebecca, and Betty Exelby. *Early Learning Environments That Work.* Beltsville, MD: Gryphon House, 2001.

Isbell, Rebecca, and Shirley Raines. "Young Children's Oral Language Production in Three Types of Play Centers." *Journal of Research in Childhood Education* 5 (Spring/ Summer 1991): 140–146.

Isenberg, Joan, and Mary Renck Jalongo. *Creative Expression and Play in the Early Childhood Curriculum.* New York: Macmillan, 1993.

Isenberg, Joan, and Nancy Quisenberry. "Play: A Necessity for All Children." *Childhood Education* 64 (February 1988): 138–145.

Isenberg, Joan, and Teresa Rosegrant. "Children and Technology." In *Selecting Educational Equipment and Materials for School and Home,* edited by Joan Moyer, 25–29. Wheaton, MD: Association for Childhood Education International, 1995.

Ivey, Bill. "The Arts Are Basic." *Teaching Music* 6 (June 1999): 56–57.

Jacobs, Heidi Hayes, ed. *Interdisciplinary Curriculum: Design and Implementation.* Washington, DC: Association for Supervision and Curriculum Development, 1989.

Jacobson, Linda. "Debate Continues over Head Start Assessment." *Education Week* 23 (March 10, 2004).

Jaggar, Angela. "Allowing for Language Differences." In *Discovering Language with Children,* edited by Gay Su Pinnell. Urbana, IL: National Council of Teachers of English, 1980.

Jaggar, Angela, and M. Trika Smith-Burke, eds. *Observing the Language Learner.* Newark, DE: International Reading Association/National Council of Teachers of English, 1985.

Jalongo, Mary Renck. "Using Recorded Music with Young Children: A Guide for Nonmusicians." *Young Children* 51 (July 1996): 6–13.

Jalongo, Mary Renck, and Mitzie Collins. "Singing with Young Children! Folk Singing for Nonmusicians." *Young Children* 40 (January 1985): 17–21.

Jaques-Dalcroze, Emile. *Rhythm, Music and Education.* Translated by L. F. Rubenstein. London, England: Hazell Watson and Viney Ltd. for the Dalcroze Society, 1921.

Jensen, Eric. *Teaching with the Brain in Mind.* Alexandria, VA: Association for Supervision and Curriculum Development, 1998.

Johns, Kenneth M., and C. Espinoza. *Management Strategies for Culturally Diverse Classrooms.* Fastback #396. Bloomington, IN: Phi Delta Kappa Educational Foundation, 1996.

Johnston, Lynne, and Joy Mermin. "Easing Children's Entry to School: Home Visits Help." *Young Children* 49 (July 1995): 62–68.

Jones, Elizabeth. "Inviting Children into the Fun: Providing Enough Activity Choices Outdoors." *Child Care Information Exchange* 70 (December 1989): 15–19.

Jones, Elizabeth, and John Nimmo. *Emergent Curriculum.* Washington, DC: National Association for the Education of Young Children, 1994.

Jones, Hazel A., and Steven F. Warren. "Enhancing Engagement in Early Language Teaching." *Teaching Exceptional Children* 23 (Summer 1991): 48–50.

Jones, Rebecca. "Involving Parents Is a Whole New Game: Be Sure You Win!" *American School Board Journal* 88 (September 2001): 18–22.

Jones, Vernon F., and Louise S. Jones. *Comprehensive Classroom Management: Motivating and Managing Students.* 3rd ed. Boston: Allyn & Bacon, 1990.

Kamii, Constance. *Number in Preschool and Kindergarten.* Washington, DC: National Association for the Education of Young Children, 1982.

Kamii, Constance, and Georgia DeClark. *Young Children Reinvent Arithmetic: Implications of Piaget's Theory.* New York: Teachers College Press, 1985.

Kamii, Constance, and Rheta DeVries. *Physical Knowledge in Preschool Education.* Englewood Cliffs, NJ: Prentice-Hall, 1978.

Kamii, Constance, and Rheta DeVries. *Physical Knowledge in Preschool Education: Implications of Piaget's Theory.* Rev. ed. Englewood Cliffs, NJ: Prentice-Hall, 1993.

Kamii, Constance, and Linda Joseph. *Young Children Continue to Reinvent Arithmetic—2nd Grade: Implications of Piaget's Theory.* New York: Teachers College Press, 1989.

Kamii, Constance, and Mieko Kamii. "Why Achievement Testing Should Stop." In *Achievement Testing in the*

Early Grades: The Games Grown-Ups Play, edited by Constance Kamii, 15–39. Washington, DC: National Association for the Education of Young Children, 1990.

Katz, Lilian. "Engaging Children's Minds: The Implications of Research for Early Childhood Education." In *A Resource Guide to Public School Early Childhood Programs*, edited by Cynthia Warger. Alexandria, VA: Association for Supervision and Curriculum Development, 1988.

Katz, Lilian. Keynote speech. Oregon Association of School Administrators Conference of Kindergarten Teachers and Elementary Principals, Salem, Oregon, 1986.

Katz, Lilian. *More Talks with Teachers*. Urbana, IL: ERIC Clearinghouse on Elementary and Early Childhood Education, 1984.

Katz, Lilian. "The Professional Early Childhood Teacher." *Young Children* 39 (September 1984): 3–10.

Katz, Lilian, and Sylvia C. Chard. *Engaging Children's Minds: The Project Approach*. Norwood, NJ: Ablex, 1989.

Katz, Lilian, and Diane E. McClellan. *Fostering Children's Social Competence: The Teacher's Role*. Washington, DC: National Association for the Education of Young Children, 1997.

Keller, Bess. "Parent Communication." *Education Week* 23 (May 5, 2004): 34.

Kellogg, Rhoda. *Analyzing Children's Art*. Palo Alto, CA: National Press Books, 1970.

Kennedy, David K. "After Reggio Emilia: May the Conversation Begin!" *Young Children* 51 (July 1996): 24–27.

Kent, Judith F., and Jennie Rakestraw. "The Role of Computers in Functional Language: A Tale of Two Writers." *Journal of Computing in Childhood Education* 5 (1994): 329–337.

Kieff, Judith. "Preferences of Mothers of At Risk and Peer Model Children for Parent Involvement Strategies." Doctoral dissertation, Oregon State University, 1990.

Kieff, Judith, and Renee Casbergue. *Playful Learning and Teaching: Integrating Play into Preschool and Primary Programs*. Boston: Allyn & Bacon, 2000.

Kieff, Judith, and Karyn Wellhousen. "Planning Family Involvement in Early Childhood Programs." *Young Children* 55 (May 2000): 18–25.

Kilmer, Sally J., and Helenmarie Hofman. "Transforming Science Curriculum." In *Reaching Potentials: Transforming Early Childhood Curriculum and Assessment*, vol. 2, edited by S. Bredekamp and T. Rosegrant, 43–63. Washington, DC: National Association for the Education of Young Children, 1995.

King, Margaret, and Dan Gartrell. "Building an Encouraging Classroom with Boys in Mind." *Young Children* 58 (July 2003): 33–37.

King, Martha L. "Language: Insights from Acquisition." *Theory Into Practice* 26 (1987): 358–363.

Kingsbury, Nancy M., and Joan C. Hall. "Provision of a Health Education Program for Preschoolers: A Demonstration Project Using Volunteers." *Early Childhood Development and Care* 36 (July 1988): 91–100.

Klesius, Janell P., and Priscilla L. Griffith. "Interactive Storybook Reading for At-Risk Learners." *Reading Teacher* 49 (April 1996): 552–590.

Koff, Susan R. "Toward a Definition of Dance Education." *Childhood Education* 77 (Fall 2000): 27–31.

Kohn, Alfie. *The Schools Our Children Deserve: Moving beyond Traditional Classrooms and "Tougher Standards."* Boston: Houghton Mifflin, 1999.

Kokoski, Teresa M., and Nancy Downing-Leffler. "Boosting Your Science and Math Programs in Early Childhood Education: Making the Home-School Connection." *Young Children* 50 (July 1995): 35–39.

Kostelnik, Marjorie, Laura Stein, Alice P. Whiren, and Anne K. Soderman. *Guiding Children's Social Development*. 2nd ed. Albany, NY: Delmar, 1993.

Kozol, Jonathan. *The Shame of the Nation: The Restoration of Apartheid Schooling in America*. New York: Crown, 2005.

Krajcik, Joseph S., Charlene M. Czerniak, and Carl Berger. *Teaching Children Science: A Project-Based Approach*. Boston: McGraw-Hill, 1999.

Kramer, Rita. *Maria Montessori: A Biography*. New York: G. P. Putnam's Sons, 1976.

Krashen, Stephen. "Looking for Bilingual Answers." *American Language Review* 4 (January/February 2000a): 16–19.

Krashen, Stephen D. *Second Language Acquisition and Second Language Learning*. New York: Pergamon Press, 1981.

Krashen, Stephen D. *Three Arguments against Whole Language and Why They Are Wrong*. Portsmouth, NH: Heinemann, 1999.

Krashen, Stephen. "What Does It Take to Acquire Language?" *ESL Magazine* 3 (May/June 2000b): 22–23.

Kratcoski, Annette Manning, and Karyn Bobkoff Katz. "Conversing with Young Language Learners in the Classroom." *Young Children* 53 (May 1998): 30–33.

Krechevsky, M. *Project Spectrum: Preschool Assessment Handbook*. New York: Teachers College Press, 1998.

Kreidler, William J. *Teaching Conflict Resolution through Children's Literature*. New York: Scholastic, 1994.

Kritchevsky, Sybil, and Elizabeth Prescott. *Planning Environments for Young Children: Physical Space*. Washington, DC: National Association for the Education of Young Children, 1969.

Kuehn, Christine. "Inventing: Creative Sciencing." *Childhood Education* 65 (Fall 1988): 5–7.

Labinowicz, Ed. *The Piaget Primer: Thinking, Learning, Teaching*. Menlo Park, CA: Addison-Wesley, 1980.

Langone, John, D. Michael Malone, and Tina Kinsley. "Solutions for Young Children with Developmental Concerns." *Infants and Young Children* 16 (April 1999): 65–78.

Lasky, E. Z., and K. Klopp. "Parent-Child Interactions in Normal and Language-Disordered Children." *Journal of Speech and Hearing Disorders* 47 (1982): 7–18.

Leatzow, Nancy, Carol Neuhauser, and Liz Wilmes. *Creating Discipline in the Early Childhood Classroom*. Provo, UT: Brigham Young University Press, 1983.

Leff, S. S., T. J. Power, P. H. Manz, T. E. Costigan, and L. A. Nabors. "School-Based Aggression Prevention Programs for Young Children: Current Status and Implications for Violence Prevention." *School Psychology Review* 30 (2001): 344–363.

Leitch, M. Laurie, and Sandra S. Tangri. "Barriers to Home–School Collaboration." *Educational Horizons* 66 (Winter 1988): 70–74.

Lenters, Kimberly. "No Half Measures: Reading Instruction for Young Second-Language Learners." *Reading Teacher* 58 (December/January 2005): 328–336.

Leonard, Ann Marie. *I Spy Something! A Practical Guide to Classroom Observations of Young Children.* Little Rock, AR: Southern Early Childhood Association, 1997.

Leppo, Marjorie L. *Healthy from the Start: New Perspectives on Childhood Fitness.* Teacher Education Monograph 15. ERIC Document Reproduction Service 352357. 1993.

Levin, Diane E. "Beyond Banning War and Superhero Play: Meeting Children's Needs in Violent Times." *Young Children* 58 (May 2003): 60–63.

Levin, I., F. Wilkening, and Y. Dembo. "Development of Time Quantification: Integration of Beginnings and Endings in Comparing Durations." *Child Development* 55 (1984): 2160–2172.

Levine-Epstein, Marcy. "What Happens When Students Take the Lead in Parent Conferences?" *Pro Principal* 16 (November 2003): 1–2.

Lewis, Anne C. "Hi Ho, Hi Ho, It's Off to Tests We Go." *Phi Delta Kappan* 84 (2003): 483–484.

Lillard, Paula P. *Montessori: A Modern Approach.* New York: Schocken Books, 1972.

Lindfors, Judith Wells. *Children's Language and Learning.* Englewood Cliffs, NJ: Prentice-Hall, 1980.

Lino, Mark, Peter Basiotis, Shirley A. Gerrior, and Andrea Carlson. "The Quality of Young Children's Diets." *Family Economics and Nutrition Review* (2002): 52–62.

Loomis, Catherine, and Jane Wagner. "A Different Look at Challenging Behavior." *Young Children* 60 (March 2005): 94–99.

Love, Ida H., and Daniel Levine. *Performance Ratings of Teacher Aides with and without Training and Follow-Up in Extending Reading Instruction.* ERIC Document Reproduction Service 349294. 1992.

Lowenfeld, Viktor, and W. Lambert Brittain. *Creative and Mental Growth.* 7th ed. New York: Macmillan, 1982.

Lowenthal, Barbara. "Teaching Social Skills to Preschoolers with Special Needs." *Childhood Education* 72 (Spring 1996): 137–140.

Lowenthal, Barbara. "Useful Early Childhood Assessment: Play-Based, Interviews and Multiple Intelligences." *Early Child Development and Care* 129 (February 1997): 43–49.

Luke, Jennifer L., and Catherine M. Myers. "Toward Peace: Using Literature to Aid Conflict Resolution." *Childhood Education* 71 (Winter 1994/1995): 66–69.

Lund, Kathryn A., and Candace S. Bos. "Orchestrating the Preschool Classroom: The Daily Schedule." *Teaching Exceptional Children* 14 (December 1981): 120–125.

Lundberg, Ingvar, Jergen Frost, and Ole-Peter Petersen. "Effects of an Extensive Program for Stimulating Pho-

nological Awareness in Preschool Children." *Reading Research Quarterly* 23 (Summer 1988): 263–284.

Lunzer, E. "Intellectual Development in the Play of Young Children." *Educational Review* 11 (1959): 205–217.

Lyon, G. Reid. "Overview of Reading and Literacy Initiatives." Statement to Committee on Labor and Human Resources. Washington, DC: National Institutes of Health, 1998.

Lyons, John B. "Do School Facilities Really Impact a Child's Education?" University of Georgia, College of Education. 2001. Available online: www.coe.uga.edu/sdpl/articlesandpapers/lyons/html (Retrieved May 21, 2005).

Machen, Sandra M., Janell D. Wilson, and Charles E. Notar. "Parental Involvement in the Classroom." *Journal of Instructional Psychology* 32 (January 2005): 13–17.

Madsen, Nancy. "Diversity in Music Education." *Illinois Music Educator* (Winter 2004): 50–51.

Malaguzzi, Loris. "For an Education Based on Relationships." *Young Children* 49 (November 1993): 9–12.

Malina, R. M. "Motor Development in the Early Years." In *The Young Child: Reviews of Research*, vol. 3, edited by S. G. Moore and C. R. Cooper, 11–229. Washington, DC: National Association for the Education of Young Children, 1982.

Malkusak, Tony, Jean Schappet, and Bruya Lawrence. "Turning Accessible Playgrounds into Fully Integrated Playgrounds: Just Add a Little Essence." *Parks and Recreation* 37 (May 2002): 66–71.

Marantz, Mady. "Fostering Prosocial Behavior in the Early Childhood Classroom: Review of the Research." *Journal of Moral Education* 17 (January 1988): 27–39.

Marchand, Nancy E., and Robert J. McDermott. "'Mouse Calls': A Storytelling Approach to Teaching First Aid Skills to Young Children." *Journal of School Health* 56 (December 1986): 453–454.

Marcon, Rebecca A. "Positive Relationships between Parent School Involvement and Public School Inner City Preschoolers' Development and Academic Performance." *School Psychology Review* 28 (1999): 395–413.

Marion, Marian. "Guiding Young Children's Understanding and Management of Anger." *Young Children* 52 (November 1997): 62–67.

Martin, Anne. "Teachers and Teaching." *Harvard Educational Review* 58 (November 1988): 488–501.

Martin, Bill, Jr. "Celebrating Language." Seminar sponsored by the School of Education, Oregon State University, Corvallis, Oregon, Summer 1986.

Martin, Sue. *Developmentally Appropriate Evaluation: Convincing Students and Teachers of the Importance of Observation as Appropriate Evaluation of Children.* ERIC Document Reproduction Service 391601. 1996.

Marxen, Carol E. "Push, Pull, Toss, Tilt, Swing: Physics for Young Children." *Childhood Education* 71 (Summer 1995): 212–216.

Maslow, Abraham H. *Motivation and Personality.* New York: Harper and Row, 1954.

Mayeux, Lara, and Antonius H. N. Cillessen. "Development of Social Problem-Solving in Early Childhood: Stability, Change, and Association with Social

Competency." *Journal of Genetic Psychology* 164 (February 2003): 153–173.

McAfee, Oralie, and Deborah Leong. *Assessing and Guiding Young Children's Development and Learning.* 2nd ed. Boston: Allyn & Bacon, 1997.

McArdle, F. "Art in Early Childhood: The Discourse of 'Proper' Teaching." Doctoral dissertation, Queensland University of Technology, Brisbane, 2001.

McCarthy, Jan. "Reggio Emilia: What Is the Message for Early Childhood Education?" *Contemporary Education* 66 (Spring 1995): 139–142.

McClintic, Susan V. "Conservation—A Meaningful Gauge for Assessment." *Arithmetic Teacher* 35 (February 1988): 12–14.

McCracken, Janet B. *Valuing Diversity: The Primary Years.* Washington, DC: National Association for the Education of Young Children, 1993.

McDonald, Dorothy T. *Music in Our Lives: The Early Years.* Washington, DC: National Association for the Education of Young Children, 1979.

McDonald, Dorothy T., and Gene M. Simons. *Musical Growth and Development: Birth through Six.* New York: Schirmer Books, 1989.

McGregor, Lynn, Maggie Tate, and Ken Robinson. *Learning through Drama.* Portsmouth, NH: Heinemann, 1987.

McIntyre, Margaret. *Early Childhood and Science.* Washington, DC: National Science Teachers Association, 1984.

McNeely, S. L. *Observing Students and Teachers through Objective Strategies.* Boston: Allyn & Bacon, 1997.

McNeill, David. "Developmental Psycholinguistics." In *The Genesis of Language,* edited by Frank Smith and George Miller. Cambridge, MA: MIT Press, 1966.

McQuillan, Jeff. *The Literacy Crisis: False Claims, Real Solutions.* Portsmouth, NH: Heinemann, 1998.

McWayne, Christine, Virginia Hampton, John Fantuzzo, Heather Cohen, and Yumko Sekino. "A Multivariate Examination of Parent Involvement and the Social and Academic Competence of Urban Kindergarten Children." *Psychology in the Schools* 41 (March 2004): 363–377.

Meisels, Samuel J. "Should We Test 4-Year-Olds?" *Pediatrics* 113 (May 2004): 1401–1402.

Meisels, Samuel J. "Uses and Abuses of Developmental Screening and School Readiness Testing." *Young Children* 42 (January 1987): 4–6, 68–73.

Meisels, Samuel J., et al. "New Evidence for the Effectiveness of the Early Screening Inventory." *Early Childhood Research Quarterly* 8 (September 1993): 327–346.

Meisels, Samuel J., Fong-Ruey Liaw, Aviva Dorfman, and Regena F. Nelson. "The Work Sampling System: Reliability and Validity of a Performance Assessment for Young Children." *Early Childhood Research Quarterly* 10 (1995): 277–296.

Meriwether, Linda. "Math at the Snack Table." *Young Children* 52 (July 1997): 69–73.

Merrion, Margaret Dee, and Marilyn Curt Vincent. *A Primer on Music for Non-Musician Educators.* Fastback 270. Bloomington, IN: Phi Delta Kappa Educational Foundation, 1988.

Micklo, Stephen J. "Math Portfolios in the Primary Grades." *Childhood Education* 73 (Summer 1997): 194–199.

Midjaas, C. L. "Use of Space." In *Instructional Leadership Handbook,* edited by J. W. Keefe and J. M. Jenkins. Reston, VA: National Association of Secondary School Principals, 1984.

Miller, Cheri Sterman. "Building Self-Control: Discipline for Young Children." *Young Children* 40 (November 1984): 15–19.

Miller, S. "The Facilitation of Fundamental Motor Skill Learning in Young Children." Doctoral dissertation, Michigan State University, 1978.

Million, June. "Getting Teachers Set for Parent Conferences." *Communicator* (National Association of Elementary School Principals) 28 (February 2005): 5–6.

Mitchell, Anne, and Judy David. *Explorations with Young Children: A Curriculum Guide from the Bank Street College of Education.* Mt. Rainier, MD: Gryphon, 1992.

Mitchell, Lucy S. "Making Young Geographers Instead of Teaching Geography." *Progressive Education* 5 (July/August/September 1928): 217–223.

Monroe, Eula E., and Robert Panchyshyn. "Vocabulary Considerations for Teaching Mathematics." *Childhood Education* 72 (Winter 1994/1995): 80–83.

Montessori, Maria. *Dr. Montessori's Own Handbook.* New York: Frederick A. Stokes, 1914.

Mooney, Margaret E. *Reading to, with, and by Children.* Katonah, NY: Richard C. Owen, 1990.

Moore, Margaret A., Peggy L. Hart, and Peggy Daisey. "Making the Science Literacy Connection: After-School Science Clubs." *Childhood Education* 80 (Summer 2004): 180–186.

Morrow, Lesley M., and Muriel K. Rand. "Promoting Literacy During Play by Designing Early Childhood Classroom Environments." *Reading Teacher* 44 (February 1991): 396–402.

Murray, Paula L., and Richard E. Mayer. "Preschool Children's Judgments of Number Magnitude." *Journal of Educational Psychology* 80 (June 1988): 206–209.

Murata, Nathan M., and Julienne K. Maeda. "Structured Play for Preschoolers with Developmental Delays." *Early Childhood Education Journal* 29 (Summer 2002): 237–240.

Music Educators National Conference (MENC). *Opportunity-to-Learn Standards for Music Instruction: Grades PreK–12.* Reston, VA: Author, 1999. Available online: www.menc.org/publication/books/techstan.htm.

Music Educators National Conference (MENC). *The School Music Program: A New Vision.* Reston, VA: Author, 1994. Available online: www.menc.org/publication/books/prek12st.html.

Music Educators National Conference (MENC). *The Value and Quality of Arts Education: A Statement of Principles.* Reston, VA: Author, January 1999. Available online: www.menc.org/information/prek12/principl.html.

Myhre, Susan. "Enhancing Your Dramatic-Play Area through the Use of Prop Boxes." *Young Children* 48 (July 1993): 6–11.

National Academies Press. *National Science Education Standards: An Overview.* Washington, DC: Author, 2006.

Available online: www.nap.edu/readingroom/books/nses/overview.html#content.

National Association for Sport and Physical Education (NASPE). *National Standards for Physical Education.* Reston, VA: Author, 2004. Available online: www.aahperd.org/naspe/template.cfm?template=ns_index.html.

National Association for the Education of Young Children (NAEYC). "NAEYC Position Statement: Technology and Young Children—Ages Three through Eight." *Young Children* 51 (September 1996): 11–16.

National Association for the Education of Young Children (NAEYC). "NAEYC Position Statement on Standardized Testing of Young Children 3 through 8 Years of Age." *Young Children* 43 (March 1988): 42–47.

National Association for the Education of Young Children. *Early Childhood Curriculum, Assessment, and Program Evaluation.* Washington, DC: Author, 2003.

National Association for the Education of Young Children (NAEYC)/National Council of Teachers of Mathematics (NCTM). *Early Childhood Mathematics: Promoting Good Beginnings.* Washington, DC: Author, 2002.

National Association for the Education of Young Children (NAEYC)/National Council of Teachers of Mathematics (NCTM). "Learning Paths and Teaching Strategies in Early Mathematics." *Young Children* 58 (2003): 41–43. Available online: www.naeyc.org/about/positions/pdf/mathchart.pdf.

National Council for Accreditation of Teacher Education (NCATE). *NCATE Standards, Procedures, and Policies for the Accreditation of Professional Units.* Washington, DC: NCATE, 1987.

National Council for the Social Studies (NCSS). *Curriculum Standards for Social Studies: Expectations of Excellence.* Washington, DC: NCSS, 1998.

National Council for the Social Studies (NCSS). *National Standards for Social Studies Teachers.* Washington, DC: Author, 1997. Available online: www.socialstudies.org/standards/teachers/vol1.

National Council for the Social Studies (NCSS), Task Force on Standards for Teaching and Learning in the Social Studies. *A Vision of Powerful Teaching and Learning in the Social Studies: Building Social Understanding and Civic Efficacy.* Washington, DC: Author, 1992. Available online: www.socialstudies.org/positions/powerful.

National Council of Teachers of Mathematics (NCTM). *Standards for Discussion.* 2000. Available online: www.nctm.org.

National Reading Panel. *Report of the National Reading Panel: Teaching Children to Read: An Evidence-Based Assessment of the Scientific Research Literature on Reading and Its Implications for Reading Instruction.* Washington, DC: National Institute of Child Health and Human Development/National Institute for Literacy, 2000.

National Research Council. *National Science Education Standards.* Washington, DC: National Academy Press, 1996.

Neely, Linda P. "Practical Ways to Improve Singing in Early Childhood Classrooms." *Young Children* 47 (July 2002): 80–83.

Neisworth, John T., and Stephen J. Bagnato. "The MisMeasure of Young Children: The Authentic Assessment Alternative." *Infants and Young Children* 17 (March 2004): 198–222.

Neisworth, John T., and Thomas J. Buggey. "Behavior Analysis and Principles in Early Childhood Education." In *Approaches to Early Childhood Education,* 2nd ed., edited by Jaipaul Roopnarine and James E. Johnson. New York: Macmillan, 1993.

Nelson, Katherine. "Structure and Strategy in Learning to Talk." *Monographs of the Society for Research in Child Development* 38 (1973): 149.

Nelson, R. G. "Which Is the Best Kindergarten?" *Principal* 79 (May 2000): 38–41.

Neuman, Susan B. "Becoming a Reader." *Scholastic Parent and Child* 12 (April/May 2005): 64–65.

Neuman, Susan B., and Kathy Roskos. "Bridging Home and School with a Culturally Responsive Approach." *Childhood Education* 70 (Summer 1994): 210–214.

Neuman, Susan B., and Kathleen A. Roskos. *Language and Literacy Learning in the Early Years.* Fort Worth, TX: Harcourt Brace Jovanovich, 1993.

New, Rebecca. "Excellent Early Education: A City in Italy Has It." *Young Children* 45 (September 1990): 4–10.

Nicolson, S., and S. G. Shipstead. *Through the Looking Glass: Observations in the Early Childhood Classroom.* New York: Merrill, 1994.

Novick, Rebecca. "Supporting Early Literacy Development: Doing Things with Words in the Real World." *Childhood Education* 76 (Winter 1999/2000): 70–75.

O'Brien, Thomas C., and Ann Moss. "Real Math?" *Phi Delta Kappan* 86 (December 2004): 292–296.

Ockelford, Adam, Graham Welch, and Sally Zimmerman. "Music Education for Pupils with Severe or Profound and Multiple Difficulties—Current Provision and Future Need." *British Journal of Special Education* 29 (April 2002): 178–182.

Odoy, Hillary Ann, and Sarah Hanna Foster. "Creating Play Crates for the Outdoor Classroom." *Young Children* 52 (September 1997): 12–16.

Ogle, Donna M. "The Know, Want to Know, Learn Strategy." In *Children's Comprehension of Text,* edited by K. D. Muth, 205–223. Newark, DE: International Reading Association, 1989.

Ohanian, Susan. "Goals 2000: What's in a Name?" *Phi Delta Kappan* 81 (January 2000): 344–355.

Oken-Wright, Pamela. "Show and Tell Grows Up." *Young Children* 43 (1988): 52–58.

Opitz, Michael F. "Cultural Diversity + Supportive Text = Perfect Books for Beginning Readers." *Reading Teacher* 52 (May 1999): 888–890.

Owens, Caroline V. "Conversational Science 101: Talking It Up!" *Young Children* 54 (September 1999): 4–9.

Pagni, David. "You're Never Too Old (or Too Young) to Use a Calculator." *Elementary Mathematician* 1 (December 1987): 10–11.

Paley, Vivian Gussey. "Finding a Place for Fantasy Play." *Parent and Child* 12 (March 2004): 57–59.

Pangrazi, Robert P., and Victor P. Dauer. *Dynamic Physical Education for Elementary School Children.* 10th ed. New York: Macmillan, 1992.

Pangrazi, Robert P., and Victor P. Dauer. *Movement in Early Childhood and Primary Education*. Minneapolis, MN: Burgess, 1981.

Parette, Howard P., Jr., Nancy S. Dunn, and Debra R. Hoge. "Low-Cost Communication Devices for Children with Disabilities and Their Family Members." *Young Children* 50 (September 1995): 75–81.

Parten, Mildred B. "Social Participation among Preschool Children." *Journal of Abnormal and Social Psychology* 27 (July/September 1932): 243–269.

Pattnaik, Jyotsna. "Learning about the 'Other': Building a Case for Intercultural Understanding among Minority Children." *Childhood Education* 79 (Summer 2003): 204–211.

Patton, Mary M., and Teresa M. Kokoski. "How Good Is Your Early Childhood Science, Mathematics, and Technology Program? Strategies for Extending Your Curriculum." *Young Children* 51 (July 1996): 38–44.

Paulson, F. Leon, Pearl R. Paulson, and Carol A. Meyer. "What Makes a Portfolio a Portfolio?" *Educational Leadership* 48 (February 1991): 60–63.

Pellegrini, Anthony D. *Applied Child Study: A Developmental Approach*. Hillsdale, NJ: Lawrence Erlbaum Associates, 1987.

Pellegrini, Anthony D., and Brenda Boyd. "The Role of Play in Early Childhood Development and Education: Issues in Definitions and Function." In *Handbook of Research on the Education of Young Children*, edited by Bernard Spodek, 105–121. New York: Macmillan, 1993.

Pena, Delores C. "Parent Involvement: Influencing Factors and Implications." *Journal of Educational Research* 94 (September/October 2000): 42–55.

Peregoy, S. F., and Owen F. Boyle. *Reading, Writing, and Learning in ESL*. New York: Addison Wesley Longman, 2004.

Perlmutter, Jane C., and Louise Burrell. "Learning through 'Play' as Well as 'Work' in the Primary Grades." *Young Children* 50 (July 1995): 14–21.

Persellin, Diane. "Teaching Songs to Young Children: What Do Music-Teacher Educators Say?" *General Music Today* 17 (January 2003): 18–28.

Pestalozzi, Johann Heinrich. *How Gertrude Teaches Her Children*. Translated by Lucy E. Holland and Francis C. Turner. Syracuse, NY: C. W. Bardeen, 1894.

Pestalozzi, Johann Heinrich. *Leonard and Gertrude*. Translated and abridged by Eva Channing. Boston: D.C. Heath, 1885.

Peter, Melanie. "Drama, Narrative and Early Learning." *British Journal of Special Education* 30 (January 2003): 21–27.

Petersen, Susan C. "The Sequence of Instruction in Games: Implications for Developmental Appropriateness." *Journal of Physical Education, Recreation and Dance* 63 (August 1992): 36–39.

Phyfe-Perkins, Elizabeth. "Children's Behavior in Preschool Settings: A Review of Research Concerning the Influence of the Physical Environment." In *Current Topics in Early Childhood Education*, vol. 3, edited by L. Katz et al. Norwood, NJ: Ablex, 1980.

Piaget, Jean. *The Child's Conception of Number*. London: Routledge and Kegan Paul, 1952a.

Piaget, Jean. "Development and Learning." In *Piaget Rediscovered*, edited by R. Ripple and V. Rockcastle. Ithaca, NY: Cornell University Press, 1964.

Piaget, Jean. *The Language and Thought of the Child*. 3rd ed. London: Routledge and Kegan Paul, 1959.

Piaget, Jean. *The Origins of Intelligence in Children*. New York: International Universities Press, 1952b.

Piaget, Jean. *Play, Dreams and Imitation in Childhood*. New York: W. W. Norton, 1962.

Piaget, Jean. *Science of Education and the Psychology of the Child*. New York: Orion Press, 1970.

Piaget, Jean, and Barbel Inhelder. *The Psychology of the Child*. Translated by Helen Weaver. New York: Basic Books, 1969.

Pickle, Barbara. *Increasing Safety Awareness of Preschoolers through a Safety Education Program*. ERIC Document Reproduction Service 310880. 1989.

Piper, Terry. *Language for All Our Children*. New York: Merrill, 1993.

Pogrow, Stanley. "Success for All Does Not Produce Success for Students." *Phi Delta Kappan* 82 (September 2000): 67–80.

Politis, Charlotte. "When Parents Won't Get Involved." *Early Childhood Today* 18 (January/February 2004): 4.

Potts, R., A. C. Huston, and J. C. Wright. "The Effects of Television Form and Violent Content on Boys' Attention and Social Behavior." *Journal of Experimental Child Psychology* 41 (1986): 1–17.

Prescott, Elizabeth, Elizabeth Jones, and Sybil Kritchevsky. *Group Day Care as a Child-Rearing Environment*. Washington, DC: Children's Bureau, Social Security Administration, Department of Health, Education and Welfare, 1967.

Price, Gary Glen. "Research in Review: Mathematics in Early Childhood." *Young Children* 44 (May 1989): 53–58.

Purcell-Gates, V. "Stories, Coupons, and the TV Guide—Relationships Between Home Literacy Experiences and Emergent Literacy Knowledge." *Reading Research Quarterly* 31(4) (1996): 406–428.

Ramsburg, Dawn. "The Debate over Spanking." *ERIC Digest*. ERIC Document Reproduction Service ED 405139. 1997.

Ramsey, Patricia G. *Teaching and Learning in a Diverse World: Multicultural Education for Young Children*. New York: Teachers College Press, 1998.

Ransbury, Molly Kayes. "Friedrich Froebel 1782–1982: A Reexamination of Froebel's Principles of Childhood Learning." *Childhood Education* 59 (November/December 1982): 101–105.

Readdick, Christine A., and Patricia Bartlett. "Vertical Learning Environments." *Childhood Education* 71 (Winter 1994/1995): 86–90.

Readdick, Christine A., and Jennifer J. Park. "Achieving Great Heights: The Climbing Child." *Young Children* 53 (November 1998): 14–19.

Reardon, S. Jeanne. "A Collage of Assessment and Evaluation from Primary Classrooms." In *Assessment and Evaluation in Whole Language Programs*, edited by Bill Harp. Boston: Christopher Gordon, 1991.

Reifel, Stuart, and June Yeatman. "From Category to Context: Reconsidering Classroom Play." *Early Childhood Research Quarterly* 8 (1993): 347–367.

Retting, Michael A. "Cultural Diversity and Play from an Ecological Perspective." *Children and Schools* 24 (July 2002): 189–200.

Richards, Leah. "Measuring Things in Words: Language for Learning Mathematics." *Language Arts* 67 (January 1990): 14–25.

Richards, Mary Helen. *Mary Helen Richards Teaches: The Child in Depth.* Portola Valley, CA: Richards Institute of Music Education and Research, 1969.

Richardson, Kathy. "Assessing Understanding." *Arithmetic Teacher* 35 (February 1988): 39–41.

Rickards, Debbie, and Earl Cheek, Jr. *Designing Rubrics for K–6 Classroom Assessment.* Norwood, MA: Christopher Gordon, 1999.

Rightmeyer, Elizabeth C. "Democratic Discipline: Children Creating Solutions." *Young Children* 58 (July 2003): 38–45.

Ringgenberg, Shelly. "Music as a Teaching Tool: Creating Story Songs." *Young Children* 58 (September 2003): 76–79.

Rivkin, Mary S. "Problem Solving through Outdoor Play." *Early Childhood Today* 15 (April 2001): 36–42.

Robertson, Shari Brand, and Susan Ellis Weismer. "Effects of Treatment on Linguistic and Social Skills in Toddlers with Delayed Language Development." *Journal of Speech, Language & Hearing Research* 42 (October 1999): 1234+.

Robinson, Sandra L. "The Grading Ritual: Unreliable and Unsuitable—But Unalterable?" *Young Children* 52 (July 1997): 86–87.

Rogers, Cosby S., and Sandra S. Morris. "Reducing Sugar in Children's Diets: Why? How?" *Young Children* 41 (July 1986): 11–16.

Rogers, Dwight L., and Dorene D. Ross. "Encouraging Positive Social Interaction among Young Children." *Young Children* 41 (March 1986): 12–17.

Rogers, Fred, and Hedda B. Sharapan. "Helping Parents, Teachers, and Caregivers Deal with Children's Concerns about War." *Young Children* 46 (March 1991): 12–13.

Rollins, Pamela R., Barbara A. Pan, Gina Conti-Ramsden, and Catherine E. Snow. "Communicative Skills in Children with Specific Language Impairments: A Comparison with Their Language-Matched Siblings." *Journal of Communication Disorders* 27 (June 1994): 189–206.

Roopnarine, Jaipaul, and Alice S. Honig. "Research in Review: The Unpopular Child." *Young Children* 40 (September 1985): 59–64.

Roopnarine, Jaipaul L., and James E. Johnson. *Approaches to Early Childhood Education.* Columbus, OH: Merrill, 2000.

Roser, Nancy L. "A Place for Everything and Literature in Its Place." *The New Advocate* 14 (Summer 2001): 211–249.

Roskos, K., and S. Neuman. "Play Settings as Literacy Environments: Their Effects on Children's Literacy Behaviors." In *Children's Emergent Literacy: From Research to Practice,* edited by D. F. Lancy, 251–264. Westport, CT: Praeger Press, 1994.

Ross, Dorothy G. *Stanley Hall: The Psychologist as Prophet.* Chicago: University of Chicago Press, 1972.

Ross, James G., and Russell R. Pate. "The National Children and Youth Study II: A Summary of Findings." *Journal of Physical Education, Recreation and Dance* 58 (November/December 1987): 51–56.

Ross, Michael E. "Science Their Way." *Young Children* 55 (March 2000): 6–13.

Rousseau, Jean-Jacques. *Emile.* Translated by Barbara Foxley. 1780. Reprint, New York: E. P. Dutton, 1950.

Routman, Regie. *Conversations.* Portsmouth, NH: Heinemann, 2000.

Rubin, K., G. Fein, and V. Vanderberg. "Play." In *Carmichaels's Manual of Child Psychology: Social Development,* edited by E. Hetherington. New York: Wiley, 1983.

Rubin, Renee, and Veronica G. Carlan. "Using Writing to Understand Bilingual Children's Literacy Development." *Reading Teacher* 58 (May 2005): 728–739.

Ruiz, Nadeen T. "A Young Deaf Child Learns to Write: Implications for Literacy Development." *Reading Teacher* 49 (November 1995): 206–217.

Rule, Audrey C., and Manuel T. Barrera. "Science Object Boxes: Using Object Boxes to Promote Hands-On Exploration of Both Concrete and Abstract Science Topics." *Science and Children* 37 (October 1999): 30–37+.

Safford, Phillip L. *Integrated Teaching in Early Childhood: Starting in the Mainstream.* White Plains, NY: Longman, 1989.

Samaras, Anastasia. "Children's Computers." *Childhood Education* 72 (Spring 1996): 133–136.

Sanacore, Joseph. "Genuine Caring and Literacy Learning for African American Children." *Reading Teacher* 57 (May 2004): 744–753.

Santos, Rosa M. "Ensuring Culturally and Linguistically Appropriate Assessment of Young Children." *Young Children* 59 (January 2004): 48–50.

Scarborough, Hollis S. "Very Early Language Deficits in Dyslexic Children." *Child Development* 61 (1990): 1728–1743.

Schickedanz, Judith. "Views of Literacy Development: Then and Now." Paper presented at the annual conference of the National Association for the Education of Young Children, Anaheim, CA, 1988.

Schickedanz, J. A., D. I. Schickedanz, and P. D. Forsyth. *Toward Understanding Children.* Boston: Little, Brown, 1982.

Schiller, Marjorie. "An Emergent Art Curriculum That Fosters Understanding." *Young Children* 50 (March 1995): 33–38.

Schiller, Pam, and Joan Townsend. "Early Childhood: Science All Day Long: An Integrated Approach." *Science and Children* 23 (October 1985): 34–36.

Schirrmacher, Robert. "Talking with Young Children about Their Art." *Young Children* 41 (July 1986): 3–7.

Schmidt, Patricia R. "Working and Playing with Others: Cultural Conflict in a Kindergarten Literacy Program." *Reading Teacher* 48 (February 1995): 404–412.

Schreiber, Mary E. "Lighting Alternatives: Considerations for Child Care Centers." *Young Children* 51 (May 1996): 11–13.

Schwartz, Sydney. "Calendar Reading: A Tradition That Begs Remodeling." *Teaching Children Mathematics* 1 (October 1994): 104–109.

Schweinhart, Lawrence J. *Lifetime Effects: The High/Scope Perry Preschool Study through Age 40.* Ypsilant, MI: High Scope Foundation, 2005.

Schweinhart, Lawrence J. "Observing Young Children in Action: The Key to Early Childhood Assessment. *Young Children* 48 (July 1993): 29–33.

Scott, Deborah, Brenda Williams, and Kathy Hyslip. "Mathematics as Communication." *Childhood Education* 69 (Fall 1992): 15–18.

Sears, N. C., and L. L. Medearis. "Educating Teachers for Family Involvement with Young Native Americans." Manuscript, East Central University, Ada, OK, 1993.

Sears, Sue, Cathy Carpenter, and Nancy Burstein. "Meaningful Reading Instruction for Learners with Special Needs." *Reading Teacher* 47 (August 1994): 632–638.

Seefeldt, Carol. "Transforming Curriculum in Social Studies." In *Reaching Potentials: Transforming Curriculum and Assessment,* vol. 2, edited by S. Bredekamp and T. Rosegrant. Washington, DC: National Association for the Education of Young Children, 1995b.

Seefeldt, Vern. "Physical Fitness in Preschool and Elementary School-Aged Children." *Journal of Physical Education, Recreation and Dance* 55 (November/December 1984): 33–37.

Sgroi, Laura A. et al. "Assessing Young Children's Mathematical Understandings." *Teaching Children Mathematics* 1 (January 1995): 275–277.

Shedler, Jonathan, and Jack Block. "Adolescent Drug Use and Psychological Health: A Longitudinal Inquiry." *American Psychologist* 45 (May 1990): 612–630.

Sheldon, Kristyn. "'Can I Play Too?' Adapting Common Classroom Activities for Young Children with Limited Motor Abilities." *Early Childhood Education Journal* 24 (February 1996): 115–120.

Shriver, Mark D., and Jack J. Kramer. "Parent Involvement in an Early Childhood Special Education Program: A Descriptive Analysis of Parent Demographics and Level of Involvement." *Psychology in the Schools* 30 (July 1993): 255–263.

Shure, Myrna B. "Bullies and Their Victims: A Problem-Solving Approach to Prevention." *Brown University Child & Adolescent Behavior Letter* 16 (October 2000): 1–3.

Shuy, Roger. "Language as a Foundation for Education: The School Context." *Theory Into Practice* 26 (1987): 166–174.

Slavin, Robert E., et al. "Success for All: A Summary of Research." *Journal of Education for Students Placed at Risk* 1 (January 1996): 41–76.

Smilansky, Sara. "Can Adults Facilitate Play in Children? Theoretical and Practical Considerations." In *Play: The Child Strives toward Self-Realization,* edited by G. Engstrom, 39–50. Washington, DC: National Association for the Education of Young Children, 1971.

Smilansky, Sara, and Leah Shefatya. *Facilitating Play.* Gaithersburg, MD: Psychosocial and Educational Publications, 1990.

Smith, Frank. "Why Systematic Phonics and Phonemic Awareness Instruction Constitute an Educational Hazard." *Language Arts* 77 (November 1999): 150–155.

Smith, Jane Diane, Denise Heffner, and Tom Algozzine. "Using Portfolio Assessments with Young Children Who Are at Risk for School Failure." *Preventing School Failure* 48 (2003): 1.

Smith, John A. "Singing and Songwriting Support Early Literacy Instruction." *Reading Teacher* 53 (May 2000): 646.

Smith, Peter K., Rebecca Smees, and Anthony D. Pellegrini. "Play Fighting and Real Fighting: Using Video Playback Methodology with Young Children." *Aggressive Behavior* 30 (2004): 164–173.

Smith, S. S. *Early Childhood Mathematics.* Boston: Allyn & Bacon, 2001.

Snow, Catherine E., M. Susan Burns, and Peg Griffin. *Preventing Reading Difficulties in Young Children.* Washington, DC: National Academy Press, 1998.

Sorohan, Erica G. "Playgrounds Are Us." *Executive Educator* (August 1995): 28–32.

Soundy, Cathleen S., and Nancy L. Stout. "Talk: Fostering the Emotional and Language Needs of Young Learners." In *Spotlight on Young Children and Language,* edited by Derry Koralek (pp. 13–17). Washington, DC: National Association for the Education of Young Children, 2003.

Spencer, J. P., and G. Schöner. "Bridging the Representational Gap in the Dynamic Systems Approach to Development." *Developmental Science* 6 (2003): 392–412.

Spidel, Jo. "Working with Parents of the Exceptional Child." In *Parents as Partners in Education,* 2nd ed., edited by Eugenia Hepworth Berger. Columbus, OH: Merrill, 1987.

Spodek, Bernard. *Early Childhood Education.* Englewood Cliffs, NJ: Prentice-Hall, 1973.

Stahl, Steven A., Ann M. Duffy-Hester, and Katherine A. D. Stahl. "Everything You Wanted to Know about Phonics (but Were Afraid to Ask)." *Reading Research Quarterly* 33 (July/August/September 1998): 338–355.

Staley, Lynn. "Beginning to Implement the Reggio Philosophy." *Young Children* 53 (May 1998): 20–25.

Staley, Lynn, and Penelope A. Portman. "Red Rover, Red Rover, It's Time to Move Over!" *Young Children* 55 (January 2000): 67–72.

Standing, E. M. *Maria Montessori: Her Life and Work.* New York: Academy Guild Press, 1957.

Standing, E. M. *The Montessori Method: A Revolution in Education.* Fresno, CA: Academy Library Guild, 1962.

Steele, Marcee. "Teaching Science to Students with Learning Problems in the Elementary Classroom." *Preventing School Failure* 49 (Fall 2004): 19, 21.

Stegelin, Dolores. A. "Making the Case for Play Policy: Research-Based Reasons to Support Play-Based Environments." *Young Children* 60 (March 2005): 76–85.

Steinfels, Margaret O'Brien. *Who's Minding the Children? The History and Politics of Day Care in America.* New

York: Simon & Schuster, 1973 (as quoted in Grubb 1989).

Stewart, Janice P. "Teacher-Mediated Learning for Young Readers: Successful Strategies with Predictable Book Reading." *Reading Horizons* 36, no. 2 (1995): 131–147.

Stone, Janet I. "Early Childhood Math: Make It Manipulative." *Young Children* 42 (September 1987): 16–23.

Stone, Sandra J. "Integrating Play into the Curriculum." *Childhood Education* 72 (Winter 1995/1996): 104–107.

Stone, Sandra J. *Understanding Portfolio Assessment: A Guide for Parents.* Wheaton, MD: Association for Childhood Education International, 1995.

Storch, Stacey A., and Grover J. Whitehurst, G. J. "Oral Language and Code-Related Precursors to Reading: Evidence from a Longitudinal Model." *Developmental Psychology* 38 (2002): 934–947.

Strickland, Dorothy S. "Emergent Literacy: How Young Children Learn to Read." *Educational Leadership* 47 (March 1990): 18–23.

Sullivan, Molly. *Feeling Strong, Feeling Free: Movement Exploration for Young Children.* Washington, DC: National Association for the Education of Young Children, 1982.

Suthers, Louie. "Introducing Young Children to Live Orchestral Performance." *Early Child Development and Care* 90 (May 1993): 55–64.

Sutton-Smith, Brian. "The Spirit of Play." In *The Young Child at Play: Reviews of Research*, vol. 4, edited by Greta Fein and Mary Rivkin, 3–13. Washington, DC: National Association for the Education of Young Children, 1986.

Sutton-Smith, Brian. "The Struggle between Sacred Play and Festive Play." In *Play as a Medium for Learning and Development*, edited by Doris Bergen. Portsmouth, NH: Heinemann, 1988.

Swick, Kevin J., Gloria Boutte, and Irma Van Scoy. "Families and Schools Building Multicultural Values Together." *Childhood Education* 70 (Winter 1995/1996): 75–79.

Swick, Kevin J., and Shirley McKnight. "Characteristics of Kindergarten Teachers Who Promote Parent Involvement." *Early Childhood Research Quarterly* 4 (March 1989): 19–29.

Swick, Kevin J. et al. *Family Involvement in Early Multicultural Learning.* ERIC Document Reproduction Service 380240. 1995.

Sylva, Kathy, Jerome S. Bruner, and Paul Genova. "The Role of Play in the Problem-Solving of Children 3–5 Years Old." In *Play: Its Role in Development and Evolution*, edited by Jerome S. Bruner, Alison Jolly, and Kathy Sylva, 244–257. New York: Basic Books, 1976.

Sylwester, Robert. *A Celebration of Neurons: An Educator's Guide to the Human Brain.* Alexandria, VA: Association for Supervision and Curriculum Development, 1995.

Szecsi, Tunde, and Debra A. Giambo. "ESOL in Every Minute of the School Day." *Childhood Education* 81 (Winter 2004/2005): 104–106.

Tabors, Patton O. "What Early Childhood Educators Need to Know: Developing Effective Programs for Linguistically and Culturally Diverse Children and Families." *Young Children* 53 (November 1998): 20–26.

Tallal, Paula, and Mahel Rice. "Fast Forword (Computer Software): Language Disorders." *ASHA* 39 (March 1997): 12–13.

Taylor, Denny. *Beginning to Read and the Spin Doctors of Science: The Political Campaign to Change America's Mind about How Children Learn to Read.* Urbana, IL: National Council of Teachers of English, 1998.

Taylor, Judy. "How I Learned to Look at a First-Grader's Writing Progress Instead of His Deficiencies." *Young Children* 51 (January 1996): 38–42.

Taylor-Cox, Jennifer. "Algebra in the Early Years? Yes!" *Young Children* 58 (January 2003): 14–21.

Teale, W. H., and E. Sulzby. "Emerging Literacy: New Perspectives." In *Emerging Literacy: Young Children Learn to Read and Write*, edited by D. S. Strickland and L. M. Morrow (pp. 1–15). Newark, DE: International Reading Association, 1989.

Temple, Charles A., Ruth G. Nathan, Frances Temple, and Nancy A. Burris. *The Beginnings of Writing.* 3rd ed. Boston: Allyn & Bacon, 1993.

Theemes, Tracy. *Let's Go Outside! Designing the Early Childhood Playground.* Ypsilanti, MI: High/Scope Educational Research Foundation, 1999.

Thelen, E., and L. B. Smith. "Dynamic Systems Theories." In. *Handbook of Child Psychology: Volume I, Theoretical Models of Human Development*, edited by R. M. Lerner (pp. 563–634). New York: Wiley, 1998.

Thomas, A., and S. Chess. *Temperament and Development.* New York: Brunner/Mazel, 1977.

Thompson, Susan, Paula Knudson, and Darlene Wilson. "Helping Primary Children with Recess Play: A Social Curriculum." *Young Children* 52 (September 1997): 17–21.

Thomson, Barbara. "Building Tolerance in Early Childhood." *Educational Leadership* 47 (October 1989): 78–79.

Thurlow, Martha L., Patrick J. O'Sullivan, and James E. Ysseldyke. "Early Screening for Special Education: How Accurate?" *Educational Leadership* 44 (November 1986): 93–95.

Timberlake, Pat. "Classroom Holidaze." *Childhood Education* (January 1978): 128–130.

Tracy, Dyanne M. "Using Mathematics Language to Enhance Mathematical Conceptualization." *Childhood Education* 70 (Summer 1994): 221–224.

Tudor, Mary. *Child Development.* New York: McGraw-Hill, 1981.

Turkel, Susan, and Claire M. Newman. "What's Your Number? Developing Number Sense." *Arithmetic Teacher* 35 (February 1988): 53–55.

Twiss, Lindy L. "Innovative Literacy Practices for ESL Learners." *Reading Teacher* (February 1996): 412–414.

Urzua, Carole. "Doing What Comes Naturally: Recent Research in Second Language Acquisition." In *Discovering Language with Children*, edited by Gay Su Pinnell. Urbana, IL: National Council of Teachers of English, 1980.

U.S. Department of Agriculture. *The Healthy Eating Index, 1999/2000.* Washington, DC: USDA.

Van de Walle, John A. "The Early Development of Number Relations." *Arithmetic Teacher* 35 (February 1988): 15–21.

Van Hoorn, Judith, Patricia Nourot, Barbara Scales, and Keith Alward. *Play at the Center of the Curriculum.* New York: Macmillan, 1993.

Vergeront, Jeanne. *Places and Spaces for Preschool and Primary (Indoors).* Washington, DC: National Association for the Education of Young Children, 1987.

Vygotsky, Lev. *Mind in Society: The Development of Higher Psychological Functions.* Cambridge, MA: Harvard University Press, 1978.

Vygotsky, Lev. *Thought and Language.* Cambridge: MIT Press, 1962.

Wachowiak, Frank. *Emphasis Art.* 3rd ed. New York: Harper and Row, 1977.

Wadsworth, Barry J. *Piaget's Theory of Cognitive and Affective Development.* 4th ed. New York: Longman, 1989.

Ward, Christina D. "Adult Intervention: Appropriate Strategies for Enriching the Quality of Children's Play." *Young Children* 51 (March 1996): 20–24.

Wardle, Francis. "Proposal: An Anti-Bias and Ecological Model for Multicultural Education." *Childhood Education* 72 (Spring 1996): 152–156.

Wardle, Francis. "Supporting Multiracial and Multiethnic Children and Their Families." *Young Children* 56 (November 2001): 38–39.

Warren, R. *Caring: Supporting Children's Growth.* Washington, DC: National Association for the Education of Young Children, 1977.

Washington, V., and J. D. Andrews. *Children of 2010.* Washington, DC: National Association for the Education of Young Children, 1998.

Wasserman, Selma. "Serious Play in the Classroom." *Childhood Education* 68 (Spring 1992): 132–139.

Watts-Taffe, Susan, and Diane M. Truscott. "Using What We Know about Language and Literacy Development for ESL Students in the Mainstream Classroom." *Language Arts* 77 (January 2000): 258–265.

Weigel, Daniel J., Sally S. Martin, and Kimberley K. Bennett. "Ecological Influences of the Home and the Child-Care Center on Preschool-Age Children's Literacy Development." *Reading Research Quarterly* 40 (April 2005): 205–233.

Weiller, Karen H., and Peggy A. Richardson. "A Program for Kids: Success-Oriented Physical Education." *Childhood Education* 69 (Spring 1993): 133–137.

Weinstein, Carol S. "The Physical Environment of the School: A Review of the Research." *Review of Educational Research* 49 (Fall 1979): 577–610.

Weitzman, Elaine, and Janice Greenberg. *Learning Language and Loving It: A Guide to Promoting Children's Social, Language and Literacy Development in Early Childhood Settings.* Toronto, Canada: Hanen Centre, 2002.

Wells, Gordon. *Learning through Interaction: The Study of Language Development.* Cambridge, England: Cambridge University Press, 1981.

Wells, Gordon. *The Meaning Makers: Children Learning Language and Using Language to Learn.* Portsmouth, NH: Heinemann, 1986.

Wenner, George. "Relationship between Science Knowledge Levels and Beliefs toward Science Instruction Held by Preservice Elementary Teachers." *Journal of Science Education and Technology* 2 (1993): 461–468.

Whaley, Kimberlee, and Elizabeth Blue Swadner. "Multicultural Education in Infant and Toddler Settings." *Childhood Education* 66 (Summer 1990): 238–240.

Whitenack, Joy, and Erna Yackel. "Making Mathematical Arguments in the Primary Grades: The Importance of Explaining and Justifying Ideas." *Teaching Children Mathematics* 8 (May 2002): 524–528.

Whitin, David J. "Collecting Data with Young Children." *Young Children* 52 (January 1997): 28–32.

Whitin, David J. "Literature and Mathematics in Preschool and Primary: The Right Connection." *Young Children* 49 (January 1994): 4–11.

Whitmore, Kathryn F., and Yetta M. Goodman. "Transforming Curriculum in Language and Literacy." In *Reaching Potentials: Transforming Early Childhood Curriculum and Assessment* 2, edited by S. Bredekamp and T. Rosegrant, 145–166. Washington, DC: National Association for the Education of Young Children, 1995.

"Why the Testing Craze Won't Fix Our Schools." *Rethinking Schools Online* (Spring 1999), www.rethinkingschools. org/archives/13–03/edit133.htm.

Wilford, Sara. "Teacher Self-Evaluation: Building on Your Strengths." *Early Childhood Today* 19 (May 2005): 6–7.

Willig, Sharon. "General Indicators of Developmental Language Disorders." *American Speech-Language-Hearing Association* 40 (Summer 1998): 43+.

Wilson, Ruth A. "Nature and Young Children: A Natural Connection." *Young Children* 50 (September 1995): 4–11.

Wolery, Mark, and Jan S. Wilbert, eds. *Including Children with Special Needs in Early Childhood Programs.* Research Monograph of the National Association for the Education of Young Children, vol. 6. Washington, DC: NAEYC, 1994.

Woolfolk, A. *Educational Psychology.* Boston: Allyn & Bacon, 2001.

Workman, Susan H., and Jim A. Gage. "Family-School Partnerships: A Family Strengths Approach." *Young Children* 52 (May 1997): 10–14.

Worthen, S. C. *The Integrated Classroom: The Assessment-Curriculum Link in Early Childhood Education.* Englewood Cliffs, NJ: Merrill, 1996.

Wright, J. L., and D. Shade, eds. *Young Children: Active Learners in a Technological Age.* Washington, DC: National Association for the Education of Young Children, 1994.

Wright, S. "The Arts and Schooling: An Analysis of Cultural Influences." *Journal of Cognitive Education* 6 (1997): 53–69.

Wright, S. *The Arts, Young Children, and Learning.* Boston: Allyn & Bacon, 2003.

Wuertenburg, Jacque. Speech to Northern Arizona Reading Council, Flagstaff, Arizona, April 1993.

Yarrow, L. "Should Children Play with Guns?" *Parents* 58 (January 1983): 50–52.

Index

Note: Bold numbers indicate pages on which topics are identified as key terms.

Activity time, 129. *See also* Schedules/scheduling
ADA. *See* Americans with Disabilities Act
Adaptive equipment (for special-needs children), **101.** *See also* Special needs, instructional materials for
Aggression
  gender and, 24
  play and, 25, 155–156, 167–168
  social development and, 24–26
Algebra (patterns and functions), 355, 366–368
Algorithms (in mathematics), **355**
Americans with Disabilities Act (ADA), 100
Anecdotal record (as assessment strategy), 162–163, 165, 192, **210**–212
Antibias curriculum, **119.** *See also* Multicultural education
Arrival time (and behavior management), **184**–185. *See also* Behavior management
Art. *See* Creative arts; Visual arts
Art area
  instructional materials for, 87–89
  outdoor location for, 89
  planning for, 87–89
Artists (study of), 427, 428
Arts education. *See* Creative arts
Assertive discipline (system of behavior management), 192–195
Assessment, 220–235
  behavior management and, 192, 196
  child development and, 212, 221, 224
  in content areas, 224
  content-area standards and, 212
  in creative arts, 442–443
  cultural diversity and, 232–233
  curriculum planning and, 114–115, 118–119, 120, 202–203, 230–231
  as basis for decisions, 205–206, 217, 218
  definition of, **202**
  developmentally appropriate practice and, 226–227
  documentation of, 66, 207, 208
  of English language learners, 298, 343
  evaluation of, 229–230
  language of, 217, 218
  of literacy development, 337–339
  mandated goals and, 118–119
  of mathematics, 362, 378–380, 381
  multiple intelligences and, 220–221, 231
  observation and, 15, 207, 210–212, 337–339
  of oral language, 337
  organizing data from, 217–223
  parents and, 217, 218, 223–230

  of play, 156–157, 162–164, 165
  of programs, 230–231
  reporting data from, 223–230, 232
  of special-needs children, 136, 231–232
  strategies for, 162–164, 192, 207–217
  testing vs., 202. *See also* Tests/testing
  of thematic instruction, 114–115
  types of, 203, 222
  of writing, 215, 216, 337–339
Assistive technology (for communication), 289–**290**, 341
Autism (children with), 170
Autoeducation, 51, 52–53. *See also* Montessori model

Bandura, Albert, 12–13. *See also* Social learning theory
Bank Street College of Education, 43, 60, 65
Basal readers, 326
Behavior management (in classroom), 174–199
  aggression and, 24–26
  approaches to, 176–178
  assessment of, 192, 196
  behaviorist theory/model and, 6–7, 57–59
  child development and, 178, 179, 194
  cultural diversity and, 198
  curriculum planning and, 180–182, 195
  decision making involved in, 190–192
  developmentally appropriate practice and, 184, 197
  discipline and, 176–177, 178, 184, 195, 196–197
  examples of, 179–180
  gender and, 185, 198
  of groups, 188–190
  guidance and, 176, 177–178, 193, 197, 198
  instructional materials and, 182–183
  learning areas and, 94–95, 95
  learning environment and, 182–183, 195, 197
  Montessori model and, 53
  planning for, 178–186
  play and, 25, 155–156, 167–168
  preventing problems and, 180–185, 194
  punishment and, 176–177
  room arrangement and, 182–183
  rules and, 188–189, 195, 197
  schedules/scheduling and, 184–185
  self-esteem and, 178, 179, 195
  social development and, 186–188, 197
  for special-needs children, 197
  strategies for, 186–192, 103
  systems for, 192–197

Behavior-management systems, **192**–197. *See also* Behavior management
Behaviorist theory/model
  application of, 14
  on behavior management, 6–7, 57–59
  on child development, 5, 6–7, 14, 29, 69, 70
  foundations of, 57–59, 70
  goals of, 59
  on intellectual development, 29, 59
  on language development, **273**–274, 275
  schedules/scheduling for, 59, 60–61
Bilingual education, 295–299. *See also* English language learners
Blindness (children with), 169
Block play area
  instructional materials for, 87, 88, 90–91
  planning for, 87, 88, 90–91, 159–160
Bloom, Benjamin, 44, 45
Bloom's taxonomy, 45
Books
  display of, 90
  knowledge of, 339
Brain-based learning, 31. *See also* Intellectual development
Broken homes, **240**
Bronfenbrenner, Urie, 13. *See also* Ecological systems theory
Bruner, Jerome, 8, 44, 45–46, 274–275. *See also* Constructivist theory

Calculators (in mathematics instruction), 374, 380–381
Cambourne, Brian, 306–308, 342
Canter, Lee, 192–195
Center-based curriculum, 109–110. *See also* Curriculum planning; Learning areas
Chants, 287, 433
Chard, Sylvia, 67
Checklist (as assessment strategy), 163, 213–214
Child care, **46**
Child development, 2–37
  assessment and, 212, 221, 224
  behavior management and, 178, 179, 194
  emotional development. *See* Emotional development
  intellectual development. *See* Intellectual development
  language development. *See* Language development
  overview of, 15, 16–17, 70
  physical development. *See* Physical development
  play and, 22–23, 148–153, 168
  program models and, 53–55, 56, 69, 70

Child development, *continued*
   social development. *See* Social
     development
   special-needs children and, 35, 168.
     See also Special needs
   theories of, 5–15. *See also specific*
     theories
Chomsky, Noam, 274
Cinquain, 409
Classification (learning plan for), 117
Classifying (as science process skill),
   388–389, 390
Classroom environment. *See* Learning
   environment
Code switching, 281
Cognitive delays (children with), 170
Cognitive development, **29**. *See also*
   Intellectual development
Collage, 426–427
Comenius, John, 40
Commercial programs
   for language development, 281–282
   for literacy instruction, 326–327
Communicating (as science process
   skill), **389**, 390
Communication (as mathematical
   process strand), 355, **371**
Communicative competence, **269**–271
Comparing (as science process skill),
   389, 390–391
Complex unit (of play/activity), **83**, 84
Computers, 122–128
   art activity using, 445
   effective use of, 124, 125, 128
   in mathematics instruction, 374,
     380–381
   online access via, 126–127, 222–223
   selecting software for, 125–126, 127
   special-needs children and, 126
Conferences
   with parents, 218, 225–228, 246,
     248, 249
   records of, 214–215
   with students, 214–215, 228
Connections (as mathematical process
   strand), 355, 371–372
Consortium of National Arts Education
   Associations, 416, 417–418, 419,
   424, 437
Constructivist theory/model
   application of, 14
   on child development, 5, 8–10, 14, 29,
     67–69, 70
   foundations of, 60–63, 67–69, 70
   goals of, 63–69
   on intellectual development, 29
   on language development, 273,
     274–275, 276
   programs based on, 64–70. *See also*
     specific programs
   schedules/scheduling for, 67, 68–69
   on science instruction, 387–388
Content-area standards
   assessment and, 212
   for dance, 437–438
   for drama, 440–441
   English language learners and, 137
   for language development, 282
   for literacy development, 312–314
   for mathematics, 353–354
   for music, 430–431

   for science, 395–404
   thematic instruction and, 111
   for visual arts, 424–425
Content areas
   assessment in, 224
   behaviorist theory/model and, 57, 59
   curriculum planning for, 107, 108,
     110, 137, 164–166
   for English language learners, 137
   integrated curriculum and, 265
   Montessori model and, 54
   play and, 164–166
Content strands (of mathematics
   instruction), **354**–355, 356–362
Conventional spelling (stage of writing),
   333
Conversations
   with parents, 229
   records of, 214–215
   with students, 214–215, 284, 291
Corporal punishment, **177**. *See also*
   Punishment
Counting, 357–359
Craft activities, **427**–428. *See also* Visual
   arts
Creative arts, 414–419
   activities for, 444
   assessment in, 442–443
   curriculum planning and, 417, 418,
     419, 443–445, 446
   developmentally appropriate practice
     and, 443
   goals of, 417–419
   importance of, 416–417
   integrated curriculum and, 417,
     443–445, 446
   literacy and, 444–445
   literature and, 444–445
   science and, 443–444
   specialists in, 441–442
   standards for, 419
   types of. *See* Drama; Movement and
     dance; Music; Visual arts
Creativity, **416**
Cultural diversity
   assessment and, 232–233
   behavior management and, 198
   child development and, 35–36
   creative arts and, 448–449
   curriculum planning and, 136, 137.
     See also Multicultural education
   early childhood programs and, 73
   English language learners and. *See*
     English language learners
   family/families and, 13, 121, 136, 198,
     240, 262
   food and, 136
   holidays and, 136
   instructional materials and, 102, 171
   intellectual development and, 35–36
   language differences and, 254, 262,
     293–299, 341–343, 344, 448–449
   learning areas and, 102
   literacy development and, 341–343
   literature and, 136
   mathematics and, 381–382
   parent/parents and, 171, 198, 232, 254,
     258
   play and, 170–171, 262
   school segregation and, 73
   science and, 411

   teachers' awareness of, 4, 381–382,
     411, 448
   themes and, 136
Curriculum (definition of), 106
Curriculum planning, 104–139. *See also*
   Early childhood programs
   assessment of, 114–115, 118–119, 120,
     202–203, 230–231
   behavior management and, 180–182,
     195
   child development and, 19–20, 22,
     26–27, 28–29, 33–34
   content areas and, 107, 108, 110
   creative arts and, 417, 418, 419,
     443–445, 446
   curriculum design, **106**–108
   dance and, 437–438
   developmentally appropriate practice
     and, 32, 108–110, 116
   drama and, 440–441
   emotional development and, 28–29
   for English language learners, 136,
     137
   foundations of, 106–108
   integrated approach to. *See* Integrated
     curriculum
   language development and, 289
   literacy and, 308, 313–314, 340
   mathematics and, 353–356, 374–378
   music and, 429, 430–431
   organizational approaches to, 108. *See*
     also Integrated curriculum
   physical development and, 19–20
   play and, 157, 158, 161, 164–166, 167
   program goals and, 106
   schedules/scheduling and, 120
   science and, 403, 405–409
   self-esteem and, 22
   social development and, 26–27
   theoretical foundation for, 13–15
   visual arts and, 424–425

Daily class schedule, **128**. *See also*
   Schedules/scheduling
Dalcroze Eurhythmics, 434, 435, 436
Dance education, 436, **437**–438
DAP. *See* Developmentally appropriate
   practice
Data analysis and probability, 355,
   368–369, 370
Deafness (children with), 169, 341
Deficit model (of parent involvement),
   239–240
Departure time (and behavior
   management), **185**. *See also*
   Behavior management
Descriptive writing. *See also* Writing
   learning plan for, 118, 119
Developmental delays (children with),
   168, 445
Developmentally appropriate practice
   (DAP)
   assessment and, 226–227
   behavior management and, 184, 197
   creative arts and, 443
   curriculum planning and, 32, 108–110,
     116
   definition of, **4**–5
   language development and, 294
   learning environment and, 93
   literacy and, 308, 310–311, 324

mathematics and, 354
paraprofessionals and, 258
parent involvement and, 258
play and, 155
program models and, 71
schedules/scheduling and, 129
science and, 403
testing and, 206–207
Dewey, John, 40, 42–43, 44, 65, 110
Dialects, **294**–295, 342
Directed play, **142**
Discipline, **176**–177, 178, 184, 195, 196–197. *See also* Behavior management
Dispositional learning (and behavior management), **188**
Doll corner. *See* Dramatic play area
Drama, 197, **438**–441, 447–448
Dramatic play area, 87, 88, 91
Drawing (development of), 419, 420–422, 423
Drawing realism stage, **421**
Dreikurs model (of behavior management), 192, 195–195

Early childhood, definition of, **4**
Early childhood programs, 38–75
assessment of, 230–231
developmentally appropriate practice and, 71
history of, 40–46
models of, 49–50, 69–70. *See also* Behaviorist theory/model; Constructivist theory/model; Montessori model
research on, 70–72
theoretical foundations for, 49–50
types of, 46–50. *See also specific types*
Early intervention programs, 46–47, 49. *See also* Head Start
Earth/space science (as science content standard), 395, 402–404
Ecological systems theory, 6, **13**, 15
Education for All Handicapped Children Act, 48
Egocentric thought patterns, **150**
Electronic portfolios, 222–223
Emergent literacy
definition of, 282, **312**
standards and, 312
Emerging curriculum
definition of, **42**
origins of, 42
thematic instruction and, 114
Emotional development, 15, 17, 27–29
activities for, 28–29
curriculum planning and, 28–29
patterns of, 27–29
play and, 150
English language learners, **295**–299
activities for, 298–299
assessment of, 298, 343
bilingual education for, 295–299
creative arts for, 450
curriculum planning for, 136, 137
home language use by, 299
literacy development of, 341–343, 344
literature for, 344
mathematics for, 381–382
native language use by, 343, 382
reading by, 343, 344

Environment. *See* Family/families, home environment of; Learning environment
Environmental print, **305.** *See also* Print; Print-rich environment
Erikson, Erik, on psychological development, 20–21, 56
Experimenting (as science process skill), **389,** 390
Exploratory play, **148**–149

Family/families. *See also* Parent/parents
behavior modification and, 198
cultural diversity and, 13, 121, 136, 240, 262
home environment of, 42, 45, 153–154
play and, 153–154, 262
poverty among, 238–239
of special-needs children, 135, 231
structure of, 238, 239, 240
Fine arts. *See* Art
Fingerplays, 41
First-graders. *See* Five- and six-year-olds
Five- and six-year-olds, play of, 151–153, 157–158
Food
cultural diversity and, 136
snack time, 131–132
Forman, George, 8. *See also* Constructivist theory
Formative assessment, **203.** *See also* Assessment
Four Blocks (literacy program), 326–327
Fractions, 361–362
Free play, **142**
Froebel, Friedrich, 40–41, 44, 46
Full-inclusion classrooms, 290. *See also* Inclusive classes; Mainstream
Functions (as mathematical concept), 366, **367**–368
Furniture, 79, 80, 85, 183. *See also* Learning environment

Games of construction, **146**
Games with rules, **145,** 152
Gardening area, 97
Gardner, Howard, 10–12, 220–221, 231. *See also* Multiple intelligences theory
Gender
aggression and, 24
behavior management and, 185, 198
social development and, 24
Geometry and spatial sense, 162, 355, 362–363, 364
Gesell Institute, 7–8
Gifted and talented children
identification of, 4
science for, 411
Ginott model (of behavior management), 192, 195
Glasser model (of behavior management), 192, 195
Grammar, 269, 270, 277
Graphic art, 425–426
Groups
behavior management and, 188–190
time scheduled for, 131. *See also* Schedules/scheduling
Guidance, 176, 177–**178**, 193, 197, 198. *See also* Behavior management

Guided dramatization, 197
Guided listening, **434**
Guided play, **142,** 161
Guided reading, **325**–326

Handwriting, instruction in, 33–34
Hall, G. Stanley, 44
Handbooks (for parents), **246**–247
Head Start
assessment for, 205
definition of, **47**
origins of, 44, 47, 50
special-needs children in, 48
Hearing impairments (children with), 169, 341, 410, 445–446
Hierarchy of needs, 45
High/Scope, 60, 64–65, 72, 220
High-stakes testing, **205**–206, 217, 218
Hill, Patty Smith, 41–42
History and nature of science (as science content standard), 395, 404
Holidays
themes and, 136
Home visits (to parents), **247**–248
Housekeeping corner. *See* Dramatic play area
Hunt, J. McVicker, 44–45

IDEA. *See* Individuals with Disabilities Education Act
IDEA 2004, 49. *See also* Individuals with Disabilities Education Act
IEP. *See* Individualized education plan
IFSP. *See* Individualized family service plan
Illicit play, **155**–156
Incident record (as assessment strategy), 208–209, 210
Incidental learning, **117**
Inclusive classes, 72. *See also* Mainstreaming
Individualized education plan (IEP), 135, 231
Individualized family service plan (IFSP), 135, 231
Individuals with Disabilities Education Act (IDEA), provisions of, 48–49
Infants. *See* One- and two-year-olds
Instructional materials, 85–95
behavior management and, 182–183
computers. *See* Computers
cultural diversity and, 102, 171
learning areas and, 86, 87–95, 101. *See also* Learning areas
literacy and, 314–315
manipulative types of, 372–374, 386–387
for mathematics, 372–374, 380–381
Montessori model and, 51–52, 56
for play, 147, 158, 159–160, 169
program goals and, **78**
for science, 386–387
selection of, 85–86
for special-needs children, 101–102, 126, 169–170, 289–290, 341, 380–381
Instrumental play, **155**
Instruments (musical), 89–90, 433–434
Integrated curriculum, 110–115
assessment of, 114–115
creative arts and, 417, 443–445, 446

Integrated curriculum, *continued*
  foundations of, **110**–111
  language development and, 289
  literacy and, 340, 444–445
  mathematics and, 374–378, 445
  planning for, 111–114, 265
  science and, 405–409, 443–444
  social studies and, 445, 446
  for special-needs children, 135
Intellectual development, 15, 17, 29–33
  activities for, 33
  curriculum planning and, 32–33
  environment and, 32
  language development and, 272
  materials for, 33
  patterns of, 29–33
  play and, 30, 41, 148–150
  research on, 31–32
  scaffolding of, 30
  theories of, 29, 59
Intelligence
  theories of, 44
  types of, 10–12
International Reading Association (IRA)
  on literacy assessment, 337
  on literacy instruction, 308, 310–311, 337
  standards of, 282, 312–314
  teachers' standards of, 304, 309
Internet, children's use of, 126–127
Interviews
  with children, 214–215, 216
  with parents, 244, 245
  records of, 214–215, 216
IRA. *See* International Reading Association

Journal writing, **336**–337

Katz, Lilian, 67
Key experiences, 64–65
Kidwatching, **283**
Kindergarten. *See also* Five- and
    six-year-olds
  assessment in, 381
  definition of, **46**
  history of, 40–41, 44, 46–47
  mathematics in, 381
  parents' involvement in, 244
  play in, 151–152
  schedules/scheduling for, 129, 130, 134
Knowledge, types of, 9
Kodály method (of music instruction),
    434, 435
KWL charts, 408, 409

Language arts
  activities area for, 90. *See also* Library/
      listening/writing area
  play and, 164
Language, 266–271
  characteristics of, 268
  definition of, **268**, 328
  development of. *See* Language
      development
  forms of, 275
  functions of, 275
  systems of, 268–271, 279
Language acquisition, 272, 274, 275
Language delays (children with),
    290–293

Language development, 271–301
  activities for, 283–289, 292–293
  assessment of, 337
  benchmarks of, 278, 279
  cognitive development and, 272
  commercial programs for, 281–282
  curriculum planning and, 289
  holistic nature of, 279–280
  instructional materials and, 288
  integrated curriculum and, 289
  learning areas, and 288
  learning environment and, 276–282
  literacy and, 315–316, 337
  milestones in, 269, 270
  models of, 273–276
  observation of, 283
  science and, 409
  sequence of, 272–273
  special-needs children, 289–293
  standards for, 282
  strategies for, 277–278, 280
Language differences
  creative arts and, 448–450
  of parents, 254, 262
  of students, 136, 137, 293–299,
      341–343, 344. *See also* Dialects;
      English language learners
"Learned stupidity," 33
Learning. *See also* Intellectual
      development; Intelligence
  literacy and, 306, 307
  mathematics and, 350–352
  play and, 41
  science and, 387–388
  theories of, 8–10, 41, 50–53, 57–59,
      61–63
Learning areas
  behavior management and, 94–95
  cultural diversity and, 102
  instructional materials for, 86, **87**–94,
      288. *See also specific types*
  language development and, 288
  multicultural education and, 123
  schedules/scheduling for, 94
  thematic instruction and, 113
Learning centers, 87. *See also* Learning
      areas
Learning environment, 76–103
  assessment of, 78, 83–85
  behavior management and, 182–183,
      195
  computers in. *See* Computers
  examples of, 81, 82, 85, 86
  furniture in, 79, 80, 85, 183
  influence of, 51, 56, 58, 62, 66, 78, 80
  instructional materials in. *See*
      Instructional materials
  intellectual development and, 32, 42
  language development and, 276–282
  learning areas in. *See* Learning areas
  literacy and, 314–315
  multicultural education and, 121, 123
  outdoors. *See* Outdoor learning
      environment
  physical climate of, 82–83
  planning of, **78**–79
  play and, 83–84, 147, 158
  program goals and, 78–79
  room arrangement and, 78, 80–81, 82,
      182–183
  safety in, 98–101, 392

  science and, 394
  for special-needs children, 48,
      101–102, 169–170, 290
  structuring of, 79–85
  traffic patterns in, 81, 87–88, 183
  vertical space in, 80–81
Learning plans, 116–119
  definition of, **116**
  examples of, 117, 118, 119, 162, 286,
      334, 370, 409, 428
  lesson plans vs., 116
Least restrictive environment (LRE), **48**
Lesson plans, 116, 117. *See also*
      Learning plans
Letter-name (phonetic) stage (of
      writing), 332
Letters/notes (to parents), 251–252
Liberation teaching, 193. *See also*
      Behavior management
Library/listening/writing area
  instructional materials for, 87, 88–89,
      90
  literacy and, 315
  planning for, 87, 88–89, 90
Life science (as science content
      standard), 395, 399–402
Linear repetitive stage (of writing), 330
Linguistic competence, 269–271
Linguistic model (of language
      development), 273, **274**, 276
Listening
  development of, **316**
  music and, 434
Listening area. *See* Library/listening/
      writing area
Literacy, 302–347. *See also* Reading;
      Writing
  activities for, 316–326, 340
  assessment of, 337–339
  commercial programs for, 326–327
  creative arts and, 444–445
  curriculum planning and, 308,
      313–314
  definition of, **304**
  developmentally appropriate practice
      and, 308, 310–311, 324
  development of, 305–308, 310–311,
      328–329
  instructional materials and, 314–315
  integrated curriculum and, 340,
      444–445
  language development and, 315–316
  learning environment and, 314–315
  mathematics and, 376–377
  Montessori model and, 54
  program elements for, 309–329
  research on, 304–305
  science and, 406, 407–409
  self-esteem, 327–329
  standards for, 312–314
  teacher's role in, 304–308
Literature
  activities using, 284–286
  creative arts and, 444–445
  cultural diversity and, 136
  language development and, 284–287
  mathematics and, 378, 379
  multicultural sources of, 343
  read-aloud books, 318, 409
  science and, 408–409
  song picture books, 316

Logico-mathematical learning/
    knowledge, **350**–352, 387
LRE. *See* Least restrictive environment

Mainstreaming, **48**, 290. *See also*
    Inclusive classes
Make-believe (and cognitive
    development), 30. *See also* Play,
    types of
Mandated goals, **118**–119. *See also*
    Content-area standards
Manipulatives
    intellectual development and, 33, 62
    mathematics instruction and, **372**–374
    science instruction and, 386–387
Manipulatives/mathematics/games area
    instructional materials for, 87, 89, 92
    planning for, 87, 89, 92
Maslow, Abraham, 44, 45
Mastery learning, **45**
Materials. *See* Instructional materials
Mathematics, 348–383
    activities for, 356–357, 358, 359,
        360–361, 362, 363–365, 366,
        367–368, 369, 370, 371, 375, 376
    assessment of, 362, 378–380, 381
    curriculum planning for, 353–356,
        374–378. *See also* Strand model
    definition of, **350**
    developmentally appropriate practice
        for, 354
    instructional materials for, 372–374,
        380–381
    integrated curriculum and, 374–378,
        445
    learning of, 350–352
    learning area for, 87, 89, 92
    literacy and, 376–377
    literature and, 378, 379
    play and, 166, 374–376, 377
    special-needs children and, 380–381
    standards for, 353–354
    strand model for, 354–356. *See also*
        Strand model
    teaching of, 352–353
Maturationist theory
    application of, 14
    on child development, 5, **7**–8, 14
Measurement (in mathematics), 118,
    355, 363–366, 367
Measuring (as science process skill),
    389, 390–391
Memory
    types of, 9
MENC. *See* Music Educators National
    Conference
Middle childhood. *See* Seven- and
    eight-year-olds
Mitchell, Lucy Sprague, 43–44, 65
Modeling (by teachers)
    Montessori model and, 51
    of play, 156
    social learning theory and, 12–13
Money (as mathematical concept), 366
Montessori, Maria, 40, 50, 56. *See also*
    Montessori model
Montessori model, 50–56
    on child development, 53–55, 56, 69,
        70
    example of, 55, 56
    foundations of, 50–53, 70

    goals of, 53–55
    origins of, **50**
    resources about, 55
    schedules/scheduling in, 54–55
Morphemes, **268**–269
Morphology, **268**–269
Movement experiences, 90, **436**–437
Multicultural education, 119–122, 123
    characteristics of, 122
    curriculum planning for, 119–122, 123
    definition of, **119**, 120
    family/families and, 121
    goals of, 120–122
    instructional materials and, 102, 343
    learning environment and, 121, 123
    literature for, 343
Multiple intelligences theory, 5, **10**–12,
    14, 220–221, 231
Music, 428–436
    curriculum planning for, 429, 430–431
    definition of, **428**
    goals of, 429–430
    instruments, 89–90, 433–434
    learning and, 41–42
    learning area for, 87, 89–90
    literacy and, 316
    singing/songs, 287, 316, 431–433, 444,
        447
    standards for, 430–431
    teaching of, 434–435
Music area, 87, 89–90
Music Educators National Conference
    (MENC), 417–418, 419, 429
Musical instruments, 89–90, 433–434

NAEYC. *See* National Association for the
    Education of Young Children
NAME. *See* National Association for
    Music Educators
Narrative
    as assessment strategy, 208–210
    as literary form, 284–286
    as report to parents, 228
National Association for Music
    Educators (NAME), 419, 429
National Association for the Education
    of Young Children (NAEYC)
    on computer use, 124
    on developmentally appropriate
        practice, 108–109
    on early childhood, 4
    on Internet use, 126
    on literacy instruction, 308, 310–311
    origins of, 42
    on types of tests, 203–204
National Council of Teachers of English
    (NCTE) (standards of), 282, 312–314
National Council of Teachers of
    Mathematics (NCTM) Standards,
    353–354
National Science Education (NSE)
    Standards, 395–404
National Standards for Arts Education,
    419, 424, 430, 437, 440
NCLB. *See* No Child Left Behind (NCLB)
    Act
NCTE. *See* National Council of Teachers
    of English
NCTM Standards. See National Council
    of Teachers of Mathematics (NCTM)
    Standards

Negative reinforcement, 6–7
Newsletters (for parents), 229, 246
No Child Left Behind (NCLB) Act
    special-needs children and, 49
    testing and, **206**–207
Nonjudgmental attitude (of teachers
    toward parents), **239**
NSE Standards. See National Science
    Education (NSE) Standards
Number and operations, 356–359

Observation (by teachers)
    assessment and, 15, 207, 210–212,
        337–339. *See also* Assessment
    child development and, 212
    content standards and, 212
    curriculum planning and, 120
    language development and, 283
    literacy development and, 337–339
    of play, 156, 162–164, 165, 231
    of special-needs children, 231
    theoretical foundation for, 15
Observing (as science process skill), **388**,
    390–391
One- and two-year-olds
    play of, 151
One-to-one correspondence, 13–15, 357
Open-ended materials (for play),
    159–160
Operant conditioning, **6**–7
Operations on whole numbers, 360–361
Oral language
    assessment of, 337
    development of, 278, 279, **315**–316
Orff approach (to music instruction),
    434, 435
Outdoor learning environment
    art activities in, 89, 98
    curriculum planning for, 424–425
    equipment/materials for, 96–98
    physical development and, 96
    planning of, 96–100, 167–168
    play in, 167–168
    safety in, 98–101

Paraprofessionals (in classroom), 237,
    256–260, 261
Parent/parents. *See also* Family/families
    activities for, 241–242, 244–246
    assessment and, 217, 218, 223–230
    behavior modification and, 198
    communication with, 162, 217, 218,
        223–230, 232, 244, 245, 246–253,
        254
    conferences with, 218, 225–228
    cultural diversity and, 171, 198, 232,
        254, 258, 262
    education of, 254
    of English language learners, 299
    involvement in school by, 237, 238,
        239–246, 253, 254, 258
    language differences of, 254, 262
    observation by, 249, 250
    play and, 162, 171
    pressures facing, 238–239, 244
    single parents, 240
    of special-needs children, 260
    teachers' relationships with, 239–240,
        242–244
    working mothers, 239
Parent place (in school), **249**–250

Parent visits (to school), 246, 248–251
Patterns (as mathematical concept), **366**–368
Pegboard system (for learning areas), 95
Personality. *See also* Temperament
development of, 20–22. *See also* Social development
Pestalozzi, Johann, 40
Phonemic awareness, **319**–320
Phonetic stage (of writing), 332
Phonics, **320**–324
Phonology, **268,** 270
Physical climate, 82–83. *See also* Learning environment
Physical development, 15–20
activities for, 19–20
curriculum planning and, 19–20
patterns of, 15–19
play and, 96, 150
playgrounds and, 96–101
Physical disabilities (children with), 169–170, 341, 411, 447
Physical education area
instructional materials for, 87, 89, 93
planning for, 87, 89, 93
Physical environment. *See* Learning environment
Physical knowledge, **387**
Physical science (as science content standard), 395, 396–399
Piaget, Jean. *See also* Constructivist theory
on cognitive development, 29, 30–31
on early education, 60, 61, 63–64
on language development, 274–275
on learning, 8–9, 10, 40, 56, 60, 61, 350–352
on play, 146–147, 148, 150
Place value, 359–360
Play, 140–173
aggression and, 25, 155–156, 167–168
assessment of, 156–157, 162–164, 165, 231
behaviors for, 151–153, 231
child development and, 22–23, 30, 41, 96–98, 148–153
characteristics of, 142–144
content areas and, 164–166
cultural diversity and, 170–171
curriculum planning and, 157, 158, 161, 164–166, 167
definition of, **142**
developmentally appropriate practice and, 155
at home vs. school, 153–154
intellectual development and, 30, 41, 148–150
learning environment and, 83–84, 147, 158
levels of, 144–147
materials for, 147, 158, 159–160, 169, 171
mathematics and, 166, 374–376, 377
in outdoors, 167–168. *See also* Outdoor learning environment
parent/parents and, 162, 171
purposes of, 148–153
research on,149–150, 161
in school settings, 153–166, 171
social development and, 22–23, 25

teacher's roles in, 153, 154–155, 156–157, 160, 161
as teaching strategy, 160, 161
theories of, 22, 30, 44, 146–148, 150, 161
types of, 30, 142, 144–147, 155. *See also specific types*
Play with objects, 145–146
Playgrounds. *See also* Outdoor learning environment
example of, 99
physical development and, 96
planning for, 96–98
safety for, 98–101
special-needs children and, 100–101
Poetry
language development and, 287
science and, 409
Portfolios (as assessment strategy), **219**–223, 224, 232
Positive reinforcement, 6–7
Poverty (among U.S. children/families), 238–239
Practice play, **145,** 151
Pragmatics, **269,** 270
Preschematic stage (of drawing), **420**
Preschoolers. *See* Three- and four-year-olds
Presenting selected text, 324–326
Print (children's awareness/knowledge of), 305, 315, 319, 339
Print-rich environment, **315**
Printing (as art activity), 426
Problem solving
behavior management and, 188, 195
as mathematical process strand, 355, **369**–370
play and, 149
Process skill instruction (in mathematics), 372
Process strands (of mathematics instruction), **355,** 369–372
Progressive education movement, **42,** 43
Project Approach, 60, 67
Prosocial behaviors, 24. *See also* Social skills
Public Law (PL) 94-142, 48, 72
Public Law (PL) 99-456, 48, 72
Pull-out programs, **134**–135. *See also* Special needs, programs for
Punishment, 6, **176**–177, 178, 179–180. *See also* Behavior management

Questionnaire (as assessment strategy), 217
Quiet area
instructional materials for, 80, 87, 93
planning for, 80, 87, 93

Race/ethnicity
school segregation and, 73
Random-letter stage (of writing), 330–332
Rating scale (as assessment strategy), 214
Records of conversations/conferences/interviews, 214–215. *See also* Conferences; Interviews
Read-alouds, **317**–318, 409
Readiness
Montessori model and, 53

Readiness tests, 203, **205**
Reading
activities for, 316–326
assessment of, 339
commercial programs for, 326–327
cues for, 305–306
definition of, **305**
development of, 305–308, 310–311
developmentally appropriate practice and, 324
of English language learners, 343, 344
instructional materials for, 314–315
language development and, 315–316, 337
learning environment for, 314–315
play and, 164
schedules/scheduling for, 337, 338
science and, 408–409
standards for, 312–314
Reasoning and proof, 355, 371
Reflective abstraction, **352**
Reggio Emilia schools, 60, 65–67, 79, 114, 207, 417
Reinforcement (positive and negative), 6–7
Relating, inferring, and applying (as science process skills), **389**–390
Reliability (in testing), 203, **205**
Report cards, 223–225, 246
Reporting (assessment data), 223–230. *See also* Assessment
evaluation of, 229–230
forms of, 223–230
purpose of, 223
Representation (as mathematical process strand), 355, **372**
Research
on behavior management, 198
on brain, 31–32
on child development, 43–44, 45, 149–150
on literacy, 304–305
on phonics instruction, 320–321
on play, 149–150, 161
on program models, 70–72
Rhymes, language development and, 287
Room arrangement, **78,** 80–81, 82, 182–183. *See also* Learning environment
Rote memory/learning, 9
Rousseau, Jean-Jacques, 7, 40. *See also* Maturationist theory
Rubric (as assessment strategy), **215**–217
Rule-governed play, **148**–149
Rules (behavior management and), 188–189, 195, 197
Running narrative/log (as assessment strategy), 208, 209

Safety
for indoor learning environment, 98–100
for Internet use, 126–127
for playground/outdoor learning environment, 100–101
for science instruction, 392
Sand tables/sandbox area
equipment/instructional materials for, 87, 92–93, 97
planning for, 87, 92–93, 97, 160

Scaffolding
  intellectual development and, 30
  language development and, 275
Schedules/scheduling, 128–135
  adaptations to, 133
  behavior management and,
    184–185
  curriculum planning and, 120,
    128–133
  details of, 129–133, 184–185
  developmentally appropriate practice
    and, 129
  examples of, 129, 130
  instructional materials and, 94
  for kindergarten, 129, 130, 134
  program models and, 54–55, 59,
    60–61, 67, 68–69
  reading and, 337, 338
  routines in, 133, 184
  special-needs children and, 134–135
  transition times, 132–133, 185
Schematic stage (of drawing), **420**–421
School design. *See* Curriculum planning;
    Early childhood programs
School handbooks (for parents),
    246–247
Science, 384–413
  activities for, 393–394, 396–404, 408
  attitudes toward, 393
  creative arts and, 443–444
  cultural diversity and, 411
  curriculum planning for, 403,
    405–409
  definition of, **386,** 387, 391
  developmentally appropriate practice
    for, 403
  instructional materials for, 386–387,
    408–409
  integrated curriculum and, 405–409,
    443–444
  language development and, 409
  learning area for, 87, 89, 91–92
  learning of, 386–391
  learning environment for, 392
  literacy and, 406, 407–409
  literature and, 408–409
  play and, 166
  safety in, 392
  skills underlying, 388–391
  special-needs children and, 410–411
  standards for, 395–404
  teaching of, 386, 387–388, 391–404,
    405
Science and technology (as science
    content standard), 395, 404
Science as inquiry (as science content
    standard), 395, 396
Science/discovery area
  instructional materials for, 87, 89,
    91–92
  planning for, 87, 89, 91–92
Science in personal and social
    perspectives (as science content
    standard), 395, 404
Scientific process, **388**–391
Screening tests, 203, **204**
Scribbling stage
  of drawing, **420**
  of writing, 329–330
Scripted program, 326
Sculpture, 426

Second-language learners, 296. *See
    also* English language learners;
    Language differences
Segregation, 73
Self-esteem
  activities for, 22
  behavior management and, 178, 179,
    195
  curriculum planning and, 22
  literacy development and, 327–329
  social development and, 22
Self-evaluation (as assessment strategy),
    217
Semantics, **269,** 270, 306
Seven- and eight-year-olds, play of,
    152–153, 157–158
Sewing (as art activity), 427
Sex-role identification. *See also* Gender
  social development and, 26
Shared reading, **325**
Sharing time, 131, 288. *See also*
    Schedules/scheduling
Sheltered instruction, 137
Show-and-tell, 131. *See also*
    Schedules/scheduling
Sight impairments (children with), 169,
    341, 380, 410
Sight-word vocabulary, **305**–306. *See
    also* Vocabulary
Signing (and drama activities),
    447–448
Simple abstraction, **351**
Simple unit (of play/activity), **83,** 84
Singing/songs, 287, 316, 431–433, 444,
    447. *See also* Music
Single parents, 240. *See also*
    Parent/parents
SIOP (Sheltered Instruction Observation
    Protocol), 137
Skinner, B. F., 6. *See also* Behaviorist
    theory
Snack time, 131–132. *See also*
    Schedules/scheduling
Social development, 15, 16, 20–27
  activities for, 26–27
  aggression and, 24–26
  behavior management and, 186–188
  curriculum planning and, 26–27
  gender and, 24
  patterns of, 20–26
  personality and, 20–22
  play and, 22–23, 150
  relationships and, 23–24
  self-esteem and, 22
  social skills and, 23–24
Social knowledge (and behavior
    management), **188**
Social learning theory, 6, **12**–13, 14–15
Social play, 144–**145**
Social skills
  behavior management and, **186,** 197
  social development and, 23–24. *See
    also* Social development
Social studies
  creative arts and, 445, 446
  integrated curriculum and, 445, 446
Sociocultural theory, 9–10
Sociodramatic play, **146**–147, 161
Sociolinguistics, **271**
Software (selection of), 125–126, 127.
    See also Computers; Internet

Songs/singing, 287, 316, 431–433, 444,
    447
Sound–letter relationships, 306
Special needs (children with)
  assessment of, 136, 231–232
  behavior management for, 197
  computer use by, 126, 445
  creative arts and, 445–448, 449
  curriculum planning for, 135–136
  identification of, 4, 35, 49, 290–291
  families of, 135, 231
  instructional materials for, 101–102,
    126, 169–170, 289–290, 341,
    380–381, 410–411, 445
  integrated curriculum and, 135
  labeling of, 48
  language development of, 289–293
  learning environment for, 48, 101–102,
    169–170, 197, 290
  legislation providing for, 48–49, 72,
    100
  literacy development of, 340–341
  mathematics and, 380–381
  paraprofessionals working
    with, 260
  parents of, 260
  placement of, 72–73
  play of, 168–169
  playgrounds for, 100–101
  programs for, 47–49, 72–73, 134–136
  schedules/scheduling for, 134–136
  science and, 410–411
  standardized tests for, 231, 232
  types of. *See specific
    conditions/disabilities*
Specialized learning areas
  instructional materials for, 93–94
  planning for, 93–94
Specialists (in creative arts), **441**–442
Speech disabilities, 447
Spelling, 333
Standardized tests, 204, **205,** 218, 231,
    232
Standards. *See* Content-area standards
Standards for the English Language Arts,
    282, 312–314
State standards (and thematic
    instruction), **111.** *See also* Content-
    area standards
Stimulus-response theory, **6**
Storage areas
  for outdoor equipment/materials, 98
  planning for, 94, 98
Storytelling, 286–287, 318–319
Strand model (of mathematics
    instruction), **354**–372
  content strands, 354–355, 356–362
  process strands, 355, 369–372
Subject-matter approach (to curriculum
    planning), 108. *See also* Content
    areas, curriculum planning for
Summative assessment, **203.** *See also*
    Assessment
Super unit (of play/activity), **83,** 84
Symbolic play, **145**
Syntax, **269,** 306

Tally (as assessment strategy), 207–208,
    209
Teacher aides/assistants. *See*
    Paraprofessionals

Teachers
  cultural awareness of, 4
  knowledge base of, 1, 3, 265
  language use of, 292
  observations of. *See* Observation
  relationships with parents, 239–240,
    242–244
  standards for, 304, 309
  working with paraprofessionals, 237,
    256–260, 261
  working with volunteers, 237,
    253–255, 256, 257
Teaching strategies
  for behavior management, 186–192
  for play, **160,** 161
Telecommunication (with parents),
  252–253
Telephone calls (to parents), 229, 246
Temperament
  nature of, 27. *See also* Personality
Tests/testing. *See also* Assessment
  definition of, **202**
  developmentally appropriate practice
    and, 206–207
  No Child Left Behind Act and,
    206–207
  of special-needs children, 231, 232
  types of, 203–206
Thematic organization (of curriculum),
  108. *See also* Integrated curriculum
Themes, 111–115. *See also* Integrated
  curriculum
  children's interest in, 113–114, 115
  content-area standards and, 111
  evaluation of, 114–115
  holidays as, 136
  implementation of, 112–114
  learning areas and, 113
  selection of, **111**–112, 136
  for special-needs children, 135
Theories of child development. *See* Child
  development, theories of
Three- and four-year-olds, play of, 151
Time (as mathematical concept),
  365–366

Time out, 177. *See also* Behavior
  management; Punishment
Traffic patterns, **81,** 87–88, 183. *See also*
  Learning environment
Transitional spelling (stage of writing),
  333
Transitions (in schedule), **132**–133, **185.**
  See also Schedules/scheduling

Unifying concepts and processes (as
  science content standard), 395

Validity (in testing), 203, **205**
Verbal skills (and behavior
  management), **186**
Vertical space, **80**–81. *See also* Learning
  environment
Videotapes (for parents), 229, 251
Violence in schools, 25, 26, 195
Vision impairments (children with), 169,
  341, 380, 410, 445
Visual arts, 419–428
  activities for, 425–428
  craft activities vs., 427–428
  curriculum planning for, 424–425
  definition of, **419**
  development of drawing, 419,
    420–422, 423
  goals of, 422–424
  learning and, 41–42, 66
  learning area for, 87–89
  learning plan for, 428
  outdoor activities for, 89, 98
  standards for, 424–425
  teaching of, 420, 422
Vocabulary
  development of, 305–306
  learning plan for, 286
  reading and, 305–306
Volunteers (in classroom), 237, **253**–255,
  256, 257
Vygotsky, Lev
  on cultural diversity, 35
  on intellectual development, 29
  on language development, 275

on learning, 8, 9–10, 35, 60, 61, 62
on play, 30, 144, 147–148, 161
on science instruction, 387–388

Water tables/play area
  equipment/instructional materials for,
    87, 92–93, 97
  planning for, 87, 92–93, 97, 160
Weaving (as art activity), 427
Webs/webbing
  examples of, 113, 208
  theme implementation and,
    112–113
Weikart, David, 64
Whole number operations, 360–361
Withitness, **191.** *See also* Behavior
  management
Woodworking area
  instructional materials for, 87, 92
  planning for, 87, 92
Working mothers, 239. *See also*
  Parent/parents
Writing, 329–337
  assessment of, 215, 216, 337–339
  conventions of, 333, 334
  definition of, **329**
  development of, 308, 310–311,
    329–333
  instructional materials for, 90,
    314–315
  language development and, 315–316,
    337
  learning environment and,
    314–315
  learning plans for, 118, 334, 409
  process of, 335–337
  science and, 407–408, 409
  standards for, 312–314
Writing area. *See* Library/listening/
  writing area

Zone of proximal development (ZPD),
  10, 62

Photo Credits

Comstock: p. 2; Will Faller: pp. 5, 87, 132, 168, 290, 447, 478, 501; Frank Siteman: pp. 18, 23, 236;
Richard Hutchings/PhotoEdit: pp. 38, 414; Lon C. Diehl/PhotoEdit: p. 47; Will Hart: pp. 63, 204,
244, 266, 315, 317, 351, 400, 439; Lauren Shear/Photo Researchers: p. 71; Dennis MacDonald/
PhotoEdit: p. 76; Jonathan Nourok/PhotoEdit: p. 97; Michael Newman/PhotoEdit: pp. 104, 145;
David Mager/Pearson Learning Photo Studio: pp. 106, 251; Brian Smith: pp. 109, 125, 159, 211, 287;
Paul Conklin/PhotoEdit: p. 140; Corbis/Stock Market: p. 152; Myrleen Ferguson Cate/PhotoEdit:
p. 174; Tony Freeman/PhotoEdit: p. 180; Robert Harbison: pp. 183, 189, 480, 487; Laura Dwight
Photography: pp. 200, 397; Robin Sachs/PhotoEdit: p. 225; Cindy Charles/PhotoEdit: p. 241;
Lindfors Photography: pp. 280, 302, 335; David Young-Wolff/PhotoEdit: p. 312; Bill Aron/PhotoEdit:
p. 348; Will Hart/PhotoEdit: p. 360; Ariel Skelley/Bettmann/Corbis: p. 373; EyeWire/Photodisc/Getty
Images: p. 384; Corbis: p. 407; Bill Losh/Taxi/Getty Images: p. 424; Rudi Von Briel/PhotoEdit: p. 432;
Stockbyte: p. 452; Jeff Greenberg/PhotoEdit: p. 468; James Ross/Getty Images: p. 476; Rob Van
Petten/Digital Vision/Getty Images: p. 495